From Idea to Essay

A Rhetoric, Reader, and Handbook

Thirteenth Edition

From Idea to Essay
A Rhetoric, Reader, and Handbook

Jo Ray McCuen-Metherell
Emerita, Glendale Community College

Anthony C. Winkler

WADSWORTH
CENGAGE Learning·

Australia · Brazil · Japan · Korea · Mexico · Singapore · Spain · United Kingdom · United States

WADSWORTH
CENGAGE Learning

From Idea to Essay: A Rhetoric, Reader, and Handbook, Thirteenth Edition
Jo Ray McCuen-Metherell,
Anthony C. Winkler

Editor: Margaret Leslie

Development Editor: Larry Goldberg

Assistant Editor: Amy Haines

Editorial Assistant: Elizabeth Ramsey

Media Editor: Jane Tangney

Marketing Manager: Jason Sakos

Marketing Communications Manager:
Stacey Purviance

Project Management, Editorial Production:
PreMediaGlobal

Art Director: Jill Ort

Print Buyer: Betsy Donaghey

Rights Acquisition Specialist: Katie Huha

Production Service: PreMediaGlobal

Photo Researcher: PreMediaGlobal

Copy Editor: PreMediaGlobal

Cover Designer: Roycroft Design/
Ikon Images/Masterfile

Compositor: PreMediaGlobal

For product information and technology assistance, contact us at
Cengage Learning Customer & Sales Support, 1-800-354-9706
For permission to use material from this text or product,
submit all requests online at **www.cengage.com/permissions**
Further permissions questions can be emailed to
permissionrequest@cengage.com

Library of Congress Control Number: 2010940627

ISBN-13: 978-0-495-91212-5

ISBN-10: 0-495-91212-3

Wadsworth
20 Channel Center Street
Boston, MA 02210
USA

Cengage Learning is a leading provider of customized learning solutions with office locations around the globe, including Singapore, the United Kingdom, Australia, Mexico, Brazil, and Japan. Locate your local office at:
international.cengage.com/region

Cengage Learning products are represented in Canada by Nelson Education, Ltd.

For your course and learning solutions, visit **www.cengage.com**

Purchase any of our products at your local college store or at our preferred online store **www.ichapters.com**

Instructors: Please visit **login.cengage.com** and log in to access instructor-specific resources.

Printed in the United States of America
3 4 5 14 13 12

Brief Contents

Contents

Chapter 6   Drafting, Revising, and Style   83

Part V Handbook   553

Chapter 19   Grammar Fundamentals   555

Chapter 20   Correcting Common Errors   574

Preface

Which is harder to do, write a textbook from scratch or revise an old edition already established in the marketplace? The answer is that it is harder to revise an existing work than to create a new one, for the simple reason that a book that has been around as long as this one has–the first edition appeared in 1977–tends to establish constituencies for its various features. Some instructors fall in love with a certain reading or feature and fight to retain it because they know that finding a book that works in the classroom is a treasure to both student and instructor. One gives up such a work only with great reluctance. A special vellum edition that was presented to the authors to commemorate sales of 100,000 copies in its first year shows the high regard in which this book was widely held. Today books simply do not begin life so spectacularly as this one did, or continue to live on, as this one does.

Enduring Features of This Book

Books do not acquire a long shelf life without good reason. In the case of *From Idea to Essay* its longevity is due mainly to its observance of the prime directive of textbooks on writing: above all else, be useful. Look at the table of contents and you'll quickly see that this book is no mere book—it is a veritable syllabus for a writing course. Take Chapter 7, for example, which teaches narration. It opens with a story, "The Code," in which the narrator doggedly sticks to his belief that he and his dying father share a fanatical commitment to atheism that surpasses all reason. When on his death bed his father turns to him for comfort, the son can offer no other support to help the dying man enter the cold and comfortless darkness of death than an idiotic unbending code. It is to the son's credit that he comes to see what a cheerless, cruel road he had sent his father on—alone and uncomforted— and to try, in his imagination, to say the words he should have said—but, alas, too late. This moving story is followed by a poem, "Richard Cory," which deals with a similar theme—pretense in being what you're not—and the awful consequences of that lie.

But wait—as they say in television commercials that sell sinister knives with improbable Oriental names—there's more! Both the story and poem are only introductions, intended to trigger the writing assignment, which is, "Have you ever had an experience that taught you a lesson about life? Write an essay about it." But before the student has written a single word, she is treated to specific instructions on doing the assignment. The instructions are arrayed under practical terms, such as "Prewrite on the assignment," "Be consistent in your point of view," "Have a theme," and "Pace your narration to focus on important scenes." Following these instructions is the essay as written by a professional writer, in this case, "A Gift of Laughter," about a childhood misunderstanding that the writer never forgot. In sum, we show, we tell, we show again, and we exemplify a writer's treatment of the topic—all this before the student, anxious to try his hand on the topic, taps the first key on the keyboard. All the writing chapters follow this identical organization. Any serious student who wishes to learn the craft of writing will find a treasure trove of rich material in *From Idea to Essay*.

New to the Thirteenth Edition

The reviser's touch does not fall equally on every page of a revision. It is finally what the writers have learned from their audience that determines what is scrubbed and polished versus what is merely dusted and buffed. In this edition most of our changes have occurred in the first six chapters. In addition, we have introduced a *talking mascot*—a miner who is sifting through the dirt for gold and whose search parallels the students' own search for meaning as potential writers. A little whimsicality never hurt even a serious topic, and laughter itself can set off an infectious echo. Among the major changes to this edition are the following:

- We have completely rewritten Chapter 1 to update the examples and to emphasize writing for real reasons, real audiences, and real patterns.
- Chapter 4 on planning and organizing the essay now precedes the chapter on the paragraph, which has been written to be more concise and student-friendly. The first six chapters have been heavily revised and shortened.
- We have changed many of the writing examples in Chapter 6, added a student example on specific details, and referred the student writer to the instructor for consultation on using a personal style rather than the preferred academic style that is expected.
- We have replaced the debate on same-sex marriage with a cluster argument exploring religion, race, and sexual identity.

Many incidental jobs of housekeeping have been performed throughout this revision, ranging from the rewriting of student examples to the introduction of new writing tips.

Other physical changes made to this book are so numerous as to be unnoticed. Among them are the following:

- The chapter and part openers have been redesigned to entice even the most hesitant student writer to turn the pages.

- An eye-catching scriptlike font has been introduced in the redesigned table of contents that highlights the chapters and crowns our colorful mascot, the miner sifting for gold, throughout Part II on writing the essay.
- Color has been used more judiciously and in greater frequency to improve readability and highlight pedagogy, including the Writing Tips and Student Tips.

Instructor's Manual

Available for download on the book companion website, the Instructor's Manual is intended to help instructors gauge students' mastery of the text. Included are answers to all questions and self-graded exercises in the book, as well as short quizzes to test reading comprehension of the professional essays in Chapters 7 to 15.

Book Companion Website

Visit the book companion website to access valuable course resources. Resources for students include an extensive library of interactive exercises and animations that cover grammar, diction, mechanics, punctuation, research, and writing concepts, as well as a complete library of student papers and a section on avoiding plagiarism. Instructors will find sample syllabi, web resources, and a downloadable Instructor's Manual.

Acknowledgments

We have benefited from the advice given to us by many loyalist and some new users, to whom we say thanks. We are deeply grateful to the reviewers of this edition, who offered many helpful suggestions: Marina P. Agrafiotis, California University of Pennsylvania; Carol Bledsoe, Florida Gulf Coast University; John Colagrande, Jr., Miami-Dade College; Janet Crosier, Springfield Technical Community College; Meredith A. Love-Steinmetz, Francis Marion University; and Becky Lee Meadows, St. Catharine College.

Our special and deep appreciation goes to Larry Goldberg, our development editor, who suggested new essays, shared new ideas with us, prodded us to keep deadlines, and encouraged us not to lose our nerve in being creative. Trish O'Kane, our project manager, should also be commended, who worked tirelessly to shepherd this project from manuscript to printed book. Others who supported or worked on the project include Monica Eckman, executive editor; Margaret Leslie, acquisitions editor; Amy Haines, assistant editor; Elizabeth Ramsey, editorial assistant; Margaret Bridges, content project manager; Stacey Purviance, marketing communications manager; Ryan Ahern, marketing coordinator; Katie Huha, text permissions editor; Jennifer Myer Dare, image permissions editor; and Janine Tangney, associate media editor.

Jo Ray McCuen-Metherell

Anthony C. Winkler

From Idea to Essay
A Rhetoric, Reader, and Handbook

PART I

Fundamentals

Chapter 1

The Writing Process

Expository writing, the focus of this book, is writing that explains, discusses, describes, analyzes, and argues—the bulk of everyday tasks that you'll most likely be called upon to do in your career. It includes every kind of workaday writing job you can think of, ranging from memos and descriptions to evaluations, summaries, and formal proposals. In primary school you learned how to form letters and words using pen or pencil. In this class you will move beyond the physical act of writing to learning how to express your ideas and to express them well. You will learn the art and technique of expository writing—the beast of burden in the transactions of business and everyday life.

Although words can be molded into a variety of literary and grammatical forms, most of these constructions, except for a precious few, will remain modest artifacts of everyday living. It is a harsh truth that for every "Gettysburg Address" millions of graveside eulogies have been written and read without the world taking any notice. To believe that expository writing, if done well, will lead to fame and fortune is to be badly mistaken. Most expository writing is pragmatic and unglamorous.

Here is an example of the kind of expository writing you are likely to find yourself doing regularly. The note below was sent to one of your authors by a two-person sales team hoping to have made the winning bid for adding a porch room to the author's house.

Dear Mr. and Mrs. Winkler:

Thank you for your hospitality and interest in the Cool Breeze patio room project. Sam and I enjoyed our visit and hope we provided all the information needed for you to make a wise investment decision. Please let us know what you decide. Remember our warning against the use of unsuitable material in outdoor patio construction which is likely to lead to dry rot and premature damage to the structure. If you choose our company, be assured that your project will receive our personal oversight care to ensure that you will be happy with your new room and with the appropriate resistance to weathering you have the right to expect.

Here, taken from a student paper, is an example of a paragraph defining the speaker of a poem:

> You open a book and begin reading a short poem. According to the title line, it is written by one John Ball who tells you a story about the day he lost his cat. It was a miserable day, according to John Ball. He misses his cat very much, especially at bedtime when they used to snuggle together before going to sleep. Who is John Ball? He's the speaker of the poem you've just read. He's a consciousness invented by the poet as a way of mounting the poem. If you had no poem, you'd have no speaker. And if you had no speaker, you'd have no poem.

Neither sample is sophisticated or oratorical; but both examples have the advantage of clarity and directness—prized in any kind of writing but especially so in expository prose.

What Is Good Writing?

Clarity is the aim of good expository writing. There are many ways to achieve this clarity—depending on the temperament of the writer—but the surest way of all is by repeated rewriting. The irony is that many students regard rewriting as clumsy and a sign of their ineptness as writers. This is as far from the truth as the earth is from the sun. Composing with a back-and-forth movement over the emerging text is exactly how most professional writers work. They crisscross the text over and over again, making little changes with every pass, until they are satisfied. In the movies, the climactic scene of a biopic on a writer's life often shows a kind of miraculous breakthrough for the writer, who not only survives a drunken weekend but also manages to compose something eternally splendid in the process. However, this depiction is far removed from fact.

The truth is that almost all writers compose by repeatedly going back and forth over the text until they've got it right. Researchers have even given the process a name—calling it *recursive*—a word whose root meaning suggests a revisiting or bending back on the self. As a generally descriptive word of what the writing process entails, this word is accurate if not utterly precise.

If there is one universal characteristic of all good expository writing, it is the powerful effect the writing has on the reader. If it is a written argument, it will be persuasive. If it is a description, it will be vivid. If it is an explanation, it will be clear. Exactly why one word or one sentence is better than another can be explained after the fact. What is difficult to do is to say how to produce on demand such an obvious effect.

Good writing of this kind cannot be taught. It can, however, be learned. And it can be learned in a classroom such as this one, which allows students the freedom to experiment as well as the opportunity to practice. For the truth is, the more you write, the better your writing will be. The improvement, however, will be sporadic rather than slow and sustained like the gains of daily exercise. A better metaphor for the progress of the writer is the archer whose arrow is more likely to hit the target with regular practicing. But no guarantee can be given for the absolute accuracy of any one shot.

Learning to write well can also offer additional benefits that are likely to improve your performance in other classes. Mastering the art of writing well will better arm you for the day-to-day clash of contending opinion you will encounter your whole life. English Composition may strike you as an overly academic course that spends too much time nagging about picky grammatical errors and hairsplitting rules of punctuation, but it is a mistake to misjudge its usefulness.

True, the classroom is an imitation of life, not an exact duplicate. English departments teach writing by trying to mimic the conditions under which real writers work. Assignments are made, deadlines set, and an imaginary audience sometimes created for a particular writing job. However, even the most realistic scenario is sometimes overwhelmed by the improbabilities. For example, for whom does the student write? On the face of it, your instructor is your only audience and the one person you must please. But that arrangement is more complex than it appears. True, the instructor is the main reader of your work, but that relationship is similar to having a boss in the real world to whom you must submit your reports and memos. What is different is that your instructor brings an exposure to and a broad grasp of writing throughout the ages that cannot be found in the narrow field of any business or occupation. In the classroom you are also free to experiment with your writing without running the risk of being fired, which is a far harsher penalty than earning an "F."

The Process and Structure of Writing

Expository writing may be divided into two main parts: process and structure. Process is inferred rather than seen because it is the preparation made behind the scenes, before putting words down on paper. This *prewriting* process involves exploring, inventing, scribbling at random, focusing ideas, or any other way of coming to terms with the writing assignment. Structure, on the other hand, refers to the form in which the writer's ideas are molded and expressed. It could be a poem, a short story, a play, or a parable; but in a class on expository writing, the structure would most likely be an essay. Structure is as visible as a skeleton. If an idea is expressed as a poem, the layout on the page will reflect that form. More often than not, an essay will look like an essay, a poem like a poem, a short story like a short story, and so on. Whatever literary type is used will be made clear by the appropriate form.

The process of writing is remarkably similar from writer to writer. And it defies what students often think about writing and writers. Many students, for example, worry about the slow pace of composing, which they think springs from their ineptitude. In effect they say to themselves, "I can't write; that's why I keep going back over what I've written." That false conclusion is used by many students to reinforce their imagined inability to write.

How Many Drafts?

Most instructors suggest at least three. Of course, it is possible to produce a good paper with the first draft. But it is also possible, and more likely, that producing a good or excellent paper will take a dozen or more drafts. With writing, as with everything else, the harder you work, the better you will write.

Research on how writers actually compose shows that this back-and-forth movement is typical of professional writers. When we get stuck, most of us have the tendency to gaze around the room and to chew on our pens. Professional writers, in contrast, reread what they have written, making changes and corrections until they come to where they were stuck. And if they're still stuck? They do the same thing all over again, confident that eventually they'll get unstuck. This back-and-forth movement of composing is called "recursive," meaning action that is circular and comes back around again and again. One generalization we can make about the writing process is that most writers rewrite their work. Typically they will produce multiple drafts until they're satisfied. As the saying goes around English departments, "There is no writing; there's only rewriting."

Personal Versus Objective Writing

Writing may be divided into two broad categories: personal and objective. *Personal writing* is writing in which you and your feelings and opinions take center stage. Your aim is to say how you feel or think. The opinions you express in personal writing generally do not need to be supported or proved, because they are, after all, yours alone and no one else's. For instance, if you describe your fury at having to clean up your roommate's breakfast dishes every morning, no reader will ask you to provide evidence of your emotional reaction. Emotional reactions are personal and therefore do not require corroboration. With its emphasis on the self, personal writing is regarded as the easier of the two categories.

On the other hand, *objective writing* focuses impartially on a subject. It expresses and supports your opinions on the subject, but in a scholarly way, with your ego, the *I*, staying in the background. When you give an opinion, you must say why you hold it and justify it with facts and with the views of others. Most college textbooks, for instance, are examples of objective writing because the authors or editors do not allow their personal emotions to intrude on their work. They usually stick to their subjects through thick and thin, expressing neither anger nor ecstasy over any chapter or segment.

Here are some examples of personal writing topics:

The beauties I experienced camping at Yosemite

The best job I ever had

My dog Fritz and I

Why I want to master the guitar

The poverty into which I was born

Here are some objective writing topics:

Summer vacations are too long

How to find a job

What are animal rights?

The difference between soft rock and hard rock music

The effects of poverty on Detroit

The line between personal and objective subjects is not always clear. The same subject treated one way may be personal, whereas treated another way, it may be objective. Here, for example, is a personal paragraph on depression:

> When my older sister went through a bout of depression, she was not the only one who suffered. My parents agonized; her friends worried; her college instructors were mystified. In other words, all involved with my sister also suffered. It was frightening to deal with her depression because we feared that she would take her own life. I firmly believe that anyone found to be seriously depressed should be encouraged instantly to seek psychotherapy because the latest advances in psychology and medicine have produced therapy and medication that can help even the severest disorders.

Here is an objective essay on the same topic:

> According to "Health Responsibility Systems, Inc.," an electronic essay retrieved from America Online, nine million American adults suffer from some kind of depressive illness within any six-month period. Depressive illnesses torment not only the victims but also those who care for them. Parents agonize; friends worry; teachers are mystified. Everyone involved suffers. If the victim is uncommunicative and deeply pessimistic, that mood eventually spreads to the loved ones. If the victim is suicidal, that possibility inflicts terror on all around the sufferer. It is imperative that anyone seriously depressed instantly seek medical treatment because the latest advances in psychology and medicine have produced therapy and medication that can help even the most severe disorders.

Most of us prefer personal over objective writing assignments and find them easier to do. We have done them since kindergarten and have years of experience scribbling thank-you notes for birthday presents. Many student writers also find it hard to write at length without using *I*. And just as many teachers firmly believe that *I* has no business in an objective essay.

Take heart, however. Writing without the use of *I* is not hard to do once you have practiced doing so a number of times. Nor is it particularly hard to express an opinion in an objective, rather than a merely personal, way. Moreover, learning how to write objectively is a useful skill that will be of great value later on in your life as you cover legal reports, contact business partners for urgent information, or demand your constitutional rights when they are threatened. Most of the writing you will be asked to do for this book will be objective rather than personal. Even so, it is only a small step from writing Grandma a thank-you note for a birthday gift to writing a report to explain why a certain product is not selling.

Generating Ideas with Journal Writing

A journal is a personal record of your thoughts. It is not intended to be a timetable or an exact account of how your day passed. Instead, it should be a collection of your personal observations and innermost feelings. What makes a journal significant is its absolute privacy, which enables you to say exactly what you think and precisely how you feel. If you use a journal to catalog every little flea bite that happened during the course of a day, it will do you little good, now or later. Here, for example, is an excerpt from a journal kept by a woman named Elizabeth Fuller (1776–1856) that is so full of picky details as to be utterly useless:

May, 1791
1—Sabbath I went to meeting today.
2—I spun five skeins today.
3—I spun five skeins today.
4—I spun two skeins today finished the Warp for this Piece. Nathan Perry worked here this p.m.
5—I spun four skeins of tow to the piece I have been spinning. Pa went to Worchester to get the newspaper. Nathan Perry here this eve.
6—I spun four skeins today.
7—I spun four skeins today.

This journal does little more than convince us of the dullness of the writer's life. As a springboard for ideas, it is plainly useless.

What makes a journal priceless is that it tends to act as an outlet for our feelings. We often have no idea how we feel about an incident or an episode until we try to write about it. Then, for some odd reason, when we begin to scribble down our impressions, we are often surprisingly candid about how we really feel.

The first step to journal writing is to keep a notebook handy. Sometimes even scratch paper will do. Professional writers have admitted scribbling ideas on grocery bags, envelopes, and restaurant napkins—anything and anywhere. Some beginning and professional writers use an iPhone, which has a notes feature, or any cell phone or electronic device with similar capabilities. Any method of notetaking—electronic or otherwise—is acceptable, just so long as you can record your thoughts on the spur of the moment. Here are some guidelines for keeping your own journal:

1. Use your journal to record your impressions about life, not necessarily to register every single incident in it. The point is to say how you feel, not to give a strict account of what happened. Of course, if something extraordinary happens to you during the course of the day, then naturally it belongs in your journal.

2. Write on a fairly regular basis, but only when you feel like it. To become fixated about keeping a journal is to rob the process of all its fun and to turn it into yet another chore.

3. Write down anything you feel like saying. Journal writing is a kind of talking to yourself. What you write is for your eyes only; it is not intended to be read by anyone else. Here are a few examples of topics to consider writing about:

    A person, private or public, who made a remark that impressed or surprised you

    An event during the day that either hurt your feelings or made you happy

    An action or comment you regret

    A cartoon that made a point

    A striking passage in a book you are reading

The point is to connect your feelings with daily life. Once you cultivate the habit of being perfectly honest in your journal, you will be surprised at what your entries reveal about you.

You can return to the miscellaneous entries you make in your journal and consider them later as topics for full-blown writing assignments. For instance, one student wrote in his journal about his pet octopus, which he kept in an aquarium in his room. When asked to write an essay describing his favorite pet, he drew on the experiences with the octopus he had recorded in his journal. Here is one of many journal entries about Seven, the pet octopus:

May 5, 1999
    Came home from work late night and spent an hour playing with Seven. I don't know whether Seven's a boy or a girl, but I always think she's a girl. I've had her now for almost a year. She's missing a tentacle, which the man I bought her from says was

chewed off by a moray eel. She's very gentle and intelligent, and if you didn't know she had an injury, you'd never know she was handicapped the way she bravely scoots around the aquarium. After playing with her for almost an hour, I got tired and went to bed. She looked disappointed as I turned off the light.

Parts of this passage and others were incorporated into an essay on a favorite pet. Here's one paragraph of that essay:

> My favorite pet is an octopus I call Seven because she's missing an arm. The man I bought her from said the arm was eaten off by a moray eel when Seven was very young. Her mobility is only slightly disrupted by her missing arm. She is two years old and is fully grown for her species. Seven has beautiful purple tones with contrasting pink streaks. She is approximately five inches long and glides effortlessly in my forty-gallon aquarium. Seven has no hair or whiskers anywhere on her body, so her skin always feels smooth as silk. She can change the color and texture of her skin to blend with the various colors of her surroundings, but she usually remains purple. Her seven arms bear two rows of suckers on each. The suckers on her arms are very sensitive and feel like the tongue of a dog. There is a deep groove between her rows of suckers, and each arm ends with a spoonlike tip. Each of her suckers is two millimeters in length and has a sticky, filmy layer on it. Seven has a soft body with two large, complex eyes that do not protrude from her head. She has a tiny beak on her head, just below her almond-shaped eyes, that resembles the lens of a camera. With her razor-sharp vision, she flinches at any quick movement outside her aquarium. She has made herself a home by pulling two small corals together with her suckers.

A journal is not only useful in helping you develop possible writing assignments, but it can also give you a place to blow off steam or simply mull over how you feel about the events in your life. For this reason alone, keeping a journal is well worth the effort.

Assembling a Portfolio

Assembling a portfolio means gathering samples of your best work in a folder to be reviewed and judged later. The idea is to give you practice at evaluating your own writing. Even if your instructor does not require a formal portfolio, we recommend that you create one for your own use over the term of this course. Choosing your best work for a portfolio will sharpen your critical faculties and give you an editor's eye.

A portfolio will also preserve samples of your college writing long after you have left school. To the student grappling with the task of mastering composition, the idea of preserving the work produced during these trying days may seem ridiculous. Trust us on this point, however. Long after you have passed the course and settled into middle age, the day will come when you will regard your student essays in a more kindly light and wish you had even saved some of them for the grandchildren who are still years away.

Writing Assignments

1. Write a brief statement in which you provide examples of the process you use for writing in college. What aspects of writing cause you the most frustration? At what point are you the most satisfied with your writing?

2. If you were to write an objective assessment of universal health care in our country, what kinds of phrases might you avoid in order to keep your essay impartial? List several and state why you would avoid them. (The internet can provide you with numerous blogs that are obviously personal reactions rather than objective assessments.)

3. What steps do you take before you actually begin to write an essay? In a brief passage, describe these steps and how they contribute to your efforts at writing. If you never prewrite, give a justification for your habit of plunging straight into a writing assignment. Research the methods of writing and composing practiced by any well-known writer. Describe them in a brief essay, and explain how they differ from your own.

4. Make entries in a journal over the course of a week. Then review the journal to find an entry you can use for a writing topic, and write a short essay about it.

Chapter 2

Critical Thinking, Reading, and Seeing

Thinking and reading are both necessary links in a writer's intellectual chain of being. All writers are thinkers. They engage in a systematic kind of thinking known as critical thinking. Likewise, writers are regular readers of novels, newspapers, and magazines. We have never known a writer who was not a thinker. Nor have we ever known a writer who was not a habitual reader.

Critical Thinking

Critical thinking means thinking with selectivity and judgment. Its opposite is superficial thinking characterized by laziness where propositions and viewpoints are accepted too lightly. Critical thinking does much of this assessment and evaluation by making inferences and drawing conclusions.

Students are often confused by the differences in the words *implication* and *inference*. To *imply* means to hint or indirectly suggest that something is true. To *infer* means to draw a conclusion from something we read about or heard. The implication is not based on rock solid evidence, but neither is the inference. Both, however, are legitimate means of arguing, especially of complex ideas and propositions. You may correctly imply something in what you say, and a reader or listener may incorrectly infer meaning from what someone says, but it is always incorrect to say "I imply from your words that you don't trust the candidate" or "From what you infer in your statement, you don't trust the candidate." This kind of misuse of these two words, *infer and imply*, is quite common in everyday speech. Just remember that you do not *infer* meaning from what you write anymore than you *imply* it from what you read.

The opposite of critical thinking is the habit of uncritically accepting every proposition at its face value, questioning nothing and assuming each conclusion entirely proven, even on thin or lacking evidence. No one deliberately sets out to think this way; it's simply a point of view that springs from bad habits and laziness.

Here are some tips for thinking critically.

Separate Opinion from Fact

A fact is a bit of information whose truth is verifiable. An opinion is a strictly personal belief. The distinction between the two may sometimes seem fuzzy, particularly when a person speaks with conviction about a belief. But no matter how persuasive someone is about a personal opinion, it does not qualify as a fact unless it is verifiable.

Take the example of a local pizzeria. You have a friend who considers its pizza the best in the known universe. That is not a verifiable truth for the simple reason that the universe of pizza cannot be adequately sampled, and if it could be, the sampling would be corrupted by personal opinion. On the other hand, the statement "Every Monday night Johnny's Pizza offers $2 off the price of a large pizza" is verifiable by a telephone call. If it is true, it's a fact. If it isn't true, it's a rumor or an outright lie.

Sometimes there is disagreement about whether a particular statement is fact or opinion. For example, some scientists believe that global warming is not a demonstrable fact. Others point to the warming effect on the earth because of the corresponding build-up of carbon dioxide in the atmosphere. Where the truth lies is still unresolved. The critical thinker takes into account both sides and tries to determine which viewpoint is better supported by the evidence.

One of the first questions a critical thinker should ask is what motive a writer or speaker has for making a statement. If there is a self-serving motive, the critical thinker will question the validity and sincerity of the message. For example, someone trying to sell you an SUV may go on at length about its off-road capabilities and its ability to deal with bad weather conditions. What that person probably won't tell you is what a gas hog the SUV is and how difficult it is to park and maneuver such a bulky vehicle around town.

Faced with deciding whether a statement is an opinion or a fact, the critical thinker must move to check its verifiability. If the statement is not verifiable, it cannot be considered a fact. However, sometimes fact and opinion are reversed by history. An example is Galileo's observation made 350 years ago that the Earth revolves around the sun, which at the time was regarded as a heretical opinion. For daring to suggest what was contrary to the teachings of the church, Galileo was forced by threats to make a humiliating public retraction. Three hundred and fifty years later, the pope formally apologized and admitted that Galileo was right.

Some issues are so complex that the distinction between fact and opinion seems perpetually muddled. Take, for example, the debate over Social Security. Is it really going bankrupt, as some insist, or have the latest increases in taxes been enough to ensure the survival of the system? Even when you dig through the numbers and examine all the projections, it is difficult to come to a definitive conclusion. Other issues are so specialized as to leave the determination of fact or opinion entirely to the experts. DNA testing, whose analysis depends on the services and testimonies of experts, is one such issue. Because DNA analysis is always done by experts rather than amateurs, a case frequently depends entirely on the testimony of specialists whose opinion is regarded, by default, as fact. In such cases, you are at the mercy of the expert, but in our complex world that has become a common condition.

The whole point of critical thinking is to question the assumption and reasoning behind a proposition or argument. For example, in a letter to the editor a reader wrote that condoms "have a 22% failure rate in preventing pregnancy and a 15% failure rate in preventing HIV." No source is cited for these numbers, and since the writer belongs to an organization that opposes the distribution of condoms to teenagers, the critical thinker will automatically question the accuracy and origin of these statistics.

No number sounds more impressive than a statistic. No number is more frequently twisted to throw a favorable light on one side of an issue. For example, the sample statistic about condoms can serve another purpose. That condoms are successful 85% of the time in stopping the transmission of HIV might strike us as reason enough to urge their distribution (15% failure means 85% success), especially when we recognize that engaging in sex without condoms is one of the major ways of spreading HIV. Statistics can be as deceptive as the sales pitches of snake oil salesmen, and critical thinkers are smart to take such numbers with a grain of salt.

■ *Exercise*

Decide which statement is a fact and which is an opinion in each pair of statements that follows. Be prepared to discuss your choice in class.

1. a. Muslims tend to be extremists in their religious pursuits.
   b. Muslims believe in one God, Allah, and in Muhammad, his prophet.

2. a. Mao Zedong helped found the Chinese Communist Party in 1921 and led the Long March of 1934–1935 through China.
   b. Mao Zedong was a Chinese hero whom everyone should admire for his devotion to the poverty-ridden people of China.

3. a. Men are better cooks than women.
   b. Paul Bocuse has received many awards for his creative French cuisine.

4. a. Carl Sandburg wrote a poem comparing fog to a cat slithering around the corner of a building.
   b. People who live in foggy areas of the world are usually mentally depressed.

5. a. Between 2000 and 2010, the U.S. faced some enormous challenges, such as the terrorist attack on the twin towers in New York (2001), reporter Daniel Pearl being kidnapped and murdered in Pakistan (2002), Hurricane Katrina striking New Orleans (2005), and the U.S. economy plunging to its lowest level since the Great Depression (2008).
   b. The 2000s should be called the Decade of Broken Dreams or the Decade from Hell because so many horrible things happened in the world to discourage both the young and the elderly.

6. a. Prague is undoubtedly the most beautiful city in the modern world.
   b. Prague is the capital of the Czech Republic.

7. a. A tsunami is the most frightening and destructive force in nature.
   b. In January 2005 a tsunami killed more than 250,000 people in Indonesia, India, Thailand, and Sri Lanka.

8. a. The fact that in 2009 U.S. medical schools admitted as many female as male applicants proves that women physicians are considered just as valuable or competent as men.
   b. It's about time our country recognize that women have finally shattered the glass ceiling that for many years has prevented them from being as successful as men.

9. a. The Belle Epoque was one of our country's most glamorous and exciting periods—a time when the super wealthy in the U.S. imitated their European counterparts by living self-centered and lavish lifestyles in huge mansions situated on prime property in several parts of the country.
   b. In its 2010 Cartier exhibit of Belle Epoque jewellery, the San Francisco Palace of the Legion of Honour displayed twelve rooms filled with diamond tiaras, necklaces, watches, and other pieces, owned by wealthy customers like Consuela Vanderbilt, the Duchess of Windsor, and Gloria Swanson.

10. a. No one, including those who kill savagely in the heat of passion, deserves the death penalty, which is a vestige of barbaric times when individual human life had little worth.
    b. On December 14, 2004, a jury sentenced a mentally ill man to death by lethal injection for murdering his wife and unborn child.

Critical Reading

Critical reading, a blood relation of critical thinking, **compels you** to see both sides of an issue, to recognize the bias in an opinion, and to welcome new ideas. It is the direct opposite of the kind of leisurely reading people do on the beach in summer. Critical reading is active, energetic, and focused. While this kind of reading is demanding, it is also rewarding. Here are some guidelines to help you read critically.

Understand What You Read

How many times have you read a book for pleasure and come across a passage that you didn't understand? Chances are that has happened to you at some point with every book you've ever read. And chances are that you just moved on without rereading the passage and trying to get its meaning.

The critical reader, however, never lets an incomprehensible passage pass. If it is necessary to look up an unfamiliar word or to ask a friend to explain what the writer is trying to say, the critical reader will do it. The golden rule of critical reading is therefore this: Understand what you read.

Look for Biases and Hidden Prejudices

Biases and prejudices are part of the human condition. An atheist to whom a fertilized human egg is a soulless clump of cells will enthusiastically support stem cell research. The same research will be bitterly opposed by a Christian fundamentalist who believes that the fertilized egg has an inborn soul.

An opponent who has a strong bias for or against the topic is not entirely unexpected and may even give you an advantage if you can expose the bias as illogical. There is no law that stipulates that every idea has to be logically consistent with every other, but people do prefer arguments and arguers to be clear and open about their biases.

Don't Be Seduced by Phony Claim

Phony claims, common in advertising, also crop up often in arguments. For example, we once heard a television evangelist argue that male homosexuality was instigated by Satan. We've also heard pop psychologists argue that male homosexuality springs from a domineering mother. Neither claim is substantiated by research. Some homosexuals were raised in families dominated by the mother; so were some heterosexuals. And no research has yet been able to establish even a tenuous link between sexual preference and Satan. Come to think of it, no research has been able to isolate Satan in a test tube.

Annotate Your Reading

The best way to read critically is to jot down your reactions to the material in the margin of the book you're reading. We're not encouraging you to deface books that are not your own. You should never write in the margins of a rare book, such as the one that came down to you from your grandparents. Common sense also advises against writing in the margin of any book that you plan to resell.

In other cases, though, we encourage you to write in your own books. Jotting down your reactions in the margins of a book keeps you actively involved in grasping the writer's meaning. Many reading experts encourage this practice, which requires you to pause and think about what the writer is saying. Basically, you should record your first reactions to the reading. Later, when you return to this reading, your notes will remind you of this initial reaction. For an example of the kinds of notes you might make, see the poem on page 18.

The notes you make are for your personal use and do not need to be grammatical, witty, or in your best style. They can be one-word interjections, such as "Nonsense!" beside a paragraph whose ideas you disagree with. What you are after is a brief response—the margin of a typical book is not big enough for anything else. But since your marginal notes are intended only for your personal use, you can use any kind of shorthand you want to express your reactions.

Here are some other suggestions for approaching the readings in this book so they will help produce specific ideas for your own writing:

- **Stop and reread any passage that grabs your attention.** If you especially like the way the writer expressed a particular idea, say so, even if you write only "Wow!"

- **If you agree or disagree with the writer, say so and why.** Try to apply the writer's ideas, thoughts, and recollections to your own experiences.

- **Make a list of key ideas that you might explore in an essay.** For instance, reading Ernest Hemingway's short story "In Another Country" might generate a discussion about how "shell-shocked" soldiers were once treated versus how veterans suffering from "traumatic battle fatigue" are treated today.

- **Ask some basic questions about the work.** For example, what support does the author offer for the thesis? Is this support adequate and convincing? What is it lacking?

- **Don't be intimidated by the fact that the author is published.** Writers make fools of themselves as much on the printed page as on the handwritten one. For instance, Hemingway wrote rhapsodic passages about the beauty of bull fighting, a lot of which today would strike a proponent of animal rights as utter nonsense. If you are one of them, express yourself here and now.

- **Point to noteworthy stylistic effects in the material—symbols, metaphors, similes, or vivid images.** For instance, the poem "Richard Corey" (p. 18) uses the expression "he glittered when he walked." You might note this strong metaphor. In Luigi Pirandello's short story "War" (p. 410), you could mention how the train functions as a symbolic microcosm of society. On the other hand, if you think an image is over the top, don't be afraid to say so. Remember, you're writing for yourself; as a critical thinker, you're entitled to your opinion.

- **Pay attention to the tone of the writing, which will indicate the writer's attitude toward the subject.** For example, in Pirandello's "War" the grandiose speech made by the bereaved father about how his son died like a happy patriot in the war uses an ironic tone; that is, the father is not being truthful or saying what he really means. His true feelings become apparent only at the end of the story, when he realizes that his son is dead and gone forever and he breaks into "harrowing, heartrending, uncontrollable sobs."

Writing notes in the margins of a book is a freewheeling practice. You can write anything you desire. There's no right way or wrong way to do it. You can underline key ideas, draw check marks or exclamation points next to ideas you find debatable, and jot down questions when you are puzzled. All these techniques are part of reading actively rather than passively. They allow you to hold a conversation with the text and, indirectly, with the author. They make reading fun!

POEM

EDWIN ARLINGTON ROBINSON

Richard Cory

Edwin Arlington Robinson (1869–1935) was regarded during his lifetime as the greatest U.S. poet. He was born in Head Tide, Maine, and educated at Harvard University. His many volumes of verse include The Children of the Night (1897), The Man Who Died Twice (1924; Pulitzer Prize), and Tristram (1928; Pulitzer Prize). Robinson, who never married, lived a life of quiet reclusiveness, spending many of his summers in New Hampshire at the MacDowell Colony for artists and writers.

[annotation: I must never forget that looks are deceptive.]

1 Whenever Richard Cory went down town,
We people on the pavement looked at him:
He was a gentleman from sole to crown,
Clean favored, and imperially slim.

[annotation: This dude reminds me of Dennis, the son of my orthopedic surgeon.]
[annotation: ordinary people]

2 And he was always quietly arrayed,
And he was always human when he talked;
But still he fluttered pulses when he said,
"Good-morning," and he glittered when he walked.

[annotation: He wore conservative clothes.]
[annotation: Amazing image]

3 And he was rich—yes, richer than a king—
And admirably schooled in every grace:
In fine, we thought that he was everything
To make us wish that we were in his place.

[annotation: Howard Hughes, in the movie Aviator, is this kind of person.]

4 So on we worked, and waited for the light,
And went without the meat, and cursed the bread;
And Richard Cory, one calm summer night,
Went home and put a bullet through his head.

[annotation: big success]
[annotation: Wow! I didn't expect this ending.]
[annotation: Image of how most people struggle to make ends meet.]

■ *Exercise*

After studying the following passages, explain in writing the prejudice or bias that underlies each statement.

1. Since Jack underwent a triple heart bypass last year, he should not be appointed chair of our Language Arts Division.
2. No kid under the age of 21 should be allowed to seek medical treatment for a sexually transmitted disease, have an abortion, or buy contraceptives without at least one parent's authorization.

3. You know, his father is German, so you can imagine how strictly the poor guy was brought up.

4. Swimming ten laps in a pool five days a week is the best exercise for your heart.

5. Fred loves ballet, and he makes his living sewing women's clothes. Isn't it obvious that he is gay?

6. If the U.S. Government had not supported UNSCOP'S 1948 creation of a formal state of Israel, the Jihadist movement would never have evolved.

7. Everyone needs at least eight hours of sleep per night. I can't function unless I sleep at least eight hours.

8. Enroll in Professor Fowler's class. He is a marvelous economics professor. He rarely gives any student an F.

9. She wears a silver ring on her tongue and has a huge giraffe tattoo above her panty line. Now, can you just imagine what kind of mother brought her up?

10. Don't elect him president of our class. Save him for playing in the band at our senior party. His African-American background makes him a great player of the blues.

Critical Seeing

Critical seeing means seeing the whole picture—with both your eyes and your brain. Doing this in today's world is an act of self-defense. Ours is a visual world that constantly bombards us with images intended to influence our judgment. We see images on billboards, on the internet, in magazines, in newspapers, and on that mother of all image generators, television. At some point during the day someone will try to influence us with a visual image.

This unending flow of images is not necessarily bad. An image, whether a picture, a drawing, or a sign, can be informative, even lifesaving. You would be foolish, for example, to ignore a sign that warns against a slippery roadway with the image of a skidding car. What we need to do as we make our way through an increasingly visual world is learn how to react rationally to images so that we can benefit from them without being over influenced. In broad strokes, then, here are some questions to ask yourself as you cope with visual images.

1. **What is the purpose of the visual image?** Behind every published image is a motive. Most of the time the image is intended to get us to buy a product or service. Occasionally an image will serve a double purpose. For example, a highway billboard may advertise a restaurant while announcing an upcoming exit. Many images, however, have no particular point beyond being highly political, even preachy. The trick is to find the

purpose behind the image. For example, Pablo Picasso's mural, *Guernica,* is a strong protest against the savage bombing of that small Basque village by the Nazis on April 26, 1937. If you did not know the purpose behind it, this odd mural would seem a meaningless jumble.

2. **What is the pitch behind the image?** Behind every commercial image is a pitch. It may be for a new car, a brand of underwear, a cell phone plan, or a vacation spot. In any case, be aware that advertisers stack their images with catchy themes and attractive figures, often at the expense of reality. You must weigh what is shown against the reality you instinctively know. No matter what an image might suggest, you will not be whisked away to an upscale neighborhood pool teeming with stylish jet-setters if you wear a certain brand shirt.

3. **What is the context of the image?** A photograph in a newsmagazine has an entirely different context than a photograph in a brochure advertising a luxury car. Often a news photograph reflects the energy of real life and radiates a spontaneous urgency. A brochure, on the other hand, has the deliberateness of a posed and rehearsed shot that is likely to make the car look better than it does in real life. Knowing the context enriches an image with meaning. For example, the famous photograph of the leveled ruins of Hiroshima, Japan, following the August 6, 1945, atomic bombing would be meaningless if you did not know the context.

4. **What information does the image communicate?** Prose communicates with words; images communicate with graphics. A photo of the scrawny child of a migrant worker may communicate the plight of these often exploited people and the harsh conditions under which they generally live. A work of art may communicate an idea, an emotional moment, or a novel view of familiar objects. *The Starry Night* by Vincent van Gogh shows us the stars as spectacular, whirling spirals of light, communicating the unique vision of its painter.

5. **What does the image mean to me?** Our reactions to images are so personal that we express them as feelings rather than as judgments. The usual comment made about an image is either "I like it" or "I don't like it." To have a certain feeling about an image is fine—artwork, in particular, often provokes highly individualistic responses. But it is more insightful if you also know why you like or dislike a particular visual image. What, exactly, did a particular image bring to mind that made you like or dislike it? What does your reaction say about you or the image?

6. **What is the subtext of the image?** Some images have a *subtext*—a message that is implied but not openly stated. Sometimes this subtext is meant to be funny. For example, a 1988 cartoon by *Far Side* creator Gary Larson shows in the foreground a sign that says "Bates Motel," and in the background, a wooden house on the hill with three figures silhouetted against

the topmost window. One of the figures is saying in a balloon, "Say hello to our new houseguest, Mother." The text of the cartoon reads, "What really happened to Elvis." Unsaid in the subtext is the twisted answer—that Elvis was killed by the insane mother of Norman Bates, the main character in the movie *Psycho*. If you didn't know about the movie *Psycho,* you would entirely miss the subtext, as well as the humor, of this cartoon.

Throughout this book you will occasionally be asked to write a paragraph or an essay about an image. Such an assignment might seem novel to you, but it really is only a variation on the typical writing topic. You organize your material in the same way, use the same grammar, and more or less proceed through the same number of drafts—at least three. The main difference is that in writing about an image, you draw most of your supporting detail from the image itself.

Here are some practical ideas on how to write about visual material such as works of art, news photos, magazine and newspaper ads, and cartoons.

Responding to a Work of Art

No artist goes to the trouble of creating a work in the hope of getting a neutral response. Art is meant to affect people both emotionally and intellectually. Here are some guidelines for reacting to a work of art with both your heart and your brain:

- **Look carefully at the work, taking in everything about it, from top to bottom and from side to side.** Pay particular attention to its title, which might give you a clue to what the artist means. The title is particularly important in abstract paintings, where the image is based on an artist's imagination rather than on reality. The title of the painting shown on page 22, *The Senate*, gives the viewer a major clue to its subject matter. Once you have read this title, the corpulent man at the center of the painting, hands flung in the air and mouth wide open as he renders some rhetorical bombast, takes on a particular meaning. He is most likely a senator with an ax to grind.

- **Pay particular attention also to the body language of the person or people in the painting.** *Body language* means the impression a person gives by a facial expression or way of sitting, standing, or slumping. For example, the central figure in *The Senate* is standing up to give a passionate speech in the fierce style of King Lear or Winston Churchill. In sharp contrast, the other men in the almost empty chamber are indifferent to the speaker. One, slumped in one chair with his feet up on another, seems utterly bored with the orator. Another is reading a newspaper and ignoring the speaker's ranting. In the back of the room, we glimpse another apathetic figure—this one engrossed in a paper, perhaps waiting his turn to speak.

William Gropper (1897–1977). *The Senate.* 1935. Oil on canvas, 25 1/8″ × 33 1/8″. Gift of A. Conger Goodyear (180, 1936). Digital Image © The Museum of Modern Art/Licensed by SCALA/Art Resource

When you are writing, you should support your opinions by referring specifically to facts about the image. For example, if you're writing an essay about this painting, you should not merely say that the central figure is giving a speech and that no one is listening. You should clarify what visual evidence in the image leads you to this conclusion. Giving reasons to support your conclusion is no more than you would be asked to do in any other essay, but in an essay interpreting a painting or drawing your reasons and evidence must come from the image itself.

- **Respond both emotionally and intellectually.** Some writing assignments require objectivity from the writer. A paper about art is not one of them. Art demands both an intellectual and an emotional response. Do you like the work, or do you hate it? Share your feelings with the reader and say what specifically you like or dislike about the painting or drawing. A work of art makes its point through the use of color, shading, setting, and lines. In

The Senate, for instance, the desks, chairs, and papers all are squares that surround the rotund orator. The room is not the ornate chamber we are used to seeing on television, and the fat senator is neither appealing nor charming. Most people who study this painting find it a comical poke at a sacred U.S. institution, the Senate.

- **Check with the experts.** We all have our own feelings and opinions about any work of art. But it is at least interesting to see how they correspond with the views of experts. Art books and the internet can help you plumb the meaning of a complex or subtle work of art. You might also consult friends who regularly visit museums and art exhibitions. *The Senate* was painted in 1935 by William Gropper, an American painter who greatly admired the work of the French caricaturist, Honoré Daumier. According to Peter Self, an art professor at the University of California, Berkeley, Gropper, a harsh critic of the political establishment, painted *The Senate* to satirize the bombast, boredom, self-centeredness, and disaffection of Capitol Hill politicians.

■ *Exercise*

Using the internet as a research aid, choose a painting by one of your favorite artists. If you have no favorite, find a painting by one of the following: Sandro Botticelli, Sanzio Raphael, Auguste Renoir, Max Ernst, Diego Rivera, Alphonse Mucha, Pablo Picasso, Jacob Lawrence, Edward Hopper, Barbara Hepworth, Rosa Bonheur, or Mary Cassatt. Write an essay of approximately 300 words analyzing the work of art you chose. Use the guidelines supplied here.

Responding to a Photo

A photo and a painting are both visual images, and your responses to both are likely to be similar. Photos are usually more up to date and topical than paintings for the simple reason that it is easier to take a photograph than to paint a picture. Every day of our lives we are exposed to photos of every kind. We see so many everywhere around us that we sometimes forget how powerful a photograph can be. In writing about a photo, you should follow these guidelines:

- **Find the context for the photo.** When was the photo taken, and what does it show? Without this kind of context, it is difficult to react to any photo, much less write about it. For example, the image on p. 24 reveals the scene of an apparent disaster. It is a photo of the panic that took place following the catastrophic earthquake that struck Haiti on January 12, 2010. Most likely, now that you know what the photo is about, your reaction is quite different than it was when you thought you were looking at the aftermath of some unidentified mayhem. Like most Americans, you probably

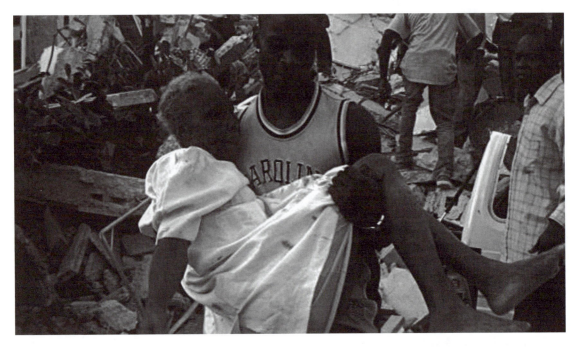

Clarens Renois/AFP/Getty Images

watched the news on television for days or weeks following the temblor's occurrence—hoping that the search teams would save as many victims as possible.

- **Ask what the photo means to you.** It is possible for a photo to trigger a response that is based completely on emotion rather than on fact. For example, if you have a deadly allergy to wasps, your reaction to a photograph of a wasp nest is likely to be one not of appreciation, but of horror. To someone who had an unhappy childhood, a photograph of a crying child is likely to bring back bad memories. No matter how you react, if you focus on details in the photograph itself, your interpretation of it will at least be grounded in fact.

- **Be honest about how the photo made you feel and why.** There's no right way or wrong way to respond to a photograph. Because every viewer brings to a photograph a unique background and a unique set of eyes, disagreements in interpretation are to be expected. An argument about the details of a photograph may be settled by a careful study of the photograph itself. On the other hand, arguments about interpretation are not so easily resolved. But this disagreement is not necessarily bad. Visual images are supposed to make us think. And if this thinking leads us to a spirited discussion, then the photograph has served its purpose.

■ *Exercise*

Leafing through present and past issues of a newspaper or a magazine such as *Time, Newsweek,* or *U.S. News & World Report,* find a news photo that depicts some modern disaster. Once you have settled on a photo, write a brief essay describing it and interpreting its meaning and importance. Attach the photo or a copy of it to your essay.

Responding to an Advertisement

Canadian writer Stephen Leacock called advertising "the science of arresting the human intelligence long enough to get money from it." Although this view may seem cynical, the hard fact is that advertising sells thousands of products, from toilet tissue to cemetery plots. Virtually everything we do—from the way we vote to the concerts we attend—is influenced by advertising. Here are some ideas to help you cope with advertising graphics:

- **Be clear about what is being advertised.** Most magazine and newspaper images are straightforward about identifying their products. But sometimes the message of an image is subtle and indirect rather than obvious—for example, advertisements for deodorant products. One typical theme of such advertisements shows passengers in an elevator shunning one among them who, as we gather, stinks. Of course, that is only an implication. Advertisers walk a thin line between making their pitch and insulting their potential patrons.

   As another example, an ad might show a man in an obviously miserable mood, coughing and holding a handkerchief to his mouth. The caption below "ZICAM" (an allergy medication) suggests relief. A similar haziness often overlies the images used to sell beauty products. An ad for Covergirl eye makeup lures the reader with the words "Smoky Shadowblast—like having a makeup artist at your fingertips." Often the virtues of these products are expressed in roundabout words known as *euphemisms,* a term that simply means saying something vaguely rather than bluntly.

- **Notice the associations with the product being made by the visual image.** A luxury car, for example, is typically shown parked in front of a mansion, linking the car with conspicuous wealth. An expensive watch appears on a wrist against the background of a colorful sailing regatta. A pickup truck advertised for its toughness is shown, covered with mud and driven by a cowboy, out on the range where a fence is being repaired. These images are all stacked to suggest that successful people wear this watch, wealthy people drive this car, and tough men drive this truck. What you will never see is the expensive luxury car parked in front of a broken-down shack. You're also not likely to see the mud-covered truck at a tea party or being driven by a scrawny-looking person dressed in business attire. An ad for Starbucks coffee is an example. It shows a young woman curled up in a comfortable armchair with a mug of coffee at her side, reading the newspaper. The heading says: "Welcome to Starbucks. Shoes optional," inviting viewers to take off their shoes, relax, and get cozy while sipping Starbucks coffee. Before cigarette manufacturers were banned from advertising on television, the tobacco company Philip Morris, which produced the brand Marlboro, associated its label with handsome, brawny, leather-clad cowboys dubbed "Marlboro men." In an ironic twist of fate, two of these rugged models, Wayne McLaren and David McLean, died of lung cancer.

The advertisement on page 27 combines humor with marketing. The purpose of the ad is to hook the reader into associating the product "FRESH STEP® litter" with the image of a cat who is every inch an adorable, finicky lady. She is wiggling in cross-legged desperation on a shiny floor, luminous eyes gazing into space, obviously needing to visit her litter box but not knowing where it is because, as the caption indicates: "It's hard to find your litter box if you can't smell it." Notice that the only words explaining the function of the product are "Odor Eliminating Carbon," printed in a red circle on a box of FRESH STEP® litter. The reader is given no details about the effectiveness of FRESH STEP® litter or its chemical formula. Presumably it contains carbon, but what does that contribute? Obviously, the FRESH STEP® litter company and its marketing staff want you to remember FRESH STEP® litter and its cute feline spokespet every time you get ready to purchase some kitty litter deodorant. They figure that a pretty picture is worth a thousand scientific explanations of how to get rid of bad odors in a litter box. This is a captivating twist, something advertisers like to use in an attempt to lure the public to buy their products.

- **Watch for inversion of reality in the image.** Many advertising images are inversions of reality—meaning they turn the truth on its head. For example, it is well known that cigarettes are a terrible health hazard and that people who smoke are more likely to end up with cancer than people who don't smoke. The very opposite of that truth is typically the theme of cigarette advertising images: they show only people who appear to be in robust health, rugged and tough. Similarly, advertising images used to sell candy and desserts never show an overweight person eating them—they show only people who are lean and trim.

- **Pay attention to exaggeration in the image.** Nearly all advertising is exaggeration. No company puts out images of its products that are not flattering. One brand of gasoline from Exxon Mobil Corp. uses the image of a sprinting tiger to dramatize how well it will make your car run. A soft-drink brand from Coca-Cola features a polar bear as its spokesanimal. Polar bears and tigers get starring roles in advertisements because they enjoy good press in the public consciousness. On the other hand, the vulture and the rat—both of which rank low in public esteem—represent no corporation. In any event, advertising photos are invariably doctored to make everyone associated with the product look better. Be aware of this fact, and you're likely to be more resistant to the pitch.

It's hard to find your litter box if you can't smell it.   freshstep.com

Jill Greenberg Studio. FRESH STEP® is a registered trademark of The Clorox
Pet Products Company. Copyright © 2010, The Clorox Pet Products Company.
Reprinted with permission.

■ *Exercise*

Find an advertisement, either online or in a magazine, that demonstrates the
typical gimmicks used by advertisers. Write a one-page analysis of the ad using the
guidelines suggested previously.

Responding to a Cartoon

Some cartoons are amusing; some are grim but touching; some are satirical. Many give us a revealing view of ourselves. For example, a recent cartoon showed a car crashing through a fence, scattering people and animals in its path. On the front door of the car is the lettering "As the Crow Flies Cab Co." Many of us long to travel "as the crow flies," meaning in a straight line. This cartoon shows us the destruction and havoc that would result if we literally traveled that way. In responding to cartoons, you need to bear the following in mind:

- **What is the purpose of the cartoon?** Most cartoons have no deeper purpose than to amuse. An example of a humorous cartoon is one which shows a triumphant woman who, having just swatted a fly, cries with delight, "Got him!" She is surrounded by broken furniture, shattered lamps, cracked walls, and other damage she did in trying to kill the fly. From behind the doorjamb a man peeps out at her cautiously. The situation is humorous partly for itself and partly because it is recognizable. Many of us have gone into a similar frenzy trying to kill a fly, mosquito, cockroach, or other pest.

- **Be clear about the subject of the cartoon.** Many cartoons are topical, dealing with current issues. An example is the cartoon shown below.

Bruce Eric Kaplan/Cartoon Bank

Here Cupid is seen pouting on a cloud because so many couples on earth are now publishing their personality profiles on the internet through online dating services instead of meeting spontaneously at a party, pub, college, or some other traditional place. The message is clearly a satirical comment on the current fad of calculated dating via the computer. Cupid is angry because technology once again has replaced nature.

- **Understand the context of the cartoon.** Political cartoons, sometimes called caricatures because they exaggerate the known physical features of their target, are especially dependent on context. The cartoon shown below is an example of a political cartoon. It shows an old ship, presumably one used to transport slaves, under sail. In the next panel is a modern ship named *U.S. Corporations,* also at sea. The caption under the slave ship is "Taking the slaves to work," and under the modern ship, "Taking the work to slaves." The cartoonist is objecting to the tendency of American corporations to ship jobs to countries where the wages are lower. The implication is that the modern practice is simply another kind of slavery.

- **Some cartoons, even those intended as fun, can be quite subtle.** One of our favorite cartoons shows two figures that look like they've been created by a cubist artist. (Cubism, an art style that began in 1904, portrays the human figure in geometric segments.) In this cartoon the two figures have necks of squiggles, crescent moons for faces, and one huge round eye each.

Taking the Slaves to work   Taking the work to Slaves

Used with permission of Joe Sharpnack.

These two art creatures are standing in a museum before a conventional painting of an ordinary-looking man. Pointing a curlicue finger at the painting, one of the creatures is sniffing scornfully, "Even I can paint better than that!" This is exactly what lovers of conventional art often say about abstract compositions. Normality in art, as the cartoon slyly tells us, is relative. Keep these questions in mind when you analyze a cartoon:

What is the cartoon poking fun at?

What criticism of the subject is implied?

What kind of humor is used—angry or lighthearted?

What is the main point of the cartoon? (State it in one sentence.)

■ *Exercise*

Find a cartoon that makes you laugh while it points out a serious flaw in society. In a 300-word essay, describe the cartoon so that your reader can visualize it, and then explain its underlying intent. Evaluate the cartoonist's view by stating why you agree or disagree with it.

Using Internet Images in Your Papers

The internet is a treasure trove of images found in different media and celebrating all occasions. Once the richness and ease of use of this collection had become apparent, students began including these images as a way of emphasizing a point. To find appropriate images for use in your papers, enter the title or your theme into any search engine. For example, we entered "images of Charles Bukowski" and were immediately directed to a collection of photographs of the American poet. As you do the search, bear the following points in mind:

1. Double check that you have the correct image. Internet labeling is notorious for being unreliable.
2. Keep your caption close to the image.
3. If you're using a painted portrait, make sure you give the artist credit.
4. If you have any questions about using an image found on the internet, check with your instructor.
5. Don't use images just because you can. The most important part of your paper is your writing. Any image should add weight, not fluff, to your paper.
6. Before you go to the trouble of checking for images, confirm with your instructor that the use of imagery is acceptable in your paper.

■ *Exercise*

Choose one of the following topics and prepare to write a paper on it. Your first step is to research the topic enough to download an appropriate image from the internet. After finding such an image, describe it in detail and state what role it will play in your paper.

- Philanthropists of the Industrial Age in the United States
- The dangers of global warming
- The unsuccessful retreat of the Nez Perce Indians under Chief Joseph
- The art of French impressionism
- The modern role of Swiss guards
- The evolution of the totem pole among Native Americans of the Northwest
- The Haitian revolution and Jean-Bertrand Aristide

Writing Assignments

1. Write a paragraph in which you offer two personal examples of opinion versus fact.
2. Focus on an issue from your local newspaper, and summarize your opinion about it.
3. Write a paragraph of appreciation for one of your best-loved works of art.
4. Compare and contrast the advertisements in an upscale magazine, such as *The New Yorker* or *National Geographic*, with those from one of the tabloids.
5. Write an essay about your favorite cartoonist, giving examples of his or her work.

Chapter 3

Elements of Writing

The work of a writer can be so varied and complex as to be nearly impossible to classify. But no matter the subject, length, or topic, almost all writing will consist of two major elements: the *material elements* that a reader can see—*words*, and *paragraphs* arranged on paper; and the *abstract elements* which a reader can't see—*purpose*, *audience*, and *pattern*. To one extent or another, all of these elements will play a part in creating and shaping the work.

Purpose

Formal writing always has a purpose. This purpose may be implied in the presentation of the material or announced in the opening lines. Whether hinted at or trumpeted aloud, the purpose of a work will eventually begin to exercise control over an emerging composition. Of course, the writer may foolishly forget the purpose or decide not to follow it for one reason or another, which will surely bring the writing to ruin. Forgetting one's purpose is a common mistake that writers make. Assuming, however, that you avoid that trap, your purpose can be triggered by various grammatical structures, ranging from a simple sentence to a question. Here are some examples of the variety of ideas that can lead to a writer's purpose.

> *A question:* If sanity and insanity exist, how shall we know them? (The purpose is to explain how to recognize sanity or insanity.)
>
> *A plain statement*: Whenever we tend to become completely absorbed in an enterprise or an idea, it is a good thing to stand off from it now and again and look at it from the most dispassionate point of view. (The purpose is to prove the importance of remaining objective when gripped by an idea.)
>
> *Two opening sentences:* The teacher has a very peculiar job. It is easy in some ways, and difficult in others. (The purpose is to reveal the paradoxical nature of teaching.)

Having a clear purpose for writing benefits both the writer and the reader. The writer starts out with a makeshift map that depicts the limits of the coverage.

Purpose, used this way, tells the writer where to go and where not to. Likewise, it informs the reader what thematic ground the writer intends to cover. If the writer describes the writing's purpose as a description of summer in Vietnam, the reader has every reason to expect that and not coverage of summer in Antarctica.

Practical readers expect that communication, particularly in writing, will be good for something other than an idle "hello." It is partly our culture that inclines us to feel that writing must never be inane and partly a long literary history described and commemorated by the written word. However we came to this expectation of writing, it exists in our culture and reverberates even in freshman composition assignments for classroom writing. You must have a purpose when you write.

Some students over the years have pointed out that the purpose of writing is an invented one in freshman composition classes. We have had students argue that the only purpose that exists in freshman composition is to pass the course. That, of course, may be a short-range purpose, but it is worthless as a means of helping you write well. What a writer should get from a well-conceived purpose is a guide for choosing words, sentences, and details. Purpose, in this sense, means the writer's intent and hopes for the essay. Your purpose may not be formally articulated either to yourself or to your reader. But it still exerts as much control over what you write and how you express yourself as any other element in your composition.

Whatever the subject, most of your writing in a composition class will be in the form of an *essay*, a term coming from the French word *essai,* meaning "attempt." Nowadays *essay* is used to refer to a variety of nonfiction prose whose common purpose is to express a writer's viewpoint or opinion on a topic. Here is an example of how purpose works to give shape to your essay.

Say you have an assignment to write about a childhood memory. Hundreds of memories churn about in your brain—so many, in fact, that you have no idea where to begin. Because it is a rainy day and you feel gloomy, you decide on a grim purpose: to recount the most miserable day of your entire childhood. With that one decision, you have narrowed the possibilities; you can block out all recollections of childhood merriment, and zoom in on details and adjectives that tell how miserable you felt on that one day of gloom. With this clear purpose in mind, you know exactly what not to say, if not what to say.

If your purpose is to expose the greed of Christmas, you know that you should blast the materialism of the season and Santa's wasteful ways. On the other hand, if you decide to write about Christmas as the most joyful season of the year, then you know to dust off the warmhearted images of sugarplums and gift giving. Purpose gives you a point to stick to and a track to stay on. Beginning without a clear purpose almost always results in an essay that seems pointless. Here, for example, is the opening paragraph of an essay whose writer began with no clear sense of purpose:

> Christmas is a tradition many people celebrate throughout the world. The word *Christmas* comes from an early English phrase *Cristes Maesse,* meaning "Mass of Christ." Christmas day is one of many holidays. The word *holiday* comes from the Anglo-Saxon word *holig daeg,* or "holy day." However, many people lose sight of the fact that Christmas is a holy day. People are too busy with the artificial part of

Christmas to remember the birth of Jesus. Moreover, Christmas is offensive to certain religions who do not believe in Jesus as God's son incarnate. For instance, Jews and Muslims find gift giving on December 25 inappropriate. I think the American Civil Liberties Union is correct in banning crèches and other Christian symbols from store windows during the holiday season.

If you detect a certain pointlessness to this paragraph, as if the writer were searching for a direction, you are right. Lacking a clear purpose, the writing is adrift. When we asked the student writer about this paragraph, she admitted that she had plunged into writing it without thinking about what she wanted to say.

What am I trying to say? What effect do I hope to achieve? What main point do I want to make? Begin your essay by asking and answering these questions honestly. Knowing what you are trying to do in the essay will narrow your choices of language and details and help you achieve a working focus.

In Chapter 4, we cover various techniques that can help you find the purpose of your essay and state it in a clear thesis statement.

Audience

It is always better to tailor your work to a specific audience, especially if you know something about the readers for whom you are writing. Tailoring your work means presenting it in a style and form appropriate to its readers. For example, for what kind of audience do you think the writer intended the following paragraph?

Ordinary life experiences that apparently involve manifestations of psi (i.e., telepathy, clairvoyance, precognition, or psychokinesis) can be of great psychological intensity and meaning, sometimes to the point of producing an experience of insight and spiritual blessedness at one extreme, or suffering, fear of going crazy, and maladaptive behavior at the other extreme. Psychological help may occasionally be required. In the past and, unfortunately still too often in the present, such help was often irrelevant or worsened the client's state.

This passage is taken from the *Journal of the American Society for Psychical Research* and aimed at an audience of professional parapsychologists—students and researchers of the paranormal. Some telltale signs are its complex syntax (the opening sentence is fifty-two words long) and technical vocabulary (the writer assumes that the reader already knows the meaning of *telepathy, clairvoyance, precognition,* and *psychokinesis*). We can infer the intended readers of this writing by noting the assumptions the writer has obviously made about them.

Who are my readers? What do they know about my subject? What am I trying to say to them, and how can I best say it? These are the questions a writer asks before beginning an assignment. If you are writing for readers in a particular discipline, you might have to learn the jargon, the preferred habits of expression, and the ethics of language practiced in that particular field. Sometimes, you might even find yourself in a conflict between the demands of a new field and the style of writing you have learned from your earlier training. Social scientists, for example, are known for writing prose that shatters rules English majors have been taught to follow—avoid long, tortured sentences; use words with Anglo-Saxon roots rather than Latin whenever possible; prefer the active over the passive voice; and so forth. To social scientists, on the other hand, the writing of English majors may seem merely pretty or overly poetic. All writers occasionally find themselves having to adapt to their audiences. Many writers make this adaptation without thinking, in the same way that you instinctively know that a letter to your mother should not sound like one meant for your banker, and vice versa.

The Instructor as Audience

For whom, then, does the student write? The answer is, of course, for the audience assigned by the instructor. But how can that be, when typically only the instructor reads and marks the papers? And what adjustments for audience can students be expected to make when they are always writing for the same instructor?

In fact, the instructor in the classroom realistically reflects the working conditions of professional writers. This book, for example, although written for an audience of students, must first be approved by the publisher's editor, who will review and evaluate it. A dual audience is similarly found throughout the world of business. For example, you might be asked to write a sales brochure aimed at an audience of vendors, but the sales manager will have the final say over your copy. Additionally, college instructors represent what we might label "an audience with well-educated sensibilities." This lofty description merely means that the typical English instructor is widely versed in general knowledge and up-to-date in the various issues sweeping the country like forest fires, making him or her practically the ideal audience that the beginning writer could want.

Pattern

In the beginning is the idea; in the end is the essay. *Pattern* is the specific rhetorical strategy you use to develop your idea into an essay. The suggestion that an essay has a preconceived or ideal pattern into which it can fit is abhorrent to many teachers of writing. They believe that form emerges naturally out of content during the act of composition the way a tree emerges out of a seed in the garden. To their minds, no other pattern exists.

We do not ideologically belong to either faction in this debate. We think that the rhetorical modes—as these preexisting forms or patterns are called—serve a useful function by allowing the student a second way of conceptualizing the writing task. Having a rhetorical pattern in mind for the ideas you're trying to express is a help, not a hindrance.

There are nine rhetorical patterns that are most commonly taught in freshman composition. They are *narration, description, example, definition, comparison/ contrast, process, classification/division, causal analysis,* and *argumentation.* Sometimes a writing assignment is worded in such a way as to require the use of a particular rhetorical pattern. But sometimes the choice of the pattern to use may be left up to the student writer. For instance, your instructor may ask you to write an essay *narrating* a dangerous incident in your life, or an essay *defining* terrorism, or an essay *contrasting* rap music with hip-hop. Or the assignment may simply ask you to "give an account of" some historic battle, which is really a *process* essay. A psychology assignment may not call for a "definition," but it may ask "What are the symptoms of dementia?" An economics test might not include a "causal analysis" question, but it might well ask you to "trace the problems leading up to the 2009 banking crisis in the United States." Here are assignments whose wording is linked to the most appropriate patterns of development. Ask these questions and then watch the patterns emerge:

Question	Pattern
What happened?	Narration
What is the dominant impression?	Description
What are some typical instances of it?	Example
What is it? What does it mean?	Definition
How are they alike? How do they differ?	Comparison/contrast
How did it happen? How does it work?	Process
To what type/category does it belong?	
Into what kinds is it divided?	Classification/division
What caused it to happen? What was its effect?	Causal analysis
Why am I for it? Why am I against it?	Argumentation

 *Writing Tip*

Using The Rhetorical Patterns

The rhetorical patterns exist to help you write better, more clearly, with sharpened focus and heightened emphasis. As you mature as a writer and gain self-confidence, you will naturally find yourself getting better at adapting these abstract strategies to your needs.

Patterns of writing provide structure for both individual paragraphs and entire essays. For now, we will briefly define each strategy and illustrate its structure and techniques in a single-paragraph example.

Narration

A paragraph or essay developed by narration tells a story, sometimes from the first-person point of view and sometimes from the third-person point of view. Here is an example of a paragraph developed by narration from the first-person point of view:

> Every morning I lay on the floor in the front parlor watching her door. The blind was pulled down to within an inch of the sash so that I could not be seen. When she came out on the doorstep my heart leaped. I ran to the hall, seized my books and followed her. I kept her brown figure always in my eye and, when we came near the point at which our ways diverged, I quickened my pace and passed her. This happened morning after morning. I had never spoken to her, except for a few casual words, and yet her name was like a summons to all my foolish blood.
>
> —James Joyce, "Araby"

The details are specific and the sequence fast-paced and clear. The recurring use of "I" tells us that the story is narrated from the first-person point of view. Furthermore, the event recounted—young, unreturned love—is one with which most readers can identify. Chapter 7 teaches how to develop an entire essay by narration.

Description

A paragraph or essay developed by description uses a dominant impression as a central theme to unify its descriptive details. In the following passage, the dominant impression of Braggioni is of an expensively dressed, grossly fat man. We have italicized specific words that support this impression.

> Braggioni catches her glance solidly as if he had been waiting for it, leans forward, *balancing his paunch* between his spread knees, and sings with tremendous emphasis, weighing his words. He has, the song relates, no father and no mother, nor even a friend to console him; lonely as a wave of the sea he comes and goes, lonely as a wave. His *mouth opens round* and yearns sideways, his *balloon cheeks* grow oily with the labor of song. He *bulges* marvelously in his *expensive garments*. Over his *lavender collar, crushed upon a purple necktie, held by a diamond hoop;* over his ammunition belt of *tooled leather worked in silver, buckled cruelly* around his *gasping middle;* over the *tops of his glossy yellow shoes Braggioni swells* with *ominous ripeness,* his mauve *silk hose stretched taut,* his ankles bound with the stout leather thongs of his shoes.
>
> —Katherine Anne Porter, "Flowering Judas"

Without a dominant impression, a passage of description runs the risk of becoming overwhelmed by irrelevant details. Chapter 8 teaches the use of a dominant impression in writing a descriptive essay.

Example

A paragraph or essay developed by *example* begins with a generalization, which it then supports with specific cases. The examples must be to the point, vivid, supportive of the generalization, and clearly connected to it by an introductory phrase such as *for example* or *for instance*. Here is a case in point:

> Temperaments are so various that there may be even more than "nine and sixty ways" of writing books. Rousseau, for example, could not compose with pen in hand: but then Chateaubriand could not compose without. Wordsworth did it while walking, riding, or in bed; but Southey, only at his desk. Shakespeare, we are told, never blotted a line; Scott could toss first drafts unread to the printer; Trollope drilled himself, watch on desk, to produce two hundred and fifty words every quarter of an hour; Hilaire Belloc, so Desmond MacCarthy once told me, claimed to have written twenty thousand of them in a day; and in ten days Balzac could turn out sixty thousand.
>
> —F. L. Lucas, *Style*

The generalization occurs in the first sentence, which also introduces the main idea the paragraph intends to document. Following the generalization are examples of various methods of composing used by ten different authors. Chapter 9 takes up the use of examples as a strategy in the writing of essays.

Definition

A paragraph or essay developed by definition focuses on specifying the characteristics of the subject—first by showing the general category it belongs to and then by distinguishing it from other items in the same category. Here is an example:

> Chemistry is that branch of science which has the task of investigating the materials out of which the universe is made. It is not concerned with the forms into which they may be fashioned. Such objects as chairs, tables, vases, bottles, or wires are of no significance in chemistry; but such substances as glass, wool, iron, sulfur, and clay, as the materials out of which they are made, are what it studies. Chemistry is concerned not only with the composition of such substances, but also with their inner structure.
>
> —John Attend Timm, *General Chemistry*

The writer first places chemistry in the category of science and then differentiates it from other scientific disciplines by the nature and content of its study. A definition may be short like this one or considerably longer when the subject is a more abstract and complex term such as love or justice. Chapter 10 teaches the development of an essay by definition.

Comparison/Contrast

Comparison/contrast paragraphs and essays examine items for similarities and differences. The items are compared on certain specific bases, and the writer alternates from one to the other, indicating either similarities or differences through the use of appropriate phrases such as *on the other hand, likewise, similarly, though*, and *but*. In the following example, terms indicating comparison/contrast are in italics:

> The way in which culture affects language becomes clear by *comparing* how the English and Hopi languages refer to H_2O in its liquid state. English, like most other European languages, has only one word—"water"—and it pays no attention to what the substance is used for or its quantity. The Hopi of Arizona, *on the other hand,* use "pahe" to mean the large amounts of water present in natural lakes or rivers, and "keyi" for the small amounts in domestic jugs and canteens. English, *though,* makes other distinctions that Hopi does not. The speaker of English is careful to distinguish between a lake and a stream, between a waterfall and a geyser; *but* "pahe" makes no distinction among lakes, ponds, rivers, streams, waterfalls, and springs.
>
> —Peter Farb, *Man at the Mercy of His Language*

The basis of this comparison/contrast between English and Hopi—the way these languages refer to water—is given early in the paragraph. After announcing this basis, the writer then catalogs the similarities and differences between the English and Hopi languages on this one item. Chapter 11 discusses comparison/contrast as it applies to the development of an entire essay.

Process

Process refers to any writing that gives step-by-step instructions on how to do something or how something happened. For instance, a process essay might give instructions on how to bake a cake, how to create and maintain dreadlocks, how to use an Apple iPhone, or how to play the recorder. It could also explain the steps taken in refurbishing the Statue of Liberty, the strategies used by Ulysses Grant to win the battle of Fort Donelson in 1862, or how firefighters in 2009 put out a runaway fire in the Sierras. The following example instructs the reader in how to change a tire.

> If you are a motorist, sooner or later you'll get a flat tire and need to put on the spare. It's a pesky job that can be done safely and fairly quickly if you follow some simple rules. First, make sure you pull off the road in a safe spot that makes your vehicle visible and does not expose you to traffic. If you have passengers, ask them to get out of the car. A surprising number of people have been killed over the years while changing a tire on the roadside. Second, now is a good time to use your hazard lights as well as those emergency caution signs and flares you've been toting around. Once satisfied that you're safe from passing traffic, take the spare tire out of your trunk as well as the tools you'll need, such as the lug wrench and the car jack.

On a Roll?

If ever you find yourself on a roll but moving somewhat away from your chosen writing pattern, don't worry. Abiding by some ideal form is not your aim. Expressing yourself is. Straying from the form is no big deal, so long as you stick to the point.

> Be sure the car is in gear and the emergency brake set. Remove the hubcap, if necessary, and loosen the lug nuts. Once the nuts are just barely loose, jack up the car following the directions in the owner's manual. Make sure you have enough clearance to put a fully inflated tire on. Finish taking off the lug nuts and remove the tire. In the process of doing so, never ever stick your legs or other limbs under the jacked-up car that might be injured if the car should fall off the jack. Once the tire is on, tighten the lug nuts until they're barely snug and lower car on the jack until the tread of the tire is touching ground. Do not attempt to tighten the nuts while the car is still jacked up, as the effort might cause the car to roll off the jack. Do not over tighten the nuts or you might strip them. Put away your tools and the punctured tire, remove all the emergency warning signs, and you'll be on your way again.—Student essay

Other than the occasional muddling of the sequence, students generally have no trouble writing process paragraphs or essays. For further instruction in this strategy, see Chapter 12.

Classification

To *classify* means to divide something and group its elements into major categories and types. For a classification to be useful, it must be based on a single principle, and it must be complete. For instance, say you had to write a paragraph or essay classifying students according to their year in college. If your classification included only freshmen, sophomores, and seniors, it would violate the requirement of completeness by omitting juniors. On the other hand, if your scheme included freshmen, sophomores, juniors, seniors, fraternity members, and nonfraternity members, it would no longer be based on a single principle. The first four categories refer to the student's year in college, whereas the fifth and sixth refer to membership or nonmembership in campus organizations. Here is an example of a paragraph developed by classification:

> A few words about the world's reaction to the concentration camps: the terrors committed in them were experienced as uncanny by most civilized persons. It came

as a shock to their pride that supposedly civilized nations could stoop to such inhuman acts. The implication that modern man has such inadequate control over his cruelty was felt as a threat. Three different psychological mechanisms were most frequently used for dealing with the phenomenon of the concentration camp: (a) its applicability to man in general was denied by asserting (contrary to available evidence) that the acts of torture were committed by a small group of insane or perverted persons; (b) the truth of the reports were denied by ascribing them to deliberate propaganda. This method was favored by the German government, which called all reports on terror in the camps horror propaganda *(Greuelpropaganda)*; (c) the reports were believed, but the knowledge of the terror was repressed as soon as possible.

—Bruno Bettelheim, *The Informed Heart*

The author first specifies the principle of the classification—the psychological mechanisms used to deal with human cruelty. He then completes the classification by listing the mechanisms. Chapter 13 teaches how to develop an entire essay by classification.

Causal Analysis

Causal analysis attempts to relate two events by asserting that the occurrence of one event is the reason for the occurrence of the other: a car engine blew up because it lacked oil; a woman slipped and fell because the pavement was slippery; a dog got rabies because it was bitten by a rabid raccoon. Each of these statements asserts a causal relationship between two events.

While cause relates two events by asserting one event as the reason for the other, effect relates two events by asserting one event as the result of another. If you write an essay giving as a reason for your father's bitterness his failure to fulfill his ambition to be a doctor, you are analyzing cause. If you write an essay analyzing what happens to a person who fails to fulfill a lifelong career ambition, you are analyzing effect. Both essays nevertheless would be considered examples of causal analysis.

Consider this paragraph, which analyzes why our age has no "giants":

Why have giants vanished from our midst? One must never neglect the role of accident in history; and accident no doubt plays a part here. But too many accidents of the same sort cease to be wholly accidental. One must inquire further. Why should our age not only be without great men but even seem actively hostile to them? Surely one reason we have so few heroes now is precisely that we had so many a generation ago. Greatness is hard for common humanity to bear. As Emerson said, "Heroism means difficulty, postponement of praise, postponement of ease, introduction of the world into the private apartment, introduction of eternity into the hours measured by the sitting-room clock." A world of heroes keeps people from living their own private lives.

—Arthur M. Schlesinger, Jr., *The Decline of Heroes*

The following paragraph analyzes the effects of changes in the sun's nuclear balance:

> Inevitably, the solar nuclear balances will change. The hydrogen will be used up, converted into helium. The sun's core will start to burn helium in a struggle for life. The heat will increase, the sun will grow redder and swell, on the way to being a red giant star. As it expands it will bring biblical fire and brimstone to the inner planets. Mercury, Venus will melt and drop into the expanding plasma; on earth, all life will be gone long before the oceans boil and vaporize and the rocks are smelted down.
>
> —Lennard Bickel, *Our Sun: The Star We Live In*

Student-written causal analyses sometimes suffer from *dogmatism*—an authoritative stating of opinion as fact without providing sufficient evidence. Cause and effect often have a complex and frail association, which you should assert with caution. For more on how to write a causal analysis, see Chapter 14.

Argumentation

Argumentation, the final strategy for developing a paragraph or an essay, involves persuading the reader to the writer's viewpoint. Such a paragraph or essay will often be a combination of the strategies discussed so far, simultaneously analyzing cause, describing, giving examples, comparing/contrasting, and defining. Unlike a paragraph or essay developed by one single pattern, the argumentative paragraph or essay has no single strategy of development but is recognizable instead by its intent. Here, for example, is a paragraph that argues that the "positive attitude" for which Americans are known all over the world is not rooted in real happiness:

> There is an anxiety…in the heart of American positive thinking. If the generic "positive thought" is correct and things are really getting better, if the arc of the universe tends toward happiness and abundance, then why bother with the mental effort of positive thinking? Obviously, because we do not fully believe that things will get better on their own. The practice of positive thinking is an effort to pump up this belief in the face of much contradictory evidence. Those who set themselves up as instructors in the discipline of positive thinking—coaches, preachers, and gurus of various sorts—have described this effort with terms like "self-hypnosis," "mind control," and "thought control." In other words, it requires deliberate self-deception, including a constant effort to repress or block out unpleasant possibilities and "negative" thoughts. The truly self-confident, or those who have in some way made their peace with the world and their destiny within it, do not need to expend effort censoring or otherwise controlling their thoughts. Positive thinking may be a quintessentially American activity, associated in our minds with both individual and national success, but it is driven by a terrible insecurity.
>
> —Barbara Ehrenreich, Bright-Sided

In presenting her argument, the writer resorts to a variety of strategies. She *defines* "positive thinking," she cites *examples* of groups who teach the positive attitude, she *contrasts* individuals who are truly confident with those who need thought control, and finally she mentions insecurity as the *cause* of positive thinking. A paragraph or essay developed by argumentation will more often than not employ more than one strategy. See Chapter 15 for more on argumentation.

Blending Rhetorical Patterns

The rhetorical patterns are helpful guidelines for a beginning writer and should never be used to solely and rigidly dictate the final draft of your paragraph or essay. You should never stifle any spontaneous and apt phrasing merely because it does not conform to a particular rhetorical pattern. To do so is to behave like Procrustes of Greek mythology, who cut off the legs of passersby to make them fit into his short bed.

Many paragraphs or essays do more or less conform to one strategy of development or another, but complex works routinely blend several strategies. Here is an example from John W. Gardner's *Excellence*, an influential book on education:

> We are a long, long way from understanding the complexities of individual motivation. We understand very imperfectly, for example, the inner pressures to excel which are present in some children and absent in others. We don't really know why, from earliest years, some individuals seem indomitable, while others are tossed about by events like the bird in a badminton game. Differences in energy and other physiological traits are partially responsible. Even more important may be the role of early experiences—relations with brothers and sisters, early successes and failures. We know, for example, that high standards may be a means of challenging and stimulating the child or, depending on the circumstances, a means of frightening and intimidating him.
>
> —John W. Gardner, *Excellence*

Example

Contrast

Cause

Example

An essay is written with a dominant purpose conceived in the mind of the writer. But a translation of this dominant purpose onto the page generally requires many different kinds of paragraphs. It is a little like building a brick house. One uses not only brick but also cement, lumber, sheetrock, tiles, and wire. Yet when the building is finished, it is indisputably a brick house, though constructed of many different kinds of materials. Essays likewise have distinct and recognizable purposes. Some are intended primarily to describe; others set out to narrate; still others are written to analyze cause. Yet most are constructed of many different kinds of paragraphs.

Practical Applications
of the Rhetorical Strategies

Some students believe that what they are taught in English courses has little useful-ness in the outside world. To dismiss this myth, we have selected some examples of real-world applications of the writing strategies discussed in this book. All examples actually happened.

1. You have applied for a job with a large multinational corporation and have passed successfully through a battery of screening tests. The candidates have been narrowed to a field of five. As a basis for final selection, the human resources psychologist has asked each applicant to write an essay about his or her greatest personal success. You sit down and try to think. Then you begin to write.

   Purpose: To persuade the psychologist that you are the one for the job

   Pattern: Narration

2. You are a social worker responsible for supervising the living conditions in some state-supported nursing homes for the elderly. You find unsani-tary living conditions at one nursing home and file a stop-payment order against it to cut off its state funding. Your supervisor asks you to explain the conditions at this nursing home in support of your action.

   Purpose: To convince the state to withdraw aid from this nursing home

   Pattern: Description

3. As a vocal member of your PTA group, you listen with horror as school district officials propose curriculum changes that you are convinced will lower the standard of education. You are opposed to the changes because you have read of other districts in which such changes have not been ben-eficial. You meet with other parents who share your view, and a committee is formed. You are asked to find examples of other districts where similar changes have produced no advantages.

   Purpose: To persuade the school district not to make the proposed changes in the curriculum

   Pattern: Example

4. You work as a textbook salesperson for a college publisher. A sociology book published by your company is being criticized by the professors us-ing it because it lacks a section on deviance. You report this to your editor, who fires back a memo asking you to find out exactly what the professors mean by "deviance."

   Purpose: To acquaint the editor with the professors' complaint about the text

   Pattern: Definition

5. You are employed in the accounting division of a major department store. An employee has made a suggestion for changing the method of reporting daily income. Your boss likes the idea but is uncertain whether it would be enough of an improvement over the existing method to justify the change. You are asked to write a comparison of this new method with the existing one.

    Purpose: To persuade the boss to adopt the new reporting method

    Pattern: Comparison/contrast

6. Mad about creamy chocolate pudding, you have perfected the ideal recipe. Neither riches nor fame can tempt you to share it. Love, however, does. You sit down to write out the recipe for your beloved.

    Purpose: To share your recipe for perfect chocolate pudding with a friend

    Pattern: Process

7. You work in the counseling office of a major university where entering freshmen are required to take an English test. The university is planning new English classes for its freshmen, and you are assigned to write a report dividing and classifying the incoming freshmen according to their English placement scores.

    Purpose: To gather data to help with curriculum planning

    Pattern: Classification

8. Your firm specializes in the manufacture of household brushes. Sales of one item—a plastic brush designed as a bathroom grout cleaner—have slumped badly. Your boss assigns you to find out why.

    Purpose: To find out why sales of this brush have fallen

    Pattern: Causal analysis

9. You and eleven other jurors have listened for two weeks to a procession of witnesses. Along with four other jurors, you become convinced of the defendant's guilt, but to your amazement and dismay, the remaining jurors have come to exactly the opposite view. Undecided himself, the foreman asks each group to prepare a written argument outlining its reasons for believing in the defendant's guilt or innocence. Your group assigns you to argue its viewpoint.

    Purpose: To persuade your fellow jurors to vote in favor of a guilty verdict

    Pattern: Argument

Writing Assignments

1. Write a brief passage explaining the practical advantages of knowing how to use the various writing patterns.

2. In a brief passage, explain to your reader why it is important (or irrelevant) to have a definite purpose to govern your writing.

3. Using the writing pattern most suited to your purpose, develop a passage on the topic of making intimate friends at college. In choosing your pattern, be sure to think about your purpose and the audience you wish to address.

4. Explain in your own words how the audience for whom you write will dictate the purpose and pattern of your writing. Use two or three examples to clarify your view.

5. To what kind of audience would the following topics most likely appeal? Describe each audience and suggest a purpose for developing the topic into an essay. (If you need to increase your knowledge of these subjects, explore the internet.)
   a. Mozart's view of human nature as reflected in his operas
   b. The bitter aspects of Mark Twain's humor
   c. How the Nobel Prize came about
   d. Why TV wrestling has attracted so many fans

6. Name the purpose you would adopt in order to turn the following word clusters into an essay:
   a. Some pediatricians think a baby's cries have specific meanings.
      Some psychiatrists think our genes predestine us completely.
      Internists disagree on the cure for indigestion.
      My gynecologist does not believe in hormone replacement.
   b. Little kids spend hours sitting in front of the TV or computer.
      Too many parents reward their kids' good behavior with candy bars.
      What has happened to basket ball hoops or soccer balls in neighborhoods?
      A balanced diet of protein, vegetables, grains, and fruit is important for the nutrition of growing children while growing up.
   c. Intuition is not real insight.
      Intuition is having a hunch or a suspicion.
      Facts are different from intuition.
      Many people claim to have a sixth sense about events.
   d. Energy efficiency
      Energy security
      Energy diversity
      Better CO_2 management

Chapter 4

Planning and Organizing the Essay

Your goal is to write a successful essay. To do that, you need to take several preliminary steps, some of which may suit your style of writing, some of which may not. For example, we do not all organize the same way nor to the same degree. Some of us, in fact, hate all kinds of organizing and would simply prefer to get started on the actual process of writing. Then again, some teachers like to see the steps you took in dreaming up the topic and developing it into the final essay. Whatever you do, don't do, or even plan to do, it is a good idea to get your teacher's approval before doing it.

Finding a Topic

The first thing you have to do, on your way to writing an essay, is to find your topic. We assume at this point that you already have a subject in mind—meaning a broad area that you intend to cover in your essay. The topic is always a miniaturization of the subject. Often, the subject is too ponderous or long to fit in an essay. Finding a shorter version will save you a lot of grief in the actual writing, as it is as hard to write about a subject that is too big as it is to write about a topic that is too small.

Our primary suggestion for finding a topic is that you write about what you know. Commonsense tells us that it is surely easier to write about a subject we know intimately than to tackle one about which we know nothing. With the known subject, it is easier to find appropriate details, to understand what to emphasize and what to skip, and to summarize your position in a thesis.

If you cannot write about what you know, the next best approach is to know about what you write. Before you pen a single word, read about the topic and consult campus experts on it for their opinions. If you are writing a paper about the problems of people with disabilities, you might interview disabled students for a real-world glimpse into the difficulties they face daily. Similarly, if you are doing an essay on law enforcement, you could enliven it by including the views of a criminology professor or by interviewing and quoting someone who is or has been a police officer.

Many students, finding the internet unmatched as a rich source of views and opinions on practically all topics, go there first in their research. Simply find a search engine that you like and dip into that. Don't be afraid to experiment with the wording of your searches. Remember the search engine is merely a piece of dumb technology and not a faultfinding editor who is eager to criticize the wording of your queries. It understands you about as well as a stop sign understands a passing motorist.

What are you looking for at this first step of writing a paper? In a broad sense, you're looking for some topic you can get your teeth into. It should be a topic that you are drawn to or have a natural interest in. It should not be a topic that you find humdrum or boring or you think will be a snap to do. Pick a topic that fails to generate a sense of excitement about what you have to do and you'll regret it later. Writing anything can be a chore; writing on a topic you secretly dislike can be murder.

The Controlling Idea

Once you have nailed down your basic topic, you can move on to focusing on a *controlling idea*. As the main thought behind your essay, the controlling idea is in effect a snapshot of what the essay will do—argue, narrate, describe, classify, and so forth. If the topic is the direction in which you must sail your ship, your controlling idea is the exact compass point where you intend to make landfall. Naturally, the controlling idea will always be smaller and more focused than the topic. Likewise, to be useful, the topic will always be smaller than the subject.

At this point we come to another ideological fork in the road. The people who believe in writing as a process would argue that you should not try to cram an idea into the ready-made mold of a paragraph. In the normal process of composition, they argue, what you're trying to say will assume a form that emerges from the writing. Adherents of the opposite point of view claim otherwise and look for an ideal structure into which opinion may be molded and expressed.

The following list will give you an idea of the relationship between a topic and the controlling idea based on it:

Topic	Controlling idea
The sport of golf	The origin of the word "golf"
Extinction of wild animals	How to save Kenya's Northern white Rhinos from extinction
New dangers of smoking	The relationship between smoking and macular degeneration

In this and the preceding chapter we write about the interaction of purpose, pattern, and controlling idea as if they were static parts of the essay. That, of course, is merely for the sake of discussion. In fact, the essay is a diverse and dynamic mixture of these elements, and any suggestion to the contrary is merely academic. But to give you a more realistic idea of how these separate elements come together and interact, consider three hypothetical approaches to an essay on farming:

Purpose: To explain the decline of agriculture as a college major

Pattern: Write an analysis of the causes that have led to the decline of agricultural majors in college.

Controlling idea: The low margin of profit for agricultural products and the harshness of the farming lifestyle as they impact farming as a career

Purpose: To give the reader a vivid picture of a day in a farmer's life

Pattern: Write an essay describing life on the farm.

Controlling idea: Golden fields with the sweet smell of freshly mowed hay, ramshackle outbuildings used for storage, and the dimly lit lobbies of agricultural cooperatives

Purpose: To illustrate the appeal of farming

Pattern: Give two examples that illustrate the appeal of farm life.

Controlling idea: The excitement during planting and the reward of harvesting

Notice that in every case the chosen purpose dictates the best pattern and also influences the controlling idea. Later in the chapter, we shall discuss the *thesis* of an essay, closely related to the controlling idea and often confused with it. This is the sort of planning and shaping a writer does during the prewriting phase and even while actually writing the work.

Writing Assignments

1. Using Google or Yahoo as your search engine, plug in the keywords "space shuttle disasters," and come up with at least two appropriate controlling ideas for an essay.

2. Explain in a paragraph any adaptations you might make in writing for different instructors.

3. Write a paragraph about the first time you consciously sat down to write anything in a formal context and did it successfully.

4. Write a paragraph on the usefulness or irrelevance of a controlling idea to your particular writing habits.

5. Using the term "depression," try to narrow it down to three different topics, with a controlling idea for each.

Prewriting Activities

Prewriting refers to all the preliminary steps a writer might take in preparing to write. It includes randomly thinking about the topic, systematically gathering information about it, and sketching out a possible controlling idea and structure for the essay. Even those writers not temperamentally inclined to prewrite can benefit from at least thinking about the topic before committing pen to paper or fingers to keyboard. Professional writers often spend more time on prewriting than on actual writing.

Part of the prewriting quest is to find an opinion or point of view to which you feel particularly committed. Dig and search until you find a vein of ore that makes you scream "Eureka!" Writing about that will invest your words with the energy and voice you need to make your point. Making that discovery, however, may require you to engage in one or more of the following prewriting activities.

Freewriting

Freewriting means writing on the assignment creatively and without restrictions. Your goal is to put down every random idea, notion, thought, or opinion that pops into your head about the general subject. First you write down the assignment, word for word, on the top of the paper. Then you begin the freewriting. If you get stuck, write *I'm stuck* and keep going. Here's an example of freewriting on the following assignment: *Write a classification essay about a force, a group, a system, a ritual, or an emotion.*

> What is a force? What is a system? Do I want to write about a force, a system, a group, or an emotion? What emotion? Rituals, rituals, what are rituals? I picture religious robes and candles burning in various church nooks and crannies, I hear voices chanting in unison, responding to the priest. Hmmmm. What group? I'm stuck. Name some emotions? I don't want to write about groups. Rituals? What rituals? Who has rituals? There's the ritual of the lecture, of grading, of classroom interaction. I feel stuck. Keep writing! Keep writing!

Usually freewriting reveals a predisposition, a slight leaning toward one topic over all others. Follow that hunch in another freewriting session.

> *Religious rituals.* We have many in our church. The services are loaded with rituals. The sacraments are rituals. The relationship between priest and laypeople is governed by rituals. The behavior of the congregation is governed by rituals.

Now you have a better idea of what you want to do—you want to focus your essay on the rituals of your church. One way to do this is to ask yourself a question about one of the items on the list. The answer to this question, if complete enough, can be the controlling idea of your essay.

For example, you might ask this question about the sacramental rituals mentioned: *What kinds of sacramental rituals does my church use?* Your answer might be as follows:

> The seven sacraments of the Greek Orthodox Church are Holy Baptism, Holy Chrism, Holy Communion, Holy Confession, Holy Marriage, Holy Unction, and Holy Orders.

And that can be the controlling idea or thesis of an essay classifying the sacramental rituals practiced by your church.

Talking

Talking about the assigned subject with yourself—or better yet, with a willing friend—can help you find a suitable topic. What we have in mind is purposeful talk, where you or your friend asks pointed questions aimed at ferreting out particular subtopics you might find appealing in your chosen subject. In our own college days this kind of talk came under the heading of "a rap session" and were found to be quite productive in massaging opinions that could be used as topics.

If this glorification of talk example strikes you as a little too pat, remember that we are interested in imparting the point that talking systematically to yourself or a friend about the subject can reveal subtopics that you might otherwise have missed. And you might be surprised at how this back-and-forth chat works. Bear in mind that the purpose of talking out an essay was the same then as now. The overwhelming aim was to turn up subtopics and minor points that might otherwise be overlooked. Remember to keep the conversation focused on the essay and resist the temptation to stray from the point. You might be surprised at how well this tactic works for you as it did for your grandparents.

Clustering

Clustering is freewriting done in the style of a doodle. It is simply a diagram of possible subtopics that you might include in your essay. It is also a method of narrowing a broad subject into a manageable topic. Here is how clustering works: You begin by drawing a rectangle in the middle of the page and filling it in with your subject. Let us say you are assigned to write an essay on hypocrisy. Your basic diagram will look like this:

```
+-----------------------+
|                       |
|      hypocrisy        |
|                       |
+-----------------------+
```

Then you add smaller boxes attached to the main rectangle by spokes. In each smaller box, you write one of the question words—who, what, when, where, and why—then scribble below each box some tentative answers and ideas. The resulting diagram might look like this:

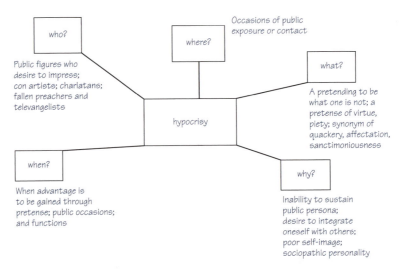

Conscientiously answer the questions in the satellite boxes—providing appropriate facts, figures, examples, anecdotes, and testimonials—and you will have the bare-bones details necessary for writing your essay.

You can also use a cluster to plan an essay on a narrowed subject that you have decided to treat with a particular strategy. For example, let us say that you decide to write an essay on hypocrisy, using the strategy of definition. (For more on definition, see Chapter 10.) You can then develop a cluster showing the lexical meaning of hypocrisy as well as other obvious subtopics you might also cover. Here is an example:

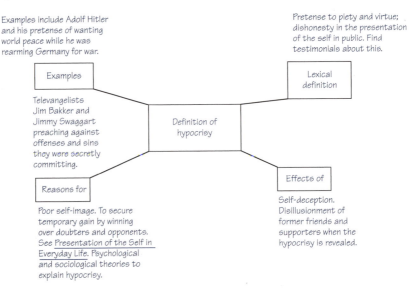

Whether you find your narrowed topic through freewriting, talking, or clustering, be sure to always write about what you know, or at least know about what you write. Imagination is a wonderful faculty, but in expository writing there simply is no substitute for the familiarity and details suggested by actual contact with a topic.

Writer's Block

Writer's block is a supposed condition in which afflicted writers are said to be unable to freely express their opinions on paper. In movies, the scenario usually features a rumpled writer hunched over a desk, straining vainly to write, with clumps of manuscript discarded on the floor testifying to the futility of the effort. We say it is a supposed condition because we think writer's block is a misnomer.

In fact, writers are seldom blocked from saying what they believe and desperately want to say; they are more typically blocked when they try to say what they do not want to say or when they have nothing to say. What passes for writer's block is usually nothing more than writer's emptiness.

We are speaking, of course, of expository prose, in which writers try to express themselves factually on a topic, not of fiction, which is altogether another kettle of fish. With expository prose, there are several common reasons for so-called writer's block.

Psychological Reasons

Naturally, we cannot tailor a textbook to address every psychological cause of writer's block. But as teachers, we know that the most common cause is a professed hatred of writing, often brought about by a bad experience with a past instructor or an underrated idea of one's own talent.

The good writer is not one who dashes off fifty pages at one sitting and never makes a mistake. That creature is mainly a figment of scriptwriters' imaginations and rarely exists in real life. Indeed, testimony from notable writers down through the ages tells us that writing is a chore, a labor; that it is slow and agonizing work; and that it involves repeated rewriting, stopping, and starting. If this is the way you work, you are not a bad writer but merely a typical one.

Physical Reasons

Among the physical factors that can contribute to writer's block are the use of poor equipment or the choice of an inappropriate site for composing.

Writing with a pen or a typewriter can be sheer labor compared with writing on a computer. Some writers who are eruptive composers can find themselves frustrated if they are forced to gush through the capillary of a pen. The solution to this problem is to get and use a computer. Many modern college libraries make computers available for free or at low cost.

As for finding an appropriate site for writing, the best place is not always a quiet alcove overlooking a peaceful vista with birds dutifully chirping in the background. Some writers do indeed favor such an ideal setting, but others prefer the hustle and bustle of Starbucks, sipping lattes, their laptops at the ready. You know where you do your best writing, and you should try to stick with that setting.

The Internal Editor

Within each of us, the theory goes, is an internal editor who sits in silent judgment of our every sentence. This editor consists of every grammatical lesson we ever learned, every red-inked comment we ever received in the margins of our papers. It is the collection of all we think we know about writing. And sometime this internal editor becomes so severe a critic that we simply cannot produce a single line that we like.

The solution often recommended to shut up a fault-finding internal editor is simply to sit down and write. Or do as the writer William Stafford recommends: Whenever you feel blocked, simply lower your standards. Write without looking back; put everything down exactly as it occurs to you. Later, you can always go back and sift through and edit what you have written. Often, this tactic is effective in silencing a too-severe internal editor.

But the technique that works for us no matter what the cause of the so-called block is a simple and effective one: rereading our work. If we do not find the problem on the first rereading pass, we reread the work again, changing words and sentences here and there. And if necessary, we reread it again. Nothing is better for writing than rereading, and all conscientious writers incessantly and repeatedly reread every page they have written until they are satisfied. This technique is tedious but miraculously effective. Try it next time you feel blocked while writing an essay.

Finding Your Thesis

The thesis has a simple function in life, and that is to answer the question: What is this all about? For the thesis exists only as a statement of what you're trying to do in a written passage and how you're doing it. In the thesis, you declare where you're going, what you intend to do, how you feel about a certain subject—in short, you give a synopsis of what's coming.

The usefulness of the thesis lies in its limiting effect on a writer's efforts. As writers, all of us know how utterly vast the blank page can be, especially when we are groping toward our initial topic and have only a vague idea of what we want to write. It is then that a well-worded thesis can help point us in one direction and provide us with a useful limit for our thinking and writing.

The Too-Narrow or Too-Broad Thesis

Many mishaps can occur to a sentence as it journeys from the writer's brain, where it hatched as an idea for a topic, onto the page, where it becomes a thesis. Two errors are particularly common: writing an overly narrow thesis or writing an overly broad thesis.

A thesis that is overly narrow usually leaves the writer scrambling for something to say, causing the wordiness known affectionately as "padding." Here is an example of what we mean by an overly narrow thesis:

> Hundreds of northside commuters have to drive their cars south to the city every weekday morning.

To test for an overly narrow thesis, consider whether it leaves anything of significance to argue or assert. So hundreds of northside commuters drive south to work every day? And hundreds more drive north, and possibly another few hundred drive east and west. So what? We are left to fill in the blanks around a dead-end utterance. Here is a much improved version:

> Hundreds of northside commuters have to drive their cars south to the city every weekday morning because public transportation is not available from the suburbs of Atlanta.

Now we have room for argument. We can show how we are squandering precious energy through the folly of encouraging the lone commuter; we can point out how the northern suburbs of Atlanta, and the city itself, will eventually suffer economically and culturally from the lack of public transportation.

The overly broad thesis, in contrast, does not choke off argument with its littleness; instead, it rather overwhelms the writer with its bigness. Here is an example:

> This paper will explain the reasons wars are fought.

Utterly impossible. A book may take a stab at such an enormous topic; a five-hundred-word essay would be a pinprick. Worse yet, the effort at writing a small essay on a big topic can easily seduce a writer into composing generalities.

The simplest way of gauging whether your topic—as summarized in your thesis—is too big for your essay is to check it using library or internet reference sources. A topic such as the causes of war is likely to generate scores of references, which ought to warn you that you may be biting off more than you can chew. Remember that a five-hundred-word essay can, at best, only nibble on a topic. Use your commonsense. For example, the student who initially attempted to write an essay about war changed the thesis to how his father felt about serving in Vietnam—a topic that is certainly more manageable in a short essay.

Refining the Thesis

The thesis will not always occur to you before you start to write the essay; nor will it always automatically emerge from your prewriting efforts. Sometimes, writing about a topic is the only way to discover how you really feel about it. The ideal, however, is to have a preliminary thesis that gives you a firm idea of what you want to say.

Let us say, for example, that you are asked to write about your activities of the past year. How do you discover and refine the thesis for an essay on such a topic?

First, begin by asking yourself some questions about the past year: What did I mainly do during the past year? How did I feel most of the time? Did I learn anything different or was I stuck in a rut? Have I suffered constant upheavals, or have I led a calm existence? Has my family approved of me or not?

After playing with these questions and others, you hit on the following crudely worded ideas:

1. Most of the time, I have been hassled with money worries.
2. Basically, it's been deadly dull, which I can't stand, making me so bored day in and day out.
3. The last year spent learning frugality
4. Major upheavals have caused me to sink or swim as I met various Waterloos.
5. Why have I felt so guilty all year?
6. The first six months were misery. The second six months were ecstasy.

Our thesis should implicitly answer the underlying question that led to it. And the answer to that underlying question will, in turn, logically suggest the best development for your essay. Consider the following revisions:

1. Meeting my monthly expenses on a budget of $300 has kept me anxious and depressed all year.

The word *hassled* has been refined to *anxious and depressed. Money worries* have been more specifically identified as *monthly expenses.* The phrase *on a budget of $300* helps explain the writer's anxiety and worry. The underlying question: Meeting what monthly expenses has kept me anxious and depressed? Develop by *example*.

2. Because of the deadly routine of my studies and work, the past year has been unbearably boring.

Incoherence is the main problem with the original version; the reader gets the general meaning but has to guess where the essay is leading. The underlying question behind the more pointed and purposeful revision: Why has the past year been so boring? Develop by *causal analysis*.

3. Over the last year, I have learned the meaning of frugality.

The original version is a sentence fragment. Through rewording, we have turned the fragment into a complete sentence. The underlying question: What have I learned about the meaning of frugality over the past year? Develop by *definition* or *narration*.

4. Major upheavals required difficult decisions from me this past year.

The original version misuses a figure of speech. Waterloo was a famous battle-field; one cannot sink or swim in it. Figures of speech tend to blur meaning and should be avoided in wording a controlling idea. The underlying question: What major upheavals required difficult decisions? Develop by *narration* or *examples*.

5. Because of several serious errors in judgment, I felt guilt ridden most of last year.

Our new version simply turns a question into an answer, thereby giving better direction to the content of the essay. The underlying question: Why have I felt guilty all year? Develop by *causal analysis*.

6. In contrast to my misery during the first six months of the year, I spent the second six months in a glorious, ecstatic mood.

The original version suggests two unrelated controlling ideas that tend to tug the reader in separate directions. Blended together in a single thesis, these two statements now answer the underlying question: How did my first six months contrast with the second? Develop by *comparison/contrast*.

From this discussion, we can propose six guidelines for writing good controlling ideas. Your controlling idea should:

1. Predict the content of your essay as specifically as possible without wasting words.
2. Be clear and coherent.
3. Be stated in one complete sentence.
4. Be free from figures of speech.
5. Be a statement, not a question.
6. Move toward a single point, not diverge into two or more ideas.

The Informal Outline

The informal outline is a rough sketch of the main points of your essay—of what you intend to say in it and the sequence of the points you mean to cover. It is also a dying form. Many instructors no longer require one for a formal or informal paper. Generations of students who grew up on the computer find the elaborate requirements of outlining oppressive. Some students, if an outline of the paper is required, do it after the fact—that is to say, they write the paper first and then extract an outline from what they have written. In short, the computer age which gives us instantaneity and immediacy has come to regard the practice of outlining as another generation's clunker.

With the outline having declined in popularity, our treatment of it will skim only the major principles. Here is an example of a basic simple outline, covering an essay contrasting two friends. It is an informal outline not intended for submission to the instructor but for the writer's own use. To the left of her entries, she has noted the successive points on which her contrast will be based:

Controlling idea: My two <u>closest</u> friends, John and Mark, are nearly exact opposites in their handling of money.

Attitude toward money:	I.	John has contempt for money.
		Mark has reverence for money.
Willingness to spend money:	II.	John spends without hesitation.
		Mark comparison shops.
Items to be bought:	III.	John buys what he wants.
		Mark buys what he can afford.

If you wish to abandon altogether the numbering system used in outlines, you can simply make a *jot list* of your essay. This is a list on which you jot down your main points with perhaps a note or two about what details to include under each point as support. Jot lists are personal creations that are never submitted to an instructor and may consequently be as neat, messy, or scribbled over as you like, just so long as they help you plan better. An example of a jot list a student did for an essay recounting the effects of a stroke is shown here.

Controlling idea: A stroke affects the victim, the victim's family, and the long-range plans of the victim and the family.

Effects of a stroke

Physical effects on the victim

    Impairment of physical functions.
    Slurred speech. Memory lapses.

Effects on the family

    Loss of former living standard. Decline in income.
    Increased care and attention must be given to the victim.

Effects on long-range plans

> College plans must be changed.
> Vacation plans must be postponed.

Another informal outline is a diagrammatic one, such as the following example, which resembles a computer programmer's flowchart:

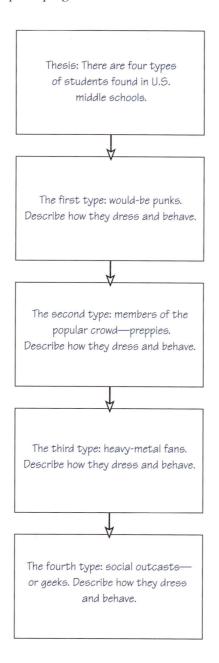

Every rectangle represents a single paragraph, and the arrows show the linkages between them. In each rectangle, the student scribbled down the main points she intended to cover. You can also use a separate index card for each major entry, giving you the flexibility to add or discard entries as the need arises without having to redo the entire outline. Computer software specifically for flowcharting is also readily available.

The Formal Outline

The *formal outline* subdivides the controlling idea of the essay into smaller ideas, which are then developed in separate paragraphs. The currently accepted form of outlining uses Roman numerals, capital letters, and Arabic numerals to order ideas according to their importance. The major principle behind the outline is the equal ranking of ideas of equal importance. Consider this sample outline:

Thesis

I. Main idea
  A. Subidea
  B. Subidea
    1. Subdivision of subidea
    2. Subdivision of subidea

II. Main idea
  A. Subidea
  B. Subidea
    1. Subdivision of subidea
    2. Subdivision of subidea

A typical outline keeps subdividing larger ideas into smaller ones. This, of course, means that every subdivided idea must have at least two subcategories, because it is impossible to divide anything into fewer than two parts.

The following example is known as a *three-level outline* because it has three levels of entries designated by a Roman numeral, a capital letter, and an Arabic numeral. Longer papers use the more complex *four-level outline,* whose shell is shown here:

Thesis

I. Main idea
  A. Subidea
    1. Division of a subidea
    2. Division of a subidea
      a. Minor idea
      b. Minor idea

The Sentence Outline Versus the Topic Outline

You can write either a *sentence outline* or a *topic outline*. All entries in a sentence outline are full sentences, whereas the entries in a topic outline consist of single words or phrases. The following excerpts illustrate the difference.

TOPIC OUTLINE

Thesis: Two primary problems confronting adolescents are extreme dependence on family and the search for personal identity.

  I. Extreme dependence on family
    A. Financial
    B. Emotional

 II. Search for personal identity
    A. Between childhood and adulthood
    B. Difficulty of finding self in today's world
    C. Blurred social standards
    D. No official rites of passage to adulthood

SENTENCE OUTLINE

Thesis: Two primary problems confronting adolescents are extreme dependence on family and the search for personal identity.

  I. Adolescents are extremely dependent on their families.
    A. Because jobs for the young don't pay well, adolescents have to depend on parents for financial support.
    B. Because parents have always provided emotional stability, adolescents feel lost without parental support.

Writing Tip

Outlining After Writing

If you do not outline before you write, consider outlining after you have written. Occasionally, especially if you're writing about a complex subject, an outline will give you a broad view of your essay that might show some weakness. For such an outline, you do not need to observe all the fussy rules of outlining. A simple listing of your main topics will do the job.

II. Adolescents are perplexed by their search for an identity in a changing world.
   A. They are torn between acting as children and acting as adults.
   B. It is difficult for adolescents to form ideals or goals when their world is in an upheaval.
   C. Blurred social standards cause frustration and consequent insecurity in adolescents.
   D. Without official rites of passage to adulthood, adolescents in American society must establish their own rites to account for their emerging identities.

Writing Assignments

1. In a paragraph, explain the organizing methods that you find most useful in writing essays.
2. Write a paragraph on the value of talking out a writing topic with a friend.
3. Write a paragraph about any experience you have had with writer's block.
4. Write a paragraph about the usefulness, or lack of usefulness, of formal outlines.
5. Explain in a paragraph the planning, or lack of it, that goes into your own essay writing.

Chapter 5

The Paragraph

Paragraph comes from the middle Latin word *paragraphus,* meaning *a sign that designates a separate part*. The concept of the paragraph emerged before the invention of the printing press when all writing was still done on continuous papyrus scrolls and copied by an elite army of fussy clerks known as scribes. Out of these humble origins came the idea of the paragraph—a mark inserted in the margins of a manuscript to indicate the appearance of new idea or a significant twist in an old one. Nowadays in practice the idea of the *paragraphus* more or less remains unchanged. What has changed is the marginal mark, which has been replaced by the familiar five space indentation of the first line. The survival of the paragraph throughout the centuries is no doubt due to the usefulness of the concept of dividing a discussion into its separate parts. In that sense, the paragraph is a miniature essay, concerned with expressing a single idea. The sentences of a paragraph have three basic functions:

They state the topic of the paragraph.

They support the topic sentence.

They make smooth and coherent transitions or segues between ideas.

The Topic Sentence

The *topic sentence*—usually the lead sentence of the paragraph—does the job of trumpeting the topic of the paragraph. Here is an example of a typical paragraph, with the topic sentence italicized:

> *All good narratives make a point*. But this point does not have to be profound, preachy, or moralistic. Nor does it have to be an ideological and far-fetched declaration, such as "Communists deserve to go to hell" or "Eat vegetables lest you die." However, your narration must have a point—be it simple or deep, hinted or trumpeted. "My first date was a repulsive experience"; "Skydiving is not for the timid"; "Catching a rainbow in a photograph of Stonehenge was a thrilling accomplishment." Each of these modest assertions could easily be the point of a separate narration.

Topic sentence

The paragraph, in effect, is the means by which ideas may be packaged on the page according to their importance. The reader does not have to search through a jumble of words for the significant points but is guided to them by the familiar paragraph indentation.

Sentences That Back Up the Topic Sentence

You have a topic sentence and proclaim it clearly and concisely. What you must do next is to supply proof that will make your point convincing. By "proof" we do not have in mind what geometry means by that word. Instead, the proof you need to supply falls under the heading of "specific or supporting details," terms that more or less have the same meaning. If, for instance, you say that a recently released movie is a *tense drama,* you have to furnish the details that provide support for this claim—its memorable performances, its taut script, and its unforgettable set design. Here is an example of the use of supporting or specific details in a paragraph:

Topic sentence

> *No more stupid apology for pain has ever been devised than that it elevates*. It is an explanation due to the necessity of justifying pain from the Christian point of view. Pain is nothing more than a signal given by the nerves that the organism is in circumstances hurtful to it; it would be as reasonable to assert that a danger signal elevates a train. But one would have thought that the ordinary observation of life was enough to show that in the great majority of cases, pain, far from refining, has an effect which is merely brutalising. An example in point is the case of hospital in-patients: physical pain makes them self-absorbed, selfish, querulous, impatient, unjust and greedy; I could name a score of petty vices that it generates, but not one virtue. Poverty also is pain. I have known well men who suffered from that grinding agony of poverty which befalls persons who have to live among those richer than themselves; it makes them grasping and mean, dishonest and untruthful. It teaches them all sorts of detestable tricks. With moderate means they would have been honorable men, but ground down by poverty they have lost all sense of decency.

Supporting details

> —W. Somerset Maugham, *The Summing Up*

The sentences that follow the topic sentence are supporting details. In the preceding paragraph, we learn that pain brings out the worst in people, making them grasping or mean and causing them to lose "all sense of decency." The topic sentence is always more general and broader than the details that back it up. Without supporting details of the right kind, your topic sentence will seem unconvincing and weak.

Sentences Used in Transitions Between Concepts and Ideas

A paragraph will occasionally move from one idea to the next, making a transition necessary. Consider the following two paragraphs on the subject of how much a hometown can change in thirty years:

> Sights have changed: there is a new precision about street and home, a clearing away of chicken yards, cow barns, pigeon-crested cupolas, weed lots and coulees, the dim and secret adult-free rendezvous of boys. An intricate metal "jungle gym" is a common backyard sight, the back swing uncommon. There are wide expanses of clear windows designed to let in the parlor light, fewer ornamental windows of colored glass designed to keep it out. Attic and screen porch are slowly vanishing and lovely shades of pastel are painted upon the new houses, tints that once would have embarrassed farmer and merchant alike.
>
> Sounds have changed: I heard not once the clopping of a horse's hoof, nor the mourn of a coyote. I heard instead the shriek of brakes, the heavy throbbing of the once-a-day Braniff airliner into Minot, the shattering sirens born of war, the honk of a diesel locomotive which surely cannot call to faraway places the heart of a wakeful boy like the old steam whistle in the night.
>
> —Eric Sevareid, *This Is Eric Sevareid*

The first paragraph deals with changes in sights, the second paragraph with changes in sounds. It is as if the writer had said to the reader, "Listen, I'm going to tell you how much my hometown has changed. First, I'm going to tell you about the sights." Then, when he is done with that topic, he nudges the reader, as if to say, "Now I am going to tell you about the sounds."

If you look hard enough, you'll find that every sentence in a paragraph is being used directly or indirectly for one of these three reasons—either to state the topic sentence, to provide backup for the topic sentences, or to make smooth transitions between ideas.

More about the Topic Sentence

Topic sentences are as variable as any other sentence and in real life do not practice a slavish orthodoxy to form. Some topic sentences, for example, are developed over two paragraphs. Here is an example with the topic sentence italicized:

> *For the past century or so, we've been performing an open-ended experiment on ourselves, extending the day, shortening the night, and short-circuiting the human body's sensitive response to light.* The consequences of our bright new world are

more readily perceptible in less adaptable creatures living in the peripheral glow of our prosperity. But for humans, too, light pollution may take a biological toll. At least one new study has suggested a direct correlation between higher rates of breast cancer in women and the nighttime brightness of their neighborhoods.

Topic sentence   In the end, humans are no less trapped by light pollution than the frogs in a pond near a brightly lit highway. Living in a glare of our own making, we have cut ourselves off from our evolutionary and cultural patrimony—the light of the stars and the rhythms of day and night. *In a very real sense, light pollution causes us to lose sight of our true place in the universe, to forget the scale of our being, which is best measured against the dimensions of a deep night with the Milky Way—the edge of our galaxy—arching overhead.*

—Verlyn Kinkenborg, "Our Vanishing Night,"
National Geographic, November, 2008.

In this case, the topic sentence is placed at the end of the second paragraph because in that strong position it can wrap up the controlling idea, namely that modern society is harming itself through light pollution. Developing an idea over two or more paragraphs gives a writer the advantage of taking a slower pace that allows supporting details and informative or humorous asides to be blended into the discussion.

Topic Sentence Implied

Finally, not all paragraphs are written with definite topic sentences. Indeed, many paragraphs have topic sentences that are not stated but are merely implied. Here is an example:

The little crowd of mourners—all men and boys, no women—threaded their way across the market-place between the piles of pomegranates and the taxis and the camels, wailing a short chant over and over again. What really appeals to the flies is that the corpses here are never put into coffins, they are merely wrapped in a piece of rag and carried on a rough wooden bier on the shoulders of four friends. When the friends get to the burying-ground, they hack an oblong hole a foot or two deep, dump the body in it and fling over it a little of the dried-up, lumpy earth, which is like broken brick. No gravestone, no name, no identifying mark of any kind. The burying-ground is merely a huge waste of hummocky earth, like a derelict building-lot. After a month or two no one can even be certain where his own relatives are buried.

—George Orwell, "Marrakech"

Orwell's details are already so vivid and gripping that no formal topic sentence is necessary.

An implied topic sentence is most commonly found in paragraphs that come in the middle of an essay and add information to it. Here is an example:

Neurotic, self-loathing, arrogant, and vociferous, Kepler was drubbed with tiresome regularity by his classmates. He fared little better once out in the world, where he tried but failed to become a Lutheran minister. He sought solitude in marriage, but his wife, he said with the bleak objectivity of a born observer, "was simple of mind and fat of body . . . stupid, sulking, lonely, melancholy." Kepler tried to make a living casting horoscopes, but was seldom paid. He spent much of his time trekking from one court to another to plead for his fee, drawing titters from the flunkies when he appeared in his baggy, food-stained suit, tripping over himself with apologies and explanations, getting nowhere. His lifetime earnings could not have purchased the starglobe in Tycho's library.

—Timothy Ferris, *Coming of Age in the Milky Way*

Implied in this paragraph is the topic sentence *Kepler was the most unlikely of men to be a world-class astronomer,* or something to that effect, echoing a theme that occurred earlier in the essay.

However, the implied topic sentence, so common in the essays of professionals, is seldom encouraged in student paragraphs. For the beginner, the safest course is to create paragraphs whose topic sentences make the writer's aim and meaning immediately clear.

The Shape of the Paragraph

The paragraph is often graphically represented as resembling an overstuffed sandwich. In this portrayal, the process and pattern factions of rhetorical theory once again face off. Process believes that the shape or form of the paragraph is not predetermined but is arrived at through the trial and error of the composing process. On the other hand, the other side (pattern) argues that it is possible for a writer to conceptualize an ideal form for the paragraph and then use it as a mold for writing. This is an abstract squabble that has no effect upon the writer. Any theory of writing that strikes at the heart of composing itself is bound to influence the working habits of the everyday writer. Writing is a complex business, so complex that we would be startled to learn that either side—process or pattern—had swept the day. The fact is that both sides contain a modicum of truth but not enough to categorically declare a winner.

The following odd-looking shape reminds us that paragraphs typically begin and end with a generalization, between which are crammed more specific assertions.

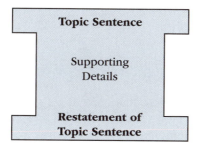

Here is such a paragraph:

Topic sentence

Supporting
details

Summary
sentence

By a strange perversity in the cosmic plan, the biologically good die young. Species are not destroyed for their shortcomings but for their achievements. The tribes that slumber in the graveyards of the past were not the most simple and undistinguished of their day but the most complicated and conspicuous. The magnificent sharks of the Devonian period passed with the passing of the period, but certain contemporaneous genera of primitive shellfish are still on Earth. Similarly, the lizards of the Mesozoic era have long outlived the dinosaurs who were immeasurably their biologic betters. Illustrations such as these could be endlessly increased. The price of distinction is death.

—John Hodgdon Bradley, "Is Man an Absurdity?"

Topic Sentence in the Middle

Some paragraphs are found buried somewhere in the middle of an essay, where the argument is the thickest. A transition sentence or two, a little discussion, and the topic sentence of the paragraph is forced to take a seat somewhere in the middle pews. What is important, however, is not where the topic sentence is actually placed, but how adequately it has been developed and proved. Consider this paragraph:

Topic sentence

As long as women were brought up and educated very differently from men and as long as their whole mode of life was different, it was safe and suitable to uphold the traditional beliefs as to certain mental sex differences. But as the differentiation in the education of the two sexes lessened, so has the differences in their abilities and interests. *Today the survival of some of these stereotypes is a psychological straitjacket for both sexes.* Witness the fact that some 40 per cent of women undergraduates have confessed (the proportion was confirmed in two studies on widely separated college campuses) that they have occasionally "played dumb" on dates; that is, concealed some academic honor, pretended ignorance of a subject, "threw games," played down certain skills in obedience to the unwritten law that the man must be superior in those particular areas. If he *were* superior, the stratagem would not be necessary. "It embarrassed me that my 'steady' in high school," recalled a college junior in an interview, "got worse marks than I. A boy should naturally do better in school. I would never tell him my marks and would often ask him to help me with my homework." Confront the belief "a boy should naturally do better in school" with the fact that marks of high school girls are generally somewhat superior to those of boys, probably because girls study more conscientiously. Could a surer recipe for trouble be invented?

—Mirra Komarovsky, "The Bright Girl's Dilemma," *Women in the Modern World*

In sum, although the topic sentence will typically occur at the beginning of a paragraph, sometimes it will also be found crouching in the middle or bringing up the rear. The essay written so that every topic sentence dutifully comes at the beginning of every paragraph would soon seem tiresome and mechanical. You would be smart to write paragraphs whose topic sentences vary not only in wording, but also in placement.

Characteristics of the Paragraph

Paragraphs vary widely in shape, style, length, and complexity, but all good paragraphs have *unity, coherence,* and *completeness.*

Unity

Good paragraphs have *unity*, meaning that they do not beat about the bush; they approach the subject directly, moving toward the main point of the topic sentence without distraction. To be unified, a paragraph must stick to its main point and never stray from it. For example, if your topic sentence commits you to writing about the anguish you felt when your German shepherd died, then any description of pets in general or a world without pets would ruin the focus that unity provides.

All writers occasionally stray from the topic sentence, but most of the time they catch and correct this mistake during revision. Staying with your main point sometimes even requires you mercilessly to discard compelling but pointless details. There is, moreover, an ancient rule of thumb that might help you achieve unity: Each new sentence of a paragraph should begin with old information and end by adding something new. Consider, as an example, the practice of this rule in the following paragraph:

> Mathematicians discovered that there were various series of numbers, each one smaller than the one before, which, if added together, come to a total that equals pi exactly. The only trouble is that *the series of numbers* goes on and on and on and on and never comes to an end. *This means if you add up* the first eight numbers of the series you come close to pi; if you add up the first 16 you come closer; if you add up the first 32 you come still closer and so on—but you never get it exactly. *What's more, the numbers are* mathematically complicated and it takes time to work out exactly what each *successive number is.*
>
> —Isaac Asimov, "Mathematicians Look for a Piece of Pi"

In the preceding paragraph we have italicized phrases that hark back to old information. The rest of the respective sentences add something new. Observe this rule in your own writing, and your paragraphs are likely to be unified.

Coherence

A well-written paragraph has *coherence*: its sentences are not only clear, logical, and grammatically correct, but they are also arranged so that the reader easily understands the flow of ideas. Perhaps the best way to achieve coherence is to think of your paragraph as a single unit rather than a succession of sentences. The focal point of the unit is the topic sentence, which all other sentences of the paragraph should work coherently to support. Here are some important guidelines for creating coherent paragraphs:

Avoid mixed constructions.   Sentences have built-in predictable patterns and structures. For example, when we hear a sentence that begins *If you don't play the lottery,* we might anticipate it to end, *you can't expect to win.* But we never expect a sentence that begins *If you don't play the lottery* to end with *winning is hopeless.* Such a sentence can be understood, but not as quickly and as easily as the sentence whose ending follows the pattern predicted by its beginning. Sentences that begin with one structural pattern but jump to another are called *mixed constructions.* Here are some examples of *mixed construction* with their corrections:

Mixed   Bowing to the pressure of special interests is a sure way for a politician to lose respect.

Improved   Bowing to the pressure of special interests is a sure way for a politician to lose the respect of his voters.

or

Mixed   Whereas parents insist on stifling their children's independence, they encourage rebellion.

Improved   When parents insist on stifling their children's independence, they encourage rebellion.

Correcting all mixed constructions in your paragraphs will immediately improve their coherence.

Use pronouns that refer only to clear antecedents.   Here is an example of incoherence resulting from poor pronoun reference:

Everybody today wants psychological advice so that *they* will tell *them* what to do. But *that's* a way of avoiding *your* problems and losing *one's* sense of responsibility, *which* is the only healthy way to survive.

A careless and inconsistent use of pronouns jumbles the ideas. The passage simply does not stick together properly. To whom do *they* and *them* refer? What does *that's* stand for? Why is there a sudden shift from *everybody* to *your* and yet another shift to *one's*? Finally, *which* seems to refer to *responsibility,* creating further confusion. Now observe the revision:

Everybody today wants psychological advice from a counselor who will tell him or her what to do. But relying on counseling is a way of avoiding problems and losing one's sense of responsibility; without responsibility a happy life is impossible.

(See the *Handbook,* p. 566, for an explanation of antecedents.)

Use similar grammatical structures to achieve balance in a sentence.   This practice is called *parallelism*. The use of parallelism could improve the following sentence:

> Walking a beat, riding in patrol cars, and the work of an undercover agent are all dangerous aspects of police work.

Walking and *riding* are similar in form, but *the work of an undercover agent* breaks the pattern. The following is an improvement:

> Walking a beat, riding in patrol cars, and doing undercover work are all dangerous aspects of police work.

> (For a fuller explanation of parallelism, see pp. 598–602 in the *Handbook*.)

Use transition words to help the reader move easily through your paragraph. Transition words identify the logical connection between two parts of a sentence. They help the reader move smoothly from one idea to another. For example:

She searched and searched for her purse. She could not find it.   *Too abrupt*

She searched and searched for her purse, but she could not find it.   *Improved*

Romance may express itself in a variety of ways. A man may send a woman   *Too abrupt*
a dozen long-stemmed roses. A husband may plan and cook a gourmet
meal.

Romance may express itself in a variety of ways. For example, a man may send   *Improved*
a woman a dozen long-stemmed roses. Or, as a romantic gesture, a husband
may plan and cook a gourmet meal.

When you choose a transition word, be certain of the type of signal you wish to send the reader—addition, contrast, specification, or conclusion. (See conjunctions in the *Handbook,* pp. 570–571.)

Repeat key words to attract and hold your reader's attention.   Notice the effective repetition of the word *dance* in the following excerpt from Hans Christian Andersen's *The Red Shoes:*

> The shoes would not let her do what she liked: when she wanted to go to the right, they *danced* to the left. When she wanted to *dance* up the room, the shoes *danced* down the room, and then down the stairs, through the streets and out of the town gate. Away she *danced,* and away she had to *dance,* right into the dark forest. Something shone up above the trees and she thought it was the moon, for it was a face, but it was the old soldier with the red beard. He nodded and said, "See what pretty *dancing* shoes!"

Metro Imagery

If you are in the mood for some kind of image to explain the role of the paragraph, then you can imagine the sentences as the individual box cars of an underground metro. When the locomotive appears, it is always followed by several compartments. The locomotive, of course, is the main point of the paragraph—its topic sentence. The compartments are the supporting details.

> This frightened her terribly and she wanted to throw off the red shoes, but they stuck fast. She tore off her stockings, but the shoes had grown fast to her feet. So off she *danced,* and off she had to *dance,* over fields and meadows, in rain and sunshine, by day and by night, but at night it was fearful.

The repetition of the word *dance* holds the reader's attention and reinforces the point of the fairy tale—that the red shoes were magical.

Completeness

There are no rules governing the length of an adequately developed paragraph. The topic sentence must guide you. The topic sentence *A pig is ugly* could probably be supported in one-hundred words; on the other hand, *Poverty is ugly* might require at least three-hundred words. The more restricted and narrow the topic sentence, the shorter the paragraph required. To write effective, complete paragraphs, you need to distinguish between generalizations and specific details. A generalization is a broad statement, such as "In the nineteenth century infectious diseases often killed people." A specific detail is more narrow, such as "Pneumonia and influenza were major threats to young and old people." Our point is that when you write your topic sentence, which is a broad statement, you need to support it with specific details. Exactly what kinds of supporting details you should use in your paragraphs will vary with your subject, but as a general rule, it is better to write in specifics than in generalities. Any writer who pens a sentence such as "Cigarette smoke contains many dangerous gases" will not sound as believable as one who writes that "Cigarette smoke contains a variety of dangerous gases, including carbon monoxide, formaldehyde, and hydrogen cyanide."

Journalistic Paragraphs

A specialized kind of paragraph has evolved from news reporting. Often, this sort of paragraph is no more than a sentence or two long, is entirely lacking in supporting details, and is intended to present only the bare bones of a case. This *journalistic paragraph* is written to be gulped down at a glance by a reader crowded in a bus or squashed between commuters in a subway. Students of journalism are instructed to answer five questions as succinctly as possible—who what, when, where, and how. Here are three examples of journalistic paragraphs:

> San Francisco—the liberal, left-coast city conservatives love to mock—could be undergoing a transformation when it comes to homeless people. Although the city would still be a poor choice for a pep rally for the war in Iraq, indications are that the residents have had it with aggressive panhandlers, street squatters, and drug users.
>
> —*San Francisco Chronicle,* Oct. 9, 2007, A-1

> When Tobias "Bags of Money" Boyland went looking for a new career after serving 13 years in prison for armed robbery and drug dealing, he quickly found something that suited his sensibilities: He opened a collection agency.
>
> —*Enterprise Record,* Jan. 6, 2010, 8A

> Administrators at Stevenson High School in Lincolnshire spiked Friday's, edition of the school's award-winning newspaper because of concerns over stories on drinking and smoking by honor students, teen pregnancy, and shoplifting, the editor-in-chief said. Advocates of press freedom bashed the decision to halt publication.
>
> —*Chicago Tribune,* Nov. 20, 2009, front page

Transitions Between Paragraphs

An essay consists of ideas united around a central thesis and expressed in separate paragraphs. And it is the responsibility of the careful writer to link these separate paragraphs with their individual freight of ideas into a seamless train of thought. Among the several common techniques used to link paragraphs are *repetition, transitional words and phrases, transitional questions,* and *bridging sentences.*

Repetition

Paragraphs may be linked by repeating in their initial sentences some word or phrase that is common and equally important to both. Here is an example:

> I have experienced *loneliness* many times in my life, but until recently I lived my *loneliness* without being aware of it. In the past I tried to overcome my sense of

isolation by plunging into work projects and entering into social activities. By keeping busy and by committing myself to interesting and challenging work, I never had to face, in any direct or open way, the nature of my existence as an isolated and solitary individual.

I first began to awaken to the meaning of *loneliness,* to feel *loneliness* in the center of my consciousness, one terrible day when my wife and I were confronted with the necessity of making a decision . . .

—Clark E. Moustakas, "The Terror and Love in Loneliness"

Repetition of the word *loneliness* in the initial sentences serves to link the paragraphs.

Transitional Words and Phrases

The English language is rich in ready-made phrases that writers routinely use to link paragraphs. Here is an example:

In every cultivated language there are two great classes of words which, taken together, comprise the whole vocabulary. First, there are those words with which we become acquainted in ordinary conversation, which we learn, that is to say, from the members of our own family and from our familiar associates, and which we should know and use even if we could not read or write. They concern the common things of life, and are the stock in trade of all who speak the language. Such words may be called "popular," since they belong to the people at large and are not the exclusive possession of a limited class.

On the other hand, our language includes a multitude of words which are comparatively seldom used in ordinary conversation. Their meanings are known to every educated person, but there is little occasion to employ them at home or in the market-place.

—J. B. Greenough and G. L. Kittredge, "Learned Words and Popular Words"

The italicized phrase, *on the other hand,* links the two paragraphs, the first of which discusses popular words and the second, learned words.

Bridging Sentences

Some paragraph transitions consist of an initial bridging sentence that both sums up what went before and anticipates what comes after. Here is an example of such a sentence (in italics), describing the execution of Mary, Queen of Scots:

Briefly, solemnly, and sternly they delivered their awful message. They informed her that they had received a commission under the great seal to see her executed, and she was told that she must prepare to suffer on the following morning.

She was dreadfully agitated. For a moment she refused to believe them. Then, as the truth forced itself upon her, tossing her head in disdain and struggling to control herself, she called her physician and began to speak to him of money that was owed to her in France. At last it seems that she broke down altogether, and they left her with fear either that she would destroy herself in the night, or that she would refuse to come to the scaffold, and that it might be necessary to drag her there by violence.

—James Anthony Froude, "The Execution of Mary, Queen of Scots"

Bridging sentences are widely used in modern journalism and are especially favored by many popular magazines, such as *Time.*

Using Varied Paragraph Transitions

Sometimes the continuity of theme is strong enough between two paragraphs to require no formal transition. However, if the new paragraph introduces an entirely new idea or a significantly different wrinkle to an old one, you may need a transition. Common sense must be your guide. All writers eventually develop signature traits in their styles—and one could be a fondness for, say, the bridging sentence transition. But to overuse the same kind of paragraph transition is to risk boring your reader. The ideal is to use a variety of paragraph transitions, as this excerpt does (transitions in italics):

Let us, *for example,* examine the case of a man I will call Victor Clauson. He is a junior executive with a promising future, a wife who loves him, and two healthy children. Nevertheless he is anxious and unhappy. He is bored with his job, which he believes saps his initiative and destroys his integrity; he is also dissatisfied with his wife, and convinced he never loved her. Feeling like a slave to his company, his wife, and his children, Clauson realizes that he has lost control over the conduct of his life.

Is this man "sick"? And if so, what can be done about it? At least half a dozen alternatives are open to him. He could throw himself into his present work or change jobs or have an affair or get a divorce. Or he could develop a psychosomatic symptom such as headaches and consult a doctor. Or, as still another alternative, he could seek out a psychotherapist. Which of these alternatives is the *right* one for him? The answer is not easy.

—Thomas S. Szasz, M.D., "What Psychiatry Can and Cannot Do"

Using a variety of transitional devices, ranging from a transitional phrase to questions to a bridging sentence, this writer produces paragraphs that cover his theme in bright and lively sequence.

Beginning and Ending Paragraphs

Beginning and ending paragraphs are two specialized variations on the paragraph, and consequently are somewhat different in structure from the usual workhorse paragraph found in the thick of an essay. Since they open and close the essay, these paragraphs should be carefully crafted to have an impact. Following are some examples of opening strategies to consider.

Begin with a memorable personal experience.   From an essay about being trapped and almost executed by vigilantes in the South:

> I was born and raised in rural upstate New York, but who I am began with a younger brother's death in a hunting accident when I was twelve and he was eight. I held the gun that killed him. But if my life began at twelve with my brother's sudden, violent death, then my end, determined by the trajectory of that harsh beginning, could easily have taken place a scant six years later, when, in June 1965, I was kidnapped at gunpoint by vigilantes near the small town of Hayneville, Alabama.
>
> —Gregory Orr, "Return to Hayneville, *The Virginia Quarterly Review,*
> Summer 2008.

Begin with a question.   From an essay defining poverty:

> You ask me what is poverty? Listen to me. Here I am, dirty, smelly, and with no "proper" underwear on and with the stench of my rotting teeth near you. I will tell you. Listen to me. Listen without pity. I cannot use your pity. Listen with understanding. Put yourself in my dirty, worn-out, ill-fitting shoes, and hear me.
>
> —Jo Goodwin Parker, "What Is Poverty?"

Begin with a thought-provoking quotation.   From an essay on our obsession with numbers:

> "The very hairs of your head," says Matthew 10:30, "are all numbered." There is little reason to doubt it. Increasingly, everything tends to get numbered one way or another, everything that can be counted, measured, averaged, estimated or quantified. Intelligence is gauged by a quotient, the humidity by a ratio, the pollen by its count, and the trends of birth, death, marriage and divorce by rates. In this epoch of runaway demographics, society is as often described and analyzed with statistics as with words. Politics seems more and more a game played with percentages turned up by pollsters, and economics a learned babble of ciphers and indexes that few people can translate and apparently nobody can control. Modern civilization, in sum, has begun to resemble an interminable arithmetic class in which, as Carl Sandburg put it, "numbers fly like pigeons in and out of your head."
>
> —Frank Trippett, "Getting Dizzy by the Numbers"

Begin by answering the question posed by your title.   From an essay on the future of marriage titled "Does Marriage Have a Future?"

> The answer to this question is an unequivocal yes. The future of marriage is, I believe, as assured as any human social form can be....
>
> —Jessie Bernard, "Does Marriage Have a Future?"

Begin with a surprising statement.   From an essay arguing for the superiority of women over men:

> Physically and psychically women are by far the superiors of men. The old chestnut about women being more emotional than men has been forever destroyed by the facts of two great wars....
>
> —Ashley Montagu, "Women As the Superiors of Men"

Ending Paragraphs

Take leave of your audience with an emphatic exit. Do not timidly shrink or fade, as does this conclusion:

> And so, the reasons I have just cited are why animal experimentation is wrong.

No writer can expect to inspire a reader with such a sloppy conclusion. Here is an improved version:

> Researchers defend their work on animals scientifically on the basis of the similarities between animals and people, but then they defend this same work morally on the basis of their differences. Well now, they cannot have it both ways. Besides, the differences are not so clear-cut. Some animals have a more highly developed intelligence than some human beings. Ponder this question: If we were to be discovered by some more intelligent creatures in the universe, would they have the right to experiment on us?

There are as many ways to end a paragraph as to begin one. Here are some suggestions and examples for climactic endings.

End with an incisive summary.   From a student essay listing the causes of why the Japanese are acquiring more global competence than are Americans:

> In sum, the Japanese spend eleven million dollars a year on study abroad for their students, as opposed to our four million dollars; the Japanese introduce foreign languages into their elementary school curriculum whereas we usually wait until high school; and the Japanese reveal an enormous curiosity about successful countries and their way of doing things. We had better start improving our own global competence by imitating the Japanese attitude or we could decline into a second-class nation.

The key to writing clever beginning paragraphs and emphatic closing ones is rewriting. Seldom does a zippy opening or climactic ending drop into a writer's lap. It is through repeated digging into the material, through rewriting, that the writer will most likely unearth a gem suitable for the beginning or ending.

The Relationship Between the Beginning and the Ending

No simple relationship exists between the beginning and the ending of an essay that may be expressed in a formula. But there is a geometric shape that more or less applies to the essay, and it is a circle. Typically, essays hark back to their beginnings in their endings. The final paragraph may decisively evoke the essay's opening or may only vaguely hint at it. Or, for that matter, the ending may atypically make no mention at all of the beginning.

Nevertheless, it is true that many essays will circle back to their beginnings in their endings. And many will do so imagistically, by alluding in the final paragraph to an image that occurred in the essay's opening. Here is an example of an essay that does so almost precisely:

THE ENDING

While I was still a boy, I came to the conclusion that there were three grades of thinking; and since I was later to claim thinking as my hobby, I came to an even stranger conclusion—namely, that I myself could not think at all.

I must have been an unsatisfactory child for grownups to deal with. I remember how incomprehensible they appeared to me at first, but not, of course, how I appeared to them. It was the headmaster of my grammar school who first brought the subject of thinking before me—though neither in the way, nor with the result he intended. He had some statuettes in his study. They stood on a high cupboard behind his desk. One was a lady wearing nothing but a bath towel. She seemed frozen in an eternal panic lest the bath towel slip down any farther, and since she had no arms, she was in an unfortunate position to pull the towel up again. Next to her crouched the statuette of a leopard, ready to spring down at the top drawer of a filing cabinet labeled A–AH. My innocence interpreted this as the victim's last, despairing cry. Beyond the leopard was a naked, muscular gentleman, who sat, looking down, with his chin on his fist and his elbow on his knee. He seemed utterly miserable.

THE ENDING

If I were to go back to the headmaster's study and find the dusty statuettes still there, I would arrange them differently. I would dust Venus and put her aside, for I have come to love her and know her for the fair thing she is. But I would put *The Thinker,* sunk in his desperate thought, where there were shadows before him—and at his back, I would put the leopard, crouched and ready to spring.

—William Golding, "Thinking as a Hobby"

The opening paragraphs of this classic essay use statuettes to represent and classify thinking into three distinct types, an image to which the ending also pointedly returns. This is a nearly perfect example of a final paragraph achieving closure by repeating an image with which the essay opened. Many essays use their conclusions to hark back to their openings, but few do so as neatly. Here is a final paragraph that hints at the opening but only indirectly:

THE ENDING

When I have been dead 10 years and a family comes to tend the flowers on the grave next to mine, and they talk about the latest pitiful inequity plaguing their town, they will hear a rattling from my grave and can properly say: "That's Jim again. His knee is still jerking."

—James Michener, "We Can Create a Decent Society"

After opening the essay by describing the low into which liberals had fallen during the Reagan years, the author proceeds to identify himself unashamedly only as a knee-jerk liberal. The playful image of his knee still jerking in the grave nicely rounds off the discussion.

■ *Exercises*

1. Identify the topic sentence in each of the following paragraphs, and state whether the material moves from the specific to the general or from the general to the specific.

    a. You get milk from a cow without killing it. You get wool from the sheep without killing it. Two of the strongest animals in the jungle are vegetarians—the elephant and the gorilla. The first two years are the most important years of a man's life, and during that period he is not involved with eating meat. If you suddenly become very ill, there is a good chance you will be taken off a meat diet. So it is a myth that killing is necessary for survival.

    —Dick Gregory, "If You Had to Kill Your Own Hog"

    b. If you enjoy working out the strategy of games, tic-tac-toe or poker or chess; if you are interested in the frog who jumped up three feet and fell back two in getting out of a well, or in the fly buzzing between the noses of two approaching cyclists, or in the farmer who left land to his three sons; if you have been captivated by codes and ciphers or are interested in crossword puzzles; if you like to fool around with numbers; if music appeals to you by the sense of form which it expresses—then you will enjoy logic. You ought to be warned, perhaps. Those who take up logic get glassy-eyed and absent-minded. They join a fanatical cult. But they have a good time. Theirs is one of the most durable, absorbing and inexpensive of pleasures. Logic is fun.

    —Roger W. Holmes, *The Rhyme of Reason*

c. Computers, it is often said, manipulate symbols. They don't deal with numbers directly, but with symbols that can represent not only numbers but also words and pictures. Inside the circuits of the digital computer these symbols exist in electrical form, and there are just two basic symbols—a high voltage and a low voltage. Clearly, this is a marvelous kind of symbolism for a machine; the circuits don't have to distinguish between nine different shades of gray but only between black and white, or, in electrical terms, between high and low voltages.

—Tracy Kidder, *The Soul of a New Machine*

d. The intensity and depth of his concentration were fantastic. When battling a recalcitrant problem, he worried it as an animal worries its prey. Often, when we found ourselves up against a seemingly insuperable difficulty, he would stand up, put his pipe on the table, and say in his quaint English, "I will a little tink" (he could not pronounce "th"). Then he would pace up and down, twirling a lock of long, graying hair around his forefinger.

—Banesh Hoffmann, "My Friend, Albert Einstein"

2. Identify the pattern used in each of the following paragraphs.

a. The "human condition" may be defined as a measure of the extent to which the potential for living is realized under the limitations of the inborn genes and of the environment of the Earth. Full potential means adequate food, shelter, clothing, education, and health care, plus useful and creative work and leisure for every normal baby born. The slums of Calcutta or Rio, the ghettos of the West, represent a potential close to zero.

—Stuart Chase, Two Cheers for Technology

b. Illiterates cannot travel freely. When they attempt to do so, they encounter risks that few of us can dream of. They cannot read traffic signs and, while they often learn to recognize and to decipher symbols, they cannot manage street names which they have not seen before. The same is true for bus and subway stops. While ingenuity can sometimes help a man or woman to discern directions from familiar landmarks, buildings, cemeteries, churches, and the like, most illiterates are virtually immobilized. They seldom wander past the streets and neighborhoods they know. Geographical paralysis becomes a bitter metaphor for their entire existence.

—Jonathan Kozol, "The Human Cost of an Illiterate Society"

c. Lenin, with whom I had a long conversation in Moscow in 1920, was, superficially, very unlike Gladstone, and yet, allowing for the difference of time and place and creed, the two men had much in common. To begin with the differences: Lenin was cruel, which Gladstone was not; Lenin had no respect for tradition, whereas Gladstone had a great deal; Lenin considered all means legitimate for securing the victory of his party, whereas for Gladstone politics was a game with certain rules that must be observed. All these differences, to my mind, are to the advantage of Gladstone, and accordingly Gladstone on the whole had beneficent effects, while Lenin's effects were disastrous. In spite of all these dissimilarities, however, the points of resemblance were quite as profound. Lenin supposed himself to be an atheist, but in this he was mistaken. He thought that the world was governed by the dialectic, whose instrument he was; just as much as Gladstone, he conceived of himself as the human agent of a superhuman Power. His ruthlessness and unscrupulousness were only as to means, not as to ends; he would not have been willing to purchase personal power at the expense of apostasy. Both men derived their personal force from this unshakable conviction of their own rectitude. Both men, in support of their respective faiths, ventured into realms in which, from ignorance, they could only cover themselves with ridicule—Gladstone in Biblical criticism, Lenin in philosophy.

—Bertrand Russell, *Unpopular Essays*

Writing Assignments

1. Write a paragraph about some common superstitions in modern life. Begin with a personal experience.

2. Write two paragraphs about the importance of *confidentiality*. Make sure that you have a clear transition from one paragraph to the next.

3. Write a paragraph showing the difference between *ignorance* and *stupidity*. After completing your paragraph, review it to ensure that it is complete.

4. In a paragraph, describe how you feel after studying all evening. Be sure to stick to your topic sentence and prove it adequately.

5. In a paragraph, state the probable reasons for the popularity of Google, Inc., the billion-dollar internet company. Place your topic sentence at the beginning of the paragraph.

6. Pretending that you are writing for a newspaper, write five paragraphs reporting an event that happened in your community.

7. Write the opening paragraph for an essay about receiving a poorer grade than you expected on one of your major course exams. Begin the paragraph with a question.

8. In a single paragraph, argue for or against having mothers stay at home while they have small children. Begin the paragraph with an appropriate statistic or a quotation from an expert.

9. Write a single paragraph listing the steps involved in any process with which you are familiar. Begin with a general statement about the process. (For example, "Reconciling a checkbook requires concentration.")

10. In a paragraph, describe any jogger you have observed. Place your topic sentence at the end of your paragraph.

Rewriting Assignment

The following paragraph is incomplete because its does not fulfill its promise to show that the author's roommate had a dysfunctional family. Collaborate with another student in your class, and complete the paragraph so that it is convincing. You may use fictional support for the topic sentence. Take turns with your partner in supplying effective examples.

My roommate Joe's family is dysfunctional in the way all of the siblings interact with constant hostility toward each other. Last November, I was invited to have Thanksgiving with this family. From the time I entered the house until I said goodbye, the two brothers and sisters kept quarreling. Their attitude ruined the entire celebration for me.

Chapter 6

Drafting, Revising, and Style

Drafting, the attempt at actually writing the essay, usually begins after the research and reading have all been done and almost always after a thesis has been devised. We recommend a minimum of three drafts. The first draft should simply get something down on paper. Revise this for macro errors and you end up with the second draft. After editing and proofreading this second draft, you type up or print out the final draft for submission.

Pointers on Drafting

Although writers and their methods are infinitely varied, there are still some time-tested practices that can help anyone write a better draft.

Keep Your Audience in Mind

Write down on a note card or sheet of paper a statement of what you are writing, for whom, and for what effect. For example, if you are writing a paper aimed at persuading a landlubber audience about the joys of sailing, you might jot down the following: *five-hundred-word essay on sailing aimed at novices to convince them to take up the sport.* We firmly believe that no writer ever went broke remembering the overall aims of an assignment.

Keep Your Purpose in Mind

You may begin with one purpose and have every intention of keeping it, but during the drafting you discover a better and more energetic aim for your essay. If so, go with the energy. Creativity is exactly what drafting is meant to bring out. You are a sculptor trying to find a stone to chisel. Your first draft will be the raw stone. You will do the chiseling during revising and editing.

Organize Your Main Points

An easy way to make a rough outline of your essay is to write down your main points on separate index cards. You may also jot down supporting details on each card. Shuffle the cards to reflect the order of presentation of your points. Experiment with rearranging the cards until you are satisfied that you have the best and most emphatic sequence. Then begin the writing.

Include Ample Specific Details

If you pack details or examples behind your points, your paragraphs will seem solid and substantial. If you do not, they will seem like this one—vague and empty:

> Thinking back into the history of music, one can still hear the peaceful melodies of Bach and Beethoven—sounds to soothe the soul, not torment the mind. As words were added to the music, song developed and warmed our hearts. From the 1960s and 1970s came songs of love and despair, tunes to portray fun in the sun, and choruses of rhyme and reason. Each of these songs either contained deep sentiment or meaning or simply provided easy listening or a light beat to dance to. Again there were songs to provide thought and fun and to ease the mind. Then came the 1980s.

The problem with this paragraph—from an actual student essay—is not its language, which is conventional and easy to read, nor its style, which is straightforward. Instead, the problem is emptiness of content. What love songs of the 1960s and 1970s does the writer mean? With a little effort, he or she could have named some— "You Send Me" by Sam Cooke, "Michelle" by the Beatles, "The First Time Ever I Saw Your Face" by Roberta Flack—and sounded impressively authoritative. That is what you must try hard to do in your draft.

Write in Any Sequence You Prefer

We are tediously linear writers. We begin with the first word and slog a path doggedly through to the last. But that is not necessarily the best way for all writers to work. You may, as you begin your draft, have the words for a brilliant ending paragraph come tumbling into your head. In that case, write the last paragraph first. Do what works best for you. You can always adjust the sequence later.

Be Patient

It is rare for a writer to breeze through a first draft without repeatedly stopping and starting. Do not delude yourself, as some do, into believing that the faltering progress of your draft marks you as an inept writer. If anything, it signals that your working habits are normal and healthy. Writing is always rough going at first. Dorothy Canfield Fisher, a seasoned writer, compared starting to write with a baseball pitcher warming up his arm. Keep on writing and your prose, like a pitcher's curve ball, is bound to get better.

Use a Computer

Most of your writing will probably be done on a computer. In that case, we recommend two tricks that we practice ourselves in our own writing.

The first is to edit not only on the screen but also on the actual printed page. When you are nearly satisfied with your text, print it out and edit it with a pencil or pen. In doing so, you not only get a lifelike view of your text that a screen equivalent cannot match, but you also preserve your original in case you later decide to restore some or all of it.

The second technique is to create a file for saving large erasures or deletions. Many computers save the last change in a buffer and allow you to reinstate it with a few keystrokes, but the material is typically lost when you turn off the machine. If you create a file and save your erasures, you can reinstate this text if you decide later that it is not so bad after all. You might also store the separate drafts for later comparison.

The First Draft

The text you produce in drafting will be clumsy, scrawled over, and perhaps occasionally incoherent. Good. That is exactly how a first draft should look and read. This process of self-discovery should be eye-opening.

To give you a realistic idea of the successive steps involved in producing a paper, we will follow an actual student paper through three stages: a *draft*, a *revision*, and a final editing for *style*. The assignment was to write a paper that answered the question *Who am I?* A student named Alfredo Silva agreed to let us peer over his shoulder during the entire process.

Peanuts: © 1972 United Features Syndicate, Inc. Reprinted by permission.

Following is Alfredo's draft, annotated by the marginal comments of his instructor.

STUDENT ESSAY—FIRST DRAFT

Alfredo Silva

Who Am I?

Try for a more captivating opening that answers the question.

1   My professional goal is to be a history teacher and help children of Mexican de~~c~~ent [s] to become successful. In my fantasies I see Nobel Prize-winning immunologists with surnames such as Gomez or Castillo. I also see brown-skinned, brown-eyed senators, Supreme Court justices, university presidents, journalists, and CEOs of conglomerates. These ~~persons,~~ [leaders—women as well as men—] whom I have taught, would be dedicating their lives to improving our country's morality, customs, political system, philosophy, and education. ~~These leaders~~ [They] would in turn set strong examples for all of the young people to follow. In the society of

Repeat key words.

my (vision,) racial violence, high school dropouts, teenage pregnancies, and drug abuse have vanished.

2   Although I know that my (aspiration) [vision] cannot be realized overnight, I am firmly convinced that education is the ~~basis~~ [bedrock] of any significant social change. Knowledge of what went wrong is the most powerful start for righting what is wrong. To cause change (we) [ref] must join forces. As a unit we can accomplish more than we can as individuals. We can compliment [e] each other's ~~weaknesses~~ [talents, shore up each other's weaknesses,] and therefore be strong as a whole. Through cooperation we as a people can ~~defend ourselves~~ [guard] against losing our identity or our [Hispanic] culture, while still promoting an American way of life. This country has a lot to offer all of its citizens, including Hispanics. In turn, Hispanics can contribute to maintaining a reputation for the United States as a great place to call home. I have thought of other careers, even contemplating law, accounting, and nursing. Yet, I have settled on being a history teacher,

because - - - -

3   The Hispanic community needs history teachers. Our children need to know that the pain and suffering of my ancestors was in the pursuit of liberties that we would not otherwise have. They need to know the immeasurable courage of people like Patrick

Too vague. Replace with more specific motivation that you feel.

Henry, who cried out, "Give me liberty or give me death!" They need to know about people who believed so much in this country that they were willing to die for it so that future freedom would be guaranteed to anyone wanting it enough.

4   ~~Personally, I consider myself~~ *I am also* a romantic extrovert. I come from a family of seven

siblings, so *emotional* relationships ~~have always been easy for~~ *are familiar to* me. I was taught always to be

open and honest with my feelings. As I was growing up, I found that this honesty and

straightforwardness were not always appreciated. I turned to writing poems in an

effort to express myself in subtle ways. Eventually I began using poetry to sort out the

confusion I felt after *certain* events in my life began to affect me greatly. For me writing in verse is a

~~very~~ spiritual experience. In my poems I ask many questions that I did not know I had.

Sometimes an inspiring thought ~~will enter~~ my mind, or a striking image will appeal to

my emotions. I will *then* be bound to my desk for hours, trying to figure out ~~exactly how~~ I feel

and how to express the feeling.

Here you need to provide further explanation.

Were you hurt? Did people turn on you?

Provide an example.

What Questions?

Avoid this vague word.

5   Although I am continually struggling to find out who I am, I think the answer

may lie in the pages of my tattered notebooks in which I unburden my heart and my

mind. An important aspect of a happy life is peace of mind, which can be found in

communication. Poetry is my clue to the mystery of who I am, for it is through it that I

communicate my wants and needs.

Try to clinch your ending. Give it some punch.

Revising the First Draft

The big elements of the essay—especially the paragraph—should be your focus during the revision. Later, you can worry about grammar, spelling, and punctuation; for now, your aim should be the repair of any major structural flaws in the larger parts of the essay. We recommend the following checklist:

1. Check your opening paragraph.
2. Check your sequence of points.
3. Check for adequate examples and details.
4. Check paragraph transitions.

Check Your Opening Paragraph

Check to see if the style and tone of the opening paragraph fit in with the rest of the paper. For example, here is an opening paragraph that begins in typically wooden fashion:

> The concept of an unmarried woman choosing to have a baby and raise it by herself has become increasingly prevalent. There is much publicity on celebrities

having children out of wedlock. In the last several years, this concept has wrongly been made to be a glamorous and stylish way of life. An unmarried woman who purposely has a child out of wedlock is selfish, immature, and clearly not able to make a rational decision on her own.

Realizing that she had written this before she had found her voice for the essay, the writer made these revisions:

> Today it has become almost common for an unmarried woman to choose to have and raise a baby alone. With much publicity, many celebrities have had children out of wedlock, their example making single motherhood seem a glamorous and stylish way of life. My own feeling is that an unmarried woman who purposely has a child out of wedlock is selfish, immature, and clearly not able to make a rational decision on her own.

This is a brisker and more direct opening. (See "Put a Personal Voice in the Writing" on pp. 95–96.) You should also revise your paragraph, if necessary, to give it a catchier opening. See Chapter 4 for some suggestions about how to pep up your opening paragraph.

Check Your Sequence of Points

One easy way to assure that the ideas in your essay follow a proper sequence, as we suggested in Chapter 4, is to make an after-the-fact rough outline of the essay—checking to make sure that you covered your major points in the order announced in the thesis. For example, the opening paragraph just cited charges the unmarried mother with being *selfish, immature, and clearly not able to make a rational decision on her own*. If the last of these points—the alleged irrationality of the unwed mother—were covered first, the essay would seem awkwardly amiss, with a topsy-turvy development. Readers expect a writer to follow the order in which topics are named in the thesis.

Check for Adequate Examples and Details

Check your paragraph for completeness. (For a discussion of completeness, see p. 72 in Chapter 5.) Sometimes an anecdote or extended example is all that is needed to beef up an otherwise empty paragraph. This first draft of the essay against unwed mothers illustrates a lack of detail.

> Although many women feel that intentionally having a child out of wedlock has become acceptable, they clearly do not have any sense of logic. The woman is only thinking of herself and therefore basing her decisions on very selfish reasons. They are evading the real issues for having a child. A child is something created by a man and a woman who want to show their love for each other, and for a baby. The unwed mother cannot see the future, only the present she feels she needs to have a child for reasons such as she is getting older, or is not seriously involved with a man now or in the immediate future.

Its other problems aside, this paragraph needs the bite of an example. When a peer-editing group pointed this out to the writer, she made the following revision:

> Although many women feel that intentionally having a child out of wedlock has become acceptable or even enviable, they clearly do not have any sense of logic. These women only think of themselves and therefore base their decisions on very selfish reasons. My sister, for example, had a baby fourteen years ago with a man she knew only briefly and has never kept up with. Now the child is asking questions about her father, and my sister has no answers for her. She cannot tell her daughter that she deliberately used the man only to get pregnant and without telling him of her intentions. She cannot admit that she does not know where he is because she didn't care for him then or now. If she tells the truth, she will be setting a terrible moral example. Meanwhile, my niece is asking more and more questions every day.

The poignant example makes this a much more effective paragraph.

Check Paragraph Transitions

During the heat of composition, writers often forget to link paragraphs carefully. You may find that you need to add a bridging sentence or transitional phrase. (See pp. 74–75 in Chapter 5 for examples.)

Achieving Style

"Have something to say, and say it as clearly as you can. That is the only secret of style." So wrote Matthew Arnold (1822–1888), the English poet and critic. Indeed, it is hard to imagine a more crucial component of style than clarity. And it is impossible to imagine how witless and muddled writing can seem stylish.

Here is an example of what we mean by muddled writing:

> Cloverdale College's planning efforts have made a serious attempt to stress the city's key barometer as being the future direction of its youth, seeking primarily to diffuse the painful alienation by struggling to build cooperation among diverse groups with efforts like its multicultural curriculum having developed subject matter that encourages students in becoming acquainted with cultural diversity and to appreciate it.

This paragraph is murky because its single sentence is too long and overburdened. More sentences, and simpler ones, are needed. Here is a possible rewrite:

> In studying the future, Cloverdale College has tried to use its students as the key barometer for all planning efforts. It has particularly focused on the painful alienation felt by individual cultural groups on campus, such as Armenians, Koreans, or Hispanics. It has also developed multicultural classes whose course content builds cooperation among diverse cultural groups by teaching students to appreciate the advantages of cultural diversity.

Writing Tip

Do You Have Style?

Style does not have the same meaning in writing as it does in fashion. To have style in fashion can mean to be fancy or frilly. Style in writing, on the other hand, means expressing yourself in a way that is uniquely you. In other words, to achieve a good style, above all else, be yourself.

The key to writing clearly—and consequently, with a dab of style—is to unravel tangled sentences and reduce them to shorter and more straightforward units. And the cause of muddled writing is usually a combination of three factors: The writer does not understand the subject, believes that language should reflect an imagined self-importance, or simply does not know how to edit.

Whatever the cause, however, some basic principles of editing can help transform muddled writing into clear prose.

Express Action in Verbs Rather Than Nouns

Noun constructions tend to make actions seem as if they were impersonal objects, rather than freely made choices, and have consequently found favor in the writing of education committees and government panels. Verbs, on the other hand, add directness, briskness, and accountability—which is why they have fallen into disfavor in the prose of collective bodies.

Student writers sometimes use such constructions to fudge any opinion they feel tentative or insecure about bluntly expressing. Instead of writing *This poet writes an annoyingly abstract line that, even after it is deciphered, often seems empty and pointless,* they will write *The abstractness of this poet and her work has sometimes been noted.* Strictly as a matter of style, however, the bluntness of the first sentence is always preferable to the fuzziness of the second.

Avoid the Passive Voice

English has two voices: the active and the passive. In the *active voice,* actor and action are clearly linked through a straightforward verb: *Jim smashed Susie's pumpkin with a hammer.* In the *passive voice,* on the other hand, the actor is often disguised by the construction of the verb and may even altogether disappear: *Susie's pumpkin was smashed with a hammer.* The culprit of this deed, *Jim,* lurks unnamed in the passive verb.

Most of the time, you are better off writing in the active voice. Your prose will be cleaner, more direct, and vastly easier to read than if you did otherwise. On the other hand, in some rare instances the passive voice is justified, especially when an action is more significant than its actor. Here is an example:

> In 2008 a series of unsolved murders in the South were traced to a nomadic drifter held in the slaying of a young woman named Meredith Emerson, whose body was found in the mountains near the start of the Appalachian Trail.

What is more important here is not who traced the connection between the murders and the drifter, but that the connection was made.

Of the two voices, the active is the more vigorous and definitely the one you should ordinarily use. Instead of writing *More space is needed in the parking lot to accommodate the massive number of commuting students,* it is better to write *The massive number of commuting students need more space to park.*

Be Brief and to the Point

A sentence may be grammatical but still graceless, as is this one:

> During this same time period Elizabeth Murray Smith insisted on having a "prenuptial agreement," a legal document, with her husband, written so that her husband could not acquire all her wealth after they were married.

The writer uses unnecessary words in the original. Trimmed down, the sentence loses no meaning yet is considerably clearer:

> During this same period Elizabeth Murray Smith insisted on a prenuptial agreement to prevent her husband from acquiring all of her wealth after they were married.

For the sake of brevity, you should use as few words as possible, not stating what is already obvious to the reader from the context. You should also avoid overburdening your sentences with too many parenthetical asides, such as this writer uses:

> Douglass was, of course, unaware that ultimately war would be the result of that awakening of the South, but from the days of the Wilmot Proviso, *past the terrible disappointment of the passage of the vile, abominable Fugitive Slave Act, the foulest component of the loathsome Compromise of 1850,* through to his abandonment in 1856 of what was left of the Liberty Party, *the Radical Abolitionist Party of Gerrit Smith, in favor of the rising Republican Party,* Douglass was exhilarated by the thought that men of goodwill like Garret Smith—*and Frederick Douglass*—would somehow persuade legislators to use the law to end slavery.
>
> —William S. McFeely, *Frederick Douglass*

If we eliminate the parenthetical information, we are left with a more straightforward and readable sentence:

> Douglass was, of course, unaware that ultimately war would be the result of that awakening of the South, but from the days of the Wilmot Proviso through to his abandonment in 1856 of what was left of the Liberty Party, Douglass was exhilarated by the thought that men of goodwill like Gerrit Smith would somehow persuade legislators to use the law to end slavery.

Many writers have the mistaken idea that fatter sentences are more dazzling to readers than leaner ones. But that belief is a myth. All writing improves on a diet high on directness and low on redundancy, triteness, and grandiosity.

Redundancy.   *Redundancy* refers to the use of unnecessarily repetitious language. One common redundancy in the English language is the overuse of *word pairs,* such as *true and accurate, long and hard, willing and able, hope and trust,* and *basic and fundamental.* These deadwood pairs, which roll effortlessly off the pen out of sheer habit, only glut the sentence. Instead of writing *We hope and trust she will come,* simply write *We hope she will come.* In other words, choose only one word in the pair.

Another redundancy occurs through the use of *words whose meaning is implicit in an earlier word,* for example, writing that a table is *round in shape* when *round* obviously implies *shape.* Other redundancies of this kind are *few in number* (*few* already implies *number*), *red in color* (*red* is always a *color*), and *future hopes* (*hope* always involves the *future*).

Triteness.   *Triteness* is the use of stale expressions and prepackaged phrases. Sometimes the prudent use of colloquial phrases can add an endearing and democratic

Writing Tip

Need Help with Checking Your Work?

The saying "One good deed deserves another" applies to the written word. If you have a friend who is also in a writing class, consider swapping papers for the final check. Writers often can't see their own mistakes and tend to become overly fond of their own words. A friend, on the other hand, has no ego invested in your writing and is likely to tell you the plain truth. Naturally, you are expected to do the same for your friend's writing. If no friend is available to help you edit, try going over your paper while pretending that it was written by someone else. That way you might be more objective or detached.

tone to writing. But most of the time, prepackaged phrases and expressions such as *worth her weight in gold, as clear as day,* and *the burning question* are merely annoying. If you cannot think of an original metaphor, it is better to write down what you have to say plainly without using any of these lame phrases. Instead of writing *the order was clear as the living day,* write merely *the order was clear.*

Each of the following commonly used prepackaged phrases should be turned into a single word:

in this day and age	today
owing to the fact that	because
despite the fact that	although
if it should happen that	if
on the occasion of	when
in anticipation of	before
subsequent to	after
concerning the matter	about
it is necessary that	must

Grandiosity.   *Grandiosity* is an annoying fondness for big words over common ones. In prose, plainer is usually better, and in college papers especially, which the harried instructor must read reams of, a simpler style is always greeted with reward and gratitude. Moreover, the common word is usually the more effective. Listen to this passage from a student college application:

> As I apply to your college, I am cognizant of the fact that doing so is in response to my ancient reveries of attaining an education in an environment completely supportive of my educational objectives and a campus affording me the best in learning environments.

Pity the screening committee that must wade through this stilted passage. It is not likely to be impressed. How much more convincing and human to have sounded plain and simple, as this student did:

> Since I was a child, I have dreamed of attending Mount Sinai College, where my father earned his degree in American history. I have always loved your campus for its rustic beauty, and I especially value the emphasis your program places on personal instruction. I am convinced that I will get a first-rate education at your college.

Grandiosity can be avoided if you say what you have to say in plain and simple English. Doing so will mean using a plain but precise diction. Here are some examples of pompous terms to avoid, along with their more common synonyms:

terminate	end
facilitate	help
ascertain	find out

endeavor	try
inception	beginning, start
envisage	see
transpire	happen
incisive	biting
conflagrant	burning
traverse	cross

Our personal bugaboo, which we think deserves special mention, is the use of *utilize* when *use* is meant. *Utilize* your common sense; use *use* if you mean *use*.

Vary Sentence Types

Variety is the spice of style. Passages that monotonously begin with the same word or use the same sentence type and length are stultifying to read. Here is an example:

> There are two basic personality descriptions that can be used to describe people of all walks of life. There is, for example, the Type A personality, who is described as aggressive and driven. There is also the Type B personality, who is described as laid-back and optimistic. There are profound differences between the two types of personalities that scientists are just beginning to find out.

Notice that all the sentences of this paragraph unremittingly open with the same word, *there,* which creates a monotonous effect. This is how the student rewrote the passage:

> People of all walks of life can be classified into two basic personality types. The Type A personality is described as a person who is aggressive and driven. In sharp contrast is the Type B personality, who is habitually laid back and optimistic. Between the two types of personalities exist profound differences science is just beginning to discover.

We think it generally lazy to begin two sentences in a row with the same word, unless it is being done deliberately for emphasis, and inexcusable to begin three in a row with the same opening.

Edit Awkward Language

Mishaps of style caused by awkwardness of language and phrasing can easily be remedied with simple editing. Here is an example:

> His victories at Fort Henry and Donelson demonstrated to Sherman that if the Union put its mind to it, it could achieve success.
>
> —John F. Marszalek, *Sherman: A Soldier's Passion for Order*

In this sentence, two *it*'s with different meanings are awkwardly kissing. Simple rewriting entirely removes this inelegance:

> His victories at Fort Henry and Donelson demonstrated to Sherman that a determined Union could achieve success.

or

> His victories at Fort Henry and Donelson demonstrated to Sherman that if the Union made up its mind, it could achieve success.

Another common source of awkwardness is overuse of the same preposition in a single sentence. Here is an example:

> The Christmas dinner was filled *with* chatter *with* all the relatives *with* children.

or

> He was thinking *of* resigning his job *of* which he was very proud because *of* the cuts in the budget.

Only a pittance of rewriting is required to remove the awkwardness from these two sentences:

> The Christmas dinner was filled *with* the chattering of the relatives and their children.
> Although proud of his job, he was contemplating resigning over budget cuts.

Finally, there is the awkwardness of unintentional internal rhymes, which can make even a somber passage seem ridiculously flippant. Here is a sentence that is often quoted as a classic example of this miscue:

> Hence no force however great can stretch a cord however fine into an horizontal line which is accurately straight: there will always be a bending downwards.
> —William Whewell, *Elementary Treatise on Mechanics*

Here *great* rhymes with *straight* and *fine* with *line*. One possible rewrite is to eliminate the rhyming words in favor of unrhymed synonyms:

> Hence no force however powerful can stretch a cord however thin into a horizontal line which is accurately straight: there will always be a bending downwards.

Put a Personal Voice in the Writing

Every writer begins a new assignment by groping to find just the right voice for the piece. This problem of finding the right voice is especially acute for the student writer with no particular sense of commitment to the topic. Here is an example of what we mean:

> Financial debt is a dangerous situation. Once the victim of debt has been overcome by creditors, he or she may lose all options for redeeming the bad credit risk. No one will want to lend money; therefore bankruptcy could be the inevitable consequence. Debt is caused by many circumstances, which include unemployment, lack of effective budgeting, and mismanagement of credit.

The problem with this paragraph is not grammatical but rhetorical: It has no definite voice and no personality—it might have been penned by an unfeeling robot. We infer that the writer does not care about the topic, is bored with it, but is dutifully cobbling together some sentences in hopes of fulfilling the assignment. A bit more soul and emotional interest plugged into the paragraph would improve it considerably. See if you agree:

> Financial debt is a malignant trap. It is like the spider's web that holds the struggling fly. The victim of debt can be destroyed by creditors like the merciless spider devouring her prey. We often wonder why in the world so many people get wrecked by debt. Clearly, it can happen more easily than we think. Debt can be caused by many circumstances, which include unemployment, lack of budgeting, and pure lack of discipline.

Here is an example of an opening paragraph with a personal voice. In it, the writer clearly knows who she is and what she believes and quite plainly intends to tell us:

> Do blondes have more fun? Perhaps, if being stereotyped as bubbly, cheap, and stupid can be considered fun. However, most of the time, these accusations and idiotic beliefs are as shallow as the people practicing them.

The voice behind this paragraph is indignant, aroused, and opinionated—someone who is clearly sick to death of the stereotypes of the dumb blonde. And the snap in the writing mainly comes from the writer's impassioned commitment to her viewpoint.

How do you project a personal voice in your writing? You do so by being yourself and stating your opinions honestly. If the assigned topic is one that does not appeal to you particularly, you learn about it until you can choose one side over the other. Take different approaches to the subject until you can stake out an honest claim that expresses your viewpoint. Writers always write better when they have something to say, and writers are more likely to have something to say when they care about the topic.

Of course, some essays—especially research papers—require a purely objective, academic voice using only formal language and reciting only stiff-necked opinion. If so, you would have to either take another class or get permission from your teacher to write a different kind of paper. To find yourself in that circumstance is not the end of the world. If you're like everyone else, once you have left school you might even find yourself writing for someone who hates you and your work, in which case going through something similar in school will help you survive this ordeal.

Following is Alfredo's revision of his first draft, including the comments of his instructor.

STUDENT ESSAY—SECOND DRAFT

Alfredo Silva

Who Am I?

1   I have a dream: I would like to become the bard of my community. In the Middle Ages, bards and troubadours related the history of their people through poetry and song. In some past life I may have been a bard because the longing to be one keeps rolling over me in a familiar wave. I am a Mexican Don Quixote--filled with idealism for the future of my people. In my fantasies I see Nobel Prize-winning immunologists with surnames such as Gomez or Castillo. I also see brown-skinned, brown-eyed senators, Supreme Court justices, university presidents, journalists, and CEOs of conglom*e*rates.
These ~~persons~~ leaders—women as well as men—~~would be~~ *are* dedicating their lives to improving our country's morality, customs, political system, philosophy, and education. They would in turn set strong examples for all the young people to follow. In the society of my vision, racial violence, high school dropouts, teenage pregnancy, and drug abuse have vanished.

Lovely beginning—much more captivating than the original

Sp

2   While I know that my dream cannot be realized overnight, I am firmly convinced that education is the bedrock ~~and cornerstone~~ of any significant social change. Knowledge of what went wrong is the ~~most powerful~~ *necessary* start for righting *ing point* what is wrong. To cause change we Hispanics must join forces because as a unit we can accomplish more than we can as individuals. We can complement each other's talents, shore up each other's weaknesses, and therefore be strong as a whole. Through cooperation we ~~as a people~~ can guard against losing our Hispanic identity or our culture, while still promoting an American way of life. This country has ~~a lot~~ *rich treasures* to offer all of its citizens,

Redundant logic

including Hispanics. In turn, Hispanics can ~~contribute to maintaining a~~ [help foster the] reputation ~~for~~ [of]

the United States as a great place to call home. I have thought of other careers, even

contemplating law, accounting, and nursing. Yet, I have settled on being a history

teacher because in that profession I can best reveal to my people what sacrifices

Americans made in order to ensure ~~the pursuit of liberty for everyone~~ [life, liberty, and the pursuit of happiness for all.]

Be more direct. 3
/ Sp

[I have a dark side to my personality.]
~~In my self observation, my darkest side stares me in the face~~. I am competi[i]tive

to an almost destructive point. For instance, I play tennis, soccer, and basketball for

recreation and to release tension. I vent much of my frustration through sweat and even

through blood. Of course, I am careful not to hurt anyone but myself. As an athlete

I am my worst enemy as much as I am my best friend. In fact, on the court and on the

field, I am often transformed into a ~~different kind of person~~ [brutal competitor]. I believe that through this

Be specific
about this
transformation.

[metamorphosis]
physical ~~catharsis~~ I can more easily deal with the tedium and toil of everyday life.

[Consequently I often]
~~That leads me to the problem~~ of find~~ing~~ myself apologizing for ~~conduct that is, what we say,~~

[conduct]
unsportsmanlike. Some may say that a sport is only a game, but to me sports teach many

of life's necessary lessons--that getting ahead requires a competitive edge, that teamwork

is often an excellent shortcut to success, and that we control our own destinies.

4   I am also a romantic extrovert. I come from a family of seven siblings, where

emotional relationships were familiar staples of my family life. I was taught always to be

[But]
open and honest with my feelings. ~~As~~ I was growing up, I found that this openness and

honesty were not always appreciated. Quite often they were either misinterpreted or

[mad]
rejected. For instance, in my early teen years I once told a girl on whom I had a ~~powerful~~

[H]
crush, "~~Like~~, hey, I'd like to spend the rest of my life with you." Well, she was so repulsed

that she never spoke to me again, and to this day the sight of this girl fills me with

[boldly informed]
embarrassment. On another occasion I ~~told~~ a teacher that I had difficulty concentrating

in his class because it was so boring. The result? I was promptly ushered to the front of

the class, where I was forced to answer questions even though I never raised my hand

Redundant

~~once~~. Gradually I turned to writing poems in an effort to express myself in subtle ways.

Eventually I began using poetry to sort out the confusion I felt after certain events in my life,

such as my father['s] ~~having a serious~~ stroke and my close friend['s] ~~dying in a car accident~~ [death], tore me apart inside. For me writing poetry is a spiritual experience. In my poems, I ask many questions that I did not know I had, such as "What purpose does education have for me?" "Why do people lie?" "When will I die?" Sometimes an inspiring thought will enter my mind, or a striking image will appeal to my emotions. I will then be bound to my desk for hours, trying to figure out exactly how I feel and how to express the feeling in a poem. Although I am continually struggling to find out who I am, I think the answer may lie in the pages of my tattered poetry notebooks in which I unburden my heart and my mind. An important aspect of a happy life is peace of mind, which can be found in communication. Poetry is my clue to the mystery of who I am, for it is through it that I communicate my wants and needs.

5   In a sense I am an ordinary person, but my love for the Hispanic people energizes me and makes me want to be an inspiration to others. I am convinced that an ordinary person can become an extraordinary person when he gives unselfishly and with passion.

> Find an ending that clinches the essay. Make it brief; sometimes less is more.

I am an ordinary man, but I have extraordinary dreams.

Editing the Second Draft

Now is the time to check your grammar and punctuation. If you have any questions, you can refer to the grammar section at the end of this book. Now is also the time to check spelling, verify facts, and ensure that both sentences and paragraphs are coherent. You should also *proofread* the paper for any typing miscues.

Pay particular attention to these common micro errors:

1. Check subject-verb agreements.
2. Check pronoun antecedents. Watch for errors such as *The garden **implements** were so carefully concealed that no one could find **it**.*
3. *Check for comma splices and misuse of fragments.*
4. Check for use of the wrong word—for example, ***Their** are many bargains to be found in the thrift shop.*
5. Check for faulty diction and overuse of grand words.

When you are finished with this mechanical overhaul of spelling, grammar, logic, and rhetoric, give the whole paper a final critical reading to make sure that it hangs together and is both logical and convincing.

Peer Review

As the name suggests, peer review is a process of having your work critiqued by fellow students before you submit it. Most journals use peer review to judge the fitness for publication of submitted manuscripts. The bread-and-butter evaluation is done by a panel of scholars who are up-to-date on work being done in the field or on the subject. For judging papers and experiments, peer review has become the standard procedure throughout the world of business and academia.

Peer review allows your fellow students to help you evaluate your work. The process is not meant to be an exercise in one-upmanship. Rather, the job of the reviewing students is to praise the strengths of your paper and offer remedies for its weaknesses. For peer review to work, honesty is required of both the reader and writer or the process will be a flop. The reviewer who gushes, "This is great; you deserve a Pulitzer Prize," is just as worthless as the one who says, "Wow! I can't understand a word you're trying to say."

Another hurdle to clear is that reviewers must overcome a natural reluctance to pass judgment on the writing of a fellow student. The writer whose work is being reviewed, on the other hand, must not take personally any remarks made about the work. You're all working for a common good—to become better writers—and you must accept the process of peer review as a means to that end.

Peer Editing

Peer editing is a hands-on session between the writer and reviewers. It is usually done in one of two ways—verbal review or written review. We shall look at both of these methods.

Verbal review.   Five students (or any other uneven number in case of disagreement) should sit in a circle. Each student reviewer is given a copy of the essay to be reviewed as well as a list of things to look for. The session begins with the writer reading the essay aloud while group members follow along with their copies, making notes of their reactions in the margin of the essay. Once the reading is finished, the group should critique the essay with particular emphasis on the following points:

1. Main idea
2. Details to support the main idea
3. Order of writing
4. Words
5. Mechanics (grammar, spelling, punctuation, capitalization)

Main idea.   The author of the essay moves down the list, asking questions like, "Is my main idea clear?" to which anyone in the group can respond. A free-flowing discussion of each point should then follow, with students offering suggestions on how to improve any weaknesses or complimenting the writer on any strengths. Wherever possible, panel members should offer specific suggestions for change. The same process should be used on every point on the list so that the essay is systematically discussed.

Details to support the main idea.   Scanty details are often a common fault of student work. Panel members should therefore focus on this point. It is unlikely that the main idea will be too cluttered with supporting details to make sense, but if this should be the case, members should suggest a remedy to the writer.

Order of writing.   Peer reviewers need to check the general sequence of the essay, making sure that all segments follow each other in logical order. The paragraphs of an essay must contain a topic sentence that supports the main point of the essay, and the sentences of each paragraph must support the paragraph's topic sentence. Typically, some reviewers will object to paragraphs being too skimpy or not arranged in an emphatic sequence. A misstep like this can often be remedied by the suggestions of peer reviewers. One reviewer might suggest, "Paragraph two needs a better example." Another might recommend a stronger transition between two paragraphs. This give-and-take benefits both the writer and the reviewers.

Words.   Some words are lively and suitable for the occasion. Others are over-dressed or otherwise ill equipped for use in a particular context. A peer reviewer can help you gauge the punch of your vocabulary and help suggest livelier word choices.

Mechanics.   At this point, you will be lucky if you had a fussy peer reviewer who can recognize sentence fragments, comma splices, fused sentences, misplaced apostrophes, and other sins of mechanics. If you make grammatical errors, you should try to master the principle behind them so you can avoid repetition of the same mistake in another paper.

Written review.   The simplest way to have written peer reviews is for the teacher to hand each student in the class a "Peer Review Worksheet." Then each student exchanges his or her essay with a fellow student, who sits down and reads it carefully. After reading the essay, the peer fills out the "Peer Review Worksheet." Two sample worksheets follow, one for a paragraph and one for an entire essay:

Peer Review Worksheet for a Paragraph

Author's name _____

1. The topic sentence of this paragraph is

_____

_____

2. Here is the detail I liked best:

_____

_____

3. The paragraph is (too skimpy/ too bloated/ just right) [circle one].

4. All of the sentences in the paragraph relate to the topic sentence. (yes/no) [circle one]. If you circled "no," then list the part that breaks the unity of the paragraph:

_____

_____

5. Other comments:

_____

_____

Peer reviewer's name: _____

_____

Peer Review Worksheet for an Essay

Name of author:_____

Answer the questions as briefly as possible.

1. What is the thesis of the essay? Is it clear? Did it capture your interest?

2. How well do the paragraphs support the thesis of the essay?

3. Which paragraph(s) could use more details? Which is (are) bloated?

4. How coherent is the essay? Could you follow the order of the writing? What transitions, if any, do you suggest?

5. Which words, if any, would you replace? If you can suggest a better word, do so.

6. If this were your essay, what changes would you make before handing it in? Be specific.

7. What overall impression do you have of this essay?

Peer reviewer's name: _____

_____

Silva 1

Alfredo Silva

Professor McCuen

English 101

November 13, 2000

Who Am I?

1   I have a dream: I would like to become the bard of my
community. In the Middle Ages, bards and troubadours related
the history of their people through poetry and song. In some past
life I may have been a bard because the longing to be one keeps
rolling over me in a familiar wave. I am a Mexican Don Quixote--
filled with idealism for the future of my people. In my fantasies I
see Nobel Prize-winning immunologists with surnames such as
Gomez or Castillo. I also see brown-skinned, brown-eyed senators,
Supreme Court justices, university presidents, journalists, and
CEOs of conglomerates. These leaders--women as well as men--are
dedicating their lives to improving our country's morality, customs,
political system, philosophy, and education. They set strong
examples for all the young people to follow. In the society of my
vision, racial violence, high school dropouts, teenage pregnancy,
and drug abuse have vanished.

2   While I know that my dream cannot be realized overnight,
I am firmly convinced that education is the bedrock of any
significant social change. Knowledge of what went wrong is the
necessary starting point for righting what is wrong. To cause

Silva 2

change we Hispanics must join forces because as a unit we can accomplish more than we can as individuals. We can complement each other's talents, shore up each other's weaknesses, and therefore be strong as a whole. Through cooperation we can guard against losing our Hispanic identity or our culture, while still promoting an American way of life. This country has rich treasures to offer all of its citizens, including Hispanics. In turn, Hispanics can help foster the reputation of the United States as a great place to call home. I have thought of other careers, even contemplating law, accounting, and nursing. Yet, I have settled on being a history teacher because in that profession I can best reveal to my people what sacrifices Americans made in order to ensure life, liberty, and the pursuit of happiness for all.

3   I have a dark side to my personality. I am competitive to an almost destructive point. For instance, I play tennis, soccer, and basketball for recreation and to release tension. I vent much of my frustration through sweat and even through blood. Of course, I am careful not to hurt anyone but myself. As an athlete I am my worst enemy as much as I am my best friend. In fact, on the court and on the field, I am often transformed into a brutal competitor. I believe that through this physical metamorphosis, I can more easily deal with the tedium and toil of everyday life. Consequently, I often find myself apologizing for unsportsmanlike conduct. Some may say that a sport is only a game, but to me sports teach many of life's necessary lessons--that getting ahead requires a competitive edge, that teamwork is often an excellent shortcut to success, and that we control our own destinies.

4   I am also a romantic extrovert. I come from a family of seven siblings, where emotional relationships were familiar staples of my family life. I was taught always to be open and honest with my feelings. But as I was growing up, I found that this openness and honesty were not always appreciated. Quite often they were either misinterpreted or rejected. For instance, in my early teen years, I once told a girl on whom I had a mad crush, "Hey, I'd like to spend the rest of my life with you." Well, she was so repulsed that she never spoke to me again, and to this day, the sight of this girl fills me with embarrassment. On another occasion I boldly informed a teacher that I had difficulty concentrating in his class because it was so boring. The result? I was promptly ushered to the front of the class, where I was forced to answer questions even though I never raised my hand. Gradually I turned to writing poems in an effort to express myself in subtle ways. Eventually I began using poetry to sort out the confusion I felt after certain events in my life, such as my father's stroke and my close friend's death, tore me apart inside. For me writing poetry is a spiritual experience. In my poems, I ask many questions that I did not know I had, such as "What purpose does education have for me?" "Why do people lie?" "When will I die?" Sometimes an inspiring thought will enter my mind, or a striking image will appeal to my emotions. I will then be bound to my desk for hours, trying to figure out exactly how I feel and how to express the feeling in a poem.

Silva 4

Although I am continually struggling to find out who I am, I think

the answer may lie in the pages of my tattered poetry notebooks in

which I unburden my heart and my mind. An important aspect of a

happy life is peace of mind, which can be found in communication.

Poetry is my clue to the mystery of who I am, for it is through it that

I communicate my wants and needs.

5   I am an ordinary man, but I have extraordinary dreams.

■ Exercises

1. Rewrite the following passage from a student essay, following the guidelines given in this chapter.

There were two things I learned in karate before I learned to fight. The first thing was respect. I was told that I must salute to the Korean, United States, and our martial arts flag before entering or leaving the training hall. To acknowledge my teachers and elders such as black belts, I must also bow to them. When ever asked a question my reply of yes sir or no sir is expected of me given in a confident tone. There examples of respect are symbolic to every day life. We must respect each other countries to live a peaceful life. When we are kind and acknowledge people, there becomes a friendly atmosphere.

The second thing I learned was defensive movements. How to block a punch or a kick. How to escape being held. A few basic blocks such as low and high blocks. I was not very happy because I wanted to learn how to kick like in the movies and all I was taught was respect and defensive hand movements. Each lesson became more advanced and the escape movements became natural movements for me. By the time I learned my requirements I realized karate was for humble people that wanted to protect themselves if bothered.

Confidence in all aspects of life was gained after most advanced martial artist have trained for several years. After receiving the next belt, breaking bricks or several boards or winning a trophy in a tournament bring an unbeatable attitude. After people accomplish difficult feats, they tend to be able to overcome their fears and obstacles in life. After training in karate, they learn that they are winners.

2. Rewrite the following sentences in more direct grammar. Make sure the actor is stated as a subject and the action as a verb.
   a. His expectation was to attract young Americans to the martial art of tae kwon do.
   b. The instructor's rebuttal to the accusation was of importance to him.
   c. There was deep anger among the employees over the loss of a pay raise.
   d. Indefinite continuance of financial support for the choral group cannot be guaranteed as long as the hospital sees no great need for such entertainment.
   e. Although methods of corroborating the validity of English prerequisites have been improved, acceptance as useful by the Academic Affairs Committee of any present prerequisite is not possible.

3. In each of the following sentences, change the passive voice into active only where necessary; otherwise, leave the sentence as is.
   a. Many verses have been written by people who believe they are poets but who are merely rhymesters.
   b. Until after the election, derogatory remarks about the Democratic ticket were continually made by Professor Smith.
   c. A mock earthquake, including evacuating people from the Tower Building, creating a command post, establishing a triage area, and organizing a system of transportation, was planned by the Safety Committee.
   d. During the medieval period, man was no longer viewed as a superb creature, capable of Promethean achievements; rather, he was viewed as a pitiful being, tarnished by original sin and in need of moral redemption.
   e. The ability of women to make right executive decisions under stress has generally been underestimated by society.

4. Eliminate redundancy in each of the following sentences.
   a. In this day and age, families should limit themselves to two children in order not to overcrowd the various different countries of Planet Earth.
   b. By taking ballet dancing lessons, I have achieved a greater self-confidence in myself.
   c. All of our cities' bureaucratic agencies that provide and offer services, such as law enforcement, fire prevention, sewage disposal, and library service, cannot continue to grow, develop, and expand without higher local taxes.
   d. All of Eloise Martin's hopes and desires were based on her belief that human beings are basically and fundamentally able to set goals they can reach through dedication and by applying themselves.
   e. Suddenly, the computer graphic turned red in color and became ugly in appearance.

5. Replace the trite, prepackaged expressions in each of the following sentences.
   a. For years, Gillespie thought he was sitting on top of the world, but in the end, he went to jail for illegal drug trafficking, trapped like a mouse in his own compromised cleverness.
   b. Yes, Pete McClure should be appointed Senior Vice-President of Marketing because throughout 20 years of time, he has paid his dues to Brendon and Company by years of backbreaking work, selling to small businesses and private merchants at a time when our product was not popular.
   c. What I despise about my boss is that he simply rides roughshod over his employees in order to get the almighty dollar.
   d. Anyone who continues to buy Johnson and Smith stocks is just fishing in troubled waters.
   e. Most of the crowd attending the town meeting simply had their own axe to grind or their own beds to feather, and they were not the least concerned about whether the proposed housing development was good or bad for the neighborhood.

6. Recast each of the following sentences to eliminate grandiose diction.
   a. Various tennis coaches called to ascertain how much equipment could be appropriated on lease from the university and then transmitted to the tournament leaders.
   b. Dear Mr. Webster: I am in receipt of your letter of March 10, which endeavors to explain your absence at the last townhouse Executive Committee meeting.
   c. Surely it is incumbent upon education to facilitate the understanding by students of how to envisage life in all of its richness, its profundity, and its mystery.
   d. Prior to my arrival at Harvard, I had conceived of a campus that would be socially harsh, frigid, and filled with discordant factors, whose only compensation would be all of the knowledge I would acquire.
   e. Her visage was smiling in reverie as she reclined in the grass, reading a tome of Amy Lowell's poems.

Writing Assignments

1. Write a paragraph summing up what you try to do in writing a first draft versus a second.

2. Write a paragraph explaining what you could do to become a better writer.

3. Write a paragraph listing the advantages or disadvantages of peer review.

4. What part of the writing process do you find most difficult? Write a paragraph answering that question.

5. List three examples you would use to prove the following topic sentence: "True heroes exist today."

Peer Review Assignment

Choose a classmate with whom you will exchange the Peer Review Worksheet for an Essay after writing the assignment. First, both you and your peer will write a five-hundred-word essay offering your opinions on whether the government should cut back on general relief for the poor. Once both of you have completed decent first drafts, exchange papers with your partner and use the Peer Review Worksheet to evaluate your papers. When you have completed the form, discuss which suggestions made actually improved the paper. The original author of each paper should maintain the final say over any changes to be made.

PART II

Writing the Essay

Chapter 7

Narration

RICHARD T. GILL

The Code

Richard Thomas Gill (b. 1927) was born on Long Island, New York, and received his Ph.D. from Harvard University. A former assistant professor of economics at Harvard, Gill has presented a fifteen-part series on public television titled Economics U$A. *He was the principal bass of New York's Metropolitan Opera for over a decade and was an occasional contributor of stories to* The New Yorker *and* Atlantic Monthly. *Gill is the author of several books, among them* Economic Development: Past and Present *and* Economics and the Public Interest.

READING FOR IDEAS   Some things are better, and more dramatically, left unsaid than expressed in writing, especially in a narrative. In the moving tale that follows, for example, the writer leaves volumes unsaid about his motives and thoughts during a climactic religious exchange with his dying father. At the end of the story, he also implies what he might have said to comfort his stricken father but failed to say. Nevertheless, the narrator ends by learning a rueful lesson about the selfishness and the narrowness of a self-imposed code of conduct.

Allow the story to trigger some memories of your own and ask yourself the following questions: Has an experience ever taught me a lesson about life? What have I learned from a memorable experience?

I

1   I remember, almost to the hour, when I first began to question my religion. I don't mean that my ideas changed radically just at that time. I was only twelve, and I continued to go to church faithfully and to say something that could pass for prayers each night before I went to sleep. But I never again felt quite the same. For the first time in my life, it had occurred to me that when I grew up I might actually leave the Methodist faith.

2   It all happened just a few days after my brother died. He was five years old, and his illness was so brief and his death so unexpected that my whole family was almost crazed with grief. My three aunts, each of whom lived within a few blocks of our house, and my mother were all firm believers in religion, and they turned in unison, and without reservation, to this last support. For about a week, a kind of religious frenzy seized our household. We would all sit in the living room—my mother, my aunts, my two sisters, and I, and sometimes Mr. Dodds, the Methodist minister, too—saying prayers in low voices, comforting one another, staying together for hours at a time, until someone remembered that we had not had dinner or that it was time for my sisters and me to be in bed.

3   I was quite swept up by the mood that had come over the house. When I went to bed, I would say the most elaborate, intricate prayers. In the past, when I had finished my "Now I lay me down to sleep," I would bless individually all the members of my immediate family and then my aunts, and let it go at that. Now, however, I felt that I had to bless everyone in the world whose name I could remember. I would go through all my friends at school, including the teachers, the principal, and the janitor, and then through the names of people I had heard my mother and father mention, some of whom I had never even met. I did not quite know what to do about my brother, whom I wanted to pray for more than for anyone else. I hesitated to take his name out of its regular order, for fear I would be committed to believing that he had really died. But then I *knew* that he had died, so at the end of my prayers, having just barely mentioned his name as I went along, I would start blessing him over and over again, until I finally fell asleep.

4   The only one of us who was unmoved by this religious fervor was my father. Oddly enough, considering what a close family we were and how strongly my mother and aunts felt about religion, my father had never shown the least interest in it. In fact, I do not think that he had ever gone to church. Partly for this reason, partly because he was a rather brusque, impatient man, I always felt that he was something of a stranger in our home. He spent a great deal of time with us children, but through it all he seemed curiously unapproachable. I think we all felt constrained when he played with us and relieved when, at last, we were left to ourselves.

5   At the time of my brother's death, he was more of a stranger than ever. Except for one occasion, he took no part in the almost constant gatherings of the family in the living room. He was not going to his office that week—we lived in a small town outside Boston—and he was always around the house, but no one ever seemed to know exactly where. One of my aunts—Sarah, my mother's eldest sister—felt very definitely that my father should not be left to himself, and she was continually saying to me, "Jack, go upstairs and see if you can find him and talk to him." I remember going timidly along the hallway on the second floor and peeking into the bedrooms, not knowing what I should say if I found him and half afraid that he would scold me for going around looking into other people's rooms. One afternoon, not finding him in any of the bedrooms, I went up into the attic, where we had a sort of playroom. I remember discovering him there by the window. He was sitting absolutely motionless in an old wicker chair, an empty pipe in his hands, staring out fixedly over the treetops. I stood in the doorway for several minutes before he was aware of me. He turned as if to say something, but then, looking at me or just above my head—I was not sure which—he seemed to lose himself in his thoughts. Finally, he gave me a strangely awkward salute with his right hand and turned again to the window.

6   About the only times my father was with the rest of us were when we had meals or when, in the days immediately following the funeral, we all went out to the cemetery, taking fresh flowers or wreaths. But even at the cemetery he always stood slightly apart— a tall, lonely figure. Once, when we were at the grave and I was nearest him, he reached over and squeezed me around the shoulders. It made me feel almost embarrassed as though he were breaking through some inviolable barrier between us. He must have felt as I did, because he at once removed his arm and looked away, as though he had never actually embraced me at all.

7   It was the one occasion when my father was sitting in the living room with us that started me to wondering about my religion. We had just returned from the cemetery—two carloads of us. It was three or four days after the funeral and just at the time when, the shock having worn off, we were all experiencing our first clear realization of what had happened. Even I, young as I was, sensed that there was a new air of desolation in our home.

8   For a long time, we all sat there in silence. Then my aunts, their eyes moist, began talking about my brother, and soon my mother joined in. They started off softly, telling of little things he had done in the days before his illness. Then they fell silent and dried their eyes, and then quickly remembered some other incident and began speaking again. Slowly the emotion mounted, and before long the words were flooding out. "God will take care of him!" my Aunt Sarah cried, almost ecstatically. "Oh, yes, He will! He will!" Presently, they were all talking in chorus—saying that my brother was happy at last and that they would all be with him again one day.

9   I believed what they were saying and I could barely hold back my tears. But swept up as I was, I had the feeling that they should not be talking that way while my father was there. The feeling was one that I did not understand at all at the moment. It was just that when I looked over to the corner where he was sitting and saw the deep, rigid lines of his face, saw him sitting there silently, all alone, I felt guilty. I wanted everyone to stop for a while—at least until he had gone upstairs. But there was no stopping the torrent once it had started.

10   "Oh, he was too perfect to live!" Aunt Agnes, my mother's youngest sister, cried. "He was never a bad boy. I've never seen a boy like that. I mean he was never even naughty. He was just too perfect."

11   "Oh, yes. Oh, yes," my mother sighed.

12   "It's true," Aunt Sarah said. "Even when he was a baby, he never really cried. There was never a baby like him. He was a saint."

13   "He *was* a saint!" Aunt Agnes cried. "That's why he was taken from us!"

14   "He was a perfect baby," my mother said.

15   "He was taken from us," Aunt Agnes went on, "because he was too perfect to live."

16   All through this conversation, my father's expression had been growing more and more tense. At last, while Aunt Agnes was speaking, he rose from his chair. His face was very pale, and his eyes flashed almost feverishly. "Don't talk like that, Agnes!" he exclaimed, with a strange violence that was not anger but something much deeper. "I won't have you talking like that any more. I don't want anybody talking like that!" His whole body seemed to tremble. I had never seen him so worked up before. "Of course he was a bad boy at times!" he cried. "Every boy's bad once in a while. What do you have to change him for? Why don't you leave him as he was?"

17   "But he was such a perfect baby," Aunt Sarah said.

18   "He *wasn't* perfect!" my father almost shouted, clenching his fist. "He was no more perfect than Jack here or Betty or Ellen. He was just an ordinary little boy. He wasn't perfect. And he wasn't a saint. He was just a little boy, and I won't have you making him over into something he wasn't!"

19   He looked as though he were going to go on talking like this, but just then he closed his eyes and ran his hand up over his forehead and through his hair. When he spoke again, his voice was subdued. "I just wish you wouldn't talk that way," he said. "That's all I mean." And then, after standing there silently for a minute, he left the living room and walked upstairs.

20   I sat watching the doorway through which he had gone. Suddenly, I had no feeling for what my mother and my aunts had been saying. It was all a mist, a dream. Out of the many words that had been spoken that day, it was those few sentences of my father's that explained to me how I felt about my brother. I wanted to be with my father to tell him so.

21   I went upstairs and found him once again in the playroom in the attic. As before, he was silent and staring out the window when I entered, and we sat without speaking for what seemed to me like half an hour or more. But I felt that he knew why I was there, and I was not uncomfortable with him.

22   Finally, he turned to me and shook his head. "I don't know what I can tell you, Jack," he said, raising his hands and letting them drop into his lap. "That's the worst part of it. There's just nothing I can say that will make it any better."

23   Though I only half understood him then, I see now that he was telling me of a drawback—that he had no refuge, no comfort, no support. He was telling me that you were all alone if you took the path that he had taken. Listening to him, I did not care about the drawback. I had begun to see what a noble thing it was for a man to bear the full loss of someone he had loved.

II

24   By the time I was thirteen or fourteen I was so thoroughly committed to my father's way of thinking that I considered it a great weakness in a man to believe in religion. I wanted to grow up to face life as he did—truthfully, without comfort, without support.

25   My attitude was never one of rebellion. Despite the early regimen of Sunday school and church that my mother had encouraged, she was wonderfully gentle with me, particularly when I began to express my doubts. She would come into my room each night after the light was out and ask me to say my prayers. Determined to be honest with her, I would explain that I could not say them sincerely, and therefore should not say them at all. "Now, Jack," she would reply, very quietly and calmly, "you mustn't talk like that. You'll really feel much better if you say them." I could tell from the tone of her voice that she was hurt, but she never tried to force me in any way. Indeed, it might have been easier for me if she *had* tried to oppose my decision strenuously. As it was, I felt so bad at having wounded her that I was continually trying to make things up—running errands, surprising her by doing the dishes when she went out shopping—behaving, in short, in the most conscientious, considerate fashion. But all this never brought me any closer to her religion. On the contrary, it only served to free me for my decision *not* to believe. And for that decision, as I say, my father was responsible.

26   Part of his influence, I suppose, was in his physical quality. Even at that time—when he was in his late forties and in only moderately good health—he was a most impressive figure. He was tall and heavychested, with leathery, rough-cast features and with an easy, relaxed rhythm in his walk. He had been an athlete in his youth, and, needless to say, I was enormously proud of his various feats and told about them, with due exaggeration, all over our neighborhood. Still, the physical thing had relatively little to do with the matter. My father, by that time, regarded athletes and athletics with contempt. Now and again, he would take me into the back yard to fool around with boxing gloves, but when it came to something serious, such as my going out for football in high school, he invariably put his foot down. "It takes too much time," he would tell me. "You ought to be thinking of college and your studies. It's nonsense what they make of sports nowadays!" I always wanted to remind him of *his* school days, but I knew it was no use. He had often told me what an unforgivable waste of time he considered his youth to have been.

27   Thus, although the physical thing was there, it was very much in the background— little more, really, than the simple assumption that a man ought to know how to take care of himself. The real bond between us was spiritual, in the sense that courage, as opposed to strength, is spiritual. It was this intangible quality of courage that I wanted desperately to possess and that, it seemed to me, captured everything that was essential about my father.

28   We never talked of this quality directly. The nearest we came to it was on certain occasions during the early part of the Second World War, just before I went off to college. We would sit in the living room listening to a speech by Winston Churchill, and my father would suddenly clap his fist against his palm. "My God!" he would exclaim, fairly beaming with admiration. "That man's got the heart of a tiger!" And I would listen to the rest of the speech, thrilling to every word, and then, thinking of my father, really, I would say aloud that, of all men in the world, the one I would most like to be was Churchill.

29   Nor did we often talk about religion. Yet our religion—our rejection of religion—was the deepest statement of the bond between us. My father, perhaps out of deference to my mother and my sisters and aunts, always put his own case very mildly. "It's certainly a great philosophy," he would say of Christianity. "No one could question that. But for the rest . . ." Here he would throw up his hands and cock his head to one side, as if to say that he had tried, but simply could not manage the hurdle of divinity. This view, however mildly it may have been expressed, became mine with absolute clarity and certainty. I concluded that religion was a refuge, without the least foundation in fact. More than that, I positively objected to those—I should say those *men,* for to me it was a peculiarly masculine matter—who turned to religion for support. As I saw it, a man ought to face life as it really is, on his own two feet, without a crutch, as my father did. That was the heart of the matter. By the time I left home for college, I was so deeply committed to this view that I would have considered it a disloyalty to him, to myself, to the code we had lived by, to alter my position in the least.

30   I did not see much of my father during the next four years or so. I was home during the summer vacation after my freshman year, but then, in the middle of the next year, I went into the Army. I was shipped to the Far East for the tail end of the war, and was in

Japan at the start of the Occupation. I saw my father only once or twice during my entire training period, and, naturally, during the time I was overseas I did not see him at all.

31   While I was away, his health failed badly. In 1940, before I went off to college, he had taken a job at a defense plant. The plant was only forty miles from our home, but he was working on the night shift, and commuting was extremely complicated and tiresome. And, of course, he was always willing to overexert himself out of a sense of pride. The result was that late in 1942 he had a heart attack. He came through it quite well, but he made no effort to cut down on his work and, as a consequence, suffered a second, and more serious, attack, two years later. From that time on, he was almost completely bedridden.

32   I was on my way overseas at the time of the second attack, and I learned of it in a letter from my mother. I think she was trying to spare me, or perhaps it was simply that I could not imagine so robust a man as my father being seriously ill. In any event, I had only the haziest notion of what his real condition was, so when, many months later, I finally did realize what had been going on, I was terribly surprised and shaken. One day, some time after my arrival at an American Army post in Japan, I was called to the orderly room and told that my father was critically ill and that I was to be sent home immediately. Within forty-eight hours, I was standing in the early-morning light outside my father's bedroom, with my mother and sisters at my side. They had told me, as gently as they could, that he was not very well, that he had had another attack. But it was impossible to shield me then. I no sooner stepped into the room and saw him than I realized that he would not live more than a day or two longer.

33   From that moment on, I did not want to leave him for a second. Even that night, during the periods when he was sleeping and I was of no help being there, I could not get myself to go out of the room for more than a few minutes. A practical nurse had come to sit up with him, but since I was at the bedside, she finally spent the night in the hallway. I was really quite tired, and late that night my mother and my aunts begged me to go to my room and rest for a while, but I barely heard them. I was sure he would wake up soon, and when he did, I wanted to be there to talk to him.

34   We did talk a great deal that first day and night. It was difficult for both of us. Every once in a while, my father would shift position in the bed, and I would catch a glimpse of his wasted body. It was a knife in my heart. Even worse were the times when he would reach out for my hand, his eyes misted, and begin to tell me how he felt about me. I tried to look at him, but in the end I always looked down. And, knowing that he was dying, and feeling desperately guilty, I would keep repeating to myself that he knew how I felt, that he would understand why I looked away.

35   There was another thing, too. While we talked that day, I had a vague feeling that my father was on the verge of making some sort of confession to me. It was, as I say, only the vaguest impression, and I thought very little about it. The next morning, however, I began to sense what was in the air. Apparently, Mr. Dodds, the minister, whom I barely knew, had been coming to the house lately to talk to my father. My father had not said anything about this, and I learned it only indirectly, from something my mother said to my eldest sister at the breakfast table. At the moment, I brushed the matter aside. I told myself it was natural that Mother would want my father to see the minister at the last. Nevertheless, the very mention of the minister's name caused something to tighten inside me.

36   Later that day, the matter was further complicated. After lunch, I finally did go to my room for a nap, and when I returned to my father's room, I found him and my mother talking about Mr. Dodds. The conversation ended almost as soon as I entered, but I was left with the distinct impression that they were expecting the minister to pay a visit that day, whether very shortly or at suppertime or later in the evening, I could not tell. I did not ask. In fact, I made a great effort not to think of the matter at all.

37   Then, early that evening, my father spoke to me. I knew before he said a word that the minister was coming. My mother had straightened up the bedroom, and fluffed up my father's pillows so that he was half sitting in the bed. No one had told me anything, but I was sure what the preparations meant. "I guess you probably know," my father said to me when we were alone, "we're having a visitor tonight. It's—ah—Mr. Dodds. You know, the minister from your mother's church."

38   I nodded, half shrugging, as if I saw nothing the least unusual in the news. "He's come here before once or twice," my father said. "Have I mentioned that? I can't remember if I've mentioned that."

39   "Yes, I know. I think Mother said something, or perhaps you did. I don't remember."

40   "I just thought I'd let you know. You see, your mother wanted me to talk to him. I—I've talked to him more for her sake than anything else."

41   "Sure. I can understand that."

42   "I think it makes her feel a little better. I think—" Here he broke off, seeming dissatisfied with what he was saying. His eyes turned to the ceiling, and he shook his head slightly, as if to erase the memory of his words. He studied the ceiling for a long time before he spoke again. "I don't mean it was all your mother exactly," he said. "Well, what I mean is he's really quite an interesting man. I think you'd probably like him a good deal."

43   "I know Mother has always liked him," I replied. "From what I gather most people seem to like him very much."

44   "Well, he's that sort," my father went on, with quickening interest. "I mean, he isn't what you'd imagine at all. To tell the truth, I wish you'd talk to him a little. I wish you'd talk things over with him right from scratch." My father was looking directly at me now, his eyes flashing.

45   "I'd be happy to talk with him sometime," I said. "As I say, everybody seems to think very well of him."

46   "Well, I wish you would. You see, when you're lying here day after day, you get to thinking about things. I mean, it's good to have someone to talk to." He paused for a moment. "Tell me," he said, "have you ever . . . have you ever wondered if there wasn't some truth in it? Have you ever thought about it that way at all?"

47   I made a faint gesture with my hand. "Of course, it's always possible to wonder," I replied. "I don't suppose you can ever be completely certain one way or the other."

48   "I know, I know," he said, almost impatiently. "But have you ever felt—well, all in a sort of flash—that it *was* true? I mean, have you ever had that feeling?"

49   He was half raised up from the pillow now, his eyes staring into me with a feverish concentration. Suddenly, I could not look at him any longer. I lowered my head.

50   "I don't mean permanently or anything like that," he went on. "But just for a few seconds. The feeling that you've been wrong all along. Have you had that feeling—ever?"

51   I could not look up. I could not move. I felt that every muscle in my body had suddenly frozen. Finally, after what seemed an eternity, I heard him sink back into the pillows. When I glanced up a moment later, he was lying there silent, his eyes closed, his lips parted, conveying somehow the image of the death that awaited him.

52   Presently, my mother came to the door. She called me into the hall to tell me that Mr. Dodds had arrived. I said that I thought my father had fallen asleep but that I would go back and see.

53   It was strangely disheartening to me to discover that he was awake. He was sitting there, his eyes open, staring grimly into the gathering shadows of the evening.

54   "Mr. Dodds is downstairs," I said matter-of-factly. "Mother wanted to know if you felt up to seeing him tonight."

55   For a moment, I thought he had not heard me; he gave no sign of recognition whatever. I went to the foot of the bed and repeated myself. He nodded, not answering the question but simply indicating that he had heard me. At length, he shook his head. "Tell your mother I'm a little tired tonight," he said. "Perhaps—well, perhaps some other time."

56   "I could ask him to come back later, if you'd like."

57   "No, no, don't bother. I—I could probably use the rest."

58   I waited a few seconds. "Are you sure?" I asked. "I'm certain he could come back in an hour or so."

59   Then, suddenly, my father was looking at me. I shall never forget his face at that moment and the expression burning in his eyes. He was pleading with me to speak. And all I could say was that I would be happy to ask Mr. Dodds to come back later, if he wanted it that way. It was not enough. I knew, instinctively, at that moment that it was not enough. But I could not say anything more.

60   As quickly as it had come, the burning flickered and went out. He sank back into the pillows again. "No, you can tell him I won't be needing him tonight," he said, without interest. "Tell him not to bother waiting around." Then he turned on his side, away from me, and said no more.

61   So my father did not see Mr. Dodds that night. Nor did he ever see him again. Shortly after midnight, just after my mother and sisters had gone to bed, he died. I was at his side then, but I could not have said exactly when it occurred. He must have gone off in his sleep, painlessly, while I sat there awake beside him.

62   In the days that followed, our family was together almost constantly. Curiously enough, I did not think much about my father just then. For some reason, I felt the strongest sense of responsibility toward the family. I found myself making the arrangements for the funeral, protecting Mother from the stream of people who came to the house, speaking words of consolation to my sisters and even to my aunts. I was never alone except at night, when a kind of oblivion seized me almost as soon as my head touched the pillow. My sleep was dreamless, numb.

63   Then, two weeks after the funeral, I left for Fort Devens, where I was to be discharged from the Army. I had been there three days when I was told that my terminal leave would begin immediately and that I was free to return home. I had half expected that when I was at the Fort, separated from the family, something would break inside me. But still

no emotion came. I thought of my father often during that time, but, search as I would, I could find no sign of feeling.

64   Then, when I had boarded the train for home, it happened. Suddenly, for no reason whatever, I was thinking of the expression on my father's face that last night in the bedroom. I saw him as he lay there pleading with me to speak. And I knew then what he had wanted me to say to him—that it was really all right with me, that it wouldn't change anything between us if he gave way. And then I was thinking of myself and what I had said and what I had *not* said. Not a word to help! Not a word!

65   I wanted to beg his forgiveness. I wanted to cry out aloud to him. But I was in a crowded train, sitting with three elderly women just returning from a shopping tour. I turned my face to the window. There, silent, unnoticed, I thought of what I might have said.

■ *Vocabulary*

unison (2)	constrained (4)	intangible (27)
brusque (4)	inviolable (6)	deference (29)

■ *Questions on Meaning and Technique*

1. What was the author's childhood faith? How old was he when he thought he might give it up?

2. Why, after the death of his brother, did the narrator feel he had to bless everyone, even people whose names he had heard mentioned but whom he really didn't know?

3. What was the value of religion to the narrator's mother and aunts? Where is this stated?

4. What did the past athletic prowess of the father have to do with the code that developed between him and the narrator? How was the code related to masculinity?

5. What "intangible quality" drew the narrator to his father?

6. Examine paragraphs 30 and 32, and identify at least two devices the author uses to move the story along.

7. In paragraph 59, the narrator says of his father, "He was pleading with me to speak," and that he, the narrator, knew that his answer "was not enough." What did the narrator's father want him to say? Why didn't the narrator say it?

8. What does "The Code" have to say about role playing and about rigid beliefs in masculinity?

9. How would you characterize the father's deathbed behavior? Was he courageous? Cowardly?

10. What is the significance of the final scene and the three elderly women in the train?

EDWIN ARLINGTON ROBINSON

Richard Cory

Edwin Arlington Robinson (1869–1935) was regarded during his lifetime as the greatest U.S. poet. He was born in Head Tide, Maine, and educated at Harvard University. His many volumes of verse include The Children of the Night *(1897),* The Man Who Died Twice *(1924; Pulitzer Prize), and* Tristram *(1928; Pulitzer Prize). Robinson, who never married, lived a life of quiet reclusiveness, spending many of his summers in New Hampshire at the MacDowell Colony for artists and writers.*

READING FOR IDEAS   Behind every poem is a character whose worldview it may describe, a narrator who may be part of its plot, or a speaker who merely exists to give the poem a voice. Ask yourself who the voice behind this poem is and to what socioeconomic class and gender he or she probably belongs. Notice the implicit social differences that exist between the speaker and the subject of the poem, Richard Cory. Why does the speaker find Cory's suicide so mystifying? Ask yourself, further, whether Cory's suicide reported by a member of his own privileged class would seem as shocking.

1   Whenever Richard Cory went down town,
We people on the pavement looked at him:
He was a gentleman from sole to crown,
Clean favored, and imperially slim.

2   And he was always quietly arrayed,
And he was always human when he talked;
But still he fluttered pulses when he said,
"Good-morning," and he glittered when he walked.

3   And he was rich—yes, richer than a king—
And admirably schooled in every grace:
In fine, we thought that he was everything
To make us wish that we were in his place.

4   So on we worked, and waited for the light,
And went without the meat, and cursed the bread;
And Richard Cory, one calm summer night,
Went home and put a bullet through his head.

■ *Questions on Meaning and Technique*

1. From whose viewpoint is this poem narrated? What rhetorical advantages does this viewpoint afford the writer?

2. Why was Richard Cory the envy of those who saw him? Enumerate his enviable characteristics.

3. What is the meaning of "But still he fluttered pulses when he said, 'Good-morning'"?

4. Aside from the narrative form, what other rhetorical mode is evident in this poem?

5. What do we know about the "we" who narrate this poem? Why is it important that we have some information about them?

How to Write a Narration

Narration tells what happened. In its widest sense, *narration* includes history, biography, personal experience, travel, and fiction—in short, any writing that lays out the events of a story in a dramatic and climactic order.

Writing Assignment

Narrate an incident or experience that taught you a lesson about life. Recreate it on paper as you remember it, trying to be as animated as possible. Keep the events in the order in which they occurred. At the end of the narrative, explain what the incident or experience taught you.

Specific Instructions

Prewrite on the assignment.   The key word in this assignment is *lesson*. Your experience must not be merely gripping or tellable; it must also have taught you something, and you should be able to say what. Note, for example, that in the model Student Essay (see pp. 134–137) the writer tells us in her final paragraph that the death of her Uncle Thom taught her an "important lesson" in tolerance.

Begin your prewriting by outlining one of the most memorable experiences or adventures you have ever had. Choose the one that moves you most. If necessary and if you cannot quite decide on any particular experience, talk out the assignment with a friend or with your instructor.

Decide next on what lesson the experience taught you and express that in a sentence or two. This lesson, properly worded as a lead-in or a conclusion to your story, could become the theme for your narrative. But do not be too mechanical about it. Often it is more effective to let a conclusion unfold naturally from the story rather than to begin by slugging the reader hard over the head with it.

Narrative writing must have a consistent point of view.   *Point of view* refers to the vantage point from which a story is told. The most elemental point of view for any writer is the first-person narrator. In its simplest application, this point of view may be the writer telling the story as an *I* who lived or saw it. In a more complex application, the *I* telling the story is innocent of what the story really means. For example, this narrator from Edgar Allan Poe's "The Tell-Tale Heart" is insane but does not know it:

> TRUE!—nervous—very, very dreadfully nervous I had been and am! but why will you say that I am mad? The disease had sharpened my senses—not destroyed—not dulled them. Above all was the sense of hearing acute. I heard all things in the heaven and in the earth. I heard many things in hell. How, then, am I mad? Hearken! and observe how healthily—how calmly I can tell you the whole story.

The narrator opens by denying that he is mad, insisting that he is only nervous. Later in the tale, we get a glimpse of his madness when he tells us a sinister story about how he stalked and murdered a harmless old man who he thought possessed an "Evil Eye."

Probably the most commonly used point of view today is the *omniscient narrator.* This person sees all, hears all, and reports all, moving across time and place at will. Characters are referred to as *he* or *she,* and their actions, motives, and thoughts are related by this invisible agent who is everywhere. Few student narratives, except for those written in creative writing classes, use the omniscient point of view, because most student narrative assignments ask for a story based on personal experience, requiring the use of *I.*

In using the first-person point of view, you must decide early who you are in the story, take on the voice of your assumed character, and remain faithful to it throughout the telling. For instance, if you are relating an incident from the point of view of a young boy, the language of the story should reflect his youthfulness. It would seem odd if, having indicated to the reader that the story is to be told from a boy's point of view, you then make him sound like an elderly college professor.

Writers resort to a variety of techniques and devices to make their prose reflect their assumed characters. The most common technique is playacting: The writer simply pretends to be the person narrating the story and tries to write the way that person would write.

This passage is taken from a story narrated from the point of view of an uneducated slave. Notice how the language is used to reflect his character:

> A long time ago, in times gone by, in slavery times, there was a man named Cue. I want you to think about him. I've got a reason.
>
> He got born like the cotton in the boll or the rabbit in the pea patch. There wasn't any fine doings when he got born, but his mammy was glad to save him. Yes. He didn't get born in the Big House, or the overseer's house, or any place where the bearing was easy or the work light. No, Lord. He came out of his mammy in a field hand's cabin one sharp winter, and about the first thing he remembered was his

mammy's face and the taste of a piece of bacon rind and the light and shine of the pitch-pine fire up the chimney. Well, now, he got born and there he was.

—Stephen Vincent Benét, *Freedom's a Hard-Bought Thing*

Whatever character you choose to speak through—innocent young boy, lonely middle-aged man, or wise old woman—you must stay in that role throughout the narrative. Don't be one character in one paragraph, only to shift suddenly to another in the next. Such an abrupt change will make your story seem unbelievable. Here is an example of the sort of shift to avoid:

> Jessica and I hated all grownups. We'd climb onto my parents' four-story apartment roof, and you can bet that we were up to no good. Gosh, sometimes we'd spit down on old lady Gunther 'cause she was such a grouch about us playing on her lawn. *I find it rather nostalgic to reflect on those budding days of my youth, when life was free and easy and each day was the dawn of a new adventure.*

Notice the sudden shift from mischievous child to reflective adult in line four.

The narration must have a theme. Unlike most assignments, the narrative generally uses a theme instead of a thesis. A *theme* is a central topic of the work that functions like a thesis but is usually implied rather than stated. Basically, the main point of a narration is its theme. For example, "The Code" tells the story of a code of atheism shared by a young man and his father and how it became a barrier between them. That a rigidly held belief can have a chilling effect on human intimacy is a theme of this story, even though the author does not come out and say so. Similarly, the theme of the poem "Richard Cory" is that things are often not what they seem, but again the poet understates this nugget of wisdom. Instead, we are left wondering why a man like Richard Cory, described in all his splendor from the viewpoint of the poor, admiring townspeople, would commit suicide.

Your own narration must have a theme, or the story will seem pointless. To write a narrative with a central theme, it helps to imagine a reader on the other end of your story asking, "So what?" We are tempted to blurt, "So what?" and if the teller has no answer, to walk away in a huff. As a narrator, you are under a similar obligation to make your narration meaningful, to give it some central theme or topic that justifies its reading. Begin your narrative by asking yourself, "So what?" And be sure that by the end of your narrative you have answered that question.

Pace your narration to focus on important scenes. Every reader of fiction has encountered passages that read like this:

> The first time I saw her she was chasing a schnauzer in the park. Her hair was wind-blown and wild as she dodged pedestrians and bicyclists and ran screaming after the runaway schnauzer. Her flowered sundress billowed in furls as she tried to run in floppy leather-thonged sandals. She was as graceful and lovely as ever a woman could be. *I didn't see her for three weeks after that.* Then one Tuesday morning, as I was taking a post-digestive jog along the elm-lined footpath, I saw her again.

STUDENT TIP FOR INVENTING IDEAS

Assignment

Narrate an incident or experience that taught you a lesson about life.

How I found my topic

A few days before this assignment, I had listened to TV host Larry King interview "Dr. Phil," who believes that everyone should list on paper the ten defining moments of life—that is, those moments that had a deep and lasting influence on you. So as I was watching TV, I tried to think of one defining moment. At first I couldn't think of anything serious.

Then, suddenly I remembered the day my mother left a half-finished letter to her mother in Texas on the breakfast table. I just glanced at it (OK, I didn't glance at it; I read it.) and glimpsed two sentences: "Francine (my sister) is so beautiful that people stare at her in public. Jessica (that's me) is not beautiful, but she is our sunshine girl." That was my defining moment. All of my life I have tried to be happy and cheerful because I am supposed to be the sunshine girl, as first expressed by my mother.

I could now write my essay about why I always try to act bubbly and to smile, even when I am feeling down in the dumps. And I think I'm going to say that the lesson it taught me was—don't snoop around in other people's private letters.

—A female freshman at a four-year university in Michigan

Three sentences are devoted to a description of an encounter between the narrator and the girl in the park; then three weeks are dismissed in a single, brief sentence. Obviously, life was not suspended during those three weeks, but because that time is unimportant to the narrative, it is quickly passed over.

This is an example of *pacing*, an important and commonsense principle of narrative writing. Unimportant time, events, and scenes are dismissed as the narrative focuses on and develops in detail only what is important to its theme. For example, in "The Code," the author glosses over his enlistment in the army during wartime in this brief paragraph:

> I did not see much of my father during the next four years or so. I was home during the summer vacation after my freshman year, but then, in the middle of the next year, I went into the Army. I was shipped to the Far East for the tail end of the

war, and was in Japan at the start of the Occupation. I saw my father only once or twice during my entire training period, and, naturally, during the time I was overseas I did not see him at all.

—Richard Gill, "The Code"

Four years go up in the puff of a single sentence because nothing significant to the theme of the story occurred during that stretch of time. If the writer had included his various army adventures, he would only have diluted the dramatic drive of his narrative and ruined the climactic deathbed scene.

Common sense must guide you in selecting scenes and events to be developed in your own narration, but your basic yardstick should be the relevance of the material to your theme.

Use vivid details to describe people and places in your narrative.
People and places are the lifeblood of your narration. Make them real and distinct through the use of forceful details (see Chapter 8, "Description"). Here, for example, is how one author describes his main character, a young prodigy by the name of Wallace. Notice the wealth of specific details that the author uses:

> As a matter of fact, one look at Wallace should have been enough to tell the teachers what sort of genius he was. At fourteen, he was somewhat shorter than he should have been and a good deal stouter. His face was round, owlish and dirty. He had big, dark eyes, and his black hair, which hardly ever got cut, was arranged on his head as the four winds wanted it. He had been outfitted with attractive and fairly expensive clothes, but he changed from one suit to another only when his parents came to call on him and ordered him to get out of what he had on.
>
> —Richard Rovere, "Wallace"

Detailed *dialogue* is another technique that narration uses to infuse life in a character. In "The Code," dialogue reveals the father as a man who will not tolerate emotional and irrational beliefs. For example, when the aunts go into hysterics over the death of the author's younger brother, calling him "a perfect baby," "a saint," "too perfect to live," the father angrily reacts:

> His face was very pale, and his eyes flashed almost feverishly. "Don't talk like that, Agnes!" he exclaimed, with a strange violence that was not anger but something much deeper. "I won't have you talking like that any more. I don't want anybody talking like that!" His whole body seemed to tremble. I had never seen him so worked up before. "Of course he was a bad boy at times!" he cried. "Every boy's bad once in a while. What do you have to change him for? Why don't you leave him as he was?"
>
> —Richard Gill, "The Code"

A vivid narrative requires careful observation of people and how they live, using those details that contribute best to a clear, vigorous, and interesting story.

ALLAN SHERMAN

A Gift of Laughter

Allan Sherman (1924–1975)—American entertainer, television producer, singer, and comedy writer—was born in Chicago and attended the University of Illinois. He wrote jokes and songs for television variety shows such as The 54th Street Revue *and was co-creator of the television game show* I've Got a Secret. *In 1963, he won a Grammy Award for the song "Hello Muddah, Hello Fadduh." His books include* A Gift of Laughter: The Autobiography of Allan Sherman *(1965).*

READING FOR IDEAS In this simple but moving story, taken from Allan Sherman's autobiography, a child tries to give his distracted father a present but is cut short. Notice the simplicity of the language and the directness of the dialogue, which are woven together to present a typical episode in any family's life. Notice also the use of a flashback in telling the story and the smooth transition the narrator makes to an earlier period in his life. As you read, ask yourself what are the advantages and disadvantages of directness in storytelling.

1   "DaddydaddyDADDY!" That's how it came out—one long, excited word. He started yelling it at the top of the stairs, and by the time he bounded into the living room he really had it going good. I'd been talking to his mother about a money problem, and it stopped me mid-sentence.

2   "Robbie, *please!*" I said. Then I appealed to my wife. "Can't we just have five minutes around here without kids screaming?"

3   Robbie had been holding something behind his back. Now he swung it around for me to see. "Daddy, *look!*"

4   It was a picture, drawn in the messy crayon of a seven-year-old. It showed a weird-looking creature with one ear three times as big as the other, one green eye and one red; the head was pear-shaped, and the face needed a shave.

5   I turned on my son. "Is *that* what you interrupted me for? Couldn't you wait? I'm talking to your mother about something *important!*"

6   His face clouded up. His eyes filled with bewilderment, rage, then tears. "Awright!" he screamed, and threw the picture to the floor. "But it's *your* birthday Saturday!" Then he ran upstairs.

7   I looked at the picture on the floor. At the bottom, in Robbie's careful printing, were some words I hadn't noticed: MY DAD by Robert Sherman.

8   Just then Robbie slammed the door of his room. But I heard a different door, a door I once slammed—25 years ago—in my grandmother's house in Chicago.

9   It was the day I heard my grandmother say she needed a *football.* I heard her tell my mother there was going to be a party tonight for the whole family, and she had to have a football, for after supper.

10   I couldn't imagine *why* Grandmother needed a football. I was sure she wasn't going to play the game with my aunts and uncles.

11   She had been in America only a few years, and still spoke with a deep Yiddish accent. But Grandma wanted a football, and a football was something in *my* department. If I could get one, I'd be important, a contributor to the party. I slipped out the door.

12   There were only three footballs in the neighborhood, and they belonged to older kids. Homer Spicer wasn't home. Eddie Polonsky wouldn't sell or rent, at any price.

13   The last possibility was a tough kid we called Gudgie. It was just as I'd feared. Gudgie punched me in the nose. Then he said he would trade me his old football for my new sled, plus all the marbles I owned.

14   I filled Gudgie's football with air at the gas station. Then I sneaked into the house and shined it with shoe polish. When I finished, it was a football worthy of Grandmother's party. All the aunts and uncles would be proud. When nobody was looking I put it on the dining-room table. Then I waited in my room for Grandma to notice it.

15   But it was Mother who noticed it. "Allan!" she shouted.

16   I ran to the dining room.

17   "You know your grandmother's giving a party tonight. Why can't you put your things where they belong?"

18   "It's not mine," I protested.

19   "Then give it back to whoever it belongs to. Get it out of here!"

20   "But it's for Grandma! She said she needed a football for the party." I was holding back the tears.

21   Mother burst into laughter. "A *football* for the party! Don't you understand your own grandma?" Then, between peals of laughter, Mother explained: "Not football. Fruit bowl! Grandma needs a fruit bowl for the party."

22   I was starting to cry, so I ran to my room and slammed the door. The worst part of crying was trying to stop. I can still feel it—the shuddering, my breath coming in little, staccato jerks. And each sputtery breath brought back the pain, the frustration, the unwanted feeling that had made me cry in the first place. I was still trying to stop crying when the aunts and uncles arrived. I heard their voices (sounding very far away), and the clink-clink of Grandma's good china, and now and then an explosion of laughter.

23   After dinner, Mother came in. "Allan," she said, "come with me. I want you to see something." I followed her into the living room.

24   Grandma was walking around the room like a queen, holding out to each of the aunts and uncles the biggest, most magnificent cut-glass bowl I'd ever seen. There were grapes and bananas in it, red apples, figs and tangerines. And in the center of the bowl, all shiny and brown, was Gudgie's football.

25   Just then my Uncle Sol offered Grandma a compliment. "Esther," he said, "that's a beautiful *football*. Real *cott gless*."

26   Grandma looked at Uncle Sol with great superiority. "Sol," she said, "listen close, you'll learn something. This *cott gless* is called a *fruit boll*, not a *football*. This in the middle, this is a *football*."

27   Uncle Sol was impressed. "Very smot," he said. "Very nice. But, Esther, now tell me something. How come you got a *football* in your *fruit boll*?" He pronounced them both very carefully.

28   "Because," Grandma said, "today mine Allan brought me a nice present, this football. It's beautiful, no?"

29   Before Uncle Sol could answer, Grandma continued, "It's beautiful, yess—because from a child is beautiful, anything."

30   . . . *From a child is beautiful, anything.*

31   I picked up Robbie's picture from the floor. It wasn't bad, at that. One of my ears is a little bigger than the other. And usually, when Robbie sees me at the end of the day, I *do* need a shave.

32   I went up to his room. "Hi, Rob," I said.

33   His breath was shuddering, and his nose was running. He was packaging a cardboard box, as he always does when he Leaves Home. I held up the picture. "Say, I've been looking this over. It's very good."

34   "I don't care," he said. He threw a comic book into the box and some Erector-set pieces. "Tear it up if you want to. I can't draw, anyhow."

35   He put on his cap and jacket, picked up the box and walked right past me. I followed him with the picture in my hand.

36   When he got to the front door, he just stood there, his hand on the knob, the way he always does. I suppose he thinks of the same things I used to, whenever I Left Home. You stand there by the door, and pray they won't let you go, because you have no place to go, and if they don't want you, who does?

37   I got on my coat and joined him. "Come on," I said. "I'm going with you." And I took him by the hand.

38   He looked up at me, very scared. "Where we going?"

39   "The shopping center is open tonight," I said. "We're going to buy a frame for this picture. It's a beautiful picture. We'll hang it in the living room. After we get the frame we're going to have an ice-cream soda and I'll tell you about something."

40   "About what?"

41   "Well, you remember that old football your great-grandma keeps in the cut-glass bowl on her dining-room table?"

42   "Yes."

43   "Well, I'm going to tell you how she got it."

▪ Vocabulary

staccato (22)

▪ Questions on Meaning and Technique

1. How does the author's beginning immediately draw us into the story? What is this kind of beginning called?

2. How would you characterize the language used throughout this story? What does the use of this language contribute to the narration?

3. The narrator tells us in paragraph 1 that he wanted to talk to his wife about "a money problem." Why do you think he mentions the subject they were discussing?

4. How does the writer begin the flashback that takes him from his present life as an adult to the memories he has of being a child? What triggers the flashback?

5. In paragraph 13, the narrator tells us what the boy who owned the football wanted for it but does not reveal the details of the actual trade. Why do you think he omits those details?

6. What do you think of the adults depicted in the story? What kind of parents are they portrayed to be?

7. In paragraph 19, the mother is quoted as saying, "Then give it back to whoever it belongs to." Strictly speaking, what is grammatically wrong with this sentence? Why is this sentence still appropriate for this narrative?

8. In paragraph 33, the writer capitalizes "Leaves Home." Similarly, he capitalizes "Left Home" in paragraph 36. What is suggested by this odd capitalization?

9. What is your opinion of the quality of this story? How do you think it compares with other stories in this chapter? For what kind of audience do you think this story is intended?

STUDENT ESSAY—FIRST DRAFT

Kindra Neuman

English 3

Paradise Academy

From a journal entry

My Uncle Thom

1   ~~As~~ I am lying in bed,~~I~~ look*ing* out the ~~clear, cold-looking~~ *frosted* window at the crisp red and yellow leaves of autumn. They fly away and I wish I ~~w~~*c*ould fly the way they can. The leaves fall to the ground and then it is still. My mind wanders*,* *and* ⌐I drift back to the past, *one particular moment. As* when I was a little girl, and I seem to relive ⌐it⌐ Time stops, ~~as~~ it takes its toll because   *reference*

I miss my uncle Thom I can hear his voice so clearly: "Kindra, Get out of the street!

There's a truck coming!" He is yelling.   *He yells again. I remember as if it were happening again.*   *Better transition*

2   The three of us—my mother, Uncle Thom, and my four-year-old self—were crossing
Suddenly I stopped and refused to move.
the street. ~~I wouldn't move.~~ As the truck drew closer, I planted my feet on the crosswalk.

I was a stubborn child and I had made up my mind that I wasn't going anywhere. My

more specific wording

                                                                                                    truck
uncle had no choice but to drag me out of the way of the oncoming ~~vehicle~~. I was ~~mad~~ at

the time because I was perfectly content standing in the intersection, but Uncle Thom

saved my life. Given, it wasn't hard to move a four-year-old, but he was there for me.

3   My uncle Thom was the greatest! Since he played the piano for luxury cruises, he

                                          exotic   *all kinds of far away places*
traveled all over the world, bringing me ~~the best~~ gifts from ~~all over the globe~~. One year he

Avoid repeating "wore"
                                          silk   *Insert A*   *so*
surprised me with a blue Japanese dress. I adored it. The silk material seemed elegant,

                                                                  put on
and when I wore the dress, I felt like an Oriental princess. I ~~wore~~ this dress ~~often~~, and I

Be specific
                                                              whenever the occasion called
told everyone that my uncle Thom gave it to me.   *for a special outfit,*

4   Uncle Thom was full of happy surprises and delightful fun. Still, a mysterious element

Insert B
always seemed to lurk somewhere inside his heart and mind. Some aspect of inner peace

                                act   *—the unendurable—*
was missing, which often made him weary and glum. Then one day the unbelievable ∧

Add drama
happened. It was July 12, 2007, when Uncle Thom chose to end his life. He was forty-four

                                          Why? Why? *Insert C*
years old. He was my favorite uncle. Why did it happen? All kinds of questions tumbled

against each other, but with no real answer. The main key to the door was missing.

5   My uncle was one of six brothers. All of the brothers had just gone on a sailing

trip with their dad, my grandpa. They all had a great time. Thom had made his special

Explain fully
fruit pies in the galley of the sailboat. He had told me once that the secret ingredient to

despite the fact that they had such different personalities.
his delicious pies was rainwater. He had such a knack for saying and doing unexpected

                                                              full
things that everyone loved. My dad and he were blood brothers

whereas the other brothers were half brothers. Having the same mother and father forged

a close bond between them. My dad is a pilot, and at the time my uncle was dying from

Be specific   *this irreversible*   *self-administered*
an overdose of poison, my dad was off at work in another country. One of his half

wired him that Uncle Thom was on his deathbed,
                                                        my dad
brothers ~~told him about my uncle Thom,~~ and ~~he~~ tried desperately to get home, but it was

too late. Now my dad feels guilty. My grandparents were beside themselves with

~~agonizing~~ grief and still weep every day over the loss of their son. To everyone who knew

                superstar
him, he was a ~~Prince William~~—enormously charming and talented. Only the sky could

limit his achievements. He was the guy with the golden spoon.

Insert A
—embroidered with yellow primroses and trimmed in gold—

Insert B
Name some of these surprises and fun (skate
boarding, videos, family events)

Insert C
Those who loved him pondered and
speculated. Was if a chemical imbalance
in his brain? Was it a sense of futility?

6   So what went wrong? Why did it happen? These are the questions we all asked.∧ *I suppose they are age-old questions posed by all human beings who have faced sorrows which seemed to happen without cause.* Everyone is filled with remorse and guilt. I can't help but cry when I see my grandma and grandpa or my dad so torn up. Grandma's eyes have lost their twinkle, and I can't even conceive of the pain she and Grandpa feel.¶∧ At first, I too kept repeating, "Why?" I search∧ed for the reason behind this ~~monstrous~~ tragedy. Why ~~is~~ *was* he gone? Why would he take his own life and cause those of us who loved him such deep and lasting pain? No one gave me a straight answer, so I had to figure it out for myself. Now I think I know part of the answer. Of course, I can't claim to know exactly what demons were struggling inside Thom when he swallowed the poison, but I have a few thoughts which have served as an explanation.

my own philosophical thoughts

tense

7   First of all, in a family of devout Christians, Thom was an avowed Atheist who never allowed himself to ~~form a relationship with~~ *acknowledge* a power greater than he. I suppose he thought he could manage life ~~by submitting to his own authority~~ *on his own*. He had a reputation for getting into mischief and bad ~~stuff, which he shouldn't have~~ *habits,* but he never sought the one remedy that might have saved him from complete desolation—a belief in a Divine Force to guide him when life's path was too rough for him to trudge onward alone.

More specific word

8   In addition to having doubts about God's existence, ~~he~~ *Thom* was also gay. When he was a little boy and his friends wanted to play soccer, he wanted to dance on ice skates or to win competitions in gymnastics. In other words, his artistic temperament separated him from his peers, who ~~rebuffed~~ *avoided* him because they didn't understand him.

reference

more accurate

9   ~~Hw told me he was an atheist~~. Some of our religious friends have suggested that denying God was the reason for ~~his~~ *Thom's* desire to end life. I see his problem from a different angle. I think that since *many* ∧ people didn't accept him throughout his life, he probably thought that God wouldn't accept him either. I rather suspect that he thought he was too far gone, too far on the wrong path to turn back and to fit into society, or to even ask anyone for ~~acceptance~~ *help*.

reference

better word

10   My uncle Thom's death taught me an important lesson: I must accept people, even when they are different from me. Parents, schools, and churches should teach children early on to be tolerant of people who seem offbeat, different, and therefore easy to ignore. Surely if God exists, He accepts all human beings as part of his creation and ~~will~~ love^s them unconditionally, as he must have loved my uncle Thom.

Neuman 1

Kindra Neuman

English 3

Paradise Academy

From a journal entry

My Uncle Thom

1   I am lying in bed, looking out the frosted window at the crisp red and yellow leaves of autumn. They fly away and I wish I could fly the way they can. The leaves fall to the ground and then it is still. My mind wanders and I drift back to the past when I was a little girl, and I seem to relive one particular moment. As time stops, it takes its toll because I miss my uncle Thom. I can hear his voice so clearly: "Kindra, get out of the street! There's a truck coming!" He is yelling. He yells again. I remember the instant as if it were happening again.

2   The three of us—my mother, Uncle Thom, and my four-year-old self—were crossing the street. Suddenly I stopped and refused to move. As the truck drew closer, I planted my feet on the crosswalk. I was a stubborn child and I had made up my mind that I wasn't going anywhere. My uncle had no choice but to drag me out of the way of the oncoming truck. I threw a temper tantrum because I was perfectly content standing in the intersection, but Uncle Thom saved my life. Given, it wasn't hard to move a four-year-old, but he was there for me.

Neuman 2

3   My uncle Thom was the greatest! Since he played the piano for luxury cruises, he traveled all over the world, bringing me exotic gifts from all kinds of far away places. One year he surprised me with a blue silk Japanese dress. I adored it. The silk material—embroidered with yellow primroses and trimmed in gold—seemed elegant, and when I wore the dress, I felt like an Oriental princess. I put on this dress whenever the occasion called for a special outfit, and I told everyone that my uncle Thom gave it to me.

4   Uncle Thom was full of happy surprises and delightful fun. For instance, he taught me how to skate board; he created family videos with his piano music as background; and he always added hilarious anecdotes to every family event. Still, a mysterious element always seemed to lurk somewhere inside his heart and mind. Some aspect of inner peace was missing, which often made him act weary and glum. Then one day the unbelievable—the unendurable—happened. It was July 12, 2007, when Uncle Thom chose to end his life. He was forty-four years old. He was my favorite uncle. Why did it happen? Why? Why? Why? All kinds of questions tumbled against each other, but with no real answer. The main key to the door was missing.

5   My uncle was one of six brothers. All of the brothers had just gone on a sailing trip with their dad, my grandpa. They all had a great time. Thom had made his special fruit pies in the galley of the sailboat. He had told me once that the secret ingredient to his delicious pies was rainwater. He had such a knack for saying and doing unexpected things that everyone loved. My dad and

Neuman 3

he were best friends despite the fact that they had such different personalities. They were full blood brothers whereas the other brothers were half brothers. Having the same mother and father forged a close bond between them. My dad is a pilot, and at the time my uncle was dying from this irreversible overdose of poison, my dad was off at work in another country. One of his half brothers wired him that Uncle Thom was on his deathbed, and my dad tried desperately to get home, but it was too late. Now my dad feels guilty. My grandparents were beside themselves with grief and still weep every day over the loss of their son. To everyone who knew him, he was a superstar—enormously charming and talented. Only the sky could limit his achievements. He was the guy with the golden spoon.

6   So what went wrong? Why did it happen? These are the questions we all asked. I suppose they are age-old questions, asked by all human beings who have faced sorrows that seem to happen without cause. Everyone is filled with remorse and guilt. I can't help but cry when I see my grandma and grandpa or my dad so torn up. Grandma's eyes have lost their twinkle, and I can't even conceive of the pain she and Grandpa feel.

7   At first, I too kept repeating, "Why?" I searched for the reason behind this tragedy. Why was he gone? Why would he take his own life and cause those of us who loved him such deep and lasting pain? No one gave me a straight answer, so I had to figure it out for myself. Now I think I know part of the answer. Of course, I can't claim to know exactly what demons were struggling inside Thom when he swallowed the poison, but I have a few thoughts which have served as an explanation.

Neuman 4

8   First of all, in a family of devout Christians, Thom was an avowed atheist who never allowed himself to acknowledge a power greater than he. I suppose he thought he could manage life on his own. He had a reputation for getting into mischief and bad habits, but he never sought the one remedy that might have saved him from complete desolation—a belief in a Divine Force to guide him when life's path was too rough for him to trudge onward alone.

9   In addition to having doubts about God's existence, Thom was also gay. When he was a little boy and his friends wanted to play soccer, he wanted to dance on ice skates or to win competitions in gymnastics. He preferred to play the piano than to play contact sports. In other words, his artistic temperament separated him from his peers, who avoided him because they didn't understand him.

10   Some of our religious friends have suggested that denying God was the reason for Thom's desire to end life. I see his problem from a different angle. I think that since many people didn't accept him throughout his life, he probably thought that God wouldn't accept him either. I rather suspect that he thought he was too far gone, too far on the wrong path to turn back and to fit into society, or to even ask anyone for help.

11   My uncle Thom's death taught me an important lesson: I must accept people, even when they are different from me. Parents, schools, and churches should teach children early on to be tolerant of people who seem offbeat, different, and therefore easy to ignore. Surely if God exists, He accepts all human beings as part of his creation and loves them unconditionally, as he must have loved my uncle Thom.

ELIE WIESEL

Excerpt from *Night*

Elie Wiesel, a French-American writer and humanist (b. 1928), was born in Sighet, Romania, to a Hasidic Jewish family. In 1944, his family was deported from Hungary by the Nazis and sent first to Auschwitz and then to Buchenwald. His father, mother, and sister perished in the Nazi concentration camps. Wiesel told his harrowing story of survival in his internationally acclaimed book, Night *(1960). After World War II, Wiesel worked as a newspaper correspondent and studied at the University of Paris. He became an American citizen in 1963 and was made a professor of humanities at Boston University in 1976. He is the author of over twenty books. He was awarded the Congressional Gold Medal in 1985 and the Nobel Peace Prize in 1986.*

READING FOR IDEAS In narrating a story, a writer is often faced with deciding exactly what voice would be appropriate for telling it. If the story is basically a trivial one, the writer might choose to intensify the drama by using an especially dramatic narrative voice. Or to make up for lack of a strong plot or exotic setting, the writer might rely on rich descriptions to add punch to the tale. In this excerpt, the writer uses a direct, almost reportorial voice. The environment he describes—a Nazi concentration camp—is so horrible that there is no need to heighten the story with dramatic language. And the story he tells about the brutal death of his father is already so dramatic that using overly rich language would only detract from it. Bear in mind as you read that the author was just seventeen years old when these events occurred.

1   At the entrance to the camp, SS officers were waiting for us. We were counted. Then we were directed to the *Appelplatz.* The orders were given over the loudspeakers:

2   "Form ranks of fives! Groups of one hundred! Five steps forward!"

3   I tightened my grip on my father's hand. The old, familiar fear: not to lose him.

4   Very close to us stood the tall chimney of the crematorium's furnace. It no longer impressed us. It barely drew our attention.

5   A veteran of Buchenwald told us that we would be taking a shower and afterward be sent to different blocks. The idea of a hot shower fascinated me. My father didn't say a word. He was breathing heavily beside me.

6   "Father," I said, "just another moment. Soon, we'll be able to lie down. You'll be able to rest . . ."

7   He didn't answer. I myself was so weary that his silence left me indifferent. My only wish was to take the shower as soon as possible and lie down on a cot.

8   Only it wasn't easy to reach the showers. Hundreds of prisoners crowded the area. The guards seemed unable to restore order. They were lashing out, left and right, to no avail.

Some prisoners who didn't have the strength to jostle, or even to stand, sat down in the snow. My father wanted to do the same. He was moaning:

9   "I can't anymore . . . It's over . . . I shall die right here . . ."

10   He dragged me toward a pile of snow from which protruded human shapes, torn blankets.

11   "Leave me," he said. "I can't go on anymore . . . Have pity on me . . . I'll wait here until we can go into the showers . . . You'll come and get me."

12   I could have screamed in anger. To have lived and endured so much; was I going to let my father die now? Now that we would be able to take a good hot shower and lie down?

13   "Father!" I howled. "Father! Get up! Right now! You will kill yourself . . ."

14   And I grabbed his arm. He continued to moan:

15   "Don't yell, my son . . . Have pity on your old father . . . Let me rest here . . . a little. . . I beg of you, I'm so tired . . . no more strength . . ."

16   He had become childlike: weak, frightened, vulnerable.

17   "Father," I said, "you cannot stay here."

18   I pointed to the corpses around him; they too had wanted to rest here.

19   "I see, my son. I do see them. Let them sleep. They haven't closed an eye for so long . . . They're exhausted . . . exhausted . . ."

20   His voice was tender.

21   I howled into the wind:

22   "They're dead! They will never wake up! Never! Do you understand?"

23   This discussion continued for some time. I knew that I was no longer arguing with him but with Death itself, with Death that he had already chosen.

24   The sirens began to wail. Alert. The lights went out in the entire camp. The guards chased us toward the blocks. In a flash, there was no one left outside. We were only too glad not to have to stay outside any longer, in the freezing wind. We let ourselves sink into the floor. The cauldrons at the entrance found no takers. There were several tiers of bunks. To sleep was all that mattered.

25   WHEN I WOKE UP, it was daylight. That is when I remembered that I had a father. During the alert, I had followed the mob, not taking care of him. I knew he was running out of strength, close to death, and yet I had abandoned him.

26   I went to look for him.

27   Yet at the same time a thought crept into my mind: If only I didn't find him! If only I were relieved of this responsibility, I could use all my strength to fight for my own survival, to take care only of myself . . . Instantly, I felt ashamed, ashamed of myself forever.

28   I walked for hours without finding him. Then I came to a block where they were distributing black "coffee." People stood in line, quarreled.

29   A plaintive voice came from behind me:

30   "Eliezer, my son . . . bring me . . . a little coffee . . ."

31   I ran toward him.

32   "Father! I've been looking for you for so long . . . Where were you? Did you sleep? How are you feeling?"

33   He seemed to be burning with fever. I fought my way to the coffee cauldron like a wild beast. And I succeeded in bringing back a cup. I took one gulp. The rest was for him.

34   I shall never forget the gratitude that shone in his eyes when he swallowed this beverage. The gratitude of a wounded animal. With these few mouthfuls of hot water, I had probably given him more satisfaction than during my entire childhood . . .

35   He was lying on the boards, ashen, his lips pale and dry, shivering. I couldn't stay with him any longer. We had been ordered to go outside to allow for cleaning of the blocks. Only the sick could remain inside.

36   We stayed outside for five hours. We were given soup. When they allowed us to return to the blocks, I rushed toward my father:

37   "Did you eat?"

38   "No."

39   "Why?"

40   "They didn't give us anything . . . They said that we were sick, that we would die soon, and that it would be a waste of food . . . I can't go on . . ."

41   I gave him what was left of my soup. But my heart was heavy. I was aware that I was doing it grudgingly.

42   Just like Rabbi Eliahu's son, I had not passed the test.

43   EVERY DAY, my father was getting weaker. His eyes were watery, his face the color of dead leaves. On the third day after we arrived in Buchenwald, everybody had to go to the showers. Even the sick, who were instructed to go last.

44   When we returned from the showers, we had to wait outside a long time. The cleaning of the blocks had not been completed.

45   From afar, I saw my father and ran to meet him. He went by me like a shadow, passing me without stopping, without a glance. I called to him, he did not turn around. I ran after him:

46   "Father, where are you running?"

47   He looked at me for a moment and his gaze was distant, other worldly, the face of a stranger. It lasted only a moment and then he ran away.

48   SUFFERING FROM DYSENTERY, my father was prostrate on his cot, with another five sick inmates nearby. I sat next to him, watching him; I no longer dared to believe that he could still elude Death. I did all I could to give him hope.

49   All of a sudden, he sat up and placed his feverish lips against my ear:

50   "Eliezer . . . I must tell you where I buried the gold and silver . . . In the cellar . . . You know . . ."

51   And he began talking, faster and faster, afraid of running out of time before he could tell me everything. I tried to tell him that it was not over yet, than we would be going home together, but he no longer wanted to listen to me. He *could* no longer listen to me. He was worn out. Saliva mixed with blood was trickling from his lips. He had closed his eyes. He was gasping more than breathing.

52   FOR A RATION OF BREAD I was able to exchange cots to be next to my father. When the doctor arrived in the afternoon, I went to tell him that my father was very ill.

53   "Bring him here!"

54   I explained that he could not stand up, but the doctor would not listen. And so, with great difficulty, I brought my father to him. He stared at him, then asked curtly:

55   What do you want?"

56   "My father is sick," I answered in his place . . . "Dysentery . . ."

57   "That's not my business. I'm a surgeon. Go on. Make room for the others!"

58   My protests were in vain.

59   "I can't go on, my son . . . Take me back to my bunk."

60   I took him back and helped him lie down. He was shivering.

61   "Try to get some sleep, Father. Try to fall asleep . . ."

62   His breathing was labored. His eyes were closed. But I was convinced that he was seeing everything. That he was seeing the truth in all things.

63   Another doctor came to the block. My father refused to get up. He knew that it would be of no use.

64   In fact, that doctor had come only to finish off the patients. I listened to him shouting at them that they were lazy good-for-nothings who only wanted to stay in bed . . . I considered jumping him, strangling him. But I had neither the courage nor the strength. I was riveted to my father's agony. My hands were aching, I was clenching them so hard. To strangle the doctor and the others! To set the whole world on fire! My father's murderers! But even the cry stuck in my throat.

65   ON MY RETURN from the bread distribution, I found my father crying like a child:

66   "My son, they are beating me!"

67   "Who?" I thought he was delirious.

68   "Him, the Frenchman . . . and the Pole . . . They beat me . . ."

69   One more stab to the heart, one more reason to hate. One less reason to live.

70   "Eliezer . . . Eliezer . . . tell them not to beat me . . . I haven't done anything . . . Why are they beating me?"

71   I began to insult his neighbors. They mocked me. I promised them bread, soup. They laughed. Then they got angry; they could not stand my father any longer, they said, because he no longer was able to drag himself outside to relieve himself.

72   THE FOLLOWING DAY, he complained that they had taken his ration of bread.

73   "While you were asleep?"

74   "No. I wasn't asleep. They threw themselves on me. They snatched it from me, my bread . . . And they beat me . . . Again . . . I can't go on, my son . . . Give me some water . . ."

75   I knew that he must not drink. But he pleaded with me so long that I gave in. Water was the worst poison for him, but what else could I do for him? With or without water, it would be over soon anyway . . .

76   "You, at least, have pity on me . . ."

77   Have pity on him! I, his only son . . .

78   A WEEK WENT BY like that.

79   "Is this your father?" asked the *Blockälteste*.

80   "Yes."

81   "He is very sick."

82   "The doctor won't do anything for him."

83   He looked me straight in the eye:

84   "The doctor *cannot* do anything more for him. And neither can you."

85   He placed his big, hairy hand on my shoulder and added:

86   "Listen to me, kid. Don't forget that you are in a concentration camp. In this place, it is every man for himself, and you cannot think of others. Not even your father. In this place, there is no such thing as father, brother, friend. Each of us lives and dies alone. Let me give you good advice: stop giving your ration of bread and soup to your old father. You cannot help him anymore. And you are hurting yourself. In fact, you should be getting *his* rations . . ."

87   I listened to him without interrupting. He was right, I thought deep down, not daring to admit it to myself. Too late to save your old father . . . You could have two rations of bread, two rations of soup . . .

88   It was only a fraction of a second, but it left me feeling guilty.

89   I ran to get some soup and brought it to my father. But he did not want it. All he wanted was water.

90   "Don't drink water, eat the soup . . ."

91   "I'm burning up . . . Why are you so mean to me, my son? . . . Water . . ."

92   I brought him water. Then I left the block for roll call. But I quickly turned back. I lay down on the upper bunk. The sick were allowed to stay in the block. So I would be sick. I didn't want to leave my father.

93   All around me, there was silence now, broken only by moaning. In front of the block, the SS were giving orders. An officer passed between the bunks. My father was pleading:

94   "My son, water . . . I'm burning up . . . My insides . . ."

95   "Silence over there!" barked the officer.

96   "Eliezer," continued my father, "water . . ."

97   The officer came closer and shouted to him to be silent. But my father did not hear. He continued to call me. The officer wielded his club and dealt him a violent blow to the head.

98   I didn't move. I was afraid, my body was afraid of another blow, this time to *my* head.

99   My father groaned once more, I heard:

100   "Eliezer . . ."

101   I could see that he was still breathing—in gasps. I didn't move.

102   When I came down from my bunk after roll call, I could see his lips trembling; he was murmuring something. I remained more than an hour leaning over him, looking at him, etching his bloody, broken face into my mind.

103   Then I had to go to sleep. I climbed into my bunk, above my father, who was still alive. The date was January 28, 1945.

104   I WOKE UP AT DAWN on January 29. On my father's cot there lay another sick person. They must have taken him away before daybreak and taken him to the crematorium. Perhaps he was still breathing . . .

105   No prayers were said over his tomb. No candle lit in his memory. His last word had been my name. He had called out to me and I had not answered.

106   I did not weep, and it pained me that I could not Weep. But I was out of tears. And deep inside me, if I could have searched the recesses of my feeble conscience, I might have found something like: Free at last! . . .

■ *Vocabulary*

vulnerable (16)	cauldrons (24)	dysentery (46)
plaintive (29)	ashen (35)	recesses (103)

■ *Questions on Meaning and Technique*

1. Every now and again, a former Nazi SS member has been discovered living in the United States and has been made the subject of deportation hearings. Most of these men are now dead. What do you think should be done with leaders of any country who are found guilty of atrocities that violate human rights?

2. Examine the description in paragraph 8 of the prisoners trying to get to the showers. How would you characterize the author's approach to descriptive writing? How effective does it seem to you?

3. In paragraph 28, the author writes that when he came back to the block, the prisoners were being given black coffee. Why do you think he puts "coffee" in quotation marks?

4. Throughout the excerpt, the author keeps reproaching himself for how he treats his dying father. What is your opinion of his behavior?

5. What kind of paragraphs does the author mainly use? How effective are they in telling his story?

6. What do you find most moving about this narration?

7. What is so unusual about paragraph 69? Why would such a paragraph be unsuitable for a student essay?

8. In paragraph 77, what is your interpretation of the narrator's exclamation, "Have pity on him! I, his only son...."?

9. In paragraph 86, the author relates some advice given to him by the head of the block. What do you think of this advice? What does it say about life in a Nazi concentration camp?

10. What are some examples of the author's use of pacing in this narrative?

Writing Assignments

1. Write a narrative about a specific experience you have had with either your mother or your father.

2. Write a narrative about the best advice a relative has ever given you.

EDGAR ALLAN POE

The Tell-Tale Heart

Edgar Allan Poe (1809–1849)—American writer, poet, and critic—was born in Boston, Massachusetts. He was orphaned at an early age and raised by John Allan, a successful businessman. After a falling out with his adoptive family, Poe went to work as a clerk in Boston. His first book, Tamerlane and Other Poems, *was anonymously published in 1827 when Poe was only 18. Poe is regarded as the father of the modern short story, the inventor of the detective story, and a pioneer in the psychological depiction of characters. Among his many memorable works are "The Gold Bug," "The Murders in the Rue Morgue," and "The Fall of the House of Usher." Poe is also remembered for his poetry, especially such favorites as "The Raven," "Lenore," and "Annabel Lee."*

READING FOR IDEAS Using the first-person point of view, this story—in typical Poe fashion—takes us into the demented mind of a murderer. Notice that in the very first paragraph, the narrator insists that he is not mad, alerting us to the distinct possibility that he well may be. This type of story, in which the narrator tells more about himself than he means to, is so overused nowadays as to be practically cliché. But Poe was the first writer to try it. Notice also Poe's clever use of pacing, which focuses the story on the narrator's feelings about the old man and leads the plot to its dramatic climax. As you read, think about when you first begin to be suspicious of the narrator's sanity. What clues does the narrator's language give to his state of mind?

1   True!—nervous—very, very dreadfully nervous I had been and am! but why will you say that I mad? The disease had sharpened my senses—not destroyed—not dulled them. Above all was the sense of hearing acute. I heard all things in the heaven and in the earth. I heard many things in hell. How, then, am I mad? Hearken! and observe how healthily—how calmly I can tell you the whole story.

2   It is impossible to tell how the first idea entered my brain; but once conceived, it haunted me day and night. Object there was none. Passion there was none. I loved the old man. He had never wronged me. He had never given me insult. For his gold I had no desire. I think it was his eye! Yes, it was this! One of his eyes resembled that of a vulture—a pale blue eye, with a film over it. Whenever it fell upon me, my blood ran cold; and so by degrees—very gradually—I made my mind up to take the life of the old man, and thus rid myself of the eye forever.

3   Now this is the point. You fancy me mad. Madmen know nothing. But you should have seen *me*. You should have seen how wisely I proceeded—with what caution—with what foresight—with what dissimulation I went to work!

4   I was never kinder to the old man than during the whole week before I killed him. And every night, about midnight, I turned the latch of his door and opened it—oh, so gently! And then, when I had made an opening sufficient for my head, I put in a dark-lantern,* all closed, closed, so that no light shone out, and then I thrust in my head. Oh, you would have laughed to see how cunningly I thrust it in! I moved it slowly—very, very slowly, so that I might not disturb the old man's sleep. It took me an hour to stick my whole head within the opening so far that I could see him as he lay upon his bed. Ha!—would a madman have been so wise as this? And then, when my head was well in the room, I undid the lantern cautiously—oh, so cautiously—cautiously (for the hinges creaked)—I undid it just so much that a single thin ray fell upon the vulture eye. And this I did for seven long nights—every night just at midnight—but I found the eye always closed; and so it was impossible to do the work; for it was not the old man who vexed me, but his Evil Eye. And every morning, when the day broke, I went boldly into the chamber, and spoke courageously to him, calling him by name in a hearty tone, and inquiring how he had passed the night. So you see he would have been a very profound old man, indeed, to suspect that every night, just at twelve, I looked in upon him while he slept.

5   Upon the eighth night I was more than usually cautious in opening the door. A watch's minute hand moves more quickly than did mine. Never before that night had I *felt* the extent of my own powers—of my sagacity. I could scarcely contain my feelings of triumph. To think that there I was, opening the door, little by little, and he not even to dream of my secret deeds or thoughts. I fairly chuckled at the idea; and perhaps he heard me; for he moved on the bed suddenly, as if startled. Now you may think that I drew back—but no. His room was as black as pitch with the thick darkness (for the shutters were close fastened, through fear of robbers), and so I knew that he could not see the opening of the door, and I kept pushing on it steadily, steadily.

6   I had my head in, and was about to open the lantern, when my thumb slipped upon the tin fastening, and the old man sprang up in bed, crying out: "Who's there?"

7   I kept quite still and said nothing. For a whole hour I did not move a muscle, and in the meantime I did not hear him lie down. He was still sitting up in the bed listening;— just as I have done, night after night, hearkening the death watches in the wall.

8   Presently I heard a slight groan, and I knew it was the groan of mortal terror. It was not a groan of pain or grief—oh no!—it was the low stifled sound that arises from the bottom of the soul when overcharged with awe. I knew the sound well. Many a night, just at midnight, when all the world slept, it has welled up from my own bosom, deepening, with its dreadful echo, the terrors that distracted me. I say I knew it well. I knew what the old man felt, and pitied him, even though I chuckled at heart. I knew that he had been lying awake ever since the first slight noise, when he had turned in the bed. His fears had ever since been growing upon him. He had been trying to fancy them causeless, but could not. He had been saying to himself, "It is nothing but the wind in the chimney—it is only a mouse crossing the floor," or "it is merely a cricket which has made a single chirp." Yes, he had been trying to comfort himself with these suppositions; but he had found all in vain. *All in vain;* because Death, in approaching him, had stalked with his black

---

*A lantern whose light can be revealed or hidden by opening or closing a cover.

shadow before him, and enveloped the victim. And it was the mournful influence of the unperceived shadow that caused him to feel—although he never saw nor heard—to *feel* the presence of my head within the room.

9   When I had waited a long time, very patiently, without hearing him lie down, I resolved to open a little—a very, very little crevice in the lantern. So I opened it—you cannot imagine how stealthily, stealthily—until, at length, a single dim ray, like the thread of the spider, shot from out the crevice and fell upon the vulture eye.

10   It was open—wide, wide open—and I grew furious as I gazed upon it. I saw it with perfect distinctness—all a dull blue, with a hideous veil over it that chilled the very marrow in my bones; but I could see nothing else of the old man's face or person: for I had directed the ray, as if by instinct, precisely upon the damned spot.

11   And now—have I not told you what you mistake for madness is but over-acuteness of the senses?—now, I say, there came to my ears a low, dull, quick sound, such as a watch makes when enveloped in cotton. I knew *that* sound well, too. It was the beating of the old man's heart. It increased my fury, as the beating of a drum stimulates the soldier into courage.

12   But even yet I refrained and kept still. I scarcely breathed. I held the lantern motionless. I tried how steadily I could maintain the ray upon the eye. Meanwhile the hellish tattoo of the heart increased. It grew quicker and quicker, and louder and louder every instant. The old man's terror *must* have been extreme! It grew louder, I say, louder every moment!—do you mark me well? I have told you that I am nervous: so I am. And now at the dead hour of night, amid the dreadful silence of that old house, so strange a noise as this excited me to uncontrollable terror. Yet for some minutes longer I refrained and stood still. But the beating grew louder, louder! I thought the heart must burst. And now a new anxiety seized me—the sound would be heard by a neighbor! The old man's hour had come! With a loud yell, I threw open the lantern and leaped into the room. He shrieked once—only once. In an instant I dragged him to the floor, and pulled the heavy bed over him. I then smiled gayly to find the deed so far done. But, for many minutes, the heart beat on with a muffled sound. This, however, did not vex me; it would not be heard through the wall. At length it ceased. The old man was dead. I removed the bed and examined the corpse. Yes, he was stone, stone dead. I placed my hand upon the heart and held it there many minutes. There was no pulsation. He was stone dead. His eye would trouble me no more.

13   If you still think me mad, you will think so no longer when I describe the wise precautions I took for the concealment of the body. The night waned, and I worked hastily, but in silence. First of all I dismembered the corpse. I cut off the head and the arms and the legs.

14   I then took up three planks from the flooring of the chamber, and deposited all between the scantlings. I then replaced the boards so cleverly, so cunningly, that no human eye—not even *his*—could have detected anything wrong. There was nothing to wash out—no stain of any kind—no blood spot whatever. I had been too wary for all that. A tub had caught all—ha! ha!

15   When I had made an end of these labors, it was four o'clock—still dark as midnight. As the bell sounded the hour, there came a knocking at the street door. I went down

to open it with a light heart—for what had I *now* to fear? There entered three men, who introduced themselves, with perfect suavity, as officers of the police. A shriek had been heard by a neighbor during the night: suspicion of foul play had been aroused; information had been lodged at the police office, and they (the officers) had been deputed to search the premises.

16   I smiled—for *what* had I to fear? I bade the gentlemen welcome. The shriek, I said, was my own in a dream. The old man, I mentioned, was absent in the country. I took my visitors all over the house. I bade them search—search *well*. I led them, at length, to *his* chamber. I showed them his treasures, secure, undisturbed. In the enthusiasm of my confidence, I brought chairs into the room, and desired them *here* to rest from their fatigues, while I myself, in the wild audacity of my perfect triumph, placed my own seat upon the very spot beneath which reposed the corpse of the victim.

17   The officers were satisfied. My *manner* had convinced them. I was singularly at ease. They sat, and while I answered cheerily, they chatted familiar things. But, ere long, I felt myself getting pale and wished them gone. My head ached, and I fancied a ringing in my ears: but still they sat and chatted. The ringing became more distinct:—it continued and became more distinct: I talked more freely to get rid of the feeling: but it continued and gained definitiveness—until, at length, I found that the noise was *not* within my ears.

18   No doubt I now grew *very* pale;—but I talked more fluently, and with a heightened voice. Yet the sound increased—and what could I do? It was a *low, dull, quick sound— much such a sound as a watch makes when enveloped in cotton.* I gasped for breath— and yet the officers heard it not. I talked more quickly—more vehemently; but the noise steadily increased. Why *would* they not be gone? I paced the floor to and fro with heavy strides, as if excited to fury by the observation of the men—but the noise steadily increased. Oh, what *could* I do? I foamed—I raved—I swore! I swung the chair upon which I had been sitting, and grated it upon the boards, but the noise arose over all and continually increased. It grew louder—louder—*louder!* And still the men chatted pleasantly, and smiled. Was it possible they heard not? Ah!—no, no! They heard!—they suspected!—they *knew!*—they were making a *mockery* of my horror!—this I thought, and this I think. But anything was better than this agony! Anything was more tolerable than this derision! I could bear those hypocritical smiles no longer! I felt that I must scream or die!—and now—again!—hark! louder! louder! louder! *louder!*—

19   "Villains!" I shrieked, "dissemble no more! I admit the deed!—tear up the planks!— here, here!—it is the beating of his hideous heart!"

■ *Vocabulary*

dissimulation (3)	dismembered (13)	singularly (17)
sagacity (5)	scantlings (14)	vehemently (18)
overcharged (8)	suavity (15)	derision (18)
unperceived (8)	deputed (15)	dissemble (19)
tattoo (12)	reposed (16)	

■ *Questions on Meaning and Technique*

1. This story begins with the narrator telling us that he is not mad. Why do you think he tells us this right away?

2. In paragraph 2, the narrator assures us that he had no motive or object in mind for killing the old man. What is the point of this admission?

3. Throughout the narrative, the author uses many dashes. What does this contribute to the telling of the tale?

4. What can you deduce about the narrator from his language? How does his language help characterize him?

5. How might a reader today react to this story? How did it affect you?

6. What techniques of pacing are evident in this story? Point to specific passages that illustrate these techniques.

7. In paragraph 2, the author writes, "For his gold I had no desire." How would a modern writer be likely to phrase this sentence?

8. *Foreshadowing* is a technique of fiction where the writer hints of what is to come later. In paragraph 1, what example of foreshadowing can you find?

9. The narrator doesn't tell us how the police officers reacted upon hearing his confession. How do you suppose they reacted? Why didn't the narrator describe their reaction?

10. Throughout this story, what technique does the narrator use to emphasize his revelations?

Writing Assignments

1. Use the first-person narrative point of view to tell a story about how you were once misunderstood.

2. Narrate a ghost story or a frightening experience, using the first-person point of view.

Internet Research Assignment

Go to the internet to find the poem "Miniver Cheevy," by Edwin Arlington Robinson, the same poet who wrote "Richard Cory," (p. 136). After carefully studying the poem, write a paragraph in which you describe the character traits that Richard Cory and Miniver Cheevy have in common.

Additional Writing Assignments

1. Narrate any incident from your life in which you were forced by a role to suppress your true feelings. Describe the effect this suppression had on you.

2. Tell a ghost story or a story of some occult or unexplainable experience you have had.

3. Narrate a family conflict that illustrates how you feel about your mother and/or your father.

4. Narrate an incident that revealed to you the true nature or character of an aunt, uncle, or cousin.

5. Narrate the story of "the day everything went wrong" and how you responded to the challenge.

6. Narrate a story about an accident or mishap that you either witnessed or experienced yourself.

7. Narrate a love story or experience.

8. Robert Southey once said, "Curses are like young chickens; they always come home to roost." Narrate an experience from your life that explains or illustrates this observation.

9. Tell the story of the most thrilling and exciting day of your life.

10. Narrate a story about an experience you had with a very young child.

Rewriting Assignment

Analyze the following narrative passage, and indicate in writing what is wrong with it.

We left home midmorning and traveled through miles of snow. Found a dog lying on the ground, evidently frozen to death from lack of food and shelter. I had to get breakfast while snow flakes fell outside our cabin. Tomorrow I plan to bring out the cured salmon for breakfast. This afternoon the air was pure, but it took my putting on two sweaters and a wool coat before I stopped shivering. In the evening, two young fellows came over to play some country music on their guitars. One song was titled "I Left My Dog for You." We laughed heartily until it was time to retire and go to bed. I think I'm learning to like Alaska.

Photo Writing Assignment

Karen Moskowitz/Riser/Getty Images

Using your imagination, narrate a plausible story detailing the events that led up to this scene.

Digging for Gold or for a Story Line

It may seem odd to liken a miner's digging for gold to the kind of digging a writer must do to gather information about the topic for an essay; yet, that is exactly what we intend to do in the use of this icon throughout the coming chapters. The icon is intended to remind us that as writers we often have to dig for evidence to back up our points and that our findings are every bit as precious to our task as specks of gold are to the prospector's.

Dig deep into your topic, making notes as you go along. Stick to what you know about the subject as does the student writer of "My Uncle Thom" in explaining her uncle's suicide. Keep an open mind and allow one writing assignment to suggest another. For example, Elie Wiesel writes about the unique subject of cruelty to human beings in a concentration camp. In turn, this topic might suggest another, such as our cruelty to animals. One simple way to inspire you to dig enthusiastically on your topic is to discuss it with a friend. Sometimes a casual chat will suggest a perspective you overlooked, such as, what a scary story "The Tell-Tale Heart" by Edgar Allan Poe must have been when it was first published. Sift through the bedrock of your experiences, where specks of gold are hiding. Keep digging until you encounter a glittering idea.

Chapter 8

Description

S T O R Y

ANTON CHEKHOV

The Lament

Anton Pavlovich Chekhov (1860–1904), the son of a grocer and grandson of a serf, was a Russian physician whose stories and plays won him international acclaim during his lifetime. Among his theatrical masterpieces are The Seagull *(1898),* Uncle Vanya *(1899),* The Three Sisters *(1901), and* The Cherry Orchard *(1904). His stories are collected in* At Twilight *(1887) and* Stories *(1888).*

READING FOR IDEAS "The Lament" is the story of a poor Russian cabdriver overwhelmed by the grief of losing his only son. Read the story for a dominant impression—a central theme that unifies the descriptive details. Observe carefully the accumulation of details and how they fit into the narrative. What does the story tell you about grief, about society, and about human capacity for suffering? What is the conflict in the story? How is it finally resolved? What feelings does the story arouse in you?

1   It is twilight. A thick wet snow is twirling around the newly lighted street lamps, and lying in soft thin layers on roofs, on horses' backs, on people's shoulders and hats. The cabdriver Iona Potapov is quite white, and looks like a phantom; he is bent double as far as a human body can bend double; he is seated on his box; he never makes a move. If a whole snowdrift fell on him, it seems as if he would not find it necessary to shake it off. His little horse is also quite white, and remains motionless; its immobility, its angularity, and its straight wooden-looking legs, even close by, give it the appearance of a gingerbread horse worth a *kopek*. It is, no doubt, plunged in deep thought. If you were snatched from the plow, from your usual gray surroundings, and were thrown into this slough full of monstrous lights, unceasing noise, and hurrying people, you too would find it difficult not to think.

2   Iona and his little horse have not moved from their place for a long while. They left their yard before dinner, and up to now, not a fare. The evening mist is descending over the town, the white lights of the lamps replacing brighter rays, and the hubbub of the street getting louder. "Cabby for Viborg way!" suddenly hears Iona, "Cabby!"

3   Iona jumps, and through his snow-covered eyelashes sees an officer in a greatcoat, with his hood over his head.

4   "Viborg way!" the officer repeats. "Are you asleep, eh? Viborg way!"

5   With a nod of assent Iona picks up the reins, in consequence of which layers of snow slip off the horse's back and neck. The officer seats himself in the sleigh, the cabdriver smacks his lips to encourage his horse, stretches out his neck like a swan, sits up, and, more from habit than necessity, brandishes his whip. The little horse also stretches its neck, bends its wooden-looking legs, and makes a move undecidedly.

6   "What are you doing, werewolf!" is the exclamation Iona hears from the dark mass moving to and fro, as soon as they have started.

7   "Where the devil are you going? To the r-r-right!"

8   "You do not know how to drive. Keep to the right!" calls the officer angrily.

9   A coachman from a private carriage swears at him; a passerby, who has run across the road and rubbed his shoulder against the horse's nose, looks at him furiously as he sweeps the snow from his sleeve. Iona shifts about on his seat as if he were on needles, moves his elbows as if he were trying to keep his equilibrium, and gapes about like someone suffocating, who does not understand why and wherefore he is there.

10   "What scoundrels they all are!" jokes the officer; "one would think they had all entered into an agreement to jostle you or fall under your horse."

11   Iona looks round at the officer, and moves his lips. He evidently wants to say something, but the only sound that issues is a snuffle.

12   "What?" asks the officer.

13   Iona twists his mouth into a smile, and with an effort says hoarsely:

14   "My son, *barin*, died this week."

15   "Hm! What did he die of?"

16   Iona turns with his whole body toward his fare, and says:

17   "And who knows! They say high fever. He was three days in the hospital, and then died. . . . God's will be done."

18   "Turn round! The devil!" sounds from the darkness. "Have you popped off, old doggie, eh? Use your eyes!"

19   "Go on, go on," says the officer, "otherwise we shall not get there by tomorrow. Hurry up a bit!"

20   The cabdriver again stretches his neck, sits up, and, with a bad grace, brandishes his whip. Several times again he turns to look at his fare, but the latter has closed his eyes, and apparently is not disposed to listen. Having deposited the officer in the Viborg, he stops by the tavern, doubles himself up on his seat, and again remains motionless, while the snow once more begins to cover him and his horse. An hour, and another. . . . Then, along the footpath, with a squeak of galoshes, and quarreling, come three young men, two of them tall and lanky, the third one short and humpbacked.

21   "Cabby, the Police Bridge!" in a cracked voice calls the humpback. "The three of us for two *griveniks!*"

22   Iona picks up his reins, and smacks his lips. Two *griveniks* is not a fair price, but he does not mind whether it is a *rouble* or five *kopeks*—to him it is all the same now, so long as they are fares. The young men, jostling each other and using bad language, approach the sleigh, and all three at once try to get onto the seat; then begins a discussion as to which two shall sit and who shall be the one to stand. After wrangling, abusing each other, and much petulance, it is at last decided that the humpback shall stand, as he is the smallest.

23   "Now then, hurry up!" says the humpback in a twanging voice, as he takes his place and breathes on Iona's neck. "Old furry! Here, mate, what a cap you have! There is not a worse one to be found in all Petersburg! . . ."

24   "He-he!—he-he!" giggles Iona. "Such a . . ."

25   "Now you, 'such a,' hurry up, are you going the whole way at this pace? Are you? . . . Do you want it in the neck?"

26   "My head feels like bursting," says one of the lanky ones. "Last night at the Donkmasovs, Vaska and I drank the whole of four bottles of cognac."

27   "I don't understand what you lie for," says the other lanky one angrily; "you lie like a brute."

28   "God strike me, it's the truth!"

29   "It's as much the truth as that a louse coughs!"

30   "He, he," grins Iona, "what gay young gentlemen!"

31   "Pshaw, go to the devil!" says the humpback indignantly.

32   "Are you going to get on or not, you old pest? Is that the way to drive? Use the whip a bit! Go on, devil, go on, give it to him well!"

33   Iona feels at his back the little man wriggling, and the tremble in his voice. He listens to the insults hurled at him, sees the people, and little by little the feeling of loneliness leaves him. The humpback goes on swearing until he gets mixed up in some elaborate six-foot oath, or chokes with coughing. The lankies begin to talk about a certain Nadejda Petrovna. Iona looks round at them several times; he waits for a temporary silence, then, turning round again, he murmurs;

34   "My son . . . died this week."

35   "We must all die," sighs the humpback, wiping his lips after an attack of coughing. "Now, hurry up, hurry up! Gentlemen, I really cannot go any farther like this! When will he get us there?"

36   "Well, just you stimulate him a little in the neck!"

37   "You old pest, do you hear, I'll bone your neck for you! If one treated the like of you with ceremony one would have to go on foot! Do you hear, old serpent Gorinytch! Or do you not care a spit?"

38   Iona hears rather than feels the blows they deal him.

39   "He, he," he laughs. "They are gay young gentlemen, God bless 'em!"

40   "Cabby, are you married?" asks a lanky one.

41   "I? He, he, gay young gentlemen? Now I have only a wife and the moist ground. . . . He, ho, ho . . . that is to say, the grave. My son has died, and I am alive. . . . A wonderful thing, death mistook the door. . . . instead of coming to me, it went to my son. . . ."

42   Iona turns round to tell them how his son died, but at this moment, the humpback, giving a little sigh, announces, "Thank God, we have at last reached our destination," and Iona watches them disappear through the dark entrance. Once more he is alone, and again surrounded by silence. . . . His grief, which has abated for a short while, returns and rends his heart with greater force. With an anxious and hurried look, he searches among the crowds passing on either side of the street to find whether there may be just one person who will listen to him. But the crowds hurry by without noticing him or his trouble. Yet it is such an immense, illimitable grief. Should his heart break and the grief pour out, it would flow over the whole earth, so it seems, and yet no one sees it. It has managed to conceal itself in such an insignificant shell that no one can see it even by day and with a light.

43   Iona sees a hall porter with some sacking, and decides to talk to him.

44   "Friend, what sort of time is it?" he asks.

45   "Past nine. What are you standing here for? Move on."

46   Iona moves on a few steps, doubles himself up, and abandons himself to his grief. He sees it is useless to turn to people for help. In less than five minutes he straightens himself, holds up his head as if he felt some sharp pain, and gives a tug at the reins; he can bear it no longer. "The stables," he thinks, and the little horse, as if it understood, starts off at a trot.

47   About an hour and a half later Iona is seated by a large dirty stove. Around the stove, on the floor, on the benches, people are snoring; the air is thick and suffocatingly hot. Iona looks at the sleepers, scratches himself, and regrets having returned so early.

48   "I have not even earned my fodder," he thinks. "That's what's my trouble. A man who knows his job, who has had enough to eat, and his horse too, can always sleep peacefully."

49   A young cabdriver in one of the corners half gets up, grunts sleepily, and stretches toward a bucket of water.

50   "Do you want a drink?" Iona asks him.

51   "Don't I want a drink!"

52   "That's so? Your good health! But listen, mate—you know, my son is dead. . . Did you hear? This week, in the hospital. . . . It's a long story."

53   Iona looks to see what effect his words have, but sees none—the young man has hidden his face and is fast asleep again. The old man sighs, and scratches his head. Just as much as the young one wants to drink, the old man wants to talk. It will soon be a week since his son died, and he has not been able to speak about it properly to any-one. One must tell it slowly and carefully; how his son fell ill, how he suffered, what he said before he died, how he died. One must describe every detail of the funeral, and the journey to the hospital to fetch the dead son's clothes. His daughter Anissia has remained in the village—one must talk about her too. Is it nothing he has to tell? Surely the listener would gasp and sigh, and sympathize with him? It is better, too, to talk to women; although they are stupid, two words are enough to make them sob.

54   "I'll go and look after my horse," thinks Iona, "there's always time to sleep. No fear of that!"

55   He puts on his coat, and goes to the stables to his horse; he thinks of the corn, the hay, the weather. When he is alone, he dares not think of his son; he can speak about him to anyone, but to think of him, and picture him to himself, is unbearably painful.

56   "Are you tucking in?" Iona asks his horse, looking at its bright eyes; "go on, tuck in, though we've not earned our corn, we can eat hay. Yes! I am too old to drive—my son could have, not I. He was a first-rate cabdriver. If only he had lived!"

57   Iona is silent for a moment, then continues:

58   "That's how it is, my old horse. There's no more Kuzina Ionitch. He has left us to live, and he went off pop. Now let's say, you had a foal, you were the foal's mother, and suddenly, let's say, that foal went and left you to live after him. It would be sad, wouldn't it?"

59   The little horse munches, listens, and breathes over its master's hand. . . . Iona's feelings are too much for him, and he tells the little horse the whole story.

■ *Vocabulary*

angularity (1)	brandishes (5)
slough (1)	petulance (22)

■ *Questions on Meaning and Technique*

1. How does the title "The Lament" relate to the content of this story?

2. The death of a loved one is not the only loss probed in the story. What other sorrows are examined?

3. What is Iona's overwhelming desire throughout the story? Why does he have this desire?

4. What do all of Iona's passengers have in common?

5. In what paragraph does Iona think about the exact steps he should take in expressing his grief?

6. Examine paragraph 1, and point out some details that suggest the story will involve some kind of grief, sadness, or loss.

7. What details create the dominant impression of a father grieving for his son? Point to specific paragraphs.

8. What is the conflict of the story? How is it resolved?

P O E M

JANE KENYON

Coats

Jane Kenyon (1947–1995), American poet, was born in Michigan and educated at the University of Michigan. Her work has been published in such magazines as The New Yorker *and* New Republic *and collected in* From Room to Room *(1978) and* The Little Boat *(1986). In 1981, she was a fellow of the National Endowment for the Arts.*

READING FOR IDEAS The language of poetry is often powerfully evocative. Here, for example, with a stark economy of words, a poet evokes a vivid scene of grief, showing us a weeping man who is leaving a hospital carrying a woman's coat on a mild December day. Although the poem does not directly say so, we infer a deep connectedness between the unknown man and woman, perhaps even as husband and wife. The scene merely hints of personal sorrow and loss suffered on a lovely winter day, effectively leaving the rest to our imagination. Ask yourself what assumptions the poet makes about the man. Are her assumptions reasonable?

1   I saw him leaving the hospital
with a woman's coat over his arm.
Clearly she would not need it.
The sunglasses he wore could not
conceal his wet face, his bafflement.

2   As if in mockery the day was fair,
and the air mild for December. All the same
he had zipped his own coat and tied
the hood under his chin, preparing
for irremediable cold.

- *Vocabulary*

   irremediable (2)

- *Questions on Meaning and Technique*

   1. The poet does not personalize the man by telling us, for example, anything about his particular age and looks. Why? What does this omission add to the poem?
   2. Why was it "mockery" that "the day was fair"? From whose point of view is this line delivered?
   3. What symbolic meaning does the poem seem to impute to coats?
   4. What do you think is meant by "irremediable cold"? What kind of cold is this?
   5. What ironic implication about the protection afforded by coats does the poem make?

How to Write a Description

A *description* is a word picture of a person, place, feeling, animal, event, or thing. It may be as uncommon as a description of a faraway palace or as ordinary as a poster describing a lost dog. But no matter what word picture you're drawing, some basic techniques will work.

A vivid description supports a dominant impression with specific details. The dominant impression of a description is its central and unifying theme. In *The Godfather,* for instance, Mario Puzo bases his descriptions of all of Don Corleone's sons on the dominant impression of their resemblance to Cupid. This impression is introduced in the description of Sonny and then applied to all the other sons:

> Sonny Corleone was tall for a first generation American of Italian parentage, almost six feet, and his crop of bushy, curly hair made him look even taller. His face was that of a gross Cupid, the features even but the bow-shaped lips thickly sensual, the dimpled cleft chin in some curious way obscene.

With slightly varying details, this dominant impression accommodates a description of the Don's second son, Frederico Corleone:

> He was short and burly, not handsome but with the same Cupid head of the family, the curly helmet of hair over the round face and the sensual bow-shaped lips. Only, in Fred, these lips were not sensual but granite-like.

A contrast to this dominant impression is provided in the description of Michael Corleone, the third son:

> Michael Corleone was the youngest son of the Don and the only child who had refused the great man's direction. He did not have the heavy, Cupid-shaped face of the other children, and his jet black hair was straight rather than curly. His skin was clear olive-brown that would have been called beautiful in a girl. He was handsome in a delicate way.

Writing Assignment

Describe as vividly as you can a person, a place, or an event. Begin by picking a subject you like. If possible, accumulate details and impressions by observing your subject up close. Next, find the dominant impression of the person, place, or event, and state it in one sentence. The dominant impression of a place might be "Ben's cafe is a dingy hole in the wall." Of a person, it might be "Alicia has a delicate beauty." Of an event, it might be "The wedding was badly organized." Support this impression with details, omitting anything that might break its focus. Develop the dominant impression and selected supporting details into a well-shaped essay.

Specific Instructions

Prewrite on the assignment.   The assignment is open ended enough to give you a real choice among the allowable categories of a person, place, or event. For some lucky few, there will be no hesitation; they will immediately know what they want to tackle. Even so, they will probably need to outline and flesh out their ideas. On the other hand, if you are among those who truly have no idea what to describe or even where to begin, prewriting is one way to discover a possible topic.

STUDENT TIP FOR INVENTING IDEAS

Assignment

Describe as vividly as you can a person, a place, or an event.

How I found my topic

I am wandering through my parents' house to find a spot I can describe. I had just come back from the local grocery store, thinking I could describe it but decided it was just too ordinary. I've been thinking about this assignment all week, but every person, place, or event seemed like a bummer and just didn't turn me on. I gaze at my bedroom—too cutesy. I wander through our family room—too traditional. I head toward my dad's study but couldn't see describing that. Now I am looking through our sliding glass doors at our backyard. It is early December: the trees are completely bare, except for a few pine trees and one pomegranate tree bearing three ripe pomegranates. This is a gloomy sight. Even the squirrels are in hiding. I can't hear any birds. The only sound hitting my ears is the ominous sound of wind broadcasting more rain. Our lawn is already covered with wet leaves because of yesterday's storm. I'm in a rotten mood anyway, so I can work with this scene.

—A male junior at a four-year Midwestern college

One approach is to make a list with three headings: person, place, and event. Under each heading, jot down candidates for your description as they occur to you. For example, under the heading *Person*, you might list memorable friends, lovers, relatives, or acquaintances. Under *Place*, you might jot down your hometown, favorite hiking trail, vacation spot, or beach. Do the same under *Event* until you have exhausted your ideas. You can be as loose or as organized as you like as you make your list.

Once the list is complete, review the individual entries and decide which one you like best. Professional writers often have to write about boring topics, but there is no good reason for you to suffer in the same way. As you go over the entries under the three headings, sooner or later one is bound to capture your fancy. That is the one you should write about.

Establish the dominant impression.   Before beginning to write, you should establish the dominant impression of whatever you wish to describe. The dominant impression in a description is the equivalent of the controlling idea in other types of essays. If you decide to describe a place, visit the place and spend some time observing it. The details you observe will often suggest a suitable dominant impression. Once chosen, this dominant impression, in turn, will influence your selection of details.

For example, suppose you decide to write a description of your local airport lobby. You visit the airport and observe the following details:

1. A man's hat falls off as he races down the hall to catch his plane.

2. A sailor passionately kissing a woman suddenly looks at his watch and abruptly heads toward the escalator.

3. A little girl shrieks as an elderly woman—probably her grandmother—jerks her out of the arms of her mother to rush along toward Gate 31.

4. A fat executive comes out of the smoking area and goes huffing and puffing toward the departure gate.

5. People of all sizes, ages, and races scramble across the lobby, bumping into one another and then resuming their frantic journeys.

6. A well-manicured woman sits casually on a bench reading a magazine and looking bored.

7. Two uniformed porters belly-laugh over a joke during a lull in foot traffic.

Most of these details suggest a dominant impression of the airport as a place where people are rushed. You scribble down the following controlling idea, which includes this dominant impression: *At certain hours, the International Airport lobby is a thoroughfare for people who are rushed.*

The function of the dominant impression at this stage of the essay is to provide a standard for judging the relevance of details. Details that support the dominant impression are relevant; those that contradict it are irrelevant. Details 1 through 5, for instance, can be included because they support this dominant impression, but details 6 and 7 must be omitted because they contradict it. The dominant impression, therefore, provides a pattern that unifies the description, preventing your essay from being watered down by irrelevant details.

Focus the dominant impression.   Like the controlling idea, the dominant impression must have a focus. The following dominant impressions lack focus and need improvement:

Unfocused   Toward evening the meadow becomes eerie in its forsaken barrenness as the magpies chatter happily.

Better   Toward evening the meadow becomes eerie in its forsaken barrenness as the wind howls and groans.

Happily chattering magpies destroy the idea of "forsaken barrenness."

Unfocused   A delicate fragility was the outstanding feature of this husky old lady.

Better   A delicate fragility gave beauty to the face of this aristocratic old lady.

"Husky" ruins the impression of fragility.

Select specific and sensory details. A good dominant impression attracts details the way a whirlpool sucks water toward its center. You must not only avoid irrelevant details that blur the dominant impression of your description, but also select details that are specific and appeal to the senses.

Lack of *specific details* is the biggest mistake in student descriptions. The overwhelming tendency is to fill the page with mushy generalizations, for example:

> One could tell at a look that Chaim Sachar was poor and slovenly. He was always hungry, and as a result he would wander about with a hungry attitude. His continual poverty caused him to become stingy to the point where he would collect garbage to use as fuel for his stove, and he cooked poor meals.

The description never comes to life because the supporting details are vague. Contrast this passage with another account:

> Two small eyes, starved and frightened, peered from beneath his disheveled eyebrows; the red rims about his eyes were reminiscent of the time when he would wash down a dish of fried liver and hard-boiled eggs with a pint of vodka every morning after prayer. Now, all day long, he wandered through the marketplace, inhaling butchershop odors and those from restaurants, sniffing like a dog, and occasionally napping on porters' carts. With the refuse he had collected in a basket, he fed his kitchen stove at night; then, rolling the sleeves over his hairy arms, he would grate turnips on a grater.
>
> —Isaac Bashevis Singer, "The Old Man"

Now the portrait leaps at you, punctuated by specific details, including "disheveled eyebrows," "red rims about his eyes," and "hairy arms." The first description is a shadowy figure in a darkened room; the second is that same figure after the lights have been turned on.

Remember, too, that you can appeal to your reader through all the senses. You can make a reader see, taste, smell, touch, and hear what you are describing:

> The winter was difficult. There was no coal, and since several tiles were missing from the stove, the apartment was filled with thick black smoke each time the old man made a fire. A crust of blue ice and snow covered the window panes by November, making the rooms constantly dark or dusky. Overnight, the water on his night table froze in the pot. No matter how many clothes he piled over him in bed, he never felt warm; his feet remained stiff, and as soon as he began to doze, the entire pile of clothes would fall off, and he would have to climb out naked to make his bed once more. There was no kerosene; even matches were at a premium. Although he recited chapter upon chapter of the Psalms, he could not fall asleep. The wind, freely roaming about the rooms, banged the doors; even the mice left. When he hung up his shirt to dry, it would grow brittle and break, like glass.
>
> —Isaac Bashevis Singer, "The Old Man"

The passage uses details that appeal to the reader's senses:

Visual	"crust of *blue ice* and *snow* covered the window panes"
Auditory	"the wind, freely roaming about the room, *banged* the door"
Tactile	"No matter how many clothes he piled over him in bed, he never *felt warm*."

Use figures of speech.   To add vividness to a description, writers often use colorful words and expressions along with figures of speech, most commonly, similes and metaphors. A *simile* is a figure of speech that draws a direct comparison between two items; one thing is plainly declared to be *like* another. For example, in his famous poem "The Eagle," Alfred, Lord Tennyson, in a vivid simile, clearly likens the dive of an eagle to a thunderbolt:

> The wrinkled sea beneath him crawls;
> He watches from his mountain walls,
> And like a thunderbolt he falls.

A *metaphor* also draws a comparison, but through suggestion and without the use of a linking *like* between the compared items. Here, for example, Shakespeare compares aging to a tree in autumn:

> That time of year thou mayst in me behold
> When yellow leaves, or none, or few do hang
> Upon those boughs which shake against the cold,
> Bare ruined choirs where late the sweet birds sang.

Had the bard said, "That time of year thou mayst in me behold / When I am *like* a tree whose yellow leaves, or none, or few do hang," the figure would have been a simile.

Writers frequently mix these figures of speech in a single passage, depending on what and for whom they are writing. Here, for example, a writer describes a woman, using a combination of two similes and a metaphor:

> She was a little woman, with brown, dull hair very elaborately arranged, and she had prominent blue eyes behind invisible pince-nez. Her face was long, like a sheep's; but she gave no impression of foolishness, rather of extreme alertness; she had the quick movements of a bird. The most remarkable thing about her was her voice, high, metallic, and without inflection; it fell on the ear with a hard monotony, irritating to the nerves like the pitiless clamour of the pneumatic drill.
>
> —W. Somerset Maugham, "Rain"

A caution: Avoid obvious, trite figures of speech, such as *busy as a bee, white as a sheet,* and *big as a bear.* Worn and ineffective, such figures hit readers in the face *like a truck* and could possibly render them *dead as a doornail.* If you use figures of speech, make them as *fresh as a daisy.* Get the idea?

ALEXANDER MCCALL SMITH

Mma Ramotswe Thinks About the Land

Alexander McCall Smith (b. 1950) is a professor of medical law at Edinburgh University in Scotland. He was born in what is now known as Zimbabwe and taught law at the University of Botswana. He is the author of over fifty books on a wide range of subjects, including specialist titles such as Forensic Aspects of Sleep. *But what has endeared him most to thousands of readers are his five books about Mma Ramotswe, a delightfully plump and shrewd woman detective who drives her tiny white van all over Gaborone in order to track down missing husbands, investigate the disappearance of a loved one, or solve other problems for people in trouble. The books in the series, in chronological order, are:* The No. 1 Ladies' Detective Agency, Tears of the Giraffe, Morality for Beautiful Girls, The Kalahari Typing School for Men, *and* The Full Cupboard of Life. *The following description of sunrise in Africa is taken from the first book.*

READING FOR IDEAS If you allow your imagination to roam while you read this vivid description of a region in Africa, you can bring up a picture of some place dear to you—a spring garden, a natural pond, a camping spot, a view of towering mountains, a relative's farm—any plot of land that has secured a special corner in your heart. As you visualize this place, try to conjure up details in the same way Smith has done for Africa.

1   Mma Ramotswe drove her tiny white van before dawn along the sleeping roads of Gaborone, past the Kalahari Breweries, past the Dry Lands Research Station, and out onto the road that led north. A man leaped out from bushes at the side of the road and tried to flag her down; but she was unwilling to stop in the dark, for you never knew who might be wanting a lift at such an hour. He disappeared into the shadows again, and in her mirror she saw him deflate with disappointment. Then, just past the Mochudi turnoff, the sun came up, rising over the wide plains that stretched away towards the course of the Limpopo. Suddenly it was there, smiling on Africa, a slither of golden red ball, inching up, floating effortlessly free of the horizon to dispel the last wisps of morning mist.

2   The thorn trees stood clear in the sharp light of morning, and there were birds upon them, and in flight—hoopoes, louries, and tiny birds which she could not name. Here and there cattle stood at the fence which followed the road for mile upon mile. They raised their heads and stared, or ambled slowly on, tugging at the tufts of dry grass that clung tenaciously to the hardened earth.

3   This was a dry land. Just a short distance to the west lay the Kalahari, a hinterland of ochre that stretched off, for unimaginable miles, to the singing emptinesses of the Namib. If she turned her tiny white van off on one of the tracks that struck off from the

main road, she could drive for perhaps thirty or forty miles before her wheels would begin to sink into the sand and spin hopelessly. The vegetation would slowly become sparser, more desert-like. The thorn trees would thin out and there would be ridges of thin earth, through which the omnipresent sand would surface and crenellate. There would be patches of bareness, and scattered grey rocks, and there would be no sign of human activity. To live with this great dry interior, brown and hard, was the lot of the Batswana, and it was this that made them cautious, and careful in their husbandry.

4   If you went there, out into the Kalahari, you might hear lions by night. For the lions were there still, on these wide landscapes, and they made their presence known in the darkness, in coughing grunts and growls. She had been there once as a young woman, when she had gone with her friend to visit a remote cattle post. It was as far into the Kalahari as cattle could go, and she had felt the utter loneliness of a place without people. This was Botswana distilled; the essence of her country.

5   It was the rainy season, and the land was covered with green. Rain could transform it so quickly, and had done so; now the ground was covered with shoots of sweet new grass, Namaqualand daisies, the vines of Tsama melons, and aloes with stalk flowers of red and yellow.

6   They had made a fire at night, just outside the crude huts which served as shelter at the cattle post, but the light from the fire seemed so tiny under the great empty night sky with its dipping constellations. She had huddled close to her friend, who had told her that she should not be frightened, because lions would keep away from fires, as would super-natural beings, *tokoloshes* and the like.

7   She awoke in the small hours of the morning, and the fire was low. She could make out its embers through the spaces between the branches that made up the wall of the hut. Somewhere, far away, there was a grunting sound, but she was not afraid, and she walked out of the hut to stand underneath the sky and draw the dry, clear air into her lungs. And she thought: I am just a tiny person in Africa, but there is a place for me, and for every-body, to sit down on this earth and touch it and call it their own. She waited for another thought to come, but none did, and so she crept back into the hut and the warmth of the blankets on her sleeping mat.

8   Now, driving the tiny white van along those rolling miles, she thought that one day she might go back into the Kalahari, into those empty spaces, those wide grasslands that broke and broke the heart.

■ *Vocabulary*

deflate (1)	ochre (3)	distilled (4)
course (1)	omnipresent (3)	essence (4)
tenaciously (2)	crenellate (3)	transform (5)
hinterland (3)	husbandry (3)	constellations (6)

■ *Questions on Meaning and Technique*

1. How many dominant impressions of the land are revealed in this description? At which point does the narrator move from one impression to the next? How does he avoid confusing the reader?

2. What figure of speech does the narrator use to describe the rising sun? In your own words, explain the characteristics of the sun as Mma Ramotswe observes it? How effective is the language used?

3. What are the main characteristics of the desert face of this land? What color dominates? What happens to the vegetation as one moves toward the interior of the land?

4. Why does the narrator describe the emptiness of the Namib as "singing"? How do you interpret this figure of speech?

5. What natural phenomenon quickly transforms the sterile desert into a romantic garden? What are the details of this garden? Is this transformation realistic or did the author take literary license?

6. What philosophical thought did the visit to the cattle post engender in the narrator? What attitude does the narrator have toward the land? What clues are given to this attitude?

7. What detail is given at the start of the description to hint that Mma Ramotswe is a detective? What does the detail imply?

8. How would you label the author's style? Give examples of your label.

9. What role, if any, does the "tiny white van" play?

10. Why do you think the author contemplates a return to the Kalahari (see paragraph 8)? What would motivate her to do so?

STUDENT ESSAY—FIRST DRAFT

Shjena Erazo

Eng 105

Dr. Frusciente

University of Miami

Children and Guns: Marks of an Unscrupulous World

1 ~~If asked to characterize the most threatening, the most powerful military machine in the history of the Earth, your attempt to conjure familiar images of power and war would~~ Irrelevant

~~lead you to the American Expeditionary Force under Eisenhower, the French under Napoleon, the Macedonians under Alexander the Great, or even the Germans under~~

~~Kaiser Wilhelm II. My purpose in listing these examples is to highlight how in American society our ideas about power and war are collectively familiar in the sense that we are conditioned to be aware of certain images depicting war in a certain form.~~ This makes ~~us relatively naïve toward modern day warfare. For example, it seems that most people honestly believe that today's warfare is primarily people dropping large bombs on each other (the so called weapons of mass destruction). While this may be the United States' prime form of attack, hand to hand combat predominates in many countries. Even more shocking is the fact that children, boys and girls alike, are trained by their countries' respective governments for battle. They, of course, come out of this experience toting guns and looking for blood, because in many cases the older men have no patience for weaklings too compassionate to execute another human being on command. This is not only unfortunate, but it is absolutely inconceivable in American society. We are the people who don't want our children watching fictitious violence on television lest they grow up to be murderers and rapists. However, in the Democratic Republic of Congo, the latter are expectations of children. Little girls and boys are given machine guns and expected to do what they are told or the older men will rape and murder them. That is where the tremendous societal differences lie. Ours is a relatively conservative society and theirs an incredibly radical society. In that respect ours is the better society, as it protects children from such injustices.~~

Begin here   2   The photograph above the title of this essay is shocking and disturbing. In the foreground it depicts a beautiful black teenage girl holding an automatic firearm, ready for combat. What is most dreadful about this image is that this girl could just as easily have been holding a popsicle as this deadly weapon. What this photo does is to point out an unbridgeable gap between our society and the society to which this little girl belongs, and it is this difference that I wish to stress throughout ~~most of~~ my essay.

not necessary   3   This photo was taken in the Democratic Republic of Congo. ~~While French is considered the official language of the Democratic Republic of Congo, I don't feel morally correct in recognizing the remnants of an imperialistic venture as destructive as that of the Belgians in this region of Africa (my education comes care of *Heart of Darkness,* one of the best novels ever written).~~ I have chosen to title it in Swahili: *Salama,* or "peace."

The irony of such a title expresses my conviction that the beautiful girl holding the gun so menacingly in this photograph is innately desirous of peace. I feel that those older veterans who harvest young girls and boys to fight and kill like barbaric adults have tried their best to rip out the roots of any desire for peace in these youthful hearts and have replaced ~~them~~ *those roots* with the seeds of hatred and belligerence.   *reference*

4   At first this little girl's life may appear doomed because one might think that surely her environment has corrupted her forever so that she will never pursue peace. But I hold no such cynical belief. In fact, I am convinced that no environmental system is so strong that it can entirely eclipse nature's fundamental urges. Thus, while the war lords want to see more and more blood flow, the human heart longs for love and peace. You may judge me naïve and foolish, but I feel that optimism in the face of such hell is important. In the past, glimmers of hope have been known to trump despair. We must not lose hope.

5   In *Salama,* the young girl, dark as night and wearing a plaid shirt with a cloth draped over ~~both of~~ her shoulders stands at a window-like opening in the foreground of   *dash (for more effective punctuation)* this photograph. Her head is wrapped in a bandanna, knotted at the nape of her neck, and she holds a black machine gun in her disproportionately small hands. While her face tries to display a serious sense of purpose, the careful observer cannot miss the childlike look on her face and the innocence hiding behind her steady eyes. To her right stands a young boy in a white t-shirt displaying some sort of blue and red advertising. He too is dark-skinned and he is leaning against some unseen object. His stare is focused, but his thoughts seem to be in some other place, perhaps on the battlefield or some sort of ~~intangible~~ utopia. He also holds a black, automatic gun whose barrel rests on a brown   *redundant* boot that ~~lays~~ *lies* on the window sill that most likely was created by the blast of a powerful   *verb* explosive. Behind him is another boy, wearing a buttoned-up shirt and holding a large firearm wrapped in a white cloth. Like the other children in the photograph, he too has black skin, so black that he seems invisible, shrouded in the shadow of the photo's background. Behind the girl and to her left is the head of another child, barely visible against the pitch black background. ~~The hole through which these four children gaze~~   *Repetitive* ~~appears to be a window that has been blasted out of the concrete by some explosive.~~ These four children gazing through the carved and chipped wall opening have been

forced to grow up much faster than their counterparts in the United States. While

American children play on monkey bars and see-saws in our parks, these children hide

more vivid word   behind doors and in dark alleys, ready to ~~confront~~ the enemy and kill.
                                                                pounce on

6   *Salama,* taken by journalist Jacky Naegelen for Reuters news agency at the Hema

militia camp near the city of Bunia in the Democratic Republic of Congo, conveys a

clear message: "What is occurring in the Democratic Republic of Congo is hugely unjust

and utterly tragic." One wonders what Satanic impulse would allow such a picture to
                                                       risk the precious lives of their children by
more direct   exist. How can any nation ~~subject its children to risking their precious lives~~ fighting in
                                        these children
reference   a ruthless war when ~~they~~ should be learning how to read and write in school and to play

harmless games with their classmates?

7   Perhaps one of the worst aspects of the photo is that few people in other countries

will ever be aware of this war in which children are forced to bear arms because the

battlefield is located on the forgotten continent of Africa. A further irony exists here:

Most people mistakenly label Africa a third-world nation, choked in the mire of poverty

and ignorance. Quite to the contrary, much of Africa is well developed economically,

politically, and socially. Moreover, it bears the typical marks of a developed society—

namely the prevalence of universities, federal and local governments, and businesses.

tighten up the   Unfortunately, the conflicts that ~~often~~ lead to economic, political, and social instability are
sentence
~~also~~ present in Africa, especially in the Democratic Republic of Congo. Although *Salama*

was taken a few years ago, the violence still continues unabated as unidentified militia

groups raid innocent, peaceful villages, with the dreadful consequence that children are

encouraged to participate in these combats. It is this misguided concept of war that this

photo emphasizes. The viewer studies these youthful faces and cannot reconcile them

with the machine guns being used in a ferocious war, where gallantry does not exist.

8   Regardless of how the world views the conflict in the Congo, surely every American

feels a blast of righteous indignation and justified horror when viewing *Salama.* As U.S.

citizens, we may be accustomed to images of eighteen to twenty-something-year-old

men in camouflage suits, ~~with little American flag patches~~, holding automatic firearms
                against   *s*
tightly ~~beneath~~ their right clavicle. We may accept that they emerge straight out of

fifth-period high school trigonometry into battles of mortal consequence. This is what
we expect to see, whether we condone or condemn the implications of such men in
uniform. What also unites us, in a sense, is our general awareness of that precarious line
between a military force too immature for battle and one that is more prepared (although
we as human beings can never fully prepare ourselves for the true nature of war) for the
incredible trials and horrors ~~that are~~ inherent in war. While the line between an eighteen-
year-old recruit and a senior high school student is ~~insubstantial~~ ^{flimsy}, ~~as it is the difference~~   *word*
~~between your eighteenth birthday and the day before,~~ it is a distinction we Americans
are prepared to make.

9   In the Democratic Republic of Congo, as well as in other regions of the world, such
images and understandings do not exist in the same way as they do here. People in   *be specific*
                    ^{in the United States}
those countries do not choose to ^{acknowledge} ~~discern~~ that line between mental immaturity and
mental preparedness. As is evident in *Salama,* their policies on war seem to define
a soldier based upon physical strength (namely the ability to hold and fire a gun
effectively) rather than on mental and emotional maturity. They believe that they should
not ignore a potentially powerful military force just because its members are young.
After all, military veterans can condition children to think like soldiers, to be ruthless,
decisive, and stoic. And besides, there can be no better way to live a fulfilling life than
serving ~~your~~ ^{one's} country, ~~your~~ ^{one's} people. The problem, of course, is that such beliefs are based
on a lack of emotion and love, a heartlessness that the American people, thankfully, as a
whole, simply do not harbor.

10   In *Salama,* the reason for which these children are holding guns goes back to the
reasons most wars are fought--territorial expansion, revolution against the current
regime, economic poverty, or plain nationalism. But none of these reasons can possibly
justify what the Hema militia is doing in the Democratic Republic of Congo. Their lack of
moral qualms about using teenage girls and boys to fight for its cause is simply atrocious
and inexcusable.

11   I am inclined to believe that the world will not change unless faced with utter
catastrophe. That is to say that such egocentric leaders will remain ~~purposefully unaware~~   *redundant*

~~and~~ indifferent until their well-being, their desires, their self-centered views of life are threatened by a massive movement of altruism and philanthropy. Such a movement is not altogether impossible either, for there is a possibility (perhaps even a probability) that one day the world may collectively wake up from its sleep, from its work, from its habits and realize that the good in the world far outweighs the evil. And of course that realization would end the pictures of children with guns, ~~and wars for that matter~~ for people would turn on their televisions one day and find the Dalai Lama, the Pope, and three billion other human beings sitting upon the dirt, singing "Heck no, we won't go." And under the

punctuation weight of incredible social pressure, we would all follow suit, because ~~that's~~ that is our nature,

more formal and as we would all spread out across the land, these narcissistic leaders would come to find that no substantial piece of land was left for their dominance and no substantial group of people was available to pay them homage. So they would join the movement or wither

punctuation away, and in either case no evil would be left. But then again, I'm just musing.

S T U D E N T   E S S A Y — F I N A L   D R A F T

Erazo 1

Shjena Erazo

English 105

Professor Frusciante

University of Miami

Children and Guns: Marks of an Unscrupulous World

1   The photograph above the title of this essay is shocking and disturbing. In the foreground it depicts a beautiful black teenage girl holding an automatic firearm, ready for combat. What is most dreadful about this image is that this girl could just as easily have been holding a popsicle as this deadly weapon. What this photo does is to point out an unbridgeable gap between our society and

Erazo 2

© REUTERS/Jacky Naegelen

the society to which this little girl belongs, and it is this difference that I wish to stress throughout this essay.

2   This photo was taken in the Democratic Republic of Congo. I have chosen to title it in Swahili: *Salama*, or "peace." The irony of such a title expresses my conviction that the beautiful girl holding the gun so menacingly in this photograph is innately desirous of peace. I feel that those older veterans who harvest young girls and boys to fight and kill like barbaric adults have tried their best to rip out the roots of any desire for peace in these youthful hearts and have replaced these roots with the seeds of hatred and belligerence.

3   At first this little girl's life may appear doomed because one might think that surely her environment has corrupted her forever so that she will never pursue peace. But I hold no such cynical belief. In fact, I am convinced that no environmental system is so

Erazo 3

strong that it can entirely eclipse nature's fundamental urges. Thus, while the war lords want to see more and more blood flow, the human heart longs for love and peace. You may judge me naïve and foolish, but I feel that optimism in the face of such hell is important. In the past, glimmers of hope have been known to trump despair. We must not lose hope.

4   In *Salama*, the young girl—dark as night and wearing a plaid shirt with a cloth draped over her shoulders—stands at a window-like opening in the foreground of this photograph. Her head is wrapped in a bandanna, knotted at the nape of her neck, and she holds a black machine gun in her disproportionately small hands. While her face tries to display a serious sense of purpose, the careful observer cannot miss the childlike look on her face and the innocence hiding behind her steady eyes. To her right stands a young boy in a white t-shirt displaying some sort of blue and red advertising. He too is dark-skinned and he is leaning against some unseen object. His stare is focused, but his thoughts seem to be in some other place, perhaps on the battlefield or some sort of utopia. He also holds a black, automatic gun whose barrel rests on a brown boot that lies on the window sill that most likely was created by the blast of a powerful explosive. Behind him is another boy, wearing a buttoned-up shirt and holding a large firearm wrapped in a white cloth. Like the other children in the photograph, he too has black skin, so black that he seems invisible, shrouded in the shadow of the photo's background. Behind the girl and to her left is the head of another child, barely visible against the pitch black background.

Erazo 4

These four children gazing through the carved and chipped wall opening have been forced to grow up much faster than their counterparts in the United States. While American children play on monkey bars and see-saws in our parks, these children hide behind doors and in dark alleys, ready to pounce on the enemy and kill.

5   *Salama*, taken by journalist Jacky Naegelen for Reuters news agency at the Hema militia camp near the city of Bunia in the Democratic Republic of Congo, conveys a clear message: "What is occurring in the Democratic Republic of Congo is hugely unjust and utterly tragic." One wonders what Satanic impulse would allow such a picture to exist. How can any nation risk the precious lives of their children by fighting in a ruthless war when these children should be learning how to read and write in school and to play harmless games with their classmates?

6   Perhaps one of the worst aspects of the photo is that few people in other countries will ever be aware of this war in which children are forced to bear arms, because the battlefield is located on the forgotten continent of Africa. A further irony exists here: Most people mistakenly label Africa a third-world nation, choked in the mire of poverty and ignorance. Quite to the contrary, much of Africa is well developed economically, politically, and socially. Moreover, it bears the typical marks of a developed society—namely the prevalence of universities, federal and local governments, and businesses. Unfortunately, the conflicts that lead to economic, political, and social instability are present in Africa, especially in the Democratic Republic of Congo. Although *Salama*

Erazo 5

was taken a few years ago, the violence still continues unabated as unidentified militia groups raid innocent, peaceful villages, with the dreadful consequence that children are encouraged to participate in these combats. It is this misguided concept of war that this photo emphasizes. The viewer studies these youthful faces and cannot reconcile them with the machine guns being used in a ferocious war, where gallantry does not exist.

7   Regardless of how the world views the conflict in the Congo, surely every American feels a blast of righteous indignation and justified horror when viewing *Salama*. As U.S. citizens, we may be accustomed to images of eighteen to twenty-something-year-old men in camouflage suits, holding automatic firearms tightly against their right clavicles. We may accept that they emerge straight out of fifth-period high school trigonometry into battles of mortal consequence. This is what we expect to see, whether we condone or condemn the implications of such men in uniform. What also unites us, in a sense, is our general awareness of that precarious line between a military force too immature for battle and one that is more prepared (although we as human beings can never fully prepare ourselves for the true nature of war) for the incredible trials and horrors inherent in war. While the line between an eighteen-year-old recruit and a senior high school student is flimsy, it is a distinction we Americans are prepared to make.

8   In the Democratic Republic of Congo, as well as in other regions of the world, such images and understandings do not exist in the same way as they do here in the United States. People in those countries do not choose to acknowledge that line between mental

Erazo 6

immaturity and mental preparedness. As is evident in *Salama,*
their policies on war seem to define a soldier based upon physical
strength (namely the ability to hold and fire a gun effectively) rather
than on mental and emotional maturity. They believe that they
should not ignore a potentially powerful military force just because
its members are young. After all, military veterans can condition
children to think like soldiers, to be ruthless, decisive, and stoic. And
besides, there can be no better way to live a fulfilling life than serving
your country, your people. The problem, of course, is that such
beliefs are based on a lack of emotion and love, a heartlessness that
the American people, thankfully, as a whole simply do not harbor.

9   In *Salama,* the reason for which these children are holding
guns goes back to the reasons most wars are fought—territorial
expansion, revolution against the current regime, economic poverty,
or plain nationalism. But none of these reasons can possibly justify
what the Hema militia is doing in the Democratic Republic of
Congo. Their lack of moral qualms about using teenage girls and
boys to fight for its cause is simply atrocious and inexcusable.

10   I am inclined to believe that the world will not change unless
faced with utter catastrophe. That is to say that such egocentric
leaders will remain indifferent until their well-being, their desires,
their self-centered views of life are threatened by a massive
movement of altruism and philanthropy. Such a movement is not
altogether impossible either, for there is a possibility (perhaps even
a probability) that one day the world may collectively wake up from
its sleep, from its work, from its habits and realize that the good
in the world far outweighs the evil. And of course that realization

Erazo 7

would end the pictures of children with guns, for people would

turn on their televisions one day and find the Dalai Lama, the Pope,

and three billion other human beings sitting upon the dirt, singing

"Heck no, we won't go." And under the weight of incredible social

pressure, we would all follow suit, because that is our nature,

and as we would all spread out across the land, these narcissistic

leaders would come to find that no substantial piece of land was

left for their dominance and no substantial group of people was

available to pay them homage. So they would join the movement

or wither away, and in either case no evil would be left. But then

again, I'm just musing.

FURTHER READING

JOYCE CAROL OATES

Bonobo Momma

Joyce Carol Oates (b. 1938) has been called "America's foremost woman of letters" due partly to her prolific writing output. She has published over fifty-five novels, countless short stories, and numerous essays concerning literary subjects or social problems. In 1962, she married Raymond J. Smith, who taught English literature at the University of Windsor (Ontario) and at New York University. Until her husband's death in 2008, the couple cooperated on several literary ventures, such as editing and publishing the Ontario Review *and the* Ontario Review Books. *Oates' best-known novels are* Them *(1969),* Blackwater *(1992),* What I lived For *(1994) and* Blonde *(2000). She also published several novels under the pseudonyms of Rosamond Smith and Lauren Kelly. Since 2008, Oates has been a professor of creative writing at Princeton University.*

READING FOR IDEAS In an interview, Joyce Carol Oates admitted that she had always been attracted to failure. Certainly this attraction is obvious in the story that follows. As you read the narrator's unusual account of a luncheon date with her glamorous mother, try to understand all of the influences that have badgered this young girl since her birth. While the mother is the central character in this story, other people add shades of color that help draw a portrait of the narrator. After reaching the end of the narration, come up with a possible theme—that is, the lesson you extracted from the entire event described. Also, take special note of the various sensory details provided.

1   THAT DAY, I met my "estranged" mother in the lobby of the Carlisle Hotel on Fifth Avenue, New York City. It was a few weeks following the last in a series of surgeries to correct a congenital malformation in my spine, and one of the first days when I could walk unassisted for any distance and didn't tire too quickly. This would be the first time I'd seen my mother since Fall Fashion Week nearly two years ago. Since she'd divorced my father when I was eight years old my mother—whose professional name was Adelina—spent most of her time in Paris. At thirty she'd retired from modeling and was now a consultant for one of the couture houses—a much more civilized and rewarding occupation than modeling, she said. For the world is "pitiless" to aging women, even former *Vogue* models.

2   As soon as I entered the Carlisle Hotel lobby, I recognized Adelina waiting for me on a velvet settee. Quickly she rose to greet me and I was struck another time by the fact that my mother was so *tall*. To say that Adelina was a striking woman is an understatement. The curvature of my spine had stunted my growth and even now, after my first surgery. I more resembled a girl of eleven than thirteen. On the way to the hotel I'd become anxious that my beautiful mother might wince at the sight of me, as sometimes she'd done in the past, but she was smiling happily at me—joyously her—arms opened for an embrace. I felt a jolt of love for her like a kick in the belly that took my breath away and left me faint-headed. *Is that my mother? My—mother?*

3   Typical of Adelina, for this casual luncheon engagement with her thirteen-year-old daughter she was dressed in such a way—cream-colored coarse-knit coat, very short very tight sheath in a material like silver vinyl, on her long sword-like legs patterned stockings, and on her feet elegantly impractical high-heeled shoes—to cause strangers to glance at her, if not to stare. Her ash-blond hair fell in sculptured layers about her angular face. Hiding her eyes were stylish dark glasses in oversized frames. Bracelets clattered on both her wrists and her long thin fingers glittered with rings. In a hotel like the Carlisle it was not unreasonable for patrons to assume that this glamorous woman was *someone*, though no one outside the fashion world would have recalled her name.

4   My father too was "famous" in a similar way—he was a painter/sculptor whose work sold in the "high six figures"—famous in contemporary Manhattan art circles but little-known elsewhere.

5   "Darling! Look at *you*—such a tall girl—"

6   My mother's arms were thin but unexpectedly strong. This I recalled from previous embraces, when Adelina's strength caught me by surprise. Surprising too was the flatness of Adelina's chest, her breasts small and resilient as knobs of hard rubber. I loved her special fragrance—a mixture of flowery perfume, luxury soap, something drier and more acrid like hair bleach and cigarette smoke. When she leaned back to look at me her mouth worked

as if she were trying not to cry. Adelina had not been able to visit me in the hospital at the time of my most recent operation though she'd sent cards and gifts to my room at the Hospital for Special Surgery overlooking the East River: flowers, candies, luxurious stuffed animals and books more appropriate for a younger girl. It had been her plan to fly to New York to see me except an unexpected project had sent her to Milan instead.

7   "Your back, darling!—you are all mended, are you?—yet so *thin.*"

8   Before I could draw away Adelina unzipped my jacket, slipped her hands inside and ran her fingers down my spine in a way that made me giggle for it was ticklish, and I was embarrassed, and people were watching us. Over the rims of her designer sunglasses she peered at me with pearl-colored eyes that seemed dilated, the lashes sticky-black with mascara. "But—you are *very pretty.* Or would be if—"

9   Playfully seizing my lank limp no-color brown hair in both her beringed hands, pulling my hair out beside my face and releasing it. Her fleshy lips pouted in a way I knew to be distinctly French.

10   "A haircut, *chérie!* This very day."

11   Later I would remember that a man had moved away from Adelina when I'd first entered the lobby. As I'd pushed through the revolving door and stepped inside I'd had a vague impression of a man in a dark suit seated beside the striking blond woman on the settee and as this woman quickly rose to greet me he'd eased away, and was gone.

12   Afterward I would think *There might be no connection. Much is accident.*

13   "You're hungry for lunch, I hope? I am famished—*très petit déjeuner* this morning—'jet log'—come!"

14   We were going to eat in the sumptuous hotel restaurant. Adelina had made a "special reservation."

15   So many rings on Adelina's fingers, including a large glittery emerald on the third finger of her left hand, there was no room for a wedding band and so there was no clear sign if Adelina had remarried. My father did not speak my "estranged" mother, and I would not have risked upsetting him with childish inquiries. On the phone with me, in her infrequent calls, my mother was exclamatory and vague about her personal life and lapsed into breathless French phrases if I dared to ask prying questions.

16   Not that I was an aggressive child. Even in my desperation I was wary, hesitant. With my S-shaped spine that had caused me to walk oddly, and to hold my head at an awkward angle, and would have coiled back upon itself in ever-tighter contortions except for the corrective surgery, I had always been shy and uncertain. Other girls my age hoped to be perceived as beautiful, sexy, "hot"—I was grateful not to be stared at.

17   As the maitre d' was seating us in the restaurant, it appeared that something was amiss. In a sharp voice Adelina said, "No. I don't like this table. This is not a good table."

18   It was one of the small tables, for two, a banquette seat against a mirrored wall, close by other diners; one of us would be seated on the banquette seat and the other on the outside, facing in. Adelina didn't want to sit with her back to the room nor did Adelina want to sit facing the room. Nor did Adelina like a table so close to other tables.

19   The maitre d' showed us to another table, also small, but set a little apart from the main dining room; now Adelina objected that the table was too close to the restrooms: I hate this table!"

20   By this time other diners were observing us. Embarrassed and unhappy, I stood a few feet away. In her throaty aggrieved voice Adelina was telling the maitre d' that she'd made a reservation for a "quiet" table—her daughter had had "major surgery" just recently—what was required was a table for four, that we would not be "cramped." With (an) expression of strained courtesy the maitre d' showed my mother to a table for four, also at the rear of the restaurant, but this table too had something fatally wrong with it, or by now the attention of the other diners had become offensive to Adelina, who seized my hand and huffily pulled me away. In a voice heavy with sarcasm she said, "We will go elsewhere, *monsieur! Merci beaucoup!*"

21   Outside on Fifth Avenue, traffic was thunderous. My indignant mother pulled me to the curb, to wait for a break in the stream of vehicles before crossing over into the park. She was too impatient to walk to the intersection, to cross at the light. When a taxi passed too slowly, blocking our way, Adelina struck its yellow hood with her fist. "Go on! *Allez!*"

22   In the park, Adelina lit a cigarette and exhaled bluish smoke in luxurious sighs as if only now could she breathe deeply. Her mood was incensed, invigorated. Her wide dark nostrils widened further, with feeling. Snugly she linked her arm through mine. I was having trouble keeping pace with her but I managed not be wince in pain for I knew how it would annoy her. On the catwalk—"catwalk" had been a word in my vocabulary for as long as I could remember—Adelina had learned to walk in a brisk assured stride no matter how exquisitely impractical her shoes.

23   "Lift your head, *chérie.* Your chin. You are a pretty girl. Ignore if they stare. Who are *they*!"

24   With singular contempt Adelina murmured *they.* I had no idea what she was talking about but was eager to agree.

25   It was a sunny April day. We were headed for the Boat House Restaurant to which Adelina had taken me in the past. On the paved walk beside a lagoon excited geese and mallards rushed to peck at pieces of bread tossed in their direction, squawking at one another and flapping their wings with murderous intent. Adelina crinkled her nose. "Such a *clatter*! I hate noisy birds."

26   It was upsetting to Adelina, too, that the waterfowl droppings were everywhere underfoot. How careful one had to be, walking beside the lagoon in such beautiful shoes.

27   "Not good to feed wild creatures! And not good for the environment. You would think, any idiot would know."

28   Adelina spoke loudly, to be overheard by individuals tossing bread at the waterfowl.

29   I was hoping that she wouldn't confront anyone. There was a fiery sort of anger in my mother, that was fearful to me, yet fascinating.

30   "Excuse me, *chérie:* turn here."

31   With no warning Adelina gripped my arm tighter, pivoting me to ascend a hilly incline. When I asked Adelina what was wrong she hissed in my car, "Eyes straight ahead. Ignore if they stare."

32   I dared not glance back over my shoulder to see who or what was there.

33   Because of her enormously busy professional life that involved frequent travel to Europe, Adelina had relinquished custody of me to my father at the time of their divorce. It had been a "tortured" decision, she'd said. But "for the best, for all." She had never heard of the private girl's school in Manhattan to which my father was sending me and

alluded to it with an air of reproach and suspicion for everyone knew, as Adelina said, that my father was "stingy—*perfide*." Now when she questioned me about the school—teachers, courses, classmates—I sensed that she wasn't really listening as she responded with murmurs of *Eh? Yes? Go on!* Several times she turned to glare at someone who'd passed us saying sharply, "Yes? Is there some problem? Do I know you?"

34   To me she said, frowning, "Just look straight ahead, darling! Ignore them."

35   Truly I did not know if people were watching us—either my mother or me—but it would not have surprised me. Adelina dressed like one who expects attention, yet seemed sincere in rebuffing it. Especially repugnant to her were the openly aggressive, sexual stares of men, who made a show of stopping dead on the path to watch Adelina walk by. As a child with a body that had been deformed until recently, I'd become accustomed to people glancing at me in pity, or children starting at me in curiosity, or revulsion; but now with my repaired spine that allowed me to walk more or less normally, I did not see that I merited much attention. Yet on the pathway to the Boat House my mother paused to confront an older woman who was walking a miniature schnauzer, and who had in fact been staring at both Adelina and me, saying in a voice heavy with sarcasm, "Excuse me, *madame?* My daughter would appreciate not to be stared at. *Merci!*"

36   Inside the Boat House, on this sunny April day, many diners were awaiting tables. The restaurant took no phone reservations. There was a crowd, spilling over from the bar. Adelina raised her voice to give her name to the hostess and was told that we would have a forty-minute wait for a table overlooking the lagoon. Other tables were more readily available but Adelina wanted a table on the water: "This is a special occasion. My daughter's first day out, after major surgery."

37   The hostess cast me a glance of sympathy. But a table on the lagoon was still a forty-minute wait.

38   My disappointed mother was provided with a plastic device like a remote control that was promised to light up and "vibrate" when our table was ready. Adelina pushed her way to the bar and ordered a drink—"Bloody Mary for me, Virgin Mary for my daughter."

39   The word *virgin* was embarrassing to me. I had never heard it in association with a drink and had to wonder if my capricious mother had invented it on the spot.

40   In the crowded Boat House, we waited. Adelina managed to capture a stool at the bar, and pulled me close beside her as in a windstorm. We were jostled by strangers in a continuous stream into and out of the dining area. Sipping her blood-red drink, so similar in appearance to mine which turned out to be mere tomato juice, my mother inquired about my surgery, and about the surgeon; she seemed genuinely interested in my physical therapy sessions, which involved strenuous swimming; another time she explained why she hadn't been able to fly to New York to visit me in the hospital, and hoped that I understood. (I did! Of course) "My life is not so fixed, *chérie*. Not like your father so settled out there on the island."

41   My father owned two residences: a brownstone on West Eighty-ninth Street and, at Montauk Point at the easternmost end of Long Island, a rambling old shingleboard house. It was at Montauk Point that my father had his studio, overlooking the ocean. The brownstone, which was where I lived most of the time, was maintained by a housekeeper. My father preferred Montauk Point though he tried to get into the city at least once a week. Frequently on weekends I was brought out to Montauk Point—by hired car—but it was a

long, exhausting journey that left me writhing with back pain, and when I was there, my father spent most of the time in his studio or visiting with artist friends. It was not true, as Adelina implied, that my father neglected me, but it was true that we didn't see much of each other during the school year. As an artist/bachelor of some fame my father was eagerly sought as a dinner guest and many of his evenings both at Montauk Point and in the city were spent with dealers and collectors. Yet he'd visited me each day while I'd been in the hospital. We'd had serious talks about subjects that faded from my memory afterward—art, religion?—Whether God "existed" or was a "universal symbol"—whether there was "death" from the perspective of "the infinite universe." In my hospital bed when I'd been dazed and delirious from painkillers it was wonderful how my father's figure melted and eased into my dreams with me, so that I was never lonely. Afterward my father revealed that when I'd been sleeping he had sketched me—in charcoal—in the mode of Edvard Munch's "The Sick Child"—but the drawings were disappointing, he'd destroyed them.

42   My father was much older than my mother. One day I would learn that my father was eighteen years older than my mother, which seemed to me such a vast span of time, there was something obscene about it. My father loved me very much, he said. Still, I saw that he'd begun to lose interest in me once my corkscrew spine had been repaired, and I was released from the hospital: my medical condition had been a problem to be solved, like one of my father's enormous canvases or sculptures, and once such a problem was solved, his imagination detached from it.

43   I could understand this, of course. I understood that, apart from my physical ailments, I could not be a very interesting subject to any adult. It was a secret plan of mine to capture the attention of both my father and my mother in my life to come. I would be something unexpected, and I would excel: as an archeologist, an Olympic swimmer, a poet. A neurosurgeon.

44   At the Boat House bar, my mother fell into conversation with a man with sleek oiled hair and a handsome fox face; this man ignored me, as if I did not exist. When I returned from using the restroom, I saw the fox-faced man was leaving, and my mother was slipping a folded piece of paper into her oversized handbag. The color was up in Adelina's cheeks. She had a way of brushing her ash-blond hair from her face that reminded me of the most popular girls at my school who exuded at all times an air of urgency, expectation. "*Chérie*, you are all right? You are looking pale, I think." This was a gentle admonition. Quickly I told Adelina that I was fine. For some minutes a middle-aged couple a few feet away had been watching my mother, and whispering together, and when the woman at last approached my mother to ask if she was an actress—"Someone on TV, your face is so familiar"—I steeled myself for Adelina's rage, but unexpectedly she laughed and said no, she'd never been an actress, but she had been a model and maybe that was where they'd seen her face, on a *Vogue* cover. "Not for a while, though! I'm afraid." Nonetheless the woman was impressed and asked Adelina to sign a paper napkin for her, which Adelina did, with a gracious flourish.

45   More than a half-hour had passed, and we were still waiting to be seated for lunch. Adelina went to speak with the harried young hostess who told her there might be a table opening in another ten-fifteen minutes. "The wand will light up, ma'am when your table is ready. You don't have to check with me." Adelina said, "No? When I see other people being seated, who came after us?" The hostess denied that this was so.

Adelina indignantly returned to the bar. She ordered a second Bloody Mary and drank it thirstily. "She thinks that I'm not aware of what she's doing," my mother said. "But I'm very aware. I'm expected to slip her a twenty, I suppose. I hate that!" Abruptly then my mother decided that we were leaving. She paid the bar bill and pulled me outside with her; in a trash can she disposed of the plastic wand. Again she snugly linked her arm through mine. The Bloody Marys had warmed her, a pleasant yeasty-perfumy odor lifted from her body. The silver-vinyl sheath, which was a kind of tunic covering her legs to her mid-thighs, made a shivery sound as she moved. "Never let anyone insult you, darling. Verbal abuse is as vicious as Physical abuse." She paused, her mouth working as if she had more to say but dared not. In the Boat House she'd removed her dark glasses and shoved them into her handbag and now her pearly-gray eyes were exposed to daylight, beautiful glistening eyes faintly bloodshot, tinged with yellow like old ivory.

46   "*Chérie*, your shoulder! Your left, you carry it lower than the other. Are you aware?"

47   Quickly I shook my head *no*.

48   "You don't want to appear hunchbacked. What was he—*Quasimodo*—A terrible thing for a girl. Here—"

49   Briskly like a physical therapist Adelina gripped my wrists and pulled them over my head, to stretch me. I was made to stand on my toes, like a ballerina.

50   Adelina scolded: "I don't like how people look at you. With pity, that is a kind of scorn. I hate that!"

51   Her mouth was wide, fleshy. Her forehead was low. Her features seemed somehow in the wrong proportions and yet the effect of my mother was a singular kind of beauty, it was not possible to look away from her. At about the time of their divorce my father had painted a sequence of portraits titled *Bonobo Momma* which was his best-known work as it was his most controversial: enormous unfinished canvases with raw, primitive figures of monkey-like humanoid females. It was possible to see my beautiful mother in these simian figures with their wide fleshy mouths, low brows, breasts like dugs, swollen and flushed female genitalia. When I was older I would stare at the notorious *Bonobo Momma* in the Museum of Modern Art and I would realize that the female figure most closely resembling Adelina was unnervingly sexual, with large hands, feet, genitalia. This was a rapacious creature to inspire awe in the merely human viewer.

52   I would see that there was erotic power greater than beauty. My father had paid homage to that, in my mother. Perhaps it was his loathing of her, that had allowed him to see her clearly.

53   Approaching us on the path was a striking young women—walking with two elegant borzoi dogs—dark glasses masking half her face—in tight designer jeans crisscrossed with zippers like stitches—a tight sweater of some bright material like crinkled plastic. The girl's hair was a shimmering chestnut-red ponytail that fell to her hips. Adelina stared with grudging admiration as the girl passed us without a glance.

54   "That's a distinctive look."

55   We walked on. I was becoming dazed, light-headed. Adelina mused: "On the catwalk, it isn't beauty that matters. Anyone can be beautiful. Mere beauty is boring, an emptiness. Your father knew that, at least. With so much else he did not know, at lease he knew that. It's the walk—the authority. A great model announces 'Here I am—there is only me'."

56   Shyly I said, " 'There is only I.' "

57   "What?"

58   " 'There is only I.' You said 'me.' "

59   "What on earth are you talking about? Am I supposed to know?"

60   My mother laughed, perplexed. She seemed to be having difficulty keeping me in focus.

61   I'd meant to speak in a playful manner with Adelina, as I often did with adults who intimidated me and towered over me. It was a way of seeming younger than I was. But Adelina interpreted most remarks literally. Jokes fell flat with her, unless she made them herself, punctuated with her sharp barking laughter.

62   Adelina hailed a taxi, to take us to Tavern on the Green.

63   The driver, swarthy-skinned, with a short-trimmed goatee, was speaking on a cell phone in a lowered voice, in a language unknown to us. At the same time, the taxi's radio was on, barrage of noisy advertising. Adelina said, "Driver? Please turn off that deafening radio, will you?"

64   With measured slowness as if he hadn't quite heard her, the driver turned off his radio. Into the cell phone he muttered an expletive in an indecipherable language.

65   Sharply Adelina said, "Driver? I'd prefer that you didn't speak on the phone while you're driving. If you don't mind."

66   In the rear view mirror the driver's eyes fixed us with scarcely concealed contempt.

67   "Your cell phone, please. Will you turn it off. There's a law against taxi drivers using their cell phones while they have fares, you must know that. It's dangerous. I hate it. I wouldn't want to report you to the taxi authority."

68   The driver mumbled something indistinct. Adelina said, "It's rude to mumble, *monsieur*. You can let us off here."

69   "Ma'am?"

70   Don't pretend to be stupider than you are, *monsieur!* You understand English perfectly well. I see your name here, and I'm taking down your license number. Open this damned door. Immediately."

71   The taxi braked to a stop. I was thrown forward against the scummy plastic partition that separated us from the furious driver. Pain like an electric shock, fleeting and bright, throbbed in my spine. Adelina and the swarthy-skinned driver exchanged curses as Adelina yanked me out of the taxi and slammed the door, and the taxi sped away.

72   "Yes, I will report him! Illegal immigrant—I wouldn't be surprised."

73   We were stranded inside the park, on one of the drives traversing the park from Fifth Avenue to Central Park West. We had some distance to walk to Tavern on the Green and I was feeling light-headed, concerned that I wasn't going to make it. But when Adelina asked me if I was all right, quickly I told her that I was fine.

74   "Frankly, darling, you don't look 'fine.' You look sick. What on earth is your father thinking, entrusting you with a *housekeeper?*"

75   I wanted to protest, I loved Serena. A sudden panic came over me that Adelina might have the authority to fire her, and I would have no one.

76   "Darling, if you could walk straighter. This shoulder!—*try*. I hate to see people looking at my daughter in *pity*."

77   Adelina shook her head in disgust. Her ash-blond hair stirred in the wind, stiffly. At the base of her throat was a delicate hollow I had not seen before. The bizarre thought

came to me, I could insert my fingers into this hollow. I could push down, using all of my weight. My mother's brittle skeleton would shatter.

78   "—what? What are you saying, darling?"

79   I was trying to protest something. Trying to explain. As in a dream in which the right words won't come. Not ten feet from us stood a disheveled man with a livid boiled-beet face. He too was muttering to himself—or maybe to us—grinning and showing an expanse of obscenely pink gum. Adelina was oblivious of him. He'd begun to follow us, lurching and flapping his arms as if in mockery of my gorgeous mother.

80   Adelina chided: "You shouldn't have come out today, darling. If you're not really mended. I could have come to see you, we could have planned that. We could have met at a restaurant on the West Side."

81   Briskly Adelina was signaling for another taxi, standing in the street. She was wearing her dark-tinted glasses now. Her manner was urgent, dramatic. A taxi braked to a stop, the driver was an older man, darker-skinned than the other driver, more deferential. Adelina opened the rear door, pushed me inside, leaned into the window to instruct the driver: "Please take my daughter home. She'll tell you the address. She's just thirteen, she has had major surgery and needs to get home, right away. Make sure she gets to the actual door, will you? You can wait in the street and watch her. Here"—thrusting a bill at the driver, which must have been a large bill for the man took it from Adelina's fingers with a terse smile of thanks.

82   Awkwardly Adelina stooped to kiss my cheek. She was juggling her designer handbag and a freshly lit cigarette, breathing her flamy-sweet breath into my face. "Darling, goodbye! Take a nap when you get home. You look ghastly. I'll call you. I'm here until Thursday. *Auvoir!*"

83   The taxi sprang forward. On the curb my mother stood blowing kissed after us. In the rear view mirror the driver's narrowed eyes shifted to my face.

84   A jarring ride through the park! Now I was alone, unobserved. I wiped at my eyes. Through the smudged window beside me flowed a stream of strangers on the sidewalk— all that I knew in my life that would be permanent, and my own.

Source: Joyce Carol Oats, "Bonobo Momma." *Michigan Quarterly Review,* Winter 2009. Reprinted in *Pushcart Prize XXXIV.* Ed. Bill Henderson. N.Y. 2010, pp. 79–89.

▪ Vocabulary

couture (1)	aggrieved (19)	flourish (44)
settee (2)	catwalk (22)	humanoid (51)
curvature (2)	pivoting (31)	simian (51)
angular (3)	rebuffing (35)	indecipherable (65)
exclamatory (14)	brownstone (41)	terse (81)

▪ Questions on Meaning and Technique

1. What dominant impression do you have of Adelina? State your impression in one sentence and list the details that support this impression.

2. How does Adelina make her daughter feel? What is your character analysis of the daughter? How does she respond to her mother's attentions?

3. What is the tone and purpose revealed in paragraph 22?

4. What ironic contradiction exists between Adelina's actions or outward appearance and her inward thoughts? What is your reaction to this person, either as a woman or as a mother? Explain your response.

5. What is the meaning of paragraph 28? How important is the paragraph to the theme of the story? Give reasons for your answers.

6. What is the purpose of the reference to Edvard Munch in paragraph 41? If you are not familiar with this person, look him up on the internet. What does this reference and the reference to Quasimodo in paragraph 48 have in common?

7. How are the narrator's father and mother alike? Wherein do they differ? Of the two, whom do you consider the better parent? Explain your judgment.

8. What is the relationship of the unusual title to the rest of the story? What is your opinion of this title? Does it work or what better title might you suggest?

Writing Assignments

1. Write a description of someone with poor parenting skills in your circle of relatives or acquaintances. Be sure to supply a dominant impression that you support with vivid details. Be clear and direct in your assessment.

2. Write a descriptive portrait of your father or mother by relating some significant incident in your home life. Your essay should reflect your parent's personality as it relates to you. Consider characteristics such as gentleness, sternness, humor, tact, volatility, pride, generosity, selfishness, and love.

FURTHER READING

MAYA ANGELOU

Sister Flowers

Maya Angelou (b. 1928) is a novelist, poet, playwright, actress, composer, and singer. Her varied accomplishments have thrown her into the public limelight and have made her a much sought-after speaker and reader of her own works. She is best known for her passionate insistence that all human beings need to be tolerant and must treat all other human beings, regardless of color or race, with dignity and respect. Many of her short stories, like the one presented here, tell of black people fighting stubbornly to maintain their self-respect in a world of prejudice. Among her best-known works are I Know Why the Caged Bird Sings *(1970), from which this essay is taken,* Gather Together in My Name *(1974),* Singin' and Swingin' and Gettin' Merry Like Christmas *(1976),* Heart of a Woman *(1981), and* All God's Children Need Traveling Shoes *(1986). Angelou has also written volumes of poetry, including* Oh Pray My Wings Are Gonna Fit Me Well *(1975), and* I Shall Not Be Moved *(1991). She read her poem* "On the Pulse of Morning" *at President Bill Clinton's inauguration in 1993 and has become a role model for aspiring female writers of many minority backgrounds.*

READING FOR IDEAS   In this story, a young girl regains her self-esteem after having been raped. As you read, try to follow the steps in the narrator's progress. On paper write down the significant details that helped her achieve healing. For instance, you might record the respect with which Mrs. Flowers treats the narrator's mother despite the mother's incorrect grammar. Ask yourself what impact that respect had on the narrator. Try to determine how important respect is to the life of ordinary people.

1   For nearly a year [after I was raped], I sopped around the house, the Store, the school and the church, like an old biscuit, dirty and inedible. Then I met, or rather got to know, the lady who threw me my first life line.

2   Mrs. Bertha Flowers was the aristocrat of Black Stamps. She had the grace of control to appear warm in the coldest weather, and on the Arkansas summer days it seemed she had a private breeze which swirled around, cooling her. She was thin without the taut look of wiry people, and her printed voile dresses and flowered hats were as right for her as denim overalls for a farmer. She was our side's answer to the richest white woman in town.

3   Her skin was a rich black that would have peeled like a plum if snagged, but then no one would have thought of getting close enough to Mrs. Flowers to ruffle her dress, let alone snag her skin. She didn't encourage familiarity. She wore gloves too.

4   I don't think I ever saw Mrs. Flowers laugh, but she smiled often. A slow widening of her thin black lips to show even, small white teeth, then the slow effortless closing. When she chose to smile on me, I always wanted to thank her. The action was so graceful and inclusively benign.

5   She was one of the few gentlewomen I have ever known, and has remained throughout my life the measure of what a human being can be.

6   Momma had a strange relationship with her. Most often when she passed on the road in front of the Store, she spoke to Momma in that soft yet carrying voice, "Good day, Mrs. Henderson." Momma responded with "How you, Sister Flowers?"

7   Mrs. Flowers didn't belong to our church, nor was she Momma's familiar. Why on earth did she insist on calling her Sister Flowers? Shame made me want to hide my face. Mrs. Flowers deserved better than to be called Sister. Then, Momma left out the verb. Why not ask, "How *are* you, *Mrs.* Flowers?" With the unbalanced passion of the young, I hated her for showing her ignorance to Mrs. Flowers. It didn't occur to me for many years that they were as alike as sisters, separated only by formal education.

8   Although I was upset, neither of the women was in the least shaken by what I thought an unceremonious greeting. Mrs. Flowers would continue her easy gait up the hill to her little bungalow, and Momma kept on shelling peas or doing whatever had brought her to the front porch.

9   Occasionally, though, Mrs. Flowers would drift off the road and down to the Store and Momma would say to me, "Sister, you go on and play." As she left I would hear the beginning of an intimate conversation. Momma persistently using the wrong verb, or none at all.

10   "Brother and Sister Wilcox is sho'ly the meanest—" "Is," Momma? "Is"? Oh, please, not "is," Momma, for two or more. But they talked, and from the side of the building where I waited for the ground to open up and swallow me, I heard the soft-voiced Mrs. Flowers and the textured voice of my grandmother merging and melting. They were interrupted from time to time by giggles that must have come from Mrs. Flowers (Momma never giggled in her life). Then she was gone.

11   She appealed to me because she was like people I had never met personally. Like women in English novels who walked the moors (whatever they were) with their loyal dogs racing at a respectful distance. Like the women who sat in front of roaring fireplaces, drinking tea incessantly from silver trays full of scones and crumpets. Women who walked over the "heath" and read morocco-bound books and had two last names divided by a hyphen. It would be safe to say that she made me proud to be Negro, just by being herself.

12   She acted just as refined as whitefolks in the movies and books and she was more beautiful, for none of them could have come near that warm color without looking gray by comparison.

13   It was fortunate that I never saw her in the company of powhitefolks. For since they tend to think of their whiteness as an evenizer, I'm certain that I would have had to hear her spoken to commonly as Bertha, and my image of her would have been shattered like the unmendable Humpty-Dumpty.

14   One summer afternoon, sweet-milk fresh in my memory, she stopped at the Store to buy provisions. Another Negro woman of her health and age would have been expected to carry the paper sacks home in one hand, but Momma said, "Sister Flowers, I'll send Bailey up to your house with these things."

15   She smiled that slow dragging smile, "Thank you, Mrs. Henderson. I'd prefer Marguerite, though." My name was beautiful when she said it. "I've been meaning to talk to her, anyway." They gave each other age-group looks.

16   Momma said, "Well, that's all right then. Sister, go and change your dress. You going to Sister Flowers's."

17   The chifforobe was a maze. What on earth did one put on to go to Mrs. Flowers's house? I knew I shouldn't put on a Sunday dress. It might be sacrilegious. Certainly not a house dress, since I was already wearing a fresh one. I chose a school dress, naturally. It was formal without suggesting that going to Mrs. Flowers's house was equivalent to attending church.

18   I trusted myself back into the Store.

19   "Now, don't you look nice." I had chosen the right thing, for once. . . .

20 There was a little path beside the rocky road, and Mrs. Flowers walked in front swinging her arms and picking her way over the stones.

21 She said, without turning her head, to me, "I hear you're doing very good school work, Marguerite, but that it's all written. The teachers report that they have trouble getting you to talk in class." We passed the triangular farm on our left and the path widened to allow us to walk together. I hung back in the separate unasked and unanswerable questions.

22 "Come and walk along with me, Marguerite." I couldn't have refused even if I wanted to. She pronounced my name so nicely. Or more correctly, she spoke each word with such clarity that I was certain a foreigner who didn't understand English could have understood her.

23 "Now no one is going to make you talk—possibly no one can. But bear in mind, language is man's way of communicating with his fellow man and it is language alone which separates him from the lower animals." That was a totally new idea to me, and I would need time to think about it.

24 "Your grandmother says you read a lot. Every chance you get. That's good, but not good enough. Words mean more than what is set down on paper. It takes the human voice to infuse them with the shades of deeper meaning."

25 I memorized the part about the human voice infusing words. It seemed so valid and poetic.

26 She said she was going to give me some books and that I not only must read them, I must read them aloud. She suggested that I try to make a sentence sound in as many different ways as possible.

27 "I'll accept no excuse if you return a book to me that has been badly handled." My imagination boggled at the punishment I would deserve if in fact I did abuse a book of Mrs. Flowers's. Death would be too kind and brief.

28 The odors in the house surprised me. Somehow I had never connected Mrs. Flowers with food or eating or any other common experience of common people. There must have been an outhouse, too, but my mind never recorded it.

29 The sweet scent of vanilla had met us as she opened the door.

30 "I made tea cookies this morning. You see, I had planned to invite you for cookies and lemonade so we could have this little chat. The lemonade is in the icebox."

31 It followed that Mrs. Flowers would have ice on an ordinary day, when most families in our town bought ice late on Saturdays only a few times during the summer to be used in the wooden ice-cream freezers.

32 She took the bags from me and disappeared through the kitchen door. I looked around the room that I had never in my wildest fantasies imagined I would see. Browned photographs leered or threatened from the walls and the white, freshly done curtains pushed against themselves and against the wind. I wanted to gobble up the room entire and take it to Bailey, who would help me analyze and enjoy it.

33 "Have a seat, Marguerite. Over there by the table." She carried a platter covered with a tea towel. Although she warned that she hadn't tried her hand at baking sweets for some time, I was certain that like everything else about her the cookies would be perfect.

34   They were flat round wafers, slightly browned on the edges and butter-yellow in the center. With the cold lemonade they were sufficient for childhood's lifelong diet. Remembering my manners, I took nice little lady-like bites off the edges. She said she had made them expressly for me and that she had a few in the kitchen that I could take home to my brother. So I jammed one whole cake in my mouth and the rough crumbs scratched the insides of my jaws, and if I hadn't had to swallow, it would have been a dream come true.

35   As I ate she began the first of what we later called "my lessons in living." She said that I must always be intolerant of ignorance but understanding of illiteracy. That some people, unable to go to school, were more educated and even more intelligent than college professors. She encouraged me to listen carefully to what country people called mother wit. That in those homely sayings was couched the collective wisdom of generations.

36   When I finished the cookies she brushed off the table and brought a thick, small book from the bookcase. I had read *A Tale of Two Cities* and found it up to my standards as a romantic novel. She opened the first page and I heard poetry for the first time in my life.

37   "It was the best of times and the worst of times . . ." Her voice slid in and curved down through and over the words. She was nearly singing. I wanted to look at the pages. Were they the same that I had read? Or were there notes, music, lined on the pages, as in a hymn book? Her sounds began cascading gently. I knew from listening to a thousand preachers that she was nearing the end of her reading, and I hadn't really heard, heard to understand, a single word.

38   "How do you like that?"

39   It occurred to me that she expected a response. The sweet vanilla flavor was still on my tongue and her reading was a wonder in my ears. I had to speak.

40   I said, "Yes, ma'am." It was the least I could do, but it was the most also.

41   "There's one more thing. Take this book of poems and memorize one for me. Next time you pay me a visit, I want you to recite."

42   I have tried often to search behind the sophistication of years for the enchantment I so easily found in those gifts. The essence escapes but its aura remains. To be allowed, no, invited, into the private lives of strangers, and to share their joys and fears, was a chance to exchange the Southern bitter wormwood for a cup of mead with Beowulf or a hot cup of tea and milk with Oliver Twist. When I said aloud, "It is a far, far better thing that I do, than I have ever done . . ." tears of love filled my eyes at my selflessness.

43   On that first day, I ran down the hill and into the road (few cars ever came along it) and had the good sense to stop running before I reached the Store.

44   I was liked, and what a difference it made. I was respected not as Mrs. Henderson's grandchild or Bailey's sister but for just being Marguerite Johnson.

45   Childhood's logic never asks to be proved (all conclusions are absolute). I didn't question why Mrs. Flowers had singled me out for attention, nor did it occur to me that Momma might have asked her to give me a little talking to. All I cared about was that she had made tea cookies for *me* and read to *me* from her favorite book. It was enough to prove that she liked me.

■ *Vocabulary*

sopped (1)	textured (10)	crumpets (11)
inedible (1)	merging (10)	unmendable (13)
familiarity (3)	moors (11)	infuse (24)
benign (4)	incessantly (11)	aura (42)
unceremonious (8)	heath (11)	absolute (45)
intimate (9)	morocco (11)	

■ *Questions on Meaning and Technique*

1. Why did Mrs. Flowers make such a good impression on the narrator? What personality traits, admired by the narrator, did Mrs. Flowers display?

2. Why do you think the narrator called her grandmother "Momma" rather than "Grandma"? What striking difference between Momma and Mrs. Flowers caused enormous stress in the narrator? What was the cause of her reaction?

3. What does the narrator mean when she states, "It didn't occur to me for many years that they were as alike as sisters, separated only by formal education"? How can people be like sisters if they do not have similar educations?

4. What were some of the "lessons in life" the narrator received from Mrs. Flowers? How important were these lessons? What is one of the first lessons in life you received? What were the circumstances surrounding this lesson?

5. What was the effect on the narrator of her visit with Mrs. Flowers? In what paragraph is this effect best expressed?

6. What writing technique does the author use to support her dominant impression of Mrs. Flowers as an elegant, refined woman? Point to specific passages in the story.

7. Occasionally the author uses words or expressions that belong to a southern vocabulary. What are some of these words or expressions? Try to explain them to the class. What do these expressions add to the story?

8. From your own reading of short stories, novels, or poems, which characters have left an impression on your view of life? Explain your answer.

Writing Assignments

1. Write an essay describing a person you know who has never graduated from high school but who has nonetheless made some valuable contributions to society. Enhance your description with vivid language.

2. In "Sister Flowers" the narrator mentions that she was so intrigued by Mrs. Flowers's home that she wanted to "gobble up the room entire." Describe in vivid details a room you will never forget because it made such a deep impression on you. Begin with a dominant impression of this room.

Internet Research Assignment

On the internet, find an image of Maya Angelou. Study her face until you can come up with a descriptive word that serves as the dominant impression of this famous female novelist. Then, develop a paragraph to support this dominant impression.

Additional Writing Assignments

1. Using *dingy* as your dominant impression, write a description of an imaginary place. Support the impression with details.
2. Describe your conception of how the ideal modern man or woman should look.
3. Go to your local supermarket, notebook in hand. Observe the scene around you, and reduce it to a single dominant impression. Write down the dominant impression and some details that support it. From these notes, develop a descriptive essay.
4. Describe your favorite nature spot or scene.
5. Describe your closest friend. Begin with a dominant impression, and develop details to support it.
6. Write a description of the worshipers in a church, chapel, synagogue, or temple.
7. Develop a descriptive essay comparing your boyfriend or girlfriend to a flower, animal, or object.
8. Write a description of a seaside resort you have visited.
9. Write a description of your favorite pet, living or dead.
10. Describe the smells of the house or apartment where you spent your childhood.
11. Write a description of any country scene during autumn.

Rewriting Assignment

A student wrote the following in an essay describing people standing in line to see the movie *No Country for Old Men*.

> The line stretched clear to the end of the block and around the corner. It was filled with people who seemed either excited by the prospect of seeing this award-winning performance or irritated at having to stand in a long line to get tickets. I was particularly struck by the many weird outfits people were wearing.

Obviously, this description lacks focus and details. Rewrite it to stick to a single dominant impression bolstered by appropriate sensory details.

Photo Writing Assignment

© Adam Nadel/Polaris

The soccer team pictured here is proudly called "The Sierra Leone Amputee Soccer Team." After studying the details of this photo, write a vivid description of these invincible athletes. Begin with a dominant impression that you support with details.

Digging for Gold or for a Dominant Impression

Like the miner, who digs to unearth a nugget of gold, the descriptive writer digs to find the common element that will sum up in a dominant impression everything about the person or scene that the senses perceive. And what the senses perceive about a scene or person is not always visual but may be a blend of sound, texture, taste, and smell. Sometimes this common element will immediately become obvious to the writer. But sometimes it will be as elusive as a mother lode to the laboring miner. In either case, the only solution for the separate quests of the miner and writer, is for both to keep digging.

Wake up your senses of sight, hearing, touch, and taste. Think about what you're perceiving. Notice how in this chapter Alexander Smith focuses on the dry land of Botswana; Joyce Carol Oates, on the stuck up, self-centered mother; Maya Angelou, on the wise black woman called "Sister Flowers." In every case, the secret to good description is awareness—looking, listening, sensing, and interpreting. Buckle down and keep digging. Eventually, you'll find the treasure you're looking for. That's the moment that you'll move from idea to essay.

Chapter 9

Examples

STORY

FLOYD DELL

We're Poor

Floyd Dell (1887–1969), advocate of pacifist and liberal causes, was a prolific novelist, playwright, and short story writer. He wrote ten novels, six books of nonfiction, several plays, and an autobiography, Homecoming *(1933), from which this excerpt comes. The excerpt poignantly recounts a child's discovery that his family is poor.*

READING FOR IDEAS Read the excerpt "We're Poor," which is as self-contained and climactic as any short story. Notice the accumulation of small representative details throughout that finally lead the narrator to the numbing conclusion at the end of the narrative. After reading the narrative, ask yourself what pattern the details of your life over the past year suggest. What kind of year has it been? What has been its main theme? Try to answer these questions in a single sentence that could serve as the controlling idea for an essay.

1   That fall, before it was discovered that the soles of both my shoes were worn clear through, I still went to Sunday school. And one time the Sunday-school superintendent made a speech to all the classes. He said that these were hard times, and that many poor children weren't getting enough to eat. It was the first that I had heard about it. He asked everybody to bring some food for the poor children next Sunday. I felt very sorry for the poor children.

2   Also, little envelopes were distributed to all the classes. Each little boy and girl was to bring money for the poor, next Sunday. The pretty Sunday-school teacher explained that we were to write our names, or have our parents write them, up in the left-hand corner of the little envelopes. . . . I told my mother all about it when I came home. And my mother gave me, the next Sunday, a small bag of potatoes to carry to Sunday school. I supposed the poor children's mothers would make potato soup out of them. . . . Potato soup was good. My father, who was quite a joker, would always say, as if he were surprised,

193

"Ah! I see we have some nourishing potato soup today!" It was so good that we had it every day. My father was at home all day long and every day, now; and I liked that, even if he was grumpy as he sat reading Grant's *Memoirs*. I had my parents all to myself, too; the others were away. My oldest brother was in Quincy, and memory does not reveal where the others were: perhaps with relatives in the country.

3   Taking my small bag of potatoes to Sunday school, I looked round for the poor children; I was disappointed not to see them. I had heard about poor children in stories. But I was told just to put my contribution with the others on the big table in the side room.

4   I had brought with me the little yellow envelope, with some money in it for the poor children. My mother had put the money in it and sealed it up. She wouldn't tell me how much money she had put in it, but it felt like several dimes. Only she wouldn't let me write my name on the envelope. I had learned to write my name, and I was proud of being able to do it. But my mother said firmly, no, I must not write my name on the envelope; she didn't tell me why. On the way to Sunday school I had pressed the envelope against the coins until I could tell what they were; they weren't dimes but pennies.

5   When I handed in my envelope, my Sunday-school teacher noticed that my name wasn't on it, and she gave me a pencil; I could write my own name, she said. So I did. But I was confused because my mother had said not to; and when I came home, I confessed what I had done. She looked distressed. "I told you not to!" she said. But she didn't explain why. . . .

6   I didn't go back to school that fall. My mother said it was because I was sick. I did have a cold the week that school opened; I had been playing in the gutters and had got my feet wet, because there were holes in my shoes. My father cut insoles out of cardboard, and I wore those in my shoes. As long as I had to stay in the house anyway, they were all right.

7   I stayed cooped up in the house, without any companionship. We didn't take a Sunday paper any more, but the Barry *Adage* came every week in the mails; and though I did not read small print, I could see the Santa Clauses and holly wreaths in the advertisements.

8   There was a calendar in the kitchen. The red days were Sundays and holidays; and that red 25 was Christmas. (It was on a Monday, and the two red figures would come right together in 1893; but this represents research in the World Almanac, not memory.) I knew when Sunday was, because I could look out of the window and see the neighbors' children, all dressed up, going to Sunday school. I knew just when Christmas was going to be.

9   But there was something queer! My father and mother didn't say a word about Christmas. And once, when I spoke of it, there was a strange, embarrassed silence; so I didn't say anything more about it. But I wondered, and was troubled. Why didn't they say anything about it? Was what I had said I wanted (memory refuses to supply that detail) too expensive?

10   I wasn't arrogant and talkative now. I was silent and frightened. What was the matter? Why didn't my father and mother say anything about Christmas? As the day approached, my chest grew tighter with anxiety.

11   Now it was the day before Christmas. I couldn't be mistaken. But not a word about it from my father and mother. I waited in painful bewilderment all day. I had supper with them, and was allowed to sit up for an hour. I was waiting for them to say something. "It's time for you to go to bed," my mother said gently. I had to say something.

12   "This is Christmas Eve, isn't it?" I asked, as if I didn't know.

13   My father and mother looked at one another. Then my mother looked away. Her face was pale and stony. My father cleared his throat, and his face took on a joking look. He pretended he hadn't known it was Christmas Eve, because he hadn't been reading the papers. He said he would go downtown and find out.

14   My mother got up and walked out of the room. I didn't want my father to have to keep on being funny about it, so I got up and went to bed. I went by myself without having a light. I undressed in the dark and crawled into bed.

15   I was numb. As if I had been hit by something. It was hard to breathe. I ached all through. I was stunned—with finding out the truth.

16   My body knew before my mind quite did. In a minute, when I could think, my mind would know. And as the pain in my body ebbed, the pain in my mind began. I knew. I couldn't put it into words yet. But I knew why I had taken only a little bag of potatoes to Sunday school that fall. I knew why there had been only pennies in my little yellow envelope. I knew why I hadn't gone to school that fall—why I hadn't any new shoes—why we had been living on potato soup all winter. All these things, and others, many others, fitted themselves together in my mind, and meant something.

17   Then the words came into my mind and I whispered them into the darkness:

18   "We're poor!"

19   That was it. I was one of those poor children I had been sorry for, when I heard about them in Sunday school. My mother hadn't told me. My father was out of work, and we hadn't any money. That was why there wasn't going to be any Christmas at our house.

20   Then I remembered something that made me squirm with shame—a boast. (Memory will not yield this up. Had I said to some Nice little boy, "I'm going to be President of the United States"? Or to a Nice little girl "I'll marry you when I grow up"? It was some boast as horribly shameful to remember.)

21   "We're poor." There in bed in the dark, I whispered it over and over to myself. I was making myself get used to it. (Or—just torturing myself, as one presses the tongue against a sore tooth? No, memory says not like that—but to keep myself from ever being such a fool again: suffering now, to keep this awful thing from ever happening again. Memory is clear on that; it was more like pulling the tooth, to get it over with—never mind the pain, this will be the end!)

22   It wasn't so bad, now that I knew. I just hadn't known! I had thought all sorts of foolish things: that I was going to Ann Arbor—going to be a lawyer—going to make speeches in the Square, going to be President. Now I knew better.

23   I had wanted (something) for Christmas. I didn't want it, now. I didn't want anything.

24   I lay there in the dark, feeling the cold emotion of renunciation. (The tendrils of desire unfold their clasp on the outer world of objects, withdraw, shrivel up. Wishes shrivel up, turn black, die. It is like that.)

25   It hurt. But nothing would ever hurt again. I would never let myself want anything again.

26   I lay there stretched out straight and stiff in the dark, my fists clenched hard upon Nothing. . . .

27   In the morning it had been like a nightmare that is not clearly remembered—that one wishes to forget. Though I hadn't hung up any stocking, there was one hanging at the foot of my bed. A bag of popcorn, and a lead pencil, for me. They had done the best they could, now they realized I knew about Christmas. But they needn't have thought they had to. I didn't want anything.

■ *Questions on Meaning and Technique*

1. How would you characterize the style of this excerpt? Why do you think the author chose to write it in this style?

2. How old was the author at the time of his discovery that his family was poor? How typical of that age does he seem in the narrative?

3. What effects of poverty did the author's family experience that seem typical for families in their situation? What effects of poverty do you regard as the worst?

4. The author relates that his mother made contributions of food and money to the poor in spite of her own family's need. What does this gesture say about her?

5. Psychologists say that small children think in very concrete terms. What passages of this excerpt seem to confirm this view?

6. In paragraphs 9 and 10, how does the author dramatize his mounting sense of suspicion and foreboding about his family's true condition?

7. What effect do you think the discovery about the poverty of his family likely had on the author's later development? What effect do you think such a discovery would be likely to have on any child?

8. The author says that his body knew the truth before his mind did. Is this plausible? Why or why not?

P O E M

JOHN LENNON AND PAUL MCCARTNEY

Eleanor Rigby

John Lennon (1940–1980) and Paul McCartney (b. 1942) were the two most prolific lyricists and composers within the musical group the Beatles. Rising out of the poverty of Liverpool, England, the Beatles, a group of four young men, were introduced to the American public on the Ed Sullivan TV show in 1964, and they immediately won the hearts of teenagers and adults alike with their music and freewheeling social opinions. Today only Paul McCartney and Ringo Starr survive; John Lennon was murdered in 1980, and George Harrison died of cancer in 2002.

READING FOR IDEAS Poetry does not always sing about birds playing in the trees or the beauties of nature. Modern poetry, especially, is just as likely to focus on the inner life of human beings—their longings, sorrows, and fears. An example of this focus is the song that follows, popularized by the Beatles, a group of singers from England whose lyrical compositions revolutionized rock music. This is a sad lyric but a touching one, that continues to appeal to our emotions.

1   Ah, look at all the lonely people!
     Ah, look at all the lonely people!

2   Eleanor Rigby
     Picks up the rice in the church where a wedding has been,
     Lives in a dream.
     Waits at the window
     Wearing the face that she keeps in a jar by the door.
     Who is it for?

3   All the lonely people,
     Where do they all come from?
     All the lonely people,
     Where do they all belong?

4   Father McKenzie,
     Writing the words of a sermon that no one will hear,
     No one comes near.

5   Look at him working,
     Darning his socks in the night when there's nobody there.
     What does he care?

6   All the lonely people,
     Where do they all come from?
     All the lonely people,
     Where do they all belong?

7   Ah, look at all the lonely people!
     Ah, look at all the lonely people!

8   Eleanor Rigby died in the church and was buried along with her name,
     Nobody came.
     Father McKenzie,
     Wiping the dirt from his hands as he walks from the grave,
     No one was saved.

9   All the lonely people,
     Where do they all come from?
     All the lonely people,
     Where do they all belong?

10   Ah, look at all the lonely people!
     Ah, look at all the lonely people!

■ *Questions on Meaning and Technique*

1. What writing technique announces that this is a song rather than a poem?

2. What theme (lesson about life) can you derive from this song? State it in one sentence.

3. One example of the lonely people in this song is Eleanor Rigby. How would you portray this woman? Describe a typical day in her life as you imagine it.

4. What is the meaning of the reference to the "face that she keeps in a jar by the door"? Explain this reference in your own words.

5. Where does Father McKenzie find his purpose in life? What keeps him going? Have you known people like him? Were they all priests, or have you known the Father McKenzie type in other professions? Explain what kinds of people they are.

6. One of the questions repeated throughout is, "Where do they [the lonely people] all come from?" Is there an answer to that question? If so, what is it?

7. Another question asked about all the lonely people is, "Where do they all belong?" What is your answer to that question?

8. What end does the lyricist contrive for Eleanor Rigby? How is Father McKenzie involved in her end? What greater meaning does this twist of fate have?

9. While we cannot help but see the hopeless failure of these two creatures—Eleanor Rigby and Father McKenzie—the authors do not seem to blame them or castigate them. Whom do they subtly blame?

10. In this world filled with despair, what can we as individuals do to soften the predicament of those who are lonely and hopeless?

How to Write with Examples

An *example* is an illustration that unmistakably clarifies and enforces the point you are making. During the Middle Ages, most sermons ended with an *exemplum,* a little story that illustrated some important religious truth. Knowing that these stories would awaken dozing audiences and instill them with zeal or fear, the church priests told vivid tales about the evils of money and the dangers of disobedience. The example is still favored in prose writing as a means of proving a point or explaining an idea.

Writing Assignment

Write an essay that uses at least three extended examples to support the thesis that poverty exists in your neighborhood, town, or state.

Specific Instructions

Prewrite on the assignment.   The assignment calls for an essay that develops three extended examples of poverty in your neighborhood, town, or state. By extended example, we mean an example developed in some detail and extended over the course of several sentences or paragraphs. The following example is not extended:

> "Women's language" shows up in all levels of English. For example, women are encouraged to make far more precise discriminations in naming colors than men do. Words like "mauve," "beige," "ecru," "aquamarine," "lavender," and so on, are unremarkable in a woman's vocabulary, but largely absent from that of most men.
>
> —Robin Lakoff, "Women's Language"

Here, on the other hand, is a legitimate extended example:

> Years ago some people accused of serious crimes pleaded "insanity." Today they are often charged with it. Instead of receiving a brief jail sentence, a defendant may be branded "insane" and incarcerated *for life* in a psychiatric institution.
>
> This is what happened, for example, to a filling-station operator I will call Joe Skulski. When he was told to move his business to make way for a new shopping center, he stubbornly resisted eviction. Finally the police were summoned. Joe greeted them with a warning shot in the air. He was taken into custody and denied bail, because the police considered his protest peculiar and thought he must be crazy. The district attorney requested a pretrial psychiatric examination of the accused. Mr. Skulski was examined, pronounced mentally unfit to stand trial, and confined in the state hospital for the criminally insane. Through it all, he pleaded for the right to be tried for his offense. Now in the mental hospital he will spend years of fruitless effort to prove that he is sane enough to stand trial. If convicted, his prison sentence would have been shorter than the term he has already served in the hospital.
>
> —Thomas S. Szasz, M.D., "What Psychiatry Can and Cannot Do"

Because the topic is already specified in the wording of the assignment, the aim of your prewriting efforts should be to find the area of poverty in your neighborhood, town, or state you wish to cover and to amass specific details that you can include in your examples. If you are like most of us, you will find poverty just around the corner. As a prewriting activity, we suggest you take a drive to the affected area and look it over for yourself. Try to group your impressions under three obvious signs of poverty: perhaps the ruined state of the houses, the neglected condition of the streets, the messy appearance of the residents. Or you may prefer, instead, to illustrate poverty in your town by writing about three symptoms of it—perhaps homelessness, high unemployment, and skyrocketing crime rates.

Personal observation usually provides the most vivid details for examples, but you may be among the lucky few to live in a neighborhood and adjoining town that is entirely free of poverty. If that is the case, you will have to resort to library research to find information about poverty in your state. (Unfortunately, no state is entirely free of poverty.) Newspapers and regional magazines can usually provide you with all the facts and information you need. Again, remember to look for material that can be used in three extended examples.

Use examples that are relevant.   An example has failed if it does not help your reader see the truth of what you are saying. The following example misses the point:

> As the Bible says, there is a right time for everything—even for being born and for dying. For example, the other day I failed my social science test. The day before had been beastly hot—90 degrees in the shade—and I just didn't feel like studying, so I stretched out on the couch, fanning myself and watching TV. I guess it was my time to die intellectually because when the exam was handed back, it was decorated with a big fat F.

The example is too trivial to illustrate such a serious philosophic truth. The biblical reference deserves a more significant example. On the other hand, the following passage uses an example that is exactly to the point:

> Some people will do the strangest things to gain fame. For example, there are those who go in for various kinds of marathons, dancing or kissing or blowing bubble gum for days at a time, to get their names in the paper or in a record book of some kind. Then there are people who sit on flagpoles or who perch on the ledges of skyscrapers for a week or more, apparently enjoying the attention they receive from the crowd below. There are people who hope to be remembered by someone because they ate the most cream pies or because they collected the most bottle tops. And there are even people who seek public notice by way of setting a record for the number of articles of clothing they can put on at one time or the number they can take off. Of course, there are a few mentally twisted individuals who seek fame at the expense of other people's property or even lives, but fortunately the great majority of people satisfy their urge to be remembered in ways that produce little more damage than tired lips or a bad case of indigestion.
>
> —Sheila Y. Graham, *Writingcraft*

These examples do a good job of illustrating the idea that "Some people will do the strangest things to gain fame."

Use details to make your example vivid.   Many examples are ineffective because they are vague rather than vivid. Consider the vague and consequently boring example in this passage:

> There is no control over memory. Sometimes one remembers the most trivial details. For example, I remember trivial things about my father, about pieces of furniture in our house, and about insignificant places that I once visited. I even remember a particular shopping spree that took place a long time ago.

Writing Tip

Using the Mongrel

The example tends to be the mongrel among the patterns of development because nearly all of the rhetorical patterns will occasionally draw on examples to make a point even though the purpose of the paragraph may be something quite different, such as a comparison/contrast. For this reason, some writers about rhetoric do not feature the example as a stand-alone pattern. If you find yourself using examples in a paragraph that is meant to define, don't be surprised. That's normal for the mongrel.

Now observe how the same ideas come to life through the use of detailed examples:

> There is no control over memory. Soon you find yourself being vague about an event which seemed so important at the time that you thought you'd never forget it. Or unable to recall the face of someone who you could have sworn was there forever. On the other hand, trivial and meaningless memories may stay with you for life. I can still shut my eyes and see Victoria grinding coffee on the pantry steps, the glass bookcase and the books in it, my father's pipe rack, the leaves of the sandbox tree, the wallpaper of the bedroom in some shabby hotel, the hairdresser in Antibes. It's in this way that I remember buying the pink Milanese-silk underclothes, the assistant who sold them to me, and coming into Bond Street holding the parcel.
>
> —Jean Rhys, *The New Yorker,* April 26, 1976

Vividness is the basic difference between the first and second passages. The first passage lacks details, whereas the second is rich with them.

When necessary, establish a clear connection between your example and the point you are making.   This advice is particularly important when you begin an essay or a paragraph with an example. Consider the following:

> A 13-year-old girl has had one leg amputated, but three times a week she is put through the humiliation of being forced to change into gym shorts. Says the teacher, "Those are the rules, and there's no reason you can't keep score while the other girls play."
>
> A high school teacher accidentally bumps into the upraised hand of a girl who wants to ask a question. The teacher cries out that the girl is trying to strike her and that if it happens again, she'll call the police.
>
> A first-grade teacher forces a boy to sit all day in a wastepaper basket as punishment for being noisy. When an assistant principal orders the boy's release after 2½ hours, it is some minutes before he can stand up straight. He can barely limp to his seat.

Without a connecting comment, these examples are puzzling. The reader wonders what they are intended to illustrate. The following paragraph makes clear the connection between the examples and the point they illustrate:

> These are all documented cases of teacher ineptitude, insensitivity or brutishness. While the overwhelming majority of America's teachers are professionally competent and sensitive to children's needs, there are enough who are unfit to cause concern among both parents and school administrators.
>
> —Bernard Bard, "Unfeeling Teachers?"

Connective expressions commonly used to introduce an example are *for example, to illustrate, for instance,* and *a case in point is.* Frequently, however, writers will omit a formal connective in introducing their examples provided the context makes clear what is being illustrated:

> People who sneer at "fancy theories" and prefer to rely on common sense and everyday experience are often in fact the victims of extremely vague and sweeping hypotheses. This morning's newspaper contains a letter from a young person in Pennsylvania who was once "one of a group of teenage pot smokers. Then a girl in the crowd got pregnant. Her baby was premature and deformed and needed two operations." The newspaper's adviser to the teenage lovelorn printed that letter approvingly, as evidence that the price of smoking marijuana is high.
>
> —Paul Heyne and Thomas Johnson, *Toward Economic Understanding*

This passage clearly illustrates what is meant by "victims of . . . vague and sweeping hypotheses." No connective phrase is necessary; the connection is established by the context.

PROFESSIONAL MODEL

WENDELL BERRY

Are You All Right?

Wendell Berry (b. 1934) is one of Kentucky's most admired fiction writers and cultural critics. He is a prolific author of novels, short stories, poems, and essays. After attending Stanford University and studying under Wallace Stegner, Berry produced his first novel, Northern Coulter *(1961). A notable year for Berry was 1965, when he moved to a farm he had purchased in Kentucky. Working as a farmer—growing tobacco, corn, and small grain—provided the background for Berry's most popular works. Berry has written eleven novels and twenty-three short stories. Collected in an anthology titled* Distant Land *(2004), the short stories form a chronicle of the fictional small Kentucky town of Port William, populated with a variety of memorable characters. A theme running throughout Berry's fiction is the importance of frugality, reverence for the land, and the interconnectedness of life—a life where good neighbors are a gift to be cherished.*

READING FOR IDEAS This is the kind of writing that defies classification. It is not a short story, though it has strong narrative elements. It is not a memoir, though it relates an episode from the narrator's past. It builds to a climactic moment that is immediately deflated. Yet its pacing is suspenseful and its descriptive passages so rich and imaginative that the ending of the piece is almost unexpected. Along the way we learn about the ethic of caring that exists among hardy and self-sufficient country folk.

1   The spring work had started, and I needed a long night's rest, or that was my opinion, and I was about to go to bed, but then the telephone rang. It was Elton. He had been getting ready for bed, too, I think, and it had occurred to him then that he was worried.

2   "Andy, when did you see the Rowanberrys?"

3   I knew what he had on his mind. The river was in flood. The backwater was over the bottoms, and Art and Mart would not be able to get out except by boat or on foot.

4   "Not since the river came up."

5   "Well, neither have I. And their phone's out. Mary, when did Mart call up here?"

6   I heard Mary telling him, "Monday night," and then, "It was Monday night," Elton said to me. "I've tried to call every day since, and I can't get anybody. That's four days."

7   "Well, surely they're all right."

8   "Well, that's what Mary and I have been saying. Surely they are. They've been taking care of themselves a long time. But, then, you never know."

9   "The thing is, we don't know."

10   We knew what we were doing, and both of us were a little embarrassed about it. The Rowanberry Place had carried that name since the first deeds were recorded in the log cabin that was the first courthouse at Hargrave. Rowanberrys had been taking care of themselves there for the better part of two hundred years. We knew that Arthur and Martin Rowanberry required as little worrying about as anybody alive. But now, in venturing to worry about them, we had put them, so to speak, under the sign of mortality. They were, after all, the last of the Rowanberrys, and they were getting old. We were uneasy in being divided from them by the risen water and out of touch. It caused us to think of things that could happen.

11   Elton said, "It's not hard, you know, to think of things that could happen."

12   "Well," I said, "do you think we'd better go see about them?"

13   He laughed. "Well, we've thought, haven't we? I guess we'd better go."

14   "All right. I'll meet you at the mailbox."

15   I hung up and went to get my cap and jacket.

16   "Nobody's heard from Art and Mart for four days," I said to Flora. "Their phone's out."

17   "And you and Elton are going to see about them," Flora said. She had been eavesdropping.

18   "I guess we are."

19   Flora was inclined to be amused at the way Elton and I imagined the worst. She did not imagine the worst. She just dealt with mortality as it happened.

20   I picked up a flashlight as I went out the door, but it was not much needed. The moon was big, bright enough to put out most of the stars. I walked out to the mailbox and made myself comfortable, leaning against it. Elton and I had obliged ourselves to worry about the Rowanberrys, but I was glad all the same for the excuse to be out. The night was still, the country all silvery with moonlight, inlaid with bottomless shadows, and the air shimmered with the trilling of peepers from every stream and pond margin for miles, one full-throated sound filling the ears so that it seemed impossible that you could hear anything else.

21   And yet I heard Elton's pickup while it was still a long way off, and then light glowed in the air, and then I could see his headlights. He turned into the lane and stopped and pushed the door open for me. I made room for myself among a bundle of empty feed sacks, two buckets, and a chain saw.

22   "Fine night," he said. He had lit a cigarette, and the cab was fragrant with smoke.

23   "It couldn't be better, could it?"

24   "Well, the moon could be just a little brighter, and it could be a teensy bit warmer."

25   I could hear that he was grinning. He was in one of his companionable moods, making fun of himself.

26   I laughed, and we rode without talking up out of the Katy's Branch valley and turned onto the state road.

27   "It's awful the things that can get into your mind," Elton said. "I'd hate it if anything was to happen to them."

28   The Rowanberrys were Elton's friends, and because they were his, they were mine. Elton had known them ever since he was just a little half-orphan boy, living with his mother and older brothers on the next farm up the creek. He had got a lot of his raising by being underfoot and in the way at the Rowanberrys'. And in the time of his manhood, the Rowanberry Place had been one of his resting places.

29   Elton worked hard and worried hard, and he was often in need of rest. But he had a restless mind, which meant that he could not rest on his own place in the presence of his own work. If he rested there, first he would begin to think about what he had to do, and then he would begin to do it.

30   To rest, he needed to be in somebody else's place. We spent a lot of Sunday afternoons down at the Rowanberrys' on the porch looking out into the little valley in the summertime, inside by the stove if it was winter. Art and Mart batched there together after their mother died, and in spite of the electric lights and telephone and a few machines, they lived a life that would have been recognizable to Elias Rowanberry, who had marked his X in the county's first deed book—a life that involved hunting and fishing and foraging as conventionally as it involved farming. They practiced an old-fashioned independence, an old-fashioned generosity, and an old-fashioned fidelity to their word and their

friends. And they were hound men of the old correct school. They would not let a dog tree anywhere in earshot, day or night, workday or Sunday, without going to him. "It can be a nuisance," Art said, "but it don't hardly seem right to disappoint 'em."

31   Mart was the one Elton liked best to work with. Mart was not only a fine hand but had a gift for accommodating himself to the rhythms and ways of his partner. "He can think your thoughts," Elton said. Between the two of them was a sympathy of body and mind that they had worked out and that they trusted with an unshaken, unspoken trust. And so Elton was always at ease and quiet in Mart's company when they were at rest.

32   Art was the rememberer. He knew what he knew and what had been known by a lot of dead kinfolks and neighbors. They lived on in his mind and spoke there, reminding him and us of things that needed to be remembered. Art had a compound mind, as a daisy has a compound flower, and his mind had something of the unwary comeliness of a daisy. Something that happened would remind him of something that he remembered, which would remind him of something that his grandfather remembered. It was not that he "lived in his mind." He lived in the place, but the place was where the memories were, and he walked among them, tracing them out over the living ground. That was why we loved him.

33   We followed the state road along the ridges toward Port William and then at the edge of town turned down the Sand Ripple Road. We went down the hill through the woods, and as we came near the floor of the valley, Elton went more carefully and we began to watch. We crossed a little board culvert that rattled under the wheels, eased around a bend, and there was the backwater, the headlights glancing off it into the treetops, the road disappearing into it.

34   Elton stopped the truck. He turned off his headlights and the engine, and the quietness of the moonlight and the woods came down around us. I could hear the peepers again. It was wonderful what the road going under the water did to that place. It was not only that we could not go where we were used to going; it was as if a thought that we were used to thinking could not be thought.

35   "Listen!" Elton said. He had heard a barred owl off in the woods. He quietly rolled the window down.

36   And then, right overhead, an owl answered: "HOOOOOAWWW!"

37   And the far one said, "Hoo hoo hoohooaw!"

38   "Listen!" Elton said again. He was whispering.

39   The owls went through their whole repertory of hoots and clucks and cackles and gobbles.

40   "Listen to them!" Elton said. "They've got a lot on their minds." Being in the woods at night excited him. He was a hunter. And we were excited by the flood's interruption of the road. The rising of the wild water had moved us back in time.

41   Elton quietly opened his door and got out and then, instead of slamming the door, just pushed it to. I did the same and came around and followed him as he walked slowly down the road, looking for a place to climb out of the cut.

42   Once we had climbed the bank and stepped over the fence and were walking among the big trees, we seemed already miles from the truck. The water gleamed over the bottomlands below us on our right; you could not see that there had ever been a road in that

place. I followed Elton along the slope through the trees. Neither of us thought to use a flashlight, though we each had one, nor did we talk. The moon gave plenty of light. We could see everything—underfoot the blooms of twinleaf, bloodroot, rue anemone, the little stars of spring beauties, and overhead the littlest branches, even the blooms on the sugar maples. The ground was soft from the rain, and we hardly made a sound. The flowers around us seemed to float in the shadows so that we walked like waders among stars, uncertain how far down to put our feet. And over the broad shine of the backwater, the calling of the peepers rose like another flood, higher than the water flood, and thrilled and trembled in the air.

43   It was a long walk because we had to go around the inlets of the backwater that lay in every swag and hollow. Way off, now and again, we could hear the owls. Once we startled a deer and stood still while it plunged away into the shadows. And always we were walking among flowers. I wanted to keep thinking that they were like stars, but after a while I could not think so. They were not like stars. They did not have that hard, distant glitter. And yet in their pale, peaceful way, they shone. They collected their little share of light and gave it back. Now and then, when we came to an especially thick patch of them, Elton would point. Or he would raise his hand and we would stop a minute and listen to the owls.

44   I was wider awake than I had been since morning. I would have been glad to go on walking all night long. Around us we could feel the year coming, as strong and wide and irresistible as a wind.

45   But we were thinking, too, of the Rowanberrys. That we were in a mood to loiter and did not loiter would have reminded us of them, if we had needed reminding. To go to their house, with the water up, would have required a long walk from any place we could have started. We were taking the shortest way, which left us with the problem that it was going to be a little too short. The best we could do, this way, would be to come down the valley until we would be across from the house but still divided from it by a quarter mile or more of backwater. We could call to them from there. But what if we got no answer? What if the answer was trouble? Well, they had a boat over there. If they needed us, one of them could set us over in the boat. But what if we got no answer? What if, to put the best construction upon silence, they could not hear us? Well, we could only go as near as we could get and call.

46   So if our walk had the feeling of a ramble, it was not one. We were going as straight to the Rowanberrys' house as the water and the lay of the land would allow. After a while we began to expect to see a light. And then we began to wonder if there was a light to see.

47   Elton stopped. "I thought we'd have seen their light by now."

48   I said, "They're probably asleep."

49   Those were the first words we had spoken since we left the truck. After so long, in so much quiet, our voices sounded small.

50   Elton went on among the trees and the shadows, and I followed him. We climbed over a little shoulder of the slope then and saw one window shining. It was the light of an oil lamp, so their electricity was out, too.

51   "And now we're found," Elton said. He sang it, just that much of the old hymn, almost in a whisper.

52   We went through a little more of the woods and climbed the fence into the Rowanberrys' hill pasture. We could see their big barn standing up black now against the moonlight on the other side of the road, which was on high ground at that place, clear of the backwater.

53   When we were on the gravel we could hear our steps. We walked side by side, Elton in one wheel track, I in the other, until the road went under the water again. We were as close to the house then as we could get without a boat. We stopped and considered the distance.

54   And then Elton cupped his hands around his mouth, and called, "Ohhhhh, Mart! Ohhhhh, Art!"

55   We waited, it seemed, while Art had time to say, "Did you hear somebody?" and Mart to answer, "Well, I thought so." We saw light come to another window, as somebody picked up a lamp and opened the hall door. We heard the front door open. And then Art's voice came across the water: "Yeeeaaah?"

56   And Elton called back, "Are you aaalll riiight?"

57   I knew they were. They were all right, and we were free to go back through the woods and home to sleep.

58   But now I know that it was neither of the Rowanberrys who was under the sign of mortality that night. It was Elton. Before another April came he would be in his grave on the hill at Port William. Old Art Rowanberry, who had held him on his lap, would survive him by a dozen years.

59   And now that both of them are dead, I love to think of them standing with the shining backwater between them, while Elton's voice goes out across the distance, is heard and answered, and the other voice travels back: "Yeeeaaah!"

■ *Vocabulary*

deeds (10)	companionable (25)	comeliness (32)
venturing (10)	foraging (30)	culvert (33)
obliged (20)	conventionally (30)	repertory 39)
peepers (20)	compound (32)	swag (43)

■ *Questions on Meaning and Technique*

1. What is the connection between this story and its title? When is the connection revealed? How important is the title to the meaning of the story?

2. Who is the narrator of the story? What advantage to the reader is his point of view?

3. The story contains many vividly descriptive passages. Choose the one that appeals to you most and explain why you find it especially appealing.

4. What triggered Elton and Andy's worry about the Rowanberrys? Is the worry justified? Explain your answer.

5. What contrasting personality traits do the two Rowanberry brothers reveal? How would you summarize the kind of person each brother is?

6. What does the narrator mean when he uses the term "under the sign of mortality"? To whom does he think the term applies that night of the flood? What is ironic about his belief?

7. How does the author use sound to create mood? Give at least two examples of this technique.

8. What is the author illustrating with his story about two men walking through the woods to find out if a neighbor is out of harm's way?

Writing Assignments

1. Looking back on your experiences with people, write an extended example of what you think is true friendship. Make sure that your example is convincing.

2. Write an essay in which you offer three brief examples of the meaning of friendship. Base the example on your own experience.

STUDENT ESSAY—FIRST DRAFT

This anecdote makes a good introduction by focusing on a specific example of poverty.

The revision connects the introduction with the rest of the paper.

Tom Meade

Poverty in Atlanta

Insert A

                                                    the
[1]   People living in plush surroundings of North Atlanta may be fully isolated from

the real world of grinding poverty ~~in their great city. Poverty is undoubtedly visible~~

Insert B
~~in most third world countries, but it~~ has sifted its way into this booming city of
                                                    thought
opportunity--Atlanta. One chilling ~~fact that is~~ almost incomprehensible to most
                        that some people actually have no home, no place to live.
Atlantans is ~~the thought of someone's not have a home,~~
    What a degrading condition!

Insert A
Jan Trimble, age 50, lived in a local mental hospital during most of her adult life. Because she was not deemed dangerous to herself and others, she was forced to move to the streets two years ago when funding cuts were made at her institution. She now exists by foraging through dumpsters for food, and she finds shelter from the biting cold at night under stacks of cardboard boxes. All of her worldly goods are contained in a grimy, brown shopping bag.

Insert B
as experienced by Jan Trimble. Although newspapers and television have graphically portrayed the poverty in Third World countries such as Ethiopia and Bangladesh, they have not made equally visible the poverty that

[2]   ~~There are~~ An estimated five to ten thousand homeless people survive in Atlanta. Many of them are also plagued by other personal problems, such as alcohol, drugs, mental illness, divorce, or job loss--problems for which state agencies ~~need to take more~~ take little or no responsibility and do not begin to solve ~~in solving~~.

[3]   Working as a security guard in Atlanta, I am regularly exposed to the reality of poverty in various communities. The picture of old people hunched over picking up tin cans on the sidewalks is permanently etched in my memory. On blustery days, I have crossed paths with these people and have felt compassion as I ~~see~~ have seen their torn coats, their dirty shirts, their floppy old hats, and their dilapidated shoes worn without socks. I have instinctively drawn back from their toothless faces and reeking breath because the sight and smell was unpleasant--certainly not to be compared with the well-heeled look and pleasant scent of my family members or friends. Striking up a conversation with some of these poverty-stricken individuals is difficult ~~at times~~. They stutter and mumble. And even when one can distinguish individual words, the meanings of their sentences are untranslatable gibberish. However, they make it very clear when they are begging for money. *Move entire ¶ to end.*

[4]   One encouraging note in all this is ~~the fact~~ that there is a growing interest in helping the poor of Atlanta. For example, at a south-side elementary school gymnasium, Atlanta City Councilman Jabari Simama recently urged old-guard Black leaders to share their new-found economic gains with the poor. "Our real threat," he said, "is our failure up until now to extend opportunities to poor people." Moreover, House Speaker Tom Murphy's plan to seek five to ten million dollars in government funds for homeless shelters reassures us that perhaps something will be done soon ~~for~~ on behalf of the thousands for whom shelters do not exist. Although these funds will not be available ~~for eight months, the fact they are envisioned~~ tomorrow or even next month, envisioning them is a move in the right direction. Unfortunately, ~~no one can deny the fact that~~ far too many corpse bags will ~~be~~ continue to be filled before the project is completed. Death ~~is~~ a common, everyday occurrence for the poor.

[5]   Many of us remember reading or seeing news coverage about the pitiful demise of Nicholas Paul Burke, the twenty-three-month-old son of Mike and Anne Burke. He died at a

No new paragraph is needed. This passage simply clarifies the thesis.

Consistent tense

Details support contrast.

Editing improves logic.

Moving this paragraph to the end of the essay allows it to offer readers some hope. The last sentence is a strong ending.

Perhaps adds caution and avoids repetition of for.

Better emphasis

shelter for the homeless in a fire so intense that it drove away all would-be rescuers. Nicholas

died from a condition no medical examiner lists as a cause of death--homelessness. Nicholas

received a ~~brief~~ *paltry* funeral, paid for by a public who ~~felt guilty,~~ *wanted to expiate its general guilt for having neglected the helpless.* but much too often bodies like

~~his~~ *this child's* go unclaimed and unidentified. Faces remain nameless. Graves go unmarked.

[6]   ~~One~~ *An* irony that strikes ~~me~~ *one with force* is the juxtaposition of poverty and wealth*in Atlanta.* The grounds

of Georgia State University ~~in Atlanta is~~ *are* a good example. Here ~~the well heeled~~ *prosperous members of the* middle

class congregate habitually for picnics preceding football games. They spread out

their delicious food on tables--fried chicken, barbequed meatballs, multiple salads

of potato, beans, and macaroni. They laugh and joke as they fill their stomachs with

these delicacies, washing them down with Coca-Cola or beer. Then they wrap up the

leftovers, packing them into coolers or baskets, and head for their nice new cars that

will take them to the game just blocks away. On the way they pass the Baptist church,

where a line of shabby-looking, disheveled men ~~have gathered~~ *has formed* to wait for a bowl of soup

and a piece of bread. This group of indigents stands in sharp contrast to the group on

their way to the football game. The poor are silent; their eyes are hollow; their expression

is haggard. The affluent are laughing; their eyes sparkle with joie de vivre; their

expression is self-satisfied. While the football ~~lovers~~ *fans* had overindulged on picnic food,

these poor men had been standing around for hours, *hungrily* waiting for soup and bread.

[7]   The holidays are a time when the poor of Atlanta receive public attention. *Urgent appeals for clothes* ~~Cries for~~

~~coats~~, food, and money are issued from pulpits, *over* the radio, and *through* street ~~solicitors~~ *solicitations.*. Christmas

meals are donated in churches and rescue missions. But one wonders if the donors who

give away ~~extra~~ *superfluous* coats, canned goods, and loose cash really understand what it means to

be poor all year long and to live daily without the basic sustenance taken for granted by

the rest of society.

[8]   ~~It is clearly evident that Atlanta has a current crisis of poverty. Ignoring the crisis will~~

~~not make it disappear. In fact poverty, which is one of life's most degrading problems, is a~~

~~growing issue. Quoting from a recent motion picture. "The needs of the many outweigh~~

~~the needs of the few."~~

Margin notes:

Smoother text, more specificity about public guilt

An avoids repeating one.

Well-heeled has already been used two paragraphs earlier.

Lines don't "gather."

Italicize foreign words.

Better parallelism

With the new ending in place, this paragraph becomes surplus.

delete

Meade 1

Tom Meade

Professor Winkler

English 101

February 9, 2001

Poverty in Atlanta

1   Jan Trimble, age 50, lived in a local mental hospital during most of her adult life. Because she was not deemed dangerous to herself and others, she was forced to move to the streets two years ago when funding cuts were made at her institution. She now exists by foraging through dumpsters for food, and she finds shelter from the biting cold at night under stacks of cardboard boxes. All of her worldly goods are contained in a grimy, brown shopping bag.

2   People living in the plush surroundings of North Atlanta may be fully isolated from the real world of grinding poverty as experienced by Jan Trimble. Although newspapers and television have graphically portrayed the poverty in Third World countries such as Ethiopia and Bangladesh, they have not made equally visible the poverty that has sifted its way into this booming city of opportunity--Atlanta. One chilling thought almost incomprehensible to most Atlantans is that some people actually have no home, no place to live. What a degrading condition! An estimated five to ten thousand homeless people survive in Atlanta. Many of them are also plagued by other personal problems, such as alcohol, drugs, mental illness, divorce,

Meade 2

or job loss--problems for which state agencies take little or no responsibility and do not begin to solve.

3   Working as a security guard in Atlanta, I am regularly exposed to the reality of poverty in various communities. The picture of old people hunched over, picking up tin cans on the sidewalks, is permanently etched in my memory. On blustery days, I have crossed paths with these people and have felt compassion as I have seen their torn coats, their dirty shirts, their floppy old hats, and their dilapidated shoes worn without socks. I have instinctively drawn back from their toothless faces and reeking breath because the sight and smell were unpleasant--certainly not to be compared with the well-heeled look and pleasant scent of my family members or friends. Striking up a conversation with some of these poverty-stricken individuals is difficult. They stutter and mumble. And even when one can distinguish individual words, the meanings of their sentences are untranslatable gibberish. However, they make it very clear when they are begging for money.

4   Many of us remember reading or seeing news coverage about the pitiful demise of Nicholas Paul Burke, the twenty-three-month-old son of Mike and Anne Burke. He died at a shelter for the homeless in a fire so intense that it drove away all would-be rescuers. Nicholas died from a condition no medical examiner lists as a cause of death--homelessness. Nicholas received a paltry funeral, paid for by the public who wanted to expiate its general guilt for having neglected the helpless, but much too often bodies like this child's

Meade 3

go unclaimed and unidentified. Faces remain nameless. Graves go unmarked.

5 An irony that strikes one with force is the juxtaposition of poverty and wealth in Atlanta. The grounds of Georgia State University are a good example. Here prosperous members of the middle class congregate habitually for picnics preceding football games. They spread out their delicious food on tables--fried chicken, barbequed meatballs, multiple salads of potato, beans, and macaroni. They laugh and joke as they fill their stomachs with these delicacies, washing them down with Coca-Cola or beer. Then they wrap up the leftovers, packing them into coolers or baskets, and head for their nice new cars that will take them to the game just blocks away. On the way they pass the Baptist church, where a line of shabby-looking, disheveled men has formed to wait for a bowl of soup and a piece of bread. This group of indigents stands in sharp contrast to the group on their way to the football game. The poor are silent; their eyes are hollow; their expression is haggard. The affluent are laughing; their eyes sparkle with *joie de vivre*; their expression is self-satisfied. While the football fans had overindulged on picnic food, these poor men had been standing around for hours, hungrily waiting for soup and bread.

6 The holidays are a time when the poor of Atlanta receive public attention. Urgent appeals for clothes, food, and money are issued from pulpits, over the radio, and through street solicitations. Christmas meals are donated in churches and rescue missions. But one wonders

Meade 4

if the donors who give away superfluous coats, canned goods, and loose cash really understand what it means to be poor all year long and to live daily without the basic sustenance taken for granted by the rest of society.

7   One encouraging note in all this is that there is a growing interest in helping the poor of Atlanta. For example, at a south-side elementary school gymnasium, Atlanta City Councilman Jabari Simama recently urged old-guard Black leaders to share their new-found economic gains with the poor. "Our real threat," he said, "is our failure up until now to extend opportunities to poor people." Moreover, House Speaker Tom Murphy's plan to seek five to ten million dollars in government funds for homeless shelters reassures us that perhaps something will be done soon on behalf of the thousands for whom shelters do not exist. Although these funds will not be available tomorrow or even next month, envisioning them is a move in the right direction. Unfortunately, far too many corpse bags will be filled before the project is completed. For the poor, death will continue to be a common, everyday occurrence.

FURTHER READING

AMMON SHEA

The Keypad Solution

Published: January 22, 2010

Ammon Shea is the author of four books on obscure words in English: Depraved English *(1999),* Insulting English *(2001),* Depraved and Insulting English *(2002), and* Reading the OED *(2009)—the first three co-authored with Peter Novobatzky.*

While Shea refuses to label himself a lexicographer, he spends much of his time studying dictionaries and commenting on words. He insists that dictionaries are "fun" to read. He has been seen as "tireless" and even "obsessed" in his quest for strange words with odd meanings.

READING FOR IDEAS   What ties the essay below to student writing is its speculation about how influential texting may be in the future of what will pass as correct spelling. Will certain texting abbreviations eventually enter our dictionaries as an accepted part of spelling protocol, or will they vanish when the novelty of texting has worn out? That is a question you might enjoy pondering. How important and useful do you consider the texting style, and how permanent do you see it becoming?

1   **There is a long** and noble history of trying to change the English language's notoriously illogical system of spelling. The fact that *through, rough, dough, plough, hiccough* and *trough* all end with *-ough,* yet none of them sound the same as any of the others, is the sort of thing that has been vexing poets and learners of English for quite some time. Proponents of "fixing" this wayward orthography have included some of the most prominent names in American history. *Benjamin Franklin* suggested changing the alphabet, and *Andrew Carnegie* provided money for people to study the problem. *President Theodore Roosevelt* issued an edict in 1906 that gave the Government Printing Office a list of 300 words with new spellings: problem cases like *artisan, kissed* and *woe* were to be changed to *artizan, kist* and *wo*. Roosevelt was largely ignored by the G.P.O., and the matter was soon dropped. Although this issue has been extensively studied and argued over by these and other eminent thinkers, there has been an almost complete lack of success in effecting any substantial progress.

2   And so it is rather bizarre that the first widespread change in how people spell English words appears to have come from a group of (largely) young people sending *text messages* to one another with cellular phones and other electronic devices. You may not like seeing the phrase "LOL—U R gr8" on the page, but it is common enough that you are likely to understand it. Why have such inadvertent "reforms" succeeded where generations of dedicated intellectual attempts have not? And will they last?

3   For most of the history of the language, English speakers took a lackadaisical approach to spelling; the notion that a word should always be spelled the same way is a much more recent invention than the language itself. The standardization of English spelling began in the 16th century, and although it is unclear at exactly what point our spelling became set, what is certain is that ever since it happened, people have complained that the rules of spelling, such as they are, just don't make sense.

4   Perhaps the most successful attempt at spelling reform (at least in America) was wrought by Noah Webster, who managed to forever make Americans view the British *honour* and *theatre* as off-kilter. Some portion of Webster's determination to change *-our* to *-or* and *-re* to *-er* was due to nationalist fervor; he wanted his countrymen to break free of the orthographic bonds of their oppressors. He was noticeably less successful in

convincing Americans of the utility of many of his other ideas, like spelling *oblique* as *obleek, machine* as *masheen* and *prove* as *proov.*

5   I contacted several of the spelling-reform organizations in operation today to ask them about their feelings on adopting text-messaging shorthands as a kind of spelling reform. Alan Mole, the president of the American Literacy Council, when asked if his group had ever considered allying itself with the texters, said that it had not, although he added that text messaging "does serve the purpose of raising consciousness" about the fact "that there are different ways of making people spell." The council, which has picketed the Scripps National Spelling Bee, prefers its own phonetic method of spelling reform, called SoundSpel. The group offers a downloadable version of SoundSpel (ententetranslator.com/IDL.htm) that can instantly translate an entire novel's worth of standard English into a more spellable, if less recognizable, form.

6   The sister organization of the council, the British-based Spelling Society, does not advocate adopting texting conventions, either, but this is less surprising, because it does not advocate adopting any particular approach at all. Jack Bovill, the society's president, wrote in an e-mail message: "Our present aim is to raise awareness of the problems caused by the irregularity of English spelling. We DO NOT support solutions."

7   Whether texting conventions are supported by organized spelling reformists or not, can they possibly solve the difficulty of spelling our troublesome language? David Crystal, the author of "Txtng: The Gr8 Db8," told me in an e-mail message that "there's nothing in texting to suggest spelling reform," noting that texting relies heavily on abbreviations, which he sees as creative stylings, not systematic improvements. He added that there is very little that is new about most of the abbreviations and lexical shortenings that make texting so maddening to so many. In fact, he said, with the exception of a few recent coinages like *LOL,* "virtually all the commonly used ones can be found in English a century ago." For example, *bn* (been), *btwn* (between) and *wd* (would) can all be found in a 1942 dictionary of abbreviations.

8   Naomi Baron, a professor of linguistics at American University and author of "Always On: Language in an Online and Mobile World," shares Crystal's view. She predicts that the number of "textisms" will stop growing as people continue to develop more proficiency in using handheld devices and as the devices continue to grow more sophisticated than simple telephone touch pads. She adds that part of the appeal of texting shorthands is their novelty, and that that will fade.

9   Crystal did say that a certain amount of spelling reform might eventually come from the Internet: "People who try to impose reform 'top down' rarely succeed. But a 'bottom up' movement might well have some permanent effects." Given that the general attitude toward text messaging is that it comes from the linguistic bottom, it may well be that this *masheen*-sent lingua franca may *proov* to one day be less *obleek* than it is now.

Source: Ammon Shea, "The Keypad Solution." *The New York Times Magazine,* Jan 22, 2010. Retrieved from <New York Times.com.> Jan. 24, 2010.

■ *Vocabulary*

notoriously (1)	lackadaisical (3)	advocate (6)
orthography (1)	wrought (4)	coinages (7)
inadvertent (2)	phonetic (5)	

■ *Questions on Meaning and Technique*

1. Of the three suggestions for making English spelling more consistent, submitted by Benjamin Franklin, Andrew Carnegie, and President Theodore Roosevelt, which do you consider the most useful today? Give reasons for your choice.

2. How do you react to establishing rules for spelling? Since the idea of a uniform way of spelling words is rather new, do you think schools would be wise to be more lenient in checking the spelling of students' essays? What advantage or disadvantage might amass from deemphasizing spelling in compositions? Try to be objective in giving your answer, especially if you are a bad speller.

3. What does the author mean when he states that part of Noah Webster's motivation in unifying the spelling of American English was *nationalism?* What is your reaction to this opinion?

4. To what organizations do paragraphs 5 and 6 refer? What do these organizations have in common? How would you evaluate the worth of these organizations in terms of the author's thesis?

5. What writing technique does the author use to make his assertions hold water? How well does this technique work in this essay? Would Shea's development be as reliable without them? Why or why not?

6. What logic does the author offer for the possibility of texting shorthand becoming part of conventional English spelling? Do you agree or disagree with the author's suggestion? Give reasons for your answer.

7. According to David Crystal, what happens when people try to impose reform "top down"? In your opinion, what is the best tactic for acquiring reform in society?

8. What meaning is implied in the title of this essay?

Writing Assignments

1. Write an essay praising or criticizing the use of texting in your world. Use at least three examples and one or two allusions to support your viewpoint.

2. Write an essay in which you evaluate the importance of correct spelling to good writing. Use examples to support your argument.

DON FARRANT

The Word as Person: Eponyms

Don Farrant (b. 1924), a business writer and historian, lives in St. Simons Island, Georgia.

READING FOR IDEAS   This article is an informative catalog of eponyms—objects or events named after real people—and shows us how some famous eponyms were formed. As you read, try to think of other examples of eponyms the writer does not mention. Notice how the writer organizes his examples in a clear and orderly sequence.

1   When the Fourth Earl of Sandwich was hungry, he would ask his valet to prepare an easy-to-eat snack, instructing him to take two pieces of bread and put a slice of meat between them. The servant did as told and it was a turning point in culinary history. The earl, who lived from 1718–1792, had no way of knowing he was immortalizing himself . . . with the sandwich.

2   Our language contains many terms that were once the names of actual persons. These are eponymous words, from the noun *eponym:* "One whose name is so prominently connected with anything as to be a figurative designation for it."

3   Nellie Melba, an Australian soprano (1861–1931), also gave her name to a well-known food item. She disliked thick cuttings of bread, common at the time, considering them coarse and inelegant, and made a practice of preparing thin slices, toasted until crisp. Poor Madame Melba—little did she know she'd be better remembered by future generations for Melba toast than for her operatic achievements.

4   The long history of wearing apparel gives us some fascinating eponyms. The cardigan sweater, for example, got its name from James T. Brudenell (1797–1868), Seventh Earl of Cardigan and a British general who gained fame in the Crimean War.

5   The rich and handsome earl showed public spirit by sitting faithfully in Parliament for many years and through lengthy army service. It was he who led the famous Charge of the Light Brigade at the Battle of Balaklava in 1854. Overall, his popularity was diminished by a quarrelsome nature and his tendency to brag about his battlefield exploits. But alas, he is remembered less for that famous charge than for his fondness for a collarless jacket opening down the front, known as the cardigan sweater.

6   It was Amelia Bloomer, an American feminist, who decided young ladies should wear a costume consisting of a short skirt and loose trousers gathered at the ankles. This was dubbed a *bloomer*—and a variation, used for sports and gathered at the knee, became known as *bloomers*. Outmoded today, Amelia's creation was important enough to become a part of the language.

7   Or take the Duke of Wellington, who defeated Napoleon at Waterloo. His place in history is, of course, assured, but the Iron Duke gave a lesser-known contribution: the Wellington boot, loose at the top with a front portion which came up above the knee.

8   Transportation, too, has stirred up some interesting eponyms over the years. Back in the 19th century, George M. Pullman (1831–1897) didn't think railroad cars provided enough comfort on long trips. He introduced a special car with sleeping quarters for passengers. His name will be forever associated with the Pullman car.

9   Henry Peter Brougham (1778–1868) was a British political leader and supporter of humanitarian causes. As a member of the House of Lords, Brougham (pronounced *broom*) fought consistently for liberal policies and urged abolition of the slave trade. He was energetic and witty, but at times a bit eccentric. In the 1830s, after he was raised to the peerage and became Lord Chancellor of England, a special, four-wheel closed carriage, the brougham, was designed for him. Later, its popularity spread to the Continent and America.

10   In the arena of personal appearance, the pompadour hairstyle came to us from the Marquise de Pompadour (properly, Jeanne Antoinette Poisson, 1721–1764). A close associate of Louis XV of France, the marquise set a trend by working up a style of dressing her hair high over the forehead.

11   Inventors have done much to enrich our language with name-inspired nouns. It was a Frenchman, Louis Braille (1809–1852), who developed a system of printing in which alphabetical characters are represented by raised dots. Braille is still used the world over—all due to the dedication of a teacher who wanted to give sightless people a better chance to communicate.

12   Generations of chemistry students have used the invention of Robert W. Bunsen (1811–1899). The German professor devised a distinctive type of gas burner for laboratory work—the Bunsen burner.

13   Back in the late 18th century, a Scottish inventor named John Loudon McAdam (1756–1836) conducted road-making experiments in England. When he was general surveyor of the Bristol Turnpike Trust, he came up with a new system calling for an impervious surface over dry soil, utilizing proper drainage, a slight camber, and a compact layer of small stones. Nowadays, *macadam* is a general term for pavements or road surfaces made up of layers of crushed stone or gravel.

14   Three related words—*galvanic, galvanized,* and *galvanometer*—are eponyms all, stemming from Luigi Galvani (1737–1798), an Italian physiologist. He was a pioneer in electrophysiology and certainly a man ahead of his time. He was constantly applying electrodes to various objects, attempting to trace the path of electrical impulses.

15   Probably Galvani's most significant discovery was the electrical nature of nerve action. In textbooks today, *galvanic* means having the effect of an electric shock. *Galvanize* means either to stimulate to action or to coat iron or steel with zinc to guard against corrosion. A *galvanometer* is a device for detecting an electric current.

16   Sometimes eponyms reflect the contributor's own unattractive traits. Such is the case with Captain Charles Boycott (1832–1897), a land agent in Ireland in the 1880s, who collected rents in such a tyrannical, unbending way that he infuriated his tenants.

17   When Boycott's process servers, carrying eviction papers, were attacked by a mob, he decided to send out infantry to collect the rents. Things got worse: laborers refused to

work for the man, and he was refused accommodations while traveling. Frequently, he did not receive letters intended for him. Out of all this came the term *boycott*—a refusal to engage in relations with a person or firm in order to bring about a change in terms or a settlement of some sort.

18   When the 12th Earl of Derby originated a horse race for three-year-olds in 1779, little did he know he was starting a tradition. Called first "Derby's race at Epsom," it soon became an annual event; Derby Day is still one of the biggest sporting occasions of the year in Britain, taking place every June. In the U.S., the most heralded horse race is the Kentucky Derby, held each May at Churchill Downs. Both these events have large purses and attract crowds of more than 100,000.

19   In the world of medicine, Dr. Franz Anton Mesmer, a German physician (1734–1815), developed a deep rapport with his patients and may have used a form of hypnotism to treat them. In 1767, he joined the faculty of Vienna's Advanced Medical Center. As a physician he had many theories and although some were unsubstantiated, such as that of "magnetic body fluids," he was surely a leader in promoting close doctor-patient relationships. *Mesmerism* is still associated with casting a spell; it was, in fact, an early term for hypnotism.

20   Sailors can tell you what a Plimsoll mark is—but not many others can. It's the line on the side of a ship's hull that indicates the amount of cargo it can safely carry. It was named for Samuel Plimsoll (1824–1898), a 19th-century English reformer. Due to his insistence, Parliament passed the Merchant Shipping Act (1876), fixing compulsory limits of cargo under various ocean conditions and providing for the line on the hull. Prior to this law, vessels sometimes would be lost at sea due to overloading.

21   Anyone who has changed a light bulb knows the word *watt*—a unit of electrical power. It stems from James Watt, a Scottish engineer (1736–1819), who designed the engine which first made steam power feasible. Other devices are credited to this mechanical genius, who also did research in chemistry and metallurgy.

22   A waterproof outer garment made of rubber-coated fabric is known in many circles as a *mackintosh*—but whence the name? It derives from one Charles Macintosh (1766–1843), a British chemist and inventor who made significant contributions to chemical technology, including a procedure for producing lead and aluminum acetates. Macintosh, who tired of getting soaked every time he went out in the rain, came up with what is today his most famous invention—the raincoat which bears his name.

23   Then there's the Morse code, an orderly arrangement of dots and dashes which has played a vital role in communication history. Most of us know that the inventor of the telegraph, Samuel F. B. Morse, also gave his name to the code he devised. To his credit, Morse was an artist as well as a technician, and is today recognized as one of the best of the early American portrait painters.

24   New words come about in strange ways, giving fame, even immortality, to people who, in many cases, would rather be remembered for other things. Whether they like it or not, eponymous words are a sort of memorial—a lasting tribute to those who contributed to life, and often improved it.

■ *Vocabulary*

culinary (1)   camber (13)   feasible (21)

■ *Questions on Meaning and Technique*

1. What rhetorical strategy other than example is obviously at work in this article?

2. What underlying logic implicitly links the author's first two examples?

3. For what kind of audience do you think this article was written? What evidence from the text can you cite to support your conclusion?

4. The author uses no transition in paragraph 6 yet weighs in with a bridging sentence at the beginning of paragraph 11. What rhetorical explanation can you give for this difference?

Internet Research Assignment

On the Internet, find a photo of a religious ceremony held by citizens of Bhutan, a kingdom bordering on the Himalayas and ruled by a king. Give examples of how, in your view, the costumes portrayed are either similar or dissimilar to garb worn by members of traditional religions in our own culture such as Catholicism. Speculate on reasons for the differences or similarities.

Additional Writing Assignments

Illustrate the following with appropriate examples:

1. Getting sick in the United States can bankrupt even a well-off person.

2. Not all old people are fuddy-duddy, conservative, or timid.

3. All that glitters is not gold.

4. On the whole, movies nowadays are too gory.

5. Americans are too moralistic in their politics.

6. Many doctors emerge from medical school with an inflated and egotistic opinion of themselves and their profession.

7. Growth for its own sake is not always good, whether for institutions or businesses.

8. Some television shows are vulgar and tasteless.

9. Participation in sports is not for everyone, nor should it be.

10. Gun control can make (does not make) a difference.

Rewriting Assignment

Rewrite the following paragraph to include a clear connection between the topic sentence and the examples that support it:

> Social Security critics have my parents' generation scared to death that they will experience an impoverished old age. Many newspaper articles discuss how Social Security gobbles up too much money. A book by investment banker (and Secretary of Commerce under President Richard Nixon) Peter G. Peterson, titled *How the Coming Social Security Crisis Threatens You, Your Family, and Your Country,* seems immensely threatening. Government "think tanks" are constantly spreading the rumor that the baby boomers will not be able to collect Social Security because the system will be broke. Many rich people believe that if the elderly cannot save enough money to retire decently, then they will simply have to depend on the generosity of their children. Baby boomers deserve to know that if worse comes to worst, they won't have to starve or freeze to death.

Photo Writing Assignment

A young girl peers from among a group of burka-clad Afghan women. Santiago Lyon/AP Photo

The photo of a young girl peering from among a group of burka-clad Afghan women is an example of how a garment can represent a strong tradition. Write an essay in which you use two or three other examples of clothing that represents a tradition among some group.

Digging for Gold or for Cases

Miners use assay samples of the soil to predict the likelihood of finding gold in an exploratory dig. These samples represent the components of the soil. Similarly, in speaking or writing, an example is the use of the few to represent the many. The example plays an important role in argumentation by symbolically representing a population larger than itself and sparing the debater from being overwhelmed by the tyranny of individual instances. It is hard to imagine how reasoning as we know it would even be possible if the concept of the example did not exist. The miner might use four assay samples of the soil; the politician might cite four cases of hardship and suffering caused by the lack of health insurance among low-income populations. Both are instances of the useful shortcut nature of the example.

Just about any point you can make, whether oral or written, can be strengthened by the tactical use of examples. Wendell Berry ("Are you All Right?") illustrates the caring spirit of a river community for its own by relating in a folksy style how two friends walked all night to check on neighbors cut off by a dangerous river flood. Ammon Shea gives examples of words that are spelled entirely differently than they are pronounced and speculates about the possible effect that modern computer speech is likely to have upon orthodox spelling. Don Farrant delivers a brisk explanation and short history of eponyms, made even more fascinating by the many examples he dug up in his research. To develop a topic by examples, a good beginning is to consult one of those enormous dictionaries found on the reference shelf of your school library. That, plus access to a first rate search engine should be enough to get you started. The rest will be up to your digging.

Chapter 10

Definition

DOROTHY PARKER

Arrangement in Black and White

Dorothy Parker (1893–1967) was an American poet and short story writer. She gained a reputation as a wit while serving as drama critic for Vanity Fair *(1917–1920) and book reviewer for* The New Yorker *(1927–1933). Her first volume of poetry, which brought her instant fame, was* Enough Rope *(1926). It was followed by such volumes as* Death and Taxes *(1931) and* Not So Deep as a Well *(1936). Her short stories, which were usually satirical attacks on the ways and customs of her time, were collected and published in 1942. The story reprinted here has become a classic portrayal of early attempts of post–Civil War society to hide its racial prejudice behind insincere politeness.*

READING FOR IDEAS "Arrangement in Black and White" is a story about prejudice. As you listen to the main character in the story reveal her attitude toward blacks, ask yourself: What is prejudice? How is it acquired? How can it be stopped? From your own experience, what are some examples of prejudice? Be prepared to give a one-sentence definition of the word *prejudice*.

1   The woman with the pink velvet poppies twined round the assisted gold of her hair traversed the crowded room at an interesting gait combining a skip with a sidle, and clutched the lean arm of her host.

2   "Now I got you!" she said. "Now you can't get away!"

3   "Why, hello," said her host. "Well. How are you?"

4   "Oh, I'm finely," she said. "Just simply finely. Listen. I want you to do me the most terrible favor. Will you? Will you please? Pretty please?"

5   "What is it?" said her host.

6   "Listen," she said. "I want to meet Walter Williams. Honestly, I'm just simply crazy about that man. Oh, when he sings! When he sings those spirituals! Well, I said to

Burton, 'It's a good thing for you Walter Williams is colored,' I said, 'or you'd have lots of reason to be jealous.' I'd really love to meet him. I'd like to tell him I've heard him sing. Will you be an angel and introduce me to him?"

7   "Why, certainly," said her host. "I thought you'd met him. The party's for him. Where is he, anyway?"

8   "He's over there by the bookcase," she said. "Let's wait till those people get through talking to him. Well, I think you're simply marvelous, giving this perfectly marvelous party for him, and having him meet all these white people, and all. Isn't he terribly grateful?"

9   "I hope not," said her host.

10   "I think it's really terribly nice," she said. "I do. I don't see why on earth it isn't per-fectly all right to meet colored people. I haven't any feeling at all about it—not one single bit. Burton—oh, he's just the other way. Well, you know, he comes from Virginia, and you know how they are."

11   "Did he come tonight?" said her host.

12   "No, he couldn't," she said. "I'm a regular grass widow tonight. I told him when I left, 'There's no telling what I'll do,' I said. He was just so tired out, he couldn't move. Isn't it a shame?"

13   "Ah," said her host.

14   "Wait till I tell him I met Walter Williams!" she said. "He'll just about die. Oh, we have more arguments about colored people. I talk to him like I don't know what, I get so excited. 'Oh, don't be so silly,' I say. But I must say for Burton, he's heaps broader-minded than lots of these Southerners. He's really awfully fond of colored people. Well, he says himself, he wouldn't have white servants. And you know, he had this old colored nurse, this regular old nigger mammy, and he just simply loves her. Why, every time he goes home, he goes out in the kitchen to see her. He does, really, to this day. All he says is, he says he hasn't got a word to say against colored people as long as they keep their place. He's always doing things for them—giving them clothes and I don't know what all. The only thing he says, he says he wouldn't sit down at the table with one for a million dollars. 'Oh,' I say to him, 'you make me sick, talking like that.' I'm just terrible to him. Aren't I terrible?"

15   "Oh, no, no, no," said her host. "No, no."

16   "I am," she said. "I know I am. Poor Burton! Now, me, I don't feel that way at all. I haven't the slightest feeling about colored people. Why, I'm just crazy about some of them. They're just like children—just as easygoing, and always singing and laughing and everything. Aren't they the happiest things you ever saw in your life? Honestly, it makes me laugh just to hear them. Oh, I like them. I really do. Well, now, listen, I have this colored laundress, I've had her for years, and I'm devoted to her. She's a real character. And I want to tell you, I think of her as my friend. That's the way I think of her. As I say to Burton, 'Well, for Heaven's sakes, we're all human beings!' Aren't we?"

17   "Yes," said her host. "Yes, indeed."

18   "Now this Walter Williams," she said. "I think a man like that's a real artist. I do. I think he deserves an awful lot of credit. Goodness, I'm so crazy about music or anything, I don't care *what* color he is. I honestly think if a person's an artist, nobody ought to have any feeling at all about meeting them. That's absolutely what I say to Burton. Don't you think I'm right?"

19   "Yes," said her host. "Oh, yes."

20   "That's the way I feel," she said. "I just can't understand people being narrow-minded. Why, I absolutely think it's a privilege to meet a man like Walter Williams. Yes, I do. I haven't any feeling at all. Well, my goodness, the good Lord made him, just the same as He did any of us. Didn't He?"

21   "Surely," said her host. "Yes, indeed."

22   "That's what I say," she said. "Oh, I get so furious when people are narrow-minded about colored people. It's just all I can do not to say something. Of course, I do admit when you get a bad colored man, they're simply terrible. But as I say to Burton, there are some bad white people, too, in this world. Aren't there?"

23   "I guess there are," said her host.

24   "Why, I'd really be glad to have a man like Walter Williams come to my house and sing for us some time!" she said. "Of course, I couldn't ask him on account of Burton, but I wouldn't have any feeling about it at all. Oh, can't he sing! Isn't it marvelous, the way they all have music in them? It just seems to be right in them. Come on, let's go on over and talk to him. Listen, what shall I do when I'm introduced? Ought I to shake hands? Or what?"

25   "Why, do whatever you want," said her host.

26   "I guess maybe I'd better," she said. "I wouldn't for the world have him think I had any feeling. I think I'd better shake hands, just the way I would with anybody else. That's just exactly what I'll do."

27   They reached the tall young Negro, standing by the bookcase. The host performed introductions; the Negro bowed.

28   "How do you do?" he said.

29   The woman with the pink velvet poppies extended her hand at the length of her arm and held it so for all the world to see, until the Negro took it, shook it, and gave it back to her.

30   "Oh, how do you do, Mr. Williams," she said. "Well, how do you do. I've just been saying, I've enjoyed your singing so awfully much. I've been to your concerts, and we have you on the phonograph and everything. Oh, I just enjoy it!"

31   She spoke with great distinctness, moving her lips meticulously, as if in parlance with the deaf.

32   "I'm so glad," he said.

33   "I'm just simply crazy about that 'Water Boy' thing you sing," she said. "Honestly, I can't get it out of my head. I have my husband nearly crazy, the way I go around humming it all the time. Oh, he looks just as black as the ace of—Well. Tell me, where on earth do you ever get all those songs of yours? How do you ever get hold of them?"

34   "Why," he said, "there are so many different—"

35   "I should think you'd love singing them," she said. "It must be more fun. All those darling old spirituals—oh, I just love them! Well, what are you doing, now? Are you still keeping up your singing? Why don't you have another concert, some time?"

36   "I'm having one the sixteenth of this month," he said.

37   "Well, I'll be there," she said. "I'll be there, if I possibly can. You can count on me. Goodness, here comes a whole raft of people to talk to you. You're just a regular guest of honor! Oh, who's that girl in white? I've seen her some place."

38   "That's Katherine Burke," said her host.

39   "Good Heavens," she said, "is that Katherine Burke? Why, she looks entirely different off the stage. I thought she was much better-looking. I had no idea she was so terribly
dark. Why, she looks almost like—Oh, I think she's a wonderful actress! Don't you think
she's a wonderful actress, Mr. Williams? Oh, I think she's marvelous. Don't you?"

40   "Yes, I do," he said.

41   "Oh, I do, too," she said. "Just wonderful. Well, goodness, we must give someone else
a chance to talk to the guest of honor. Now, don't forget, Mr. Williams, I'm going to be at
that concert if I possibly can. I'll be there applauding like everything. And if I can't come,
I'm going to tell everybody I know to go, anyway. Don't you forget!"

42   "I won't," he said, "Thank you so much."

43   The host took her arm and piloted her into the next room.

44   "Oh, my dear," she said. "I nearly died! Honestly, I give you my word, I nearly passed
away. Did you hear that terrible break I made? I was just going to say Katherine Burke
looked almost like a nigger. I just caught myself in time. Oh, do you think he noticed?"

45   "I don't believe so," said her host.

46   "Well, thank goodness," she said, "because I wouldn't have embarrassed him for anything. Why, he's awfully nice. Just as nice as he can be. Nice manners, and everything.
You know, so many colored people, you give them an inch, and they walk all over you.
But he doesn't try any of that. Well, he's got more sense, I suppose. He's really nice. Don't
you think so?"

47   "Yes," said her host.

48   "I liked him," she said. "I haven't any feeling at all because he's a colored man. I felt
just as natural as I would with anybody. Talked to him as naturally, and everything. But
honestly, I could hardly keep a straight face. I kept thinking of Burton. Oh, wait till I tell
Burton I called him 'Mister'!"

■ *Vocabulary*

sidle (1)

■ *Questions on Meaning and Technique*

1. What kind of person is the main character of this story? How would you
   describe her to someone who has not read the story?

2. The woman insists blatantly that she has no racial prejudice. "I haven't any
   feeling at all," she repeatedly says. What evidence have you that she is
   wrong? Refer to specific passages in the story.

3. What are examples of the way the woman stereotypes African Americans?

4. What is Burton's attitude toward African Americans? Does it differ from the
   woman's? If so, how?

5. What is the attitude of the host toward the woman? What is his role in the
   story?

COUNTEE CULLEN

Incident

Countee Cullen (1903–1946) was born and orphaned in New York City and educated at New York University and Harvard. He was a major member of the 1920s black literary explosion known as the Harlem Renaissance. His work includes Color *(1925),* Copper Sun *(1927), and* The Ballad of the Brown Girl *(1927).*

READING FOR IDEAS Conflicting sharply with the outward simplicity of its rhyming stanzas, this poem recounts a painful childhood memory of racial hate. Ask yourself as you read: How did young children such as this bigoted Baltimorean come to absorb such loathsome attitudes so early? What kind of adult do you think this young Baltimorean bigot promises to be? And what effect do you think this ugly encounter had on the speaker?

1   Once riding in old Baltimore,
    Heart-filled, head-filled with glee,
    I saw a Baltimorean
    Keep looking straight at me.

2   Now I was eight and very small,
    And he was no whit bigger,
    And so I smiled, but he poked out
    His tongue and called me, "Nigger."

3   I saw the whole of Baltimore
    From May until December:
    Of all the things that happened there
    That's all that I remember.

■ *Questions on Meaning and Technique*

1. What is the theme of this poem? State it in one complete sentence.
2. Why do you think the little boy from Baltimore called the speaker a "nigger"? Comment on the social implications.
3. How does the title, "Incident," stress the poem's theme?
4. In stanza 2, what contrast adds a sad irony to the poem?
5. How do we know that the speaker was not prepared to encounter prejudice?
6. What would your reaction be if you witnessed the incident described in the poem?

How to Write a Definition

Definition is the method of development used whenever it is necessary to clarify the meaning of any "fuzzy" or controversial word or term. In the course of an essay or a conversation, we often use words or expressions whose meanings are perfectly obvious to us but less so to our readers or listeners. Sometimes the problem lies with the word we have used—it may be abstract or otherwise unclear, perhaps having multiple meanings. Such, for instance, is no doubt the case with the word *love*. No matter how dictionaries strain to give a single meaning to this word, their cause is a lost one. Men and women who have been blissfully in love will think the word means happiness second only to ecstasy. But for many others—husbands who have been dumped, wives who have been betrayed, lovers who have been jilted—the word will have a bitter sting. The meanings that many words have are similarly affected by our experience, making it necessary to define them in oral or written communication.

The *semantic triangle* (illustrated on p. 230) is often used to explain why some words have fuzzy meanings and others do not. Semanticists say that words evoke two responses from us. First, we may be clearly or dimly aware of the dictionary meaning of a word, which semanticists call its *referent* and which is also known as its *denotation*. For instance, the word *grapefruit* has as its referent the particular tangy citrus fruit that we all know by that name. One may point to a picture of a grapefruit or even produce an example of the fruit itself to settle an argument over what the word means. Where the referent of a word is an object or a thing, such as *grapefruit, textbook, pencil,* or *fountain pen,* the possibility of its meaning being misunderstood is lessened. Words that have visible referents are said to be *concrete;* words with invisible referents are said to be *abstract. Glove* is therefore a concrete word; *love* is an abstract word.

The second response a word evokes from us is known to semanticists as its *reference* or *connotation*—and here we are on unsteady ground. Often inseparable from our experiences with the particular word, the references of a word are those feelings and emotions it arouses. The jilted bridegroom will likely express the bitterest feelings about the word *love;* however, on the other side, the contented husband of some twenty-five years will rave enthusiastically about it. No matter how these two comb through a dictionary, they're hardly likely to reconcile their differing references about *love*. And because *love* is an abstract word with no visible referent, misunderstandings about its meaning are inevitable. It is precisely for such words that definitions are necessary.

The references of words are affected not only by personal experiences with them, but also by the meanings they have acquired through political or public usage. During the years preceding World War II, for instance, Hitler repeatedly justified his designs on other countries by citing Germany's need for *Lebensraum*—territory for political and economic expansion. Eventually, this word came to signify *German imperialism* to the Allies—something entirely different from what it meant to the Germans. Similarly, in the 1960s, the phrase *law and order,* which was then

The Semantic Triangle

Symbol (word)

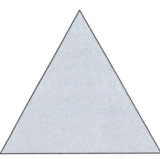

Reference (connotation)
thoughts, prejudices,
experiences associated
with the word

Referent (denotation)
what the word stands for,
the dictionary meaning

Semantic Triangle on Love
from a Contented Husband's
Point of View

Love

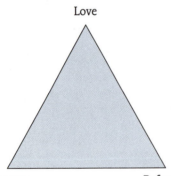

Reference
(connotation)
sharing, giving,
supporting

Referent
(denotation)
deep and
tender feeling
of affection

Semantic Triangle on Love
from a Jilted Lover's
Point of View

Love

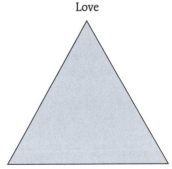

Reference
(connotation)
sham, illusion,
charade

Referent
(denotation)
deep and
tender feeling
of affection

widely bandied about, meant racial repression to some but opposition to public disorder to others. By 1968, when candidate Richard Nixon used the phrase in his nomination acceptance speech, he was obliged to add the following:

> And to those who say that law and order is the code word for racism, here is a reply: Our goal is justice—justice for every American. If we are to have respect for law in America, we must have laws that deserve respect. Just as we cannot have progress without order, we cannot have order without progress.
>
> —Richard Nixon, Nomination Acceptance Speech,
> August 8, 1968

This addition was necessary because the reference underlying this phrase had been so muddied that the phrase had become a trigger for strong feelings. Something similar has happened with the word *abortion*. The word has provoked so many vastly differing references in the minds of those who support and those who oppose abortion that it can no longer be said to have a single, clear-cut meaning.

Writing Assignment

The story and poem depict dramatic [...] them as your initial context, define *prejudice* in an e[...] rent of the word in a dictionary. Choose the definition [...] ds to your own idea of the word's meaning. Then begi[...] dice is . . . ," stating and then expanding your definiti[...]

Specific Instructions

Prewrite on the assignment.   *Prejudice* is one of those abstract words whose meaning is difficult to pinpoint. Unless you live in an ideal world and are a rare individual, you have most likely either felt or inflicted prejudice. Perhaps your girlfriend's father became prejudiced against you because he thought you were too short, too fat, too foreign, too boring, or whatever. Or your boyfriend's mother might have rejected you for similar prejudicial reasons. These incidents, used as extended examples in your essay, can shed light on the meaning of *prejudice*. Notice, for example, how chance encounters with prejudice are recounted in the sample student essay (pp. 243–247).

As for inflicting prejudice, even the saints among us have occasionally been guilty of that. Narrating these incidents of prejudice in ourselves can be painful but enlightening. You may have been prejudiced at some time in your life, for example, against fraternity members, business majors, football players, Girl Scouts, or army chaplains. Making notes about these occurrences and working them into the essay as examples can add some zest to your definition.

Note, however, that in a formal essay, you should not simply pack your definition with such personal anecdotes. You also need to research and find historical instances of prejudice to include in your essay. (See Chapter 17, "Doing the Research.") American history is a warehouse swollen with innumerable cases of personal, institutional, and corporate prejudice. Native Americans, for example, were widely regarded by westward-bound pioneers as chronic beggars who spent a good deal of their day sponging food from the wagon trains crossing the prairie. The pioneers did not understand that Native American tradition viewed food sharing as a sign of peace and friendship. Yet this entry from a pioneer woman's diary shows the prejudice that greeted this custom:

> The bucks with their bows and arrows, beaded buckskin garments and feather head gears were much in evidence and though these prairie redmen were generally friendly they were insistent beggars, often following us for miles and at mealtime disgustingly stood around and solicited food. They seldom molested us, however, but it was a case of the Indian, as well as the poor, "Ye always have with ye."
>
> —Catherine Haun, "A Woman's Trip across the Plains in 1849,"
> Manuscript Diary

This sort of example, cited in the essay with appropriate commentary, can be an enlightening inclusion in your definition of *prejudice*.

Use the etymology of a word to clarify its meaning.   The *etymology* of a word or phrase provides information about its origins and earliest meanings. The dictionary is a rich source of etymologies, which are usually given in brackets after the entries. From Webster's *New World Dictionary,* second college edition, we learn that *poet* comes from the Greek word *poietes,* meaning "one who makes"; that *prejudice* is the English equivalent of the Latin word *praejudicium,* which itself is a blend of *prae,* meaning "before," and *judicium,* meaning "judgment." The etymology usually gives a thumbnail history of the word or phrase that can throw light on its meaning. It is therefore often a good beginning point for a defining essay. Here, for example, is how one writer uses etymology to help define *botulism:*

> There are life-forms which, in the course of evolution, have developed poisons designed to kill, or to prevent themselves from being eaten. Venoms are produced by a variety of animals from jellyfish to reptiles. Plants develop a variety of poisonous substances designed to taste bad to an animal that nibbles and to kill if the animal persists.
> Pride of place, however, must be taken by the product of a bacterium which is to be found everywhere and which harms no one—ordinarily. It is *Clostridium botulinum. Clostridium* is Latin for "little spindle," which describes its shape, and *botulinum* is from the Latin word *botulus,* which means "sausage," where it has sometimes been detected.
>
> —Isaac Asimov, "World's Most Deadly Poison . . . The Botulin
> Spore," *Science Digest,* January 1972

This etymology tells us not only what the spore looks like but also where it has been found.

Even if a word or term has an unknown origin, sometimes a discussion of its probable beginnings can give a useful glimpse into its background. Here, for example, a writer speculates on where the baseball term *bullpen* came from:

> No one, much less the pitcher out there, knows quite why a bullpen is called as it is. One of the accepted theories is that the term is derived from the many Bull Durham tobacco signboards erected out beyond the outfield fences at the turn of the century. In 1909 the tobacco company put up 150 of these signs in baseball parks, the advertisements dominated by a large peaceful-looking domestic bull. Local merchants would pay up to $50 if a batter could hit the bull on the fly. Relief pitchers warmed up under or behind the sign, in an area many authorities believe began to be called the "bullpen."
>
> Others suspect the word is lifted from the prison term for the detention area where defendants waited until they stood trial, an accurate enough description of the life cycle of a relief pitcher. Yet another theory suggests that the bullpen was originally the area where fans were herded behind ropes, where they had to wait until an inning was over before being seated.
>
> —George Plimpton, "The Lore of the Bullpen"

Obviously, not all words have fascinating etymologies. Those that have been recently minted, for instance, will seem as though they sprang out of nothing, as flies were once thought to do. Most such words are Americanisms. The etymologies of such words as *hooker, blurb* (which was an arbitrary coinage), *milksop,* and *fall guy,* for instance, are not especially useful. *Horse opera* seems to have come from nowhere, and it is not especially enlightening to learn that *fiscal* comes from the Latin word *fiscus,* meaning "a basket of rushes, public chest." Yet when the etymology of a word tells something about its meaning, writers often use this information as a starting point for their definitions.

Give examples, state functions, and show effects of the defined term.   An adequate definition of a term requires more than a summary of its exact meaning. Often, it is necessary to expand on the lexical definition by giving examples, stating functions, and showing the effects of the defined term. Here, for instance, is a rather peppy paragraph from a student essay that attempts to define *love* by giving an extended example of its effects:

> Love is the pitter-patter of the heart, butterflies in the tummy, a sudden, urgent lunacy. As an example, I offer the night I met Julie. I had saved for months to go to dinner at Chez François. I had planned and saved up for a lavish dinner: oysters sauteed in olive oil; lobster steamed in wine with herb sauce; eggplant stuffed with mushrooms. I was about to order wine when I met Julie—the cocktail waitress. I took one look in her eyes and my appetite went down the tube. I know that's slang and that I should write something more elegant, but I actually felt my appetite dropping from my belly down to my toes—as if it fell down a tube—and, with a little imagination, I thought I even saw it roll out on the carpet and scurry away like a routed mouse. The rest of the night I just kept ordering one drink after another from Julie

just so I could talk to her. I ate almost none of the meal. All I did was drink, chat with Julie, and get drunk. That's love.

A more sober example can be found in an essay by the late Scottish-born scholar Gilbert Highet, who set out to define *kitsch*. First, Highet tells us that the word *kitsch* is of Russian origin, that it "means vulgar showoff, and it is applied to anything that took a lot of trouble to make and is quite hideous." Then he proceeds to make this clearer by giving examples of kitsch:

> Of course, it is found in all the arts; think of Milan Cathedral, or the statues in Westminster Abbey, or Liszt's settings of Schubert songs. There is a lot of it in the United States—for instance, the architecture of Miami, Florida, and Forest Lawn Cemetery in Los Angeles. Many of Hollywood's most ambitious historical films are superb kitsch. Most Tin Pan Alley love songs were perfect 100 per cent kitsch.
>
> —Gilbert Highet, "Kitsch"

The rest of the essay simply goes on to catalog one example after another of kitsch in literature.

Another dimension may be added to a definition by an analysis of the function of a term. For example, *sewing machine* may be defined as a mechanism that allows a tailor or a seamstress to stitch cloth together automatically. This definition may then be extended by stating specific functions, as follows:

> There are over 2,000 varieties of modern sewing machines designed for stitching processes in the great sewing industries making up clothing, boots and shoes, corsets, hats, hosiery, etc. There are machines especially designed for sewing regular or fancy shank buttons on shoes; for sewing sweat leathers into stiff felt, soft felt or straw hats; for trimming scalloping and over-edging lace curtains; for sewing silk initials, monograms or floral designs upon material at one operation. There is a seven needle machine for making seven parallel rows of fine double chain stitching simultaneously.

Writing Tip

Which Strategy to Use?

How can you tell which, or how many, of the strategies for defining you should use? There's no simple answer to this question. If the term you are defining has no referent, your essay will have to use all or most of the strategies covered in this chapter. If your subject has a referent, you can be more selective. What makes the difference is the presence or absence of a referent. *Love* has none; *lover* has one. *Lover* is therefore easier to define than *love*.

This machine is fitted with seven needles and seven loopers, and its capacity is 20,000 stitches per minute.

—*Encyclopaedia Britannica*

Clarify the definition by stating what the term is not.   To explain what a thing is, it is often convenient also to say what it is *not*. By this kind of indirection, a writer can make clear what is meant by a certain term. Here, for example, are two paragraphs taken from the essay "The Sophisticated Man" by Marya Mannes. She has already defined the *sophisticated man* as one who has acquired certain "perceptions, tastes, and attitudes." She then proceeds to these two paragraphs. The first sketches the sophisticated man in action; the second presents his opposite as a contrast:

> Would you recognize this kind of man if you saw him across the room? I think so. He's the one with an attractive woman; conservatively dressed, but easy in his clothes. His hair is trimmed close to his head, but not too close. His hands are well-groomed, but not manicured. He does not laugh loudly or often. He is looking directly at the woman he speaks to, but he is not missing the other attractive women as they enter; a flick of the eye does it. For in all ways this man is not obvious. He would no more appear to examine a woman from the ankles up than he would move his head as he read or form the words with his lips. His senses are trained and his reflexes quick. And how did they get that way? From experience, from observation, and from deduction. He puts two and two together without adding on his fingers. He is educated in life.
>
> Now what about that fellow over there—the one in the light-grey suit and the crew cut? He is telling a long story rather loudly to a girl who would rather not be hearing it. He is not, of course, aware of this, since he is not only a little tight but unaccustomed to watching the reactions of women. He will look down the front of her dress but not see the glaze in her eyes. He has not been educated in observation. He is, according to the dictionary, unsophisticated in that he is natural and simple and lacking in experience.

—Marya Mannes, "The Sophisticated Man"

By knowing what the sophisticated man is not, we have a better idea of what he is.

In defining *migraine headache,* one person noted that a migraine "is a headache so powerful that it can cause temporary blindness, terrible vomiting spells, overpowering fatigue, mental confusion, and acute sensitivity to any light or noise. While under the influence of a bad migraine, the victim may actually wish he or she could die because the pain is so devastating." She then says what a migraine is not: "In brief, a migraine is not your common variety of dull headache that can be cured with two aspirins or a cup of coffee." By providing a negative definition, the writer ensures that the reader understands the severity of migraine headaches.

Amplify the definition until the meaning is clear.   The kind of amplification that a writer should give depends, of course, on the term being defined. The only hard-and-fast rule is to give as much detail as necessary to make clear what a term or word means. Here, for example, a writer is defining *high blood pressure*. First, he says clearly what it is; then he proceeds to detail its consequences on the human body:

> In the last few years researchers have developed hard evidence that high blood pressure, if left unchecked for a few years, sharply increases the risk of a heart attack, heart failure or a stroke leading to disability and/or death. Epidemiological studies such as the Framingham study, for instance, show the rate of heart attack among men whose diastolic pressure was 105 or higher was more than twice that of men with pressures of less than 95 and three and a half times that of men with pressures of less than 85 millimeters of mercury.
>
> —Jerry Bishop, *I Think I'm Having a Heart Attack*

Use other rhetorical patterns to expand on your definition.   Where necessary or appropriate, writers will often add to their definitions by elaborating in successive paragraphs on various features, functions, and characteristics of a term. The paragraphs that follow may seem to be developed according to various methods—some may seem primarily descriptive, some essentially an analysis of effect. But each is working toward the final goal of the writer—to define a medieval *tournament* and explain its place in the life of a knight:

> Originating in France and referred to by others as "French combat" *(conflictus Gallicus),* tournaments started without rules or lists as an agreed-upon clash of opposing units. Though justified as training exercises, the impulse was the love of fighting. Becoming more regulated and mannered, they took two forms; jousts by individuals, and melees by groups of up to forty on a side, either *à plaisance* with blunted weapons or *à outrance* with no restraints, in which case participants might be severely wounded and not infrequently killed. Tournaments proliferated as the noble's primary occupation dwindled. Under the extended rule of monarchy, he had less need to protect his own fief, while a class of professional ministers was gradually taking his place around the crown. The less he had to do, the more energy he spent in tournaments artificially reenacting his role.
>
> A tournament might last as long as a week and on great occasions two. Opening day was spent matching and seeding the players, followed by days set apart for jousts, for melees, for a rest day before the final tourney, all interspersed with feasting and parties. These occasions were the great sporting events of the time, attracting crowds of bourgeois spectators from rich merchants to common artisans, mountebanks, food vendors, prostitutes, and pickpockets. About a hundred knights usually participated, each accompanied by two mounted squires, an armorer, and six servants in livery. The knight had of course to equip himself with painted and gilded armor and crested helmet costing from 25 to 50 livres, with a war-horse costing from 25 to 100 livres in addition to his traveling palfrey, and with banners and trappings and fine clothes. Though the expense could easily bankrupt him, he might also come away richer, for the loser in combat had to pay a ransom and the winner was awarded his opponent's horse and armor, which he could sell back to him or to anyone. Gain was not recognized by chivalry, but it was present at tournaments.
>
> With brilliantly dressed spectators in the stands, flags and ribbons fluttering, the music of trumpets, the parade of combatants making their draped horses prance and

champ on golden bridles, the glitter of harness and shields, the throwing of ladies' scarves and sleeves to their favorites, the bow of the heralds to the presiding prince who proclaimed the rules, the cry of poursuivants announcing their champions, the tournament was the peak of nobility's pride and delight in its own valor and beauty.

—Barbara W. Tuchman, *A Distant Mirror:*
The Calamitous 14th Century

It follows from all we have said in this section that the defining essay should give more than just a lexical meaning of a word, phrase, or term. Anyone can look in a dictionary and see the starkest, bare-bones summation of a referent. The essay that defines should give considerably more. It should show not only the mummified meaning of a term to be found in any dictionary but also the living word as it exists in the mind of the individual writer.

PROFESSIONAL MODEL

BERT B. BEACH

Fundamentalism

Bert B. Beach (b. 1928) is an author of five books and numerous articles. He is former director of the Public Affairs and Religious Liberty Department of the General Conference of Seventh-day Adventists. Beach was born in Switzerland and lived much of his life in Belgium, France, Switzerland, and Italy. Fluent in five languages, he was uniquely equipped to handle the problems of religious liberty among Christian churches in various countries. Beach has spoken and lectured all over the world on educational, religious, church-state, peace, ecumenical, and religious liberty themes. For thirty-two years he was the secretary of the Conference of Secretaries of Christian World Communion. As an American citizen, he earned a Ph.D. in history magna cum laude from the University of Paris (Sorbonne), writing his doctoral dissertation in French, titled "The Political Reconstruction in the United States, as seen by the French Diplomats and Consular Agents 1865-71." Beach is now retired and lives in Silver Spring, Maryland.

READING FOR IDEAS "Fundamentalism" and what it teaches threatens the core idea enshrined in the American Constitution—namely, that citizens have the innate right to pick and choose from among religions or, for that matter, to reject the idea of religion altogether. This state does not have the power to favor one sect or creed over another and does not have the right to meddle in the worship rites of any religion so long as the practice does not violate secular law. This open-ended right puts many of the Western democracies squarely at odds with Middle Eastern states who usually call themselves fundamentalist. Be sure to understand the reason behind fundamentalist principles and the resulting chaos it has caused and continues to cause all over the world. Ask yourself why it is that many people hate change so much that they will kill anyone who dares to question the principles upon which a new generation is building their lives. You might also think about the positive aspects of fundamentalism as they might apply today.

1   YOUR GREAT-GRANDPARENTS PROBABLY never knew the term "fundamentalism." But your children, sadly, will find it all too unavoidable.

2   "Fundamentalism," linguistically speaking, is a relatively recent entry into the vocabulary of many modern languages. In the English-speaking world, where it was first used in the 1920s in the United States, it has come to connote a broadly based traditionalist religious movement that opposes itself to the excesses and the omissions of "liberal religion" and secularity.

3   This movement began as a powerful theological and social reaction against the nineteenth- and early twentieth-century "higher criticism" of the Bible, and the concentration of "modernist" church leaders and theologians on the social and political issues of the day. Christian fundamentalists also took dead aim at the "demon of evolution," which they believed needed to be exorcised from American public education and even from institutions of higher learning.

All Around the World

4   Though the fundamentalist movement first gained international attention with the publication of a series of 12 books ("The Fundamentals") in the United States between 1910 and 1915, it quickly became apparent that the fundamentalist impulse was at work in societies other than American and religions other than Christianity. In the 80 years since the term "fundamentalism" emerged in popular discourse, both its connotation and denotation have shifted markedly. Fundamentalism can no longer be simply associated with one religion; it has become a worldwide phenomenon that has infiltrated, so to speak, all major religions and has become a dominant factor in many local or national situations.

New Equals Bad

5   Various definitions can be offered for fundamentalism, all of them containing at least an element of truth. I would agree with the church historian Martin Marty who says that fundamentalism is essentially a reaction to and fear of "*modernity.*" It is also a reaction against "*secularization.*" Most human societies in our world today are generally favorable to rapid change and pluralization.

6   The fundamentalist, in contrast, is opposed to change in general, and more specifically, to pluralism of worldviews. He (and it is generally a "he," though it may also be a "she") wants one view—always his own view—to have exclusive validity, and therefore domination and control. His worldview or religion protests—even with anger and violence—against the sweeping changes that have already overwhelmed some societies or threaten to do so. Fundamentalism as an organizing principle expresses his resentment—even rage—against the *secularization* of society, with its resulting *moral permissiveness and amoral consumer-oriented materialism and globalization.*

The cumulative effects of the eighteenth-century Enlightenment, the American (1775–1783), French (1789–1793), and Russian (1917–1919) political revolutions, and the scientific revolution of the last two centuries have resulted in diminished attention being paid, especially in the West, to moral and ultimate issues (e.g., sin, salvation, the afterlife). The focus has shifted more and more to gaining the most now from concrete material opportunities. (Some philosophic systems, such as utilitarianism, made this not only acceptable, but "good.") The trend in human societies—at least in theory, if not always in practice—is toward toleration and freedom, to "live and let live," for flexibility in dealing with sociopolitical and cultural issues.

7   Fundamentalism, it seems, is in its essence not a doctrinal phenomenon (though this is often a significant component that draws attention), but a basic outlook directed toward the current world, protesting against laissez-faire civilization. The result is often vehement, inflexible, pitiless opposition to anything new and the trampling on the human rights of the exponents of change and different opinions. Fundamentalism makes its case in blood every day, from misguided zealots who blow up abortion clinics in the name of Jesus to doctrinal fanatics who blow up villagers in the name of Allah.

What's at the Core?

8   Despite all the differences of creed and kind, there are some consistent threads running through the tapestry of fundamentalism that hold it all together: the quest for purity and perfection; the search for absolute certainty; tradition and authenticity; and the predilection for a total, global worldview that controls, or at least impacts, all aspects of life. The attention to tradition and the past—often in an illusory attempt to "restore" that which is historically unreal, which never really happened and is therefore partially false—characterizes most expressions of fundamentalism.

9   Today, fundamentalism is found in all major world religions. While the violent behavior of some of its adherents underscores that there is much to deplore in fundamentalism, thoughtful Christians tend to be sympathetic to a number of its concerns, while also avoiding its mind-set. Christians have learned that they must not idealize the past, as though life 100 or 200 years ago was wonderful, with everyone healthy, well-fed, sober, moral, justly treated, free, happy, and at peace. When Christians yearn for a "revival of primitive godliness," they are not wishing to go back and live in the distant past with all its sufferings, horrors of exploitation, and injustices. What they are seeking is the dedication and surrender to God's will exhibited by the early church.

10   The paradox of the modern world is that while scientific standards are becoming more and more precise and demands for "objectivity" ring in our ears, moral standards are becoming more vague, more situational, and increasingly imprecise. The breakdown of traditional morality, followed by growing social permissiveness, and the economic (and cultural) exploitation of Third World countries and segments of society in Western countries are the evils against which fundamentalists appropriately are protesting.

Inequality Writ Large

11   One key reason for the growth of contemporary fundamentalism is *marginalization*. Marginalization occurs when any group of people—by race, ethnicity, religion, or economic

status—is made to feel irrelevant to decision-making in their society, and excluded from participation in it. This is increasingly the case with the poor in today's world. The speed of travel and almost instant worldwide communication have placed the poverty of whole societies and their unequal social structures in close proximity to wealth and special privilege. Fundamentalism can become attractive as a form of protest for those who feel hopelessly poor, discriminated against, powerless, marginalized, and exploited.

12   Another aspect of marginalization has resulted from the global *shifts in politico-military power.* Simplifying things somewhat, we can say that prior to the seventeenth century, there were about 10 military powers, mostly all European, except the Ottoman Empire. After World War I, this number shrank to about six. Following World War II, the world knew but two superpowers—the United States and the Soviet Union. Now at the opening of the twenty-first century, there is but one superpower.

13   Fundamentalists tend to oppose shifts in international or global power relationships and object to the socioeconomic and technological changes that have caused them. An increasing number of people groups feel "out of the loop" and marginalized. Having won independence and nationhood, many young nation-states hunger for the esteem they believed would come with national identity, and feel humiliated by the economic, cultural, and occasionally military hegemony exerted over them by more powerful states. To them, it seems a kind of "new colonialism," an attempt to control their cultures and morally subvert their way of life. The resentment of the marginalized is still the most prolific breeding ground for fundamentalism.

14   Fundamentalism is also frequently *a protest against the secular national state,* a national government based on secular politics; religious neutrality grounded in some form of separation of "church and state"; democratic, representative government; and loyalty to a particular country or people. Fundamentalists object to having religion and religious leaders pushed from the power center, from the public square, to the periphery and the private home.

15   In general, fundamentalists view the secular nation both as a danger and a failure. It has not achieved social justice. It has not provided family stability, sobriety, respect, and honor. Often the result of secular national government has seemed to be greatly increased crime and divorce rates, drug culture, pornography, homosexuality, and rampant corruption in business and political life.

Going Back to "The Good Old Days"

16   Much as one might agree with some of the fundamentalist critique, one must note that there is an element of mythology and *historical blindness* in fundamentalism. While its adherents are basically against change, and dislike modernity with a vengeance, they do favor one selected change: going back to the "golden age" of tradition. For fundamentalist Muslims this means "going back" more than a thousand years. For fundamentalist Christians, "going back" can vary greatly—to the nineteenth century, to the "united" Christendom of the Middle Ages, to the time of the Church Fathers, to the first century. Some fundamentalist Jews dream of the past theocratic period and temple, or the united kingdom of David and Solomon.

17   Fundamentalists all seek in their own ways to *traditionalize,* to go back to the past, adopt the standards of the past, the theology of the pioneers, the legendary heroism of the

Teutonic knights, the fortitude of the Voortrekkers in South Africa, the firmness of the Puritans in America.

18   Many fundamentalists seek one major reactive change: they want to place their religious views at the center of life in the home, government, courts, media, schools, the military—in short, everywhere. There is a natural progression in fundamentalism toward religious extremism, and finally toward a totalitarian alliance of religion and state working hand in glove.

The Fundamentalist Paradox

19   While fundamentalism may not be as difficult to describe as, say, New Age philosophy, it also has its complexities and paradoxes. It can move in divergent and even contradictory ways. Richard Antoun's perceptive analysis puts it this way: "It can be political/apolitical, confrontational/avoiding confrontation, separationist/integrationist, concerned with orthodoxy in this world/concerned with the individual's fate in the hereafter, or concerned with the external enemy/concerned with the internal."*

20   And day's newscast reveals that fundamentalism can act—or react—in different, even diametrically opposite ways. Fundamentalists can very well hate and even fight other fundamentalists.

Each According to Its Kind

21   There are, according to some experts, at least three types of fundamentalists: (1) those who engage in direct confrontation with the state and wish to take it over and gain power by the use of every means (the end justifies the means!), including violence and terror; (2) those who want to keep some distance, autonomy, and separation from society in order to preserve, protect, and promote their purity, exclusivism, and essential identity; (3) those who "flee" the world and avoid contact as much as possible. Those with a flight or escapist mentality try to avoid state requirements such as taxes, licenses, military or civilian service, schools, memberships, and, of course, any public office. Those with a separationist mentality stay much within groups of like-minded individuals with regard to housing, education, recreation (if any), work, and social intercourse. They even tend to use a separate vocabulary, engage with their society only on points of interest, and seek converts who are similarly searching to minimize contact with a distracting world.

Life by the Book

22   While we may share with fundamentalists a "high view" of Scripture, we have learned that they tend to quote their Scriptures selectively—be it the Torah, the Bible, or the Quran—often using an out-of-context and primitive proof-text approach. Many devout fundamentalists take passages very literally, without seeing the entire perspective, and then apply them simplistically and without reflection to very different present-day situations. Some fundamentalists even rationalize extreme interpretations of their Scriptures to justify the suppression

* Richard T. Antoun, *Understanding Fundamentalism*, p. 160.

of other opinions and dissent, to support violence, the killing of innocent people, political assassinations, and the "glory of suicide-martyrdom."

23   Christianity reminds the world that God inspires his prophets, not in order to provide a weapon for intolerance and rigid dogmatism leading to persecution, but in order to give spiritual inspiration, hope, the gift of love, and reasoned guidance to all people. The truth that comes from God leads to salvation, and in the words of Jesus, "makes you free indeed."

24   From their Scriptures, Christian fundamentalists have learned that all humanity is involved in a cosmic war: salvation is at stake and so is eternity. But for the true Christian, there is no physical war—no conquest, no jihad, no crusade—between true believer and infidel, but a spiritual conflict between truth and error. There is no place for obstinate, merciless, violent intransigence, harsh punishments, or for brutal retaliation against perceived wrongs. Such human-to-human conflicts are ultimately counterfeit controversies, distractions from the spiritual battle for hearts and minds.

It All Comes Down to Freedom

25   The fundamentalist mind-set is finally unacceptable to a child of God who is created in His image as a free moral agent and committed to the teachings of Jesus. There is in fundamentalism a built-in resistance to freedom, to learning, and to creativity that opposes itself to the God who gave us all these gifts. Fundamentalism wherever found—in Tel Aviv, Tajikistan, or Toledo—reveals its taste for bigotry, for fanaticism, for rigidity and exclusiveness at a moment when the world is crying out for bridge builders and peacemakers. It revels in control—doctrinally, politically, even in the family—and justifies its refusal to dialogue and learn by its suspicions of other opinions and other faiths. While seeking to preserve the truth about God, fundamentalism ultimately gives a terribly distorted view of His character and His attitudes.

26   While we may share some of its concerns, and also look forward to the day when all things are restored to God's design, Christians will relate to fundamentalism as they do to every other human "ism." In the name of Him who died to set us free, we will build up the kingdom in His way.

27   *For not with swords, loud clashing,*
Nor roll of stirring drums.
With deeds of love and mercy,
The heavenly kingdom comes.

Source: Bert B. Beach, "Fundamentalism," *Adventist Review,* Oct. 26, 2006, pp. 8–12.

■ *Vocabulary*

linguistically (2)	laissez-faire (7)	infidel (24)
connote (2)	marginalization (11)	intransigence (24)
securality (2)	theocratic (16)	

■ *Questions on Meaning and Technique*

1. What was the original definition of "fundamentalism" in our country? What meaning has it presently acquired? What would you like the concept to mean?

2. How do fundamentalists view change? Why do you think they view change the way they do? What is your opinion of their view? Cite examples to explain your position.

3. Where do you stand on the doctrine of laissez-faire (that is, keeping hands off the beliefs of others?) What dangers, if any, do you perceive in excessive toleration or accommodation?

4. According to the author, how prevalent is fundamentalism in the major world religions? What are all fundamentalists seeking? What is acceptable in fundamentalism? What are its dangers?

5. What is the key reason for the contemporary growth of fundamentalism? What term does the author use to identify the reason? Explain the term. Among which group is the reason most obvious? Do you agree with the author's analysis? Why or why not?

6. Why do fundamentalists mistrust secular nations, where church and state are separated? What is their general view on state governments? Are they right or wrong? Give reasons for your answer.

7. What is the paradox to which the author draws attention in his discussion of how fundamentalists hate change? How effective is this argument?

8. After spending most of the essay defining fundamentalism and explaining its origin and influence, what point does the author add at the end of the essay? Who is his audience? What is his purpose? How effective is this final point?

STUDENT ESSAY—FIRST DRAFT

Cole Ollinger

Title supplied

Prejudice: Child of Ignorance

⟨Insert A⟩

The added introduction, paraphrasing Shakespeare, gives the title literary flavor and is less trite.

1   The American Heritage Dictionary defines prejudice as "the state or act of holding unreasonable preconceived judgments or convictions." The word ~~itself~~ is rooted in the Latin praejudicium, ~~loosely~~ *closely* translated as "previous judgment," an origin that remains relevant to the current popular meaning.

2   Prejudice is often confused with simple preference. *For instance,* ^Gentlemen may prefer blondes to brunettes without ~~accurately~~ being accused of showing prejudice. *Or,* ^A person ~~usually~~ *may* chooses a ~~favorite~~ *certain* style of clothing or flavor of ice cream without prejudice. These are ~~simply~~ *merely* matters of taste.

Transition added

⟨Insert A⟩ Prejudice by any other name would still be the lowest form of thinking. It squints when it looks and lies when it talks. It restrains civilization with the manacles of cruel barbarism.

[margin note: Transitional clause added *]*
[margin note: Sexist pronoun avoided *]*
[margin note: Sentence needed completion. *]*

3 (Insert B) *for instance,* If, experience has ~~guided someone~~ *convinced a driver* to purchase one ~~brand~~ *model* of car instead of another, then this person is not showing prejudice because ~~his knowledge~~ *experience* is applicable. I owned an American ~~car~~ *Ford* that ~~performed inconsistently~~ *kept breaking down;* so now I own a dependable Japanese ~~model~~ *Honda.* In this instance, I am not prejudiced, (Insert C) My father, on the other hand, buys American cars strictly out of patriotic chauvinism, ~~innately~~ *irrationally* distrusting Japanese, German, French, or any other foreign cars; ~~thus,~~ he exhibits prejudice when shopping for automobiles.

[margin note: More accurate word *]*

[margin note: Revision makes paragraph more coherent and emphatic. *]*

4 *In short, an unfavorable* ~~If a disfavorable~~ opinion or decision ~~is~~ based on ~~a study of~~ facts ~~then no prejudice~~ *is not prejudicial, but* *when it is based on pure bias, it is prejudicial.* ~~exists. For example,~~ a bank that refuses a loan to someone with ~~a~~ poor credit rating*s* has not acted with prejudice; (Insert D) ←

5 Prejudice is a common occurrence that can severely damage a particular group of people. *No ¶*

[margin note: No ¶ needed *]*

6 Recently, at a party I attended, I was the ~~focal point~~ *victim* of a relatively harmless yet annoying kind of prejudice. A group of guests had gathered in a corner to discuss books recently read. I expressed my admiration for Walker Percy's novels; then someone else brought up the Beat Generation writers, such as Allen Ginsberg and Jack Kerouac. The conversation became animated as everyone either praised or condemned the Beat writers. But for some reason, my comments were ignored. The group felt that ~~since~~ *because* I liked Walker Percy, I couldn't possibly understand the literature of the Beat Generation. In actuality, I am quite familiar with this group of writers, and the ignorant conclusions (Insert E) of the other people at the party showed prejudice. The Romans' cruel attitude toward

[margin note: New paragraph with transitional sentence needed *]*

the early Christians is an example of ~~another, much more~~ *this* brutal kind of prejudice.

[margin note: No ¶ needed *]*
[margin note: Details added *]*

7 At a time when most Romans still worshipped *Jupiter and other* mythological gods, the Christian faith was ~~considered taboo~~ *forbidden.* In their bitter scorn of Christianity, the Romans unmercifully

Insert B
Prejudice is often confused with reasoned choice.

Insert C
against American cars; I simply made a choice based on sound reasoning.

Insert D
however, a bank that refuses to give someone a loan just because that person looks poor is being prejudiced.

Insert E
While my experience was inconsequential and hurt only me, prejudice can result in enormous cruelty with global consequences. For instance,

tortured helpless Christians, *stoning, crucifying, and* forcing them to hide in caves and catacombs even though

they were doing nothing wrong.

8   In the last century, Adolf Hitler carried out a campaign of atrocities against the

Jews. Propagating the lie that Jews belonged to an inferior race, Hitler ordered them

starved, gassed, or executed. Six million people, including defenseless women and

children, died as a result of this dictator's infamous prejudice.

9   Americans have ~~been equally guilty~~ *not been free* of prejudice. To this day, blacks are still the

frequent victims of *groundless* suspicion and derision that originated over two hundred years ago.

Initially, blacks were socially and economically suppressed as slaves. Then, after finally

being given their freedom as a result of the Civil War, they were continually terrorized

by white supremacist groups like the Ku Klux Klan. Ironically, even the American

government played a role in this prejudice--clear into the 1960s--by denying blacks the

right to vote. Insensitive whites *today* continue to label blacks as "niggers" or "coons." And in

the 1988 Super Bowl game, the fact that the Washington quarterback, Doug Williams,

was a black became a burning issue, albeit one that was completely irrelevant to the

player's ability to gain a victory for his team.

	Original version is too inclusive.

10   Other minority groups have encountered ~~similar difficulties~~ *prejudice* in our country.

Americans have ~~always~~ *often* treated immigrants with hostility. ~~Again,~~ In recent history,

~~these~~ *certain immigrant* groups were given nicknames that obviously manifested prejudice *against their national origins*. Italians

were called "dagos" or "wops." Chinese were called "chinks." Japanese were

called "japs." All Irishmen were considered hopeless drunks; people from Oklahoma

were thought of as stupid and dirty; ~~and~~ Mexicans were reputed to be lazy and

undependable. An even subtler and far more damaging prejudice than this childish

name calling was the harm done by companies and individuals who, without the

slightest reason, flatly refused to hire immigrants simply because they were not

American born.

	Repetition of key word prejudice helps coherence.
	Clarifies the kind of prejudice
	Avoids needless repetition of and in same sentence

11   In the job market, women have been victims of prejudice. For many years, our

culture dictated that a woman's place was in the home; hence, women were seldom

given the chance to prove their abilities *in prestigious professions*. Men ~~in general~~ were thought to be more

	Avoids specificity and prunes deadwood

capable of success~~ful performance~~ in the corporate world. Salary figures emphasized
this point as men ~~standardly~~ *usually* earned more money than women in the same job. This
is a textbook example of prejudice. With great effort and much litigation, American
women have significantly improved their situation in recent years, but cases of
sexual prejudice linger on.

More accurate

12   Women in other parts of the world ~~have not been so fortunate~~. *continue be held back by prejudice.* In the Arabic
countries, *for example,* women are still rarely permitted to speak in public and must cover their
heads and faces with a <u>chador</u> in order to prevent themselves from ~~tempting~~ *seducing* strange
men. These women are certainly not evil temptresses, but because of a centuries-old
tradition, they are treated as if showing their faces were ~~as~~ indecorous~~, as showing
their breasts.~~

13   Prejudice occurs so often that everyone has, in some form or another, felt its
effects. Recently, I have felt the sting of prejudice from blacks. I am white, but I like
to play basketball in a predominantly black section of town. Frequently my black
teammates will not pass me the ball because of my color and because they consider

*More honest
word*

me a stranger. I have also felt the prejudice ~~against~~ *leveled at* people who are excessively tall.
Because of my height, other basketball players insist that I play close to the basket
instead of playing guard, which is my natural position. Even the playground is filled
with prejudice.

14   Another area of prejudice is product manufacture. Anyone who is taller than
six feet feels the prejudice of stores who never sell beds that are long enough
to keep a tall person's feet from dangling off the end of the mattress. People
who are left-handed also feel victimized by manufacturer prejudice because
they rarely can find golf clubs, school desks, guitars, or other items to suit
their left-handedness.

*Prunes
deadwood,
making the
conclusion
more concise*

15   Prejudice exists everywhere and ranges from petty social exclusion ~~of a person~~
to violent persecution ~~of an entire race~~. Whenever people make decisions based
on preconceived ideas--whether on the sidewalk or in the boardroom--they act
with prejudice.

Ollinger 1

Cole Ollinger

Professor Winkler

English 101

December 3, 2002

Prejudice: Child of Ignorance

1   Prejudice by any other name would still be the lowest form of thinking. It squints when it looks and lies when it talks. It restrains civilization with the manacles of cruel barbarism. *The American Heritage Dictionary* defines *prejudice* as "the state or act of holding unreasonable preconceived judgments or convictions." The word is rooted in the Latin *praejudicium*, closely translated as "previous judgment," an origin that remains relevant to the current popular meaning.

2   Prejudice is often confused with simple preference. For instance, gentlemen may prefer blondes to brunettes without being accused of showing prejudice. Or, a person may choose a certain style of clothing or flavor of ice cream without prejudice. These are merely matters of taste.

3   Prejudice is often confused with reasoned choice. If, for instance, experience has convinced a driver to purchase one model of car instead of another, then this person is not showing prejudice because experience is applicable. I owned an American Ford that kept breaking down; so now I own a dependable Japanese Honda.

Ollinger 2

In this instance, I am not prejudiced against American cars; I simply made a choice based on sound reasoning. My father, on the other hand, buys American cars strictly out of patriotic chauvinism, irrationally distrusting Japanese, German, French, or any other foreign cars; he exhibits prejudice when shopping for automobiles. A bank that refuses a loan to someone with years of bad credit ratings has not acted with prejudice; however, a bank that refuses to give someone a loan just because that person looks poor is being prejudiced. In short, an unfavorable opinion or decision based on facts is not prejudicial, but when it is based on pure bias, it is prejudicial.

4   Prejudice is a common occurrence that can damage people. Recently, at a party I attended, I was the victim of a relatively harmless yet annoying kind of prejudice. A group of guests had gathered in a corner to discuss books recently read. I expressed my admiration for Walker Percy's novels; then someone else brought up the Beat Generation writers, such as Allen Ginsberg and Jack Kerouac. The conversation became animated as everyone either praised or condemned the Beat writers. But for some reason, my comments were ignored. The group felt that because I liked Walker Percy, I couldn't possibly understand the literature of the Beat Generation. In actuality, I am quite familiar with this group of writers, and the ignorant conclusions of the other people at the party showed prejudice.

5   While my experience was inconsequential and hurt only me, prejudice can result in enormous cruelty with global consequences. For instance, the Romans' cruel attitude toward the early Christians

Ollinger 3

is an example of this brutal kind of prejudice. At a time when most Romans still worshipped Jupiter and other mythological gods, the Christian faith was forbidden. In their bitter scorn of Christianity, the Romans unmercifully tortured helpless Christians, stoning, crucifying, and forcing them to hide in caves and catacombs even though they were doing nothing wrong.

6   In the last century, Adolf Hitler carried out a campaign of atrocities against Jews. Propagating the lie that Jews belonged to an inferior race, Hitler ordered them starved, gassed, or executed. Six million people, including defenseless women and children, died as a result of this dictator's infamous prejudice.

7   Americans have not been free of prejudice. To this day, blacks are still the frequent victims of groundless suspicion and derision that originated over two hundred years ago. Initially, blacks were socially and economically suppressed as slaves. Then, after finally being given their freedom as a result of the Civil War, they were continually terrorized by white supremacist groups like the Ku Klux Klan. Ironically, even the American government played a role in this prejudice—clear into the 1960s—by denying blacks the right to vote. Insensitive whites today continue to label blacks as "niggers" or "coons." And in the 1988 Super Bowl game, the fact that the Washington quarterback, Doug Williams, was a black became a burning issue, albeit one that was completely irrelevant to the player's ability to gain a victory for his team.

Ollinger 4

8   Other minority groups have encountered prejudice in our country. Americans have often treated immigrants with hostility. In recent history, certain immigrant groups were given nicknames that obviously manifested prejudice against their national origins. Italians were called "dagos" or "wops." Chinese were called "chinks." Japanese were called "japs." All Irishmen were considered hopeless drunks; people from Oklahoma were thought of as stupid and dirty; Mexicans were reputed to be lazy and undependable. An even subtler and far more damaging prejudice than this childish name calling was the harm done by companies and individuals who, without the slightest reason, flatly refused to hire immigrants simply because they were not American-born.

9   In the job market, women have been victims of prejudice. For many years, our culture dictated that a woman's place was in the home; hence, women were seldom given the chance to prove their abilities in prestigious professions. Men were thought to be more capable of success in the corporate world. Salary figures emphasized this point as men usually earned more money than women in the same job. This is a textbook example of prejudice. With great effort and much litigation, American women have significantly improved their situation in recent years, but cases of sexual prejudice linger on.

10   Women in other parts of the world continue to be held back by prejudice. In the Arabic countries, for example, women are still rarely permitted to speak in public and must cover their heads and

Ollinger 5

faces with a *chador* in order to prevent them from seducing strange
men. These women are certainly not evil temptresses, but because
of a centuries-old tradition, they are treated as if showing their
faces were indecorous.

11   Prejudice occurs so often that everyone has, in some form
or another, felt its effects. Recently, I have felt the sting of
prejudice from blacks. I am white, but I like to play basketball
in a predominantly black section of town. Frequently my black
teammates will not pass me the ball because of my color and
because they consider me a stranger. I have also felt the prejudice
leveled at people who are excessively tall. Because of my height,
other basketball players insist that I play close to the basket
instead of playing guard, which is my natural position. Even the
playground is filled with prejudice.

12   Another area of prejudice is product manufacture. Anyone who
is taller than six feet feels the prejudice of stores who never sell
beds that are long enough to keep a tall person's feet from dangling
off the end of the mattress. People who are left-handed also feel
victimized by manufacturer prejudice because they rarely can find
golf clubs, school desks, guitars, or other items to suit their left-
handedness.

13   Prejudice exists everywhere and ranges from petty social
exclusion to violent persecution. Whenever people make decisions
based on preconceived ideas—whether on the sidewalk or in the
boardroom—they act with prejudice.

WILLIAM SPOONER DONALD

Will Someone Please Hiccup My Pat?

William Spooner Donald (1910–2002) was a career British Navy officer between 1924 and 1949 and has been a freelance writer since leaving the service. During World War II he was cited twice for gallantry under fire. A nephew of the famous Reverend William Archibald Spooner, from whose transpositions of initial syllables the term spoonerism *was derived, Donald wrote screenplays, plays, and memoirs, among them* Hong Kong Cocktail *(play, 1951),* Pickled Salts *(play, 1951),* Stand by for Action *(memoir, 1956), and* Hanky Panky in the Highlands *(play, 1968).*

READING FOR IDEAS Definitions do not have to be dour and dull, as this piece of writing shows. Nor do we have to know the name of a verbal error to make it. Whether or not we know the proper name of the mispronunciation defined in this piece, most of us have occasionally committed a *spoonerism*. Donald not only defines *spoonerism* for us, he also treats us to a brief but hilarious biography of Spooner himself. As you read, ask yourself how understatement contributes to the humor of this article. What rhetorical strategy does the author heavily rely on to advance the definition?

1   One afternoon nearly a hundred years ago the October wind gusted merrily down Oxford's High Street. Hatless and helpless, a white-haired clergyman with pink cherubic features uttered his plaintive cry for aid. As an athletic youngster chased the spinning topper, other bystanders smiled delightedly—they had just heard at first hand the latest "Spoonerism."

2   My revered relative William Archibald Spooner was born in 1844, the son of a Staffordshire county court judge. As a young man, he was handicapped by a poor physique, a stammer, and weak eyesight; at first, his only possible claim to future fame lay in the fact that he was an albino, with very pale blue eyes and white hair tinged slightly yellow.

3   But nature compensated the weakling by blessing him with a brilliant intellect. By 1868 he had been appointed a lecturer at New College, Oxford. Just then he would have been a caricaturist's dream with his freakish looks, nervous manner, and peculiar mental kink that caused him—in his own words—to "make occasional felicities in verbal diction."

4   Victorian Oxford was a little world of its own where life drifted gently by; a world where splendid intellectuals lived in their ivory towers of Latin, Euclid, and Philosophy; a world where it was always a sunny summer afternoon in a countryside, where Spooner admitted he loved to "pedal gently round on a well-boiled icicle."

5   As the years passed, Spooner grew, probably without himself being aware of the fact, into a "character." A hard worker himself, he detested idleness and is on record as having rent some lazybones with the gem, "You have hissed all my mystery lessons, and completely tasted two whole worms."

6   With his kindly outlook on life, it was almost natural for him to take holy orders; he was ordained a deacon in 1872 and a priest in 1875. His unique idiosyncrasy never caused any serious trouble and merely made him more popular. On one occasion, in New

College chapel in 1879, he announced smilingly that the next hymn would be "Number one seven five—Kinkering Kongs their Titles Take." Other congregations were treated to such jewels as ". . . Our Lord, we know, is a shoving Leopard . . ." and ". . . All of us have in our hearts a half-warmed fish to lead a better life. . . ."

7   Spooner often preached in the little village churches around Oxford and once delivered an eloquent address on the subject of Aristotle. No doubt the sermon contained some surprising information for his rustic congregation. For after Spooner had left the pulpit, an idea seemed to occur to him, and he hopped back up the steps again.

8   "Excuse me, dear brethren," he announced brightly, "I just want to say that in my sermon whenever I mentioned Aristotle, I should have said Saint Paul."

9   By 1885 the word "Spoonerism" was in colloquial use in Oxford circles, and a few years later, in general use all over England. If the dividing line between truth and myth is often only a hairsbreadth, does it really matter? One story that has been told concerns an optician's shop in London. Spooner is reputed to have entered and asked to see a "signifying glass." The optician registered polite bewilderment.

10   "Just an ordinary signifying glass," repeated Spooner, perhaps surprised at the man's obtuseness.

11   "I'm afraid we haven't one in stock, but I'll make inquiries right away, sir," said the shopkeeper, playing for time.

12   "Oh, don't bother, it doesn't magnify, it doesn't magnify," said Spooner airily, and walked out.

13   Fortunately for Spooner, he made the right choice when he met his wife-to-be. He was thirty-four years old when he married Frances Goodwin in 1878. The marriage was a happy one, and they had one son and four daughters. Mrs. Spooner was a tall, good-looking girl, and on one occasion the family went on a short holiday in Switzerland. The "genial Dean," as he was then called, took a keen interest in geology, and in no time at all he had mastered much information and many technical definitions on the subject of glaciers.

14   One day at lunchtime the younger folk were worried because their parents had not returned from a long walk. When Spooner finally appeared with his wife, his explanation was: "We strolled up a long valley, and when we turned a corner we found ourselves completely surrounded by erotic blacks."

15   He was, of course, referring to "erratic blocks," or large boulders left around after the passage of a glacier.

16   In 1903 Spooner was appointed Warden of New College, the highest possible post for a Fellow. One day walking across the quadrangle, he met a certain Mr. Casson, who had just been elected a Fellow of New College.

17   "Do come to dinner tonight," said Spooner, "we are welcoming our new Fellow, Mr. Casson."

18   "But, my dear Warden, I *am* Casson," was the surprised reply.

19   "Never mind, never mind, come along all the same," said Spooner tactfully.

20   On another occasion in later years when his eyesight was really very bad, Spooner found himself seated next to a most elegant lady at dinner. In a casual moment the latter put her lily-white hand onto the polished table, and Spooner, in an even more casual manner, pronged her hand with his fork, remarking genially, "My bread, I think."

21   In 1924 Spooner retired as Warden. He had established an astonishing record of continuous residence at New College for sixty-two years first as undergraduate, then as

Fellow, then Dean, and finally as Warden. His death in 1930, at the age of eighty-six, was a blushing crow to collectors of those odd linguistic transpositions known by then throughout the English-speaking world as Spoonerisms.

■ *Vocabulary*

plaintive (1)   idiosyncrasy (6)   obtuseness (10)
caricaturist (3)   colloquial (9)

■ *Questions on Meaning and Technique*

1. What does the title have to do with the definition in this essay?
2. What is the main technique used by the author in defining *spoonerism*?
3. Why does the author put quotation marks around *character* in paragraph 5? What does *character* mean, used in this sense?
4. Where does the author finally tell us what a *spoonerism* is? Why does he wait so long?
5. What sort of treatment do you think Spooner's odd mental kink might have received, say, in a modern business environment? Do you think it would have been treated with equal geniality and tolerance?
6. What is the point of paragraph 4, and why was making it necessary?
7. What part do you think Oxford played in the coinage of the term *spoonerism*?

Writing Assignments

1. Write a definition of the word *pun,* giving several examples.
2. Define *sarcasm* and *irony* in an essay, making a distinction between them.

 ## Internet Research Assignment

Do an Internet search on the term *ebonics*. In one paragraph, define this term by providing a lexical definition and some typical examples.

Additional Writing Assignments

Beginning with a lexical definition and extending the definition into a full essay, define one of the following terms. Be sure your essay answers the question: What is it?

alienation   respectability
fanaticism   ADHD (attention deficit hyperactivity disorder)
Google   happiness

virtue	hypocrisy
hip hop	mercy
evil	no-fault insurance

Rewriting Assignment

Choose a classmate with whom to collaborate on rewriting the skimpy definition that follows. One of you should look up the etymology of the term, and the other should state what the term is not. Then brainstorm until you come up with at least two appropriate examples that clarify the term.

Tyranny is ruling by a tyrant. No one wants to live in a tyrannical country because it allows no personal freedom. Many tyrants have ruled nations in history. Perhaps the worst was Adolf Hitler, who wanted to rid Germany of everyone who was not of the Aryan race—especially blacks and Jews—and who wanted to conquer all of Europe for himself.

Photo Writing Assignment

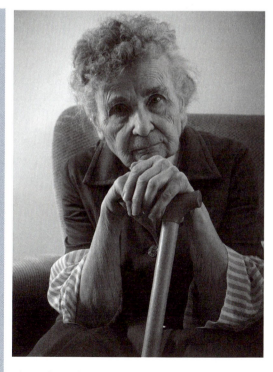

Alexander Raths 2010 / Used under license from Shutterstock.com

After carefully studying the photo of the woman with her head held in her hand, conclude what kind of emotion she is feeling. In a brief essay, define the emotion and explain it so that your reader can understand its meaning. Begin with a dictionary definition.

Digging for Gold or for Meaning

Of all the rhetorical types we will cover in these exercises, the one that fits most closely to our digging analogy is the definition. Many words over the centuries have accumulated underground meanings that make them resemble root crops like beetroot or potato. The etymology of a word is often listed by the dictionary, and it is by studying these earliest meanings that we gain a true understanding of the word's implications.

Definition gives us the chance to explain what a word really means. Ancient words have clinging to them significances and meanings that have become so lost to us that even when we see or hear the words in a familiar context, we still do not understand them. Do you recognize this line: "Fæder ure þu þe eart on heofonum"? That's the first line of the Lord's prayer in old English. The point is that with ancient words, definition becomes an urgent task that sometimes requires the writer to dig deep into meaning.

This chapter inspires a definition essay by the sheer weight of example. One can only imagine the kind of digging the writer of the essay defining *Spoonerism* had to do, to say nothing of the rich layer of clarifying terms uncovered by a new contributor, Bert B. Beach, in defining *fundamentalism*. The point is that if you don't have your meanings clear at the outset of an argument, you run the risk of having no topic, no point of contention, no argument, and no essay. Digging into the meaning of words is therefore as exciting for the writer as refining gold is for the miner. You find out what the word means and how or where it can be used, improving your vocabulary along the way. That's gold worth mining, we think.

Chapter 11

Comparison/Contrast

ANTHONY C. WINKLER

Dream House

Anthony Winkler (b. 1942) is a prolific writer of novels, textbooks, biographies, short stories, screenplays, and newspaper articles. Jamaican born and raised, he has been honored by the Jamaican government as one of the best fiction writers to reveal the heartbeat and geography of the West Indies, especially Jamaica. Although Winkler moved to California at twenty to pursue a degree in English, he never forgot his Jamaican roots and has continued, as an émigré, to write about his people, their customs, and the lusciousness of the land. His novels are filled with unusual characters—the wise, the humble, the quixotic, the superstitious, and the insane. Among Winkler's novels are: The Painted Canoe *(1984),* The Lunatic *(1987),* The Great Yacht Race *(1992),* Going Home to Teach *(1995),* The Duppy *(1999), and* The Annihilation of Fish, and Other Stories *(2004). Winkler is also the coauthor of numerous English textbooks, including this one.*

READING FOR IDEAS A good way to read this story is to reflect nostalgically on your own youth and the special places you frequented with your best friends. Perhaps no one ever built you a playhouse like the one in the following story, but you may remember a river where fish were plentiful and the water inviting, a basketball hoop hanging on someone's garage door, an orchard filled with ripe fruit, or campouts in the woods or mountains. Write down your feelings as you think about the people and places that continue to haunt you as an adult. Try to recapture the richness of these memories about specific places, people, and events.

1   My father was so clumsy that he often broke whatever he was repairing. Trying to oil a creaky screen door, he punched a hole in the mesh; replacing a single cracked pane, he ruined the mullions of a window. Part of his ineptness was god-given, but some of it came from his Jamaican upbringing that hadn't prepared him for the do-it-yourself life in America.

2   We moved from Jamaica to America when I was eight years old. In the beginning, my family—which consisted of me, my mother and father—struggled to make a home in Southern California. We didn't have much money; we didn't understand the people, their way of speech, and their outlook on life, and they didn't understand us and ours. It is hard to put into words what we found so puzzling about them, and impossible to say what they found so puzzling about us.

3   My mother had been a trauma nurse in Jamaica and, because of a nurse shortage, almost immediately found a job in a local hospital. For my father, it was like he had spontaneously generated on the day he arrived in Los Angeles and had never existed before. He had been the owner of an advertising agency in Kingston with a staff of twenty, but that didn't count in California. He had to start all over again in his 40's working the boards as a rookie graphic artist.

4   He had a good attitude, however, and he threw himself into his work and quickly made a local name for himself as a designer of imaginative logos. He became so popular that he started his own agency and soon had five employees.

5   As his company did better, we got richer, and after a series of moves, settled down in a sprawling four-bedroom home in Pasadena. It was a spacious house with a big back-yard on a quiet residential street lined on both sides with majestic live oaks. The front yard was an apron of Bermuda grass.

6   And the closest next door neighbors, whose yard shared a common fence with ours, were the Petersons.

7   The Petersons were a family of three, with a son my age whose name was Josh. We went to the same school, played baseball for the same Little League team, and hung out daily, calling ourselves the *two J's,* my name being Jessie. I got to know Josh and his family as closely as any I'd ever known.

8   Mr. Peterson was a big, gruff man whose manner said he pitied nearly everyone he met. Josh used to say that his father was handy enough to fix anything under God's sun. It took him only two weekends to single-handedly build a deck off his kitchen. He mounted the frame on sunken posts embedded in concrete, squared and leveled the floor-ing joists, and the deck just seemed to grow naturally off the back of his house like the new limb of a tree.

9   Mrs. Peterson had once been a minor actress in B-movies. Her brush with moviemak-ing had left her with a dramatic personality and a tendency to emote over every little incidental tiff. She and Mr. Peterson were always arguing over this and that—never any-thing of any great consequence, except symbolically to them. Every argument would end the same way, with Mrs. Peterson sobbing in her kitchen, and Mr. Peterson sulking in his workshop.

10   During his parents' frequent quarrels Josh would come over and take refuge in my room with me until he heard the door slam that told him that his father had angrily withdrawn, leaving his mother crying in the kitchen.

11   "Don't your parents ever fight?" he asked me one day when he was hiding from his squabbling parents.

12   I wanted to make him feel better, so I said, "Every week."

13   He perked up immediately. "Will you call me next time they fight?"

14   I said I would, but I never did. He kept asking me why. Finally, I apologized for my parents, who had lately been stubbornly getting along instead of fighting.

15   "They're just in a slump right now," I said. "But last month my mother called my father a birdbrain."

16   "What'd your father do?"

17   "He told her she was beginning to talk with a twang."

18   "Gee, they really draw blood, don't they?"

19   "That was vicious. Jamaicans hate to be told that they talk with a twang."

20   "So what'd your mother say?"

21   "She told him to go to *h e two sticks.*"

22   "What?"

23   I leaned over and whispered, "*He 2 sticks*—hell."

24   He stood up slowly like an elephant was sitting in his lap. At the door he turned and said sarcastically, "I feel much better about my mom and dad."

25   "You don't understand how bad Jamaicans feel about *h e two sticks.*"

26   The next summer Josh and I turned eleven and began sleeping on weekend nights in a tent either in his backyard or in mine. The first time we did it we were terrified by suspicious noises in the night.

27   One of us would whisper, "What's that?" to which the other would reply in a quaking voice, "I don't know."

28   We didn't sleep much that first night, and the next day at the breakfast table my father remarked that we both looked a little pale. We told him about the noises we heard and how we kept waking up.

29   He sat quietly eating for a long moment.

30   "When I was your age and I felt afraid of anything I didn't know or understand, my grandfather suggested I make up a story about it."

31   "How does that help?" I asked.

32   "It helps you to gain control over what you're afraid of. You take de thing dat terrifies you de most and put it in your story. You're telling de story. You're in charge."

33   "Being eaten by a bear frightens me," Josh said.

34   "I don't care for that, either," I remarked.

35   "A bear, eh? Dat's good because dere's no bears around here. So no matter how crazy your story bear gets, you know it can't hurt you."

36   That made a lot of sense to me and Josh, and the next time we slept in our tent and heard a funny noise, we took turns telling bear stories to explain it. The trick worked for a while, but we told such horrible stories to each other that we still felt frightened.

37   One night we so terrified ourselves that we started yelling for help. It was only after we had made a racket loud enough to rouse the dead that my father got up and stumbled to the mouth of our tent with a flashlight and asked what was wrong. Mr. Peterson never woke up.

38   After my father had returned to bed, Josh said, "You know what we need? A playhouse."

39   It took me only a blink to realize he was right.

40   What we each needed was our own playhouse. We could take turns visiting each other. The more we talked about it the more excited we got. We didn't fall asleep until the moon was hopelessly webbed in the thick limbs of an oak tree.

41   We picked out the perfect spot in our respective yards for our house and began begging our fathers to build it.

42   From the very start I knew that my father would be incapable of building my playhouse. I could tell from his reaction that he thought that I was asking him to walk on water.

43   For a while, neither father did anything. Then one Saturday Mr. Peterson abruptly began working on Josh's dream house.

44   His threw himself into the job methodically, and for the next few weeks in the evenings and weekends the whole neighborhood could hear him sawing and pounding away energetically.

45   Right in the spot Josh had selected for a house, the stick frame of a playhouse rose up on tiptoe among the trees. It was, to me and Josh, a riveting sight to see the house miraculously begin to take shape, and we would've spent endless hours out with Mr. Peterson while he was building it if he had let us. But the first time he caught us hanging around watching, he told us bluntly to get lost or he would stop working.

46   So we sat on the side of my yard and watched him from afar as he built Josh's dream house.

47   Mr. Peterson worked with the fierce concentration of a gifted handyman, and the house began to shape up with the logic of carpentry. It was a splendid playhouse, with an upstairs and a downstairs. Its roof was shingled with cedar. Its exterior walls had overlapping wood siding. The second floor balcony was railed and connected to the downstairs by an exterior staircase.

48   When it was being built, I began to badger my father into getting started on my house, and almost every week I got in a dig at him by mentioning the wonderful job Mr. Peterson was doing on Josh's house. He would wince and say something to excuse himself about how busy he was and how he meant to begin next weekend if nothing came up.

49   But something always came up.

50   In the meantime, Mr. Peterson finished the house for Josh, and one weekend as he packed his tools away, he yelled for Josh and me to come and have a look.

51   We went and stood there before the house, stupefied. In our eyes, it was palatial, the most glorious house that ever was. That first night we slept in it we could hardly tell when we were awake or dreaming.

52   The next day Mr. Peterson and Mrs. Peterson had a particularly bitter quarrel. Mr. Peterson packed his bags, flung them in the trunk of his Mercedes so hard that one suitcase burst open, and drove away, leaving Mrs. Peterson sobbing in the kitchen.

53   After his father left, Josh became depressed and avoided the playhouse completely. He refused to even go inside it.

54   In my view, we were worse off than before. Now we had a house but one Josh wouldn't use. I wanted my own playhouse worse than ever. I nagged my father mercilessly about it. Sometimes I said some unkind things to spur him on, but all I did was hurt his feelings.

55   One night I went to his office and found him sketching a house on a yellow legal pad.

56   "Is that my house?" I asked eagerly.

57   He nodded sadly.

58   "Are you going to build it?"

59   "I'm going to try," he said. "I don't know if I can do it, though."

60   "Describe it for me," I said sitting in an easy chair.

61   He began to describe it. He was very vivid, and I got caught up in his words. He said it would be a single-story house and would be built with knotty pine lumber. He asked me to close my eyes and imagine what it would look like.

62   To help us imagine it, we went outside to the spot in our yard where I wanted my house built, and we sat on the grass where the floor would be laid.

63   It was a typical August night in Pasadena—the stars smothered under a muddy run-off of light and smog from Los Angeles, and only a planet or two bobbing overhead like specks of fat in the primordial soup.

64   "Here is where you can put your sleeping bags," my father said, showing me a spot in the thick nap of Bermuda grass.

65   We heard a rustling sound and Josh appeared at the fence peering through the hedge.

66   "What're you doing?" he asked.

67   "Checking out the house my father built," I said.

68   "What house?"

69   "We're imagining what it's like," my father said softly.

70   "Can I come over and imagine, too?"

71   "Sure," my father said.

72   So Josh climbed the fence, and for the next hour, the three of us sat on the grass inside my imaginary house and talked about what we would do in it and how it would look.

73   The chalky night of Southern California ghosted by like an old clipper ship under full sail, and so engrossed were we in the imaginary house that it was long past midnight before we finally staggered off to bed.

74   The next weekend we took our sleeping bags and slept in a tent we set up on the floor of my house. We made a game of imagining that we were inside my house and surrounded by walls of knotty pine. It seemed ridiculous at first, but there was something exhilarating about being in a house that was imaginary, and we spent a peaceful night in spite of some horrible bear stories we told to each other about being devoured in our sleep.

75   The next day we were pretending to be inside our house when Mummy, who was weeding nearby, asked us what we were doing.

76   "Playing in our house," I said.

77   "What house?"

78   "Only three people in the whole world can see it, Mummy," I boasted.

79   "Your father built it, didn't he?" she muttered, resuming her weeding.

80   "Boy," Josh whispered, "this is one totally awesome house."

81   My father was what made it so awesome.

82   He spent hours with us in our house. Some weekends he slept in our tent inside our dream house and took part in telling bear stories. Without him, our belief in the invisible house would not have survived the opposition of a contradicting world. But his backing added a legitimacy that made our dream house seem real.

83   Josh was still grieving over his departed father, so my father took him under his wing that summer as if he were a second son. He took us to Dodger baseball games, fishing off the Santa Monica pier, and camping at Lake Arrowhead. Josh became my brother; my father became my best friend; and the house only the three of us could see deepened our relationship with a mystical bond stronger than blood.

84   One night my father outdid himself and told the story of a bear of such awesome savagery that even with him here, Josh and I began shaking. Seeing how terrified his story had made us, he said, "Of course, de bear was unable to get in because of de knotty pine walls."

85   We sat very still. The night was cool and dry, and from the nearby San Bernardino Freeway came the ceaseless droning of traffic—constant, shrill and unvarying like the flat line alarm of an electrocardiogram.

86   Josh finally said, "Of course, de bear was unable to get in because of de knotty pine walls," in a voice that mimicked my father's accent perfectly. I thought he was mocking my father, but I quickly saw that he was reciting as an admirer would the words of a beloved poet.

87   A week later Josh was riding his bike on the street when a speeding car knocked him down. He was taken to the hospital and lay on the brink of death in intensive care for two weeks. Because my mother was a trauma nurse at that hospital, my father was allowed regular visits to his bedside. He went to see him almost every day.

88   Josh gradually recovered and was released from the hospital. I visited him as soon as he came home. He was still in traction from a back injury and had the puffy, whitish look of an old mushroom. For a while we talked about nothing and tried our best to pretend that he was well again. Then he got serious.

89   "I think your father saved my life," he said in a weak voice.

90   "How?"

91   "I was having a dream about something bad trying to get into my room. I opened my eyes and saw your father standing there. You know what he said to me?"

92   "No. What?"

93   He said, "Remember, de bear can't get in because of de knotty pine walls."

94   He said it had sounded so ridiculous that he almost laughed. But after my father had left, Josh began to think about our dream house and its knotty pine walls. He was thinking hard about what my father had said when a nurse came in to check his IV drip.

95   "De bear can't get in because of de knotty pine walls," Josh mumbled at her.

96   "Of course not, honey!" she said cheerfully, used to delusional ravings from her semi-comatose patients. "No bears allowed in here!"

97   "I think it was death trying to get me," he whispered. "But it couldn't because of de knotty pine walls that your father built."

98   I didn't know what to say, so I said lamely, "Wow! That was some dream."

99   Summer ended, and Mr. Peterson filed for divorce. Her marriage over, Mrs. Peterson decided that the house was too much for her and that she had to move into something smaller.

100   After several months on the market, the house sold and the dreaded day of Josh's moving arrived slowly but irresistibly like death from cancer. Mr. Peterson came to help with the move, and during a break for lunch, he and my father and Josh and I hung out briefly at the fence.

101   "I see you never got around to building that playhouse," Mr. Peterson remarked to my father in a condescending tone of superiority.

102   Josh and I chuckled. Mr. Peterson looked annoyed.

103   "What's so funny?" he asked irritably.

104   "The house," Josh said, "is right here."

105   "Where?"

106   "Here!" Josh and I exclaimed in one voice, jumping up and down on the flooring.

107   "What's this all about?" Mr. Peterson asked my father brusquely.

108   "It's something just between me and de boys," my father said.

109   "But de bear can't get in because of de knotty pine walls," Josh sang out.

110   Mr. Peterson looked as if he suspected that he was being ridiculed.

111   "Well," he said spitefully, indicating the nearby unused playhouse, "at least I gave you a real American playhouse instead of a Jamaican voodoo one."

112   As Mr. Peterson stalked away, Josh began to cry.

113   "Dad, all you gave me was a pile of boards nailed together!" he screamed.

114   "You sound just like your mother," Mr. Peterson scornfully threw over his shoulder. He climbed in his Mercedes and roared out the driveway.

115   And that was the last I ever saw of him.

116   Josh and I passed through the preadolescent years and entered our teens gingerly like explorers stepping into unmapped territory. Girls came into our lives, and the dream house receded on the outgoing tide of childhood memories. We still keep in touch even though he's married and living in another state.

117   I graduated college, went to work as a copywriter for my father, got married and had a son. My parents continued to live in that Pasadena house for over thirty years. During that time, Josh's old house was occupied successively by the Rileys, the Jameses, the Wilsons, the Pevitts, and the Banions. The playhouse aged slowly but steadily like a grounded freighter being devoured in microscopic nibbles by the sea. Last year, the Banions, who were childless, had it torn down and removed.

118   The grass quickly recaptured the chosen spot on which the house was built, and by summer no one could tell that a splendid playhouse had once straddled that patch of land on posts of thick cedar.

119   Mummy died and went home in an urn, and my father, who says he's waiting to join her, stayed on by himself in the Pasadena house, which is too big for him. To keep him company, my seven year old son spends every day after school at his grandfather's, and between the two of them has blossomed the love that transcends generations.

120   One evening my son was oddly untalkative as we made our way home after I had picked him up at his grandfather's. Finally, he said to me in the voice of an awed seven year old, "Dad, did you know that there's a playhouse in grandpa's yard that only three people in the whole world can see?"

121   "Yes," I said. "I did know."

122   "And de knotty pine walls keep de bears out," he gushed. "That's awesome."

123   The copywriter in me hates that word *awesome*. I think it's overused to the point of meaninglessness. But it was the only word that fit this situation.

124   "Yes, son," I agreed. "Dat's totally awesome."

■ *Vocabulary*

mullions (1)	webbed (40)	savagery (84)
ineptness (1)	methodically (44)	delusional (96)
trauma (3)	riveting (45)	comatose (96)
spontaneously (3)	stupefied (51)	brusquely (107)
generated (3)	palatial (51)	voodoo (111)
gruff (8)	primordial (63)	gingerly (116)
emote (9)	legitimacy (82)	transcends (119)
incidental (9)	mystical (83)	

■ *Questions on Meaning and Technique*

1. This story is filled with comparisons and contrasts. What, in your view, are the most obvious items being contrasted? Name the items and list the points of contrast.

2. What does the playhouse symbolize for Josh and Jessie? Why is it so important to them? What is your interpretation of the meaning of the playhouse?

3. How does Mr. Peterson differ from Jessie's father? Which father appeals to you more? Give reasons for your choice.

4. Winkler peppers his story with vivid figurative language. Where in the story do some of these images occur? Point to the specific paragraphs and indicate how the image adds to the texture and meaning of the story.

5. How does the author avoid narrating tedious, irrelevant events? Why does his technique enhance, rather than diminish, the plot of the story? Does the story leave you with unanswered questions? If so, what are they?

6. How important are the two mothers in the story? What role do they play? What would happen to the story if the mothers were entirely eliminated?

7. What advantage does each playhouse—the real one and the imaginary one—have over the other? Which is your favorite? Give reasons for your choice.

8. What is the point of the dialogue beginning in paragraph 11? What does it add to the meaning of the story? What, if anything, does it tell you that you did not know before?

9. Why does the narrator insist that normally he hates the word *awesome* but that it was the only word that fit the circumstances he was describing? What other words fall into the same category as *awesome*? How can we redeem these words?

10. What role does Jessie's son play in the story? How important is his role? What would happen to the story if it had ended with the obliteration of Mr. Peterson's playhouse (paragraph 118)?

CHARLES BUKOWSKI

The Twins

Charles Bukowski (1920–1994), American poet and writer, was born in Andernach, Germany. He attended Los Angeles City College and worked at a variety of odd jobs for several years, including one long stint with the U.S. Postal Service. A prolific writer and best-selling author in West Germany, Bukowski was the author of numerous books, including Flower Fist and Bestial Wail *(1959),* Long Shot Poems for Broke Players *(1961),* Mocking Bird, Wish Me Luck *(1972),* Hollywood *(1989), and the screenplay* Barfly *(1987).*

READING FOR IDEAS With characteristic poetic abruptness, this poem tells a moving story while drawing a sharp contrast between a dead father and his grieving son. Pay attention to the title as well as the basic dramatic elements in the poem. Ask yourself where the speaker is and why. How is the son like and different from his father? What is ironic about the comparison?

1 he hinted at times that I was a bastard and I told him to listen
  to Brahms, and I told him to learn to paint and drink and not be
  dominated by women and dollars
  but he screamed at me, For Christ's sake remember your
                mother,
5 remember your country,
  you'll kill us all! . . .

  I move through my father's house (on which he owes
           $8,000 after 20
  years on the same job) and look at his dead shoes
  the way his feet curled the leather as if he were angry planting
                 roses,
10 and he was, and I look at his dead cigarette, his last
          cigarette
  and the last bed he slept in that night, and I feel I should
             remake it
  but I can't, for a father is always your master even when he's
              gone;
  I guess these things have happened time and again but I
           can't help
  thinking
15   to die on a kitchen floor at 7 o'clock in the morning
   while other people are frying eggs

is not so rough
unless it happens to you.

I go outside and pick an orange and peel back the bright
                                                    skin;
20   things are still living: the grass is growing quite well,
the sun sends down its rays circled by a Russian satellite;

a dog barks senselessly somewhere, the neighbors peek
                                        behind blinds:
I am a stranger here, and have been (I suppose) somewhat
                                                the rogue,
and I have no doubt he painted me quite well (the old
                                        boy and I
25   fought like mountain lions) and they say he left it all to
                                        some woman
in Duarte but I don't give a damn—she can have it: he was
                                                my old

man
    and he died.
inside, I try on a light blue suit
30   much better than anything I have ever worn
and I flap the arms like a scarecrow in the wind
but it's no good:
I can't keep him alive
no matter how much we hated each other.

35   we looked exactly alike, we could have been twins
the old man and I: that's what they
said. he had his bulbs on the screen
ready for planting
while I was laying with a whore from 3rd street.

40   very well. grant us this moment: standing before a mirror

    in my dead father's suit
    waiting also
    to die.

■ *Questions on Meaning and Technique*

1. How would you characterize the relationship between the speaker of the poem and his father?

2. What contrasts in lifestyle and temperament can you infer existed between this father and son?

3. How would you characterize the way the speaker feels about his dead father?

4. Although about two contrasting personalities, the poem is entitled "The Twins." In what way are the two personalities described in it twins?

5. In what way does this poem defy the traditional subject and treatment usually associated with poetry?

6. In what kind of verse is this poem written? Where is its rhyme?

7. The speaker says that he feels he should remake his father's bed but can't because "a father is always your master even when he's/gone." In what way is a "father always your master even when he's/gone"? Do you agree with this sentiment? Why or why not?

How to Write a Comparison/Contrast Paper

In the context of the English classroom, an assignment to do a comparison usually means to write about both similarities and differences. Strictly speaking, however, there is a difference between a comparison and a contrast. A *comparison* reveals the similarities and differences between two items; a *contrast* focuses only on differences. Most of our private and public decisions are based on comparison and contrast. We buy a Buick rather than a Toyota because of differences we perceive between the two cars. An executive hires one secretary rather than another because of perceived differences in their skills. A student selects one history class over another because of the varying reputations of the professors. Although often carried out on the spur of the moment, comparison is still a necessary and familiar thinking process for most of us.

Nevertheless, you should be aware that in English departments, *comparison* tends to be a blanket term used to cover both comparison and contrast. Many instructors have this more general meaning in mind when they assign a comparison. In other disciplines, *comparison* tends to mean "compare only," whereas *contrast* tends to mean the opposite—contrast only. If you have any doubt about what a comparison assignment means, ask the instructor. As for us, we use *comparison* in the sense of English departments to mean a careful discussion of both similarities and differences.

Writing Assignment

Compare and contrast two people who are totally different. Base your essay on the contrast between the attitudes they represent, taking into account such factors as attitude toward money, treatment of people, purpose in life, dependence on others, and any other important basis for comparison. Place the controlling idea at the end of the introductory paragraph, making sure that it expresses the general areas of contrast you will treat in your essay—for example, *Mark and John differ in their cultural values, their treatment of people, and their goals in life.*

Specific Instructions

Prewriting on the assignment.   The first step in prewriting about the topic is to make a list of likely subjects for your essay. Think of two acquaintances or friends or public figures you would like to compare/contrast. Because the aim is to gain fresh insight into your subjects through the process of matching them up against each other, you should select significant bases for the comparison/contrast. These bases or criteria should reveal telling, rather than trivial, similarities and differences. For example, a comparison between Franklin Delano Roosevelt and Abraham Lincoln based on similarities in physical appearance would end up drawing trivial conclusions. On the other hand, if you used domestic policy accomplishments as your base, the search for similarities and differences would lead to more significant revelations about two of history's most admired presidents.

Once you have selected your subjects, begin your list by heading two columns with their names. To the left, set down the bases for your comparison/contrast. Remember to use significant, rather than trivial, bases. The writer of the student essay in this chapter decided to use the bases of appearances, manners, and recreational activities. Here is how his blank list looked:

Aben Tuasso   *James Greenlaw*

Appearances:

Manners:

Recreation:

Once you have prepared this blank list, you merely fill in the details point by point under each column, which you will later work into your paragraphs.

Working from this kind of list promises a fair comparison that deals equally with both subjects. It is easy to see from this list, for example, whether you have more details on one subject or the other or whether you have entirely overlooked gathering material about, say, James's recreational activities. Such omissions are harder to spot in the essay itself.

Limit your essay to major bases for comparison.   No doubt there are countless bases for comparing people—looks, talent, charm, intelligence, creativity, ability to make friends, athletic skill, and so on. However, rambling over the infinity of differences and similarities you see between John and Mark will not necessarily give your essay structure, emphasis, or clarity. To write a structured, emphatic, and clear comparison of your two acquaintances, select the major points of difference and similarity between them and restrict your essay to a contrast based on these elements. Once chosen and expressed in your controlling idea, these bases will give your essay unity and structure. You should not violate this unity and structure by slipping into areas not mentioned in the controlling idea.

The following paragraph begins by announcing a comparison of two girls on the basis of looks, personality, and physical strength and lives up to its promise:

Kora and Shery, though best friends, were as different as winter and summer in their looks, personality, and physical strength. Kora was tall and dark, with snappy black eyes and long silken braids that fell to her hips, whereas Shery looked almost frail, with soft blue eyes and a halo of golden curls framing her delicate face. Kora wasn't afraid of anyone or anything—not even Mr. Threllkeld, the burly principal. Without the slightest abashment she could confront even the town mayor and demand that he schedule the spring prom in the civic auditorium. Strangers didn't exist for Kora. She greeted them as she would an old acquaintance, without fear or reticence. On the other hand, Shery was painfully shy. To speak up in class was a nightmare for her, as could be seen from her high blush and whispered answers. She hated meeting new people and would always wait for Kora to take over the conversation. If someone she hardly knew attempted a conversation with her, she would begin to stammer, look confused, and eventually excuse herself and hurriedly leave. Then, too, Kora was physically stronger than Shery. The boys often asked her to practice basketball or baseball with them because she could hit a basket and swing a bat as well as any other tenth-grader. Unlike Kora, Shery feared any physical adventure. When Kora playfully threw her a basketball, Shery would cover her face with her hands and dodge it. When coaxed to go swimming, skating, or climbing, Shery would say, "I'm too chicken." Kora and Shery attracted each other as opposites, not as kindred spirits.

Controlling idea

Looks

Personality

Physical strength

Decide on the organization of your comparison.   There are two ways to organize a comparison assignment—vertically or horizontally. For example, you intend to compare John, who is rich, with Mark, who is poor, on the basis of their attitude toward money. Organized *vertically,* the elements of your outline would look like this:

    I. John has the rich boy's contempt for money.
        A. He expects it to be there when he needs it.
        B. He never hesitates over a purchase.
        C. He buys what he wants.

   II. Mark has the poor boy's respect for money.
        A. He knows it is hard to come by.
        B. He hesitates and lingers over a purchase.
        C. He buys what he can afford.

Vertical organization requires that you first write about John on points A, B, and C, and then contrast Mark with John on these same points, as in this example:

Having always lived a life of luxury and comfort, John has a rich boy's contempt for money. He expects it to be there when he needs it; he sees it as having only a utility value, enabling him to do what he likes. He never lingers or hesitates over a purchase. For him, the object of shopping is not to agonize over the amount to be spent but simply to find the best, most suitable object that will satisfy all his wants. He has a high regard for quality and a low regard for expense. He buys what suits him best, whether it is the most or least expensive item in the store.

How Do You Find the Right Topic?

The comparison/contrast essay is fairly easy to write if you follow the suggestions given in the chapter. Probably the hardest thing about this assignment is finding the right topic. Some of the best essays of this mode that we've read have been comparisons/contrasts written about subjects the writer knew well. When an assignment tends to be cut-and-dry, as most comparisons/contrasts are, it helps to at least have a shot of energy that comes from writing about subjects that you know well and like.

Mark, on the other hand, has the poor boy's respect for money. It was not always there when he needed it; what little money he has acquired has cost him in labor, sweat, and drudgery. He spends an endless amount of time on shopping trips, carefully comparing prices, quality, and value and listening patiently to sales spiels and technical explanations. For him, the aim of shopping is to buy the most for the least. He regards expense on a par with quality and usually ends up buying not his first choice or even his second but sometimes his third, or fourth, or even fifth, the purchase always being dictated by his budget and seldom by quality.

Here is an outline of this same contrast organized *horizontally*:

John has contempt for money; Mark has respect for money.

John buys without hesitation; Mark hesitates and compares prices.

John buys what he wants; Mark buys what he can afford.

Here is the horizontally organized written contrast:

Having lived a life of luxury and comfort, John has the rich boy's contempt for money. Mark, on the other hand, has the poor boy's reverence for it. John expects money to be there when he needs it and sees it as having a utility value, enabling him to do as he pleases. Mark, however, knows that money is not always there when he needs it and that what little money he has acquired has cost him in labor, sweat, and drudgery. A pronounced difference shows up in their behavior on shopping trips. John never lingers or hesitates over a purchase; he shops for what he wants, buying always the most suitable, the best object that will satisfy all his wants. It is just the opposite with Mark. For him, shopping means acquiring the most for the least. He must choose his purchases not by quality alone but also by expense. Frequently he ends up buying not his first choice, or even his second or third, but his fourth or fifth choice, in every case the acquisition being dictated by budget, rather than by quality. John buys the best if it suits him; Mark, to the contrary, buys what he can afford.

Use indicators to show comparison/contrast.   A good comparison should be sprinkled with *indicators* that signal similarities and differences. For example:

Similarity	*Contrast*
likewise	but
the same as	yet
too/also	however
similarly	nevertheless
in like manner	on the contrary
	contrary to
	unlike
	the opposite of

The most common student error in comparison/contrast essays is to leave out the indicators and not complete the comparison. Consider the following:

> Benjamin Franklin was a more positive American than was Jonathan Edwards. For example, he had a much more developed sense of humor, as revealed in the numerous funny anecdotes in his autobiography. He could laugh at his own mistakes and at the stupidity of the world in general. Furthermore, he was much more successful in his work, becoming famous all over the world as an inventor, writer, and statesman. Then, too, Franklin was more optimistic about America. His writings reflect confidence and security in America's future; they indicate an innate pride in America's potential as well as its accomplishments.

As you can see, this comparison is hopelessly lopsided. Claiming to draw a contrast between Benjamin Franklin and Jonathan Edwards, the writer tells us only about Franklin, leaving us to guess about Edwards. Perhaps the student simply forgot that he was comparing two figures and that he was therefore obliged to give each equal treatment. However, one way to avoid this sort of lapse is to sprinkle the text mechanically and consciously with indicators that force a complete comparison with equal treatment to all parties:

> Benjamin Franklin was a more positive American than was Jonathan Edwards. First, Franklin had a developed sense of humor. He could laugh, as revealed in the numerous funny anecdotes of his autobiography. *In contrast,* the diaries of Jonathan Edwards are filled with passages in which he weeps and moans over his own sinful condition and the general wickedness of the world. Second, Benjamin Franklin was successful in everything he attempted, achieving worldwide fame as an inventor, writer, and statesman. *On the other hand,* Jonathan Edwards was doubted by most thinkers and despised by his own congregation; he ended his ministry as an outcast in the wilderness, helping the Native Americans. Third, Franklin was a much more optimistic man than was Jonathan Edwards. His writings show great confidence

and security in America's future; they indicate an innate pride in America's potential as well as its accomplishments. *Unlike* Franklin, Edwards was burdened by a deep-seated pessimism. His sermons emphasize man's utter depravity and vileness. In his view, all men except the few elect were despicable worms and the world was damned to everlasting hell.

The second version provides a clearer contrast than the first because the contrast indicators remind the writer to treat both sides equally.

PROFESSIONAL MODEL

GILBERT HIGHET

Diogenes and Alexander

Gilbert Highet (1906–1978), Scottish-born writer and scholar, was educated at the University of Glasgow and Oxford University and became a naturalized American citizen in 1951. Highet was best known for his scholarly writings on the classics and on a wide range of literary topics. His works include The Classical Tradition *(1949) and* The Anatomy of Satire *(1962). Highet was married to novelist Helen MacInnes.*

READING FOR IDEAS This article by Highet describes a meeting between two sharply contrasting personalities in history—Alexander the Great (356–326 B.C.E.), king of Macedonia, and Greek Cynic philosopher Diogenes (c. 412–323 B.C.E.). As you read, notice how Highet organizes his contrasts and the implicit bases he uses. Notice also the tactful curtain line that Alexander uses to withdraw with face-saving dignity from the scene. What does Highet mean when he says that "Only Alexander the conqueror and Diogenes the beggar were truly free"?

1   Lying on the bare earth, shoeless, bearded, half-naked, he looked like a beggar or a lunatic. He was one, but not the other. He had opened his eyes with the sun at dawn, scratched, done his business like a dog at the roadside, washed at the public fountain, begged a piece of breakfast bread and a few olives, eaten them squatting on the ground, and washed them down with a few handfuls of water scooped from the spring. (Long ago he had owned a rough wooden cup, but he threw it away when he saw a boy drinking out of his hollowed hands.) Having no work to go to and no family to provide for, he was free. As the market place filled up with shoppers and merchants and gossipers and sharpers and slaves and foreigners, he had strolled through it for an hour or two. Everybody knew him, or knew of him. They would throw sharp questions at him and get sharper answers. Sometimes they threw jeers, and got jibes; sometimes bits of food, and got scant thanks; sometimes a mischievous pebble, and got a shower of stones and abuse. They were not quite sure whether he was mad or not. He knew they were mad, all mad, each in a different way; they amused him. Now he was back at his home.

2   It was not a house, not even a squatter's hut. He thought everybody lived far too elab-orately, expensively, anxiously. What good is a house? No one needs privacy: natural acts are not shameful; we all do the same things, and need not hide them. No one needs beds and chairs and such furniture; the animals live healthy lives and sleep on the ground. All we require, since nature did not dress us properly, is one garment to keep us warm, and some shelter from rain and wind. So he had one blanket—to dress him in the daytime and cover him at night—and he slept in a cask. His name was Diogenes. He was the founder of the creed called Cynicism (the word means "doggishness"); he spent much of his life in the rich, lazy, corrupt Greek city of Corinth, mocking and satirizing its people, and occa-sionally converting one of them.

3   His home was not a barrel made of wood: too expensive. It was a storage jar made of earthenware, something like a modern fuel tank—no doubt discarded because a break had made it useless. He was not the first to inhabit such a thing: the refugees driven into Athens by the Spartan invasion had been forced to sleep in casks. But he was the first who ever did so by choice, out of principle.

4   Diogenes was not a degenerate or a maniac. He was a philosopher who wrote plays and poems and essays expounding his doctrine; he talked to those who cared to listen; he had pupils who admired him. But he taught chiefly by example. All should live naturally, he said, for what is natural is normal and cannot possibly be evil or shameful. Live with-out conventions, which are artificial and false; escape complexities and superfluities and extravagances; only so can you live a free life. The rich man believes he possesses his big house with its many rooms and its elaborate furniture, his pictures and expensive clothes, his horses and his servants and his bank accounts. He does not. He depends on them, he worries about them, he spends most of his life's energy looking after them; the thought of losing them makes him sick with anxiety. They possess him. He is their slave. In order to procure a quantity of false, perishable goods he has sold the only true, lasting good, his own independence.

5   There have been many men who grew tired of human society with its complications, and went away to live simply—on a small farm, in a quiet village, in a hermit's cave, or in the darkness of anonymity. Not so Diogenes. He was not a recluse, or a stylite, or a beatnik. He was a missionary. His life's aim was clear to him; it was "to restamp the currency." (He and his father had once been convicted for counterfeiting, long before he turned to philosophy, and this phrase was Diogenes' bold, unembarrassed joke on the subject.) To restamp the currency; to take the clean metal of human life, to erase the old false conventional markings, and to imprint it with its true values.

6   The other great philosophers of the fourth century before Christ taught mainly their own private pupils. In the shady groves and cool sanctuaries of the Academy, Plato dis-coursed to a chosen few on the unreality of this contingent existence. Aristotle, among the books and instruments and specimens and archives and research-workers of his Lyceum, pursued investigations and gave lectures that were rightly named *esoteric*, "for those within the walls." But for Diogenes, laboratory and specimens and lecture halls and pupils were all to be found in a crowd of ordinary people. Therefore he chose to live in Athens or in the rich city of Corinth, where travelers from all over the Mediterranean world constantly came and went. And, by design, he publicly behaved in such ways as to

show people what real life was. He would constantly take up their spiritual coin, ring it on a stone, and laugh at its false superscription.

7   He thought most people were only half-alive, most men only half-men. At bright noonday he walked through the market place carrying a lighted lamp and inspecting the face of everyone he met. They asked him why. Diogenes answered, "I am trying to find a *man.*"

8   To a gentleman whose servant was putting on his shoes for him, Diogenes said, "You won't be really happy until he wipes your nose for you: that will come after you lose the use of your hands."

9   Once there was a war scare so serious that it stirred even the lazy, profit-happy Corinthians. They began to drill, clean their weapons, and rebuild their neglected fortifications. Diogenes took his old cask and began to roll it up and down, back and forward. "When you are all so busy," he said, "I felt I ought to do *something!*"

10   And so he lived—like a dog, some said, because he cared nothing for privacy and other human conventions, and because he showed his teeth and barked at those whom he disliked. Now he was lying in the sunlight, as contented as a dog on the warm ground, happier (he himself used to boast) than the Shah of Persia. Although he knew he was going to have an important visitor, he would not move.

11   The little square began to fill with people. Page boys elegantly dressed, spearmen speaking a rough foreign dialect, discreet secretaries, hard-browed officers, suave diplomats, they all gradually formed a circle centered on Diogenes. He looked them over, as a sober man looks at a crowd of tottering drunks, and shook his head. He knew who they were. They were the attendants of the conqueror of Greece, the servants of Alexander, the Macedonian king, who was visiting his newly subdued realm.

12   Only twenty, Alexander was far older and wiser than his years. Like all Macedonians he loved drinking, but he could usually handle it; and toward women he was nobly restrained and chivalrous. Like all Macedonians he loved fighting; he was a magnificent commander, but he was not merely a military automaton. He could think. At thirteen he had become a pupil of the greatest mind in Greece, Aristotle. No exact record of his schooling survives. It is clear, though, that Aristotle took the passionate, half-barbarous boy and gave him the best of Greek culture. He taught Alexander poetry; the young prince slept with the *Iliad* under his pillow and longed to emulate Achilles, who brought the mighty power of Asia to ruin. He taught him philosophy, in particular the shapes and uses of political power: a few years later Alexander was to create a supranational empire that was not merely a power system but a vehicle for the exchange of Greek and Middle Eastern cultures.

13   Aristotle taught him the principles of scientific research: during his invasion of the Persian domains Alexander took with him a large corps of scientists, and shipped hundreds of zoological specimens back to Greece for study. Indeed, it was from Aristotle that Alexander learned to seek out everything strange which might be instructive— jugglers and stunt artists and virtuosos of the absurd he dismissed with a shrug; but on reaching India he was to spend hours discussing the problems of life and death with naked Hindu mystics, and later to see one demonstrate Yoga self-command by burning himself impassively to death.

14   Now, Alexander was in Corinth to take command of the League of Greek States which, after conquering them, his father Philip had created as a disguise for the New Macedonian Order. He was welcomed and honored and flattered. He was the man of the hour, of the century: he was unanimously appointed commander-in-chief of a new expedition against old, rich, corrupt Asia. Nearly everyone crowded to Corinth in order to congratulate him, to seek employment with him, even simply to see him: soldiers and statesmen, artists and merchants, poets and philosophers. He received their compliments graciously. Only Diogenes, although he lived in Corinth, did not visit the new monarch. With that generosity which Aristotle had taught him was a quality of the truly magnanimous man, Alexander determined to call upon Diogenes. Surely Diogenes, the God-born, would acknowledge the conqueror's power by some gift of hoarded wisdom.

15   With his handsome face, his fiery glance, his strong supple body, his purple and gold cloak, and his air of destiny, he moved through the parting crowd, toward the Dog's kennel. When a king approaches, all rise in respect. Diogenes did not rise, he merely sat up on one elbow. When a monarch enters a precinct, all greet him with a bow or an acclamation. Diogenes said nothing.

16   There was silence. Some years later Alexander speared his best friend to the wall, for objecting to the exaggerated honors paid to His Majesty; but now he was still young and civil. He spoke first, with a kindly greeting. Looking at the poor broken cask, the single ragged garment, and the rough figure lying on the ground, he said, "Is there anything I can do for you, Diogenes?"

17   "Yes," said the Dog. "Stand to one side. You're blocking the sunlight."

18   There was silence, not the ominous silence preceding a burst of fury, but a hush of amazement. Slowly, Alexander turned away. A titter broke out from the elegant Greeks, who were already beginning to make jokes about the Cur that looked at the King. The Macedonian officers, after deciding that Diogenes was not worth the trouble of kicking, were starting to guffaw and nudge one another. Alexander was still silent. To those nearest him he said quietly, "If I were not Alexander, I should be Diogenes." They took it as a paradox, designed to close the awkward little scene with a polite curtain line. But Alexander meant it. He understood Cynicism as the others could not. Later he took one of Diogenes' pupils with him to India as a philosophical interpreter (it was he who spoke to the naked *saddhus*). He was what Diogenes called himself, a *cosmopolites*, "citizen of the world." Like Diogenes, he admired the heroic figure of Hercules, the mighty conqueror who labors to help mankind while others toil and sweat only for themselves. He knew that of all men then alive in the world only Alexander the conqueror and Diogenes the beggar were truly free.

■ *Vocabulary*

squatter (2)	superfluities (4)	fortifications (9)
Cynicism (2)	recluse (5)	barbarous (12)
satirizing (2)	stylite (5)	supranational (12)
degenerate (4)	Lyceum (6)	mystics (13)
maniac (4)	superscription (6)	ominous (18)

■ *Questions on Meaning and Technique*

1. What bases govern Highet's comparison of Diogenes and Alexander?

2. How does Highet present his comparison—vertically or horizontally?

3. In what paragraph does Highet first shift from one character to another? How is the shift accomplished?

4. What other contrast is drawn besides the contrast between Diogenes and Alexander? Point to specific passages.

5. What is the analogy used in paragraph 10?

6. What are some characteristics that Diogenes and Alexander share?

7. What are the most outstanding contrasts between the old philosopher and the young emperor?

STUDENT ESSAY—FIRST DRAFT

Randy Varney

Aben and James

This sentence works better at the end of the essay.

Adds needed information about the Maori

1   ~~People's social backgrounds affect their characters.~~ Aben Tuasso lives in a small Maori tribe on New Zealand's North Island. Aben's village is located on the shore of the Tasman Sea. He is single and twenty-six years old. His lifestyle is somewhat primitive

Insert A

and simple. Across the world ‸from New Zealand in Boston, lives another young single man, James Greenlaw. His address is in a wealthy, snobbish community, where the average adult drives a luxury

Insert B

car and enjoys all of the modern conveniences people in his class are expected to own. ‸
                                                                                have
The social backgrounds of these two men ~~has~~ ‸ caused a marked difference in their

      their   their recreational activities.
appearance, ‸ mannerisms, and ~~hobbies.~~

Insert A

Sheltered from rain, wind, and occasional volcanic eruptions by a traditional Polynesian hut, Aben exists as if Captain James Cook had never brought English modernization to his part of the world. Protected by an eighteenth-century political treaty that guarantees the Maori that they can continue to live according to their tribal traditions, without interference from the British Crown, he today still leads a pristine life, herding sheep among beeches, palms, and bushy undergrowth—as did his forebears centuries ago.

Insert B

As a promising young city lawyer, he boards trains and planes in a hectic race for prestige and power.

2   Aben and James~~s looks~~ *are* set ~~them~~ completely apart *by their looks*. Aben's tribal custom requires

males over eighteen to wear black lava-lavas, ~~a~~ cloths the size of ~~a~~ large bath towels,

wrapped around the waist, and have colorful tattoos engraved with burning charcoal over

most of their bodies. *The purpose of this style is to retain the general look of a fiercely brave warring tribe.* Unlike Aben, James dresses in expensive clothing designed by his

~~own~~ tailor. In his society this dress code exemplifies success. James's social status

enables him to avoid hard manual labor, which accounts for his fair complexion and his

manicured fingernails. To keep sinewy and fit, James exercises one hour a day in his

personal exercise room, filled with gleaming equipment that he can pump, push, or pull.

~~On the other hand.~~ Aben's darkly tanned, muscular body is the result of many hours

spent spear fishing in the bay, canoeing down rivers, and climbing jagged cliffs along

the seashore. His hands and feet bear thick calluses. *Move to * above*

3   Their mannerisms *of Aben and James* are *also* distinctly different. Aben grunts and stares coldly when he

is approached by another person. In his society an arrogant attitude connotes superior

manliness. He continually tries to impress the tribal women of his village by engaging

in physical combat with the other males of his tribe. James has an entirely different

approach toward people in his environment. Following the etiquette of his peers, he

greets new acquaintances with a smile, a warm handshake, and a deferential bow.

He impresses a woman by taking her to an elegant restaurant and then to the opera

or ballet. He dazzles his peers with his sophisticated style, his fluent command of

three languages, and his Harvard law degree. One similarity between these otherwise

different young men is that both are ambitious and reveal a fervent drive to excel. Aben

does it by bringing home trophies tracked down with his bow and arrow whereas James

does it by winning different court cases. Both Aben and James desire to be the best.

4   Comparing Aben and James's ~~hobbies~~ *recreational activities* also reveals some fascinating differences.

Aben enjoys hunting with a bow and arrow and swimming in turbulent waters. He loves

diving for pearls deep beneath the surface of the sea. On special evenings, he joins his

fellow villagers in the "Haka," a ritual war dance, performed around a blazing fire. This

lusty dance is accompanied by loud singing and energetic foot stomping. When the

fire begins to die and only glowing coals are left, Aben swiftly volunteers to walk across

Marginal notes:

Smoother wording

Keep with description of Aben's looks.

Makes transition to manners more precise

Better term

Details added

the hot coals in order to demonstrate his unqualified bravery. How different are James's
                          lounge on a living room sofa,   ing
hobbies from those of Aben! James loves to read the works of Sir Walter Scott while
                  recorded on an expensive compact disc   is
listening to a Beethoven or Mozart symphony. On weekends he ~~can~~ inevitably ~~be~~ seen
                                                         with fellow sportsmen
at the country club, where he will play a round of golf or a polo match. James also loves

to play the violin, which he started to master at the age of six.   Insert C

This sentence adds texture to the conclusion.

5   A person's ~~social~~ background truly determines his or her character. If Aben and
                       birth and

James were to switch social backgrounds, would they adapt? Would James become a

fire dancer? Would Aben play the violin?

  Insert C

Aben and James are clear examples of this incontrovertible truth. Both men are young, vigorous, and
ambitious, but their lifestyles have bred them into two totally different people.

STUDENT ESSAY—FINAL DRAFT

Varney 1

Randy Varney

Professor Winkler

English 101

February 25, 2002

Aben and James

1   Aben Tuasso lives in a small Maori tribe on New Zealand's

North Island. Aben's village is located on the shore of the Tasman

Sea. He is single and twenty-six years old. His lifestyle is somewhat

primitive and simple. Sheltered from rain, wind, and occasional

volcanic eruptions by a traditional Polynesian hut, Aben exists as if

Captain James Cook had never brought English modernization to

his part of the world. Protected by an eighteenth-century political

treaty that guarantees the Maori that they can continue to live

Varney 2

according to their tribal traditions, without interference from the
British Crown, he today still leads a pristine life, herding sheep
among beeches, palms, and bushy undergrowth—as did his
forebears centuries ago. Across the world from New Zealand, in
Boston, lives another young single man, James Greenlaw. His address
is in a wealthy, snobbish community, where the average adult drives
a luxury car and enjoys all of the modern conveniences people in
his class are expected to own. As a promising young city lawyer, he
boards trains and planes in a hectic race for prestige and power. The
backgrounds of these two men have caused a marked difference in
their appearance, their mannerisms, and their recreational activities.

2   Aben and James are set completely apart by their looks.
Aben's tribal custom requires males over eighteen to wear black
lava-lavas, cloths the size of large bath towels, wrapped around the
waist, and have colorful tattoos engraved with burning charcoal
over most of their bodies. The purpose of this style is to retain the
general look of a fiercely brave warring tribe. Aben's darkly tanned,
muscular body is the result of many hours spent spear fishing in
the bay, canoeing down rivers, and climbing jagged cliffs along
the seashore. His hands and feet bear thick calluses. Unlike Aben,
James dresses in expensive clothing designed by his tailor. In his
society this dress code exemplifies success. James's social status
enables him to avoid hard manual labor, which accounts for his fair
complexion and his manicured fingernails. To keep sinewy and fit,
James exercises one hour a day in his personal exercise room, filled
with gleaming equipment that he can pump, push, or pull.

3   The manners of Aben and James are also distinctively different. Aben grunts and stares coldly when he is approached by another person. In his society an arrogant attitude connotes superior manliness. He continually tries to impress the tribal women of his village by engaging in physical combat with the other males of his tribe. James has an entirely different approach toward people in his environment. Following the etiquette of his peers, he greets new acquaintances with a smile, a warm handshake, and a deferential bow. He impresses a woman by taking her to an elegant restaurant and then to the opera or ballet. He dazzles his peers with his sophisticated style, his fluent command of three languages, and his Harvard law degree. One similarity between these otherwise different young men is that both are ambitious and reveal a fervent drive to excel. Aben does it by bringing home trophies tracked down with his bow and arrow whereas James does it by winning difficult court cases. Both Aben and James desire to be the best.

4   Comparing Aben and James's recreational activities also reveals some fascinating differences. Aben enjoys hunting with a bow and arrow and swimming in turbulent waters. He loves diving for pearls deep beneath the surface of the sea. On special evenings, he joins his fellow villagers in the "Haka," a ritual war dance, performed around a blazing fire. This lusty dance is accompanied by loud singing and energetic foot stomping. When the fire begins to die and only glowing coals are left, Aben swiftly volunteers to walk across the hot coals in order to demonstrate his unqualified bravery. How different are James's hobbies from those of Aben! James loves

Varney 4

to lounge on a living room sofa, reading the works of Sir Walter

Scott while listening to a Beethoven or Mozart symphony recorded

on an expensive compact disc. On weekends he is inevitably seen

at the country club, where he will play a round of golf or a polo

match with fellow sportsmen. James also loves to play the violin,

which he started to master at the age of six.

5   A person's birth and background truly determine his or her

character. Aben and James are clear examples of this incontrovertible

truth. Both men are young, vigorous, and ambitious, but their

lifestyles have bred them into two totally different people. If Aben and

James were to switch social backgrounds, would they adapt? Would

James become a fire dancer? Would Aben play the violin?

FURTHER READING

BRUCE CATTON

Grant and Lee: A Study in Contrasts

Bruce Catton (1899–1978) continues to be regarded as one of the best historians of the American Civil War. His books include Mr. Lincoln's Army *(1952),* Glory Road *(1952),* A Stillness at Appomattox *(1953), which won a Pulitzer Prize, and* This Hallowed Ground *(1956).*

READING FOR IDEAS When two generals have confronted each other during an important war, historians are bound to write about them from two contrasting points of view. In the case of the essay that follows, the contrast is between two important generals who fought each other during the American Civil War. One is Ulysses S. Grant (1822–1885), commander in chief of the Union army and later, eighteenth president of the United States; the other is Robert E. Lee (1807–1870), the general in chief of the Confederate armies, who after fierce fighting eventually surrendered his forces to Grant in April 1865. As you read, note the strategy used by the author to draw his comparison/contrast of these two famous men.

1   When Ulysses S. Grant and Robert E. Lee met in the parlor of a modest house at Appomattox Court House, Virginia, on April 9, 1865, to work out the terms for the surrender of Lee's Army of Northern Virginia, a great chapter in American life came to a close, and a great new chapter began.

2   These men were bringing the Civil War to its virtual finish. To be sure, other armies had yet to surrender, and for a few days the fugitive Confederate government would struggle desperately and vainly, trying to find some way to go on living now that its chief support was gone. But in effect it was all over when Grant and Lee signed the papers. And the little room where they wrote out the terms was the scene of one of the poignant, dramatic contrasts in American history.

3   They were two strong men, these oddly different generals, and they represented the strengths of two conflicting currents that, through them, had come into final collision.

4   Back of Robert E. Lee was the notion that the old aristocratic concept might somehow survive and be dominant in American life.

5   Lee was tidewater Virginia, and in his background were family, culture, and tradition . . . the age of chivalry transplanted to a New World which was making its own legends and its own myths. He embodied a way of life that had come down through the age of knighthood and the English country squire. America was a land that was beginning all over again, dedicated to nothing much more complicated than the rather hazy belief that all men had equal rights and should have an equal chance in the world. In such a land Lee stood for the feeling that it was somehow of advantage to human society to have a pronounced inequality in the social structure. There should be a leisure class, backed by ownership of land; in turn, society itself should be keyed to the land as the chief source of wealth and influence. It would bring forth (according to this ideal) a class of men with a strong sense of obligation to the community; men who lived not to gain advantage for themselves, but to meet the solemn obligations which had been laid on them by the very fact that they were privileged. From them the country would get its leadership; to them it could look for the higher values—of thought, of conduct, of personal deportment—to give it strength and virtue.

6   Lee embodied the noblest elements of this aristocratic ideal. Through him, the landed nobility justified itself. For four years, the Southern states had fought a desperate war to uphold the ideals for which Lee stood. In the end, it almost seemed as if the Confederacy fought for Lee; as if he himself was the Confederacy . . . the best thing that the way of life for which the Confederacy stood could ever have to offer. He had passed into legend before Appomattox. Thousands of tired, underfed, poorly clothed Confederate soldiers, long since past the simple enthusiasm of the early days of the struggle, somehow considered Lee the symbol of everything for which they had been willing to die. But they could not quite put this feeling into words. If the Lost Cause, sanctified by so much heroism and so many deaths, had a living justification, its justification was General Lee.

7   Grant, the son of a tanner on the Western frontier, was everything Lee was not. He had come up the hard way and embodied nothing in particular except the eternal toughness and sinewy fiber of the men who grew up beyond the mountains. He was one of a body of men who owed reverence and obeisance to no one, who were self-reliant to a fault, who cared hardly anything for the past but who had a sharp eye for the future.

8   These frontier men were the precise opposites of the tidewater aristocrats. Back of them, in the great surge that had taken people over the Alleghenies and into the opening Western country, there was a deep, implicit dissatisfaction with a past that had settled into grooves. They stood for democracy, not from any reasoned conclusion about the proper ordering of human society, but simply because they had grown up in the middle of democracy and knew how it worked. Their society might have privileges, but they would be privileges each man had won for himself. Forms and patterns meant nothing. No man was born to anything, except perhaps to a chance to show how far he could rise. Life was competition.

9   Yet along with this feeling had come a deep sense of belonging to a national community. The Westerner who developed a farm, opened a shop, or set up in business as a trader, could hope to prosper only as his own community prospered—and his community ran from the Atlantic to the Pacific and from Canada down to Mexico. If the land was settled, with towns and highways and accessible markets, he could better himself. He saw his fate in terms of the nation's own destiny. As its horizons expanded, so did his. He had, in other words, an acute dollars-and-cents stake in the continued growth and development of his country.

10   And that, perhaps, is where the contrast between Grant and Lee becomes most striking. The Virginia aristocrat, inevitably, saw himself in relation to his own region. He lived in a static society which could endure almost anything except change. Instinctively, his first loyalty would go to the locality in which that society existed. He would fight to the limit of endurance to defend it, because in defending it he was defending everything that gave his own life its deepest meaning.

11   The Westerner, on the other hand, would fight with an equal tenacity for the broader concept of society. He fought so because everything he lived by was tied to growth, expansion, and a constantly widening horizon. What he lived by would survive or fall with the nation itself. He could not possibly stand by unmoved in the face of an attempt to destroy the Union. He would combat it with everything he had, because he could only see it as an effort to cut the ground out from under his feet.

12   So Grant and Lee were in complete contrast, representing two diametrically opposed elements in American life. Grant was the modern man emerging; beyond him, ready to come on the stage, was the great age of steel and machinery, of crowded cities and a restless, burgeoning vitality. Lee might have ridden down from the old age of chivalry, lance in hand, silken banner fluttering over his head. Each man was the perfect champion of his cause, drawing both his strengths and his weaknesses from the people he led.

13   Yet it was not all contrast, after all. Different as they were—in background, in personality, in underlying aspiration—these two great soldiers had much in common. Under everything else, they were marvelous fighters. Furthermore, their fighting qualities were really very much alike.

14   Each man had, to begin with, the great virtue of utter tenacity and fidelity. Grant fought his way down the Mississippi Valley in spite of acute personal discouragement and profound military handicaps. Lee hung on in the trenches at Petersburg after hope itself had died. In each man there was an indomitable quality . . . the born fighter's refusal to give up as long as he can still remain on his feet and lift his two fists.

15   Daring and resourcefulness they had, too; the ability to think faster and move faster than the enemy. These were the qualities which gave Lee the dazzling campaigns of Second Manassas and Chancellorsville and won Vicksburg for Grant.

16   Lastly, and perhaps greatest of all, there was the ability, at the end, to turn quickly from war to peace once the fighting was over. Out of the way these two men behaved at Appomattox came the possibility of a peace of reconciliation. It was a possibility not wholly realized, in the years to come, but which did, in the end, help the two sections to become one nation again . . . after a war whose bitterness might have seemed to make such a reunion wholly impossible. No part of either man's life became him more than the part he played in their brief meeting in the McLean house at Appomattox. Their behavior there put all succeeding generations of Americans in their debt. Two great Americans, Grant and Lee, very different, yet under everything very much alike. Their encounter at Appomattox was one of the great moments of American history.

■ *Vocabulary*

virtual (2)	embodied (6)	diametrically (12)
fugitive (2)	sanctified (6)	burgeoning (12)
poignant (2)	obeisance (7)	
deportment (5)	tenacity (11)	

■ *Questions on Meaning and Technique*

1. What does the author mean when he writes that Grant and Lee brought the Civil War to its "virtual" finish? What would be the opposite of *virtual*?

2. According to paragraph 2, what was the "chief support" the Confederate government had lost? Why was it impossible for it to continue without this support?

3. What is the meaning of paragraph 4? Why does this one sentence merit an entire paragraph?

4. Does our present society have an aristocracy or have we become one enormous middle class, where everyone is equal? Explain your answer.

5. What does the author mean when he states that Grant "was everything Lee was not"? Which of the two men appeals to you more? Give reasons for your answer.

6. The author connects Lee to the past and Grant to the future. Explain this connection as you understand it. Which kind of leader do you believe we need today—a Lee type or Grant type? Explain your answer.

7. How does the author go about developing the contrast between Lee and Grant? How effective is he?

8. Is the essay a contrast only, or are there passages indicating that the two men shared certain character traits? What traits, if any, did Lee and Grant share?

9. Do you consider the meeting at Appomattox one of the great moments in history? Is it important for students to be aware of this meeting that took place so long ago? Or should they spend more time studying present-day politics and terrorism?

10. Grant is known for his support of economic growth and expansion. Do you favor continued growth and expansion, or are there values that mean more to you? Explain your answer.

Writing Assignments

1. Write an essay in which you propose the idea that a country can benefit from the presence of a privileged class.

2. Using Catton's essay as a model, write an essay in which you compare and contrast two present-day political leaders.

FURTHER READING

DOROTHY WEST

The Richer, the Poorer

*Dorothy West (1908–1995) was born in Boston, the daughter of an emancipated slave. As a teenager, she moved to Harlem, New York, where in 1926 she joined a group of writers, of which she was the youngest. Because of her obvious literary talent and dynamic personality, she became the driving force in a movement now known as the Harlem Renaissance. Her first story, "The Typewriter," won her second place in a national contest sponsored by the Urban League's Opportunity Magazine. After her involvement in a Russian film produced by the Communist party about racial discrimination in the United States, West was attacked by numerous critics, who felt that her association with the Communists was an act of subversion. Among her best-known works are two novels—*The Living Is Easy *(1948) and* The Wedding *(1993), written when she was eighty-five and sponsored by Jacqueline Kennedy Onassis, who admired West's writings. Not long after* The Wedding, *West produced a compilation of her short stories, titled* The Richer, the Poorer, *from which the following sketch is taken.*

READING FOR IDEAS This short story focuses on the lives of two sisters, Lottie and Bess, and their sharply contrasting approaches to life. Lottie is a squirrel preparing for the coming rainy days by living modestly and cautiously. Bess, on the other hand, lives for the moment, takes chances, and splurges without regard to the future. As you read this comparison of two women, try to analyze how dreams, love, and desire can transform lives. Ask yourself what gift you would most desire from life. Use your ideas as a possible springboard for a comparison/contrast essay.

1   Over the years Lottie had urged Bess to prepare for her old age. Over the years Bess had lived each day as if there were no other. Now they were both past sixty, the time for summing up. Lottie had a bank account that had never grown lean. Bess had the clothes on her back, and the rest of her worldly possessions in a battered suitcase.

2   Lottie had hated being a child, hearing her parents' skimping and scraping. Bess had never seemed to notice. All she ever wanted was to go outside and play. She learned to skate on borrowed skates. She rode a borrowed bicycle. Lottie couldn't wait to grow up and buy herself the best of everything.

3   As soon as anyone would hire her, Lottie put herself to work. She minded babies, she ran errands for the old.

4   She never touched a penny of her money, though her child's mouth watered for ice cream and candy. But she could not bear to share with Bess, who never had anything to share with her. When the dimes began to add up to dollars, she lost her taste for sweets.

5   By the time she was twelve, she was clerking after school in a small variety store. Saturdays she worked as long as she was wanted. She decided to keep her money for clothes. When she entered high school, she would wear a wardrobe that neither she nor anyone else would be able to match.

6   But her freshman year found her unable to indulge so frivolous a whim, particularly when her admiring instructors advised her to think seriously of college. No one in her family had ever gone to college, and certainly Bess would never get there. She would show them all what she could do, if she put her mind to it.

7   She began to bank her money, and her bankbook became her most private and precious possession.

8   In her third year of high school she found a job in a small but expanding restaurant, where she cashiered from the busy hour until closing. In her last year of high school the business increased so rapidly that Lottie was faced with the choice of staying in school or working full time.

9   She made her choice easily. A job in hand was worth two in the future.

10   Bess had a beau in the school band, who had no other ambition except to play a horn. Lottie expected to be settled with a home and family while Bess was still waiting for Harry to earn enough to buy a marriage license.

11   That Bess married Harry straight out of high school was not surprising. That Lottie never married at all was not really surprising either. Two or three times she was halfway persuaded, but to give up a job that paid well for a homemaking job that paid nothing was a risk she was incapable of taking.

12   Bess's married life was nothing for Lottie to envy. She and Harry lived like gypsies, Harry playing in second-rate bands all over the country, even getting himself and Bess stranded in Europe. They were often in rags and never in riches.

13   Bess grieved because she had no child, not having sense enough to know she was better off without one. Lottie was certainly better off without nieces and nephews to feel sorry for. Very likely Bess would have dumped them on her doorstep.

14   That Lottie had a doorstep they might have been left on was only because her boss, having bought a second house, offered Lottie his first house at a price so low and terms so reasonable that it would have been like losing money to refuse.

15   She shut off the rooms she didn't use, letting them go to rack and ruin. Since she ate her meals out, she had no food at home, and did not encourage callers, who always expected a cup of tea.

16   Her way of life was mean and miserly, but she did not know it. She thought she lived frugally in her middle years so that she could live in comfort and ease when she most needed peace of mind.

17   The years, after forty, began to race. Suddenly Lottie was sixty, and retired from her job by her boss's son, who had no sentimental feeling about keeping her on until she was ready to quit.

18   She made several attempts to find other employment, but her dowdy appearance made her look old and inefficient. For the first time in her life Lottie would gladly have worked for nothing, to have some place to go, something to do with her day.

19   Harry died abroad, in a third-rate hotel, with Bess weeping as hard as if he had left her a fortune. He had left her nothing but his horn. There wasn't even money for her passage home.

20   Lottie, trapped by the blood tie, knew she would not only have to send for her sister, but take her in when she returned. It didn't seem fair that Bess should reap the harvest of Lottie's lifetime of self-denial.

21   It took Lottie a week to get a bedroom ready, a week of hard work and hard cash. There was everything to do, everything to replace or paint. When she was through the room looked so fresh and new that Lottie felt she deserved it more than Bess.

22   She would let Bess have her room, but the mattress was so lumpy, the carpet so worn, the curtains so threadbare that Lottie's conscience pricked her. She supposed she would have to redo that room, too, and went about doing it with an eagerness that she mistook for haste.

23   When she was through upstairs, she was shocked to see how dismal downstairs looked by comparison. She tried to ignore it, but with nowhere to go to escape it, the contrast grew more intolerable.

24   She worked her way from kitchen to parlor, persuading herself she was only putting the rooms to rights to give herself something to do. At night she slept like a child after a long and happy day of playing house. She was having more fun than she had ever had in her life. She was living each hour for itself.

25   There was only a day now before Bess would arrive. Passing her gleaming mirrors, at first with vague awareness, then with painful clarity, Lottie saw herself as others saw her, and could not stand the sight.

26   She went on a spending spree from the specialty shops to beauty salon, emerging transformed into a woman who believed in miracles.

27   She was in the kitchen basting a turkey when Bess rang the bell. Her heart raced, and she wondered if the heat from the oven was responsible.

28   She went to the door, and Bess stood before her. Stiffly she suffered Bess's embrace, her heart racing harder, her eyes suddenly smarting from the onrush of cold air.

29   "Oh, Lottie, it's good to see you," Bess said, but saying nothing about Lottie's splendid appearance. Upstairs Bess, putting down her shabby suitcase, said, "I'll sleep like a rock

tonight," without a word of praise for her lovely room. At the lavish table, top-heavy with turkey, Bess said, "I'll take light and dark, both," with no marveling at the size of the bird, or that there was turkey for two elderly women, one of them too poor to buy her own bread.

30   With the glow of good food in her stomach, Bess began to spin stories. They were rich with places and people, most of them lowly, all of them magnificent. Her face reflected her telling, the joys and sorrows of her remembering, and above all, the love she lived by that enhanced the poorest place, the humblest person.

31   Then it was that Lottie knew why Bess had made no mention of her finery, or the shining room, or the twelve-pound turkey. She had not even seen them. Tomorrow she would see the room as it really looked, and Lottie as she really looked, and the warmed-over turkey in its second-day glory. Tonight she saw only what she had come seeking: a place in her sister's home and heart.

32   She said, "That's enough about me. How have the years used you?"

33   "It was me who didn't use them," said Lottie wistfully. "I saved for them." I saved for them. I forgot the best of them would go without my ever spending a day or a dollar enjoying them. That's my life story in those few words, a life never lived.

34   "Now it's too near the end to try."

35   Bess said, "To know how much there is to know is the beginning of learning to live. Don't count the years that are left us. At our time of life it's the days that count. You've too much catching up to do to waste a minute of a waking hour feeling sorry for yourself."

36   Lottie grinned, a real wide-open grin, "Well to tell the truth, I felt sorry for you. Maybe if I had any sense I'd feel sorry for myself, after all. I know I'm too old to kick up my heels, but I'm going to let you show me how. If I land on my head, I guess it won't matter; I feel giddy already, and I like it."

■ *Vocabulary*

indulge (6)	miserly (16)	dismal (23)
frivolous (6)	threadbare (22)	intolerable (23)

■ Questions on Meaning and Technique

1. The entire essay revolves around the meaning of being "poor" or "rich." Explain how the author plays with the meaning of these two words.

2. Which of the two sisters was rich and which was poor? Explain your answer.

3. What attracted Bess to her high school beau? Do you think they were happy together? Why or why not?

4. What technique does the author use to prepare her readers for the change that eventually will transform Lottie? Point to specific instances of this technique.

5. What is the most ironic part of Lottie's life?

6. What is the one flaw that mars Bess's life? Is Bess justified in her sadness?

7. What force motivates Lottie to send for her sister after Harry dies? How does her decision affect her life?

8. What kind of life do you imagine the two sisters leading once Bess started to live with Lottie? Suggest some specific activities.

9. Dorothy West, the author of this story, was African American and lived in Harlem, New York. In what ways might her race and neighborhood have influenced the theme of this story?

Writing Assignments

1. Compare and contrast two acquaintances—one rich and one poor (in monetary terms). First compare the two in terms of their lifestyles; then, compare them in terms of how content and happy they seem. Begin your essay with a thesis that expresses the contrast; then develop your essay either horizontally or vertically as described in this chapter.

2. Write an essay in which you weigh the importance of money and material goods or comforts. Use some appropriate examples to support your thesis.

 ## Internet Research Assignment

Go to the Internet to find some articles about the future of Social Security in the United States. Then write an essay in which you contrast two of the views that seem to recur most often.

Additional Writing Assignments

1. Develop an essay based on the following controlling idea: *Ignorance is different from stupidity.*

2. Compare and contrast two love affairs you have had.

3. Write an essay contrasting *envy* and *jealousy.*

4. Compare and contrast *respectability* and *self-respect.*

5. Write an essay comparing and contrasting any two teachers you have had.

6. Based on your travels throughout the United States and abroad, choose two cities or towns that strike you as completely different from each other. Write an essay contrasting the two.

7. Compare and contrast *erotica* and *pornography.*

8. Write an essay specifying the differences between a *romantic* versus a *realistic* novel or movie.

9. From your general knowledge of U.S. history, contrast the eighteenth and twentieth centuries on three bases—hygiene, education, and women's rights—supplying examples that stress the differences.

10. Compare and contrast the *law-abiding person* and the *moral person.*

Rewriting Assignment

Here is an incomplete sketch for an essay contrasting a *bicycle* and a *motorcycle*. Complete the sketch so that you could, if required, write a well-organized essay on the subject.

> *Thesis:* Whereas a bicycle is perceived by most people as a tool of fitness and sport, a motorcycle is usually perceived as a symbol of male chauvinism and social rebellion.

	Bicycle	*Motorcycle*
1. Purpose		
2. Cost		
3. Symbol		

Photo Writing Assignment

© Brendan Smialowski/Getty Images

Write a paragraph in which you contrast the future life of the wounded soldier portrayed here with the life of a soldier who survived war service without a serious injury. As you search for contrast bases, consider these factors: the emotional effects of being wounded, the amount of patriotism displayed, or the severity of the sacrifice made.

Digging for Gold or Likenesses and Differences

What is the difference between mining gold and writing an essay developed by comparison/contrast? The two appear so utterly different that a smart writer will avoid the analogy. Nevertheless, gold miners, like writers, do use comparison and contrast while mining. For example, veteran gold miners see the difference between iron pyrite—commonly known as fools' gold—and the real thing. They contrast rich ore with poor ore to find a vein of gold. Offhand, the strongest similarity between the gold miner and the writer is digging, a technique they both use to discover the aim of their search.

Each essay included in this chapter's collection is based on items that can be compared and contrasted. For example, Anthony Winkler's "Dream House" compares an imaginary house with a real one and leaves it to the reader to decide which is the better one. Gilbert Highet teaches us history by telling the story of two famous Greeks, one a gentle philosopher, the other a world conqueror. Bruce Catton compares and contrasts two Civil War heroes, General Lee and General Grant. Ending this collection is a comparison/contrast between two sisters, one a penny pincher all her life, the other a spendthrift.

Keep digging. There's a lot to learn. Both the writer and the gold miner may learn that a careful scrutiny of the environment can reveal differences or similarities which ultimately lead to genuine karats or genuine ideas. Moreover, the gold miner may discover that the presence of pyrite in a mine shaft is a sure sign that real gold is lurking nearby—just as the writer may discover that among the many useless ideas swarming in one's head lies the one idea that can be developed into a fine essay.

Chapter 12

Process

STORY

JOHN STEINBECK

How Mr. Hogan Robbed a Bank

John Steinbeck (1902–1968), American novelist and writer, was known mainly for his sociological novels about the poor and downtrodden of American society. Born in Salinas, California, Steinbeck studied at Stanford. His novels include Tortilla Flat *(1935),* Of Mice and Men *(1937; also made into a play), and* The Grapes of Wrath *(1939; Pulitzer Prize). Steinbeck was awarded the Nobel Prize in literature in 1962.*

READING FOR IDEAS Process is the rhetorical mode that specifies the steps involved in doing some task or taking some action. It may lay out in detail how you make something or describe how something was made. Giving instructions and directions is typical of a process essay. Not typical, however, is the following satirical short story, which draws on the techniques of process writing to detail how a seemingly model citizen committed a bank robbery. Ignored or lost in this discussion is any sense of ethics or of right and wrong. It is as if the author is asking us whether the ends always justify the means. As you read through the story, you might admire the cleverness of Mr. Hogan's method even if you are put off by his ethics. Ask yourself whether the means ever justifies the ends. In other words, if the method is right, is the purpose also right? Also, think of some task you would like to accomplish and see if you can put together similar careful, easy-to-follow directions for this task.

1   On Saturday before Labor Day, 1955, at 9:04 1/2 A.M., Mr. Hogan robbed a bank. He was forty-two years old, married, and the father of a boy and a girl, named John and Joan, twelve and thirteen respectively. Mrs. Hogan's name was Joan and Mr. Hogan's name was John, but since they called themselves Papa and Mama that left their names free for the children, who were considered very smart for their ages, each having jumped a grade in school. The Hogans lived at 215 East Maple Street, in a brown-shingle house with white trim—there are two. 215 is the one across from the street light and it is the one

with the big tree in the yard, either oak or elm—the biggest tree in the whole street, maybe in the whole town.

2   John and Joan were in bed at the time of the robbery, for it was Saturday. At 9:10 A.M., Mrs. Hogan was making the cup of tea she always had. Mr. Hogan went to work early. Mrs. Hogan drank her tea slowly, scalding hot, and read her fortune in the tea leaves. There was a cloud and a five-pointed star with two short points in the bottom of the cup, but that was at 9:12 and the robbery was all over by then.

3   The way Mr. Hogan went about robbing the bank was very interesting. He gave it a great deal of thought and had for a long time, but he did not discuss it with anyone. He just read his newspaper and kept his own counsel. But he worked it out to his own satisfaction that people went to too much trouble robbing banks and that got them in a mess. The simpler the better, he always thought. People went in for too much hullabaloo and hanky-panky. If you didn't do that, if you left hanky-panky out, robbing a bank would be a relatively sound venture—barring accidents, of course, of an improbable kind, but then they could happen to a man crossing the street or anything. Since Mr. Hogan's method worked fine, it proved that his thinking was sound. He often considered writing a little booklet on his technique when the how-to rage was running so high. He figured out the first sentence, which went: "To successfully rob a bank, forget all about hanky-panky."

4   Mr. Hogan was not just a clerk at Fettucci's grocery store. He was more like the manager. Mr. Hogan was in charge, even hired and fired the boy who delivered groceries after school. He even put in orders with the salesmen, sometimes when Mr. Fettucci was right in the store too, maybe talking to a customer. "You do it, John," he would say and he would nod at the customer, "John knows the ropes. Been with me—how long you been with me, John?"

5   "Sixteen years."

6   "Sixteen years. Knows the business as good as me. John, why he even banks the money."

7   And so he did. Whenever he had a moment, Mr. Hogan went into the storeroom on the alley, took off his apron, put on his necktie and coat, and went back through the store to the cash register. The checks and bills would be ready for him inside the bankbook with a rubber band around it. Then he went next door and stood at the teller's window and handed the checks and bankbook through to Mr. Cup and passed the time of day with him too. Then, when the bankbook was handed back, he checked the entry, put the rubber band around it, and walked next door to Fettucci's grocery and put the bankbook in the cash register, continued on to the storeroom, removed his coat and tie, put on his apron, and went back into the store ready for business. If there was no line at the teller's window, the whole thing didn't take more than five minutes, even passing the time of day.

8   Mr. Hogan was a man who noticed things, and when it came to robbing the bank, this trait stood him in good stead. He had noticed, for instance, where the big bills were kept right in the drawer under the counter and he had noticed also what days they were likely to be more than other days. Thursday was payday at the American Can Company's local plant, for instance, so there would be more then. Some Fridays people drew more money to tide them over the weekend. But it was even Steven, maybe not a thousand dollars difference, between Thursdays and Fridays and Saturday mornings.

Saturdays were not terribly good because people didn't come to get money that early in the morning, and the bank closed at noon. But he thought it over and came to the conclusion that the Saturday before a long weekend in the summer would be the best of all. People going on trips, vacations, people with relatives visiting, and the bank closed Monday. He thought it out and looked, and sure enough the Saturday morning before Labor Day the cash drawer had twice as much money in it—he saw it when Mr. Cup pulled out the drawer.

9   Mr. Hogan thought about it during all that year, not all the time, of course, but when he had some moments. It was a busy year too. That was the year John and Joan had the mumps and Mrs. Hogan got her teeth pulled and was fitted for a denture. That was the year when Mr. Hogan was Master of the Lodge, with all the time that takes. Larry Shield died that year—he was Mrs. Hogan's brother and was buried from the Hogan house at 215 East Maple. Larry was a bachelor and had a room in the Pine Tree House and he played pool nearly every night. He worked at the Silver Diner but that closed at nine and so Larry would go to Louie's and play pool for an hour. Therefore, it was a surprise when he left enough so that after funeral expenses there were twelve hundred dollars left. And even more surprising that he left a will in Mrs. Hogan's favor, but his double-barreled twelve-gauge shotgun he left to John Hogan, Jr. Mr. Hogan was pleased, although he never hunted. He put the shotgun away in the back of the closet in the bathroom, where he kept his things, to keep it for young John. He didn't want children handling guns and he never bought any shells. It was some of that twelve hundred that got Mrs. Hogan her dentures. Also, she bought a bicycle for John and a doll buggy and walking-talking doll for Joan—a doll with three changes of dresses and a little suitcase, complete with play make-up. Mr. Hogan thought it might spoil the children, but it didn't seem to. They made just as good marks in school and John even got a job delivering papers. It was a very busy year. Both John and Joan wanted to enter the W. R. Hearst National "I Love America" Contest and Mr. Hogan thought it was almost too much, but they promised to do the work during their summer vacation, so he finally agreed.

II

10   During that year, no one noticed any difference in Mr. Hogan. It was true, he was thinking about robbing the bank, but he only thought about it in the evening when there was neither a Lodge meeting nor a movie they wanted to go to, so it did not become an obsession and people noticed no change in him.

11   He had studied everything so carefully that the approach of Labor Day did not catch him unprepared or nervous. It was hot that summer and the hot spells were longer than usual. Saturday was the end of two weeks heat without a break and people were irritated with it and anxious to get out of town, although the country was just as hot. They didn't think of that. The children were excited because the "I Love America" Essay Contest was due to be concluded and the winners announced, and the first prize was an all-expense-paid two days trip to Washington, D.C., with every fixing—hotel room, three meals a day, and side trips in a limousine—not only for the winner, but for an accompanying chaperone; visit to the White House—shake hands with the President—everything. Mr. Hogan thought they were getting their hopes too high and he said so.

12   "You've got to be prepared to lose," he told his children. "There're probably thousands and thousands entered. You get your hopes up and it might spoil the whole autumn. Now I don't want any long faces in this house after the contest is over."

13   "I was against it from the start," he told Mrs. Hogan. That was the morning she saw the Washington Monument in her teacup, but she didn't tell anybody about that except Ruth Tyler, Bob Tyler's wife. Ruthie brought over her cards and read them in the Hogan kitchen, but she didn't find a journey. She did tell Mrs. Hogan that the cards were often wrong. The cards had said Mrs. Winkle was going on a trip to Europe and the next week Mrs. Winkle got a fishbone in her throat and choked to death. Ruthie, just thinking out loud, wondered if there was any connection between the fishbone and the ocean voyage to Europe. "You've got to interpret them right." Ruthie did say she saw money coming to the Hogans.

14   "Oh, I got that already from poor Larry," Mrs. Hogan explained.

15   "I must have got the past and future cards mixed," said Ruthie. "You've got to interpret them right."

16   Saturday dawned a blaster. The early morning weather report on the radio said "Continued hot and humid, light scattered rain Sunday night and Monday." Mrs. Hogan said, "Wouldn't you know? Labor Day." And Mr. Hogan said, "I'm sure glad we didn't plan anything." He finished his egg and mopped the plate with his toast. Mrs. Hogan said, "Did I put coffee on the list?" He took the paper from his handkerchief pocket and consulted it. "Yes, coffee, it's here."

17   "I had a crazy idea I forgot to write it down," said Mrs. Hogan. "Ruth and I are going to Altar Guild this afternoon. It's at Mrs. Alfred Drake's. You know, they just came to town. I can't wait to see their furniture."

18   "They trade with us," said Mr. Hogan. "Opened an account last week. Are the milk bottles ready?"

19   "On the porch."

20   Hogan looked at his watch just before he picked up the bottles and it was five minutes to eight. He was about to go down the stairs, when he turned and looked back through the opened door at Mrs. Hogan. She said, "Want something, Papa?"

21   "No," he said. "No," and he walked down the steps.

22   He went down to the corner and turned right on Spooner, and Spooner runs into Main Street in two blocks, and right across from where it runs in, there is Fettucci's and the bank around the corner and the alley beside the bank. Mr. Hogan picked up a handbill in front of Fettucci's and unlocked the door. He went through to the storeroom, opened the door to the alley, and looked out. A cat tried to force its way in, but Mr. Hogan blocked it with his foot and leg and closed the door. He took off his coat and put on his long apron, tied the strings in a bowknot behind his back. Then he got the broom from behind the counter and swept out behind the counters and scooped the sweepings into a dustpan; and, going through the storeroom, he opened the door to the alley. The cat had gone away. He emptied the dustpan into the garbage can and tapped it smartly to dislodge a piece of lettuce leaf. Then he went back to the store and worked for a while on the order sheet. Mrs. Clooney came in for a half a pound of bacon. She said it was hot and Mr. Hogan agreed. "Summers are getting hotter," he said.

23   "I think so myself," said Mrs. Clooney. "How's Mrs. standing up?"

24   "Just fine," said Mr. Hogan. "She's going to Altar Guild."

25   "So am I. I just can't wait to see their furniture," said Mrs. Clooney, and she went out.

III

26   Mr. Hogan put a five-pound hunk of bacon on the slicer and stripped off the pieces and laid them on wax paper and then he put the wax paper-covered squares in the cooler cabinet. At ten minutes to nine, Mr. Hogan went to a shelf. He pushed a spaghetti box aside and took down a cereal box, which he emptied in the little closet toilet. Then, with a banana knife, he cut out the Mickey Mouse mask that was on the back. The rest of the box he took to the toilet and tore up the cardboard and flushed it down. He went into the store then and yanked a piece of string loose and tied the ends through the side holes of the mask and then he looked at his watch—a large silver Hamilton with black hands. It was two minutes to nine.

27   Perhaps the next four minutes were his only time of nervousness at all. At one minute to nine, he took the broom and went out to sweep the sidewalk and he swept it very rapidly—was sweeping it, in fact, when Mr. Warner unlocked the bank door. He said good morning to Mr. Warner and a few seconds later the bank staff of four emerged from the coffee shop. Mr. Hogan saw them across the street and he waved at them and they waved back. He finished the sidewalk and went back in the store. He laid his watch on the little step of the cash register. He sighed very deeply, more like a deep breath than a sigh. He knew that Mr. Warner would have the safe open now and he would be carrying the cash trays to the teller's window. Mr. Hogan looked at the watch on the cash register step. Mr. Kenworthy paused in the store entrance, then shook his head vaguely and walked on and Mr. Hogan let out his breath gradually. His left hand went behind his back and pulled the bowknot on his apron, and then the black hand on his watch crept up on the four-minute mark and covered it.

28   Mr. Hogan opened the charge account drawer and took out the store pistol, a silver-colored Iver Johnson .38. He moved quickly to the storeroom, slipped off his apron, put on his coat, and stuck the revolver in his side pocket. The Mickey Mouse mask he shoved up under his coat where it didn't show. He opened the alley door and looked up and down and stepped quickly out, leaving the door slightly ajar. It is sixty feet to where the alley enters Main Street, and there he paused and looked up and down and then he turned his head toward the center of the street as he passed the bank window. At the bank's swinging door, he took out the mask from under his coat and put it on. Mr. Warner was just entering his office and his back was to the door. The top of Will Cup's head was visible through the teller's grill.

29   Mr. Hogan moved quickly and quietly around the end of the counter and into the teller's cage. He had the revolver in his right hand now. When Will Cup turned his head and saw the revolver, he froze. Mr. Hogan slipped his toe under the trigger of the floor alarm and motioned Will Cup to the floor with the revolver and Will went down quick. Then Mr. Hogan opened the cash drawer and with two quick movements he piled the large bills from the tray together. He made a whipping motion to Will on the floor, to indicate that he should turn over and face the wall, and Will did. Then Mr. Hogan stepped back around the counter. At the door of the bank, he took off the mask, and as he passed the window he turned his head toward the middle of the street. He moved into the alley, walked quickly to

the storeroom and entered. The cat got in. It watched him from a pile of canned goods cartons. Mr. Hogan went to the toilet closet and tore up the mask and flushed it. He took off his coat and put on his apron. He looked out into the store and then moved to the cash register. The revolver went back into the charge account drawer. He punched No Sale and, lifting the top drawer, distributed the stolen money underneath the top tray and then pulled the tray forward and closed the register, and only then did he look at his watch and it was 9:07½.

30   He was trying to get the cat out of the storeroom when the commotion boiled out of the bank. He took his broom and went out on the sidewalk. He heard all about it and offered his opinion when it was asked for. He said he didn't think the fellow could get away—where could he get to? Still, with the holiday coming up—

31   It was an exciting day. Mr. Fettucci was as proud as though it were his bank. The sirens sounded around town for hours. Hundreds of holiday travelers had to stop at the roadblocks set up all around the edge of town and several sneaky-looking men had their cars searched.

32   Mrs. Hogan heard about it over the phone and she dressed earlier than she would have ordinarily and came to the store on her way to Altar Guild. She hoped Mr. Hogan would have seen or heard something new, but he hadn't. "I don't see how the fellow can get away," he said.

33   Mrs. Hogan was so excited, she forgot her own news. She only remembered when she got to Mrs. Drake's house, but she asked permission and phoned the store the first moment she could. "I forgot to tell you. John's won honorable mention."

34   "What?"

35   "In the 'I Love America' Contest."

36   "What did he win?"

37   "Honorable mention."

38   "Fine. Fine—Anything come with it?"

39   "Why, he'll get his picture and his name all over the country. Radio too. Maybe even television. They've already asked for a photograph of him."

40   "Fine," said Mr. Hogan. "I hope it don't spoil him." He put up the receiver and said to Mr. Fettucci, "I guess we've got a celebrity in the family."

41   Fettucci stayed open until nine on Saturdays. Mr. Hogan ate a few snacks from cold cuts, but not much, because Mrs. Hogan always kept his supper warming.

42   It was 9:05 or :06, or :07, when he got back to the brown-shingle house at 215 East Maple. He went in through the front door and out to the kitchen where the family was waiting for him.

43   "Got to wash up," he said, and went up to the bathroom. He turned the key in the bathroom door and then he flushed the toilet and turned on the water in the basin and tub while he counted the money. Eight thousand three hundred and twenty dollars. From the top shelf of the storage closet in the bathroom, he took down the big leather case that held his Knight Templar's uniform. The plumed hat lay there on its form. The white ostrich feather was a little yellow and needed changing. Mr. Hogan lifted out the hat and pried the form up from the bottom of the case. He put the money in the form and then he thought again and removed two bills and shoved them in his side pocket. Then he put the form back over the money and laid the hat on top and closed the case and shoved it back on the top shelf. Finally he washed his hands and turned off the water in the tub and the basin.

44   In the kitchen, Mrs. Hogan and the children faced him, beaming, "Guess what some young man's going on?"

45   "What?" asked Mr. Hogan.

46   "Radio," said John. "Monday night. Eight o'clock."

47   "I guess we got a celebrity in the family," said Mr. Hogan.

48   Mrs. Hogan said, "I just hope some young lady hasn't got her nose out of joint."

49   Mr. Hogan pulled up to the table and stretched his legs. "Mama, I guess I got a fine family," he said. He reached in his pocket and took out two five-dollar bills. He handed one to John. "That's for winning," he said. He poked the other bill at Joan. "And that's for being a good sport. One celebrity and one good sport. What a fine family!" He rubbed his hands together and lifted the lid of the covered dish. "Kidneys," he said. "Fine."

50   And that's how Mr. Hogan did it.

■ *Questions on Meaning and Technique*

1. What steps does Mr. Hogan take to rob the bank? State them in the order in which they occur.

2. What point does this story make?

3. What are some examples of the typical middle-class life of the Hogans?

4. What detail in paragraph 9 clearly indicates Mr. Hogan's double-standard?

5. What is your response to the sentence in paragraph 3, ". . . if you left hanky-panky out, robbing a bank would be a relatively sound venture . . ."?

P O E M

WILLIAM CARLOS WILLIAMS

Tract

William Carlos Williams (1883–1963), American poet and physician, was born in Rutherford, New Jersey, and educated at the University of Pennsylvania and the University of Leipzig. Among the most original American poets of this century, Williams wrote in a style close to the idioms and rhythms of natural speech but with a poetic edge. His works include Collected Poems *(1934),* Collected Later Poems *(1950), and* Pictures from Brueghel and Other Poems *(1963; Pulitzer Prize).*

READING FOR IDEAS "Tract" could well be considered a step-by-step process for how to perform a funeral that would be in harmony with nature. In the first stanza, notice whom the poet addresses, and be prepared to give reasons for his choice of audience. On a sheet of paper, list the instructions one by one, and explain what they mean in a philosophical and psychological sense.

1   I will teach you my townspeople
how to perform a funeral
for you have it over a troop
of artists—
unless one should scour the world—
you have the ground sense necessary.

2   See! the hearse leads.
I begin with a design for a hearse.
For Christ's sake not black—
nor white either—and not polished!
Let it be weathered—like a farm wagon—
with gilt wheels (this could be
applied fresh at small expense)
or no wheels at all:
a rough dray to drag over the ground.

3   Knock the glass out!
My God—glass, my townspeople!
For what purpose? Is it for the dead
to look out or for us to see
how well he is housed or to see
the flowers or the lack of them—
or what?
To keep the rain and snow from him?
He will have a heavier rain soon:
pebbles and dirt and what not.
Let there be no glass—
and no upholstery, phew!
and no little brass rollers
and small easy wheels on the bottom—
my townspeople what are you thinking of?

4   A rough plain hearse then
with gilt wheels and no top at all.
On this the coffin lies
by its own weight.

5   No wreaths please—
especially no hot house flowers.
Some common memento is better,
something he prized and is known by:
his old clothes—a few books perhaps—
God knows what! You realize

how we are about these things
my townspeople—
something will be found—anything
even flowers if he had come to that.
So much for the hearse.

6   For heaven's sake though see to the driver!
Take off the silk hat! In fact
that's no place at all for him—
up there unceremoniously
dragging our friend out to his own dignity!
Bring him down—bring him down!
Low and inconspicuous! I'd not have him ride
on the wagon at all—damn him—
the undertaker's understrapper!
Let him hold the reins
and walk at the side
and inconspicuously too!

7   Then briefly as to yourselves:
Walk behind—as they do in France,
seventh class, or if you ride
Hell take curtains! Go with some show
of inconvenience; sit openly—
to the weather as to grief.
Or do you think you can shut grief in?
What—from us? We who have perhaps
nothing to lose? Share with us
share with us—it will be money
in your pockets.
                              Go now
I think you are ready.

■ *Vocabulary*

dray (2)	unceremoniously (6)
memento (5)	understrapper (6)

■ *Questions on Meaning and Technique*

1. In giving advice on how to perform a funeral, what major steps does the speaker advocate? List them in the order in which they are mentioned.

2. What is the poet's general purpose in advocating this kind of funeral?

3. In stanza 2, why does the speaker suggest the "gilt wheels . . . applied fresh"?

4. Why doesn't the speaker want the coffin to ride along smoothly (stanza 3)?

5. Instead of wreaths of "hot house" flowers (stanza 5), what does the speaker suggest as a decoration for the coffin? Why?

6. What objections does the speaker have to the undertaker's driving the carriage while wearing a silk top hat (stanza 6)?

7. What is the most important thought in the final stanza?

How to Write a Process Paper

Describing a process, often called *process analysis,* is a common assignment. Some process papers focus on "how to do it" by giving step-by-step directions, such as for assembling a computer; others focus on "how it happened" by explaining how a certain situation came about, such as the shortage of heating oil during winter. Most process papers that offer directions address the reader personally by using the pronoun *you:* "Before inserting the cartridge, *you* must clean off all excess grime." But other process papers, especially those that explain how a situation happened or will happen, are developed in the *third person:* "The first step in the trend toward achieving a zero-growth society is the use of the pill, allowing women to feel secure from unwanted pregnancy."

Writing Assignment

Choose a process with which you are thoroughly familiar, and give a specific, detailed set of instructions for doing it. Here are some sample process topics:

How to detect counterfeit money

How to train a dog in obedience

How to keep a journal

How to use a GPS system

How to write a research paper

How to balance a budget

How to sail a catamaran

The assignment here involves a "how-to-do-it" process rather than a "why-it-happened" one.

Specific Instructions

Prewrite on the assignment. A process is a series of steps taken to accomplish a certain task or to do a particular job. This explanation, for example, details the steps you must take in order to write an essay about a process. If you write about how an archaeologist excavated dinosaur bones, you're not giving step-by-step instructions but you are specifying how the process of excavation was done. A history teacher might also ask you to write a process paper about the steps that led up to the First Punic War between Rome and Carthage. But for now, let us stick to the most common process—how to do something.

The first step you must take in writing a process essay is to choose a process you know well. Don't try to write about a process you don't understand down to the bare bones. In fact, the better you know the process, the more likely you are to write a good essay about it. When a process essay goes bad, the fault is usually because the writer did not understand the process well enough.

Once you have settled on a subject, you must figure out the major steps of the process involved. Most likely, these major steps will contain sub-steps that also need explaining, but the major steps should be identified first. Let us consider a process with which all of us are familiar—making a bed. What are the major steps involved? First, airing the mattress; second, smoothing and fitting the bottom sheet; third, pulling up the bedding over the bed; fourth, fitting the corners so that the bed will have a finished look; fifth, adjusting the pillows and bedspread. Each of these major steps contains some steps of its own. An outline reveals them easily:

I. Air the mattress.
   A. Throw the pillows on the floor.
   B. Pull off the flat sheets, blankets, and bedspread.
   C. Shake the sheets and blankets.

II. Smooth and fit the bottom sheet.
   A. Get rid of all lumps or wrinkles.
   B. Make sure the corners are properly tucked under.

III. Pull the bedding over the bed.
   A. Pull the flat sheet up to the headboard, allowing a two-foot overlap.
   B. Bring the blankets to within one foot of the headboard.
   C. Allow the flat sheet to fold one foot over the blankets.

IV. Fit the corners.
   A. Smooth the blankets.
   B. Tuck in the sheets and blankets at the foot of the bed.
   C. Create symmetrical corners by pulling up the ends of the bedding and tucking them in, military style.

V. Adjust the bedspread and pillows.
  A. Align the pillows at the top of the bed.
  B. Pull up the bedspread, allowing the same length to hang down on each side and at the foot.
  C. Tuck about a foot of bedspread under the pillows to create a tailored effect.

Although the process of making a bed is admittedly a dull subject, it is also one that cannot be well explained without organizing the individual steps into the sequence in which they must be performed. Writing a process is not so much a matter of finding exotic imagery or elegant words as choosing a methodical arrangement of steps that your reader can follow.

The most common failing of process papers is the writer's assumption that a step is too self-evident to be included. For instance, if you are trying to explain how to set up camp and you leave out pitching the tent because you assume that everyone already knows that maneuver, then your process will be incomplete. This kind of omission becomes especially acute if left out of directions on how to assemble something. All of us are familiar with the frustration of creating a lopsided stool or having a window shade not work because the instructions omitted a step.

We therefore recommend that in preparing for this assignment, you write a simple outline to make sure your process is clear and complete.

Begin with a clear statement of purpose.   A process paper should begin by announcing the process it intends to clarify. Here are some samples:

Assembling a dictionary involves four major steps.

The purpose of this paper is to show the easiest way to gather a good collection of rock music.

The scientific method of investigation involves several basic steps.

A few simple steps in dealing with garbage will help us win the ecological battle to save the environment.

This initial announcement alerts the reader to the purpose of a process paper, giving a context for the individual steps that follow. Such a clear statement of purpose takes the place of the thesis in a process paper.

Assemble all the information necessary to complete the process.   It is easier to give directions or explain the separate steps of a process when you have accurate and complete information about it. If the process is unfamiliar and the information not at hand, you will need to do some research. Gather *all* the information you can. It is better to assemble more information than you will actually use than to overlook a detail that might help explain a step. Collect the facts and refer to them as you write the process.

Decide on the order of your steps.   Once the facts are collected, their order of presentation usually becomes apparent from the process. For example, if you are analyzing the steps in planting camellias, common sense tells you that the first step is preparing the soil. Similarly, if you are writing a paper on how a U.S. president is elected to office, you would not begin with the inauguration but with the election of local delegates in the primaries. A reasonable way to begin a process paper is to outline all the steps in the order in which they will logically occur and to include those details necessary for a clear presentation of each step. An example of such an outline follows:

Controlling idea: Writing a book review involves three basic steps.

   I. Read the book carefully.
      A. Look for major ideas.
      B. Mark essential pages.

  II. Think about the book.
      A. Figure out the purpose of the book.
      B. Judge the book according to how well it has fulfilled its purpose.
      C. Make mental notes of both strengths and weaknesses.

 III. Write a fair review.
      A. State the purpose of the book.
      B. Give a brief summary of the book.
      C. Explain major passages, using quotations to give a flavor of the author's style.
      D. Evaluate the book.

Although a process may be extremely simple, consisting of only one or two steps, each step may be complicated by many details. For example, the process of writing good advertising copy contains two main steps but many more details:

Controlling idea: To write good advertising copy requires knowing the product and the audience well.

   I. Begin with a strong headline.
      A. Flag down all possible customers.
      B. Include key words associated with the product.
      C. Appeal to the reader's self-interest.
      D. Make the product sound new.

  II. Write the body as if you were answering someone's questions.
      A. Go straight to the point.
      B. Be factual and specific.
      C. Include testimonials.
      D. Give the reader some helpful advice.
      E. Write in colloquial language.

The outline makes the process easier to write about by highlighting each step along with its cluster of details. Without the aid of the outline, the writer could easily become confused.

Each individual step must be clear and complete.   Each step in the process must be clearly numbered and explained; one poorly explained step can confuse an entire process. For example, suppose the third step in producing an antivenom for snake bites is to collect the serum by bleeding a horse that has been injected with the venom. A clear explanation of this step, with all the necessary details beautifully aligned, is of little use if step 1—collecting the venom by milking a snake—is never explained. A clear step-by-step presentation of material is crucial in a process paper.

JIMMY SANTIAGO BACA

Coming into Language

Jimmy Santiago Baca (b. 1952) is one of the greatly admired Barrio writers, so called because they portray their environments with vigor and artistic power. An ex-convict, he taught himself to read and write while in prison, eventually winning the American Book Award for 1988. Part Chicano and part Native American, Baca was abandoned by his parents when he was two and lived with his grandparents. By the time he was five, his mother had been murdered by her second husband, his father had died of alcoholism, and Baca had been placed in an orphanage, which he escaped to survive on the streets. While in prison on a drug charge, he was confined to maximum security and later placed in isolation. Despite his tragic life, his poetry dwells on rebirth, rather than on bitterness. Among his works are the following books of poetry: Immigrants in Our Own Land *(1979),* Swords of Darkness *(1981),* What's Happening? *(1982),* Martin and Meditations on the South Valley *(1987),* Black Mesa Poems *(1989), and* Working in the Dark: Reflections of a Poet of the Barrio *(1990), from which the following essay is taken.*

READING FOR IDEAS This is the heart-rending, disturbing, yet comforting story of one man's personal journey toward poetic birth. We are taken on a journey deep into the writer's scarred soul to witness how he survived the horrors of prison, solitary confinement, and the mental ward. We share the depths of torment and the hellish despair he suffers as well as the birth of faith and hope as he finds his footing as a poet. And in the end, we experience his joy as his love of language overcomes the miseries of a childhood marked by crime, cruelty, and violence.

1   On weekend graveyard shifts at St. Joseph's Hospital I worked the emergency room, mopping up pools of blood and carting plastic bags stuffed with arms, legs, and hands to the outdoor incinerator. I enjoyed the quiet, away from the screams of shotgunned, knifed, and mangled kids writhing on gurneys outside the operating rooms. Ambulance sirens shrieked and squad car lights reddened the cool nights, flashing against the hospital walls: gray—red, gray—red. On slow nights, I would lock the door of the administration office, search the reference library for a book on female anatomy and, with my feet propped on the desk, leaf through the illustrations, smoking my cigarette. I was seventeen.

2   One night my eye was caught by a familiar-looking word on the spine of a book. The title was *450 Years of Chicano History in Pictures.* On the cover were black-and-white photos: Padre Hidalgo exhorting Mexican peasants to revolt against the Spanish dictators; Anglo vigilantes hanging two Mexicans from a tree; a young Mexican woman with rifle and ammunition belts crisscrossing her breast; César Chávez and field workers marching for fair wages; Chicano railroad workers laying creosote ties; Chicanas laboring at machines in textile factories; Chicanas picketing and hoisting boycott signs.

3   From the time I was seven, teachers had been punishing me for not knowing my lessons by making me stick my nose in a circle chalked on the blackboard. Ashamed of not understanding and fearful of asking questions, I dropped out of school in the ninth grade. At seventeen I still didn't know how to read, but those pictures confirmed my identity. I stole the book that night, stashing it for safety under the slopsink until I got off work. Back at my boardinghouse, I showed the book to friends. All of us were amazed; this book told us we were alive. We, too, had defended ourselves with our fists against hostile Anglos, gasping for breath in fights with the policemen who outnumbered us. The book reflected back to us our struggle in a way that made us proud.

4   Most of my life I felt like a target in the cross hairs of a hunter's rifle. When strangers and outsiders questioned me I felt the hang-rope tighten around my neck and the trapdoor creak beneath my feet. There was nothing so humiliating as being unable to express myself, and my inarticulateness increased my sense of jeopardy, of being endangered. I felt intimidated and vulnerable, ridiculed and scorned. Behind a mask of humility, I seethed with mute rebellion.

5   Before I was eighteen, I was arrested on suspicion of murder after refusing to explain a deep cut on my forearm. With shocking speed I found myself handcuffed to a chain gang of inmates and bused to a holding facility to await trial. There I met men, prisoners, who read aloud to each other the works of Neruda, Paz, Sabines, Nemerov, and Hemingway. Never had I felt such freedom as in that dormitory. Listening to the words of these writers, I felt that invisible threat from without lessen—my sense of teetering on a rotting plank over swamp water where famished alligators clapped their horny snouts for my blood. While I listened to the words of the poets, the alligators slumbered powerless in their lairs. Their language was the magic that could liberate me from myself, transform me into another person, transport me to other places far away.

6   And when they closed the books, these Chicanos, and went into their own Chicano language, they made barrio life come alive for me in the fullness of its vitality. I began to learn my own language, the bilingual words and phrases explaining to me my place in the universe. Every day I felt like the paper boy taking delivery of the latest news of the day.

7   Months later I was released, as I had suspected I would be. I had been guilty of nothing but shattering the windshield of my girlfriend's car in a fit of rage.

8   Two years passed. I was twenty now, and behind bars again. The federal marshals had failed to provide convincing evidence to extradite me to Arizona on a drug charge, but still I was being held. They had ninety days to prove I was guilty. The only evidence against me was that my girlfriend had been at the scene of the crime with my driver's license in her purse. They had to come up with something else. But there was nothing else. Eventually they negotiated a deal with the actual drug dealer, who took the stand against me. When the judge hit me with a million-dollar bail, I emptied my pockets on his booking desk: twenty-six cents.

9   One night in my third month in the county jail, I was mopping the floor in front of the booking desk. Some detectives had kneed an old drunk and handcuffed him to the booking bars. His shrill screams raked my nerves like a hacksaw on bone, the desperate protest of his dignity against their inhumanity. But the detectives just laughed as he tried to rise and kicked him to his knees. When they went to the bathroom to pee and the desk attendant walked to the file cabinet to pull the arrest record, I shot my arm through the bars, grabbed one of the attendant's university textbooks, and tucked it in my overalls. It was the only way I had of protesting.

10   It was late when I returned to my cell. Under my blanket I switched on a pen flashlight and opened the thick book at random, scanning the pages. I could hear the jailer making his rounds on the other tiers. The jangle of his keys and the sharp click of his boot heels intensified my solitude. Slowly I enunciated the words . . . p-o-n-d, ri-pple. It scared me that I had been reduced to this to find comfort. I always had thought reading a waste of time, that nothing could be gained by it. Only by action, by moving out into the world and confronting and challenging the obstacles, could one learn anything worth knowing.

11   Even as I tried to convince myself that I was merely curious, I became so absorbed in how the sounds created music in me and happiness, I forgot where I was. Memories began to quiver in me, glowing with a strange but familiar intimacy in which I found refuge. For a while, a deep sadness overcame me, as if I had chanced on a long-lost friend and mourned the years of separation. But soon the heartache of having missed so much of life, that had numbed me since I was a child, gave way, as if a grave illness lifted itself from me and I was cured, innocently believing in the beauty of life again. I stumblingly repeated the author's name as I fell asleep, saying it over and over in the dark: Words-worth, Words-worth.

12   Before long my sister came to visit me, and I joked about taking her to a place called Kubla Khan and getting her a blind date with this *vato* named Coleridge who lived on the seacoast and was *malias* on morphine. When I asked her to make a trip into enemy territory to buy me a grammar book, she said she couldn't. Bookstores intimidated her, because she, too, could neither read nor write.

13   Days later, with a stub pencil I whittled sharp with my teeth, I propped a Red Chief notebook on my knees and wrote my first words. From that moment, a hunger for poetry possessed me.

14   Until then, I had felt as if I had been born into a raging ocean where I swam relentlessly, flailing my arms in hope of rescue, of reaching a shoreline I never sighted. Never solid ground beneath me, never a resting place. I had lived with only the desperate hope to stay afloat; that and nothing more.

15   But when at last I wrote my first words on the page, I felt an island rising beneath my feet like the back of a whale. As more and more words emerged, I could finally rest: I had a place to stand for the first time in my life. The island grew, with each page, into a continent inhabited by people I knew and mapped with the life I lived.

16   I wrote about it all—about people I had loved or hated, about the brutalities and ecstasies of my life. And, for the first time, the child in me who had witnessed and endured unspeakable terrors cried out not just in impotent despair, but with the power of language. Suddenly, through language, through writing, my grief and my joy could be shared with anyone who would listen. And I could do this all alone; I could do it anywhere. I was no longer a captive of demons eating away at me, no longer a victim of other people's mockery and loathing, that had made me clench my fist white with rage and grit my teeth to silence. Words now pleaded back with the bleak lucidity of hurt. They were wrong, those others, and now I could say it.

17   Through language I was free. I could respond, escape, indulge; embrace or reject earth or the cosmos. I was launched on an endless journey without boundaries or rules, in which I could salvage the floating fragments of my past, or be born anew in the spontaneous ignition of understanding some heretofore concealed aspect of myself. Each word steamed with the hot lava juices of my primordial making, and I crawled out of stanzas dripping with birth-blood, reborn and freed from the chaos of my life. The child in the dark room of my heart, that had never been able to find or reach the light switch, flicked it on now; and I found in the room a stranger, myself, who had waited so many years to speak again. My words struck in me lightning crackles of elation and thunderhead storms of grief.

18   When I had been in the county jail longer than anyone else, I was made a trustee. One morning, after a fist fight, I went to the unlocked and unoccupied office used for lawyer-client meetings, to think. The bare white room with its fluorescent tube lighting seemed to expose and illuminate my dark and worthless life. And yet, for the first time, I had something to lose—my chance to read, to write; a way to live with dignity and meaning, that had opened for me when I stole that scuffed, second-hand book about the Romantic poets. In prison, the abscess had been lanced.

19   "I will never do any work in this prison system as long as I am not allowed to get my G.E.D." That's what I told the reclassification panel. The captain flicked off the tape recorder. He looked at me hard and said, "You'll never walk outta here alive. Oh, you'll work, put a copper penny on that, you'll work."

20   After that interview I was confined to deadlock maximum security in a subterranean dungeon, with ground-level chicken-wired windows painted gray. Twenty-three hours a day I was in that cell. I kept sane by borrowing books from the other cons on the tier. Then, just before Christmas, I received a letter from Harry, a charity house Samaritan who doled

out hot soup to the homeless in Phoenix. He had picked my name from a list of cons who had no one to write to them. I wrote back asking for a grammar book, and a week later received one of Mary Baker Eddy's treatises on salvation and redemption, with Spanish and English on opposing pages. Pacing my cell all day and most of each night, I grappled with grammar until I was able to write a long true-romance confession for a con to send to his pen pal. He paid me with a pack of smokes. Soon I had a thriving barter business, exchanging my poems and letters for novels, commissary pencils, and writing tablets.

21   One day I tore two flaps from the cardboard box that held all my belongings and punctured holes along the edge of each flap and along the border of a ream of state-issue paper. After I had aligned them to form a spine, I threaded the holes with a shoestring, and sketched on the cover a hummingbird fluttering above a rose. This was my first journal.

22   Whole afternoons I wrote, unconscious of passing time or whether it was day or night. Sunbursts exploded from the lead tip of my pencil, words that grafted me into awareness of who I was; peeled back to a burning core of bleak terror, an embryo floating in the image of water, I cracked out of the shell wide-eyed and insane. Trees grew out of the palms of my hands, the threatening otherness of life dissolved, and I became one with the air and sky, the dirt and the iron and concrete. There was no longer any distinction between the other and I. Language made bridges of fire between me and everything I saw. I entered into the blade of grass, the basketball, the con's eye and child's soul.

23   At night I flew. I conversed with floating heads in my cell, and visited strange houses where lonely women brewed tea and rocked in wicker rocking chairs listening to sad Joni Mitchell songs.

24   Before long I was frayed like a rope carrying too much weight, that suddenly snaps. I quit talking. Bars, walls, steel bunk and floor bristled with millions of poem-making sparks. My face was no longer familiar to me. The only reality was the swirling cornucopia of images in my mind, the voices in the air. Mid-air a cactus blossom would appear, a snake-flame in blinding dance around it, stunning me like a guard's fist striking my neck from behind.

25   The prison administrators tried several tactics to get me to work. For six months, after the next monthly prison board review, they sent cons to my cell to hassle me. When the guard would open my cell door to let one of them in, I'd leap out and fight him—and get sent to thirty-day isolation. I did a lot of isolation time. But I honed my image-making talents in that sensory-deprived solitude. Finally they moved me to death row, and after that to "nut-run," the tier that housed the mentally disturbed.

26   As the months passed, I became more and more sluggish. My eyelids were heavy, I could no longer write or read. I slept all the time.

27   One day a guard took me out to the exercise field. For the first time in years I felt grass and earth under my feet. It was spring. The sun warmed my face as I sat on the bleachers watching the cons box and run, hit the handball, lift weights. Some of them stopped to ask how I was, but I found it impossible to utter a syllable. My tongue would not move, saliva drooled from the corners of my mouth. I had been so heavily medicated I could not summon the slightest gesture. Yet inside me a small voice cried out, I am fine! I am hurt now but I will come back! I am fine!

28   Back in my cell, for weeks I refused to eat. Styrofoam cups of urine and hot water were hurled at me. Other things happened. There were beatings, shock therapy, intimidation.

29   Later, I regained some clarity of mind. But there was a place in my heart where I had died. My life had compressed itself into an unbearable dread of being. The strain had been too much. I had stepped over that line where a human being had lost more than he can bear, where the pain is too intense, and he knows he is changed forever. I was now capable of killing, coldly and without feeling. I was empty, as I have never, before or since, known emptiness. I had no connection to this life.

30   But then, the encroaching darkness that began to envelop me forced me to re-form and give birth to myself again in the chaos. I withdrew even deeper into the world of language, cleaving the diamonds of verbs and nouns, plunging into the brilliant light of poetry's regenerative mystery. Words gave off rings of white energy, radar signals from powers beyond me that infused me with truth. I believed what I wrote, because I wrote what was true. My words did not come from books or textual formulas, but from a deep faith in the voice of my heart.

31   I had been steeped in self-loathing and rejected by everyone and everything—society, family, cons, God and demons. But now I had become as the burning ember floating in darkness that descends on a dry leaf and sets flame to forests. The word was the ember and the forest was my life.

32   I was born a poet one noon, gazing at weeds and creosoted grass at the base of a telephone pole outside my grilled cell window. The words I wrote then sailed me out of myself, and I was transported and metamorphosed into the images they made. From the dirty brown blades of grass came bolts of electrical light that jolted loose my old self; through the top of my head that self was released and reshaped in the clump of scrawny grass. Through language I became the grass, speaking its language and feeling its green feelings and black root sensations. Earth was my mother and I bathed in sunshine. Minuscule speckles of sunlight passed through my green skin and metabolized in my blood.

33   Writing bridged my divided life of prisoner and free man. I wrote of the emotional butchery of prisons, and of my acute gratitude for poetry. Where my blind doubt and spontaneous trust in life met, I discovered empathy and compassion. The power to express myself was a welcome storm rasping at tendril roots, flooding my soul's cracked dirt. Writing was water that cleansed the wound and fed the parched root of my heart.

34   I wrote to sublimate my rage, from a place where all hope is gone, from a madness of having been damaged too much, from a silence of killing rage. I wrote to avenge the betrayals of a lifetime, to purge the bitterness of injustice. I wrote with a deep groan of doom in my blood, bewildered and dumbstruck; from an indestructible love of life, to affirm breath and laughter and the abiding innocence of things. I wrote the way I wept, and danced, and made love.

■ *Vocabulary*

incinerator (1)	primordial (17)	creosoted (32)
inarticulateness (4)	subterranean (20)	metamorphosed (32)
lairs (5)	Samaritan (20)	tendril (33)
extradite (8)	treatises (20)	
enunciated (10)	regenerative (30)	

▪ *Questions on Meaning and Technique*

1. Who is the voice in this essay? What kind of person does he seem to be? How do you feel about him? Why does he seem to be writing the essay?

2. The author's experience can be divided into separate, discernible steps. What are these steps? List and summarize each step as it occurs in the total process.

3. Which part of the author's artistic journey do you consider the climax of his experience, that is, the point at which he sees the possibility of language? Give reasons for your choice.

4. Where in this essay does the author reveal his poetic talent? Use specific examples of poetic utterances.

5. How can you explain the author's seeming grasp of English mechanics and grammar despite the fact that he is a school dropout?

6. How does the author indicate the passage of time?

7. If paragraph 34 were taken as the summary of the writer's life so far, then what do you consider the essence of his past? How did writing figure in this life?

8. What do you think was the reason for the author's sluggishness described in paragraph 26? Is the reason plausible? Be specific in your answer.

9. What is your opinion of the punishment meted out by the grade school teachers described in paragraph 3? Is this punishment related to the reasons Baca dropped out in ninth grade? If so, what did the punishment contribute?

10. How do you explain the title of the essay? What other title might you suggest?

Writing Assignments

1. Write an essay delineating step by step the process of how you learned something at which you now excel.

2. Suggest a step-by-step process for getting prison inmates—especially hardened criminals—interested in literature.

S T U D E N T   E S S A Y — F I R S T   D R A F T

Monica Esparza

Driving to Preserve Your Car

~~Driving~~

More precise title

1   *Amazingly*
~~It is amazing how~~ few people realize that their driving styles affect ~~how long their~~   Cuts
the durability and   their automobiles.   deadwood;
~~automobile will last and what the~~ cost of ~~operating it will be.~~ It behooves drivers to use   more concise
and safely
their cars as efficiently ‸as possible to preserve them from deterioration and accidents.

Accidents are the number one reason for junking cars.

Punctuation   2   Here are some simple instructions that, if followed, will make your car run better

and last longer.

3   First and most important, concentrate on your driving so that you make good

judgments, especially in critical circumstances. If you have driven five or ten miles and

Numbering   suddenly you can't remember where you are or where you are going, you have probably

each

instruction   been daydreaming. Wake up and concentrate on the road.

adds clarity   Second,

to the process.   4   ∧ Avoid sudden accelerations; they cause excessive wear and tear on your car by

                                              a

Cuts   unnecessarily forcing the engine. Emergencies are exceptions, but you can minimize

deadwood   e

the likelihood of their occurrence if you ~~allow yourself thinking time by~~ concentrating on

Creates   your driving environment.

subordination   Third, s   , using them

for better   5   ∧ Stay off the brakes, ~~Use the brakes~~ as seldom~~ly~~ and ~~as~~ lightly as possible. This is the

emphasis   single most important technique you can learn. Brakes waste the momentum on your car.

Adds   ⟨Insert A⟩   the flow of

necessary   ∧In all driving, try hard to match your speed to ∧traffic ~~speed~~ so that you need not step on

information   in fits and starts.

More specific   either your brakes or on the gas ~~constantly~~. Many times this is impossible, but at least

                                                        (money!)

try. By avoiding sudden stops and starts, you save more gas ∧than through most of the

expensive mechanical modifications installed on cars to save fuel.

                  Fourth, l

More direct   6   ∧ ~~L~~ooking ahead and ~~being~~ cautious~~ is important~~. Drive as smoothly as possible by

Punctuation   anticipating traffic as much as a quarter of a mile away on city streets, and as far as you

can see on country roads or on freeways.

Adds useful   Fifth, k

example to   7   ∧ ~~K~~eep your emotions under control while driving. Competitive and angry driving

drive home the   ⟨Insert B⟩

point   ⌐not only⌐increases⌐the wear and tear on your car, but also the chance of an accident.

More direct   Sixth, drive strategically.

and concise   8   ∧ ~~There is one other large area that directly affects the life of the car, and that is road~~

                          are doubtless familiar with   and

~~strategy~~. You ~~know pretty well~~ all of the shortcuts ~~as well as~~ obstacles involved in

getting from where you live to where you work because you found out by trial and error.

Your trip to work is probably well executed. Now, get into the habit of planning all trips

to unfamiliar places as well, no matter how near. Take into account ~~the fact~~ that the

⟨Insert A⟩

Moreover, they increase the risk of someone's ramming into you from the rear.

⟨Insert B⟩

For instance, when you respond with feelings of aggressive revenge to a driver that has
just cut you off, given you an obscene sign, or in some other way irritated you, your mental
acuity is sidetracked to plot a get-even act, leaving you and your car less protected. The
smarter reaction is to dismiss this numbskull from your mind so that you can stay cool
and rational at the steering wheel.

type of road on which you travel can either cost or save gas. Choose the best route. A potholed or patched road may cost up to fifteen percent fuel penalty, and stretches of loose gravel can cost up to thirty-five percent. When you have a choice, always drive on a smooth road, maintained by a concerned local highway department.

9   Finally, ~~look at~~ ^view^ yourself as the ultimate control mechanism in the machinery that transports you. Take extra precautions to become a better driver, thus ^increasing the useful lifespan of your car.^ ~~give long lasting life to your car~~.

More precise restatement of thesis

STUDENT ESSAY—FINAL DRAFT

Esparza 1

Monica Esparza

Professor McCuen

English 101

April 4, 2008

Driving to Preserve Your Car

1   Amazingly few people realize that their driving styles affect the durability and cost of their automobiles. It behooves drivers to use their cars as efficiently and safely as possible to preserve them from deterioration and accidents. Accidents are the number one reason for junking cars.

2   Here are some simple instructions that, if followed, will make your car run better and last longer.

3   First and most important, concentrate on your driving so that you make good judgments, especially in critical circumstances. If you have driven five or ten miles and suddenly you can't remember where you are or where you are going, you have probably been daydreaming. Wake up and concentrate on the road.

Esparza 2

4   Second, avoid sudden accelerations; they cause excessive wear and tear on your car by unnecessarily forcing the engine. Emergencies are exceptions, but you can minimize the likelihood of their occurrence if you concentrate on your driving environment.

5   Third, stay off the brakes, using them as seldom and lightly as possible. This is the single most important technique you can learn. Brakes waste the momentum on your car. Moreover, they increase the risk of someone's ramming into you from the rear. In all driving, try hard to match your speed to the flow of traffic so that you need not step on either your brakes or on the gas in fits and starts. Many times this is impossible, but at least try. By avoiding sudden stops and starts, you save more gas (money!) than through most of the expensive mechanical modifications installed on cars to save fuel.

6   Fourth, look ahead and be cautious. Drive as smoothly as possible by anticipating traffic as much as a quarter of a mile away on city streets, and as far as you can see on country roads or on freeways.

7   Fifth, keep your emotions under control while driving. Competitive and angry driving increases not only the wear and tear on your car, but also the chance of an accident. For instance, when you respond with feelings of aggressive revenge to a driver who has just cut you off, given you an obscene sign, or in some other way irritated you, your mental acuity is sidetracked to plot a get-even act, leaving you and your car less protected. The smarter reaction is to dismiss this numbskull from your mind so that you can stay cool and rational at the steering wheel.

Esparza 3

8   Sixth, drive strategically. You are doubtless familiar with all of the shortcuts and obstacles involved in getting from where you live to where you work because you found out by trial and error. Your trip to work is probably well executed. Now, get into the habit of planning all trips to unfamiliar places as well, no matter how near. Take into account that the type of road on which you travel can either cost or save gas. Choose the best route. A potholed or patched road may cost up to fifteen percent fuel penalty, and stretches of loose gravel can cost up to thirty-five percent. When you have a choice, always drive on a smooth road, maintained by a concerned local highway department.

9   Finally, view yourself as the ultimate control mechanism in the machinery that transports you. Take extra precautions to become a better driver, thus increasing the useful lifespan of your car.

FURTHER READING

TA-NEHISI COATES

Battle of the Big Box

Ta-Nehisi Coates (b. 1975) is a former staff writer at The Village Voice *and* Time. *He has also contributed to numerous other periodicals, including* The New York Times Magazine. *His memoir,* Beautiful Struggle *(2008), recounts the struggle of his Black Panther father, Paul Coates, and his two sons to survive in the explosive neighborhoods of Baltimore at the end of the twentieth century. The essay below comes from the January/February 2010 issue of the* Atlantic.

READING FOR IDEAS   For many historians, all acreage that borders on or covers any American battlefield is sacred and should be preserved for posterity rather than sold to entrepreneurs wanting to develop the land into a profitable plaza or strip mall. The battlefields of our Civil War have attracted special attention from guardians who wish to make sure that the descendants of Confederate or Union soldiers are able to visit the streams, woods, and meadows where more American soldiers died than during any other war, including World War II. The actual goal of the war is still in dispute, but whether it was to save the union or to free the slaves doesn't matter. What matters is the enormous bloodletting brought on by arrogant extremists and blundering politicians. That is why today most Civil War battle fields, with their graves, are state parks, commemorating such campaigns as Bull Run, Shenandoah Valley, Antietam, Fredericksburg, Chancerville, Shiloh, and Gettysburg. These battles also promoted unforgettable stories about dashing warriors like Robert E. Lee, P.G.T. Beauregard, and Nathan B. Forrest in the South, or George B. McClellan, Stonewall Jackson, and William S. Rosecrans in the North. The essay below focuses on one special battlefield in Virginia that presently is in danger of being turned into a building site for Walmart. Reading about this particular economic crusade may prod you into doing additional research about what actually happened during the battle of the Wilderness of Orange County, Virginia. You might want to explore the life of one of the soldiers mentioned above or in the essay that follows.

H I S T O R Y

BATTLE OF THE BIG BOX

Saving Hallowed Ground from Walmart

1   LAST AUGUST, I WENT slightly mad while driving through central Virginia. The roads around Richmond are sprinkled with markers delineating the region's singular place in American history—and particularly Civil War history, my latest obsession. It took all I had not to swerve off the road every time a sign celebrating Gabriel Prosser or Stonewall Jackson's arm came into view. To the chagrin of my family members who were in tow, my efforts at self-control rarely succeeded.

2   Our first day in Virginia was providence itself. Half-lost, we were wending our way through back roads when we happened upon New Market Heights. A century and a half ago, regiments of the USCT—United States Colored Troops—had engaged a Confederate force there, and won 14 Medals of Freedom.

3   I pulled our rental car to the side of the road, and treated my son and nephew to an awkward impromptu lecture on the bravery of Sergeant Major Christian Fleetwood and Private Charles Veale. It was only mildly successful—I had to talk over SUVs loudly whizzing past, and there really wasn't much to see. Parts of the battlefield had been destroyed by housing developments. Other portions, owned by the county, are closed to the public. I ordered the kids out of the car and had them read the marker aloud, in unison. They squirmed around and gave mediocre waves as I snapped pictures.

4   In my lifetime, I have floated through all manner of geekdom—comic books, sci-fi, sports, medieval history, video games. The Civil War, with its swash-buckling heroes, its staggering toll, and its consequence of emancipation, is the culmination of an unorthodox

intellectual journey. Galactus and Charlemagne are charming, but if not for Fleetwood and Veale, I might not exist. By the time I stumbled upon New Market Heights, I'd read about the battle in at least three books. But I had come to Virginia to move beyond books and render my journey through the "late unpleasantness" in 3-D. Books about everything from the caliber of every cannon fired to post-traumatic stress disorder to Civil War cuisine can't adequately capture the actual conditions under which the soldiers lived and died; they can't convey, say, the spatial reality of being caught between gunfire from two sides. Any lesson on the Battle of the Crater isn't complete until you've been to Petersburg and seen the crater for yourself. Civil War sites are the classrooms of history.

5   Unfortunately, at New Market Heights, the classroom was closed. The Civil War Preservation Trust annually presents a list of 25 battlefields that are "endangered" and "at risk" because of sprawl and development. (Last year's included New Market Heights.) But the battlefield where the war between preservation and commerce now rages most ferociously is the Wilderness, in Orange County, Virginia, where in May of 1864, the two armies took 28,000 casualties, some of them wounded men who were incinerated in a forest fire.

6   Soon, the Wilderness may also be known for everyday low prices, thanks to Walmart's plans to put a new store at the site's very doorstep. The fight has pitted locals in search of decent value ("Go find a shirt in Orange," someone told the local paper. "You can't") against preservationists from Virginia and elsewhere, including the historian James McPherson and the actor Robert Duvall, a descendant of Confederate patriot Robert E. Lee.

7   The intersection of Routes 20 and 3, where Walmart hopes to build, holds special significance. "It's at that exact place where 100,000 Union soldiers go south," says Rob Nieweg of the National Trust for Historic Preservation. "They were ordered to turn right and continue on to Spotsylvania Courthouse and the Bloody Angle, Cold Harbor, and Petersburg, and ultimately, Appomattox and the end of the Civil War. It's the best place in America to stand and understand the average Union soldier's experience, at that moment, knowing that what he fought for wasn't wasted."

8   In September, the National Trust joined a coalition of preservationists filing suit to prevent Walmart from going forward. Walmart contends that the battlefield entrance is actually a mile away, and notes that it's been in discussions about the store with the community for more than a year. "This whole process has been going on for nearly 18 months," Keith Morris, a spokesperson for Walmart, told me. "It has been a meticulous process that's been thoroughly vetted and evaluated through public hearings, and we were approved almost unanimously by the Planning Commission and the Board of Supervisors."

9   Even if the preservationists prevail, the future of the Wilderness will still be in doubt. The land is zoned for commercial development. The current fight recalls the battle, 15 years ago, when preservationists stopped Disney from building a theme park near the Manassas battlefield, in Northern Virginia, only to see the area overtaken by residential sprawl.

10   On our last day in Virginia, I drove my family out to the Wilderness. By then we'd seen the Petersburg battlefield, where the war drew to its bloody close, and Shirley Plantation, a sprawling estate along the James River, once tended by slaves. But the sheer emptiness of the Wilderness's grassland and forest made it more haunting. A ranger sitting under a canopy directed us to various portions of the park, because we'd just missed the

tour. We walked up a dirt road into the woods, and saw earthworks and trenches that had been preserved for close to 150 years. Across from there, the ranger told us, you could see an open field that Union soldiers had charged across, only to be cut down by Confederates concealed in the woods and protected by fortifications. For a fleeting moment, I could actually imagine the smell of gunpowder and sweat in the August heat, and the sense that death awaited.

11   Afterward, we drove out Orange Plank Road, east of Grant's path as he marched toward Richmond; we turned onto Route 3, and after a few miles saw an assortment of big-box stores blooming out of the horizon. We grumbled some about the spoilage of development—and then stopped at Cracker Barrel for breakfast.

Source: Ta-Nehisi Coates, "Battle of the Big Box," *The Atlantic,* Jan/Feb 2010, pp. 20–21.

■ *Vocabulary*

delineating (1)	caliber (4)	coalition (8)
chagrin (1)	cuisine (4)	meticulous (8)
impromptu (3)	preservationists (5)	vetted (8)
mediocre (3)	ferociously (5)	canopy (10)
swashbuckling (4)	incinerated (5)	spoilage (11)

■ *Questions on Meaning and Technique*

1. What process is the author tracing in this essay? Where does the process begin? Where does it end? What motivates the author?

2. What is the subject of the author's impromptu lecture given to his son and nephew? Why does the author feel compelled to give this lecture? What is the importance of the facts he relates? How would you have reacted to the author's lesson?

3. What does the author mean when he states that his mini lecture was "only mildly successful"? What frustration is clearly revealed? Do you share the author's frustration? Why or why not?

4. Although the author has read several books about the battle of New Market Heights, he believes that books have their limitations. What can books convey? What are their limitations and how can they be overcome?

5. What is the meaning of the essay's title? How does it relate to the author's thesis? Explain the title and its relationship to the thesis.

6. How is the term "everyday low prices" connected with the number 28,000? What deeper meaning is behind the connection?

7. How does the author strengthen his point of view and make it credible? Give some specific examples.

8. At the time this essay was written, what was an important step taken by the National Trust and a coalition of preservationists to stop the commercial development at the intersection of Routes 20 and 3, where Walmart planned to build a box store? How successful will this force be? Explain your view.

Writing Assignments

1. Choosing one spot in the world that is not famous but should have special meaning for posterity, describe the spot and the steps you would take to preserve it.

2. Using the internet as your research tool, describe how the Battle of the Crater was fought. Use a step-by-step approach.

FURTHER READING

PAUL ROBERTS

How to Say Nothing in 500 Words

Paul McHenry Roberts (1917–1967) was an English teacher and writer of textbooks whose work enjoyed immense popularity. He taught at San Jose State University and Cornell University and was the author of many books on English and linguistics, among them Understanding Grammar *(1954),* Patterns of English *(1956), and* Understanding English *(1958).*

READING FOR IDEAS Freshman composition, like everything else, has its share of fashions. In the 1950s, when this article was written, the most popular argument raging among student essayists was the proposed abolition of college football. With the greater social consciousness of the early 1960s, the topic of the day became the morality of capital punishment. Topics may change, but the core principles of good writing remain constant, and this essay has become something of a minor classic in explaining them. Be concrete, says Roberts; get to the point; express your opinions colorfully. Refreshingly, he even practices what he preaches. His essay is humorous, direct, and almost salty in summarizing the working habits that all good prose writers must cultivate.

1   It's Friday afternoon, and you have almost survived another week of classes. You are just looking forward dreamily to the weekend when the English instructor says: "For Monday you will turn in a five-hundred-word composition on college football."

2   Well, that puts a good hole in the weekend. You don't have any strong views on college football one way or the other. You get rather excited during the season and go to

all the home games and find it rather more fun than not. On the other hand, the class has been reading Robert Hutchins in the anthology and perhaps Shaw's "Eighty-Yard Run," and from the class discussion you have got the idea that the instructor thinks college football is for the birds. You are no fool. You can figure out what side to take.

3   After dinner you get out the portable typewriter that you got for high school graduation. You might as well get it over with and enjoy Saturday and Sunday. Five hundred words is about two double-spaced pages with normal margins. You put in a sheet of paper, think up a title and you're off:

Why College Football Should Be Abolished

College football should be abolished because it's bad for the school and also for the players. The players are so busy practicing that they don't have any time for their studies.

4   This, you feel, is a mighty good start. The only trouble is that it's only thirty-two words. You still have four hundred and sixty-eight to go, and you've pretty well exhausted the subject. It comes to you that you do your best thinking in the morning, so you put away the typewriter and go to the movies. But the next morning you have to do your washing and some math problems, and in the afternoon you go to the game. The English instructor turns up too, and you wonder if you've taken the right side after all. Saturday night you have a date, and Sunday morning you have to go to church. (You can't let English assignments interfere with your religion.) What with one thing and another, it's ten o'clock Sunday night before you get out the typewriter again. You make a pot of coffee and start to fill out your views on college football. Put a little meat on the bones.

Why College Football Should Be Abolished

In my opinion, it seems to me that college football should be abolished. The reason why I think this to be true is because I feel that football is bad for the college in nearly every respect. As Robert Hutchins says in his article in our anthology in which he discusses college football, it would be better if the colleges had race horses and had races with one another, because then the horses would not have to attend classes. I firmly agree with Mr. Hutchins on this point, and I am sure that many other students would agree too.

One reason why it seems to me that college football is bad is that it has become too commercial. In the olden times when people played football just for the fun of it, maybe college football was all right, but they do not play football just for the fun of it now as they used to in the old days. Nowadays college football is what you might call a big business. Maybe this is not true at all schools, and I don't think it is especially true here at State, but certainly this is the case at most colleges and universities in America nowadays, as Mr. Hutchins points out in his very interesting article. Actually the coaches and alumni go around to the high schools and offer the high school stars large salaries to come to their colleges and play football for them. There was one case where a high school star was offered a convertible if he would play football for a certain college.

Another reason for abolishing college football is that it is bad for the players. They do not have time to get a college education, because they are so busy playing football. A football player has to practice every afternoon from three to six and then he is so tired that he can't concentrate on his studies. He just feels like dropping off to sleep after dinner, and then the next day he goes to his classes without having studied and maybe he fails the test.

5   (Good ripe stuff, so far, but you're still a hundred and fifty-one words from home. One more push.)

    Also I think college football is bad for the colleges and the universities because not very many students get to participate in it. Out of a college of ten thousand students only seventy-five or a hundred play football, if that many. Football is what you might call a spectator sport. That means that most people go to watch it but do not play it themselves.

6   (Four hundred and fifteen. Well, you still have the conclusion, and when you retype it, you can make the margins a little wider.)

    These are the reasons why I agree with Mr. Hutchins that college football should be abolished in American colleges and universities.

7   On Monday you turn it in, moderately hopeful, and on Friday it comes back marked "weak in content" and sporting a big "D."

8   This essay is exaggerated a little, not much. The English instructor will recognize it as reasonably typical of what an assignment on college football will bring in. He knows that nearly half of the class will contrive in five hundred words to say that college football is too commercial and bad for the players. Most of the other half will inform him that college football builds character and prepares one for life and brings prestige to the school. As he reads paper after paper all saying the same thing in almost the same words, he wonders how he allowed himself to get trapped into teaching English when he might have had a happy and interesting life as an electrician or a confidence man.

9   Well, you may ask, what can you do about it? The subject is one on which you have few convictions and little information. Can you be expected to make a dull subject interesting? As a matter of fact, this is precisely what you are expected to do. This is the writer's essential task. All subjects, except sex, are dull until somebody makes them interesting. The writer's job is to find the argument, the approach, the angle, the wording that will take the reader with him. This is seldom easy, and it is particularly hard in subjects that have been much discussed: College Football, Fraternities, Popular Music, Is Chivalry Dead? and the like. You will feel that there is nothing you can do with such subjects except repeat the old bromides. But there are some things you can do which will make your papers, if not throbbingly alive, at least less insufferably tedious than they might otherwise be.

Avoid the Obvious Content

10   Say the assignment is college football. Say that you've decided to be against it. Begin by putting down the arguments that come to your mind: it is too commercial, it takes the students' minds off their studies, it is hard on the players, it makes the university a kind of circus instead of an intellectual center, for most schools it is financially ruinous. Can you think of any more arguments, just off hand? All right. Now when you write your paper, *make sure that you don't use any of the material on this list.* If these are the points that leap to your mind, they will leap to everyone else's too, and whether you get a "C" or a "D" may depend on whether the instructor reads your paper early when he is fresh and tolerant

or late, when the sentence "In my opinion, college football has become too commercial," inexorably repeated, has brought him to the brink of lunacy.

11   Be against college football for some reason or reasons of your own. If they are keen and perceptive ones, that's splendid. But even if they are trivial or foolish or indefensible, you are still ahead so long as they are not everybody else's reasons too. Be against it because the colleges don't spend enough money on it to make it worthwhile, because it is bad for the characters of the spectators, because the players are forced to attend classes, because the football stars hog all the beautiful women, because it competes with baseball and is therefore un-American and possibly Communist-inspired. There are lots of more or less unused reasons for being against college football.

12   Sometimes it is a good idea to sum up and dispose of the trite and conventional points before going on to your own. This has the advantage of indicating to the reader that you are going to be neither trite nor conventional. Something like this:

> We are often told that college football should be abolished because it has become too commercial or because it is bad for the players. These arguments are no doubt very cogent, but they don't really go to the heart of the matter.

13   Then you go to the heart of the matter.

Take the Less Usual Side

14   One rather simple way of getting into your paper is to take the side of the argument that most of the citizens will want to avoid. If the assignment is an essay on dogs, you can, if you choose, explain that dogs are faithful and lovable companions, intelligent, useful as guardians of the house and protectors of children, indispensable in police work—in short, when all is said and done, man's best friends. Or you can suggest that those big brown eyes conceal, more often than not, a vacuity of mind and an inconstancy of purpose; that the dogs you have known most intimately have been mangy, ill-tempered brutes, incapable of instruction; and that only your nobility of mind and fear of arrest prevent you from kicking the flea-ridden animals when you pass them on the street.

15   Naturally personal convictions will sometimes dictate your approach. If the assigned subject is "Is Methodism Rewarding to the Individual?" and you are a pious Methodist, you have really no choice. But few assigned subjects, if any, will fall in this category. Most of them will lie in broad areas of discussion with much to be said on both sides. They are intellectual exercises, and it is legitimate to argue now one way and now another, as debaters do in similar circumstances. Always take the side that looks to you hardest, least defensible. It will almost always turn out to be easier to write interestingly on that side.

16   This general advice applies where you have a choice of subjects. If you are to choose among "The Value of Fraternities" and "My Favorite High School Teacher" and "What I Think about Beetles," by all means plump for the beetles. By the time the instructor gets to your paper, he will be up to his ears in tedious tales about a French teacher at Bloombury High and assertions about how fraternities build character and prepare one for life. Your views on beetles, whatever they are, are bound to be a refreshing change.

17   Don't worry too much about figuring out what the instructor thinks about the subject so that you can cuddle up with him. Chances are his views are no stronger than yours.

If he does have convictions and you oppose him, his problem is to keep from grading you higher than you deserve in order to show he is not biased. This doesn't mean that you should always cantankerously dissent from what the instructor says; that gets tiresome too. And if the subject assigned is "My Pet Peeve," do not begin, "My pet peeve is the English instructor who assigns papers on 'my pet peeve.'" This was still funny during the War of 1812, but it has sort of lost its edge since then. It is in general good manners to avoid personalities.

Slip Out of Abstraction

18   If you will study the essay on college football [near the beginning of this essay], you will perceive that one reason for its appalling dullness is that it never gets down to particulars. It is just a series of not very glittering generalities: "football is bad for the colleges," "it has become too commercial," "football is big business," "it is bad for the players," and so on. Such round phrases thudding against the reader's brain are unlikely to convince him, though they may well render him unconscious.

19   If you want the reader to believe that college football is bad for the players, you have to do more than say so. You have to display the evil. Take your roommate, Alfred Simkins, the second-string center. Picture poor old Alfy coming home from football practice every evening, bruised and aching, agonizingly tired, scarcely able to shovel the mashed potatoes into his mouth. Let us see him staggering up to the room, getting out his econ textbook, peering desperately at it with his good eye, falling asleep and failing the test in the morning. Let us share his unbearable tension as Saturday draws near. Will he fail, be demoted, lose his monthly allowance, be forced to return to the coal mines? And if he succeeds, what will be his reward? Perhaps a slight ripple of applause when the third-string center replaces him, a moment of elation in the locker room if the team wins, or despair if it loses. What will he look back on when he graduates from college? Toil and torn ligaments. And what will be his future? He is not good enough for pro football, and he is too obscure and weak in econ to succeed in stocks and bonds. College football is tearing the heart from Alfy Simkins and, when it finishes with him, will callously toss aside the shattered hulk.

20   This is no doubt a weak enough argument for the abolition of college football, but it is a sight better than saying, in three or four variations, that college football (in your opinion) is bad for the players.

21   Look at the work of any professional writer and notice how constantly he is moving from the generality, the abstract statement, to the concrete example, the facts and figures, the illustrations. If he is writing on juvenile delinquency, he does not just tell you that juveniles are (it seems to him) delinquent and that (in his opinion) something should be done about it. He shows you juveniles being delinquent, tearing up movie theatres in Buffalo, stabbing high school principals in Dallas, smoking marijuana in Palo Alto. And more than likely he is moving toward some specific remedy, not just a general wringing of the hands.

22   It is no doubt possible to be too concrete, too illustrative or anecdotal, but few inexperienced writers err this way. For most the soundest advice is to be seeking always for the picture, to be always turning general remarks into seeable examples. Don't say,

"Sororities teach girls the social graces." Say, "Sorority life teaches a girl how to carry on a conversation while pouring tea, without sloshing the tea into the saucer." Don't say, "I like certain kinds of popular music very much." Say, "Whenever I hear Gerber Sprinklittle play 'Mississippi Man' on the trombone, my socks creep up my ankles."

Get Rid of Obvious Padding

23   The student toiling away at his weekly English theme is too often tormented by a figure: five hundred words. How, he asks himself, is he to achieve this staggering total? Obviously by never using one word when he can somehow work in ten.

24   He is therefore seldom content with a plain statement like "Fast driving is dangerous." This has only four words in it. He takes thought, and the sentence becomes:

> In my opinion, fast driving is dangerous.

Better, but he can do better still:

> In my opinion, fast driving would seem to be rather dangerous.

If he is really adept, it may come out:

> In my humble opinion, though I do not claim to be an expert on this complicated subject, fast driving, in most circumstances, would seem to be rather dangerous in many respects, or at least so it would seem to me.

Thus four words have been turned into forty, and not an iota of content has been added.

25   Now this is a way to go about reaching five hundred words, and if you are content with a "D" grade, it is as good a way as any. But if you aim higher, you must work differently. Instead of stuffing your sentences with straw, you must try steadily to get rid of the padding, to make your sentences lean and tough. If you are really working at it, your first draft will greatly exceed the required total, and then you will work it down, thus:

> It is thought in some quarters that fraternities do not contribute as much as might be expected to campus life.
> Some people think that fraternities contribute little to campus life.

> The average doctor who practices in small towns or in the country must toil night and day to heal the sick.
> Most country doctors work long hours.

> When I was a little girl, I suffered from shyness and embarrassment in the presence of others.
> I was a shy little girl.

> It is absolutely necessary for the person employed as a marine fireman to give the matter of steam pressure his undivided attention at all times.
> The fireman has to keep his eye on the steam gauge.

26   You may ask how you can arrive at five hundred words at this rate. Simple. You dig up more real content. Instead of taking a couple of obvious points off the surface of the

topic and then circling warily around them for six paragraphs, you work in and explore, figure out the details. You illustrate. You say that fast driving is dangerous, and then you prove it. How long does it take to stop a car at forty and at eighty? How far can you see at night? What happens when a tire blows? What happens in a head-on collision at fifty miles an hour? Pretty soon your paper will be full of broken glass and blood and headless torsos, and reaching five hundred words will not really be a problem.

Call a Fool a Fool

27   Some of the padding in freshman themes is to be blamed not on anxiety about the word minimum but on excessive timidity. The student writes, "In my opinion, the principal of my high school acted in ways that I believe every unbiased person would have to call foolish." This isn't exactly what he means. What he means is, "My high school principal was a fool." If he was a fool, call him a fool. Hedging the thing about with "in-my-opinion's" and "it-seems-to-me's" and "as-I-see-it's" and "at-least-from-my-point-of-view's" gains you nothing. Delete these phrases whenever they creep into your paper.

28   The student's tendency to hedge stems from a modesty that in other circumstances would be commendable. He is, he realizes, young and inexperienced, and he half suspects that he is dopey and fuzzy-minded beyond the average. Probably only too true. But it doesn't help to announce your incompetence six times in every paragraph. Decide what you want to say and say it as vigorously as possible, without apology and in plain words.

29   Linguistic diffidence can take various forms. One is what we call *euphemism.* This is the tendency to call a spade "a certain garden implement" or women's underwear "unmentionables." It is stronger in some areas than others and in some people than others but it always operates more or less in subjects that are touchy or taboo: death, sex, madness, and so on. Thus we shrink from saying "He died last night" but say instead "passed away," "left us," "joined his Maker," "went to his reward." Or we try to take off the tension with a lighter cliché: "kicked the bucket," "cashed in his chips," "handed in his dinner pail." We have found all sorts of ways to avoid saying *mad:* "mentally ill," "touched," "not quite right upstairs," "feebleminded," "innocent," "simple," "off his trolley," "not in his right mind." Even such a now plain word as *insane* began as a euphemism with the meaning "not healthy."

30   Modern science, particularly psychology, contributes many polysyllables in which we can wrap our thoughts and blunt their force. To many writers there is no such thing as a bad schoolboy. Schoolboys are maladjusted or unoriented or misunderstood or in the need of guidance or lacking in continued success toward satisfactory integration of the personality as a social unit, but they are never bad. Psychology no doubt makes us better men and women, more sympathetic and tolerant, but it doesn't make writing any easier. Had Shakespeare been confronted with psychology, "To be or not to be" might have come out, "To continue as a social unit or not to do so. That is the personality problem. Whether 'tis a better sign of integration at the conscious level to display a psychic tolerance toward the maladjustments and repressions induced by one's lack of orientation in one's environment or—" But Hamlet would never have finished the soliloquy.

31   Writing in the modern world, you cannot altogether avoid modern jargon. Nor, in an effort to get away from euphemism, should you salt your paper with four-letter words.

But you can do much if you will mount guard against those roundabout phrases, those echoing polysyllables that tend to slip into your writing to rob it of its crispness and force.

Beware of Pat Expressions

32   Other things being equal, avoid phrases like "other things being equal." Those sentences that come to you whole, or in two or three doughy lumps, are sure to be bad sentences. They are no creation of yours but pieces of common thought floating in the community soup.

33   Pat expressions are hard, often impossible to avoid, because they come too easily to be noticed and seem too necessary to be dispensed with. No writer avoids them altogether, but good writers avoid them more often than poor writers.

34   By "pat expressions" we mean such tags as "to all practical intents and purposes," "the pure and simple truth," "from where I sit," "the time of his life," "to the ends of the earth," "in the twinkling of an eye," "as sure as you're born," "over my dead body," "under cover of darkness," "took the easy way out," "when all is said and done," "stand up and be counted," "gave him the best years of her life," "worked her fingers to the bone." Like other clichés, these expressions were once forceful. Now we should use them only when we can't possibly think of anything else.

35   Some pat expressions stand like a wall between the writer and thought. Such a one is "the American way of life." Many student writers feel that when they have said that something accords with the American way of life or does not they have exhausted the subject. Actually, they have stopped at the highest level of abstraction. The American way of life is the complicated set of bonds between a hundred and eighty million ways. All of us know this when we think about it, but the tag phrase too often keeps us from thinking about it.

36   So with many another phrase dear to the politician: "this great land of ours," "the man in the street," "our national heritage." These may prove our patriotism or give a clue to our political beliefs, but otherwise they add nothing to the paper except words.

Colorful Words

37   The writer builds with words, and no builder uses a raw material more slippery and elusive and treacherous. A writer's work is a constant struggle to get the right word in the right place, to find that particular word that will convey his meaning exactly, that will persuade the reader or soothe him or startle or amuse him. He never succeeds altogether—sometimes he feels that he scarcely succeeds at all—but such successes as he has are what make the thing worth doing.

38   There is no book of rules for this game. One progresses through everlasting experiment on the basis of ever-widening experience. There are few useful generalizations that one can make about words as words, but there are perhaps a few.

39   Some words are what we call "colorful." By this we mean that they are calculated to produce a picture or induce an emotion. They are dressy instead of plain, specific instead of general, loud instead of soft. Thus, in place of "Her heart beat," we may write, "Her heart *pounded, throbbed, fluttered, danced.*" Instead of "He sat in his chair," we may say, "He *lounged, sprawled, coiled.*" Instead of "It was hot," we may say, "It was *blistering, sultry, muggy, suffocating, steamy, wilting.*"

40   However, it should not be supposed that the fancy word is always better. Often it is as well to write "Her heart beat" or "It was hot" if that is all it did or all it was. Ages differ in how they like their prose. The nineteenth century liked it rich and smoky. The twentieth has usually preferred it lean and cool. The twentieth century writer, like all writers, is forever seeking the exact word, but he is wary of sounding feverish. He tends to pitch it low, to understate it, to throw it away. He knows that if he gets too colorful, the audience is likely to giggle.

41   See how this strikes you: "As the rich, golden glow of the sunset died away along the eternal western hills, Angela's limpid blue eyes looked softly and trustingly into Montague's flashing brown ones, and her heart pounded like a drum in time with the joyous songs surging in her soul." Some people like that sort of thing, but most modern readers would say, "Good grief," and turn on the television.

Colored Words

42   Some words we would call not so much colorful as colored—that is, loaded with associations, good or bad. All words—except perhaps structure words—have associations of some sort. We have said that the meaning of a word is the sum of the contexts in which it occurs. When we hear a word, we hear with it an echo of all the situations in which we have heard it before.

43   In some words, these echoes are obvious and discussable. The word *mother,* for example, has, for most people, agreeable associations. When you hear *mother* you probably think of home, safety, love, food, and various other pleasant things. If one writes, "She was like a mother to me," he gets an effect which he would not get in "She was like an aunt to me." The advertiser makes use of the associations of *mother* by working it in when he talks about his product. The politician works it in when he talks about himself.

44   So also with such words as *home, liberty, fireside, contentment, patriot, tenderness, sacrifice, childlike, manly, bluff, limpid.* All of these words are loaded with associations that would be rather hard to indicate in a straightforward definition. There is more than a literal difference between "They sat around the fireside" and "They sat around the stove." They might have been equally warm and happy around the stove, but *fireside* suggests leisure, grace, quiet tradition, congenial company, and *stove* does not.

45   Conversely, some words have bad associations. *Mother* suggests pleasant things, but *mother-in-law* does not. Many mothers-in-law are heroically lovable and some mothers drink gin all day and beat their children insensible, but these facts of life are beside the point. The point is that *mother* sounds good and *mother-in-law* does not.

46   Or consider the word *intellectual.* This would seem to be a complimentary term, but in point of fact it is not, for it has picked up associations of impracticality and ineffectuality and general dopiness. So also such words as *liberal, reactionary, Communist, socialist, capitalist, radical, schoolteacher, truck driver, undertaker, operator, salesman, huckster, speculator.* These convey meaning on the literal level, but beyond that—sometimes, in some places—they convey contempt on the part of the speaker.

47   The question of whether to use loaded words or not depends on what is being written. The scientist, the scholar try to avoid them; for the poet, the advertising writer, the public speaker, they are standard equipment. But every writer should take care that they do not

substitute for thought. If you write, "Anyone who thinks that is nothing but a Socialist (or Communist or capitalist)" you have said nothing except that you don't like people who think that, and such remarks are effective only with the most naive readers. It is always a bad mistake to think your readers more naive than they really are.

Colorless Words

48   But probably most student writers come to grief not with words that are colorful or those that are colored but with those that have no color at all. A pet example is *nice*, a word we would find it hard to dispense with in casual conversation but which is no longer capable of adding much to a description. Colorless words are those of such general meaning that in a particular sentence they mean nothing. Slang adjectives like *cool* ("That's real cool") tend to explode all over the language. They are applied to everything, lose their original force, and quickly die.

49   Beware also of nouns of very general meaning, like *circumstances, cases, instances, aspects, factors, relationships, attitudes, eventualities*, etc. In most circumstances you will find that those cases of writing which contain too many instances of words like these will in this and other aspects have factors leading to unsatisfactory relationships with the reader resulting in unfavorable attitudes on his part and perhaps other eventualities, like a grade of "D." Notice also what *etc.* means. It means "I'd like to make this longer, but I can't think of any more examples."

■ *Vocabulary*

contrive (8)	cogent (12)	diffidence (29)
bromides (9)	vacuity (14)	repressions (30)
inexorably (10)	cantankerously (17)	limpid (41)

■ *Questions on Meaning and Technique*

1. How does the author's opening draw us in? Comment on the effectiveness of his technique.

2. How did the student proceed with writing the essay on college football? Do you regard the author's description of this hypothetical attempt as exaggerated, or does it strike you as true to life? How does it compare with your own attempts at writing essays?

3. Do you think the "D" allegedly earned by the essay on college football is overly harsh or deserved? Justify your answer.

4. A characteristic of this famous essay is the hold it manages to exert over most readers. How does the author achieve this effect?

5. The author advises that you list the arguments that come immediately to mind on a topic and then never use any of them. How do you think the

author would reply to the objection that a student might deeply believe in one of the clichéd arguments on the list?

6. The author urges the student writer always to take the less usual side of a topic. Do you think this advice ethical? Why or why not?

7. What purpose do the questions at the beginning of paragraph 9 serve?

8. In paragraph 22, the author suggests that "Whenever I hear Gerber Sprinklittle play 'Mississippi Man' on the trombone, my socks creep up my ankles" is better than "I like popular music very much." What objection might an English instructor raise to the Sprinklittle sentence?

Writing Assignments

1. Inverting Roberts's approach, write an essay titled "How to Say Something in 500 Words." Like Roberts, use examples to support your thesis.

2. Write an essay in which you outline the proper steps involved in writing a journal entry and using it later in a fully developed essay.

Internet Research Assignment

The internet is full of advice on how to improve your life—by using certain foods, creams, exercises, pieces of equipment, or psychological activities. Find a process and list the steps required to master this process. Include all steps suggested. If you think a step is missing or superfluous, make a note of this opinion at the end of your list. Also indicate whether you found the process sensible, useful, and valuable.

Additional Writing Assignments

1. You would like to have a balanced budget at the end of each month. Write a process paper on how to set up your ledger sheets. Use an approach that suits your spending needs and style.

2. Write a "how-to" process paper on the way your state senators are elected.

3. Write a process paper on how to prepare for a trip to a foreign country.

4. Renting a room or an apartment often proves disastrous for students. Write a process paper indicating how to rent an appropriate room or apartment.

5. Choose your favorite hobby or sport, and write a process paper on how to excel at this activity.

6. Pretend that you are planning your wedding. Develop a process essay in which you analyze chronologically the major steps involved.

7. If you were a first-grade teacher, what events would you plan for the first hour of school? Explain them in a process essay that could serve as a lesson plan.

8. Through library research, accumulate the proper information to write an essay in which you describe the major events that led to one of the following: the Battle of Waterloo, the bombing of Pearl Harbor, the Vietnam War, or the Velvet Revolution in the Czech Republic.

9. Write a process essay suggesting the steps someone must take to overcome one of the following bad habits: eating too many desserts, smoking, talking without listening, being stingy.

Rewriting Assignment

The following process paragraph is somewhat fuzzy because the steps for washing a fancy T-shirt are not clearly separated one from the other nor are they all in sequence. Also, some steps contain deadwood and poor pronoun references. Rewrite the paragraph to clearly number each step in sequence and to clarify the language where necessary.

Are you attracted to T-shirts that have rhinestones, sequins, patches, or embroidery attached to them? I am and can't resist buying them when they are on sale. Often friends give me fancy T-shirts for my birthday or Christmas because they know I love them. But here is the downside: They can be disastrous to wash. From experience and expert counsel, I have learned the safest way to wash a fancy T-shirt. First, place it in cool water so the colors don't fade. (This is important.) Oh, and hand wash it in your bathroom sink; never use a washing machine. Let it soak for two or three minutes. The water should have ¼ cup of Woolite soap in it. I forgot. Before you place the T-shirt in the water, turn it inside out so as to preserve all of the artwork. Now, swish the T-shirt back and forth in the water. Then squeeze it gently a few times. If you see any spots, rub them with Woolite until they disappear. Now pull the T-shirt out of the sink and hold it up until most of the water has dripped into the sink. Wrap it in a soft terry towel to dry it further. Finally, lay it out flat on a dry towel placed on a flat surface until it is dry. When it is dry, you can iron it gently while it is inside out. Your T-shirt is clean and ready to turn right side out again and hang up in your closet.

Photo Writing Assignment

© AMe Photo/Getty Images

Write an essay explaining the best and most efficient way to accomplish a common household chore such as washing dishes, making a bed, cleaning the bathroom, or sewing on a button. List the steps in logical order so that anyone can follow your process. Make sure that you don't leave out an obvious step.

Digging for Gold or for Steps

In the metaphorical universe, everything is related to everything else. Without the belief in our outlook, we would have difficulty trying to explain the relationship between writing a process paper and mining for gold. However, more than one poet has pointed out the intricate interconnectedness of all the nearly infinite parts of the universe. The poet Madeleine L'Engle (1918–2007) put it this way, "Thou canst not disturb a flower without the troubling of a star."

In the practical world, process is the rhetorical form that explains the sequence involved in an action or that relates step by step a certain history. So, the miner finds a site, starts digging, splitting, sifting, and evaluating. In this chapter on process we have a story ironically told, that tells how a solid citizen, Mr. Hogan, committed a bank robbery and got away with it. The poem "Tract" is equally fussy in giving instructions on how to stage a funeral while the "Battle of the Big Box" recounts with historical precision an environmental clash between big business and preservationists. Gold miners are more interested in what they can take from the earth than in leaving intact what is already there, and on this particular score are likely to differ from writers.

Many teachers regard process as the simplest of all writing forms, but this reputation seems to us to be undeserved. Some processes are indeed simple—instructions for baking a cake, for example—but others, particularly in science, can be sophisticated and involved. Likewise relating some tangled episode of history can stretch the skills of any writer. In either case, be assured that digging into your subject may not result in a gold strike but can decidedly help you understand and unravel a complex process.

Chapter 13

Classification/Division

KURT VONNEGUT, JR.

Harrison Bergeron

Kurt Vonnegut, Jr. (1922–2007), was a writer whose science fiction, fantasy, and political satire have been especially popular on college campuses. During World War II, he was a prisoner of war in Germany, an experience reflected in many of his novels and essays. Among his best-known works are **The Sirens of Titan** *(1961),* **Cat's Cradle** *(1963),* **Slaughterhouse Five** *(1969),* **Breakfast of Champions** *(1972),* **Slapstick** *(1976),* **Jailbird** *(1979), and* **Bluebeard** *(1990).*

READING FOR IDEAS   Science fiction imagines a world whose physical limitations and conditions are different than those that govern our own reality. In this imaginary place, characters act out their lives under circumstances that are invented to dramatize human dilemmas. The fictional world is always an imagined variation of our own world that throws some light upon it. In the story that follows, for example, the author asks us to imagine what our world would be like if everyone's complete equality were the law of the land. What would our lives be like under conditions requiring a mass leveling of all intelligence and talents? What does the story teach you about possible future trends, especially related to individuality? Try to classify the handicaps described, and think about the chances of that kind of equality ever succeeding.

1   The year was 2081, and everybody was finally equal. They weren't only equal before God and the law. They were equal in every which way. Nobody was smarter than anybody else. Nobody was better looking than anybody else. Nobody was stronger or quicker than anybody else. All this equality was due to the 211th, 212th, and 213th Amendments to the Constitution, and to the unceasing vigilance of agents of the United States Handicapper General.

2   Some things about living still weren't quite right, though. April, for instance, still drove people crazy by not being springtime. And it was in that clammy month that the H-G men took George and Hazel Bergeron's fourteen-year-old son, Harrison, away.

3   It was tragic, all right, but George and Hazel couldn't think about it very hard. Hazel had a perfectly average intelligence, which meant she couldn't think about anything except in short bursts. And George, while his intelligence was way above normal, had a little mental handicap radio in his ear. He was required by law to wear it at all times. It was tuned to a government transmitter. Every twenty seconds or so, the transmitter would send out some sharp noise to keep people like George from taking unfair advantage of their brains.

4   George and Hazel were watching television. There were tears on Hazel's cheeks, but she'd forgotten for the moment what they were about.

5   On the television screen were ballerinas.

6   A buzzer sounded in George's head. His thoughts fled in panic, like bandits from a burglar alarm.

7   "That was a real pretty dance, that dance they just did," said Hazel.

8   "Huh?" said George.

9   "That dance—it was nice," said Hazel.

10   "Yup," said George. He tried to think a little about the ballerinas. They weren't really very good—no better than anybody else would have been anyway. They were burdened with sash-weights and bags of birdshot, and their faces were masked, so that no one, seeing a free and graceful gesture or a pretty face, would feel like something the cat drug in. George was toying with the vague notion that maybe dancers shouldn't be handicapped. But he didn't get very far with it before another noise in his ear radio scattered his thoughts.

11   George winced. So did two out of the eight ballerinas.

12   Hazel saw him wince. Having no mental handicap herself, she had to ask George what the latest sound had been.

13   "Sounded like somebody hitting a milk bottle with a ball peen hammer," said George.

14   "I'd think it would be real interesting, hearing all the different sounds," said Hazel, a little envious. "All the things they think up."

15   "Um," said George.

16   "Only, if I was Handicapper General, you know what I would do?" said Hazel. Hazel, as a matter of fact, bore a strong resemblance to the Handicapper General, a woman named Diana Moon Glampers. "If I was Diana Moon Glampers," said Hazel, "I'd have chimes on Sunday—just chimes. Kind of in honor of religion."

17   "I could think, if it was just chimes," said George.

18   "Well—maybe make 'em real loud," said Hazel. "I think I'd make a good Handicapper General."

19   "Good as anybody else," said George.

20   "Who knows better'n I do what normal is?" said Hazel.

21   "Right," said George. He began to think glimmeringly about his abnormal son who was now in jail, about Harrison, but a twenty-one-gun salute in his head stopped that.

22   "Boy!" said Hazel, "that was a doozy, wasn't it?"

23   It was such a doozy that George was white and trembling, and tears stood on the rims of his red eyes. Two of the eight ballerinas had collapsed to the studio floor, were holding their temples.

24   "All of a sudden you look so tired," said Hazel. "Why don't you stretch out on the sofa, so's you can rest your handicap bag on the pillows, honeybunch." She was referring to the forty-seven pounds of birdshot in a canvas bag, which was padlocked around George's neck. "Go on and rest the bag for a little while," she said. "I don't care if you're not equal to me for a while."

25   George weighed the bag with his hands. "I don't mind it," he said. "I don't notice it any more. It's just a part of me."

26   "You've been so tired lately—kind of wore out," said Hazel. "If there was just some way we could make a little hole in the bottom of the bag, and just take out a few of them lead balls, just a few."

27   "Two years in prison and two thousand dollars fine for every ball I took out," said George. "I don't call that a bargain."

28   "If you could just take a few out when you came home from work," said Hazel. "I mean—you don't compete with anybody around here. You just set around."

29   "If I tried to get away with it," said George, "then other people'd get away with it—and pretty soon we'd be right back to the dark ages again, with everybody competing against everybody else. You wouldn't like that, would you?"

30   "I'd hate it," said Hazel.

31   "There you are," said George. "The minute people start cheating on laws, what do you think happens to society?"

32   If Hazel hadn't been able to come up with an answer to this question, George couldn't have supplied one. A siren was going off in his head.

33   "Reckon it'd fall all apart," said Hazel.

34   "What would?" said George blankly.

35   "Society," said Hazel uncertainly. "Wasn't that what you just said?"

36   "Who knows?" said George.

37   The television program was suddenly interrupted for a news bulletin. It wasn't clear at first as to what the bulletin was about, since the announcer, like all announcers, had a serious speech impediment. For about half a minute, and in a state of high excitement, the announcer tried to say, "Ladies and gentlemen—"

38   He finally gave up, handed the bulletin to a ballerina to read.

39   "That's all right—" Hazel said to the announcer, "he tried. That's the big thing. He tried to do the best he could with what God gave him. He should get a nice raise for trying so hard."

40   "Ladies and gentlemen—" said the ballerina, reading the bulletin. She must have been extraordinarily beautiful because the mask she wore was hideous. And it was easy to see that she was the strongest and most graceful of all the dancers, for her handicap bags were as big as those worn by two-hundred-pound men.

41   And she had to apologize at once for her voice, which was a very unfair voice for a woman to use. Her voice was warm, luminous, timeless, melody. "Excuse me—" she said, and she began again, making her voice absolutely uncompetitive.

42   "Harrison Bergeron, age fourteen," she said in a grackle squawk, "has just escaped from jail, where he was held on suspicion of plotting to overthrow the government. He is a genius and an athlete, is under handicapped, and should be regarded as extremely dangerous."

43   A police photograph of Harrison Bergeron was flashed on the screen upside down, then sideways, upside down again, then right side up. The picture showed the full length of Harrison against a background calibrated in feet and inches. He was exactly seven feet tall.

44   The rest of Harrison's appearance was Halloween and hardware. Nobody had ever borne heavier handicaps. He had outgrown hindrances faster than the H-G men could think them up. Instead of a little ear radio for a mental handicap, he wore a tremendous pair of earphones, and spectacles with thick wavy lenses. The spectacles were intended to make him not only half blind, but to give him whanging headaches besides.

45   Scrap metal was hung all over him. Ordinarily, there was a certain symmetry, a military neatness to the handicaps issued to strong people, but Harrison looked like a walking junkyard. In the race of life, Harrison carried three hundred pounds.

46   And to offset his good looks, the H-G men required that he wear at all times a red rubber ball for a nose, keep his eyebrows shaved off, and cover his even white teeth with black caps at snaggletooth random.

47   "If you see this boy," said the ballerina, "do not—I repeat, do not—try to reason with him."

48   There was the shriek of a door being torn from its hinges.

49   Screams and barking cries of consternation came from the television set. The photograph of Harrison Bergeron on the screen jumped again and again, as though dancing to the tune of an earthquake.

50   George Bergeron correctly identified the earthquake, and well he might have—for many was the time his own home had danced to the same crashing tune. "My God—" said George, "that must be Harrison!"

51   The realization was blasted from his mind instantly by the sound of an automobile collision in his head.

52   When George could open his eyes again, the photograph of Harrison was gone. A living, breathing Harrison filled the screen.

53   Clanking, clownish, and huge, Harrison stood in the center of the studio. The knob of the uprooted studio door was still in his hand. Ballerinas, technicians, musicians, and announcers cowered on their knees before him, expecting to die.

54   "I am the Emperor!" cried Harrison. "Do you hear? I am the Emperor! Everybody must do what I say at once!" He stamped his foot and the studio shook.

55   "Even as I stand here—" he bellowed, "crippled, hobbled, sickened—I am a greater ruler than any man who ever lived! Now watch me become what I *can* become!"

56   Harrison tore the straps of his handicap harness like wet tissue paper, tore straps guaranteed to support five thousand pounds.

57   Harrison's scrap-iron handicaps crashed to the floor.

58 Harrison thrust his thumbs under the bar of the padlock that secured his head harness. The bar snapped like celery. Harrison smashed his headphones and spectacles against the wall.

59 He flung away his rubber-ball nose, revealed a man that would have awed Thor, the god of thunder.

60 "I shall now select my Empress!" he said, looking down on the cowering people. "Let the first woman who dares rise to her feet claim her mate and her throne!"

61 A moment passed, and then a ballerina arose, swaying like a willow.

62 Harrison plucked the mental handicap from her ear, snapped off her physical handicaps with marvelous delicacy. Last of all, he removed her mask.

63 She was blindingly beautiful.

64 "Now—" said Harrison, taking her hand, "shall we show the people the meaning of the word dance? Music!" he commanded.

65 The musicians scrambled back into their chairs, and Harrison stripped them of their handicaps, too. "Play your best," he told them, "and I'll make you barons and dukes and earls."

66 The music began. It was normal at first—cheap, silly, false. But Harrison snatched two musicians from their chairs, waved them like batons as he sang the music as he wanted it played. He slammed them back into their chairs.

67 The music began again and was much improved.

68 Harrison and his Empress merely listened to the music for a while—listened gravely, as though synchronizing their heartbeats with it.

69 They shifted their weights to their toes.

70 Harrison placed his big hand on the girl's tiny waist, letting her sense the weightlessness that would soon be hers.

71 And then, in an explosion of joy and grace, into the air they sprang!

72 Not only were the laws of the land abandoned, but the law of gravity and the laws of motion as well.

73 They reeled, whirled, swiveled, flounced, capered, gamboled, and spun.

74 They leaped like deer on the moon.

75 The studio ceiling was thirty feet high, but each leap brought the dancers nearer to it.

76 It became their obvious intention to kiss the ceiling.

77 They kissed it.

78 And then, neutralizing gravity with love and pure will, they remained suspended in air inches below the ceiling, and they kissed each other for a long, long time.

79 It was then that Diana Moon Glampers, the Handicapper General, came into the studio with a double-barreled 10-gauge shotgun. She fired twice, and the Emperor and the Empress were dead before they hit the floor.

80 Diana Moon Glampers loaded the gun again. She aimed it at the musicians and told them they had ten seconds to get their handicaps back on.

81 It was then that the Bergeron's television tube burned out.

82 Hazel turned to comment about the blackout to George. But George had gone out into the kitchen for a can of beer.

83   George came back in with the beer, paused while a handicap signal shook him up. And then he sat down again. "You been crying?" he said to Hazel.

84   "Yup," she said.

85   "What about?" he said.

86   "I forget," she said. "Something real sad on television."

87   "What was it?" he said.

88   "It's all kind of mixed up in my mind," said Hazel.

89   "Forget sad things," said George.

90   "I always do," said Hazel.

91   "That's my girl," said George. He winced. There was the sound of a riveting gun in his head.

92   "Gee—I could tell that one was a doozy," said Hazel.

93   "You can say that again," said George.

94   "Gee—" said Hazel, "I could tell that one was a doozy."

■ *Vocabulary*

unceasing (1)	doozy (22)	consternation (49)
vigilance (1)	impediment (37)	cowered (53)
transmitter (3)	luminous (41)	capered (73)
sash-weights (10)	grackle (42)	gamboled (73)
winced (11)	calibrated (43)	
glimmeringly (21)	symmetry (45)	

■ *Questions on Meaning and Technique*

1. To classify the handicaps presented in this story, what general categories would you list? Why?

2. Which handicap, if any, do you consider the most harmful to society? Give reasons for your answer.

3. How do George and Hazel differ? What importance is attached to their differences?

4. What is *equality*, as defined in Vonnegut's story? What is the narrator's point of view about the kind of equality described? Rely on specific passages to support your answer.

5. In your opinion, can a society succeed whose mission is to achieve the kind of equality described in this story? Why or why not?

6. What purposes does the opening paragraph serve? What is the narrator's tone?

7. What difference would it make if the story were narrated from Harrison's point of view?

8. How does the author achieve a sense of movement in the studio scene (paragraphs 69–75)?

WILLIAM SHAKESPEARE

All the World's a Stage

From *As You Like It* (Act 2, Scene 7)

William Shakespeare (1564–1616) is generally considered the greatest literary genius of the English language. Despite his world renown, little is known about Shakespeare's personal life. Born in Stratford-upon-Avon, England, the son of a successful businessman who also held the office of alderman and bailiff, Shakespeare probably attended the local grammar school, where he learned some Latin and Greek. At the age of 18, he married Anne Hathaway, eight years his senior, who bore him three children. The vast legacy of his writing includes thirty-six plays, 154 sonnets, and five epic poems.

READING FOR IDEAS This poem was taken from one of Shakespeare's most popular comedies, *As You Like It*. This excerpt is from a monologue spoken by Jacques, a melancholy gentleman who has escaped court politics to live in the forest. He views life as a meaningless process of decay governed by inexorable time. In this speech, Jacques divides life into stages with each stage dominated by a type of man.

1   All the world's a stage,
    And all the men and women merely players.
    They have their exits and their entrances,
    And one man in his time plays many parts,
5   His acts being seven ages. At first, the infant,
    Mewling and puking in the nurse's arms.
    Then the whining schoolboy, with his satchel
    And shining morning face, creeping like snail
    Unwillingly to school. And then the lover,
10   Sighing like furnace, with a woeful ballad
    Made to his mistress' eyebrow. Then a soldier,
    Full of strange oaths and bearded like the pard,[1]
    Jealous in honour, sudden and quick in quarrel,
    Seeking the bubble reputation
15   Even in the cannon's mouth. And then the justice,
    In fair round belly with good capon lin'd,
    With eyes severe and beard of formal cut,
    Full of wise saws and modern instances;
    And so he plays his part. The sixth age shifts

---

[1]Leopard.

20   Into the lean and slipper'd pantaloon,
        With spectacles on nose and pouch on side;
        His youthful hose, well sav'd, a world too wide
        For his shrunk shank, and his big manly voice,
        Turning again toward childish treble, pipes
25   And whistles in his sound. Last scene of all,
        That ends this strange eventful history,
        Is second childishness and mere oblivion,
        Sans[2] teeth, sans eyes, sans taste, sans everything.

————————
[2]French for "without."

■ *Vocabulary*

mewling (line 6)	pantaloon (line 20)	treble (line 24)
puking (line 6)	pouch (line 21)	
capon (line 16)	shank (line 23)	

■ *Questions on Meaning and Technique*

1. In the first line, what metaphor is used to describe life? What other metaphor might be appropriate? Why?

2. What name can you give to each of the seven stages of life as depicted by Jacques? Classify each character into the proper stage.

3. What does the simile "Sighing like furnace" (line 10) reveal?

4. What characteristics typify the soldier? Are these characteristics typical of soldiers today? Why or why not?

5. In the final lines, how does Jacques portray life? Do you agree with his portrayal? Give reasons for your answer.

How to Write a Classification/Division Paper

Classification or division means sorting people, objects, data, or ideas into various types and groups. It is a method of thinking that helps to impose order on the enormous jumble in the world. Classification and division are so closely related that writers often use them together because they are opposite sides of the same coin.

Classification means placing an individual part into a category with other similar parts, whereas *division* means separating a large subject into divisible parts. Biologists, for example, classify a wolf as a canine (dog family), whereas a tiger is classified as a feline (cat family). The field of anthropology is divided into the subfields of archaeology, ethnography, and linguistics, whereas botany classifies every plant into the family to which it belongs. In each case, an attempt is made to impose order by division or classification—that is, reducing the many to the few.

As civilized humans, we are entirely addicted to thinking by classification/division. We carry classes, types, and categories on the tips of our tongues. A car is not merely a car; it is a coupe, a sedan, or a convertible—classified by body type. Its engine is a four, a six, or an eight—classified by number of cylinders. Its make is either domestic or foreign—classified by country of manufacture—giving rise to further sub-typing as a Ford, Chevrolet, Mercedes, Toyota, or another kind of car. With little reflection, almost all of us can see similar groupings and categories lurking about the simplest object. What type of person is he? we commonly ask, presuming that people can be sorted into recognizable types.

Writing Assignment

After reading Kurt Vonnegut's "Harrison Bergeron" (pp. 333–338), classify all the handicaps in our society by placing them in appropriate categories and illustrating each type with examples. Somewhere in your opening paragraph, provide a clear statement of your classifications. For instance, you might write, "All handicaps in our society can be classified into one of three types—catastrophic, severe, or mild." Then develop this controlling idea by discussing each type of handicap individually and vividly. Your final paragraph might include your views about whether such handicaps help or hinder society.

Specific Instructions

Prewriting on the assignment.   Before putting any of your ideas on paper, clarify for yourself what the term *handicap* means. The dictionary tells us that it means "a deficiency that prevents or restricts normal achievement." With this definition in mind, you might make a list of deficiencies you have encountered. Keep your thoughts rolling by writing them down, uncensored, on paper. Your list might start out like this:

Students with dyslexia

People in wheelchairs

Chronic laziness

Deafness

Self-centeredness

Mental retardation

ADD (Attention Deficit Disorder)

Phobias

Being physically unattractive

Lacking social skills

Compulsive dishonesty

Chronic rudeness

Having a grating personality

Anorexia nervosa

Bulimia

Blindness

Manic depression

Lack of self-discipline

Make your list as long as you like. Then analyze it for ways to group the handicaps. Even the brief list here reveals quickly that some handicaps are physical—dyslexia, paralysis, mental retardation, ugliness, and blindness—whereas other handicaps are emotional—laziness, phobias, ADD (Attention Deficit Disorder), lack of self-discipline, and certain eating disorders, such as anorexia and bulimia. Then again, some handicaps seem to result from moral lapses—self-indulgence, dishonesty, arrogance, chronic rudeness. Almost any list you compile will allow you to cluster the entries into groups of related items. Your classification will be well on its way as soon as you have drawn your groups and filled them with approximately the same number of handicaps to keep the categories balanced rather than lopsided.

Once your groups have been chosen, you have a ready-made thesis:

Handicaps that make it difficult for individuals to fulfill their life's ambitions fall mostly into three areas—physical, emotional, and moral.

Because the assignment also asks you to draw some conclusion from having classified handicaps, you need to think about your views on the subject. Do handicaps have to be defeating, or can they actually spur someone on to heroic feats? Can talents be developed regardless of handicaps? Would our society be better off if no one had a handicap? All these questions will help you clarify your own attitudes so that you can end your paper with a strong concluding statement.

Base your classification on a single principle.   In the classification/division essay, as in most nonfiction writing, clarity and intensity are children of a pure purpose. If you set out to do one thing and one thing only in an essay, you have a good chance of successfully doing it. But if you try to do two or three different things at once—unless you are a highly skilled writer—you are most likely to do badly.

To be clear and consistent, a classification/division should therefore be made according to a single principle. Once you have selected a principle for making your division, you should concentrate exclusively on developing the categories yielded. You should not, halfway through, switch to another principle that is likely to create further categories. For example, if you were writing an essay classifying cars according to their body types and suddenly switched to a classification based on number of cylinders, overlapping categories would result. Some SUVs have eight

STUDENT TIP FOR INVENTING IDEAS

Assignment

Classify all handicaps in our society by placing them in appropriate categories and illustrating each type with examples.

How I found my topic

At first I thought this was an impossible assignment. I didn't even have a clue about how to begin. I tried to think of all handicaps that there are in the world. But all I could think of were such ordinary handicaps as being wheelchair-bound or deaf or blind and stuff like that. I just couldn't make a start, and time was running out.

Then one night as I was having dinner with my parents, my father told the story about a school friend of his who was a brilliant basketball player but had never played for the school team. He said that playing in public freaked him out. He just couldn't do it. Yet, according to my father, his friend was the best three-point shooter he'd ever seen. That set off something in my head.

After dinner, I began to make a list of possible categories for handicaps. The first was a self-imposed handicap, and my example would be my father's basketball friend. The second one that occurred to me was a handicap imposed by nature, like a birth defect. The third was obvious: a handicap caused by an accident. I had my three categories. I was ready to write.

—A female junior at a four-year university in Georgia

cylinders; so do some sedans and some convertibles. The effect would be a double count. The choice of a classification/division principle is sometimes dictated by the wording of an assignment, but often is left entirely to the writer. An essay that divides and classifies is as much a thinking as a writing assignment. Say, for example, that you are asked to write an essay classifying/dividing people. Numerous principles could be used for sorting them into categories. You could, for instance, choose degree of intimacy as your selection principle, in which case you might have an opening sentence like this:

> Three major kinds of relationships tie people to each other: acquaintance, friendship, and love.

So far, so good. If you stick to degree of intimacy as your dividing principle, you will have an essay that is at least structurally sound. But another criterion, yielding entirely different categories, could have been used. You could, for instance, have chosen to classify/divide the people you know on the basis of their politics, in which case your thesis might have read:

> Most people fall into one of four different political groups: radical, liberal, conservative, and indifferent.

Or you might have classified people on the basis of socioeconomic class:

> People are classifiable into three distinct socioeconomic classes, each with its own values and peculiar ways of behaving: lower class, middle class, and upper class.

Or humorously, on the basis of physique:

> My friends, relatives, and acquaintances fall neatly into three groups: the were-fats, the are-fats, and the will-be-fats.

In sum, you may make an entirely different essay out of the same assignment, depending on the principle you use to classify/divide.

But which principle should you have used? That is an unanswerable question. It depends entirely on what you can do and on what purpose you wish to achieve in your essay. If you are the solemn sort who writes serious essays, you would probably do well classifying people by their politics. If you are the jolly sort and can write in a humorous vein, you might tackle the essay that lumps people into fat categories. If you are the affectionate sort who values friendship, you might use degree of intimacy as your dividing principle. What matters in a serious essay is that you use an important principle for classifying/dividing and that you practice it consistently throughout. In other words, if you were doing a classification of books on the best-seller list, you should not base your essay on a principle as trivial as, say, whether the books had pictures in them. Such an essay, if meant to be serious, would be unintentionally humorous.

Finally, the use of a single principle for classification/division should be observed in the essay as a whole as well as in individual paragraphs. Here, for instance, are three paragraphs, each based on a single principle of division:

> There are five venereal diseases, all of which can cause death. Three of these have been eliminated by modern medicine, while the other two, syphilis and gonorrhea, are on the rise once more all over the world. Both of these diseases are mainly contracted through sexual relations. These germs spread to all parts of the body and, therefore, anything the infected person uses is possibly an immediate carrier. These germs can spread to another human by an open cut if it comes in contact with the germs of an infected person.
>
> The symptoms of these diseases are usually disregarded by their victims. In infectious syphilis there are three definite stages, with a few weeks lapsing between the

first two. The first stage consists of a hard chancre (SHANKer) sore in the genital area. The second stage is a rash accompanied by headaches, fever, sore throat, or loss of hair. The third stage, after a seemingly dormant period of 10 to 25 years, makes its presence known by rendering its victim blind, crippled, insane, sterile, or dead.

Unlike its counterpart, gonorrhea's latent stages are more easily noticed by its victims. The first symptom is usually a burning pain during urination. The remaining factors of this disease are similar to those of syphilis, and the results are equally as devastating.

—Mary Kathrine Wayman, "The Unmentionable Diseases," *Contemporary American Speeches,* 1969

The first paragraph is a classification/division of kinds of venereal diseases; the second, of symptoms of syphilis; the third, of symptoms of gonorrhea. Because it is based on a single principle of classification/division, each paragraph is purposeful and clear.

Divide the whole pie.   Once you have been given a subject to classify/divide, be sure you discuss the entire subject. Don't leave out a single piece. For example, if you were to classify literature into short story, drama, and poetry, a significant category would be missing: the novel. The entire subject must be included if a classification/division is to be complete.

But sometimes, especially when the classification/division is of an abstract subject whose parts are not readily apparent, it is left to the writer to give an illusion of completeness. For example, consider this paragraph:

There are three kinds of book owners. The first has all the standard sets and best-sellers—unread, untouched. (This deluded individual owns wood-pulp and ink, not books.) The second has a great many books—a few of them read through, most of them dipped into, but all of them as clean and shiny as the day they were bought. (This person would probably like to make books his own, but is restrained by a false respect for their physical appearance.) The third has a few books or many—every one of them dog-eared and dilapidated, shaken and loosened by continual use, marked and scribbled in from front to back. (This man owns books.)

—Mortimer J. Adler, "How to Mark a Book," *Saturday Review,* July 6, 1940

The division, the categories yielded, and the entire subject are obviously personal. One cannot pounce on this piece of writing as if one knew with absolute certainty exactly what kinds of book owners there are in the world. Yet the paragraph contains recognizable types and gives the illusion of completeness. What we mean to illustrate is simply that classification/division, especially of an abstract subject, is a highly imaginative exercise. It is less a question of *being* right in such a division and more a matter of *seeming* right. The preceding paragraph contains a sensible division supported by appropriate detail and delivered in a sparklingly clear style, all of which combine to give it a sense of authenticity.

Make each category in a classification separate from the others.   A classification whose groups overlap acquires a fuzziness that is the mark of a bad essay. Notice the overlapping teaching methods here:

    a. Lecture

    b. Discussion

    c. Question–answer

Question–answer and discussion overlap: There is no clear distinction between them. A discussion lesson may involve questions and answers, and a question–answer lesson may involve discussion. The classification should either be limited to lecture and discussion or include a third, clearly separate group:

    a. Lecture

    b. Discussion

    c. Quizzes

Give equal importance to each segment of the classification.   Balance plays an important role in a classification/division essay. You must not cover one group with elaborate details while barely mentioning the other. Treat each group with equal emphasis or your essay will become obviously lopsided.

Do a Personal Division

If you have a choice, stick to a personal division. If your topic is of your own invention and your categories are consistently and sensibly created, you cannot be accused of faulty thinking. If you write a formal classification/division, however, you not only have to worry about being clear, you also have the obligation to cover all the known types of your topic. Better to divide and classify your friends (a personal topic) than the various kinds of sea urchin life (a formal topic).

RUSSELL BAKER

The Plot Against People

Russell Baker (b. 1925) is a Pulitzer Prize–winning journalist who began his career as a reporter for the Baltimore Sun *and later moved to the prestigious* New York Times. *His last column was in 1998. In 1982, he captured a large reading audience with his autobiography,* Growing Up, *which appealed to the middle-class generation of the 1940s and 1950s because it reflected that era so accurately and with nostalgia. This work was followed with another autobiography,* The Good Times *(1989). But Baker is best known for his informal essays—like the one here—about life in the United States.*

READING FOR IDEAS   In a humorous tone, Baker appeals to a common human frustration—dealing with inanimate objects that seem to defy our desires for using them. He begins by dividing these objects into three easily recognized categories. Then he continues by supplying examples of each category, and these, too, are instantly recognized. Notice how soon (in the opening paragraph) the author announces his purposes and how carefully he follows the rules for classification/ division. The result is clarity and simplicity within the context of laughter.

1   Inanimate objects are classified scientifically into three major categories—those that break down, those that get lost, and those that don't work.

2   The goal of all inanimate objects is to resist man and ultimately to defeat him, and the three major classifications are based on the method each object uses to achieve its purpose. As a general rule, any object capable of breaking down at the moment when it is most needed will do so. The automobile is typical of the category.

3   With the cunning peculiar to its breed, the automobile never breaks down while entering a filling station which has a large staff of idle mechanics. It waits until it reaches a downtown intersection in the middle of the rush hour, or until it is fully loaded with family and luggage on the Ohio Turnpike. Thus it creates maximum inconvenience, frustration, and irritability, thereby reducing its owner's lifespan.

4   Washing machines, garbage disposals, lawn mowers, furnaces, TV sets, tape recorders, slide projectors—all are in league with the automobile to take their turn at breaking down whenever life threatens to flow smoothly for their enemies.

5   Many inanimate objects, of course, find it extremely difficult to break down. Pliers, for example, and gloves and keys are almost totally incapable of breaking down. Therefore, they have had to evolve a different technique for resisting man.

6   They get lost. Science has still not solved the mystery of how they do it, and no man has ever caught one of them in the act. The most plausible theory is that they have developed a secret method of locomotion which they are able to conceal from human eyes.

7   It is not uncommon for a pair of pliers to climb all the way from the cellar to the attic in its single-minded determination to raise its owner's blood pressure. Keys have been known to burrow three feet under mattresses. Women's purses, despite their great weight, frequently travel through six or seven rooms to find hiding space under a couch.

8   Scientists have been struck by the fact that things that break down virtually never get lost, while things that get lost hardly ever break down. A furnace, for example, will invariably break down at the depth of the first winter cold wave, but it will never get lost. A woman's purse hardly ever breaks down; it almost invariably chooses to get lost.

9   Some persons believe this constitutes evidence that inanimate objects are not entirely hostile to man. After all, they point out, a furnace could infuriate a man even more thoroughly by getting lost than by breaking down, just as a glove could upset him far more by breaking down than by getting lost.

10   Not everyone agrees, however, that this indicates a conciliatory attitude. Many say it merely proves that furnaces, gloves and pliers are incredibly stupid.

11   The third class of objects—those that don't work—is the most curious of all. These include such objects as barometers, car clocks, cigarette lighters, flashlights and toy-train locomotives. It is inaccurate, of course, to say that they *never* work. They work once, usually for the first few hours after being brought home, and then quit. Thereafter, they never work again.

12   In fact, it is widely assumed that they are built for the purpose of not working. Some people have reached advanced ages without ever seeing some of these objects—barometers, for example—in working order.

13   Science is utterly baffled by the entire category. There are many theories about it. The most interesting holds that the things that don't work have attained the highest state possible for an inanimate object, the state to which things that break down and things that get lost can still only aspire.

14   They have truly defeated man by conditioning him never to expect anything of them. When his cigarette lighter won't light or his flashlight fails to illuminate, it does not raise his blood pressure. Objects that don't work have given man the only peace he receives from inanimate society.

■ *Vocabulary*

inanimate (1)	burrow (7)	illuminate (14)
plausible (6)	conciliatory (10)	

■ *Questions on Meaning and Technique*

1. On what implausible idea is the tongue-in-cheek attitude of this essay based? What conclusion does the author reach?

2. What basis does Baker use for his classification? What other basis can you suggest?

3. What is the purpose of the disagreement described in paragraph 10? How important is it to know which side is right?

4. How does Baker indicate that he is moving from the first to the second category of objects? Where does the shift take place?

5. What words or phrases does the author use to make inanimate objects appear to be human?

6. Why do you think inanimate objects often infuriate humans? Is there a solution to this problem? If so, what is it? If there is no solution, how should humans adjust to the inevitable?

7. Considering that so many objects tend to break down, do you believe that society would be better off with fewer inanimate objects to contend with? Why or why not?

8. What is the purpose of Baker's brief opening paragraph?

STUDENT ESSAY—FIRST DRAFT

David Beckham

Handicaps

Insert A

1   ~~Every human being could be said to have a handicap of some sort. These handicaps could be divided into three handicaps could be divide into three categories intellectual handicaps. No one is likely to be immune from one or more of these handicaps.~~

2   Intellectual handicaps ~~come~~ *exist* in a wide variety of types. The type most immediately thought of by most people is stupidity, ~~and it is certainly a handicap,~~ *—not to be confused with ignorance.* *Stupidity* is often ~~characterized by being~~ made the butt of jokes by the slightly less stupid. ~~persons in one's environment. Indeed,~~ *Although* stupidity is a difficult handicap, ~~but~~ it is far from the only intellectual handicap a person can ~~labor under~~ *have*. Brilliance, ~~for example~~ *ironically*, is another intellectual handicap. The brilliant person may be able to ~~see~~ *grasp* immediately the

Margin note (right): Rewrite to create a more gripping opening. Also, add one more category— "aesthetic handicaps"— to complete the classification. This paragraph needs tightening throughout.

Insert A

Kurt Vonnegut, Jr., began his disturbing futuristic fantasy, "Harrison Bergeron," with some descriptive remarks: "The year was 2081, and everybody was finally equal. They weren't only equal before God and the law. They were equal in every which way." This amazing state of affairs was due to the tireless efforts, Vonnegut tells us, of the "United States Handicapper General." Well, it is only the last decade of the twentieth century, and everybody is already handicapped. No one is likely to be immune from all of these handicaps, and these handicaps can be divided into four categories: intellectual handicaps, emotional handicaps, physical handicaps, and aesthetic handicaps.

cause, effect, and cure of a particular problem at school or at work, but be unable

communicate this insight to anyone else. ←

Moving this passage up makes for better logic.

to ~~get anyone else to understand what is so obvious to this keen intellect~~. This trait

foster

alone can cause unpopularity with one's associates and ~~frustration~~ with one's self.

Such   *likely to cause serious resentment from those who are part of the problem*

~~Brilliance is apt to subject one to hostility of a far less humorous kind than stupidity~~

Use quotation marks to indicate usage.

~~does~~ Another broad subdivision of intellectual handicap might be called the "skewed

intellect." For this sufferer, the problem is one of seeing what other people see in a

quite different light. ~~Mark Twain's humor provides numerous examples of this type of

mind. From these few examples it is obvious that the possible intellectual handicaps

are many and varied.~~   ⟨Insert B⟩

in society today.

3   Emotional handicaps abound ~~within the human population of the earth~~. The two

Rewrite for more correct language and for conciseness.

most obvious are excessive emotionalism and inadequate emotional response. ~~In the~~

Excessively emotional people burst into tears at the slightest provocation—a delightful sunset,

~~first case, the sufferer, and anyone in the immediate area, is apt to be damp with the~~

a disheveled beggar, or a delicate hummingbird.

~~copious tears shed over all the sadness and misery that meets the eye at every turn.~~

~~This sad case suffers for everyone more or less equally, and quickly becomes a bore to~~

Correct subject-verb disagreement.

inadequate

~~anyone who must remain associated with him or her.~~ The emotionally ~~unresponsive~~,

Rewrite for smoothness, concreteness, and less awkwardness in avoiding sexist language

conversely, ~~are shunned because they~~ display little or no human feeling, ~~for anyone,~~ no

straits confront them.   *The earthquake victim, the lonely orphan,*

matter ~~in~~ what dire ~~straights they made be found. This unfeeling defective seems to~~

the jobless person—all receive the same cold shoulder.

~~believe that he or she is not, or should not be affected by the suffering of anyone else in~~

Delete so as not to belabor the point.

~~any circumstance.~~ ~~Beyond these broad categories lie almost infinite varieties of more

narrow emotional handicaps. The person who is obsessive about a pet snake, for

instance, or the person who is focused on saving the walrus to the exclusion of all other

earthly problems can be said to manifest an unfortunate emotional handicap.~~

usually

4   Physical handicaps draw ~~a lot of~~ attention because they are ~~often~~ obvious.

for example,

Paraplegics and quadriplegics have, clearly recognizable handicaps, for which,
                              ∧

in the United States at least, much public accommodation has been made.

⟨Insert B⟩

*Mark Twain said that being a director of an accident insurance company in Hartford gave him a whole
new outlook on accidents. When he added the statement that "There is nothing quite so seraphic as
the expression on the face of a newly maimed accident victim when he reaches into his vest pocket and
finds his accident ticket still intact," Twain was clearly displaying the "skewed intellect."*

But consider the closely related to the physical, yet differentiated from it, is the

seven footers ~~that can't~~ *who cannot* walk upright through a normal door and the four footers

~~that can't~~ *who cannot* reach the top two shelves anywhere*,* these people, too, have physical

handicaps. The ninety-seven pound weakling who ~~can't~~ *is unable to* open the doors at public

buildings and the muscle-bound weight lifter who splits the seams in his *or her* jacket when

offering assistance are alike physically handicapped. ~~The aforementioned~~ *These* examples

are obvious because they involve the ~~mechanical~~ *observable* operations of life. A ~~closely related~~ ¶

handicap*,* ~~is the~~ *closely related to the physical, yet differentiated from it, is the* aesthetic handicap*.* ~~which must be differentiated from the physical~~.

5   Excessive ugliness or beauty, which ~~effects~~ *a*ffects the way others react to one, is a handicap

as ~~significant~~ *damaging* as intellectual or emotional handicaps. In fact, aesthetic handicaps often lead

to concatenations of problems with the intellect and emotions. And by the way, ~~the~~ *facial* features

are not the only possible aesthetic handicap. Fat can certainly be an aesthetic handicap, as

can body odor, halitosis, shrillness of voice, or even misplaced regional accents.

6   In ~~sum~~ *truth*, we all labor under some kind of handicap. That ~~fact~~ provides a sort of balance *does not make everyone equal, but it does*

among the members of the human species. Rather than concerning ourselves with trying

to make everyone equal, *we should relish the diversity that exists. Moreover, the recognition that each* ~~it would behoove us to learn to appreciate the handicaps with~~ *of us is handicapped can lead us to admiration and respect for the accomplishments of others.* ~~which others live. Doing so might make our own particular difficulties more tolerable.~~

Margin notes:
Correct comma splice.

Avoid sexist language.

New paragraph is needed for new idea.

No paragraph

Improve diction. Rewrite to expand on topic sentence.

Delete final sentence because it introduces a new idea that is never developed.

STUDENT ESSAY—FINAL DRAFT

Beckham 1

David Beckham

Professor McCuen

English 101

Handicaps

1   Kurt Vonnegut, Jr., began his disturbing futuristic fantasy,

"Harrison Bergeron," with some descriptive remarks: "The year was

Beckham 2

2081, and everybody was finally equal. They weren't only equal
before God and the law. They were equal in every which way." This
amazing state of affairs was due to the tireless efforts, Vonnegut
tells us, of the "United States Handicapper General." Well, it is
only the first decade of the twenty-first century, and everybody
is already handicapped. No one is likely to be immune from all of
these handicaps, and these handicaps can be divided into four
categories: intellectual handicaps, emotional handicaps, physical
handicaps, and aesthetic handicaps.

2   Intellectual handicaps exist in a wide variety of types. The type
immediately thought of by most people is stupidity—not to be confused with ignorance. Stupidity is often made the butt of jokes by
the slightly less stupid. Although stupidity is a difficult handicap,
it is far from the only intellectual handicap a person can have. Brilliance, ironically, is another intellectual handicap. The brilliant person may be able to grasp immediately the cause, effect, and cure
of a particular problem but be unable to communicate this insight
to anyone else. Such brilliance is likely to cause serious resentment
from those who are part of the problem. This trait alone can cause
unpopularity with one's associates and foster frustration within
one's self. Another broad subdivision of intellectual handicap might
be called the "skewed intellect." For this sufferer, the problem is
one of seeing what other people see in a quite different light. Mark
Twain said that being a director of an accident insurance company
in Hartford gave him a whole new outlook on accidents. When he

Beckham 3

added the statement that "There is nothing quite so seraphic as
the expression on the face of a newly maimed accident victim
when he reaches into his vest pocket and finds his accident ticket
still intact," Twain was clearly displaying the "skewed intellect."

3   Emotional handicaps abound in society today. The two most
obvious are excessive emotionalism and inadequate emotional
response. Excessively emotional people burst into tears at the
slightest provocation—a delightful sunset, a disheveled beggar, or
a delicate hummingbird. The emotionally inadequate, conversely,
display little or no human feeling, no matter what dire straits
confront them. The earthquake victim, the lonely orphan, the
jobless person—all receive the same cold shoulder.

4   Physical handicaps draw attention because they are usually
obvious. Paraplegics and quadriplegics, for example, have clearly
recognizable handicaps, for which, in the United States at least,
much public accommodation has been made. But consider the
seven footers who cannot walk upright through a normal door and
the four footers who cannot reach the top two shelves anywhere;
these people, too, have physical handicaps. The ninety-seven
pound weakling who is unable to open the doors of public buildings
and the muscle-bound weight lifter who splits the seams in his
or her jacket when offering assistance are alike physically handicapped. These examples are obvious because they involve the
observable mechanical operations of life.

5   A handicap closely related to the physical, yet differentiated
from it, is the aesthetic handicap. Excessive ugliness or beauty,

Beckham 4

which affects the way others react to one, is a handicap as damaging as intellectual or emotional handicaps. In fact, aesthetic handicaps often lead to concatenations of problems with the intellect and
emotions. And by the way, facial features are not the only possible
aesthetic handicap. Fat can certainly be an aesthetic handicap, as
can body odor, halitosis, shrillness of voice, or even misplaced regional accents.

6   In truth, we all labor under some kind of handicap. That does
not make everyone equal, but it does provide a sort of balance
among the members of the human species. Rather than concerning
ourselves with trying to make everyone equal, we should relish
the diversity that exists. Moreover, the recognition that each one
of us is handicapped can lead us to admiration and respect for the
accomplishments of others.

FURTHER READING

MARTIN LUTHER KING, JR.

Three Types of Resistance to Oppression

Martin Luther King, Jr. (1929–1968), was an American clergyman and African-American civil rights leader of the 1960s. He was born in Atlanta and educated at Morehouse College, Crozer Theological Seminary, and Boston University. Dr. King advocated a philosophy of passive resistance to the evils of segregation and racial inequality in American society. In 1964, Dr. King won the Nobel Peace Prize.

READING FOR IDEAS In 1956, Martin Luther King gained a major victory in the battle for civil rights when the bus system of Montgomery, Alabama, was desegregated due to a boycott by blacks. Dr. King's philosophy of nonviolent resistance, as outlined in the following selection, led to his arrest on numerous occasions and eventually to his assassination on April 4, 1968. Although Dr. King is primarily making an argument, notice how his use of division/classification helps structure the entire piece. As you study King's principles, ask yourself what stand you are willing to take on this matter.

1   Oppressed people deal with their oppression in three characteristic ways. One way is acquiescence: the oppressed resign themselves to their doom. They tacitly adjust themselves to oppression, and thereby become conditioned to it. In every movement toward freedom some of the oppressed prefer to remain oppressed. Almost 2800 years ago Moses set out to lead the children of Israel from the slavery of Egypt to the freedom of the promised land. He soon discovered that slaves do not always welcome their deliverers. They become accustomed to being slaves. They would rather bear those ills they have, as Shakespeare pointed out, than flee to others that they know not of. They prefer the "flesh-pots of Egypt" to the ordeals of emancipation.

2   There is such a thing as the freedom of exhaustion. Some people are so worn down by the yoke of oppression that they give up. A few years ago in the slum areas of Atlanta, a Negro guitarist used to sing almost daily: "Been down so long that down don't bother me." This is the type of negative freedom and resignation that often engulfs the life of the oppressed.

3   But this is not the way out. To accept passively an unjust system is to cooperate with that system; thereby the oppressed become as evil as the oppressor. Noncooperation with evil is as much a moral obligation as is cooperation with good. The oppressed must never allow the conscience of the oppressor to slumber. Religion reminds every man that he is his brother's keeper. To accept injustice or segregation passively is to say to the oppressor that his actions are morally right. It is a way of allowing his conscience to fall asleep. At this moment the oppressed fails to be his brother's keeper. So acquiescence—while often the easier way—is not the moral way. It is the way of the coward. The Negro cannot win the respect of his oppressor by acquiescing; he merely increases the oppressor's arrogance and contempt. Acquiescence is interpreted as proof of the Negro's inferiority. The Negro cannot win the respect of the white people of the South or the peoples of the world if he is willing to sell the future of his children for this personal and immediate comfort and safety.

4   A second way that oppressed people sometimes deal with oppression is to resort to physical violence and corroding hatred. Violence often brings about momentary results. Nations have frequently won their independence in battle. But in spite of temporary victories, violence never brings permanent peace. It solves no social problem; it merely creates new and more complicated ones.

5   Violence as a way of achieving racial justice is both impractical and immoral. It is impractical because it is a descending spiral ending in destruction for all. The old law of an eye for an eye leaves everybody blind. It is immoral because it seeks to humiliate the opponent rather than win his understanding; it seeks to annihilate rather than to convert. Violence is immoral because it thrives on hatred rather than love. It destroys community and makes brotherhood impossible. It leaves society in monologue rather than dialogue. Violence ends by defeating itself. It creates bitterness in the survivors and brutality in the destroyers. A voice echoes through time saying to every potential Peter, "Put up your

sword." History is cluttered with the wreckage of nations that failed to follow this command.

6   If the American Negro and other victims of oppression succumb to the temptation of using violence in the struggle for freedom, future generations will be the recipients of a desolate night of bitterness, and our chief legacy to them will be an endless reign of meaningless chaos. Violence is not the way.

7   The third way open to oppressed people in their quest for freedom is the way of nonviolent resistance. Like the synthesis in Hegelian philosophy, the principle of nonviolent resistance seeks to reconcile the truths of two opposites—acquiescence and violence—while avoiding the extremes and immoralities of both. The nonviolent resister agrees with the person who acquiesces that one should not be physically aggressive toward his opponent; but he balances the equation by agreeing with the person of violence that evil must be resisted. He avoids the nonresistance of the former and the violent resistance of the latter. With nonviolent resistance, no individual or group need submit to any wrong, nor need anyone resort to violence in order to right a wrong.

8   It seems to me that this is the method that must guide the actions of the Negro in the present crisis in race relations. Through nonviolent resistance the Negro will be able to rise to the noble height of opposing the unjust system while loving the perpetrators of the system. The Negro must work passionately and unrelentingly for full stature as a citizen, but he must not use inferior methods to gain it. He must never come to terms with falsehood, malice, hate, or destruction.

9   Nonviolent resistance makes it possible for the Negro to remain in the South and struggle for his rights. The Negro's problem will not be solved by running away. He cannot listen to the glib suggestion of those who would urge him to migrate en masse to other sections of the country. By grasping his great opportunity in the South he can make a lasting contribution to the moral strength of the nation and set a sublime example of courage for generations yet unborn.

10   By nonviolent resistance, the Negro can also enlist all men of good will in his struggle for equality. The problem is not a purely racial one, with Negroes set against whites. In the end, it is not a struggle between people at all, but a tension between justice and injustice. Nonviolent resistance is not aimed against oppressors but against oppression. Under its banner consciences, not racial groups, are enlisted.

11   If the Negro is to achieve the goal of integration, he must organize himself into a militant and nonviolent mass movement. All three elements are indispensable. The movement for equality and justice can only be a success if it has both a mass and militant character; the barriers to be overcome require both. Nonviolence is an imperative in order to bring about ultimate community.

12   A mass movement of militant quality that is not at the same time committed to nonviolence tends to generate conflict, which in turn breeds anarchy. The support of the participants and the sympathy of the uncommitted are both inhibited by the threat that bloodshed will engulf the community. This reaction in turn encourages the opposition to threaten and resort to force. When, however, the mass movement repudiates violence while moving resolutely toward its goal, its opponents are revealed as the instigators and

practitioners of violence if it occurs. Then public support is magnetically attracted to the advocates of nonviolence, while those who employ violence are literally disarmed by overwhelming sentiment against their stand.

■ *Vocabulary*

acquiescence (1)	legacy (6)	anarchy (12)
tacitly (1)	Hegelian (7)	inhibited (12)
corroding (4)	perpetrators (8)	repudiates (12)
annihilate (5)	unrelentingly (8)	

■ *Questions on Meaning and Technique*

1. What is the basis of division in this selection?
2. What are the three characteristic ways in which oppressed people deal with their oppression?
3. What did Moses discover about the nature of slaves?
4. What is the author's criticism of acquiescence? What moral objection does he raise against it?
5. Why does the author object to violence? Why does he regard it as immoral?
6. How does nonviolent resistance reconcile the truths of two opposites? What are these opposites?
7. To what noble height does the author claim nonviolent resistance will raise the Negro?
8. What three elements are indispensable for successful nonviolent resistance?
9. According to King, what will Negroes gain by repudiating violence while resolutely moving toward their goal?

Writing Assignments

1. Write an essay in which you divide types of oppressors. Use your imagination and reasoning to choose the principle on which you base your division.
2. Write an essay in which you classify people who are oppressed, placing them in the proper categories to which they belong. For instance, one type might be the poor; another type might be people with disabilities; yet another type might be the revolutionary. Be sure to include all types that belong in the general subject being classified.

LARS EIGHNER

On Dumpster Diving

Lars Eighner (b. 1948) is a homeless person who made good. He became known in the literary world when he published his memoir Travels with Lizbeth: Three Years on the Road and on the Streets *(1993). Readers became fond of Lizbeth and felt cheated of stories about her when she died in 1998. However, Eighner has continued to write fiction as well as essays. He has acquired a new dog, Wilma, who, readers hope, will be featured in future writings by Eighner. "On Dumpster Diving" is an explanation of the kind of life Eighner led when he was forced to nourish himself and his dog from the refuse of other people.*

READING FOR IDEAS It might be difficult for you to imagine a literate vagrant digging through dumpsters to find enough food to keep him and his dog from starving. You probably thought that such a human being would have neither the vocabulary nor the mental acuity to write an essay about the culture and economics of dumpster exploration. But the essay below clearly indicates that an educated person can find himself in such dire poverty that resorting to food and objects discarded by the more fortunate members of society becomes part of his mode of survival. As you read, notice how the author meticulously classifies the kinds of eatable refuse and the types of scavengers who rummage around in dumpsters. Try to understand the cultural implications involved.

1   Long before I began Dumpster diving I was impressed with Dumpsters, enough so that I wrote the Merriam-Webster research service to discover what I could about the word "Dumpster." I learned from them that "Dumpster" is a proprietary word belonging to the Dempster Dumpster company.

2   Since then I have dutifully capitalized the word although it was lowercased in almost all of the citations Merriam-Webster photocopied for me. Dempster's word is too apt. I have never heard these things called anything but Dumpsters. I do not know anyone who knows the generic name for these objects. From time to time, however, I hear a wino or hobo give some corrupted credit to the original and call them Dipsy Dumpsters.

3   I began Dumpster diving about a year before I became homeless.

4   I prefer the term "scavenging" and use the word "scrounging" when I mean to be obscure. I have heard people, evidently meaning to be polite, using the word "foraging," but I prefer to reserve that word for gathering nuts and berries and such which I do also according to the season and the opportunity. "Dumpster diving" seems to me to be a little too cute and, in my case, inaccurate because I lack the athletic ability to lower myself into the Dumpsters as the true divers do, much to their increased profit.

5   I like the frankness of the word "scavenging," which I can hardly think of without picturing a big black snail on an aquarium wall. I live from the refuse of others. I am a scavenger; I think it a sound and honorable niche, although if I could I would naturally prefer to live the comfortable consumer life, perhaps—and only perhaps—as a slightly less wasteful consumer owing to what I have learned as a scavenger.

6   While my dog Lizbeth and I were still living in the house on Avenue B in Austin, as my savings ran out, I put almost all my sporadic income into rent. The necessities of daily life I began to extract from Dumpsters. Yes, we ate from Dumpsters. Except for jeans, all my clothes came from Dumpsters. Boom boxes, candles, bedding, toilet paper, medicine, books, a typewriter, a virgin male love doll, change sometimes amounting to many dollars: I acquired many things from the Dumpsters.

7   I have learned much as a scavenger. I mean to put some of what I have learned down here, beginning with the practical art of Dumpster diving and proceeding to the abstract.

8   What is safe to eat?

9   After all, the finding of objects is becoming something of an urban art. Even respectable employed people will sometimes find something tempting sticking out of a Dumpster or standing beside one. Quite a number of people, not all of them of the bohemian type, are willing to brag that they found this or that piece in the trash. But eating from Dumpsters is the thing that separates the dilettanti from the professionals.

10   Eating safely from the Dumpsters involves three principles: using the senses and common sense to evaluate the condition of the found materials, knowing the Dumpsters of a given area and checking them regularly, and seeking always to answer the question "Why was this discarded?"

11   Perhaps everyone who has a kitchen and a regular supply of groceries has, at one time or another, made a sandwich and eaten half of it before discovering mold on the bread or got a mouthful of milk before realizing the milk had turned. Nothing of the sort is likely to happen to a Dumpster diver because he is constantly reminded that most food is discarded for a reason. Yet a lot of perfectly good food can be found in Dumpsters.

12   Canned goods, for example, turn up fairly often in the Dumpsters I frequent. All except the most phobic people would be willing to eat from a can even if it came from a Dumpster. Canned goods are among the safest of foods to be found in Dumpsters, but are not utterly foolproof.

13   Although very rare with modern canning methods, botulism is a possibility. Most other forms of food poisoning seldom do lasting harm to a healthy person. But botulism is almost certainly fatal and often the first symptom is death. Except for carbonated beverages, all canned goods should contain a slight vacuum and suck air when first punctured. Bulging, rusty, dented cans and cans that spew when punctured should be avoided, especially when the contents are not very acidic or syrupy.

14   Heat can break down the botulin, but this requires much more cooking than most people do to canned goods. To the extent that botulism occurs at all, of course, it can occur in cans on pantry shelves as well as in cans from Dumpsters. Need I say that home-canned goods found in Dumpsters are simply too risky to be recommended.

15   From time to time one of my companions, aware of the source of my provisions, will ask, "Do you think these crackers are really safe to eat?" For some reason it is most often the crackers they ask about.

16   This question always makes me angry. Of course I would not offer my companion anything I had doubts about. But more than that I wonder why he cannot evaluate the condition of the crackers for himself. I have no special knowledge and I have been wrong before. Since he knows where the food comes from, it seems to me he ought to assume some of the responsibility for deciding what he will put in his mouth.

17   For myself I have few qualms about dry foods such as crackers, cookies, cereal, chips, and pasta if they are free of visible contaminates and still dry and crisp. Most often such things are found in the original packaging, which is not so much a positive sign as it is the absence of a negative one.

18   Raw fruits and vegetables with intact skins seem perfectly safe to me, excluding of course the obviously rotten. Many are discarded for minor imperfections which can be pared away. Leafy vegetables, grapes, cauliflower, broccoli, and similar things may be contaminated by liquids and may be impractical to wash.

19   Candy, especially hard candy, is usually safe if it has not drawn ants. Chocolate is often discarded only because it has become discolored as the cocoa butter de-emulsified. Candying after all is one method of food preservation because pathogens do not like very sugary substances.

20   All of these foods might be found in any Dumpster and can be evaluated with some confidence largely on the basis of appearance. Beyond these are foods which cannot be correctly evaluated without additional information.

21   I began scavenging by pulling pizzas out of the Dumpster behind a pizza delivery shop. In general prepared food requires caution, but in this case I knew when the shop closed and went to the Dumpster as soon as the last of the help left.

22   Such shops often get prank orders, called "bogus." Because help seldom stays long at these places pizzas are often made with the wrong topping, refused on delivery for being cold, or baked incorrectly. The products to be discarded are boxed up because inventory is kept by counting boxes: A boxed pizza can be written off; an unboxed pizza does not exist.

23   I never placed a bogus order to increase the supply of pizzas and I believe no one else was scavenging in this Dumpster. But the people in the shop became suspicious and began to retain their garbage in the shop overnight.

24   While it lasted I had a steady supply of fresh, sometimes warm pizza. Because I knew the Dumpster I knew the source of the pizza, and because I visited the Dumpster regularly I knew what was fresh and what was yesterday's.

25   The area I frequent is inhabited by many affluent college students. I am not here by chance; the Dumpsters in this area are very rich. Students throw out many good things, including food. In particular they tend to throw everything out when they move at the end of a semester, before and after breaks, and around midterm when many of them despair of college. So I find it advantageous to keep an eye on the academic calendar.

26   The students throw food away around the breaks because they do not know whether it has spoiled or will spoil before they return. A typical discard is a half jar of peanut

butter. In fact nonorganic peanut butter does not require refrigeration and is unlikely to spoil in any reasonable time. The student does not know that, and since it is Daddy's money, the student decides not to take a chance.

27   Opened containers require caution and some attention to the question "Why was this discarded?" But in the case of discards from student apartments, the answer may be that the item was discarded through carelessness, ignorance, or wastefulness. This can sometimes be deduced when the item is found with many others, including some that are obviously perfectly good.

28   Some students, and others, approach defrosting a freezer by chucking out the whole lot. Not only do the circumstances of such a find tell the story, but also the mass of frozen goods stays cold for a long time and items may be found still frozen or freshly thawed.

29   Yogurt, cheese, and sour cream are items that are often thrown out while they are still good. Occasionally I find a cheese with a spot of mold, which of course I just pare off, and because it is obvious why such a cheese was discarded, I treat it with less suspicion than an apparently perfect cheese found in similar circumstances. Yogurt is often discarded, still sealed, only because the expiration date on the carton had passed. This is one of my favorite finds because yogurt will keep for several days, even in warm weather.

30   Students throw out canned goods and staples at the end of semesters and when they give up college at midterm. Drugs, pornography, spirits, and the like are often discarded when parents are expected—Dad's day, for example. And spirits also turn up after big party weekends, presumably discarded by the newly reformed. Wine and spirits, of course, keep perfectly well even once opened.

31   My test for carbonated soft drinks is whether they still fizz vigorously. Many juices or other beverages are too acid or too syrupy to cause much concern provided they are not visibly contaminated. Liquids, however, require some care.

32   One hot day I found a large jug of Pat O'Brien's Hurricane mix. The jug had been opened, but it was still ice cold. I drank three large glasses before it became apparent to me that someone had added the rum to the mix, and not a little rum. I never tasted the rum and by the time I began to feel the effects I had already ingested a very large quantity of the beverage. Some divers would have considered this a boon, but being suddenly and thoroughly intoxicated in a public place in the early afternoon is not my idea of a good time.

33   I have heard of people maliciously contaminating discarded food and even handouts, but mostly I have heard of this from people with vivid imaginations who have had no experience with the Dumpsters themselves. Just before the pizza shop stopped discarding its garbage at night, jalapeños began showing up on most of the discarded pizzas. If indeed this was meant to discourage me it was a wasted effort because I am native Texan.

34   For myself, I avoid game, poultry, pork, and egg-based foods whether I find them raw or cooked. I seldom have the means to cook what I find, but when I do I avail myself of plentiful supplies of beef which is often in very good condition. I suppose fish becomes disagreeable before it becomes dangerous. The dog is happy to have any such thing that is past its prime and, in fact, does not recognize fish as food until it is quite strong.

35   Home leftovers, as opposed to surpluses from restaurants, are very often bad. Evidently, especially among students, there is a common type of personality that carefully

wraps up even the smallest leftover and shoves it into the back of the refrigerator for six months or so before discarding it. Characteristic of this type are the reused jars and margarine tubs which house the remains.

36   I avoid ethnic foods I am unfamiliar with. If I do not know what it is supposed to look like when it is good, I cannot be certain I will be able to tell if it is bad.

37   No matter how careful I am I still get dysentery at least once a month, oftener in warm weather. I do not want to paint too romantic a picture. Dumpster diving has serious drawbacks as a way of life.

38   I learned to scavenge gradually, on my own. Since then I have initiated several companions into the trade. I have learned that there is a predictable series of stages a person goes through in learning to scavenge.

39   At first the new scavenger is filled with disgust and self-loathing. He is ashamed of being seen and may lurk around, trying to duck behind things, or he may try to dive at night.

40   (In fact, most people instinctively look away from a scavenger. By skulking around, the novice calls attention to himself and arouses suspicion. Diving at night is ineffective and needlessly messy.)

41   Every grain of rice seems to be a maggot. Everything seems to stink. He can wipe the egg yolk off the found can, but he cannot erase the stigma of eating garbage out of his mind.

42   That stage passes with experience. The scavenger finds a pair of running shoes that fit and look and smell brand new. He finds a pocket calculator in perfect working order. He finds pristine ice cream, still frozen, more than he can eat or keep. He begins to understand: People do throw away perfectly good stuff, a lot of perfectly good stuff.

43   At this stage, Dumpster shyness begins to dissipate. The diver, after all, has the last laugh. He is finding all manner of good things which are his for the taking. Those who disparage his profession are the fools, not he.

44   He may begin to hang onto some perfectly good things for which he has neither a use nor a market. Then he begins to take note of the things which are not perfectly good but are nearly so. He mates a Walkman with broken earphones and one that is missing a battery cover. He picks up things which he can repair.

45   At this stage he may become lost and never recover. Dumpsters are full of things of some potential value to someone and also of the things which never have much intrinsic value but are interesting. All the Dumpster divers I have known come to the point of trying to acquire everything they touch. Why not take it, they reason, since it is all free.

46   This is, of course, hopeless. Most divers come to realize that they must restrict themselves to items of relatively immediate utility. But in some cases the diver simply cannot control himself. I have met several of these pack-rat types. Their ideas of the values of various pieces of junk verge on the psychotic. Every bit of glass may be a diamond, they think, and all that glistens, gold.

47   I tend to gain weight when I am scavenging. Partly this is because I always find far more pizza and doughnuts than water-packed tuna, nonfat yogurt, and fresh vegetables. Also I have not developed much faith in the reliability of Dumpsters as a food source, although it has been proven to me many times. I tend to eat as if I have no idea where my next meal is coming from. But mostly I just hate to see food go to waste and so I eat much more than I should. Something like this drives the obsession to collect junk.

48   As for collecting objects, I usually restrict myself to collecting one kind of small object at a time, such as pocket calculators, sunglasses, or campaign buttons. To live on the street I must anticipate my needs to a certain extent: I must pick up and save warm bedding I find in August because it will not be found in Dumpsters in November. But even if I had a home with extensive storage space I could not save everything that might be valuable in some contingency.

49   I have proprietary feelings about my Dumpsters. As I have suggested, it is no accident that I scavenge from Dumpsters where good finds are common. But my limited experience with Dumpsters in other areas suggests to me that it is the population of competitors rather than the affluence of the dumpers that most affects the feasibility of survival by scavenging. The large number of competitors is what puts me off the idea of trying to scavenge in places like Los Angeles.

50   Curiously, I do not mind my direct competition, other scavengers, so much as I hate the can scroungers.

51   People scrounge cans because they have to have a little cash. I have tried scrounging cans with an able-bodied companion. Afoot a can scrounger simply cannot make more than a few dollars a day. One can extract the necessities of life from the Dumpsters directly with far less effort than would be required to accumulate the equivalent value in cans.

52   Can scroungers, then, are people who *must* have small amounts of cash. These are drug addicts and winos, mostly the latter because the amounts of cash are so small.

53   Spirits and drugs do, like all other commodities, turn up in Dumpsters and the scavenger will from time to time have a half bottle of a rather good wine with his dinner. But the wino cannot survive on these occasional finds; he must have his daily dose to stave off the DTs. All the cans he can carry will buy about three bottles of Wild Irish Rose.

54   I do not begrudge them the cans, but can scroungers tend to tear up the Dumpsters, mixing the contents and littering the area. They become so specialized that they can see only cans. They earn my contempt by passing up change, canned goods, and readily hockable items.

55   There are precious few courtesies among scavengers. But it is a common practice to set aside surplus items: pairs of shoes, clothing, canned goods, and such. A true scavenger hates to see good stuff go to waste and what he cannot use he leaves in good condition in plain sight.

56   Can scroungers lay waste to everything in their path and will stir one of a pair of good shoes to the bottom of a Dumpster, to be lost or ruined in the muck. Can scroungers will even go through individual garbage cans, something I have never seen a scavenger do.

57   Individual garbage cans are set out on the public easement only on garbage days. On other days going through them requires trespassing close to a dwelling. Going through individual garbage cans without scattering litter is almost impossible. Litter is likely to reduce the public's tolerance of scavenging. Individual garbage cans are simply not as productive as Dumpsters; people in houses and duplexes do not move as often and for some reason do not tend to discard as much useful material. Moreover, the time required to go through one garbage can that serves one household is not much less than the time required to go through a Dumpster that contains the refuse of twenty apartments.

58   But my strongest reservation about going through individual garbage cans is that this seems to me a very personal kind of invasion to which I would object if I were a

householder. Although many things in Dumpsters are obviously meant never to come to light, a Dumpster is somehow less personal.

59   I avoid trying to draw conclusions about the people who dump in the Dumpsters I frequent. I think it would be unethical to do so, although I know many people will find the idea of scavenger ethics too funny for words.

60   Dumpsters contain bank statements, bills, correspondence, and other documents, just as anyone might expect. But there are also less obvious sources of information. Pill bottles, for example. The labels on pill bottles contain the name of the patient, the name of the doctor, and the name of the drug. AIDS drugs and antipsychotic medicines, to name but two groups, are specific and are seldom prescribed for any other disorders. The plastic compacts for birth control pills usually have complete label information.

61   Despite all of this sensitive information, I have had only one apartment resident object to my going through the Dumpster. In that case it turned out the resident was a university athlete who was taking bets and who was afraid I would turn up his wager slips.

62   Occasionally a find tells a story. I once found a small paper bag containing some unused condoms, several partial tubes of flavored sexual lubricant, a partially used compact of birth control pills, and the torn pieces of a picture of a young man. Clearly she was through with him and planning to give up sex altogether.

63   Dumpster things are often sad—abandoned teddy bears, shredded wedding books, despaired-of sales kits. I find many pets lying in state in Dumpsters. Although I hope to get off the streets so that Lizbeth can have a long and comfortable old age, I know this hope is not very realistic. So I suppose when her time comes she too will go into a Dumpster. I will have no better place for her. And after all, for most of her life her livelihood has come from the Dumpster. When she finds something I think is safe that has been spilled from the Dumpster I let her have it. She already knows the route around the best Dumpsters. I like to think that if she survives me she will have a chance of evading the dog catcher and of finding her sustenance on the route.

64   Silly vanities also come to rest in the Dumpsters. I am a rather accomplished needleworker. I get a lot of materials from the Dumpsters. Evidently sorority girls, hoping to impress someone, perhaps themselves, with their mastery of a womanly art, buy a lot of embroider-by-number kits, work a few stitches horribly, and eventually discard the whole mess. I pull out their stitches, turn the canvas over, and work an original design. Do not think I refrain from chuckling as I make original gifts from these kits.

65   I find diaries and journals. I have often thought of compiling a book of literary found objects. And perhaps I will one day. But what I find is hopelessly commonplace and bad without being, even unconsciously camp. College students also discard their papers. I am horrified to discover the kind of paper which now merits an A in an undergraduate course. I am grateful, however, for the number of good books and magazines the students throw out.

66   In the area I know best I have never discovered vermin in the Dumpsters, but there are two kinds of kitty surprise. One is alley cats which I meet as they leap, claws first, out of Dumpsters. This is especially thrilling when I have Lizbeth in tow. The other kind of kitty surprise is a plastic garbage bag tilled with some ponderous, amorphous mass. This always proves to be used cat litter.

67   City bees harvest doughnut glaze and this makes the Dumpster at the doughnut shop more interesting. My faith in the instinctive wisdom of animals is always shaken whenever I see Lizbeth attempt to catch a bee in her mouth, which she does whenever bees are present. Evidently some birds find Dumpsters profitable, for birdie surprise is almost as common as kitty surprise of the first kind. In hunting season all kinds of small game turn up in Dumpsters, some of it, sadly, not entirely dead. Curiously, summer and winter, maggots are uncommon.

68   The worst of the living and near-living hazards of the Dumpsters are the fire ants. The food that they claim is not much of a loss, but they are vicious and aggressive. It is very easy to brush against some surface of the Dumpster and pick up half a dozen or more fire ants, usually in some sensitive area such as the underarm. One advantage of bringing Lizbeth along as I make Dumpster rounds is that, for obvious reasons, she is very alert to ground-based fire ants. When Lizbeth recognizes the signs of fire ant infestation around our feet she does the Dance of the Zillion Fire Ants. I have learned not to ignore this warning from Lizbeth, whether I perceive the tiny ants or not, but to remove ourselves at Lizbeth's first pas de bourrée.[3] All the more so because the ants are the worst in the months I wear flip-flops, if I have them.

69   (Perhaps someone will misunderstand the above. Lizbeth does the Dance of the Zillion Fire Ants when she recognizes more fire ants than she cares to eat, not when she is being bitten. Since I have learned to react promptly, she does not get bitten at all. It is the isolated patrol of fire ants that falls in Lizbeth's range that deserves pity. Lizbeth finds them quite tasty.)

70   By far the best way to go through a Dumpster is to lower yourself into it. Most of the good stuff tends to settle at the bottom because it is usually weightier than the rubbish. My more athletic companions have often demonstrated to me that they can extract much good material from a Dumpster I have already been over.

71   To those psychologically or physically unprepared to enter a Dumpster, I recommend a stout stick, preferably with some barb or hook at one end. The hook can be used to grab plastic garbage bags. When I find canned goods or other objects loose at the bottom of a Dumpster I usually can roll them into a small bag that I can then hoist up. Much Dumpster diving is a matter of experience for which nothing will do except practice.

72   Dumpster diving is outdoor work, often surprisingly pleasant. It is not entirely predictable; things of interest turn up every day and some days there are finds of great value. I am always very pleased when I can turn up exactly the thing I most wanted to find. Yet in spite of the element of change, scavenging more than most other pursuits tends to yield returns in some proportion to the effort and intelligence brought to bear. It is very sweet to turn up a few dollars in change from a Dumpster that has just been gone over by a wino.

73   The land is now covered with cities. The cities are full of Dumpsters. I think of scavenging as a modern form of self-reliance. In any event, after ten years of government service, where everything is geared to the lowest common denominator, I find work that rewards initiative and effort refreshing. Certainly I would be happy to have a sinecure again, but I am not heartbroken not to have one anymore.

[3] **pas de bourrée:** A ballet step (French).

74   I find from the experience of scavenging two rather deep lessons. The first is to take what I can use and let the rest go by. I have come to think that there is no value in the abstract. A thing I cannot use or make useful, perhaps by trading, has no value however fine or rare it may be. I mean useful in a broad sense—so, for example, some art I would think useful and valuable, but other art might be otherwise for me.

75   I was shocked to realize that some things are not worth acquiring, but now I think it is so. Some material things are white elephants that eat up the possessor's substance.

76   The second lesson is of the transience of material being. This has not quite converted me to a dualist, but it has made some headway in that direction. I do not suppose that ideas are immortal, but certainly mental things are longer-lived than other material things.

77   Once I was the sort of person who invests material objects with sentimental value. Now I no longer have those things, but I have the sentiments yet.

78   Many times in my travels I have lost everything but the clothes I was wearing and Lizbeth. The things I find in Dumpsters, the love letters and ragdolls of so many lives, remind me of this lesson. Now I hardly pick up a thing without envisioning the time I will cast it away. This I think is a healthy state of mind. Almost everything I have now has already been cast out at least once, proving that what I own is valueless to someone.

79   Anyway, I find my desire to grab for the gaudy bauble has been largely sated. I think this is an attitude I share with the very wealthy—we both know there is plenty more where what we have came from. Between us are the rat-race millions who have confounded their selves with the objects they grasp and who nightly scavenge the cable channels looking for they know not what.

80   I am sorry for them.

Source: Lars Eichner, "On Dumpster Diving," *Travels with Lizbeth: Three Years on the Road and on the Streets.* N.Y. St. Martin, 1993. Reprinted in *Fifty Essays*. Ed. Samuel Cohen. N.Y. Bedford-St. Martin, 2004, pp. 107–119.

■ Vocabulary

proprietary (1)	bohemian (9)	intrinsic (45)
generic (2)	dilettanti (9)	contingency (48)
obscure (4)	phobic 12)	feasibility (49)
refuse (5)	stigma (41)	hockable (54)
sporadic (6)	dissipate (43)	abstract (74)

■ Questions on Meaning and Technique

1. What does this essay reveal about the intelligence and talent of this man who spent three years of his life homeless and scavenging in dumpsters? Is he the typical homeless beggar one encounters in the crowded centers of large cities? Explain your answer.

2. From the point of view of pattern, this essay is a well-organized classification. What are the subjects being divided, and what are their sub categories? Create an outline of the four major headings and the items classified under each heading.

3. What are some passages that add humor to an otherwise rather glum and cheerless essay? Point to specific passages and explain the humor.

4. The author claims he much prefers dumpsters to garbage cans. According to him, what is the difference? Does the author's reasoning fit his general attitude throughout the essay? Explain your answer.

5. Why does the author insist on capitalizing the word *dumpster*? Is he following a correct grammar convention, or is he making up his own rule?

6. What is the value of paragraph 10? What does it add to or detract from the essay?

7. How do we know that the author was not always a homeless scavenger? What led to his humiliating circumstances? How do you feel about the way he handled his dilemma?

8. What are some of the ethical codes the author claims to follow? Why does he think that some people would laugh at the idea of a scavenger having ethics? Do you find the idea ridiculous? Give reasons for your answer.

9. What comment does the author make about today's student papers? (See paragraph 65). What is your answer to his comment?

Writing Assignments

1. Choosing one of the following subjects, write a classification essay in which you establish at least three broad categories that do not overlap.

   a. Natural disasters

   b. National leaders

   c. Shoppers

   d. Attitudes toward universal health care

2. Divide unmotivated students into three or four different types, describing each vividly and, if possible, humorously.

Internet Research Assignment

The following comments about whether peace between Palestinians and Israelis in the Middle East is possible were taken from a message board on the Internet:

"Peace between peace-loving people and terrorism? I don't think so."

"Peace! Whatever it takes, peace! Keep working the diplomatic angle."

"As long as Israel has nukes, there will be no peace."

"There will never be peace. The hate runs too deep."

"A comet from outer space will slam into the earth . . . before they ever make peace."

"Let there be peace already!"

"Take Mahmoud Abbas seriously. . . . He could very well become the Gorbachev of the Mideast."

"Finally, now that Arafat is gone, I can see a ray of hope for peace between the Palestinians and Jews."

"Now that Iran has stepped onto the international stage, peace has become more precarious than ever."

Write an essay classifying the underlying attitudes represented by these comments. You may divide these comments by any principle you like so long as you come up with at least three groups.

Additional Writing Assignments

1. Review the architecture of your neighborhood. Then write a paper classifying the various types of buildings using such aspects as size, age, and style as a basis for creating the various categories.

2. Classify one species of domesticated animal according to three or four general types, supplying vivid examples of each type. For instance, if you are a cat lover, you might use these categories: affectionate cats, sly cats, aloof cats, vicious cats.

3. How many major kinds of entertainment are there? Who indulges in each? Write a classification essay answering these questions.

4. Think about your friends in terms of their attitudes toward church attendance. Then classify these attitudes in a way that will shed light on why people attend or do not attend church.

5. Divide current television shows into between three and five major types, supplying examples of each type.

6. Looking back over the list of teachers you have had, classify them into differ- ent types according to their personalities and ways of relating to students.

7. Humans communicate with each other by various means, some including language, some not. Classify the ways humans communicate, and supply examples of each way.

8. A *stereotype* is a classification applied unthinkingly and without taking into account individual differences. Compose a popular stereotype of one of the following: Harvard students, rock stars, male ballet dancers, car sales- persons, suburban housewives, Internet addicts.

9. All working societies pay homage to some kind of authority. Classify the major kinds of authorities, and describe the characteristics of each.

10. Clouds are a fascinating and mysterious phenomenon of nature. Divide all clouds into three or four major types, and describe each type in vivid, even poetic, language.

Rewriting Assignment

Collaborating with a classmate, rewrite the following paragraphs about "states of anxiety" until they contain no mechanical errors and read both smoothly and emphatically.

To be anxious about serious problems is normal however, many people today exaggerate their anxieties to the point of being neurotic. A person who has neurosis may be able to keep their job, but the stress from the neurosis will often lessen their effectiveness and their happiness in life. There are three main kinds of neuroses: anxi- ety, obsession-compulsion, and hysteria.

The first kind of neurosis, anxiety, causes a person to feel excessively jumpy or scarred. They have this vague sensation that someone is after them or that some catastrophe is about to happen. Sometimes their fear is attached to a specific thing or event. For instance, some neurotics can't stand to get into an elevator, others can't stand to hear an emergency siren.

Some people have obsessive-compulsive reactions, they believe, for instance, that they have cancer or heart trouble and may be dying. They will then dwell on this fear constantly. Or, they can't resist performing certain acts over and over again. Especially things like washing their hands, to never walk barefoot, or using a kleenex on a pub- lic doorknob to avoid microbes.

The third kind of neurosis is hysteria. In its worst form, the individual shows dramatic symptoms that really have no reason because nothing is wrong. They may actually suffer paralysis to the point that they must remain in bed or in a wheel chair. The hysteria may cause forgetfulness, walking in their sleep, or displaying multiple personalities. All hysteria is a way of escaping psychological problems rather than dealing with them.

Some neuroses are so mild that they are barely noticeable, but others can be life threatening and should be dealt with in a psychiatric setting.

Photo Writing Assignment

© Mark Ralston/AFP/Getty Images

In this photo, you see a full orchestra preparing to play at a symphony concert. All the instruments of an orchestra can be classified into different kinds—woodwind, percussion, brass, and string. See if you can write a paragraph placing each instrument in its proper category. Add some humor to your paragraph by indicating the sounds made by a typical kind of instrument. For instance, you might indicate that the triangle makes a cling-cling sound, that the trumpets make a toot-toot sound, or that the violins give off a nasal twang.

Digging for Gold or
for Related Types

The work of division and classification is an essential part of the miner's profession.Once the prospector has separated the gold from rock, then the work of dividing or classifying begins. Most commonly the gold is classified on the basis of size, color, or purity.

Division or classification in writing is primarily an intellectual exercise. But it is also the loose cannon from which idiotic opinions about virtually any subject are fired. For instance, a writer who asserts that "every type of blonde is flighty-flighty, but brunettes are always reflective" is being intellectually careless. Girlfriends, tools, politicians, evils, teachers, clothing. . . . the list of things that can be divided or classified is endless, but classification requires meticulous logic. Sometimes, however, a really creative writer will arrive at classifications that reveal a uniquely imaginative touch. For example, before Shakespeare concluded that every man's life has seven stages, no one else, so far as we know, had come to that speculative conclusion. It is an invented division thought up by the greatest writer who ever lived. Some classifications arrange real objects into types; others use the imagination to come up with logical but fanciful categories of the writer's own devising. In this chapter, Russell Baker's "The Plot Against the People" classifies objects into things that break, get lost, or don't work—thereby frustrating the user. When Martin Luther King, Jr. classified types of defiance by oppressed blacks, he made history because his approach was so unusual. "On Dumpster Diving" is a clear classification of the problems scavengers face when they scrounge for food.

Although you may be dividing or classifying something totally different from gold ore, the intellectual exercise is the same as that of a miner—creating categories into which you slot related sub categories And you both must begin by digging to find your subject. A good place to start is with people you know well. Ask yourself what type each person represents. Dig on.

Chapter 14

Causal Analysis

IRWIN SHAW

The Girls in Their Summer Dresses

Irwin Shaw (1913–1984), novelist, playwright, and short story writer, was born in New York City and educated at Brooklyn College. A former drama critic for The New Republic, *Shaw was known for his clear characterization and crisp plotting in the short story. He was also widely known as an author of popular novels. Many of these, such as* The Young Lions *(1948), were made into movies or, like* Rich Man, Poor Man *(1969), into highly rated television shows. His other works include* Bury the Dead *(play, 1936),* Sailor off the Bremen *(short story collection, 1939),* The Troubled Air *(1951), and* Two Weeks in Another Town *(1960).*

READING FOR IDEAS The character in a short story often knows less about his or her life than the reader does. Sometimes this lack of knowledge is necessary to the conclusion. Sometimes it is central to the fate of a character or explains a hidden dimension in a character's makeup. In this short story, for example, a wife who utterly misunderstands her husband worries needlessly about his behavior—behavior that makes sense to the reader.

1   Fifth Avenue was shining in the sun when they left the Brevoort. The sun was warm, even though it was February, and everything looked like Sunday morning—the buses and the well-dressed people walking slowly in couples and the quiet buildings with the windows closed.

2   Michael held Frances' arm tightly as they walked toward Washington Square in the sunlight. They walked lightly, almost smiling, because they had slept late and had a good breakfast and it was Sunday. Michael unbuttoned his coat and let it flap around him in the mild wind.

3   "Look out," Frances said as they crossed Eighth Street. "You'll break your neck."

4   Michael laughed and Frances laughed with him.

5   "She's not so pretty," Frances said. "Anyway, not pretty enough to take a chance of breaking your neck."

6   Michael laughed again. "How did you know I was looking at her?"

7   Frances cocked her head to one side and smiled at her husband under the brim of her hat. "Mike, darling," she said.

8   "O.K.," he said. "Excuse me."

9   Frances patted his arm lightly and pulled him along a little faster toward Washington Square. "Let's not see anybody all day," she said. "Let's just hang around with each other. You and me. We're always up to our neck in people, drinking their Scotch or drinking our Scotch; we only see each other in bed. I want to go out with my husband all day long. I want him to talk only to me and listen only to me."

10   "What's to stop us?" Michael asked.

11   "The Stevensons. They want us to drop by around one o'clock and they'll drive us into the country."

12   "The cunning Stevensons," Mike said. "Transparent. They can whistle. They can go driving in the country by themselves."

13   "Is it a date?"

14   "It's a date."

15   Frances leaned over and kissed him on the tip of the ear.

16   "Darling," Michael said, "this is Fifth Avenue."

17   "Let me arrange a program," Frances said. "A planned Sunday in New York for a young couple with money to throw away."

18   "Go easy."

19   "First let's go to the Metropolitan Museum of Art," Frances suggested, because Michael had said during the week he wanted to go. "I haven't been there in three years and there're at least ten pictures I want to see again. Then we can take the bus down to Radio City and watch them skate. And later we'll go down to Cavanagh's and get a steak as big as a blacksmith's apron, with a bottle of wine, and after that there's a French picture at the Filmarte that everybody says—say, are you listening to me?"

20   "Sure," he said. He took his eyes off the hatless girl with the dark hair, cut dancerstyle like a helmet, who was walking past him.

21   "That's the program for the day," Frances said flatly. "Or maybe you'd just rather walk up and down Fifth Avenue."

22   "No," Michael said. "Not at all."

23   "You always look at other women," Frances said. "Everywhere. Every damned place we go."

24   "Now, darling," Michael said, "I look at everything. God gave me eyes and I look at women and men and subway excavations and moving pictures and the little flowers of the field. I casually inspect the universe."

25   "You ought to see the look in your eye," Frances said, "as you casually inspect the universe on Fifth Avenue."

26   "I'm a happily married man." Michael pressed her elbow tenderly. "Example for the whole twentieth century—Mr. and Mrs. Mike Loomis. Hey, let's have a drink," he said, stopping.

27   "We just had breakfast."

28   "Now listen, darling," Mike said, choosing his words with care, "it's a nice day and we both felt good and there's no reason why we have to break it up. Let's have a nice Sunday."

29   "All right. I don't know why I started this. Let's drop it. Let's have a good time."

30   They joined hands consciously and walked without talking among the baby carriages and the old Italian men in their Sunday clothes and the young women with Scotties in Washington Square Park.

31   "At least once a year everyone should go to the Metropolitan Museum of Art," Frances said after a while, her tone a good imitation of the tone she had used at breakfast and at the beginning of their walk. "And it's nice on Sunday. There's a lot of people looking at the pictures and you get the feeling maybe Art isn't on the decline in New York City, after all—"

32   "I want to tell you something," Michael said very seriously. "I have not touched another woman. Not once. In all the five years."

33   "All right," Frances said.

34   "You believe that, don't you."

35   "All right."

36   They walked between the crowded benches, under the scrubby city-park trees.

37   "I try not to notice it," Frances said, "but I feel rotten inside, in my stomach, when we pass a woman and you look at her and I see that look in your eye and that's the way you looked at me the first time. In Alice Maxwell's house. Standing there in the living room, next to the radio, with a green hat on and all those people."

38   "I remember the hat," Michael said.

39   "The same look," Frances said. "And it makes me feel bad. It makes me feel terrible."

40   "Sh-h-h, please, darling, sh-h-h."

41   "I think I would like a drink now," Frances said.

42   They walked over to a bar on Eighth Street, not saying anything, Michael automatically helping her over curbstones and guiding her past automobiles. They sat near a window in the bar and the sun streamed in and there was a small, cheerful fire in the fireplace. A little Japanese waiter came over and put down some pretzels and smiled happily at them.

43   "What do you order after breakfast?" Michael asked.

44   "Brandy, I suppose," Frances said.

45   "Courvoisier," Michael told the waiter. "Two Courvoisiers."

46   The waiter came with the glasses and they sat drinking the brandy in the sunlight. Michael finished half his and drank a little water.

47   "I look at women," he said. "Correct. I don't say it's wrong or right. I look at them. If I pass them on the street and I don't look at them, I'm fooling you, I'm fooling myself."

48   "You look at them as though you want them," Frances said, playing with her brandy glass. "Every one of them."

49   "In a way," Michael said, speaking softly and not to his wife, "in a way that's true. I don't do anything about it, but it's true."

50   "I know it. That's why I feel bad."

51   "Another brandy," Michael called. "Waiter, two more brandies."

52   He sighed and closed his eyes and rubbed them gently with his fingertips. "I love the way women look. One of the things I like best about New York is the battalions of

women. When I first came to New York from Ohio that was the first thing I noticed, the million wonderful women, all over the city. I walked around with my heart in my throat."

53   "A kid," Frances said, "that's a kid's feeling."

54   "Guess again," Michael said, "guess again. I'm older now, I'm a man getting near middle age, putting on a little fat and I still love to walk along Fifth Avenue at three o'clock on the east side of the street between Fiftieth and Fifty-seventh Streets. They're all out then, shopping, in their furs and their crazy hats, everything all concentrated from all over the world into seven blocks—the best furs, the best clothes, the handsomest women, out to spend money and feeling good about it."

55   The Japanese waiter put the two drinks down, smiling with great happiness.

56   "Everything is all right?" he asked.

57   "Everything is wonderful," Michael said.

58   "If it's just a couple of fur coats," Frances said, "and forty-five-dollar hats—"

59   "It's not the fur coats. Or the hats. That's just the scenery for that particular kind of woman. Understand," he said, "you don't have to listen to this."

60   "I want to listen."

61   "I like the girls in the offices. Neat, with their eyeglasses, smart, chipper, knowing what everything is about. I like the girls on Forty-fourth Street at lunchtime, the actresses, all dressed up on nothing a week. I like the salesgirls in the stores, paying attention to you first because you're a man, leaving lady customers waiting. I got all this stuff accumulated in me because I've been thinking about it for ten years and now you've asked for it and here it is."

62   "Go ahead," Frances said.

63   "When I think of New York City, I think of all the girls on parade in the city. I don't know whether it's something special with me or whether every man in the city walks around with the same feeling inside him, but I feel as though I'm at a picnic in this city. I like to sit near the women in the theatres, the famous beauties who've taken six hours to get ready and look it. And the young girls at the football games, with the red cheeks, and when the warm weather comes, the girls in their summer dresses." He finished his drink. "That's the story."

64   Frances finished her drink and swallowed two or three times extra. "You say you love me?"

65   "I love you."

66   "I'm pretty, too," Frances said. "As pretty as any of them."

67   "You're beautiful," Michael said.

68   "I'm good for you," Frances said, pleading. "I've made a good wife, a good housekeeper, a good friend. I'd do any damn thing for you."

69   "I know," Michael said. He put his hand out and grasped hers.

70   "You'd like to be free to—" Frances said.

71   "Sh-h-h."

72   "Tell the truth." She took her hand away from under his.

73   Michael flicked the edge of his glass with his finger. "O.K.," he said gently. "Sometimes I feel I would like to be free."

74   "Well," Frances said, "any time you say."

75   "Don't be foolish." Michael swung his chair around to her side of the table and patted her thigh.

76   She began to cry silently into her handkerchief, bent over just enough so that nobody else in the bar would notice. "Someday," she said, crying, "you're going to make a move."

77   Michael didn't say anything. He sat watching the bartender slowly peel a lemon.

78   "Aren't you?" Frances asked harshly. "Come on, tell me. Talk. Aren't you?"

79   "Maybe," Michael said. He moved his chair back again. "How the hell do I know?"

80   "You know," Frances persisted. "Don't you know?"

81   "Yes," Michael said after a while, "I know."

82   Frances stopped crying then. Two or three snuffles into the handkerchief and she put it away and her face didn't tell anything to anybody. "At least do me one favor," she said.

83   "Sure."

84   "Stop talking about how pretty this woman is or that one. Nice eyes, nice breasts, a pretty figure, good voice." She mimicked his voice. "Keep it to yourself. I'm not interested."

85   Michael waved to the waiter. "I'll keep it to myself," he said.

86   Frances flicked the corners of her eyes. "Another brandy," she told the waiter.

87   "Two," Michael said.

88   "Yes, ma'am, yes, sir," said the waiter, backing away.

89   Frances regarded Michael coolly across the table. "Do you want me to call the Stevensons?" she asked. "It'll be nice in the country."

90   "Sure," Michael said, "call them."

91   She got up from the table and walked across the room toward the telephone. Michael watched her walk, thinking what a pretty girl, what nice legs.

■ *Questions on Meaning and Technique*

1. How does Frances feel about Michael? Why does she feel this way? State both the way she feels and the reasons for it in a single sentence that could serve as the controlling idea for an essay about the story.

2. What role do the "girls in their summer dresses" play in the story?

3. How does Michael feel toward Frances? Support your conclusion with evidence from the story.

4. How does Michael make Frances feel when he looks at other women? Why?

5. What advice would you give a wife whose husband looks at other women the way Michael does? Should she ignore him? Be happy that he enjoys beauty and life? Scold him? Flirt to get even? Why? Give your reasons.

6. What is your prediction about Michael and Frances's future together? Will they eventually divorce? Will the marriage survive? Why or why not?

7. Do you believe that Michael is unusual, or do his feelings toward women represent the feelings of most men? Explain your answer.

8. What advice might you give the young couple?

VICTOR CONTOSKI

Money

Victor Contoski (b. 1936) is a poet who was born in St. Paul, Minnesota, of Polish origin. He studied at the University of Minnesota and Ohio State for his B.A. and M.A. and received his Ph.D. from the University of Wisconsin in 1969. He has taught American literature at the University of Lodz in Poland, was a Fulbright Professor from 1963 to 1964, and was a professor of English at the University of Kansas in Lawrence. Among his works are a bilingual edition of literary criticism, titled Four Contemporary Polish Poets *(1967), and a volume of poetry,* Broken Treaties *(1973). He is the editor of* Blood of Their Blood: An Anthology of Polish-American Poetry *(1980), and has contributed essays to numerous magazines.*

READING FOR IDEAS Crucial to the understanding of the poem is the analogy being drawn. Figure out what the poet is comparing money to, and the rest of the poem's meaning will follow.

1 At first it will seem tame,
   willing to be domesticated.

2 It will nest
   in your pocket
   or curl up in a corner
   reciting softly to itself
   the names of the presidents.

3 It will delight your friends,
   shake hands with men
   like a dog and lick
   the legs of women.

4 But like an amoeba
   it makes love
   in secret
   only to itself.

5 Its food is normal
   American food.
   Fold it frequently;
   it needs exercise.

6   Water it every three days
       and it will repay you
       with displays of affection.

7   Then one day when you think
       you are its master
       it will turn its head
       as if for a kiss
       and bite you gently
       on the hand.

8   There will be no pain
       but in thirty seconds
       the poison will reach your heart.

■ *Vocabulary*

domesticated (1)   amoeba (4)

■ *Questions on Meaning and Technique*

1. What is the theme (lesson about life) of the poem, and where is it stated?
2. What is the predominant figure of speech used in the poem? How effective do you consider it? Give reasons to support your answer.
3. What allusion is used in stanza 3? Why?
4. Do you agree with the poet's opinion concerning the malevolence of money? Is it possible for money to bring true benefit to its owner? If so, how? If not, why?
5. What image of money does the second stanza use? What clue helps you recognize immediately that the reference to "it" is money?
6. Why is the destruction so sudden and so painless?

How to Write an Analysis of Cause

Causal analysis is the expression used for finding connections between events. Unconsciously, you make causal analyses every day of your life. For example, you are doing causal analysis when you try to figure out why you did poorly on an exam. You also are doing causal analysis when you decide to wear warm clothing on a mountain trip so that you won't catch a cold. In the first case, you are looking at the past to find causes; in the second case, you are looking at the future to predict results.

During your college career, you often will be required to write essays that analyze cause. Your history teacher may ask you to give the causes for the Crimean War; your health teacher may ask you to name three results of a rattlesnake bite; your meteorology teacher may ask you to cite the major causes for hurricanes.

Causal analysis can be complex. Few situations can be traced directly to a single, clear cause. It is commonplace to read about a murder trial in which noted psychiatrists and psychologists disagree vehemently about a defendant's motive and state of mind. Economists argue vainly about the causes of inflation and recession; medical professionals constantly debate the causes of cancer. Most effects have not one but several causes, and often it is difficult, if not impossible, to determine the main cause of any event.

Part of this difficulty is that an effect is often preceded by a chain of causes. For instance, what is the cause of air pollution? Industrial waste. But industrial waste is caused by industry, which is caused by the needs of an exploding population. The exploding population is caused by lack of birth control, which results in part from religious beliefs. Religious beliefs come from writings in the Bible. The Bible is the word of God. Therefore, God is the cause of air pollution.

This conclusion is obviously silly. Nonetheless, it illustrates how an attempt at tracing causation can quickly lead to absurdity and serves to warn you against drawing haphazard or hasty causal connections. Investigate your subject thoroughly, either from firsthand experience or by doing research. The causes for your parents' happy or miserable marriage can be identified through personal experience, but the causes of complex problems such as urban poverty or juvenile crime will require some research.

Writing Assignment

Write an essay analyzing the causes of a condition, event, or situation in society. First describe the condition, event, or situation. Then probe the causes, listing them one by one and making sure that each cause is directly connected to the subject being described.

Specific Instructions

Prewriting on the assignment. Before you can begin to write, you have to choose a condition, event, or situation that has occurred as the result of identifiable causes. Situations do exist to which no absolute cause can be assigned, and these will be difficult to write about in any essay. For instance, scientists are still arguing over what caused the dinosaurs to disappear and the Egyptian mummies to be so well preserved. Better to choose a subject whose causes are definite and traceable. Follow your natural inclinations. If you are of a scientific bent, write about a scientific subject. One student wrote an excellent paper on what causes fireflies to light up, explaining that the light is produced by organs located on the fly's abdomen. The student then went into details about the nerve evolvement and role of reflector cells. Another student, majoring in political science, wrote a paper identifying the control of oil production, different interpretations of Islam, and a historical distrust of one another as the major causes of quarreling among Arab states. In any case, the basic idea is to choose a subject whose causes are traceable and discussable. Here are some topics to consider:

> The growing number of homeless people in large cities
> The resistance to ordination of women as ministers or priests
> The popularity of gangs and resultant killings
> The importance of the coffee break
> The increase in school violence

Once you have chosen your topic, jot down on a piece of paper its major causes or begin the research necessary to trace them. For instance, let us assume that you want to write about the growing number of homeless people in large cities. Finding out why their numbers have increased will require some research, which, combined with experience and common sense, may lead you to the following summary:

1. Many people with mental illnesses are no longer sheltered in medical institutions.
2. Residents of large cities have become callous to the plight of homeless people.
3. Some people want the independence of roaming the streets.

Summing up these three causes could lead to this thesis for your essay:

> Three major causes contribute to the growing number of homeless people in our large cities: the government's unwillingness to shelter all mentally ill persons, callousness to the plight of homeless people, and a sense of stubborn independence on the part of these individuals.

You are now ready to begin writing the essay.

Use the proper word indicators to show causation.   Consider these examples:

Wrong	Admissions quotas based on sex, ethnic background, or age are bad. They discriminate against the capable student.
Right	Admissions quotas based on sex, ethnic background, or age are bad *because* they discriminate against the capable student.

Whether you are listing the effects or causes of a situation, warn your reader that you intend to do a causal analysis by using such expressions as *because, therefore, since, the reason is, due to, as a result, consequently,* and *thus.* Here are some examples of causal sentences:

> Chaucer is difficult to read *because* he uses antiquated English.
> *Because* living human cells are constantly breaking down, they are in a constant state of reconstructing themselves through nutrients.

Walter is talented, practices the violin five hours a day and, *as a result,* won the Luba Lefcowitz prize for violin.

The present chaos in the world may have the following *results:* the extinction of human life, a reversion to barbarism after an atomic explosion, or the peaceful establishment of a world government.

If you are listing several causes for a certain situation, it is well to number them, as in these examples:

The first cause is . . .

The second cause is . . .

The third cause is . . .

As a matter of course, professional writers often use various expressions that signal what they are about to do before they do it. If they are about to define a term, they say so. If they intend to describe a vista, they tell the reader. If they are analyzing effect, they announce this in advance. It is a commonsense strategy and one that is highly effective. Readers are more likely to comprehend a passage whose purpose is clear to them. Here, for instance, is a paragraph that analyzes

---

 STUDENT TIP FOR INVENTING IDEAS

Assignment

Write an essay analyzing the causes of a condition, event, or situation in society.

How I found my topic

When I first got this assignment, I thought to myself, everyone's going to do something big. You do something small. There's an obviously homeless man who is often found on our campus. The campus police run him off, but he just keeps coming back because there are many places that he can sneak in to sleep the night away. I decided to use him as my guinea pig.

I talked to him nearly every day, when he was around, and got to know his story about why he became homeless. It had to do with an addiction problem that he admits to. It didn't help that he saw a lot of action in Vietnam and remembers shooting a child at point-blank range. He thought the child had a bomb. He became my topic. My essay would analyze why he became homeless.

—A male sophomore at a state university in Northern California

why, after the Norman Conquest, French did not replace English as the national language in England:

> One might wonder why, after the Norman Conquest, French did not become the national language, replacing English entirely. The reason is that the Conquest was not a national migration, as the earlier Anglo-Saxon invasion had been. Great numbers of Normans came to England, but they came as rulers and landlords. French became the language of the court, the language of the nobility, the language of polite society, the language of literature. But it did not replace English as the language of the people. There must always have been hundreds of towns and villages in which French was never heard except when visitors of high station passed through.
>
> —Paul Roberts, *Understanding English*

If you are similarly analyzing the cause of a thing, or its effect, you should advise your reader that that is what you are going to do. Then you do it.

Expand on the analysis of cause.   Doing an analysis of cause often requires using a mix of writing strategies. You will almost certainly in the course of doing an essay on cause have to write paragraphs that define, describe, and exemplify. To supply background material, you may have to describe the problem, define key terms, and possibly divide and classify, even though the thrust of your essay will be to explain cause or to predict effect.

It is not surprising that this is so. Essays are written with a dominant purpose or intent conceived in the mind of the writer. But a translation of this dominant intent onto the page generally requires many different kinds of paragraphs. It is a little like baking a chocolate cake. One uses not only chocolate, but also flour, butter, baking powder, milk, eggs, and sugar. Yet when the cake comes out of the oven, it is indisputably a chocolate cake, though made of different kinds of ingredients. Essays likewise have distinct and recognizable purposes. Some are intended primarily to describe; others set out to narrate; still others are written to analyze cause. Yet most are constructed of different kinds of paragraphs.

For instance, a writer is attempting to explain why humans sleep. He is, to begin with, obliged to talk about the principal human states of mind: waking, sleeping, and dreaming. The paragraph that does this is developed by *classification/division*. But, he asks, what is sleep good for? He surveys the animal kingdom and finds that although some animals—sloths, armadillos, opossums, and bats—sleep between nineteen and twenty hours a day, there are others—such as the shrew and the porpoise—that sleep very little. He also mentions the case of some humans who require only an hour or two of sleep. The paragraph that serves up all this intriguing information has been developed by *example*. He then turns his attention to the kinds of sleep—dreaming and dreamless—and discusses the results of research into each. Again, the paragraph is developed by *classification/division*. He is now ready to suggest a reason for sleep. This paragraph is developed by causal analysis:

> Perhaps one useful hint about the original function of sleep is to be found in the fact that dolphins and whales and aquatic mammals in general seem to sleep very

---

Writing Tip

Analyze the Cause of a Local Problem

Consider writing about the cause of a local condition or problem—one that you know intimately and can write about not only from research but also from experience. For example, you can write about the causes of divorces in your neighborhood or about a problem with unleashed pets on campus, or about panhandlers harassing shoppers in the busy sections of your town. It is easier to write about a nearby problem because that enables you to interview someone about it. Many students tend to overlook the specific details that can be gathered in an interview.

---

little. There is, by and large, no place to hide in the ocean. Could it be that, rather than increasing an animal's vulnerability, the function of sleep is to *decrease* it? Wilse Webb *Analysis of cause* of the University of Florida and Ray Meddis of London University have suggested this to be the case. The sleeping style of each organism is exquisitely adapted to the ecology of the animal. It is conceivable that animals who are too stupid to be quiet on their own initiative are, during periods of high risk, immobilized by the implacable arm of sleep. The point seems particularly clear for the young of predatory animals; not only are baby tigers covered with a superbly effective protective coloration, they also sleep a great deal. This is an interesting notion and probably at least partly true. It does not explain everything. Why do lions, who have few natural enemies, sleep? The question is not a very damaging objection because lions may have evolved from animals that were not the king of beasts. Likewise, adolescent gorillas, who have little to fear, nevertheless construct nests each night—perhaps because they evolved from more vulnerable predecessors. Or perhaps, once, the ancestors of lions and gorillas feared still more formidable predators.

—Carl Sagan, *The Dragons of Eden*

The remainder of the discussion expands on this notion and finds applications of its truthfulness in the animal kingdom.

Such a paragraph mix is typical of an analysis of cause. The writer, however, must strive to keep on the straight-and-narrow path in pursuing the dominant purpose of the essay. It is all very well and good to sidestep in order to define a term or to give an example of a concept, but you must still keep to your dominant purpose—to explain cause.

Be cautious.   Don't be dogmatic or simplistic in drawing causal connections. Because very few events are sufficient in themselves to bring about a result, it is prudent to qualify your assertions with *a major cause, it appears that,* or *evidence* *indicates that*. These qualifiers show you realize that the connection between events may be probable rather than certain, and they will make you sound more credible to the reader. On the other hand, if your causal analysis is a result of a personal opinion arrived at after much research and thought, have the courage of your convictions. For example, do not say "It appears that the February, 2000 killing of Amadou Diallo, an unarmed, young black man, may have revealed excessive force used by the New York City police." Instead, say "The February, 2000 killing of Amadou Diallo, an unarmed, young black man, by New York City police adds yet another page to the U.S. history of human rights violations."

Whenever possible, focus on immediate rather than remote cause.   Causation, we pointed out earlier, has a way of multiplying back in time, with one cause leading to another and then to another, until God becomes the cause of smog. To avoid entanglement in infinity, always focus on immediate rather than remote causation. For instance, one cause of overcrowded freeways is the population explosion, but a more immediate cause is the lack of rapid transit facilities. Focusing on the immediate cause has a better chance of resulting in an effective, convincing essay. Of course, some immediate causes are too deeply rooted in remote causes for the connection to be ignored. An example is the continuing conflict between Jews and Muslims in the Middle East. Whatever immediate causes—desire for oil, a Palestinian homeland, or national sovereignty—have led to this conflict, the remote causes of the centuries-old rift between Muslim and Jew should also be discussed.

Avoid circular reasoning about cause.   The following causal statements are circular:

> The freeways are overcrowded because there are too many cars.
>
> Lung cancer is caused by the rapid and uncontrolled growth of abnormal cells in the lungs.
>
> Beauty pageants are dehumanizing because unattractive women never win them.

Each statement simply restates in the second half what is already implied in the first. Overcrowded freeways obviously have too many cars on them; lung cancer is, by definition, uncontrolled cell growth in the lungs; beauty pageants are called *beauty pageants* because they judge women for beauty. These revisions are better:

> The freeways are overcrowded because they are inadequately engineered for need and because rapid transit facilities are poor.
>
> Cigarette smoking is the major cause of lung cancer.
>
> Beauty pageants are dehumanizing because they evaluate a woman as a sex object rather than as a whole, functioning person.

Beware of ideology in assigning cause.   Here are examples of causal statements based on ideology:

> The high divorce rate in Southern California is caused by the fact that the devil has chosen this section of the country for his own and has been especially busy working among couples here.
>
> The high divorce rate in California is caused by an astrological opposition between Neptune and the Moon and by a weak but dangerous sextile relationship between Mars and the Sun.

In a complex universe, neither statement is refutable nor demonstrable, unless one is in ideological agreement with the writer. General essays on causation, however, ought not to exert any special ideological requirement on a reader.

Structuring a causal analysis essay.   A causal analysis paper can easily disintegrate into a mass of disorderly information that cannot be sorted out by the average reader. To avoid this outcome, begin your paper by asking an important question: Do I wish to emphasize cause, effect, or both? For instance, if you have chosen to write a paper on women who as children were sexually abused by males, you can decide to focus on the causes of this abuse, on its effects, or on both the causes and the effects. Now assume you have decided to cover the effects on women, rather than the causes of abuse. Begin by listing the effects you wish to consider:

1. The women's inability to relate lovingly to their partners
2. The women's excessive fear or hostility toward all men
3. The women's lack of self-esteem because of unconscious feelings that somehow they could have prevented the molestation

You have three clear effects that can be developed in the order listed. Moreover, your thesis statement can be formulated based on the three effects:

> Women who were sexually abused by men during their childhood often cannot erase the harm done at that early stage in their lives and, in fact, may have to have years of psychotherapy to counteract the effects of not being able to relate lovingly to their partners, of harboring excessive fear or hostility in relating to men in general, and of lacking a sense of self-esteem for not having prevented the molestation from taking place.

Once your thesis is in place, you can develop the essay by carefully describing the three effects, including facts, statistics, examples, case histories, and other supportive details. The structure you built will help give your essay movement and coherence.

Another way to structure the essay is to begin with molestation as an effect and then trace its causes. Here are four possible causes of molestation, listed in order of their relative importance:

1. The abuser was abused as a child
2. The abuser abuses as a substitute for trying to find love
3. The abuser victimizes a child, who is too weak to resist, thus achieving a sensc of control over the world
4. The abuser has never assimilated the normal sexual taboos of society

The thesis statement for this essay might read as follows:

> Research psychologists tell us that the major causes that drive adult males to sexually abuse young girls can be traced to these factors in the male's own development: The male was abused as a child, is trying to find love, wants to gain control over a world that victimized him, and has never assimilated the normal sexual taboos of his society.

The causal analysis essay is rooted in our elemental need to make connections between events and to understand how the events came about. A well-structured causal analysis essay may well uncover some surprising truths that help make sense of a tangled situation.

PROFESSIONAL MODEL

TENNESSEE WILLIAMS

The Catastrophe of Success

Tennessee Williams (1911–1983) was a major American playwright and one of the twentieth century's most significant literary figures. He acquired the pseudonym "Tennessee" from some college fraternity brothers because of his deep southern drawl and his Tennessee roots. Many of his best-known plays, among them A Streetcar Named Desire, *are based on his dysfunctional family, particularly his sister, Rose, an often institutionalized schizophrenic. He died at the Elysee Hotel in New York at the age of 71, due to alcoholism and drug overuse. His major plays include the following:* The Glass Menagerie *(1944),* A Streetcar Named Desire *(1947),* Cat on a Hot Tin Roof *(1955),* Suddenly, Last Summer *(1951),* Sweet Bird of Youth *(1959), and* The Night of the Iguana *(1961).*

READING FOR IDEAS The following essay is taken from Williams's memoirs and describes how fame—far from invigorating him—caused him enormous depression. As you read the essay, try to understand the tragic irony of Williams's analysis.

1   This winter marked the third anniversary of the Chicago opening of "The Glass Menagerie," an event that terminated one part of my life and began another about as different in all external circumstances as could well be imagined. I was snatched out of virtual oblivion and thrust into sudden prominence, and from the precarious tenancy of furnished rooms about the country I was removed to a suite in a first-class Manhattan hotel. My experience was not unique. Success has often come that abruptly into the lives of Americans. The Cinderella story is our favorite national myth, the cornerstone of the film industry if not of the Democracy itself. I have seen it enacted on the screen so often that I was now inclined to yawn at it, not with disbelief but with an attitude of Who Cares! Anyone with such beautiful teeth and hair as the screen protagonist of such a story was bound to have a good time one way or another, and you could bet your bottom dollar and all the tea in China that that one would not be caught dead or alive at any meeting involving a social conscience.

2   No, my experience was not exceptional, but neither was it quite ordinary, and if you are willing to accept the somewhat eclectic proposition that I had not been writing with such an experience in mind—and many people are not willing to believe that a playwright is interested in anything but popular success—there may be some point in comparing the two estates.

3   The sort of life that I had had previous to this popular success was one that required endurance, a life of clawing and scratching along a sheer surface and holding on tight with raw fingers to every inch of rock higher than the one caught hold of before, but it was a good life because it was the sort of life for which the human organism is created.

4   I was not aware of how much vital energy had gone into this struggle until the struggle was removed. I was out on a level plateau with my arms still thrashing and my lungs still grabbing at air that no longer resisted. This was security at last.

5   I sat down and looked about me and was suddenly very depressed. I thought to myself, this is just a period of adjustment. Tomorrow morning I will wake up in this first-class hotel suite above the discreet hum of an East Side boulevard and I will appreciate its elegance and luxuriate in its comforts and know that I have arrived at our American plan of Olympus. Tomorrow morning when I look at the green satin sofa I will fall in love with it. It is only temporarily that the green satin looks like slime on stagnant water.

6   But in the morning the inoffensive little sofa looked more revolting than the night before, and I was already getting too fat for the $125 suit which a fashionable acquaintance had selected for me. In the suite things began to break accidentally. An arm came off the sofa. Cigarette burns appeared on the polished surface of the furniture. Windows were left open and a rainstorm flooded the suite. But the maid always put it straight and the patience of the management was inexhaustible. Late parties could not offend them seriously. Nothing short of a demolition bomb seemed to bother my neighbors.

7   I lived on room service. But in this, too, there was a disenchantment. Some time between the moment when I ordered dinner over the phone and when it was rolled into my living room like a corpse on a rubber-wheeled table, I lost all interest in it. Once I ordered a sirloin steak and a chocolate sundae, but everything was so cunningly disguised on the table that I mistook the chocolate sauce for gravy and poured it over the sirloin steak.

8   Of course all this was the more trivial aspect of a spiritual dislocation that began to manifest itself in far more disturbing ways. I soon found myself becoming indifferent

to people. A well of cynicism rose in me. Conversations all sounded as if they had been recorded years ago and were being played back on a turntable. Sincerity and kindliness seemed to have gone out of my friends' voices. I suspected them of hypocrisy. I stopped calling them, stopped seeing them. I was impatient of what I took to be inane flattery.

9   I got so sick of hearing people say, "I loved your play!" that I could not say "thank you" any more. I choked on the words and turned rudely away from the usually sincere person. I no longer felt any pride in the play itself but began to dislike it, probably because I felt too lifeless inside ever to create another. I was walking around dead in my shoes and I knew it, but there were no friends I knew or trusted sufficiently, at that time, to take them aside and tell them what was the matter.

10   This curious condition persisted about three months, till late spring, when I decided to have another eye operation mainly because of the excuse it gave me to withdraw from the world behind a gauze mask. It was my fourth eye operation, and perhaps I should explain that I had been afflicted for about five years with a cataract on my left eye which required a series of needling operations and finally an operation on the muscle of the eye. (The eye is still in my head. So much for that.)

11   Well, the gauze mask served a purpose. While I was resting in the hospital, the friends whom I had neglected or affronted in one way or another began to call on me and now that I was in pain and darkness, their voices seemed to have changed, or rather that unpleasant mutation which I had suspected earlier in the season had now disappeared and they sounded now as they had used to sound in the lamented days of my obscurity. Once more they were sincere and kindly voices with the ring of truth in them and that quality of understanding for which I had originally sought them out.

12   As far as my physical vision was concerned, this last operation was only relatively successful (although it left me with an apparently clear black pupil in the right position, or nearly so) but in another, figurative way, it had served a much deeper purpose.

13   When the gauze mask was removed, I found myself in a readjusted world. I checked out of the handsome suite at the first-class hotel, packed my papers and a few incidental belongings, and left for Mexico, an elemental country where you can quickly forget the false dignities and conceits imposed by success, a country where vagrants innocent as children curl up to sleep on the pavements and human voices, especially when their language is not familiar to the ear, are soft as birds'. My public self, that artifice of mirrors, did not exist here, and so my natural being was resumed.

14   Then, as a final act of restoration, I settled for a while at Chapala to work on a play called "The Poker Night," which later became "A Streetcar Named Desire." It is only in his work that an artist can find reality and satisfaction, for the actual world is less intense than the world of his invention, and consequently his life, without recourse to violent disorder, does not seem very substantial. The right condition for him is that in which his work is not only convenient but unavoidable.

15   For me a convenient place to work is a remote place among strangers where there is good swimming. But life should require a certain minimal effort. You should not have too many people waiting on you, you should have to do most things for yourself. Hotel service is embarrassing. Maids, waiters, bellhops, porters and so forth are the most embarrassing people in the world for they continually remind you of inequities which we accept as the proper thing. The sight of an ancient woman gasping and wheezing as she drags a heavy

pail of water down a hotel corridor to mop up the mess of some drunken over privileged guest is one that sickens and weighs upon the heart and withers it with shame for this world in which it is not only tolerated but regarded as proof positive that the wheels of Democracy are functioning as they should without interference from above or below. Nobody should have to clean up anybody else's mess in this world. It is terribly bad for both parties, but probably worse for the one receiving the service.

16   I have been corrupted as much as anyone else by the vast number of menial services which our society has grown to expect and depend on. We should do for ourselves or let the machines do for us, the glorious technology that is supposed to be the new light of the world. We are like a man who has bought a great amount of equipment for a camping trip, who has the canoe and the tent and the fishing lines and the axe and the guns, the mackinaw and the blankets, but who now, when all the preparations and the provisions are piled expertly together, is suddenly too timid to set out on the journey but remains where he was yesterday and the day before and the day before that, looking suspiciously through white lace curtains at the clear sky he distrusts. Our great technology is a God-given chance for adventure and for progress which we are afraid to attempt. Our ideas and our ideals remain exactly what they were and where they were three centuries ago. No. I beg your pardon. It is no longer safe for a man even to declare them!

17   This is a long excursion from a small theme into a large one which I did not intend to make, so let me go back to what I was saying before.

18   This is an oversimplification. One does not escape that easily from the seduction of an effete way of life. You cannot arbitrarily say to yourself: I will now continue my life as it was before this thing, Success, happened to me. But once you fully apprehend the vacuity of a life without struggle you are equipped with the basic means of salvation. Once you know this is true, that the heart of man; his body and his brain are forged in a white-hot furnace for the purpose of conflict (the struggle of creation) and that with the conflict removed, the man is a sword cutting daisies, that not privation but luxury is the wolf at the door and that the fangs of this wolf are all the little vanities and conceits and laxities that Success is heir to—why, then with this knowledge you are at least in a position of knowing where danger lies.

19   You know, then, that the public Somebody you are when you "have a name" is a fiction created with mirrors and that the only somebody worth being is the solitary and unseen you that existed from your first breath and which is the sum of your actions and so is constantly in a state of becoming under your own volition—and knowing these things, you can even survive the catastrophe of Success!

20   It is never altogether too late, unless you embrace the Bitch Goddess, as William James called her, with both arms and find in her smothering caresses exactly what the homesick little boy in you always wanted, absolute protection and utter effortlessness. Security is a kind of death, I think, and it can come to you in a storm of royalty checks beside a kidney-shaped pool in Beverly Hills or anywhere at all that is removed from the conditions that made you an artist, if that's what you are or were or intended to be. Ask anyone who has experienced the kind of success I am talking about—What good is it? Perhaps to get an honest answer you will have to give him a shot of truth serum, but the word he will finally groan is unprintable in genteel publications.

21   Then what is good? The obsessive interest in human affairs, plus a certain amount of compassion and moral conviction, that first made the experience of living something that must be translated into pigment or music or bodily movement or poetry or prose or anything that's dynamic and expressive—that's what's good for you if you're at all serious in your aims. William Saroyan wrote a great play on this theme, that purity of heart is the one success worth having. "In the time of your life—live!" That time is short and it doesn't return again. It is slipping away while I write this and while you read it, and the monosyllable of the clock is Loss, loss, loss, unless you devote your heart to its opposition.

■ *Vocabulary*

catastrophe (title)	inoffensive (6)	figurative (12)
oblivion (1)	inexhaustible (6)	conceits (13)
prominence (1)	demolition (6)	vagrants (13)
precarious (1)	disenchantment (7)	restoration (14)
tenancy (1)	inane (8)	inequities (15)
eclectic (2)	affronted 11)	vacuity (18)
plateau (4)	mutilation (11)	
stagnant (5)	obscurity (11)	

■ *Questions on Meaning and Technique*

1. According to the author, what is the astounding and ironic part about suddenly becoming famous? Which, if any, of your acquaintances have suffered similar effects? Tell their story.

2. How does Williams use poetic language to enhance his writing? Cite at least three examples from the essay and indicate how they work.

3. How did the author react to people who told him how much they loved his play? How do you explain this reaction?

4. What incident temporarily changed the author's attitude toward people? Explain what happened to him externally as well as internally.

5. What follows Williams's description of his eye surgery? Is this next passage relevant or does it intrude onto the main point of the essay? Explain your answer.

6. What is Williams's opinion on the worth of machinery in our modern age? How should human beings relate to it? Do you agree with Williams's opinion?

7. Why did Williams leave to work in Chapala? How does Williams explain his move? Do you agree with his observations about work? Why or why not?

8. According to Williams, what conditions are necessary for creative writing? Do you think these conditions apply to all artists? Explain your answers.

9. What is Williams's conclusion to his philosophical musings about success and creativity? See if you can word it in one sentence.

Writing Assignments

1. Write an essay in which you analyze the effects of fame and luxury on certain people whom you have observed. Begin with a thesis and support it with appropriate details.

2. Write an essay in which you imagine suddenly receiving a large fortune in money. Describe the kind of life you would lead. Would you continue working? Would you move to another place? What would your attitude be toward your friends and other people?

STUDENT ESSAY—FIRST DRAFT

Ryyan Joye

English 1200

East Carolina University

The Coffee Virgin

1   "What is so magical about a cup of coffee?" I had asked myself this question

repeatedly

~~over and over again for many years~~ without knowing the answer. Coffee seemed to be   *cut deadwood*

what got millions of people worldwide going in the morning. For years I had observed

virtues

TV commercials, billboards, magazine ads, and store signs—all raving about the ~~glories~~   *word*

of coffee. Even when I traveled to South America, I couldn't escape the commercials

extoling coffee. However, I had never experienced first hand the joy or importance of a

cup of coffee. Because I had never tasted this brew, fearing that it might turn me into an

addict I decided to put an end to my innocence by driving down the street to where   *^,*

"America's best cup of coffee" is made—Starbucks.

2   It was a chilly Sunday afternoon, and, brimming with curiosity, ~~I was walking past~~

~~the two pillars in front of the Starbucks building. Cars zoom by behind me on Greenville~~   *unnecessary*
details
~~Boulevard, and the large shopping plaza sign, "La Promenade" looms to my left. Empty~~

~~tables and chairs sit lonely in the cold, and~~ I found myself walking through the arch of

the café, pulling the door open by its silver handle, and stepping inside a large,

attractive room. I was immediately greeted by a rush of warm air, the gentle sound of

music, and the rich smell of coffee beans. On my left, two couches with greenish gray

cushions were separated by an oval, wooden table ~~that was~~ cluttered with newspapers

tighten up the writing

and magazines. ~~Light is streaming in on the table from a large window on the western~~ ~~wall.~~ Next to my right hip, a cylindrical trash can rested comfortably on the sepia

tense

                                                                    stood
tiled floor. A news rack housing *The New York Times* ~~stands~~ next to the trash can.

Behind the news rack was a table on which I spotted assorted dishware holding such

trimmings as half and half, cinnamon, sugar, nutmeg, straws, stirrers, and napkins.

tense

                                                           were
Shelves laden with every imaginable coffee machine ~~are~~ situated in direct view of any

customer seated nearby. Also in close range, on another shelf, I saw the top eighteen

Starbucks coffees displayed in shiny brown sacks, standing silently, like respectful

soldiers.

Does not advance the narrative

3   ~~A wooden, rectangular table — located in between the Starbucks counter and a small~~

~~seating area—is behind the stand. A three-inch wooden panel runs around the walls of~~

~~Starbucks. Above the panel, the wall is painted a pastel green and it has jade wall~~

~~treatment below the panel.~~

4   "Can I help you?" asked a polite voice from behind the main counter. My eyes were

tense

                                                                       was
met by those of a Starbucks employee who engaged my attention. She ~~is~~ shorter than

case/tense

     I   *was*
~~me~~ and ~~is~~ wearing black pants, a hunter green shirt, and a green Starbucks apron,

tense

                                                            was
on which was embroidered "Kendra." Her streaked brown hair ~~is~~ pulled back into a

fashionable ponytail with ringlets cascading down to her jaw line. I looked at her and

explained somewhat sheepishly, "I have never had a cup of coffee and would like to

observe the café and interview customers to figure out what coffee I should try." With a

smile that revealed a hint of disbelief, she answered, "Oh, please have a seat, and when

you're ready, just come up to me and place your order." Well, so far my experiment

tense

had not been   *turning around and walking*
~~was certainly not~~ unpleasant. "Thank you," I said, ~~and turn around and walk~~ to an

tenses

                took   *could*   *was*
empty wooden table. I ~~take~~ the chair on the left side of the table so I ~~can~~ monitor who ~~is~~

coming through the door.

5   A man with a graying brown beard, wearing a black Nissan jacket, suddenly

bounded through the door and over to the counter, where he picked up an empty cup.

tense

       walked   *picked*   *poured*
He ~~walks~~ to the condiment table, ~~picks~~ up one of the shakers, and ~~pours~~ some powdery

word

                          sauntered
substance into his cup. Then he ~~walked casually~~ back towards the service counter,

tense

                         paid
where he ordered a drink and ~~pays~~ for it. "Here's my chance," I told myself. Screwing up

my courage, I got his attention and asked shyly, "Excuse me, Sir, but what coffee did you order?"

Ah," he answered with the tone of true a connoisseur, "I always order a double-shot cappuccino because it ~~really~~ gives me a lightning bolt of new energy." I asked him what he sprinkled into the cup, and he explained that it was cinnamon and sugar. "It's smokin'," he cried out. I instinctively retreated from this concentrated coffee drink, fearing that it would cause me jitters and a quickened heart beat.

Notice paragraph indentation and punctuation for dialogue

6   ~~While Kendra makes his drink, I notice that the Starbucks has a drive-thru window. Melissa, another employee of Starbucks, is speaking into her headset to communicate with the customer. The wall juts out a little as I scan the area to the right of the drive thru. The sanitation score, 96.0, is set inside a black frame. Hanging on the wall are three boards. The board to the far left has the list of beverages such as lattes, teas, and hot chocolates. The board in the center is black and the special of the day is written on it in neon markers. On the far right, the Whole Bean board displays the "real" coffees. week, decaf Verona a combination of Latin American and Indian coffees. A one pound bag cost more than ten dollars.~~

too many unnecessary details

7   A gust of ~~old~~ (cold) air suddenly ~~enters~~ (swept through) the coffee shop when a woman wearing a black sweater, black pants, black boots, and a black jacket made her striking appearance. After she ordered a "grande white cappuccino," I felt an immediate kinship with her and asked if I could interview her about her drink. She agreed amiably and introduced herself as Layne Johnson. She explained to me that she was a big fan of Starbucks and came in to get a drink ~~two times~~ (twice) a day every day of the week! When I asked what drink she would suggest to a first-time coffee drinker like myself, she narrowed her eyes, wrinkled her forehead, and tightened her lips as if deep in thought. "As a virgin coffee drinker, ~~I think~~ you should try a white chocolate mocha—just to get your feet wet. Everyone loves the white chocolate mocha. Later you can add some diversity to it." She then picked up her own cup of waiting coffee and promptly sat down to read a book titled *Love, Sex, and Marriage Through the Ages*, probably her homework for a psychology class. I began to form some important insights into the mythological effect(s) of coffee. It evidently even helped students to enjoy their homework.

better vocabulary

word

Dangling

plural

conjunction
tense

      as if   *had*

8   It seemed ~~like~~ Layne, brought business and movement with her, because shortly after she had arrived, many more people began entering Starbucks. An older couple shopped around for a bag of coffee; a group of friends chatted loudly near the stand adjacent to me; a man rushed into the men's restroom; and the man who had been sitting in front of me packed up his belongings and left.

Adds
nothing,
so delete

9   ~~I began speaking with the group of three friends. They were older ladies, their ages probably ranging from forty to fifty. I asked them what drink they would suggest a first-time coffee drinker have. They spoke amongst themselves and finally decided that the house blend would be the best. They ordered their drinks and one of the ladies ordered a hot chocolate. When I questioned her about this, she explained that she had stopped drinking coffee years ago.~~

10   Eventually, a lull in the business occurred, and I went to the counter for a closer inspection of the muffins and cookies. While I looked at the prices, a girl came in and stood next to me to order her drink. I told her that I was a first-time coffee drinker and asked her what she recommended that I drink. She immediately touted the white chocolate mocha. "It's the queen of coffee drinks," she insisted fervently. She then asked Kendra to give me a sample. Kendra gave me more than a sample; she gave me my very own complimentary cup of white chocolate mocha. I was perilously ~~on my way~~ *close* to losing my coffee virginity. What would be the results, I wondered.

succinct

logical
sequence
tense

studied   *Then,*

11   I stood and ~~sipped~~ the sweet-smelling mocha from the tall Starbucks cup, I took a

is

tiny sip and swirled it around in my mouth. "Yum! This ~~will~~ not ~~be~~ difficult to tolerate," I said to myself. After another two sips, followed by a full gulp, I was in love. Kendra asked me if I liked the drink, and I replied. "It's to die for." Melissa, Kendra's co-worker, told me that white chocolate mocha was also her favorite drink. It seemed to me that it should be the favorite drink of all people in the entire world. The effect was soothing, full, and opulent; moreover, it dripped of sumptuousness comfort. I sat back in my chair to enjoy the rest of the white chocolate mocha.

12   After drinking my first cup of coffee, I now understand the causes behind everyone's attachment to coffee. I understand why everyone seems to like waking up to

wordy

it every morning. Although most people drink coffee for energy ~~in the morning~~, or for the delicious ~~smell~~ *odor* it gives out, coffee is more than just caffeine. Its effects are downright   *better word*

seductive as well as multi faceted. For some, holding a cup of coffee in their hand

promotes relaxation while they ~~accomplishing~~ certain intellectual tasks. For others, it is   *tense*

a tradition, a routine, *Many others simply* ~~Yet others;~~ like the atmosphere it creates among friends, and the

warmth it provides during cold weather. Finally, I had come to understand the causes

behind all of the hype about coffee. I too would join the army of coffee drinkers because I

had been awakened to its allure. I was no longer a coffee virgin.

S T U D E N T   E S S A Y — F I N A L   D R A F T

Joye 1

Ryyan Joye

English 1200

East Carolina University

The Coffee Virgin

1   What is so magical about a cup of coffee?" I had asked myself

that question repeatedly for many years without knowing the

answer. Coffee seemed to be what got millions of people worldwide

going in the morning. For years I had observed TV commercials, bill-

boards, magazine ads, and store signs—all raving about the virtues

of coffee. Even when I traveled to South America, I couldn't escape

the commercials extolling coffee. However, I had never experienced

first hand the joy or importance of a cup of coffee. Because I had

never tasted this brew, fearing that it might turn me into an addict, I

decided to put an end to my innocence by driving down the street to

where "America's best cup of coffee" is made—Starbucks.

2   It was a chilly Sunday afternoon and, brimming with curiosity, I

found myself walking through the arch of the café, pulling the door open by its silver handle, and stepping inside a large, attractive room. I was immediately greeted by a rush of warm air, the gentle sound of music, and the rich aroma of coffee beans. On my left, two couches with greenish gray cushions were separated by an oval, wooden table, cluttered with newspapers and magazines. Next to my right hip, a cylindrical trash can rested comfortably on the sepia tiled floor. A news rack housing *The New York Times* stood next to the trash can. Behind the news rack was a table on which I spotted assorted dishware, holding such trimmings as half and half, cinnamon, sugar, nutmeg, straws, stirrers, and napkins. Shelves laden with every imaginable coffee machine were situated in direct view of any customer seated nearby. Also in close range, on another shelf, I saw the top eighteen Starbucks coffees displayed in shiny brown sacks, standing silently, like respectful soldiers.

3   "Can I help you?" asked a polite voice from behind the main counter. My eyes were met by those of a Starbucks employee who engaged my attention. She was shorter than I and was wearing black pants, a hunter green shirt, and a green Starbucks apron, on which was embroidered the name "Kendra." Her streaked brown hair was pulled back into a fashionable ponytail with ringlets cascading down to her jaw line. I looked at her and explained somewhat sheepishly, "I have never had a cup of coffee and would like to observe the café and interview customers to figure out what coffee I should try." With a smile that revealed a hint of disbelief, she answered, "Oh, please have a seat, and when you're ready, just come up to me and place your order." Well, so far my

Joye 3

experiment had not been unpleasant. "Thank you," I said, turning around and walking to an empty wooden table. I took the chair on the left side of the table so I could monitor who was coming through the door.

4   A man with a graying brown beard, wearing a black Nissan jacket, suddenly bounded through the door and over to the counter, where he picked up an empty cup. He walked to the condiment table, picked up one of the shakers, and poured some powdery substance into his cup. Then he sauntered back towards the service counter, where he ordered a drink and paid for it. "Here's my chance," I told myself. Screwing up my courage, I got his attention and asked shyly, "Excuse me, Sir, but what coffee did you order?"

5   "Ah," he answered with the tone of a connoisseur, "I always order a double-shot cappuccino because it really gives me a lightning bolt of new energy." I asked him what he sprinkled into the cup, and he explained that it was cinnamon and sugar. "It's smokin'," he cried out. I instinctively retreated from his concentrated coffee drink, fearing that it would cause me jitters and a quickened heart beat.

6   A gust of cold air suddenly swept through the coffee shop when a woman wearing a black sweater, black boots, and a black jacket made her striking appearance. After she ordered a "grande white cappuccino," I felt an immediate kinship with her and asked if I could interview her about her drink. She agreed amiably and introduced herself as Layne Johnson. She explained to me that she

Joye 4

was a big fan of Starbucks and came in to get a drink twice a day every day of the week! When I asked what drink she would suggest to a first-time coffee drinker like myself, she narrowed her eyes, wrinkled her forehead, and tightened her lips as if deep in thought. "As a virgin coffee drinker, you should try a white chocolate mocha—just to get your feet wet. Everyone loves the white chocolate mocha. Later you can add some diversity to it." She then picked up her own waiting cup of coffee and promptly sat down to read a book titled *Love, Sex, and Marriage Through the Ages*, probably her homework for a psychology class. I began to form some important insights into the mythological effects of coffee. It evidently even helped students to enjoy their homework.

7   It seemed as if Layne had brought business and movement with her, because shortly after she had arrived, many more people began entering Starbucks. An older couple shopped around for a bag of coffee, a group of friends chatted loudly near the stand adjacent to me, a man rushed into the men's restroom, and the man who had been sitting in front of me packed up his belongings and left.

8   Eventually, a lull in the business occurred, and I went to the counter for a closer inspection of the muffins and cookies. While I looked at the prices, a girl came in and stood next to me to order her drink. I told her that I was a first-time coffee drinker and asked her what she recommended that I drink. She immediately touted the white chocolate mocha. "It's the queen of coffee drinks," she insisted fervently. She then asked Kendra to give me a sample.

Joye 5

Kendra gave me more than a sample; she gave me my very own complimentary cup of white chocolate mocha. I was perilously close to losing my coffee virginity. What would be the results, I wondered.

9   I stood and studied the sweet-smelling mocha from the tall Starbucks cup. Then, I took a tiny sip and swirled it around in my mouth. "Yum! This is not difficult to tolerate," I said to myself. After another two sips, followed by a full gulp, I was in love. Kendra asked me if I liked the drink, and I replied. "It's to die for." Melissa, Kendra's co-worker, told me that the white chocolate mocha was her favorite drink. It seemed to me that it should be the favorite drink of all people in the entire world. I sat back in my chair to enjoy the rest of the white chocolate mocha.

10   After drinking my first cup of coffee, I now understand the causes behind everyone's attachment to coffee. I understand why everyone likes waking up to it every morning. Although most people drink coffee for energy or for the delicious odor it gives out, coffee is more than just caffeine. Its effects are downright seductive as well as multifaceted. For some, holding a cup of coffee in their hand promotes relaxation while they accomplish certain intellectual tasks. For others, it is a tradition, a routine. Many others simply like the atmosphere it creates among friends, and the warmth it provides during cold weather. Finally, I had come to understand the causes behind all of the hype about coffee. I too would join the army of coffee drinkers because I had been awakened to its allure. I was no longer a coffee virgin.

STEPHEN KING

Why We Crave Horror Movies

Stephen King (b. 1947) is a prolific writer of horror books and movies that have scared and captivated millions of readers and viewers. Among his blockbuster hits are such modern favorites as Carrie *(1974),* The Shining *(1977), and* The Green Mile *(1999). Before breaking out as a popular writer, King taught high school English. Stephen is the 2003 recipient of the National Book Foundation's Medal for Distinguished Contribution to American Letters.*

READING FOR IDEAS   King dares us to face our true inner selves and admit we are all partly crazy and watch horror movies to find release from our internal nightmares. As you read, think of other motives for watching horror movies. Ask yourself if watching horror really is an excellent way to get rid of pent-up negative emotions or if other more calming influences might work better.

1   I think that we are all mentally ill: those of us outside the asylums only hide it a little better—and maybe not all that much better, after all. We've all known people who talk to themselves, people who sometimes squinch their faces into horrible grimaces when they believe no one is watching, people who have some hysterical fear—of snakes, the dark, the tight place, the long drop . . . and, of course, those final worms and grubs that are waiting so patiently underground.

2   When we pay four or five bucks and seat ourselves at tenth-row center in a theater showing a horror movie, we are daring the nightmare.

3   Why? Some of the reasons are simple and obvious. To show that we can, that we are not afraid, that we can ride this roller coaster. Which is not to say that a really good horror movie may not surprise a scream out of us at some point, the way we may scream when the roller coaster twists through a complete 360 or plows through a lake at the bottom of the drop. And horror movies, like roller coasters, have always been the special province of the young; by the time one turns 40 or 50, one's appetite for double twists or 360-degree loops may be considerably depleted.

4   We also go to re-establish our feelings of essential normality; the horror movie is innately conservative, even reactionary. Freda Jackson as the horrible melting woman in *Die, Monster, Die!* confirms for us that no matter how far we may be removed from the beauty of a Robert Redford or a Diana Ross, we are still light-years from true ugliness.

5   And we go to have fun.

6   Ah, but this is where the ground starts to slope away, isn't it? Because this is a very peculiar sort of fun indeed. The fun comes from seeing others menaced—sometimes killed. One critic has suggested that if pro football has become the voyeur's version of combat, then the horror film has become the modern version of the public lynching.

7   It is true that the mythic, "fairy tale" horror film intends to take away the shades of gray. . . . It urges us to put away our more civilized and adult penchant for analysis and to become children again, seeing things in pure blacks and whites. It may be that horror movies provide psychic relief on this level because this invitation to lapse into simplicity, irrationality and even outright madness is extended so rarely. We are told we may allow our emotions a free rein . . . or no rein at all.

8   If we are all insane, then sanity becomes a matter of degree. If your insanity leads you to carve up women like Jack the Ripper or the Cleveland Torso Murderer, we clap you away in the funny farm (but neither of those two amateur-night surgeons was ever caught, heh-heh-heh); if, on the other hand your insanity leads you only to talk to yourself when you're under stress or to pick your nose on the morning bus, then you are left alone to go about your business . . . though it is doubtful that you will ever be invited to the best parties.

9   The potential lyncher is in almost all of us (excluding saints, past and present; but then, most saints have been crazy in their own ways), and every now and then, he has to be let loose to scream and roll around in the grass. Our emotions and our fears form their own body, and we recognize that it demands its own exercise to maintain proper muscle tone. Certain of these emotional muscles are accepted—even exalted—in civilized society; they are, of course, the emotions that tend to maintain the status quo of civilization itself. Love, friendship, loyalty, kindness—these are the emotions that we applaud, emotions that have been immortalized in the couplets of Hallmark cards. . . .

10   When we exhibit these emotions, society showers us with positive reinforcement; we learn this even before we get out of diapers. When, as children, we hug our rotten little puke of a sister and give her a kiss, all the aunts and uncles smile and twit and cry, "Isn't he the sweetest little thing?" Such coveted treats as chocolate-covered graham crackers often follow. But if we deliberately slam the rotten little puke of a sister's fingers in the door, sanctions follow—angry remonstrance from parents, aunts and uncles; instead of a chocolate-covered graham cracker, a spanking.

11   But anticivilization emotions don't go away, and they demand periodic exercise. We have such "sick" jokes as, "What's the difference between a truckload of bowling balls and a truck-load of dead babies?" (You can't unload a truckload of bowling balls with a pitchfork . . . a joke, by the way, that I heard originally from a ten-year-old.) Such a joke may surprise a laugh or a grin out of us even as we recoil, a possibility that confirms the thesis: If we share a brotherhood of man, then we also share an insanity of man. None of which is intended as a defense of either the sick joke or insanity but merely as an explanation of why the best horror films, like the best fairy tales, manage to be reactionary, anarchistic, and revolutionary all at the same time.

12   The mythic horror movie, like the sick joke, has a dirty job to do. It deliberately appeals to all that is worst in us. It is morbidity unchained, our most base instincts let free, our nastiest fantasies realized . . . and it all happens, fittingly enough, in the dark. For those reasons, good liberals often shy away from horror films. For myself, I like to see the most aggressive of them—*Dawn of the Dead,* for instance—as lifting a trap door in the civilized forebrain and throwing a basket of raw meat to the hungry alligators swimming around in that subterranean river beneath.

13   Why bother? Because it keeps them from getting out, man. It keeps them down there and me up here. It was Lennon and McCartney who said that all you need is love, and I would agree with that.

14   As long as you keep the gators fed.

■ *Vocabulary*

asylums (1)	menaced (6)	remonstrance (10)
squinch (1)	voyeur's (6)	recoil (11)
grimaces (1)	mythic (7)	anarchistic (11)
innately (4)	penchant (7)	morbidity (12)
reactionary (4)	immortalized (9)	

■ *Questions on Meaning and Technique*

1. What does the author mean when he begins his essay by announcing that "we are all mentally ill"? Do you buy this basic assumption about us? Give reasons for your answer.

2. According to King, what is the reason we gladly pay the admission price for a ticket to see a horror movie? Explain what he means. If you disagree with King, then what do you think is the reason so many people go to see horror films?

3. What analogy does the author use to explain the feeling a viewer has when he or she watches a horror movie? Does the analogy work for you? What other analogy could you use?

4. What does King mean by the terms *essential normality, conservative,* and *reactionary* as used in paragraph 4? Explain each term as you understand it. Give examples if needed.

5. In what way, according to the author, do horror movies turn us back into children? Do you agree with the author's view? Why or why not?

6. What literary device does King use in paragraph 9 to explain why watching horror movies can help us control dangerous emotions? Is the device effective? Why or why not?

7. What are some examples of the author's occasional use of informal English and even slang in this essay? What effect does this mixture of English levels produce? Does it bother you or do you like it? Point to specific passages that you find either effective or not effective.

8. What, according to King, makes the difference between the insanity of a normal person and that of someone in jail or in a mental hospital? What distinction do you make? Provide an example to make your case.

9. What implied promise resides in the title of this essay? Do you think the author fulfilled the promise? Support your answer with evidence from the essay.

10. According to King, why do we need to exercise the body of unacceptable emotions, such as fear, anger, violence? Do you agree with his method, or do you think there are better ways to handle these emotions?

Writing Assignments

1. Write an essay giving the reasons why watching horror movies is a waste of time at best and psychologically harmful at worst.

2. Remembering a horror movie you once saw, write an essay about any special effects that impressed you. Be sure to provide enough details so the reader can understand your essay.

FURTHER READING

WILLIAM MAXWELL

Nearing Ninety

William Maxwell (1908–2000) was known both as an editor (for the prestigious New Yorker) and as a fiction writer. In the early 1930s, he was also an English professor at the University of Illinois. His first novel, Right Center of Heaven, *was published to strong critical acclaim in 1934. It was followed by five other novels:* They Came Like Swallows *(1937),* The Folded Leaf *(1946),* Time Will Darken It *(1949), and* So Long, See You Tomorrow, *published in 1989 when Maxwell was 81 years old. His short stories have been printed in numerous anthologies and collections.*

READING FOR IDEAS   Ninety is something of a milestone span. Most people do not get to live that long and are curious about what is it like to have experienced such longevity. The author is direct and candid about how turning ninety affected him. His outlook is strongly flavored with a mid-western atmosphere and sensitivity. Refreshingly absent is any evangelical pitch for a certain lifestyle or diet or exercise routine. We get the impression that turning ninety is as mystifying to him as it would seem to us. As John Lennon said, "Life is what happens to you when you're busy doing something else."

1   Out of the corner of my eye I see my ninetieth birthday approaching. It is one year and six months away. How long after that will I be the person I am now?

2   I don't yet need a cane, but I have a feeling that my table manners have deteriorated. My posture is what you would expect of someone addicted to sitting in front of a typewriter, but it was always that way. "Stand up straight," my father would say to me. "You're all bent over like an old man." It didn't bother me then and it doesn't now, though I agree that an erect carriage is a pleasure to see, in someone of any age.

3   I have regrets but there are not very many of them and, fortunately, I forget what they are. I forget names, too, but it is not yet serious. What I am trying to remember and can't, quite often my wife will remember. And vice versa. She is in and out during the day, but I know she will be home when evening comes, and so I am never lonely. Long ago,

a neighbor in the country, looking at our flower garden, said, "Children and roses reflect their care." This is true of the very old as well.

4   Though there have been a great many changes in the world since I came into it on August 16, 1908, I try not to deplore. It is not constructive and there is no point in discouraging the young by invidious comparisons with the way things used to be.

5   I am not — I think I am not — afraid of dying. When I was seventeen I worked on a farm in southern Wisconsin, near Portage. It was no ordinary farm and not much serious farming was done there, but it had the look of a place that has been lived in, and loved, for a good long time. I was no more energetic than most adolescents, but the family forgave my failures and shortcomings and simply took me in, let me be one of them. The farm had come down in that family through several generations, from the man who had pioneered it to a woman who was so alive that everything and everybody seemed to revolve around her personality. She lived well into her nineties and then one day told her oldest daughter that she didn't want to live anymore, that she was tired. Though I was not present but only heard about it in a letter, this remark reconciled me to my own inevitable extinction. I could believe that enough is enough. One must also, if possible, reconcile oneself to life. To horrors (the number of legless peasants in Cambodia) that if you allowed yourself to think about them more than briefly would turn your heart to stone.

6   Because I actively enjoy sleeping, dreams, the unexplainable dialogues that take place in my head as I am drifting off, all that, I tell myself that lying down to an afternoon nap that goes on and on through eternity is not something to be concerned about. What spoils this pleasant fancy is the recollection that when people are dead they don't read books. This I find unbearable. No Tolstoy, no Chekhov, no Elizabeth Bowen, no Keats, no Rilke. One might as well be—

7   Before I am ready to call it quits, I would like to reread every book I have ever deeply enjoyed, beginning with Jane Austen and Isaac Babel and Sybille Bedford's *The Sudden View* and going through shelf after shelf of the bookcases until I arrive at the autobiographies of William Butler Yeats. As it is, I read a great deal of the time. I am harder to please, though. I see flaws in masterpieces. Conrad indulging in rhetoric when he would do better to get on with it. I would read all day long and well into the night if there were no other claims on my time. Appointments with doctors, with the dentist. The monthly bank statement. Income tax returns. And because I don't want to turn into a monster, people. Afternoon tea with X, dinner with the Y's. Our social life would be a good deal more active than it is if more than half of those I care about hadn't passed over to the other side. However, I remember them. I remember them more, and more vividly, the older I get.

8   I did not wholly escape the amnesia that overtakes children around the age of six, but I carried along with me more of my childhood than, I think, most people do. Once, after dinner, my father hitched up the horse and took my mother and me for a sleigh ride. The winter stars were very bright. The sleigh bells made a lovely sound. I was bundled up to the nose, between my father and mother, where nothing, not even the cold, could get at me. The very perfection of happiness.

9   At something like the same age, I went for a ride, again with my father and mother, on a riverboat at Havana, Illinois. It was a sidewheeler and the decks were screened, I suppose as protection against the mosquitoes. Across eight decades the name of the steamboat comes back to me—the Eastland—bringing with it the context of disaster.

A year later, at the dock in Chicago, too many of the passengers crowded on one side of the boat, waving goodbye, and it rolled over and sank. Trapped by the screens everywhere, a great many people lost their lives. The fact that I had been on this very steamboat, that I had escaped from a watery grave, I continued to remember all through my childhood.

10   I have liked remembering almost as much as I have liked living. But now it is different, I have to be careful. I can ruin a night's sleep by suddenly, in the dark, thinking about some particular time in my life. Before I can stop myself, it is as if I had driven a mineshaft down through layers and layers of the past and must explore, relive, remember, reconsider, until daylight delivers me.

11   I have not forgotten the pleasure, when our children were very young, of hoisting them onto my shoulders when their legs gave out. Of reading to them at bedtime. Of studying their beautiful faces. Of feeling responsible for their physical safety. But that was more than thirty years ago. I admire the way that, as adults, they have taken hold of life, and I am glad that they are not materialistic, but there is little or nothing I can do for them at this point, except write a little fable to put in their Christmas stocking. Our grandchild is too young to respond to any beguiling but his mother and father's. It will be touch and go whether I live long enough for us to enjoy being in each other's company.

12   "Are you writing?" people ask—out of politeness, undoubtedly. And I say, "Nothing very much." The truth but not the whole truth—which is that I seem to have lost touch with the place that stories and novels come from. I have no idea why.

13   I still like making sentences.

14   Every now and then, in my waking moments, and especially when I am in the country, I stand and look hard at everything.

■ *Vocabulary*

erect (2)	reconciled (5)	context (9)
deplore (4)	inevitable (5)	materialistic (11)
pioneered (5)	amnesia (8)	beguiling (11)

■ *Questions on Meaning and Technique*

1. Which of the effects related to old age and mentioned in the essay does the author find most unbearable? Explain your answer.

2. What technique does the author use in paragraph 2? What is the purpose? How effective is it?

3. How does the author treat the concept of regrets? What for him is fortunate about old age and regrets? Do you agree with his view? Why or why not?

4. Why do you think the author tries not to "deplore" the changes that have taken place in society over the span of his life? What motivates him to make this statement? What is your reaction?

5. Dying concerns all people, even the young. How do you feel about Maxwell's view that perhaps death is like taking a long, pleasant nap? If you have a similar or completely different view, describe and explain it.

6. What does Maxwell say he wants to do before he dies? Is his desire commendable or can you think of something better to do if you were close to death? Explain your answer.

7. The author admits that he needs to socialize occasionally rather than be a well-read recluse. Why does he believe that socializing is important? Do you agree with the author? Give reasons for your answer.

8. What are some of the peak experiences of his life, listed by the author? Looking back on your own life, what are at least three peak experiences you remember with great clarity?

9. What is the meaning of the final sentence of this essay? What do you think Maxwell intends it to mean?

Writing Assignments

1. Using Maxwell's recollection of childhood as your springboard, write an essay in which you describe two or three childhood memories that have remained with you to this day. Discuss the effect they have on you when you think of them as an adult looking back in time.

2. Write an essay in which you explore the causes underlying Maxwell's writing about what it is like to be old. What rewards do you believe he reaped from exploring this topic? Who might benefit from his thoughts?

Internet Research Assignment

With the help of some research, write a causal analysis on one of the following historical events:

   a. The Salem witch trials

   b. The Aaron Burr–Alexander Hamilton duel

   c. The explosion of the space shuttle *Challenger*

   d. The creation of labor unions

   e. The 1930s depression

   f. The Civil Rights movement of the 1960s

Additional Writing Assignments

1. Why do students seek a higher education? Write a causal analysis in which you offer the most important causes that drive students to continue their education, often beyond college into graduate school.

2. Write an essay in which you analyze the influence (effects) of your closest friend on your life. Be sure to supply vivid examples to enhance your essay.

3. What do you consider the major causes of the recent increase in drug trafficking and associated crimes? Develop an essay in which you deal with this question.

4. Think of a public figure whom you most dislike or distrust. Describe the trait that makes you dislike him or her, and find reasons for this trait. State both the trait and reasons for it in your thesis.

5. Political actions always have an effect on society—good or bad. Analyze the effect of one of the following political actions, were it to take place: national sales tax to replace income tax, free housing for all poor people, capital punishment for all first-degree murderers, compulsory military service for women, legalization of drugs, automobile taxes based on fuel consumption.

6. Explore the major causes for the high dropout rate in college. Summarize these causes in your thesis, and develop them into an essay.

7. Explore the major causes of the high divorce rate in the United States.

8. Most major cities in the United States are becoming increasingly culturally diverse, owing to large-scale immigration. Write an essay in which you explore the effects of this cultural diversity.

9. Write an essay analyzing the causes or effects of the escalating rate of obese people in the United States.

10. Write an essay analyzing the good or bad effects of any recent medical discovery, such as pacemakers, antidepressant medications, laser surgery, or genetic cloning.

11. Write an essay delineating the causes or effects of the explosion of social networking (e.g. Facebook, MySpace, Twitter, YouTube) in today's global environment.

12. Write an essay stating the reasons some people refuse to learn how to use a computer. (Or state the major effects of using a computer.)

Rewriting Assignment

A student has decided to write a causal analysis paper giving the reasons some women fall in love with men who are in prison for violent crimes. From thinking and reading about the subject, the student writes down the random thoughts listed here. Rewrite these thoughts into a sentence outline that includes at least three main topics. Begin with an appropriate thesis statement.

It's amazing how many women fall in love with prison inmates.

The men have committed violent crimes—even murder.

These women give and give—writing letters, contacting lawyers, bringing to prison items like photos, food, or reading materials.

I read in the newspaper that Richard Ramirez ("Night Stalker"), Ted Bundy (serial killer in Florida), and David Berkowitz ("Son of Sam") had lovers contacting them from outside of prison.

Even Timothy McVeigh, the Oklahoma City bomber, received offers of marriage while in prison.

What could possibly attract these women to such dreadful men? Are they crazy? Are they ignorant? Are they masochistic?

Possible motives:

Inmates offer perverted romance.

They have been betrayed into believing that the prisoner was not guilty.

Some of these men are brilliant.

They just fell in love like anyone else.

They had a father who was either often absent or didn't care—or never had a father.

Love from a distance adds to excitement and romance.

The woman feels that she's a Mother Teresa, helping someone who is down and out.

Whatever the motive, the situation is dangerous.

Bruce Ayres/Stone/Getty Images

Photo Writing Assignment

Causal analysis attempts to find physical or psychological connections between events to establish the reasons that something happened. Try to imagine a connection between the plight of the family in this photo and the society in which we live. Write an essay exploring the causes of the extreme poverty and other conditions depicted.

Digging for Gold or for Causes and Consequences

James Boswell, regarded by many as the greatest biographer ever, and Samuel Johnson, literary critic who was the subject of Boswell's groundbreaking *Life of Johnson*, went for a walk one evening. During their ramble, Boswell mentioned the name of a philosopher who believed that cause and effect were an illusion and asked Johnson how he could refute that man's complex arguments. Johnson replied, "I refute him thus!" and sent a stone flying across the road with a brisk kick. The result was a dramatic demonstration of cause and effect.

Compared to the writer, who must often scratch for cause and effect, the miner has daily confirmation that most things are propelled by physical principles of causation and its consequences. Pick the right spot to dig your mine and you'll be rewarded with a strike. Make a mistake and choose the wrong spot and your labor will have been in vain. This is cause and effect classically at work.

The writer, on the other hand, sometimes digs for material evidence to support a theory of cause and sometimes for intangible elements, such as motive or opportunity that might explain what happened. Often the possibilities lead to a dead-end and add no clarity to any conclusions. For example, in "The Girls in Their Summer Dresses," Frances, the young wife, is wrong in surmising that her husband looks at other women because he is planning to be unfaithful. The poem "Money" makes a blanket charge against money that is too glib to be universal. We cannot help but believe that Tennessee Williams would stop mewling about the "catastrophe of success" if he would reincarnate and try a taste of failure. Stephen King, in contrast, carefully probes the effect of horror movies on people and tries to explain the draw of the dark side; an equally moderate note is struck by William Maxwell, who writes about the effects of turning ninety.

Cause and effect are possibly the hardest of all phenomena to write about. In some instances, a simple relationship can be found to explain why something happened—a partygoer gets sick after drinking too much wine. But finding the cause for persistent alcohol abuse is not so easy and seldom solvable by snap judgments. The first case is characteristic of what the miner does; the second, with all its complexities and uncertainties, falls to the lot of the writer. In any case, you should always choose the logical reason to explain the cause of something rather than try to peer at reality through the colored spectacles of wishful thinking and hocus-pocus.

Chapter 15

Argumentation

STORY

LUIGI PIRANDELLO

War

Luigi Pirandello (1867–1936), Italian author and playwright, is regarded as one of the great playwrights of the twentieth-century European theater. Born in Sicily, Pirandello became professor of Italian literature at the Normal College for Women in Rome. He wrote seven novels and nearly three hundred stories, but he is best known for his grotesquely humorous plays such as Right You Are If You Think You Are *(1922),* The Pleasure of Honesty *(1923), and* Six Characters in Search of an Author *(1922). Pirandello won the Nobel Prize for literature in 1934.*

READING FOR IDEAS To lead off a chapter on argumentation with a short story may strike the reader as an odd choice, but the fact is a short story can be structured to support one point of view or another in an argumentative way. This short story, for example, "War" by Luigi Pirandello is antiwar and makes that point decisively in this tale of a random collection of passengers in a railway car, all of who have been affected by the war. The hub of the argument is a simple question: Is the war worth the cost in young lives? Decide for yourself whether or not it is.

1   The passengers who had left Rome by the night express had had to stop until dawn at the small station of Fabriano in order to continue their journey by the small old-fashioned local joining the main line with Sulmona.

2   At dawn, in a stuffy and smoky second-class carriage in which five people had already spent the night, a bulky woman in deep mourning was hoisted in—almost like a shapeless bundle. Behind her—puffing and moaning, followed her husband—a tiny man, thin and weakly, his face death-white, his eyes small and bright and looking shy and uneasy.

3   Having at last taken a seat he politely thanked the passengers who had helped his wife and who had made room for her; then he turned round to the woman trying to pull down the collar of her coat, and politely inquired:

4   "Are you all right, dear?"

5   The wife, instead of answering, pulled up her collar again to her eyes, so as to hide her face.

6   "Nasty world," muttered the husband with a sad smile.

7   And he felt it his duty to explain to his traveling companions that the poor woman was to be pitied for the war was taking away from her her only son, a boy of twenty to whom both had devoted their entire life, even breaking up their home at Sulmona to follow him to Rome, where he had to go as a student, then allowing him to volunteer for war with an assurance, however, that at least for six months he would not be sent to the front and now, all of a sudden, receiving a wire that he was due to leave in three days' time and asking them to go and see him off.

8   The woman under the big coat was twisting and wriggling, at times growling like a wild animal, feeling certain that all those explanations would not have aroused even a shadow of sympathy from those people who—most likely—were in the same plight as herself. One of them, who had been listening with particular attention, said:

9   "You should thank God that your son is only leaving now for the front. Mine has been sent there the first day of the war. He has already come back twice wounded and been sent back again to the front."

10   "What about me? I have two sons and three nephews at the front," said another passenger.

11   "Maybe, but in our case it is our only son," ventured the husband.

12   "What difference can it make? You may spoil your only son with excessive attentions, but you cannot love him more than you would all your other children if you had any. Paternal love is not like bread that can be broken into pieces and split amongst the children in equal shares. A father gives all his love to each one of his children without discrimination, whether it be one or ten, and if I am suffering now for my two sons, I am not suffering half for each of them but double . . . "

13   "True . . . true . . . " sighed the embarrassed husband, "but suppose (of course we all hope it will never be your case) a father has two sons at the front and he loses one of them, there is still one left to console him . . . while . . . "

14   "Yes," answered the other, getting cross, "a son left to console him but also a son left for whom he must survive, while in the case of the father of an only son if the son dies the father can die too and put an end to his distress. Which of the two positions is the worse? Don't you see how my case would be worse than yours?"

15   "Nonsense," interrupted another traveler, a fat, red-faced man with bloodshot eyes of the palest gray.

16   He was panting. From his bulging eyes seemed to spurt inner violence of an uncontrolled vitality which his weakened body could hardly contain.

17   "Nonsense," he repeated, trying to cover his mouth with his hand so as to hide the two missing front teeth. "Nonsense. Do we give life to our children for our own benefit?"

18   The other travelers stared at him in distress. The one who had had his son at the front since the first day of the war sighed: "You are right. Our children do not belong to us, they belong to the Country. . . . "

19   "Bosh," retorted the fat traveler. "Do we think of the Country when we give life to our children? Our sons are born because . . . well, because they must be born and when they come to life they take our own life with them. This is the truth. We belong to them but they never belong to us. And when they reach twenty they are exactly what we were at their age. We too had a father and mother, but there were so many other things as well . . . girls, cigarettes, illusions, new ties . . . and the Country, of course, whose call we would have answered—when we were twenty—even if father and mother had said no. Now, at our age, the love of our Country is still great, of course, but stronger than it is the love for our children. Is there any one of us here who wouldn't gladly take his son's place at the front if he could?"

20   There was a silence all round, everybody nodding as to approve.

21   "Why then," continued the fat man, "shouldn't we consider the feelings of our children when they are twenty? Isn't it natural that at their age they should consider the love for their Country (I am speaking of decent boys, of course) even greater than the love for us? Isn't it natural that it should be so, as after all they must look upon old boys who can not move any more and must stay at home? If Country exists, if Country is a natural necessity, like bread, of which each of us must eat in order not to die of hunger, somebody must go to defend it. And our sons go, when they are twenty, and they don't want tears, because if they die, they die inflamed and happy (I am speaking, of course, of decent boys). Now, if one dies young and happy, without having the ugly sides of life, the boredom of it, the pettiness, the bitterness of disillusion . . . what more can we ask for him? Everyone should stop crying; everyone should laugh, as I do . . . or at least thank God—as I do—because my son, before dying, sent me a message saying that he was dying satisfied at having ended his life in the best way he could have wished. That is why, as you see, I do not even wear mourning. . . . "

22   He shook his light fawn coat as to show it; his livid lip over his missing teeth was trembling, his eyes were watery and motionless, and soon after he ended with a shrill laugh which might well have been a sob.

23   "Quite so . . . quite so . . ." agreed the others.

24   The woman who, bundled in a corner under her coat, had been sitting and listening had—for the last three months—tried to find in the words of her husband and her friends something to console her in her deep sorrow, something that might show her how a mother should resign herself to send her son not even to death but to a probable danger of life. Yet not a word had she found amongst the many which had been said . . . and her grief had been greater in seeing that nobody—as she thought—could share her feelings.

25   But now the words of the traveler amazed and almost stunned her. She suddenly realized that it wasn't the others who were wrong and could not understand her but herself who could not rise up to the same height of those fathers and mothers willing to resign themselves, without crying, not only to the departure of their sons but even to their death.

26   She lifted her head, she bent over from her corner trying to listen with great attention to the details which the fat man was giving to his companions about the way his son had fallen as a hero, for his King and his Country, happy and without regrets. It seemed to her

that she had stumbled into a world she had never dreamed of, a world so far unknown to her and she was so pleased to hear everyone joining in congratulating that brave father who could so stoically speak of his child's death.

27   Then suddenly, just as if she had heard nothing of what had been said and almost as if waking up from a dream, she turned to the old man, asking him: "Then is your son really dead?"

28   Everybody stared at her. The old man, too, turned to look at her, fixing his great, bulging, horribly watery light gray eyes, deep in her face. For some little time he tried to answer, but words failed him. He looked and looked at her, almost as if only then—at that silly incongruous question—he had suddenly realized at last that his son was really dead—gone forever—forever. His face contracted, became horribly distorted; then he snatched in haste a handkerchief from his pocket and, to the amazement of everyone, broke into harrowing, heartrending, uncontrollable sobs.

■ *Vocabulary*

livid (22)	incongruous (28)
stoically (26)	harrowing (28)

■ *Questions on Meaning and Technique*

1. What is the controlling idea of the story? State it in one brief sentence.
2. What is the fat man's pretended attitude toward the loss of a son at war? How does this contrast with his real attitude?
3. The story contains little action. What is the conflict of the story?
4. What exactly triggers the sudden change in the fat man's attitude?
5. Is there any hint earlier in the story that the fat man was not as sure of his argument as he claimed to be? Explain your answer.
6. How would you counter the fat man's argument?

POEM

JAMES MICHIE

Dooley Is a Traitor

James Michie (1927–2007), a British poet and translator, was for many years director of the Bodley Head Ltd., a British publishing company, and was a lecturer at London University. Michie's work includes Possible Laughter *(1959),* The Odes of Horace *(translation; 1964), and* The Epigrams of Martial *(translation; 1973).*

READING FOR IDEAS In the following poem, a convicted murderer advances an ironic argument against going to war. Compare his argument with your own. Try to come up with a clear view of how you feel about soldiers being compelled to fight wars. Are some causes worth killing for? Is it cowardly to hate war and perhaps refuse to carry arms?

1   "So then you won't fight?"
"Yes, your Honour," I said, "that's right."
"Now is it that you simply aren't willing,
Or have you a fundamental moral objection to killing?"
Says the judge, blowing his nose
And making his words stand to attention in long rows.
I stand to attention too, but with half a grin
(In my time I've done a good many in).
"No objection at all, sir," I said.
"There's a deal of the world I'd rather see dead
Such as Johnny Stubbs or Fred Settle or my last landlord, Mr. Syme.
Give me a gun and your blessing, your Honour, and I'll be killing them all the time.

2   But my conscience says a clear no
To killing a crowd of gentlemen I don't know.
Why, I'd as soon think of killing a worshipful judge,
High-court, like yourself (against whom, God knows, I've got no grudge
So far), as murder a heap of foreign folk.
If you've got no grudge, you've got no joke
To laugh at after." Now the words never come flowing

3   Proper for me till I get the old pipe going.
And just as I was poking
Down baccy, the judge looks up sharp with "No smoking,
Mr. Dooley. We're not fighting this war for fun.
And we want a clearer reason why you refuse to carry a gun.
This war is not a personal feud, it's a fight
Against wrong ideas on behalf of the Right.
Mr. Dooley, won't you help to destroy evil ideas?"

4   "Ah, your Honour, here's
The tragedy," I said. "I'm not a man of the mind.
I couldn't find it in my heart to be unkind
To an idea. I wouldn't know one if I saw one. I haven't one of my own.

5   So I'd best be leaving other people's alone."
"Indeed," he sneers at me, "this defence is
Curious for someone with convictions in two senses.
A criminal invokes conscience to his aid
To support an individual withdrawal from a communal crusade.
Sanctioned by God, led by the Church, against a godless, churchless nation!"

6   I asked his Honour for a translation.
      "You talk of conscience," he said. "What do you know of the Christian creed?"
      "Nothing, sir, except what I can read,
      That's the most you can hope for from us jail-birds.
      I just open the Book here and there and look at the words.
      And I find when the Lord himself misliked an evil notion
      He turned it into a pig and drove it squealing over a cliff into the ocean,

7   And the loony ran away
      And lived to think another day.
      There was a clean job done and no blood shed!
      Everybody happy and forty wicked thoughts drowned dead.
      A neat and Christian murder. None of your mad slaughter
      Throwing away the brains with the blood and the baby with the bathwater.

8   Now I look at the war as a sportsman. It's a matter of choosing
      The decentest way of losing.
      Heads or tails, losers or winners,
      We all lose, we're all damned sinners.
      And I'd rather be with the poor cold people at the wall that's shot
      Than the bloody guilty devils in the firing-line, in Hell and keeping hot."
      "But what right, Dooley, what right," he cried,
      "Have you to say the Lord is on your side?"
      "That's a dirty crooked question," back I roared.
      "I said not the Lord was on my side, but I was on the side of the Lord."
      Then he was up at me and shouting.

9   But by and by he calms: "Now we're not doubting
      Your sincerity, Dooley, only your arguments,
      Which don't make sense." ('Hullo,' I thought, 'that's the wrong way round.
      I may be skylarking a bit, but my brainpan's sound.')
      Then biting his nail and sugaring his words sweet:
      "Keep your head, Mr. Dooley. Religion is clearly not up your street.
      But let me ask you as a plain patriotic fellow
      Whether you'd stand there so smug and yellow
      If the foe were attacking your own dear sister."
      "I'd knock their brains out, mister,
      On the floor," I said. "There," he says kindly, "I knew you were no pacifist.

10   It's your straight duty as a man to enlist.
      The enemy is at the door." You could have downed
      Me with a feather. "Where?" I gasp, looking round.
      "Not this door," he says angered. "Don't play the clown.
      But they're two thousand miles away planning to do us down.
      Why, the news is full of the deeds of those murderers and rapers."

"Your Eminence," I said, "my father told me never to believe the papers
But to go by my eyes.
And at two thousand miles the poor things can't tell the truth from lies."

11   His fearful spectacles glittered like the moon: "For the last time what right
Has a man like you to refuse to fight?"
"More right," I said, "than you.
You've never murdered a man, so you don't know what it is I won't do.
I've done it in good hot blood, so haven't I the right to make bold
To declare that I shan't do it in cold?"
Then the judge rises in a great rage
And writes DOOLEY IS A TRAITOR in black upon a page
And tells me I must die.
"What, me?" says I.
"If you still won't fight."
"Well, yes, your Honour," I said, "that's right."

■ Questions on Meaning and Technique

1. What is the controlling idea of Dooley's objection to fighting in the war?

2. What is the judge's counter to Dooley's position?

3. When the judge tries to trick Dooley by bringing up the Christian creed (stanza 6), what does Dooley answer? Why?

4. When the judge tries to trick Dooley again by asking what he would do if an enemy were suddenly to attack Dooley's sister (stanza 9), what is Dooley's answer?

5. Characterize Dooley's logic. How does his logic differ from that of the judge?

6. According to Dooley, who wins in a war?

7. What evidence supports either Dooley's or the judge's argument?

8. Dooley is a confessed murderer. How does this affect his view about war?

How to Write an Argument

An argument is a discussion in which opposing views are expressed on a particular subject. To write an effective argument, you must reason logically, support your case by evidence, and anticipate the opposition. In a spoken debate, all these things may take place in the give-and-take of arguing. But in a written debate, the writer must not only air personal views but must also raise and disprove any likely counterclaims by the other side.

Some arguments convince because of the merits of their evidence; others, because they are persuasively presented. Unfortunately, the merit of an argument is not necessarily related to its rightness. Many crooks have been glib and convincing in advancing their fraudulent schemes and views, whereas many saints have had their ideas rejected for lack of persuasiveness. In short, to write or state a convincing argument, you need to be more than just right; you also need to know how to argue persuasively.

Writing Assignment

Think of a current social or political problem or issue and write an argument taking one side or the other on it.

> Begin with a controlling idea that clearly expresses your opposition or support. Once expressed, the controlling idea should be supported by logic, evidence, and expert testimony; moreover, the argument should take into account the expected replies of the opposition.

Specific Instructions

Prewrite on the assignment.   A good way to get started on this assignment is to sit with a friend and discuss the issues of today that really bother you. Ask yourself what changes you would like to see in your home state, city, school, or society. What reforms do you feel most strongly about? You will have a better chance of writing a successful essay if you choose an issue to which you have some emotional commitment.

The last time we asked our classes to suggest some "hot" issues, the following topped the list: terrorism, corporate fraud, toxic waste, population control, immigration policy, racial profiling by the police, equal pay for equal work, peace in the Middle East, drug use and abuse, obscenity on the internet, and global warming.

These, of course, are big issues. You might be more interested in some narrower or more focused issues, such as uncontrolled development in your neighborhood, vandalism of a public park, a dangerous intersection, or the lack of a streamlined registration process for your college classes. Whether your focus is on a big or little issue, you should avoid any argument that rests mainly on belief and for which logical proof does not or cannot exist. You may feel strongly that the unborn fetus has a soul, but proving that scientifically or logically is impossible.

Base your argument on sound premises.   A premise is a basic assertion that serves as the starting point of an argument. Consider, for example, the premise of a speech given by Benjamin Franklin at the Constitutional Convention held in 1787. The convention was debating whether executive officers of the newly minted federal government should be paid for their services. Franklin made an impassioned speech against the idea of payment, beginning with the following premise:

> Sir, there are two passions which have a powerful influence in the affairs of men. These are ambition and avarice . . . the love of power and the love of money. Separately, each of these has great force in prompting men to action: but when united in view of the same object, they have in many minds the most violent effect.

The premise of Franklin's argument consists of his assertions about the wicked influences of ambition and avarice—avarice is excessive greed for riches. He then proceeds to give examples of what he foresaw as the harmful consequences of salaried federal offices on these weaknesses in human nature. Greedy candidates would seek office, not for love of country but for love of money. The best would not be called upon to serve, only the greediest. Once Franklin's premise is aired, the remainder of the argument consists mainly of demonstrating the harm that payment to federal officers would do to the national character.

The premise of an argument has often been compared to the foundation of a house. It is the fundamental point that the argument makes and attempts to prove; it is also the point at which an opponent will most likely strike. For instance, a possible reply to Franklin's argument would argue that good people are as much motivated by patriotism, morality, and/or duty as they are by money and ambition. And, no doubt, a strong argument could be waged on both sides, for it is the nature of premises that consist of grand assertions about human nature to be slippery and hard to prove or disprove.

Premises are as varied and complex as the individuals who assert them. We hold premises about the effects of the planets on our lives, about the causes of the common cold, or about global warming. Some premises, like Franklin's, are plainly stated in the body of an argument, whereas others are merely implied.

Here, for example, are the theses of various arguments whose premises are implied:

Thesis	A prime reason for the increase in crime has been the reduced severity of jail sentences.
Implied premise	Severe jail sentences deter crime.
Thesis	Abortion is a great wickedness that is in blatant opposition to the laws of God.
Implied premise	A God exists whose laws must be obeyed.
Thesis	We oppose school vouchers because they will eventually destroy public education while favoring private schools.
Implied premise	The use of vouchers favors private schools.

A *premise*, we said, is a summary assertion about reality. Capital punishment deters crime, energy policies impact global warming, sunspots affect the world's economy—used as the launching points of arguments, these and other generalizing statements become premises. But how do we come to believe such generalizations?

We do so by two reasoning processes—*induction* and *deduction,* two natural thought patterns everyone uses to draw conclusions and to make decisions.

Induction.   Induction is thinking that arrives at a general principle from particular facts or experiences. Take the case of Mr. Cochran, a gourmet cook. One day, he made a mistake and stewed beef in tea, which he mistook for broth. He discovered, to his surprise, that the meat turned out especially tender. A week later, he deliberately repeated his error, with the same tender and tasty result. More trials confirmed a conclusion that Mr. Cochran had begun to suspect: Meat stewed in tea is tenderized.

Though homespun and trivial, the example of Mr. Cochran uses virtually the same method of induction practiced by scientists. Whether conducted in the kitchen by a gourmet cook or in the laboratory by a scientist, induction involves investigating specific cases and drawing general conclusions from them. Here, for instance, is a newspaper report of a medical finding derived from the inductive method:

> Thousands of children are needlessly denying themselves milk and other common foods because of allergies they don't have, a research team at the National Jewish Hospital and Research Center has concluded. *)* Conclusion
>
> Dr. Charles D. May and Dr. S. Allan Bock, co-directors of a major clinical and research program in food allergies at the Denver hospital, said that of 71 children they have studied who were thought to have food allergies, only 25 actually had such allergies.
>
> "That isn't to say that there aren't children who are allergic to such things as strawberries, tomatoes, and chocolate," Bock said, "but it apparently is very much less common than people think."
>
> In the NJH research, which is continuing, children between the ages of 3 and 16 are "challenged" with food to which they are believed to be allergic, and their reactions are observed. *Inductive method used to reach conclusion*
>
> Possible bias is eliminated through the use of a double-blind technique in which neither the children nor the observers know what the patients are getting. The food is given to the patients in the form of opaque capsules. Only the person supervising the test knows what is in each capsule. It could be milk, shrimp, tomato, or one of two placebos—known whimsically as "spider teeth" and "bat wings."
>
> The capsules are administered initially in small doses, but the dosage is increased gradually, and the patients' reactions are monitored and their reactions recorded hour by hour.
>
> "These techniques . . . sometimes indicate that the patient can safely eat small amounts of food which, in larger quantities, might trigger reactions."
>
> But the most significant result of the study so far is the revelation that possibly only one-third of children thought to have food allergies actually have such allergies. *Discussion of the conclusion*
>
> This result caused May and Bock to become concerned that some people may be living with "unwarranted restrictions on optimal nutrition" because of an incorrect diagnosis of food sensitivity.
>
> The research, if its findings are confirmed by further testing, could mean that many "allergy sufferers" can enjoy more palatable and nourishing diets.
>
> —"Doctors Find Two-Thirds of 'Allergic' Kids Aren't,"
> *Atlanta Constitution*, March 19, 1979, p. 13A

Mr. Cochran drew his conclusions about the tenderizing qualities of tea after a number of experiments. Similarly, from the study of only seventy-one children, the doctors concluded that *thousands* of children thought to have allergies do not. In both cases, random samples are taken that represent characteristics of the whole. Mr. Cochran assumes that if tea tenderizes stewed meat in fifteen trials, it will do so in other instances; the doctors assume that if only twenty-five percent of a random sample of children thought to have allergies actually do, then this percentage should also apply to the larger population.

During the course of your own life, you will, without question, use induction in your everyday reasoning. It may be as simple as this: Every time you eat spicy food, you get sick. You conclude, inductively, that you shouldn't eat spicy food. Study the following box to understand induction.

Characteristics of Inductive Reasoning

1. Inductive reasoning moves from the specific to the general, beginning with the observation of specific facts or experiences and then drawing a general conclusion.

2. Induction leads to new truths by using old observations to make new ones.

3. An inductive conclusion is reliable only if the facts and observations leading to it are also reliable.

Deduction.   Deduction, the opposite of induction, moves from general to specific observations. A general principle, once discovered, is useful only if it can be applied to different cases. Consider, for instance, the possible reaction of a doctor familiar with the Denver hospital research to whom a mother has brought a child she suspects has a food allergy. The doctor's first response is likely to be of doubt based on this reasoning: "Only twenty-five percent of the children thought to have allergies in the Denver experiment actually did; therefore, it is unlikely that this particular child has a food allergy." Using this logic, the doctor will probably try to find some other cause for the mother's worry, rather than subject the child to expensive and time-consuming allergy tests.

This reasoning is an example of a syllogism, an equation that is commonly used to make deductions from general principles. Many syllogisms deduce truths about unknowns by classifying them under categories whose properties are known. The syllogism proposed by the Greek philosopher Socrates is a classic example:

Major premise	All men are mortal.
Minor premise	Socrates is a man.
Conclusion	Therefore Socrates is mortal.

Once identified as belonging to the category of "man," Socrates immediately assumes the known properties of that category, which include mortality.

On paper, this rather clear-cut example of a syllogism is hardly likely to puzzle anyone. But not all deductive reasoning is as clean and simple. Here, for instance, is a piece of pure deductive reasoning that consists of a complicated series of syllogistic steps made in rapid succession:

> Freud once told the story of how an East European Jew . . . observed in the train which was taking him home to his village a young man who seemed to be going there too. As the two sat alone in the compartment, the Jew, puzzled about the stranger, began to work things out: "Only peasants and Jews live there. He is not dressed like either, but still, he is reading a book, so he must be Jewish. But why to our village? Only fifty families live there, and most are poor. Oh, but wait, Mr. Shmuel, the merchant, has two daughters: one of them is married, but for the other he has been seeking a husband. Mr. Shmuel is rich, and lately has acquired airs, so he would not want anyone from the village for his daughter. He must have asked the marriage broker to find a son-in-law from the outside. But Mr. Shmuel is old and cannot travel to meet a new family, so he would probably want a son-in-law from a family he knows. This means it would have to be one that had lived in the village but moved away. Who? The Cohen family had a son. Twenty years ago they moved to Budapest. What can a Jewish boy do there? Become a doctor. Mr. Shmuel would like a doctor in the family. A doctor needs a large dowry. The boy opposite is neat, but not well dressed. Dr. Cohen. But in Budapest, Cohen wouldn't do. Probably changed his name. In Budapest? To Kovacs—a name which comes as naturally to Hungarians as Cohen to Jews."
>
> As the train drew into the village station, the old Jew said to the young man: "Excuse me, Dr. Kovacs, if Mr. Shmuel is not waiting for you at the station, I'll take you to his home and introduce you to your betrothed." Replied the astonished young man: "How do you know who I am and where I'm going? Not a word has passed between us."
>
> "How do I know?" said the old man with a smile. "It stands to reason."
>
> —David Abrahamsen, *Nixon Versus Nixon*

This is the sort of reasoning with which Sherlock Holmes made a name for himself. Using a series of premises that he had formulated from his life in the village, the old man was able to deduce the unknown from the known.

In practice, our daily processes of reasoning consist of innumerable leaps of induction and deduction. When you observe, year after year, that anyone who goes out into the rain gets wet, you are reasoning inductively, but when you decide to wear a raincoat to keep you from getting wet in the rain, you are reasoning deductively. Both forms of reasoning are essential parts of how we think. Over-reliance on deductive reasoning alone can lead to bigoted, stereotyped thinking because it is only a matter of time before the premises we have accumulated in our heads become stale and inaccurate. On the other hand, thinkers who live entirely by induction and will accept no premise unless personally discovered would hardly be able to function in the modern world. In an extreme example, such a Doubting Thomas about to swim in strange water might ignore a local's warning about a riptide because they haven't verified its existence through personal experiment. In such a case, deductive reasoning might save your life; inductive reasoning might drown you.

The following box summarizes the way deduction works.

Characteristics of Deductive Reasoning

1. Deductive reasoning moves from the general to the specific.
2. A deductive argument consists of three parts: major premise, minor premise, and conclusion.
3. A deductive argument is valid if the conclusion logically follows from the premises.
4. A deductive conclusion may be judged true or false depending on whether the premises are true or false. If both premises are true, the conclusion must be true.

Avoiding logical fallacies.   In the ideal world, arguments would focus entirely on the issues, which debaters would calmly and logically discuss. Alas, on our erring planet, arguments are often ruined by unfair tactics and statements that have become well enough known to be classified as logical fallacies. A *logical fallacy* is a statement that is misleading, false, or deceptive. Here are the most common logical fallacies:

Arguing in circles.   An argument is illogical if its conclusion merely repeats its major premise. Such an argument is said to *beg the question* or to be *circular*. Here is an example:

> The Bible is the word of God. How do I know it is the word of God? Because in verse after verse the Old as well as the New Testament tells us that it is God speaking. When God says it's His word, that's good enough for me.

In effect, the speaker says that the Bible is the word of God because God says so in the Bible. A variation on this same error follows:

> "The citizens of New York are more sophisticated than the citizens of Los Angeles."
> "How do you know?"
> "Because New Yorkers are far less crude and boorish."

Or, in other words, New Yorkers are more sophisticated than Angelenos because New Yorkers are more sophisticated. In a circular argument, the writer simply repeats what needs to be proved.

The red herring.   The term comes from a hunting trick where the strong scent of a herring was sometimes used to distract hounds on the trail of game. This fallacy is also called *ignoring the question* or *dodging the issue*. It is a favorite tactic of dishonest debaters. Here is an example of the red herring tactic:

> Now certain government leaders tell us that we must not display nativity scenes in our store windows at Christmas time. The question is, do we want to be governed by godless people?

That is not the question at all, nor does it follow that people opposed to nativity scenes are godless; they may simply be sensitive to religions other than Christianity.

Oversimplification. This argument often convinces gullible people, who like uncomplicated answers to all problems. But most issues are complex and cannot be easily solved. Oversimplification tends to leave out important relevant facts and is commonly used in political debates. Here is an example:

> If our government would simply stockpile an adequate number of tents for people evacuated during a natural disaster, we would solve the problem of displaced people.

Stockpiling thousands of tents would not guarantee that displaced people would have access to the tents and could survive in them contentedly. Some agency would have to organize and oversee the distribution of the tents and would have to organize the tent community. Many natural disasters are too complex for such flip solutions.

Attacking the person, also called *Ad hominem*. Here the argument attacks the person instead of the issue as in this example:

> Don't give Mr. Finchley a penny when he tries to collect money for a mobile unit to be used by the school to teach students fire prevention. Mr. Finchley is an avowed atheist who lives openly with a mistress. How can you trust him with your money?

Focus and Fairness

Stay focused on the issue of your argument and you'll have no problem with logical fallacies. The basic principle behind all logical reasoning is fairness. The opposite principle—unfairness—is at the root on many logical fallacies. If you concentrate on what you're trying to prove and stick to the facts with a cool head, your argument is likely to be made stronger by your tone of reasonableness. This does not mean that you can't anticipate the opposition. You can and should, but you don't have to do so by using smear tactics.

Entirely overlooked are the pros and cons of the usefulness of the mobile unit.

Appealing to popular opinion, also called *Ad populum*.   This tactic tries to create an appeal to popular, though irrelevant, sentiments:

> Virgil Pettis is bound to be a wonderful president. He overcame polio when he was a teenager, and he has always stuck up for the rights of little people and victims of tyranny. He is a man cut from the cloth of Lincoln and Jefferson.

This argument hopes to dazzle voters by appeals to pity and patriotism, rather than by the candidate's abilities, experience in government, or intelligence. But the sad truth is a wonderful person can also be a rotten president.

False analogy.   Comparing something to something else may be useful in explaining a process. For instance, you might say to a friend, "Look, rollerblading is like ice skating; both skills require balance." However, the naïve belief that because two items are alike in some ways, they must therefore be alike in all ways often leads to a faulty analogy. Here is an example:

> If you have cancer, chances are you got it because you have a downhearted attitude. If you really want to get better, you need a positive attitude. Curing cancer is like any other challenge in life—if you think you can beat it, you can do it. If you think you cannot beat it, most likely the disease will overcome your defenses.

Two faulty analogies are used in this argument. First, there is no reliable reason for believing that people's attitude determines whether or not they'll develop cancer. To think that is to subscribe to an unproven theory. Second, while a positive attitude may help you get over the terrible side effects of chemotherapy, no convincing evidence exists that attitude alone can cure cancer.

Hasty generalization.   This fallacy is also popularly known as jumping to conclusions. Usually the jump is based on flimsy evidence. Consider this example:

> No one should vote for Senator X. He supported giving medical care to the children of illegal immigrants; believe me, the next thing he will do is give green cards to anyone who sneaks through our borders.

As the saying goes, "One swallow does not a summer make." If you encounter two—or even three—drunken persons weaving down the street, you shouldn't assume that the town is filled with drunkards.

Be hardheaded in your use of evidence.   To argue logically, you need to support your opinions with evidence such as facts, examples, experience, authorities' opinions, and statistics. Most of the topics you will write about in an argumentative paper will therefore require some research—either in the library or on the internet. And the details you cite to support your views will determine the force of your argument. Here are some examples of unsupported and supported arguments:

Unsupported	Hot dogs are horrible things to eat and have been proven to be very bad for you because they are very high in fat and chemicals.
Supported	According to the U.S. Department of Agriculture, since 1937 the frankfurter has gone from 19% fat and 19.6% protein to 28% fat and only 11.7% protein. (The rest is water, salt, spices, and preservatives.) This deterioration is yet another of technology's ambiguous gifts.

—"The Decline and Fill of the American Hotdog," Time

Unsupported	People can reduce and lose weight. Many celebrities, including well-known actors, athletes, and politicians, have successfully lost weight. If they can, so can everyone.
Supported	People can reduce and lose weight. Alfred Hitchcock went from 365 lbs. to a weight of 200 lbs. by eating only steak and cutting down on liquor; Jackie Gleason scaled down from 280 lbs. to 221 lbs. Maria Callas likewise went from a tumorous 215 lbs. to a trim 135 lbs. Even Lyndon Johnson, when he was Vice President, lost 31 lbs. in less than 10 weeks after being elected to the post in 1961.

—Jean Meyer, Overweight: Causes, Cost, and Control

The credibility of an argument often depends on its specific details. As a general rule, if you back up what you say with facts, your case is likely to seem more believable. But facts are not the only kind of specifics you can cite. Sometimes a topic will require other kinds of details, such as descriptions or your personal impressions. For example, an essay opposing beauty contests will probably not sway your reader if it cites only facts. Arguing that beauty contests degrade women is not a point that facts can prove, particularly if the reader believes that such pageants put women on a pedestal. And rattling off facts about the number of beauty contests held in the United States is hardly likely to change that person's mind. What you must do is draw a sharp picture, using graphic detail, showing the ugly side of beauty contests. Here are two examples of arguments against beauty contests. The first is weak in its use of details:

I am against beauty pageants because they degrade women. They show the superficial side of the contestants. They never really evaluate the inside person. The whole deal is about bosoms and legs. Then all the women watching the contestants feel inferior because they don't feel as beautiful and desirable as the girls up on the stage. To me that is degrading womanhood. When the time comes for the winner to receive the flowers and the crown, I feel depressed that our country wastes its time and money on beauty pageants.

Although the argument starts out with a strong controlling idea, its details are weak.

The following has a better beginning and is sharper and more specific in the use of details:

> I am against beauty pageants because they degrade women. By degrade, I mean they force women to be less than what they really are. What the audience sees is a beautifully proportioned smiling mannequin, parading gracefully up and down a light-flooded ramp, to the tune of some lilting band music. Her smile is fixed, her beauty is lacquered. The master of ceremonies asks her some inane question, such as "How does it feel to be a runner-up in the Miss Rootbeer of Indiana Contest?" The mannequin chirps a delighted giggle and spreads her lips into a wide smile that exhibits gleamingly white teeth. If the girl has an I.Q., the judges could never discern it because she is treated as if she were made of plastic, not flesh and blood. Each year, 150 such pageants are held in California alone, sponsored as advertising by big companies that sell everything from oranges to toothpaste. And in each pageant, between ten and fifty girls must go through this degrading demotion to mannequin status. The last pageant I attended was the Miss International Trade competition. And when the girls walked out on stage, I almost expected them to jump through circus hoops held by the M.C., some honey-voiced executive who stood to gain from the advertising of the pageant.

This second argument is stronger than the first because its details effectively hammer home the grotesqueness of beauty contests.

Quote authorities.   An argument is strengthened by the supporting testimony of an authority who agrees with its views. Usually, such an authority will have a reputation for being knowledgeable, fair, and objective on a particular subject. You find such experts by checking sources such as the *Readers' Guide to Periodical Literature,* encyclopedias, *Who's Who?* and other reference books.

Here are some examples of how testimonial evidence may be incorporated into an argument:

No authority	Thomas Jefferson was not the moral saint students study in grade school.
With authority	Thomas Jefferson, far from being the moral saint studied by grade school students, was a man attracted to forbidden women, as indicated by Fawn Brodie's intimate history entitled *Thomas Jefferson.*

Relevant personal experience may also be used as testimonial evidence. For example, an argument against the legalization of marijuana may quote a former user of the drug who has had bad experiences with it. Or an argument against the welfare system may cite the case of a mother of four who has been badly served by the system. Even your own personal experience, if relevant, can be used as support for an argument. Here's an example:

No authority	The quality of medical care in the United States varies with how much you can afford to pay and how quickly you can demonstrate your ability to pay. Accident victims are sometimes turned away by hospitals because they have no insurance or proof of financial ability to pay.
	The quality of medical care in the United States varies with how much you can afford to pay and how quickly you can demonstrate your ability to pay.
With the authority of personal experience	Last summer, for instance, while climbing El Capitan in Yosemite, I fell and broke my leg. I was rescued by a group of passing hikers and driven to the nearest hospital, which refused to admit me because I had no proof of insurance. I was dressed in mountain climbing gear and sported a five-day growth of stubble on my face; my clothes had been shredded by the fall. To all appearances, I was a penniless tramp. Before the admitting nurse could dispatch me to a county hospital, one of the hikers, a well-known businessman in the area, vouched for my ability to pay. Only then was I admitted.

In sum, testimonial evidence allows you to pack your argument with opinions that support your own views. Moreover, it permits you to add a human dimension to what might otherwise be a cut-and-dried recital of facts, figures, and statistics. What makes this hiking story better evidence than someone's belief in something (alien abduction, for instance) is that it can be verified.

Anticipate the opposition.   A strong argument anticipates the opposition by identifying and answering its objections. This strategy makes it clear that your own position is held, not in ignorance, but with full awareness of the other side. Citing and rejecting the opposing point of view also effectively silences an opponent's thunder. In the following argument against the wasteful extravagance of paper grocery bags, notice how the writer anticipates two major arguments of the opposition:

> Can you believe that in the most well-educated, cultured nation in the world, we consume and destroy a vital part of our natural resources without a second thought? Consider the average brown paper grocery bag, which is made from the pulp of trees. One of our most vital resources is transformed into a convenience that is used no place else in the world with such careless extravagance as here in the United States. And for what? To move groceries from store to car to home—to be used briefly as a trash bag and then to be pulverized by chemical action into a city sewage plant. How foolish and spoiled we are. A billion tons of lovely trees are destroyed annually, just to satisfy our compulsive need for convenience. How shallow we are to make this trade-off from lush green beauty to tacky brown bags. One day in the future, people will have to look at pictures to be reminded that the Ozark Mountains were breathlessly beautiful in the fall as the deep green leaves turned to shimmering gold. Personal memories they will not have.

Of course, the big industries try to make us think that high living standards are more important than beauty. For example, George I. Kneeland, Chairman of the Board and Executive Officer of the St. Regis Paper Company, insists that "providing the highest possible standard of living for America is an urgent national priority." But I ask, what kind of value system is it that places higher priority on a trivial convenience than on the survival of Mother Earth?

Another argument is that paper is biodegradable and consequently not as polluting as plastic. But plastic bags do not have to be the substitute. People all over the world adapt to grocery carts, fishnet bags, or cloth containers. We could get into the habit of doing this, too, and we would be stopping our insane path of ecological mass murder.

Persuasion and argumentation.   *Persuasion* and *argumentation,* often assumed to be identical twins, are in fact only kissing cousins. A persuasive argument is usually logical. However, a logical argument is not always persuasive. To be persuasive, an argument must do more than cite evidence and argue logically. It must also appeal to the emotions, values, and beliefs of an audience. Here are pairs of statements on the same topic that illustrate the difference between argumentation and persuasion:

Argumentation	Our legislators should pass laws to protect helpless children.
Persuasion	So long as we are without laws that protect innocent children from hunger, physical and emotional abuse, and disease, there's no true love in the world.
Argumentation	The incidence of rape has been growing.
Persuasion	The incidence of rape has been growing, with devastating consequences to some women that last a lifetime.
Argumentation	Because of the stock market drop, many pensioners have suffered a loss of income.
Persuasion	Because of the stock market drop, many pensioners have suffered a loss of income, requiring sacrifices sometimes as extreme as cutting back to two meals a day.

The first arguments are all clear and focused but without emotional appeal. They seem to call for a recital of facts and statistics. The same arguments, worded persuasively, require facts and statistics also, but add the component of emotion. In the third example, for instance, the cutback in income of the elderly is dramatized by the image of two old people having less to eat because of the decline in the stock market. This picture, coupled with a citing of the usual facts, is more compelling than any straightforward argument by itself.

A persuasive argument, in short, supplements facts, statistics, and evidence with emotional appeal. Persuasion, however, must be used with caution. Emotional appeal is no substitute for reasoned argument or solid evidence. But used in small doses, emotional appeal can starkly dramatize an outcome or condition in a way that evidence and facts alone cannot.

Here is an example of an argument with persuasive appeal. The speaker is trying to convince an audience to donate blood for people who have hemophilia. A hemophiliac himself, the speaker spends the first half of his speech explaining factually what hemophilia is—reciting statistics about its incidence and symptoms.

Then, to dramatize the awfulness of the disease, he resorts to an emotional appeal, using his own experience with the pain of hemophilia:

> Because medical science had not advanced far enough, and fresh blood not given often enough, my memories of childhood and adolescence are memories of pain and heartbreak. I remember missing school for weeks and months at a stretch—of being very proud because I attended school once for four whole weeks without missing a single day. I remember the three long years when I couldn't even walk because repeated hemorrhages had twisted my ankles and knees to pretzel-like forms. I remember being pushed to my table. I remember sitting in the dark empty classroom by myself during recess while the others went out in the sun to run and play. And I remember the first terrible day at the big high school when I came on crutches and built-up shoes carrying my books in a sack around my neck.
>
> But what I remember most of all is the pain. Medical authorities agree that a hemophilic joint hemorrhage is one of the most excruciating pains known to mankind. To concentrate a large amount of blood into a small compact area causes a pressure that words can never hope to describe. And how well I remember the endless pounding, squeezing pain. When you seemingly drown in your own perspiration, when your teeth ache from incessant clenching, when your tongue floats in your mouth and bombs explode back of your eyeballs, when darkness and light fuse into one hue of gray, when day becomes night and night becomes day—time stands still—and all that matters is that ugly pain. The scars of pain are not easily erased.

The emotional quality of this appeal adds to the persuasiveness of the argument that people with hemophilia deserve to get blood donations.

Common knowledge and specific knowledge.   Some essays may be based entirely on a writer's memory and need no outside sources for support. For example, a narrative essay on a narrow escape you had as a child will rely on details only you can provide. You do not have to look up anything in the library to tell such a highly personal story. An argument, however, is a public debate that requires you to provide support for your opinions. Writing an argumentative essay will probably mean doing research in the library or on the internet. (See pages 484–485, which cover how to do research on the internet.) And when you find a fact and cite it in your paper, you have to document where you got it from. Inevitably, the question arises, what do you have to document?

The answer is you do not have to document common knowledge, but you do have to document specific knowledge. *Common knowledge* means knowledge that the average person is presumed to have. For example, this statement is common knowledge: "In 1863, as sixteenth president of the United States, Abraham Lincoln delivered his Gettysburg Address, expressing sorrows at the necessity of war." Such a statement requires no documentation (telling the source of this information). Here are other examples of common knowledge:

Parochial schools are schools supported by a church.

Zeus is the Olympic god of Greek mythology.

Japan is made up of four main islands: Hokkaido, Honshu, Shikoku, and Kyushu.

The Colorado River forms a wildly majestic gorge, called the Grand Canyon, as it twists through parts of Arizona.

Specific knowledge, on the other hand, consists of facts and opinions that are not commonly known. You found them somewhere—in a book, a magazine, a CD or DVD, a pamphlet, or online. When you cite an item of specific knowledge, you must document it.

Telling the difference between the two kinds of knowledge mainly takes common sense. Common knowledge is probably something you have known all your life; specific knowledge is something that you learned from a particular source. For example, if you say in a psychology paper that some people have schizophrenia, you do not need to document that. It is common knowledge. But if you add that some people with schizophrenia are also catatonic, that is, they make purposeless movements, have exaggerated mannerisms, and often appear to be in a stupor, then you need to say where you got this information. You could introduce the information this way, giving both title and page number of the source: "According to the 15th edition of *Harrison's Principles of Internal Medicine,* edited by E. Braunwald et al., one subtype of schizophrenia is the catatonic person who performs purposeless movements, engages in exaggerated mannerisms, or often appears to be in a stupor (pp. 2554–2557)."

For information on how to document sources cited in research papers, see Chapter 18.

PROFESSIONAL MODEL

ISAAC ASIMOV

The Case Against Man

Isaac Asimov (1920–1992) was a Russian-born American biochemist, educator, and prolific writer. He was best known for his science fiction works, among them I, Robot *(1950),* The Caves of Steel *(1954),* The Gods Themselves *(1973),* Out of Everywhere *(1990), and* Atom: A Journey across the Subatomic Cosmos *(1991). A popularizer of science, Asimov authored over one hundred books and a staggering variety of articles on nearly every imaginable topic. Answering the questions at the end of the essay below will help you understand the author's philosophical approach and can help you formulate your own ideas about the growth of population and the survival of humankind.*

READING FOR IDEAS   The idea of stopping the population explosion is not new and, in fact, has been proposed by numerous organizations concerned with the inability of our planet to continue feeding and housing the growing masses of humans. Asimov's statistics are frightening and convincing. As you read, ask yourself what you are willing to do to avoid the coming catastrophe. What plan would you be willing to follow? Would your friends go along with your plan? If not, how could you sway them to your side?

1   The first mistake is to think of mankind as a thing in itself. It isn't. It is part of an intricate web of life. And we can't think even of life as a thing in itself. It isn't. It is part of the intricate structure of a planet bathed by energy from the Sun.

2   The Earth, in the nearly 5 billion years since it assumed approximately its present form, has undergone a vast evolution. When it first came into being, it very likely lacked what we would today call an ocean and an atmosphere. These were formed by the gradual outward movement of material as the solid interior settled together.

3   Nor were ocean, atmosphere, and solid crust independent of each other after formation. There is interaction always: evaporation, condensation, solution, weathering. Far within the solid crust there are slow, continuing changes, too, of which hot springs, volcanoes, and earthquakes are the more noticeable manifestations here on the surface.

4   Between 2 billion and 3 billion years ago, portions of the surface water, bathed by the energetic radiation from the Sun, developed complicated compounds in organization sufficiently versatile to qualify as what we call "life." Life forms have become more complex and more various ever since.

5   But the life forms are as much part of the structure of the Earth as any inanimate portion is. It is all an inseparable part of a whole. If any animal is isolated totally from other forms of life, then death by starvation will surely follow. If isolated from water, death by dehydration will follow even faster. If isolated from air, whether free or dissolved in water, death by asphyxiation will follow still faster. If isolated from the Sun, animals will survive for a time, but plants would die, and if all plants died, all animals would starve.

6   It works in reverse, too, for the inanimate portion of Earth is shaped and molded by life. The nature of the atmosphere has been changed by plant activity (which adds to the air the free oxygen it could not otherwise retain). The soil is turned by earthworms, while enormous ocean reefs are formed by coral.

7   The entire planet, plus solar energy, is one enormous intricately interrelated system. The entire planet is a life form made up of nonliving portions and a large variety of living portions (as our own body is made up of nonliving crystals in bones and nonliving water in blood, as well as of a large variety of living portions).

8   In fact, we can pursue the analogy. A man is composed of 50 trillion cells of a variety of types, all interrelated and interdependent. Loss of some of those cells, such as those making up an entire leg, will seriously handicap all the rest of the organism: serious damage to a relatively few cells in an organ, such as the heart or kidneys, may end by killing all 50 trillion.

9   In the same way, on a planetary scale, the chopping down of an entire forest may not threaten Earth's life in general, but it will produce serious changes in the life forms of the region and even in the nature of the water runoff and, therefore, in the details of geological structure. A serious decline in the bee population will affect the numbers of those plants that depend on bees for fertilization, then the numbers of those animals that depend on those particular bee-fertilized plants, and so on.

10   Or consider cell growth. Cells in those organs that suffer constant wear and tear—as in the skin or in the intestinal lining—grow and multiply all life long. Other cells, not so exposed, as in nerve and muscle, do not multiply at all in the adult, under any

circumstances. Still other organs, ordinarily quiescent, as liver and bone, stand ready to grow if that is necessary to replace damage. When the proper repairs are made, growth stops.

11   In a much looser and more flexible way, the same is true of the "planet organism" (which we study in the science called ecology). If cougars grow too numerous, the deer they live on are decimated, and some of the cougars die of starvation, so that their "proper number" is restored. If too many cougars die, then the deer multiply with particular rapidity, and cougars multiply quickly in turn, till the additional predators bring down the number of deer again. Barring interference from outside, the eaters and the eaten retain their proper numbers, and both are the better for it. (If the cougars are all killed off, deer would multiply to the point where they destroy the plants they live off, and more would then die of starvation than would have died of cougars.)

12   The neat economy of growth within an organism such as a human being is sometimes—for what reason, we know not—disrupted, and a group of cells begins growing without limit. This is the dread disease of cancer, and unless that growing group of cells is somehow stopped, the wild growth will throw all the body structure out of true and end by killing the organism itself.

13   In ecology, the same would happen if, for some reason, one particular type of organism began to multiply without limit, killing its competitors and increasing its own food supply at the expense of that of others. That, too, could end in the destruction of the larger system—most or all of life and even of certain aspects of the inanimate environment.

14   And this is exactly what is happening at this moment. For thousands of years, the single species Homo sapiens, to which you and I have the dubious honor of belonging, has been increasing in numbers. In the past couple of centuries, the rate of increase has itself increased explosively.

15   At the time of Julius Caesar, when Earth's human population is estimated to have been 150 million, that population was increasing at a rate such that it would double in 1,000 years if that rate remained steady. Today, with Earth's population estimated at about 4,000 million (26 times what it was in Caesar's time), it is increasing at a rate which, if steady, will cause it to double in 35 years.

16   The present rate of increase of Earth's swarming human population qualifies Homo sapiens as an ecological cancer, which will destroy the ecology just as surely as any ordinary cancer would destroy an organism.

17   The cure? Just what it is for any cancer. The cancerous growth must somehow be stopped.

18   Of course, it will be. If we do nothing at all, the growth will stop, as a cancerous growth in a man will stop if nothing is done. The man dies and the cancer dies with him. And, analogously, the ecology will die and man will die with it.

19   How can the human population explosion be stopped? By raising the deathrate, or by lowering the birthrate. There are no other alternatives. The deathrate will rise spontaneously and finally catastrophically, if we do nothing—and that within a few decades. To make the birthrate fall, somehow (almost *any* how, in fact), is surely preferable, and that is therefore the first order of mankind's business today.

20   Failing this, mankind would stand at the bar of abstract justice (for there may be no posterity to judge) as the mass murderer of life generally, his own included, and mass disrupter of the intricate planetary development that made life in its present glory possible in the first place.

21   Am I too pessimistic? Can we allow the present rate of population increase to continue indefinitely, or at least for a good long time? Can we count on science to develop methods for cleaning up as we pollute, for replacing wasted resources with substitutes, for finding new food, new materials, more and better life for our waxing numbers?

22   Impossible! If the numbers continue to wax at the present rate.

23   Let us begin with a few estimates (admittedly not precise, but in the rough neighborhood of the truth).

24   The total mass of living objects on Earth is perhaps 20 trillion tons. There is usually a balance between eaters and eaten that is about 1 to 10 in favor of the eaten. There would therefore be about 10 times as much plant life (the eaten) as animal life (the eaters) on Earth. There is, in other words, just a little under 2 trillion tons of animal life on Earth.

25   But this is all the animal life that can exist, given the present quantity of plant life. If more animal life is somehow produced, it will strip down the plant life, reduce the food supply, and then enough animals will starve to restore the balance. If one species of animal life increases in mass, it can only be because other species correspondingly decrease. For every additional pound of human flesh on Earth, a pound of some other form of flesh must disappear.

26   The total mass of humanity now on Earth may be estimated at about 200 million tons, or one ten-thousandth the mass of all animal life. If mankind increases in numbers ten thousandfold, then Homo sapiens will be, *perforce*, the only animal species alive on Earth. It will be a world without elephants or lions, without cats or dogs, without fish or lobsters, without worms or bugs. What's more, to support the mass of human life, all the plant world must be put to service. Only plants edible to man must remain, and only those plants most concentratedly edible and with minimum waste.

27   At the present moment, the average density of population of the Earth's land surface is about 73 people per square mile. Increase that ten thousandfold and the average density will become 730,000 people per square mile, or more than seven times the density of the workday population of Manhattan. Even if we assume that mankind will somehow spread itself into vast cities floating on the ocean surface (or resting on the ocean floor), the average density of human life at the time when the last nonhuman animal must be killed would be 310,000 people per square mile over all the world, land and sea alike, or a little better than three times the density of modern Manhattan at noon.

28   We have the vision, then, of high-rise apartments, higher and more thickly spaced than in Manhattan at present, spreading all over the world, across all the mountains, across the Sahara Desert, across Antarctica, across all the oceans; all with their load of humanity and with no other form of animal life beside. And on the roof of all those buildings are the algae farms, with little plant cells exposed to the Sun so that they might grow rapidly and, without waste, form protein for all the mighty population of 35 trillion human beings.

29   Is that tolerable? Even if science produced all the energy and materials mankind could want, kept them all fed with algae, all educated, all amused—is the planetary high rise tolerable?

30   And if it were, can we double the population further in 35 more years? And then double it again in another 35 years? Where will the food come from? What will persuade the algae to multiply faster than the light energy they absorb makes possible? What will speed up the Sun to add the energy to make it possible? And if vast supplies of fusion energy are

added to supplement the Sun, how will we get rid of the equally vast supplies of heat that will be produced? And after the icecaps are melted and the oceans boiled into steam, what?

31   Can we bleed off the mass of humanity to other worlds? Right now, the number of human beings on Earth is increasing by 80 million per year, and each year that number goes up by 1 and a fraction percent. Can we really suppose that we can send 80 million people per year to the Moon, Mars, and elsewhere, and engineer those worlds to support those people? And even so, merely remain in the same place ourselves?

32   No! Not the most optimistic visionary in the world could honestly convince himself that space travel is the solution to our population problem, if the present rate of increase is sustained.

33   But when will this planetary high-rise culture come about? How long will it take to increase Earth's population to that impossible point at the present doubling rate of once every 35 years? If it will take 1 million years or even 100,000, then, for goodness sake, let's not worry just yet.

34   Well, we don't have that kind of time. We will reach that dead end in no more than 460 years.

35   At the rate we are going, without birth control, then even if science serves us in an absolutely ideal way, we will reach the planetary high-rise with no animals but man, with no plants but algae, with no room for even one more person, by A.D. 2430.

36   And if science serves us in less than an ideal way (as it certainly will), the end will come sooner, much sooner, and mankind will start fading long, long before he is forced to construct that building that will cover all the Earth's surface.

37   So if birth control *must come by* A.D. 2430 at the very latest, even in an ideal world of advancing science, let it come *now,* in heaven's name, while there are still oak trees in the world and daisies and tigers and butterflies, and while there is still open land and space, and before the cancer called man proves fatal to life and the planet.

■ Vocabulary

quiescent (10)	decimated (11)	waxing (21)
ecology (11)	catastrophically (19)	fusion (30)

■ Questions on Meaning and Technique

1. What is the author's main argument? Where is it explicitly stated? What advantage does such placement have?

2. According to Asimov, what conditions will prevail on earth by A.D. 2430 if matters keep going the way they are?

3. How does the author use cancer as a way to clarify the problem of ecological imbalance?

4. What similarities does the author draw between the life processes of a person and those of the planet?

5. What do the statistics and mathematical calculations add to the argument?

6. According to the author, why is moving to other planets not a plausible answer?

7. Do you agree with Asimov's sense of urgency? What other world problem, if any, do you consider more important? Why?

8. What techniques of persuasion does Asimov use in his essay? Point to specific passages.

STUDENT ESSAY—FIRST DRAFT

Benjamin Goldberg

Honors Accelerated Rhetoric 123

University of Iowa

Connecting the Dots: Racism, Sexism, and Prejudice in Modern America

1   ~~Since the dawn of time~~ *At one time or another* most people have been significantly affected by oppression. Racial and religious hatred has been a part of ~~our~~ *America's* history since the foundation of the first colonies. True, America has undoubtedly progressed since the 1700s. Women ~~now~~ have the right to vote and own land, classrooms and public transportation are ~~now~~ no longer segregated, *and* more people are ~~now~~ receiving their basic human rights. This progress, while notable, ~~just doesn't cut it~~ *is not nearly enough* *than in the past.* Racism, sexism, and anti-Semitism were modernized in tandem with the United States. *Today oppression* ~~Oppression~~ can take many forms. It is not always an overt and recognizable act, ~~that is easy to recognize~~. Rather, modern oppression ~~is more subtle~~ *recruits the weapon of subtlety.* Racism, sexism, anti-Semitism, and other forms of oppression have evolved into an interconnected and pervasive *system of advantage* that ~~effects~~ *affects* nearly all facets of American life. *No italics*

2   In a *system of advantage*, there are people who benefit from the system and ~~those who don't.~~ *people who suffer because of the system.* Those with the "right" or "default" race, religion, sex, etc. receive opportunities and advantages that people considered as "other" do not receive. Society places value in certain identity characteristics (for instance, being white, male, heterosexual, Christian, and wealthy). When people who do not fit into these categories are labeled as "other," it becomes possible to regulate levels of wealth, power, and opportunity without actually appearing racist, sexist, and unjust.

3   I myself benefit from ~~it,~~ *this system,* often without even knowing it, because I am a white male. In Peggy McIntosh's article ~~*White Privilege: Unpacking the Invisible Knapsack,*~~ "White Privilege: Unpacking the Invisible Knapsack," she

Margin notes:

Avoid clichés

Avoid slang; watch punctuation

Redundant

stronger, active language; more descriptive

Wrong word

Clarification

Quote marks around article titles

creates a "privilege list" discussing her advantages as a white person. This concept is

Use italics in place of underlining

known as white privilege: white people benefiting from their whiteness even if they

~~their profit. For instance, as a~~

are unaware of ~~it. As a~~ white person, I can express how I feel without it being labeled

the "white" opinion. I can walk around alone at night reasonably certain that I won't be

attacked or harassed (this could also be attributed to me being a six foot five male). I can

be reasonably certain that I will get housing anywhere I want to ~~live. The people I'm with~~

See note next to insert, below

~~will probably love me.~~ When I study history, I am taught that people who look like me

created civilization. I can ~~deal with~~ handle a difficult situation without being called a "credit to

my race." The advantages are numerous.

Consistent point of view— first person

4   This privilege concept is evident in all socially constructed forms of oppression.

White privilege, male privilege, straight privilege, and Christian privilege are all

different mechanisms operating within the same system of advantage. For instance,

as a Jew

~~As a Jewish person~~ I cannot be sure that I will get ~~off of~~ time off from school or work because of

religious holidays. True, most public schools and institutions are not allowed to bar

you from celebrating a religious holiday, but that is beside the point. Attendance is not

required during religious holidays, but no matter the situation class is still being missed.

What if there is a test that day? What if especially important or challenging material is

being covered that you can't afford to miss? ~~I've~~ I have chosen class over religious observances

No contractions

could not

many times simply because I ~~couldn't~~ afford to miss the scheduled material. In this

Grammar

I am

instance, Christian students are more advantaged than ~~myself~~ because they will always

have their important holidays during sanctioned school breaks.

Cut dead wood, watch punctuation Clearer text and better transition between sentences.

5   Despite our nation's ~~large and substantial~~ progress, race, religion, class, and gender

The difference is that oppression

continue to matter in the United States. ~~Oppression~~ has turned towards the modern and

the subtle. Oppression as a system of advantage is not as easily recognized as an act of

blatant racial hatred because often times people benefit from the system of advantage

without being aware of their privileges. I am not saying all white people are racist. I am

not saying all men are sexist. Rather, oppression and prejudice are no longer consistent

in their forms. Educating ourselves on increasingly complex notions of multiculturalism

Clearer conclusion

toward genuine equality. We have simply not yet finished our task.

and diversity is the key to moving ~~forward. We are simply not yet finished~~.

More formal and precise language

Insert

I can socially interact with people knowing they will most likely be neutral or pleasant to me.

Goldberg 1

Benjamin Goldberg

Honors Accelerated Rhetoric 123

University of Iowa

Connecting the Dots: Racism, Sexism, and

Prejudice in Modern America

1   At one time or another most people have been significantly

affected by oppression. Racial and religious hatred has been a

part of America's history since the foundation of the first colonies.

True, America has undoubtedly progressed since the 1700s.

Women have the right to vote and own land, classrooms and

public transportation are no longer segregated, and more people

are receiving their basic human rights than in the past. This

progress, while notable, is not nearly enough. Racism, sexism,

and anti-Semitism were modernized in tandem with the United

States. Today oppression can take many forms. It is not always an

overt and recognizable act. Rather, modern oppression recruits the

weapon of subtlety. Racism, sexism, anti-Semitism, and other forms

of oppression have evolved into an interconnected and pervasive

system of advantage that affects nearly all facets of American life.

2   In a system of advantage, there are people who benefit

from the system and people who suffer because of the system.

Those with the "right" or "default" race, religion, sex, etc. receive

opportunities and advantages that people considered as "other" do

not receive. Society places value in certain identity characteristics

Goldberg 2

(for instance, being white, male, heterosexual, Christian, and wealthy). When people who do not fit into these categories are labeled as "other," it becomes possible to regulate levels of wealth, power, and opportunity without actually appearing racist, sexist, and unjust.

3   I myself benefit from this system, often without even knowing it, because I am a white male. In Peggy McIntosh's article "White Privilege: Unpacking the Invisible Knapsack," she creates a "privilege list" discussing her advantages as a white person. This concept is known as *white privilege*: white people benefiting from their whiteness even if they are unaware of their profit. For instance, as a white person, I can express how I feel without it being labeled the "white" opinion. I can walk around alone at night, reasonably certain that I won't be attacked or harassed (this could also be attributed to me being a six-foot-five male). I can be reasonably certain that I will get housing anywhere I want to live. I can socially interact with people, knowing they will most likely be neutral or pleasant to me. When I study history, I am taught that people who look like me created civilization. I can handle a difficult situation without being called a "credit to my race." The advantages are numerous.

4   This *privilege concept* is evident in all socially constructed forms of oppression. White privilege, male privilege, straight privilege, and Christian privilege are all different mechanisms operating within the same system of advantage. For instance, as a

Goldberg 3

Jew I cannot be sure that I will get time off from school or work because of religious holidays. True, most public schools and institutions are not allowed to bar you from celebrating a religious holiday, but that is beside the point. Attendance is not *required* during religious holidays, but no matter the situation, class is still being missed. What if there is a test that day? What if especially important or challenging material is being covered that you can't afford to miss? I have chosen class over religious observances many times simply because I could not afford to miss the scheduled material. In this instance, Christian students are more advantaged than I am because they will always have their important holidays during sanctioned school breaks.

5   Despite our nation's progress, race, religion, class, and gender continue to matter in the United States. The difference is that oppression has turned toward the modern and the subtle. Oppression as a system of advantage is not as easily recognized as an act of blatant racial hatred because oftentimes people benefit from the system of advantage without being aware of their privileges. I am not saying all white people are racist. I am not saying all men are sexist. Rather, oppression and prejudice are no longer consistent in their forms. Educating ourselves on increasingly complex notions of multiculturalism and diversity is the key to moving toward genuine equality. We have simply not yet finished our task.

Work Cited

McIntosh, Peggy. "White Privilege: Unpacking the Invisible Knapsack." 1988. Women: Images and Realities. A Multicultural Anthology. Ed. Amy Kesselman, Lily D. McNair, and Nancy Schniedewind. New York: McGraw, 2008. Print.

FURTHER READING

JUDY SYFERS

I Want a Wife

Judy Syfers (now Brady) (b. 1937) is a freelance writer best known for the essay reprinted here, which has become a feminist manifesto. Born in San Francisco, Syfers earned a Bachelor of Fine Arts degree in painting at the University of Iowa. She traveled to Cuba in 1973 to study class relationships as a means of understanding how social change can occur.

READING FOR IDEAS "I Want a Wife" has become over the years an unofficial manifesto of the feminist movement. Often reprinted in textbooks on all subjects, it strikes just the right note of sarcasm and anger. Taking the stereotypical definition of a wife in the 1970s, Syfers gives us a list of chores and obligations that wives of the day were expected to fulfill and shows us with delicious irony that anyone would love to have such a dutiful mule around the house. Though she exaggerates for effect, Syfers's dramatization of the work wives were expected to do is truthful enough to drive home her main point—that when it comes to working partnerships in marriage, men get the better deal. As you read, ask yourself whether the expectations of wives today have been realistically lessened or whether the same conditions that Syfers describes still exist in modern marriages.

1   I belong to that classification of people known as wives. I am a Wife. And, not altogether incidentally, I am a mother.

2   Not too long ago a male friend of mine appeared on the scene fresh from a recent divorce. He had one child, who is, of course, with his ex-wife. He is obviously looking for another wife. As I thought about him while I was ironing one evening, it suddenly occurred to me that I, too, would like to have a wife. Why do I want a wife?

3   I would like to go back to school so that I can become economically independent, support myself, and, if need be, support those dependent on me. I want a wife who will work and send me to school. And while I am going to school I want a wife to take care of my children. I want a wife to keep track of the children's doctor and dentist appointments. And to keep track of mine, too. I want a wife to make sure that my children eat properly and are kept clean. I want a wife who will wash the children's clothes and keep them mended. I want a wife who is a good nurturant attendant to my children, who arranges for their schooling,

makes sure they have an adequate social life with their peers, takes them to the park, the zoo, etc. I want a wife who takes care of the children when they are sick, a wife who arranges to be around when the children need special care, because, of course, I cannot miss classes at school. My wife must arrange to lose time at work and not lose the job. It may mean a small cut in my wife's income from time to time, but I guess I can tolerate that. Needless to say, my wife will arrange and pay for the care of the children while my wife is working.

4   I want a wife who will take care of my physical needs. I want a wife who will keep the house clean. A wife who will pick up after me. I want a wife who will keep my clothes clean, ironed, mended, replaced when need be, and who will see to it that my personal things are kept in their proper place so that I can find what I need the minute I need it. I want a wife who cooks the meals, a wife who is a good cook. I want a wife who will plan the menus, do the necessary shopping, prepare the meals, serve them pleasantly, and then do the cleaning up while I do my studying. I want a wife who will care for me when I am sick and sympathize with my pain and loss of time from school. I want a wife to go along when our family takes a vacation so that someone can continue to care for me and my children when I need a rest and change of scene.

5   I want a wife who will not bother me with rambling complaints about a wife's duties. But I want a wife who will listen to me when I feel the need to explain a rather difficult point I have come across in my course of studies. And I want a wife who will type my papers for me when I have written them.

6   I want a wife who will take care of the details of my social life. When my wife and I are invited out by my friends, I want a wife who will take care of the babysitting arrangements. When I meet people at school that I like and want to entertain, I want a wife who will have the house clean, prepare a special meal, serve it to me and my friends, and not interrupt when I talk about the things that interest me and my friends. I want a wife who will have arranged that the children are fed and ready for bed before my guests arrive so that the children do not bother us. I want a wife who takes care of the needs of my guests so that they feel comfortable, who makes sure that they have an ashtray, that they are passed the hors d'oeuvres, that they are offered a second helping of the food, that their wine glasses are replenished when necessary, that their coffee is served to them as they like it.

7   And I want a wife who knows that sometimes I need a night out by myself.

8   I want a wife who is sensitive to my sexual needs, a wife who makes love passionately and eagerly when I feel like it, a wife who makes sure that I am satisfied. And, of course, I want a wife who will not demand sexual attention when I am not in the mood for it. I want a wife who assumes the complete responsibility for birth control, because I do not want more children. I want a wife who will remain sexually faithful to me so that I do not have to clutter up my intellectual life with jealousies. And I want a wife who understands that my sexual needs may entail more than strict adherence to monogamy. I must, after all, be able to relate to people as fully as possible.

9   If, by chance, I find another person more suitable as a wife than the wife I already have, I want the liberty to replace my present wife with another one. Naturally, I will expect a fresh, new life; my wife will take the children and be solely responsible for them so that I am left free.

10   When I am through with school and have a job, I want my wife to quit working and remain at home so that my wife can more fully and completely take care of a wife's duties. *My God, who wouldn't want a wife?*

▪ *Vocabulary*

nurturant (3)	entail (8)
replenished (6)	adherence (8)

▪ *Questions on Meaning and Technique*

1. On what premise is Syfers's argument based? What is your opinion of this premise? Give reasons for your answer.
2. What is the author's tone throughout the essay? What does her tone contribute to the piece?
3. What pronoun does the author keep associating with the word *wife*? What does this association achieve?
4. What kinds of evidence does the author use to support her argument? How strong do you consider the evidence?
5. How fair is the author's assessment of what husbands expect of their wives?
6. If you were to give the other side of the story, what list of contributions made by a husband could you provide?
7. Syfers's essay was first published in 1970. What changes, if any, have taken place since then?
8. What burden regarding a wife's sexual role does the author describe? Do you agree with her? Why or why not?
9. What is the effect of the final sentence? Why is it italicized?
10. What are the characteristics you would most want from a spouse, male or female? Provide examples of each characteristic.

Writing Assignments

1. Using Syfers's essay as a model, write an essay titled "I Want a Husband."
2. Write an essay in which you list the gains as well as the losses women have experienced in the last fifty years.

FURTHER READING

ANNA QUINDLEN

Playing God on No Sleep

Anna Quindlen (b. 1952) is an American novelist, journalist, and opinion columnist, whose New York Times *column titled "Public and Private" won her the prestigious Pulitzer Prize in 1992. Although Quindlen nowadays spends most of her time writing novels, she continues to contribute a bi-weekly column to* Newsweek *magazine. She is known for her forceful and sometimes biting criticism of the fast-paced and increasingly materialistic life here in the United States. Among her best-known novels are the following:* Object Lessons *(1991),* One True Thing *(1997),* Black and Blue *(1998), and* Blessings *(2002). Three of her novels—*One True Thing, Black and Blue, *and* Blessings*—have been turned into movies. Quindlen lives in Manhattan and is in great demand as a speaker. She is married to an attorney and has three children.*

READING FOR IDEAS The essay that follows takes on a special kind of authenticity when one realizes that Quindlen is writing from her personal experience as a mother with three children, trying to juggle a career as a writer with that of a wife and mother.

1   So a woman walks into a pediatrician's office. She's tired, she's hot and she's been up all night throwing sheets into the washer because the smaller of her two boys has projectile vomiting so severe it looks like a special effect from "The Exorcist." Oh, and she's nauseated, too, because since she already has two kids under the age of 5 it made perfect sense to have another, and she's four months pregnant. In the doctor's waiting room, which sounds like a cross between an orchestra tuning loudly and a 747 taking off, there is a cross-stitched sampler on the wall. It says GOD COULD NOT BE EVERYWHERE SO HE MADE MOTHERS.

2   This is not a joke, and that is not the punch line. Or maybe it is. The woman was me, the sampler real, and the sentiments it evoked were unforgettable: incredulity, disgust and that out-of-body feeling that is the corollary of sleep deprivation and adrenaline rush, with a soupcon of shoulder barf thrown in. I kept reliving this moment, and others like it, as I read with horrified fascination the story of Andrea Yates, a onetime nurse suffering from postpartum depression who apparently spent a recent morning drowning her five children in the bathtub. There is a part of my mind that imagines the baby, her starfish hands pink beneath the water, or the biggest boy fighting back, all wiry arms and legs, and then veers sharply away, aghast, appalled.

3   But there's another part of my mind, the part that remembers the end of a day in which the milk spilled phone rang one cried another hit a fever rose the medicine gone the car sputtered another cried the cable out "Sesame Street" gone all cried stomach upset full diaper no more diapers Mommy I want water Mommy my throat hurts Mommy I don't feel good. Every mother I've asked about the Yates case has the same reaction. She's appalled; she's aghast. And then she gets this look. And the look says that at some forbidden level she understands. The look says that there are two very different kinds of horror here. There is the unimaginable idea of the killings. And then there is the entirely imaginable idea of going quietly bonkers in the house with five kids under the age of 7.

4   The insidious cult of motherhood is summed up by the psychic weight of the sampler on that doctor's wall. We are meant to be all things to small people, surrounded by bromides and soppy verse and smiling strangers who talk about how

lucky we are. And we are lucky. My children have been the making of me as a human being, which does not mean they have not sometimes been an overwhelming and mind-boggling responsibility. That last is the love that dare not speak its name, the love that is fraught with fear and fatigue and inevitable resentment. But between the women who cannot have children and sometimes stare at our double strollers grief-stricken, and the grandmothers who make raising eight or ten sound like a snap and insist we micromanage and overanalyze, there is no leave to talk about the dark side of being a surrogate deity, omniscient and out of milk all at the same time.

5   The weight was not always so heavy. Once the responsibility was spread around extended families, even entire towns. The sociologist Jessie Bernard has this to say: "The way we institutionalize motherhood in our society—assigning sole responsibility for child care to the mother, cutting her off from the easy help of others in an isolated household, requiring round-the-clock tender, loving care, and making such care her exclusive activity—is not only new and unique, but not even a good way for either women or—if we accept as a criterion the amount of maternal warmth shown—for children. It may, in fact, be the worst."

6   It has gotten no better since those words were written 25 years ago. Worse, perhaps, with all the competing messages about what women should do and be and feel at this particular moment in time. Women not working outside their homes feel compelled to make their job inside it seem both weighty and joyful; women who work outside their homes for pay feel no freedom to be ambivalent because of the *sub rosa* sense that they are cutting parenting corners. All of us are caught up in a conspiracy in which we are both the conspirators and the victims of the plot. In the face of all this "M is for the million things she gave me" mythology it becomes difficult to admit that occasionally you lock yourself in the bathroom just to be alone.

7   The great motherhood friendships are the ones in which women can admit this quietly to one another, over cups of tea at a table sticky with spilt apple juice and littered with markers without tops. But most of the time we keep quiet and smile. So that when someone is depressed after having a baby, when everyone is telling her that it's the happiest damn time of her life, there's no space to admit what she's really feeling. So that when someone does something as horrifying as what Andrea Yates did, there is no room for even a little bit of understanding. Yap yap yap, the world says. How could anyone do that to her children?

8   Well, yes. But. I'm imagining myself with five children under the age of 7, all alone after Dad goes off to work. And they're bouncing off the walls in that way little boys do, except for the baby, who needs to be fed. And fed. And fed again. And changed. The milk gets spilled. The phone rings. Mommy, can I have juice? Mommy, can I have lunch? Mommy, can I go out back? Mommy, can I come in? And I add to all that depression, mental illness, whatever was happening in that house. I'm not making excuses for Andrea Yates. I love my children more than life itself. But just because you love people doesn't mean that taking care of them day in and day out isn't often hard, and sometimes even horrible. If God made mothers because he couldn't be everywhere, maybe he could have met us halfway and eradicated vomiting, and colic too, and the hideous sugarcoating of what we are and what we do that leads to false cheer, easy lies and maybe sometimes something much, much worse, almost unimaginable. But not quite.

■ *Vocabulary*

projectile (1)	adrenaline (2)	micromanage (4)
sampler (1)	soupcon (2)	surrogate (4)
sentiments (2)	veers (2)	omniscient (4)
evoked (2)	insidious (4)	isolated (5)
incredulity (2)	bromides (4)	criterion (5)
corollary (2)	soppy (4)	ambivalent (6)
deprivation(2)	fraught (4)	eradicated (8)

■ *Questions on Meaning and Technique*

1. What argumentative point does the author make in her essay? Try to express her thesis in one sentence.

2. Why does the story of Andrea Yates impress the author? What is the author's reaction to the Yates tragedy? According to her, what reaction do most mothers have?

3. What is the author trying to explain as she deals with the Yates story? What is your opinion of the author's strategy?

4. What does Quindlen resent about the role mothers are expected to play? How is this role imposed on them? How do you see the role of a good mother? What is the source of your view of this role? Explain yourself.

5. In paragraph 3, how does the author treat grammar? What is the resulting effect?

6. What does Quindlen mean by the "insidious cult of motherhood"? Explain in your own words what you think she means. Give an example of a "bromide" or a "soppy verse" and examine the effect on society.

7. A good argument can be bolstered by expert testimony. Where in her essay does Quindlen use expert testimony to support her thesis? What point does this testimony make? Do you agree? Why or why not?

8. What tone does Quindlen use in her final paragraph? What purpose does it serve? How do you react to the tone?

9. What technique does the author use to wrap up her argument?

Writing Assignments

1. Write an essay in which you argue for free care or some other help for mothers burdened with numerous children. Follow the guidelines for argumentation given in this chapter.

2. Write an essay arguing in favor of birth control for couples who do not have the financial or emotional resources to have multiple children. Follow the guidelines for argumentation given in this chapter.

Cluster Discussion: Understanding Diversity

The world is a complex boarding house occupied by billions of people, many of whom are unlike us in looks, ambitions, beliefs, and lifelong desires. Yet it is the nature of human beings to seek out the companionship of those with whom we can identify, and to avoid, wherever possible, those who are markedly different. Psychologists and those who try to understand human nature talk about "bonding," as if human relationships were held together by glue, and use other terms from psychology to depict why and how human beings get together. But at the basis of it all is this simple truth: We tend to like those who look like us, talk like us, and believe as we do. We tend to avoid the company of those whom we perceive as different.

To make matters worse is the fact that our galactic home—this lovely, rounded, shiny, blue earth—is a temporary dwelling where we are permitted to abide only for a short while before vanishing into the eternal darkness from which none has ever returned. In 2009, for most of us our term of residence in the boarding house hovered around 68.9 years, and while this is not an inflexible number—some few people do live to be over 100 years old—the absolute and unbreakable principle is that we live here for a short while and then we are gone from here forever.

When we contemplate this mysterious, fleeting, and sputtering thing we call life, we soon come to realize that while we are here, we might as well try to get along with our fellow boarders. Really, the more we dig into the inner being of our fellow humans, the more we see that they are remarkably like us, suffering from the same fears, exulting in the same joys, and longing for the same blessings. What we thought made them different from us usually turns out to be misunderstood and superficial variations in being. He or she is more like us than different from us.

The three short stories that follow represent three important facets of diversity in our society. "Soap and Ambergris" was written by a native Saudi Arabian who has first-hand knowledge of the evils connected with rigid and extreme religious beliefs. The narrator in the story witnesses the senseless shooting of a young woman who has in some mysterious way shamed the family patriarch. "Mixed-Blood Stew" is written from the point of view of a mixed-race girl whose forbearers were auctioned off as slaves and are still treated with prejudice. Influenced by her proud grandmother, she rejoices in the glorious diversity of Irish, Choctaw, Seminole, Anglo, and African blood that courses through her ancestral lines. "First" is the personal memory of an adult male looking back on his first attraction to another male. He was five years old, and his mother's reaction inflicted a lasting wound.

These stories are not presented as dramatic arguments for or against any viewpoint, but reading them should lead us to such questions as these: "Where do we find the solutions to the extremist's interpretation of God's will?" "How do we rid our hearts of racism?" "When do homosexuals become our true brothers or sisters?" They should also bring to the honest reader a feeling of recognition that the heart telling the story on the page is little different from the one reading about it.

YOUSEF AL-MOHAIMEED

(TRANSLATED BY ANTHONY CALDERBANK)

Soap and Ambergris

Yousef Al-Mohaimeed (b. 1964) is an award-winning writer and journalist. He has written several novels in Arabic, and has been translated into English, Russian, German, and Spanish. Al-Mohaimeed was born in Riyadh, Saudi Arabia, and was thus deeply aware of Sharia Law and other social rules that dominated the Middle East. After joining the faculty at King Saud University, he became involved in politics and edited a magazine titled Hiwar *(Dialogue), for which he was openly criticized and accused of publishing politically provocative material. Eventually the magazine was banned, and Al-Mohaimeed barely escaped expulsion from the University. In 1989, he published his first collection of short stories,* Zahira La Musha Laha *(An Afternoon Without Pedestrians), which was withdrawn from the market after a well-known religious leader dubbed it "immoral." Censure and disapproval have not stopped Al-Mohaimeed from continuing to publish and from becoming one of the most exciting of a wave of writers emerging from Saudi Arabia. Among his most popular novels are* Laghat Mawta *(The Dead's Gossip, 2003),* Fikhakh Al Ra'iha *(Wolves of the Crescent Moon, 2003),* Al Qarura *(The Bottle, 2004), and* Nozhat Addolphin *(The Dolphin's Excursion, 2006). In 2009, he received the Pushcart Prize for "Soap and Ambergris," which he adapted from his forthcoming novel,* Munira's Bottle, *and which is reprinted below. While many of Al-Mohaimeed's writings were banned in the Middle East, they were acclaimed with praise and enthusiasm in western countries.*

READING FOR IDEAS When you enter the story below, you will find yourself in a world you may find impossible to comprehend, and you will doubtless be disturbed by the dark and mysterious ritual depicted. What kind of society is represented? Who dominates and who submits? What role does each character play in the stark drama exposed so graphically? Only if you can answer these questions truthfully, can you judge the outcome of the story. As the title of our discussion states, our goal is to understand rather than praise or damn. Some internet research into Sharia Law may help you shed light on this complex story.

1   I live in a small, single-story house in Al-Atayef Quarter. My husband didn't leave me anything, apart from a mud house that shakes when the thunder crashes and the rain pours. I live off the kindness of other Muslims, either from charity or zakat. I wash the dead for Allah's sake, and take whatever kindness or generosity the family of the deceased offers in return.

2   One day, an hour before the afternoon prayer call, I heard a knock at the door. It was a bearded man, his beard full of gray hair. He spent quite a while asking Allah to preserve

me and grant me a long life before asking me to go with him to wash the corpse of a deceased woman. He said, by way of reassurance, that there was another woman with him in the car so it would be lawful for me to go with him. Anyway I was comfortable with the man. There was a look of goodness and faith in the features of his face.

3   I quickly put on my abaya and picked up my equipment and followed him into the street. I got into the back seat of a pickup truck, a Datsun or a Hilux, I can't remember. I sat next to a young woman who didn't return my greeting. She was wrapped in black and made a gesture with her index finger as if she were saying "la ilaha illa allah" inaudibly. The car set off and I uttered a blessing for the dead woman and asked Allah to have mercy on her soul. I asked Allah to grant them patience and consolation but I never heard the voice of the woman next to me at all. She never even said "Amen." Not a single cry or sob, and her body didn't shake with weeping.

4   The driver, the old sheikh, was calm and composed. He drove carefully, never went too fast. When we had been going for a while I asked him, "Is the place far?" He didn't answer. When I asked him the third time he said, "Put your trust in Allah, woman! We're almost there."

5   I stole a glance at the woman's feet. She was wearing cheap black plastic shoes and her heel and the side of her leg that showed under the abaya almost glowed they were so white. I noticed a gold ring with a zircon on her middle finger and felt convinced that she really was a woman. I had begun to fear that she was in fact a man in an abaya, and that the two of them had hatched some plot against me and were spiriting me out of the city. The man who was driving didn't look like someone who would do such a thing, but then we're always hearing how criminals can mislead their victims by acquiring innocent, honest, and noble features.

6   Suddenly, after sitting with these doubts and misgivings a while, I realized we were heading down a steep hill to the west of the city, and there was nothing around us save the hills and the highway heading to Taif. I noticed a black barrel of water in the back of the pickup, lunging left and right, and I knew that things were indeed grave, and that my end might well have been near. But I decided to hide my fear and remain calm. I asked the woman next to me if the dead woman was her mother. She didn't answer. I said quickly, stammering with dread, "May Allah reward you handsomely," as if it were my own funeral, and I was asking Him to have mercy on me and my life as its end rapidly approached.

7   After a short while during which we heard nothing but the hum of the car as it devoured the tarmac I ventured to speak to her again. "My daughter, say you take refuge in Allah from Satan!" But she didn't. She didn't say a word. I reached out my hand to touch hers, and the coldness of her palm made me jump. The driver snarled, "Shut up, woman! Take refuge from Satan yourself, and don't take my mind off the road."

8   I was silent, but my heart was not. It trembled like a bird chased by marksmen from tree to tree. I thought maybe the woman was dead and had just been propped up in the back seat, and this man was the killer. But then why did he want her washed and buried? A murderer doesn't care if he stuffs his victim in a rubbish bag and throws it into a cesspit or a well or any other place.

9   The car turned onto a paved desert road. The sun was now to the left. The driver never hesitated or slowed down to check the road in front of him. He clearly knew it well, or was someone well versed in the secrets of the desert, the hills, wadis, and dunes. Yes for

sure he knew the trees and found his way by the lay of the land and the acacia and the shafallah and the rimth and ghada trees. A man like that would never lose his way, not even at night. The daughters of Na'sh, the stars of Ursa would lead him, and the Pleiades, and Canopus and Bellatrix, and the morning star which all desert dwellers know.

10   He drove the car between two huge mountains and approached a sand dune. I remember how surprised I was that there could be a sand dune there on such rocky ground. Anyway he stopped the car and opened the back door for the woman who I'd imagined might be a corpse and would fall to the ground. But she got out slowly, calmly, obediently, and walked in front of him without closing the door. He walked behind her with deliberate steps as she headed with amazing posture and serenity towards the sand dune. Once they were on top of the dune he moved in front of her and she followed him down the other side. I saw their bodies gradually disappear until all I could see was the woman's head. Then that disappeared too without turning back once to look at me. It was as if she had made some resolute decision, or as if she were drugged and in a trance. She didn't say a word or interact with anything around her at all. My questions hadn't had any effect on her whatsoever.

11   After a few moments, as I sat alone in the car with the door open, I heard a gunshot shatter the silence of the mountains. Even now years later I hear the echo of gunshots in my little mud house and wake up terrified in the middle of the night. I don't know if there were three shots, one after the other, or if the echo bouncing round the mountains made it seem like the shots were repeated. My heart thumped wildly, as if it would fly out of my rib cage, and a shiver passed up my neck and made my hair stand on end. It was as if not a single drop of blood remained in my body.

12   After a few minutes, which seemed like an eternity, I spotted somebody coming into view from behind the hill. It was him, plodding heavily along as if he was dragging his outrageous crime behind him, as if he was dragging a million murdered people. He untied the barrel of water from the back of the pickup. "Get out!" he ordered. I couldn't refuse, or even speak. I got out and walked behind him as he rolled the barrel along in front of him. He reminded me to bring my bag with my washing tackle: soap and oils and musk and ambergris and other things. I was like the young woman had been a short while before, following behind him, stupefied and silent. I did not look back, just followed his huge feet as they sank into the sand and he lifted them out again with considerable strength and power.

13   As I walked down the other side of the dune I saw her, spread out on the sand, still wearing her abaya. I began my work, taking particular care to mop up the blood that had flowed from her chest. When he reached the bottom of the dune he must have turned round and seen her silent and submissive eyes, waiting to go to eternal death. Then he shot her, the most important thing in his life. And now he was digging in the dust with the spade he had carried over his shoulder. He wept incessantly and wailed like a woman and his beard soaked up the copious tears. When the grave was finished we wrapped the young woman in her abaya. As he was placing her in the hole, he slipped and fell in on top of her. He began to howl inconsolably. I was afraid he might do something to himself so I began to ask Allah to have mercy on her soul and I said some prayers and consoled him. After it got dark he took me home.

Source: Yousef Al-Mohaimeed, "Soap and Ambergris," *Pen America*. Reprinted in *Pushcart Prize XXXIV*. Ed. Bill Henderson. N.Y. 2010, pp. 443–446.

■ *Vocabulary*

abaya (3)	wadis (9)	copious (13)
inaudibly (3)	resolute (10)	inconsolably (13)
tarmac (7)	musk (12)	
cesspit (8)	ambergris (12)	

■ *Questions on Meaning and Technique*

1. What is this story about? Where does it take place? Who are the major characters? What details establish the mood of the narration?

2. What is the meaning of the title? Why isn't the story titled "Murder in the Desert" or something more obviously connected to the plot? If you don't know what ambergris is, look up the word in a dictionary.

3. What is your view of the young woman's behavior all through the narration? Why does she act the way she does? Describe and explain her motivation and her action. How do you think the woman should have reacted? Be specific.

4. What does the narrator's economic circumstance tell you about Muslim society? What paradox is evident in the society? What is your reaction to the paradox?

5. What effect does the description of the woman in paragraph 10 have on you? Describe your reaction. What, if anything, does this description add to the theme of the story?

6. How many times is "abaya" mentioned in the story? What, if anything, does this piece of clothing signify in the story? How do western women often react to the abaya?

7. What is the man's reaction to the woman's death? How do you interpret his reaction? Is it sincere or spurious? With what impression are you left after reading to the end?

Writing Assignments

1. Write an essay arguing against Sharia Law as it affects Muslim women in the Arab world. If you are not familiar with the concept, look it up on the internet or at the library. Be sure to follow the guidelines for proper argumentation, such as making your point clear, using strong evidence, avoiding logical fallacies, and anticipating the opposition.

2. Write an argument attacking or defending one of the following rights for women:

    a. The right of a woman to keep her maiden name after marriage.

    b. The right of a woman to choose to have an abortion.

    c. The right of a woman to earn the same as a man for doing the same job.

    d. The right of a woman to join the military and bear arms.

    e. The right of a woman not to be physically victimized by her husband.

UNDERSTANDING DIVERSITY IN SKIN COLOR

JEWELL PARKER RHODES

Mixed-Blood Stew

Jewell Parker Rhodes (1954) is one of several up and coming African American authors to influence American literature. Originally from Pittsburgh, Parker grew up wanting to be an actress, but instead followed her instinct to write. She has written three novels: Voodoo Dreams *(1995),* Magic City *(1997), and* Douglass' Women *(2003). Her work has appeared in* Ms Magazine *and other popular and literary publications. She has been anthologized in* Children of the Night: Best Short Stories by Black Writers *and* The Black Short Story in the Americas and Europe. *Rhodes has been nominated for the Pushcart Prize and has won fellowships for Yaddo and the National Endowment for the arts. She is presently a professor of creative writing and American literature at Arizona State University.*

READING FOR IDEAS This memoir should get readers to ponder their own lineages. As Americans—or at least dwellers in the United States of America—how many of us are pure anything? We have a long history of diverse racial lines. The old melting pot was always a mixture of international races. We are indeed a mixed-blood stew. Although we may check the square next to "Caucasian," "Asian," "Hispanic," or "African American" on questionnaires, it is doubtful that our bloodlines are pure. Thus, we must ask ourselves, "Where do we go from here? How do we best take advantage of the various talents that course through our bloodlines?" As you read the following personal account, think about the beauty and brainpower of being a hybrid. There is much to contemplate here. Notice how the author's unorthodox use of fragments reinforces her unique style.

1   It was an old document. Rough parchment, yellowed and withered. I was all of 10, on the threshold of womanhood, digging in my mother's closet, trying to find clues about why my mother abandoned me when I was an infant, why she returned to claim me when I was 9. On this sweltering, summer day, I found a treasure trove of documents—birth certificates, Social Security cards with various names, paycheck stubs and blurred photographs of my mother with strangers. But I knew I'd discovered something special when I uncovered the fragile sheet sandwiched between cardboard and tissue paper.

2

SLAVE AUCTION
Various goods and animals to be auctioned,
including one healthy male, a woman (good cook), and child.
Wright Plantation
Respectable offers only

3   "What are you doing?"

4   My hands trembled, but rather than retreating, I asked, "What this?"

5   "I don't like you going through my things." She took the package from my hand and laid it on the bed.

6   "That your family?" I asked. Of course they were my family, too. But Mother had been gone so long I couldn't help thinking of her as separate from me.

7   Almost whispering, Mother traced the dulled letters with her fingers. "The good cook. She was my great-grandmother. The man, her husband. The child, my grandmother. Master Wright sold them like cattle. When slavery ended, my folks claimed Master's name because they were his kin."

8   *Kin*, I knew, was a code word for rape. Race-mixing. Miscegenation. The child was mulatto. The "healthy male" who raised her wasn't her father. Nonetheless, the small family, lucky to be sold together, took Wright's name and created another, darker limb of his family tree.

9   For a brief moment, I thought Mother would slap me. Or ground me. Or scream, making me cower, cover my ears.

10   "This is mine," she said and layered the auction sheet beneath tissue paper and taped the cardboard shut.

11   But I knew she was wrong—it was mine, too—part of my blood. I reached out to give her a hug, but Mother pulled away.

12   "Don't touch my things again."

13   After Mother left I had a vision of a handsome black man and woman riding on a wagon perch with a yellow-brown girl between them. When the child's hand clasped a parent's, did she ever wonder about her lighter skin? About the faces stirring inside her blood?

14   Mother had the auction sheet framed but never hung it. Until her death it remained shelved in a closet—a buried reminder of what my mother considered a secret. What was worth hiding from neighbors' and her children's eyes. Wipe away roots. Mother created herself full-blown, sprung from the head of Zeus. Mother was all charm, respectability; in her mind her people arrived on the Mayflower, never anchored belowdecks in a slave-ship's hold.

15   I'd always known mysterious people were stirring in my blood.

16   During the nine years of my mother's absence, my paternal grandmother raised me. Raised me in the A.M.E. Methodist Church and in a community with its own special

rainbow. Red-toned Miss Chalmers, sandy-faced Willie, black-beyond-midnight Reverend, and ivory-skinned Mrs. Jackson. Dozens of words described our myriad colors: *Chocolate. Coffee. Café au lait. High yellow. Indigo. Bronze.* Street-corner boys whistled at the parade of sepia girls. Proud church women declared our deacons "fine, righteous black men." And on Easter Sundays, with pastels adorning black and brown bodies, I knew each and every one of us was beautiful.

17   "African-American people, like all people, be rich within themselves," my grandmother said. We grandkids—my sister, Tonie, my cousin Aleta and I—sitting on porch steps, sucking on salted ice or feeding grass to lightning bugs trapped inside a jar, would listen as Grandmother, her voice rising and falling like a sermon, told us tales of ourselves.

18   "We come from Georgia. Before that—Africa. White folks didn't understand there be thousands of tribes. Each with its own history. Slavers thought anybody with black skin be ignorant, be blank slates for them to write upon and breed. Foolishness."

19   "Hun-hunh," we testified, drawing people with white chalk, printing our names in block letters. If it was especially hot and humid, we'd pretend we were in church and fan ourselves with newspapers folded like accordions.

20   "Once black folks could fly. They came from a special tribe with magic words. One day when Master worked them too hard, beat them too long, they played their bodies like drums. Foot-stomping. Hand-clapping. Chest- and thigh-beating. Sent the message, 'Tonight. We fly.'

21   "Come midnight, when day blends into the next, they strapped their babies on their backs, whispered their magic, and lifted off the ground like crows. Blackbirds in the sky. Sailing high across the fields and above the seas."

22   "How come we couldn't fly?" I asked.

23   "Somebody needed to tell the tale. Like I be telling you. Like one day you be telling your children."

24   Tonie giggled. "I ain't marrying."

25   I elbowed my sister, declaring, "I'll tell."

26   Tonie rolled her eyes, stuck out her tongue.

27   Grandmother laughed, patting my back, making me feel special.

28   "White folks used to say one drop of black blood makes you a slave. Made it a law, too. Sheer foolishness. Pepper in the pot makes everything taste better. Can't use just salt."

29   "You saying we a stew?"

30   "Yes. The best kind. Mixed-blood stew."

31   Then Grandmother, noticing the sky filled with twinkling stars and a crescent moon, shooed us to bed and dreams of clouds cradling us. Dreams of ancestors flying, filling a pot with laughter and love.

32   Grandmother's tales were better than my mother's silence. Cross-racial diversity didn't imply any shame, only grace.

33   One summer Grandmother blessed us with a vacation trip to Georgia. We grandkids frolicked, skipped across grass, marveling at homes made of wood rather than brick. Marveling at one-story houses with acres of pecan and orange trees. Our three-story home had an L-shaped yard of concrete and just enough dirt for a rose bush, which rarely bloomed.

34   Blood memories of that southern visit still stir me. I remember glimpsing my great-grandmother, half Seminole, half black, sitting in the middle of her bed, wearing a white flannel gown. She was so frail I thought her a ghost. So silent I thought her mute.

35   I stood in the doorway watching her brush, over and over again, her long strands of black silk. Hair so long she could sit on it. Hair so dark it gleamed like polished rock.

36   For three days I watched her with each setting sun. Finally I asked, "Why does she do it, Grandmother? What for?"

37   "She's afraid water will make her catch cold. So she brushes away the dirt. Stroke by stroke."

38   "Hmmm," I murmured, my eyes sparkling.

39   "Don't you think it," answered Grandmother, knowing I dreaded shampoos and the hot comb pressing my kinky hair flat.

40   Grandfather, not to be outdone by Grandmother's line, had his own stories to tell.

41   "Seminole be all right. But I got Choctaw and Irish in me."

42   Sunday afternoons he'd be in his familiar spot, sitting at the head of the dining-room table, smoking a pipe and sipping Iron City beer. He'd grab anyone who passed by and tell his ancestral stories.

43   "In the '20s, Irish come to the Pittsburgh steel mills. Stood the heat 'like niggers,' some say. I say they stood the heat like men who appreciated an extra dollar at the end of the day." Then he'd jab his pipe. "Negroes got 50 cents.

44   "My Irish grand-dad, nearly bald, freckled all over, fell in love with my grandmother, who had some white in her from a generation before. She had Choctaw, too. Warrior blood. My grandmother's mama already had several of Master's children. One year, to spite him, she got pregnant by an Indian. Master was fit to be tied."

45   "So what all that blood makes me?"

46   He laughed, his mouth wide like a neighing horse. "Someone smart. Someone with the best of the best."

47   "Oh," I exhaled while Grandfather slapped his leg, his laughter ending in a fit of coughing.

48   As decades passed, our ethnic group kept changing, shifting, melding into more beautiful and varied gumbos, mixed-blood stews. Each marriage, each baby born yielded new blood.

49   White Americans insisted our bloodlines were uncomplicated. "One drop of black blood" had historical resonance.

50   In contemporary terms "one drop" meant bigots and Klansmen, thick-headed police-men and ignorant folk could kick, beat, lynch, verbally abuse you, regardless. There was no measure for diversity.

51   It was always white versus black.

52   Even when whites confronted a technically Anglo/Irish/Choctaw/Cherokee/African girl. A nigger was a nigger was a nigger . . . even when she, like me, was an assistant pro-fessor at the University of Maryland walking home from educating young minds, enjoying the sunshine and startled into fury at being called a nigger by the frat-house boys.

53   I always wanted to know the bloodlines of my tormentors. How white was their whiteness? What secrets lived in their veins? Did delving into generations yield Asian, Pacific Islander, Hispanic and African, too? And if we went back to the beginning, the early dawn of our species, wasn't Lucy their mother, too?

54   In 1954 I was born and Emmett Till, 12, was murdered for speaking slang ("Hey, Baby") to an adult white woman. His mother insisted his coffin be open so everybody could see the battering of her baby boy.

55   Till's death sparked the birth of the civil rights movement. African-Americans demanded justice. Unity was our strength. But like wily and gifted tricksters, proud

marchers knew they embodied "the other," embodied, in each and every one of them, some drop, *one drop* of Anglo-American blood.

56   Even a child knows there is no pure color. Everything comes from a mix. And like artists African-Americans have always embraced the mix, even when some of our blood mirrored our tormentors.

57   Living in my grandmother's house, I often dreamed about the faces inside my blood. As a child, stepping onto the bathtub rim, leaning against the bathroom sink, I'd stare into the mirror, pinching my skin. Freckles sprinkled across my nose—Irish? Black, slightly slanted eyes—Seminole? Hair curled tight about my face—African? For hours I tried to account for how each part of me revealed the light and dark shadows in my blood.

58   In school I learned about Dick and Jane (who came to America from nowhere) and read all the tales about white families, rural and urban, rich and poor, living happily ever after in white houses with white picket fences. Fences that kept children like me out. Literature, I had discovered, was only about white lives. I smiled, kept reading nevertheless, for I knew my own joy and happiness being a brown girl raised in my grandmother's and grandfather's house.

59   One afternoon after my eighth birthday, I passed the dining-room table. A newspaper cutting lay in the center of it.

60   "That's your father's daddy," said Grandmother, coming to stand behind me.

61   "That's Grandfather Thornton?"

62   "No. I was married before. This is your father's daddy."

63   "He's white."

64   "He's dead."

65   A sad-eyed man seemed to stare right through me. He was in a naval uniform, handsome, with a high forehead like mine and a squared-off chin like Daddy's. Name given: "Lieutenant J. Parker." Bold headline: "Served valiantly in the war." Plain print: "Age 56, survived by his wife and four kids."

66   "My grandfather's white?"

67   "Or else so light he passed. It wasn't clear. One time he told me he was French Canadian. Another time he said he was colored. Another time, Southern white."

68   I exhaled, excited by the revelation.

69   Grandmother turned away from the photo but left it on the dining-room table. I could see her down the short hallway, opening our freezer and pulling out Grandfather's (should I still call him that?) white shirts, all balled up and half frozen. "They iron better this way," Grandmother always told me.

70   I watched her lumber down the hallway, then into the living room to set up her ironing station. She turned the TV to the afternoon movies. Both Grandmother and I liked to watch Bette Davis in "Jezebel," Bob Hope in "Going Down to Rio," and Lon Chaney in "Abbott and Costello Meet Frankenstein."

71   I painted my bedroom red and black, hung fishnets from the ceiling, propped African spears and masks against the wall. A strobe light flickered in the corner, making every movement seem like two. Jimi Hendrix and the Jefferson Airplane blared from my stereo. I was celebrating my bloodlines, and for me, a black flower child was not a contradiction. I wore a bushy Afro and leopard prints with love beads and a lei. My Huey Newton print scared my mother more than the incense. My support of the Olympians' black-power salute frightened her more than the potential of my doing hard drugs at a pool party in a neighbor's back yard.

72   Mother kicked me out of the house. "Go," she said; Father said nothing. I flew from California back to Pittsburgh, to my birthplace, to Grandmother and Grandfather Thornton.

73   I think now that my mother couldn't accept herself. It was as though her shame that her family came from a plantation, that her grandmother was a mixed child of rape, still unsettled her. There was no lens to make the past less frightening, less upsetting to her sense of decorum. She wasn't an Uncle Tom or a white wanna-be. Rather, she was proud of her racial heritage, but her pride was bound up with the etiquette of a white world that was a figment of the '50s. Like Booker T. Washington, Mother thought if she worked hard enough, adopted the tastes of white middle-class culture, then she would be accepted. This desire for acceptance was her weakness, an insidious insecurity, an illogical belief that what she was—a mixed-blood, New-World African-American—was something to be ashamed of.

74   I say what she was was just fine. A special mix of humanity shaped my mother as it shaped and continues to shape us all. Mother's fears wouldn't let her embrace all the recesses and twists of her blood. Instead she established categories that contradicted themselves: Being black was fine; being a descendent of slaves was not fine. Being lovely like Lena Horne was fine; being descended from a white Master wasn't. If she could she would have suppressed half the blood that made her.

75   Sometimes I dreamed Mother and I were sitting on the bed, side by side, reflected in a wardrobe mirror. "See," she'd say to me. "You look just like me."

76   And I would nod, saying, "There's plenty of good ghosts in our blood."

77   "Yes," she'd answer, and just like a child's (a Native American's?) ritual of bonding, we'd prick our fingers, press them flesh to flesh, blood to blood, swearing, "Always." Swearing our ties couldn't be unbound. But I woke knowing Mother would have preferred purity. Being of mixed blood was too complicated for her. From either racial side, she thought she was being judged, could never be at ease. Her behavior became more and more rigid. Friendships, familial relations became a trial.

78   Mother surfaced periodically in my life, most memorably when she questioned the wisdom of my marrying a white man (Lucy's pale child from the North: British, Norwegian and Scotch-Irish). "Think of the children," she said.

79   True to form Mother did not call or write to congratulate me when I gave birth to a daughter. Nor did she call or write to congratulate me when I gave birth to a son.

80   One child light. One child dark.

81   My greatest fear is that one day someone will shout out to my son, "Nigger, what are you doing with that white girl?"

82   In the meantime I tell them to celebrate rivers, the roar of people, faces, histories stirring in their blood.

83   My census category is African-American. It always has been. Yet this category doesn't deny all the people in my blood, my genes, bubbling beneath my skin. I pass it all on. That's what Grandmother taught me.

84   In the 2000 census, millions of Americans checked more than one ethnic category. Native American. Hispanic. Anglo. Pacific Islander.

85   I think this is a good thing. All blood runs red.

Source: Jewell Parker Rhodes, "Mixed-Blood Stew," *Creative Nonfiction 19: Diversity Dialogues*. Pittsburgh, PA, 2002, pp. 107–115.

■ *Vocabulary*

miscegenation (7)	ethnic (47)	valiantly (64)
mulatto (7)	melding (47)	flamboyant (85)
indigo (15)	gumbos (47)	decorum (89)
sepia (15)	resonance (48)	insidious (89)

■ *Questions on Meaning and Technique*

1. What is the difference in between the author's grandmother and mother's attitudes toward the family tree? Evaluate the two attitudes in terms of personal happiness or healthy psychology.

2. What does the tale about black folks being able to fly in times past add to the grandmother's influence on the author? Is this influence healthy or not? Give reasons for your answer.

3. How does the grandmother react to the belief that "one drop of black blood makes you a slave"? What is your reaction to the judgment that if a person is partially black, he or she should be categorized as black?

4. What is the meaning of paragraph 31? Explain it and state why you agree or disagree with the author.

5. In paragraph 52, what is the meaning of the question "Wasn't Lucy their mother too?" Is this a fair question? How does it pertain to the argument about racial discrimination?

6. Why does the author bring up the 1954 incident of Emmett Till? What is your response to this allusion? How white *are* the white lines of Caucasians?

7. What progress do you think has been made in race relations during the past few decades in our country? Is the word "kin" still a code word for rape (see paragraph 8)? Could Emmett Till be murdered today? What do you think can be done to put a real end to race discrimination? Give specific recommendations.

8. What does the author mean by the last sentence of her story? How does this comment relate to "Even a child knows there is no pure color"? Explain both figures of speech.

Writing Assignments

1. Write an essay about Emma Lazarus and what she contributed to the "mixed-blood stew" in our country. If you do not recognize the name, look it up in an encyclopedia or on the internet.

2. Write an argument persuading your reader that poverty and ignorance are strong contributors to racial discrimination. Or, write an argument persuading your reader that poverty and ignorance do not contribute to racial discrimination. Base your essay on sound premises, avoid logical fallacies, use irrefutable evidence, and anticipate the opposition.

UNDERSTANDING DIVERSITY IN SEXUAL ORIENTATION

RYAN VAN METER

First

Ryan van Meter is a freelance writer who grew up in Missouri, where he attended the University of Missouri-Columbia, majoring in English. For a decade after graduation, he lived in Chicago and worked in advertising as a copywriter. He holds an M.A. in creative writing from Chicago's DePaul University and an MFA in nonfiction writing from the University of Iowa. Van Meter was included in the Touchstone Anthology of Creative Nonfiction, *and has been published in several prestigious journals including the* Iowa Review, *the* Indiana Review, *and the* Gettysburg Review, *from which the story below is taken. The collection that includes "First," is titled* If You Knew Then What I Know Now *(Sarabande Books, 2011). "First" was selected for* The Best American Essays of 2009.

READING FOR IDEAS In this simple but moving story, a little boy feels punished for having expressed to his best friend the romantic feelings of love he had observed when he watched his mother's soap operas. Since the speaker relating the incident is an adult recapturing an incident from his kindergartener days, you will notice that the narrator's reactions are those of an innocent child who does not yet understand all of the nuances about love as interpreted by adults. Reading this story might be an excellent opportunity for you to scan your memory for some incident in your childhood that affected or changed your life in some way. Perhaps your childhood world too experienced a painful clash with the world of grownups. If so, what lesson did you learn? Notice how in this story, time has been telescoped to the evening when this childhood event took place.

1   Ben and I are sitting side by side in the very back of his mother's station wagon. We face glowing white headlights of cars following us, our sneakers pressed against the back hatch door. This is our joy—his and mine—to sit turned away from our moms and dads in this place that feels like a secret, as though they are not even in the car with us. They have just taken us out to dinner, and now we are driving home. Years from this evening, I won't actually be sure that this boy sitting beside me is named Ben. But that doesn't matter tonight. What I know for certain right now is that I love him, and I need to tell him this fact before we return to our separate houses, next door lo each other. We are both five.

2   Ben is the first brown-eyed boy I will fall for but will not be the last. His hair is also brown and always needs scraping off his forehead, which he does about every five minutes. All his jeans have dark squares stuck over the knees where he has worn through the denim. His shoelaces are perpetually undone, and he has a magic way of tying them with a quick, weird loop that I study and try myself, but can never match. His fingernails are ragged because he rips them off with his teeth and spits out the pieces when our moms aren't watching. Somebody always has to fix his shirt collars.

3   Our parents face the other direction, talking about something, and it is raining. My eyes trace the lines of water as they draw down the glass. Coiled beside my legs are the thick black and red cords of a pair of jumper cables. Ben's T-ball bat is also back here, rolling around and clunking as the long car wends its way through town. Ben's dad is driving, and my dad sits next to him, with our mothers in the back seat; I have recently observed that when mothers and fathers are in the car together, the dad always drives. My dad has also insisted on checking the score of the Cardinals game, so the radio is tuned to a staticky AM station, and the announcer's rich voice buzzes out of the speakers up front.

4   The week before this particular night, I asked my mother, "Why do people get married?" I don't recall the impulse behind my curiosity, but I will forever remember every word of her answer—she stated it simply after only a moment or two of thinking—because it seemed that important: "Two people get married when they love each other."

5   I had that hunch. I am a kindergartener, but the summer just before this rainy night, I learned most of what I know about love from watching soap operas with my mother. She is a gym teacher and during her months off, she catches up on the shows she has watched since college. Every summer weekday, I couldn't wait until they came on at two o'clock. My father didn't think I should be watching them—boys should be outside, playing—but he was rarely home early enough to know the difference, and according to my mother, I was too young to really understand what was going on anyway.

6   What I enjoyed most about soap opera was how exciting and beautiful life was. Every lady was pretty and had wonderful hair, and all the men had dark eyes and big teeth and faces as strong as bricks, and every week, there was a wedding or a manhunt or a birth. The people had grand fights where they threw vases at walls and slammed doors and chased each other in cars. There were villains locking up the wonderfully-haired heroines and suspending them in gold cages above enormous acid vats. And, of course, it was love that inspired every one of these stories and made life on the screen as thrilling as it was. That was what my mother would say from the sofa when I turned from my spot on the carpet in front of her and faced her, asking, "Why is he spying on that lady?"

7   "Because he loves her."

8   In the car, Ben and I hold hands. There is something sticky on his fingers, probably the strawberry syrup from the ice cream sundaes we ate for dessert. We have never held hands before; I have simply reached for his in the dark and held him while he holds me. I want to see our hands on the rough floor, but they are only visible every block or so when the car passes beneath a streetlight, and then, for only a flash. Ben is my closest friend because he lives next door, we are the same age, and we both have little brothers who are babies. I wish he were in the same kindergarten class as me, but he goes to a different school—one where he has to wear a uniform all day and for which there is no school bus.

9   "I love you," I say. We are idling, waiting for a red light to be green; a shining car has stopped right behind us, so Ben's face is pale and brilliant.

10   "I love you too," he says.

11   The car becomes quiet as the voice of the baseball game shrinks smaller and smaller.

12   "Will you marry me?" I ask him. His hand is still in mine; on the soap opera, you are supposed to have a ring, but I don't have one.

13   He begins to nod, and suddenly my mother feels very close. I look over my shoulder, my eyes peeking over the back of the last row of seats that we are leaning against. She has turned around, facing me. Permed hair, laugh lines not laughing.

14   "What did you just say?" she asks.

15   "I asked Ben to marry me."

16   The car starts moving forward again, and none of the parents are talking loud enough for us to hear them back here. I brace myself against the raised carpeted hump of the wheel well as Ben's father turns left onto the street before the turn onto our street. Sitting beside my mom is Ben's mother, who keeps staring forward, but I notice that one of her ears keeps swiveling back here, a little more each time. I am still facing my mother, who is still facing me, and for one last second, we look at each other without anything wrong between us.

17   "You shouldn't have said that," she says. "Boys don't marry other boys. Only boys and girls get married to each other."

18   She can't see our hands, but Ben pulls his away. I close my fingers into a loose fist and rub my palm to feel, and keep feeling, how strange his skin has made mine.

19   "Okay?" she asks.

20   "Yes," I say, but by accident my throat whispers the words.

21   She asks again. "Okay? Did you hear me?"

22   "Yes!" this time nearly shouting, and I wish we were already home so I could jump out and run to my bedroom. To be back here in the dark, private tail of the car suddenly feels wrong, so Ben and I each scoot off to our separate sides. "Yes," I say again, almost normally, turning away to face the rainy window. I feel her turn too as the radio baseball voice comes back up of the quiet. The car starts to dip as we head down the hill of our street; our house is at the bottom. No one speaks for the rest of the ride. We all just sit and wait and watch our own views of the road—the parents see what is ahead of us while the only thing I can look at is what we have just left behind.

Source: Ryan van Meter, "First," *The Gettysburg Review*, Winter, 2008. Reprinted in *The Best American Essays 2009*. Ed. Robert Atwan. N.Y. Mariner Books, 2009, pp. 177–180.

■ *Vocabulary*

villains (6)   vats (6)

■ *Questions on Meaning and Technique*

1. Why is the story titled "First"? What other title might be appropriate? Explain your choice.

2. If this story is about love, whence did the narrator gather his views of love? What are these views? Explain them.

3. What is your interpretation of the first sentence of paragraph 2? How important is it to the development of the story? Could the sentence be deleted without damaging the theme of the story? Why or why not?

4. According to the mother, why do people get married? Do you think her answer was appropriate for a little boy? What answer would you have given and why? What impulse does the mother's answer trigger in the little boy?

5. Why does the little boy think he should have a ring when he asks his friend, "Will you marry me?" What does his thinking tell us about our social values or traditions? How much do you esteem or scorn these values or traditions?

6. What do you think of the little boy's mother depicted in this story? What does her reaction tell us about her?

7. In paragraph 6, the little boy says, "What I enjoyed most about soap operas was how exciting and beautiful life was." How would you describe the life of a typical soap opera? What kinds of people are the main characters? Would you model yourself after them? Why or why not?

8. Why does the narrator mention the sounds of the ball game on the radio in the background? What, if anything, does it add to the story?

9. What change in the boys' attitude did the mother's scolding produce? Explain this change.

10. The final sentence elucidates the entire experience of the narrator. What is the double meaning of "the only thing I can look at is what we have just left behind"? Why is the ending of the essay left ambiguous—without any definite resolution of the story's paradox? What is your reaction to the ending?

Writing Assignments

1. Write an argument supporting or attacking the legal right of homosexuals to marry and adopt children. Try to find expert testimony to support your thesis.

2. Write an essay in which you try to persuade your reader that homosexuals are part of the diversity in our society and should be treated with the consideration and respect we grant anyone else. Make sure that your argument rests on sound premises and solid evidence.

 ## Internet Research Assignment

Date rape is not diminishing on college campuses or in society. Write an argument in which you discuss how date rape can be reduced. The internet can help you uncover articles that display varying points of view on this subject. Who or what is to blame? Be sure to provide credible evidence for your thesis.

Additional Writing Assignments

1. Write an argument either for or against college students living in dormitories.

2. Write a paper in which you argue the urgent necessity for recycling by individual families.

3. It is often stated that television news programs give a distorted view of life because they report only the sensational. Argue for or against this proposition.

4. Should art galleries be censored for so-called pornographic exhibits? Answer this question in the form of an argument either for or against censorship of art.

5. Instructors of political science should never express their own political opinions in class. Argue for or against this proposition.

6. Experts on educational theory believe bright and slow students should be separated to learn at their own maximum levels; others feel that slow learners can learn from bright ones without causing harm to the bright. Take a position on this issue and argue it.

7. Write an argument supporting the view that the U.S. consumer is a victim of planned obsolescence.

8. Read through the opinion section in several issues of your local newspaper until you find an article containing a proposition with which you disagree. Counter with your own argument.

9. Argue either for or against living wills—that is, the idea that while individuals are still of sound mind, they should sign a legal document forbidding extraordinary medical methods should they contract an illness that puts them into a vegetative state.

10. Write an essay arguing in favor of buying U.S.-made cars to bolster the U.S. economy.

11. Write an argument persuading your readers to carry earthquake safety kits in the trunks of their cars.

12. As persuasively as you can, argue for or against a research paper requirement for freshman English.

13. There is no constitutionally mandated U.S. national language. Argue for or against amending the Constitution to make English the official language.

14. Once the U.S. government has identified another country as an enemy, should we send humanitarian aid to it in the event of a natural disaster such as an earthquake, flood, or famine? Answer in the form of a persuasive argument.

Rewriting Assignment

Here is the opening paragraph of an argument against having parents use the Home Drug Testing System, approved by the Food and Drug Administration, to test their teenagers for drug use. The paragraph needs a more gripping opening and a statement of the controlling idea. Rewrite the paragraph to include both.

Photo Writing Assignment

Pictured below are survivors of the 2005 tsunami that devastated Indonesia receiving food and other supplies at a makeshift evacuation camp in Banda Aceh. Much

AP Images/Danu Kusworo, Kompas Daily

of the U.S. government budget is used to help humanitarian causes all over the world. Write an essay in which you argue for or against our government's generosity toward foreign nations struggling to survive. Under what, if any, circumstances would you favor continuing to give aid? In arguing your case, use the guidelines given in this chapter.

Digging for Gold or for Points and Counterpoints

As we continue the gold miner metaphor in approaching argumentation, we imagine how prospectors argue to convince themselves, their employers, or their helpers that this river or that cave looks promising as a source of gold. Every logical reason is expressed in order to motivate some entrepreneur to advance the money for a particular gold mining enterprise.

Now let's shift to writing an argument for your English class. Our society is, we like to believe, free and open. We can go to church or not go to church without explaining why. We are not forced at gunpoint to dress a certain way, to follow dietary restrictions and other sacred observances for religious reasons, or to join a particular group unless we want to. We can choose for ourselves the career we will pursue, regardless of our gender, and be limited by nothing other than our aptitude or talent. If the American isn't a poster child for freedom, then perhaps the world really is flat as some still contend.

But we know that the world is round, not flat. We have pictures taken from satellites and space shuttles to prove it. No matter what you hear to the contrary, the idea of a round world is not a hoax perpetrated upon the gullible population. Yet some people continue to adamantly believe in a flat earth. That such a self-evident fact as the roundness of the world can still ignite controversy tells us something about the nature, persistence, and tenacity of belief. It also tells us that the passion that drives us to extreme fanaticism may have been earlier implanted in our hearts, on some other occasion, and for some other reasons. The point to keep in mind is that a really good argument is always based on fairness and sound judgment, not on gullibility or fanaticism.

This chapter consists of various propositions some people would regard as hot button topics that are sure to draw unfriendly fire. In his short story "War," Luigi Pirandello, a Nobel Prize laureate in literature, portrays the senseless waste of war in the sudden recognition by a father that his son, killed in battle, is gone forever. "The Case Against Man" by Isaac Asimov argues that our very extinction hangs in the balance if we can't control population growth. Both Judy Syfers and Anna Quindlen argue that too much is required of women striving to be good wives or good mothers, while also holding down jobs to help support the family. Student writer Ben Goldberg argues that despite all of the progress made to achieve equality in our society, a subtle and hidden kind of prejudice continues to exist.

Following these topics is a cluster of three stories about religion, skin color, and sexual orientation. This cluster discussion aims at helping the reader to understand diversity and should generate spirited debate which will not only reveal the differences between you and everyone else, but also show the common humanity that we share under the wrapping of the skin.

In sum, we believe that in terms of writing arguments on diverse elements in our society, digging for gold means searching for fair and balanced views.

The Essay Examination

Chapter 16

Preparing for the Essay Examination

How to Do Well on Essay Examinations

To excel at the essay exam requires that you (1) know your subject, (2) be able to demonstrate your knowledge in your essay, and (3) organize your answer so it is easy for an overworked grader to follow. This last observation is not meant to be cynical but is a realistic requirement the student writer must take into account when writing essay exams. Teachers who grade them are looking for particular points organized in a specific sequence. And the student who delivers these points in the expected order with a minimum of wordiness is likely to get a response of immense gratitude from any weary instructor who must plod through a stack of essays.

To perform well on essay exams, you should observe these common-sense cautions.

Read the Question Carefully, At Least Twice

The most common error students make on essay exams is to misread the question. If more than one essay answer is required, read each one so that you get an overview of the questions and are able to budget the correct time for each. Consider the following question from a History of Western Europe class:

> Define the Franco-Prussian War, placing it in its proper age, describing who the participants were, and explaining the causes that led up to it.

Implied in this question are three rhetorical objectives that the writer must meet and that the reader expects:

1. A *definition* of the Franco-Prussian war
2. A *description* of its major participants
3. An *explanation* of the causes leading up to the war

A good answer will not only present the appropriate facts but do so *exactly in the order asked* by the question. If you scramble the order of the question, you make your answer harder to read and will likely suffer a penalty. As an exam taker, your aim should be not only to deliver the answers asked for by the question but also to do so in a way that is most helpful to your reader. And once you have established that the question calls for a definition followed by a description and a causal analysis, the rest is a straightforward presentation of the facts in understandable and readable prose.

Give the Question Some Thought Before Starting to Write

In a one-hundred-yard sprint, the first runner off the block is generally the one who wins, but not so in an essay exam. Finishing before the deadline earns you no extra credit, and it is pointless to try to beat the clock by plunging as quickly as possible into the actual writing. Instead, sit back and think about the question and how you plan to answer it, including the points you must cover and the facts you intend to cite. If you have a choice of questions, answer the one you know best. And once you have made your selection, be absolutely sure that your answer sticks to the question, no matter how much you might yearn to show how much you know about a side issue. For instance, if the question asks you to explain the causes of the Civil War, do not write at length about its devastating effects. Always do *exactly* what the question asks.

Organize Your Thoughts Through Prewriting

Some students can organize their thoughts systematically and logically as they write, but most cannot and perform better on an essay exam when they prewrite. The prewriting may be as simple as jotting down on a separate piece of notepaper a few key words for all the important points. A rough outline may also be helpful, such as this one explaining the causes of the Franco-Prussian War:

I. Bismarck's desire to unify Germany

II. Napoleon III's fear of an alliance against him

III. France's fear of a Prussian prince on the Spanish throne

Exam taking is nerve wracking, and jotting down major ideas on a slip of paper can keep you from drifting or forgetting to make an important point.

Time Yourself Carefully

Because most examinations allot a time limit to every question, you cannot afford to ramble or throw in information not asked for by the question, nor will doing so get you any more points. Pay attention, therefore, to such phrases as *in a brief paragraph, in two hundred words or less,* or *in approximately two pages.* Pay particularly close attention to the number of points an answer is worth. Nothing is gained by wasting one hour on a ten-point question in a two-hour one-hundred-point examination.

Nor is anything achieved by demonstrating your knowledge on a topic not included in the question. For example, if a history question asks you to define Pickett's Charge at the Civil War Battle of Gettysburg, you will earn no bonus by throwing in details about the conduct of Union General Meade.

Using Rhetorical Strategies in Essay Examinations

Rhetorical strategies can help you to organize answers quickly during an essay exam. If you know in the abstract how to write, say, a definition, you will find it easy to write one in the particular. Some questions will clearly specify the most appropriate rhetorical strategy to be used in an answer, but others will not. You must look for key words in the essay question that will tell you which strategy to use in your answer. Here are some examples of essay examination questions, followed by a discussion of the best strategies for answering them.

FROM LITERATURE

Question

Typical of many of Shakespeare's plays, *Othello* is filled with dramatic irony. Point out at least three *instances* of this technique in the play, and *discuss* how they intensify the conflict or suspense.

Although the key words in this question are *instances* and *discuss,* common sense tells us that the logical opening for an essay answering this question is to define *dramatic irony,* which occurs in a play when the audience knows something that the stage character does not. Having defined dramatic irony, you can then cite three specific examples of it in *Othello*. The question further asks for a *discussion* of how dramatic irony intensifies conflict or suspense. *Discuss* is a catch-all term that often masks the use of various possible strategies—example, effect, argument, and so on. In this case, the question is asking that you demonstrate the *effect* of specific instances of irony on the dramatic tension in the play. In other words, you need to show how Othello's blindness to his wife's virtue intensifies emotion in the audience watching the tragic unfolding of events in the play.

FROM U.S. HISTORY

Question

Use one paragraph to answer the following questions: What is the Federal Reserve System? How did it originate? What is its purpose?

A question that begins with *What is . . . ?* almost always requires the strategy of *definition*. Your answer might begin as follows: "The Federal Reserve System is the central banking authority for the United States," which gives a nuts-and-bolts definition of the system. The second part of the question, on the *origin* and *purpose* of the Federal Reserve System, calls for an unclassifiable response based partly on narration. You might write, "It originated in 1913 as part of the Federal Reserve Act, and its purpose is to stimulate economic activity by buying securities and allowing banks to expand and thus to increase their money lending. The system may also slow down economic activity by selling securities and thus contracting bank reserves and reducing lending. Moreover, the system controls the interest rates at which member banks may borrow from it."

Because the question asks for an answer in only a single paragraph, you must stick to the required length and curb any urge to gush for pages.

FROM ART HISTORY

Question

Using *Park in Tangier, The Purple Robe,* and *Seated Blue Nude* as examples, *show* how Henri Matisse's experimentation with color eventually led to the Fauve movement.

Show as used in this question is a synonym for *describe*. A good way to begin the answer is to describe in specific detail how color is used in the Matisse paintings named. You should also describe how Matisse's paintings foreshadowed the Fauves, a group of painters, such as Derain, Braque, and Rouault, who were devoted to the use of violent, uncontrolled, brilliant color.

FROM GEOGRAPHY

Question

What major powers competed for influence in the Caribbean region in the eighteenth century, and what territories did they acquire? What were these colonial powers seeking?

Buried in this question is an implicit *division and classification* of the powers that colonized the Caribbean and the territories they captured. You must divide the Caribbean into the various Spanish, British, Dutch, and French colonies. The second part of the question—what the colonial powers were seeking—can be answered by a strategy of *causal analysis* specifying the reasons behind these Caribbean acquisitions. Notice that the wording of this question does not make it particularly clear which rhetorical strategy you should use. But with a little thought, you can easily infer the most appropriate strategy.

FROM SOCIOLOGY

Question

From your own experience or from reading the newspaper, *narrate* an incident that illustrates the unresponsive bystander syndrome in densely populated urban areas.

This question calls for a *narration* from your own experience (see Chapter 8). But if it is to be answered with purpose, the incident chosen must be paced to show

how and why people in large cities might witness a crime or an accident and refuse to help or get involved. You must avoid redundancy or irrelevant rambling by focusing sharply on the question.

FROM PHILOSOPHY

Question

What is *virtue* as revealed in Spinoza's *Foundations of the Moral Life* and in the Hindu *Bhagavadgita*? How do the concepts of virtue differ in each philosophy? Cite incidents from your own experience to back up the respective concepts and to indicate that you understand them.

Although it does not directly say so, this question is calling for three different strategies: the first, a *definition* of *virtue* in Spinoza and in the *Bhagavadgita;* the second, a *comparison/contrast* of the differing meanings of *virtue* in each philosophy; the third, the use of personal *examples* to illustrate your understanding of both concepts. For instance, you might begin by writing, "Spinoza defines *virtue* as self-preservation, whereas the *Bhagavadgita* defines *virtue* as self-denial. Clearly, the two definitions stand in stark contrast to each other."

FROM CHEMISTRY

Question

(1) Differentiate, first, between starch and glycogen and, second, between cellulose and starch. (2) High-compression automobile engines that operate at high temperatures are designed to oxidize hydrocarbons completely to carbon dioxide and water. In the process of attempting to completely oxidize the hydrocarbons, a non-carbon-containing pollutant is produced. What types of compounds are produced, and why do high-compression engines favor the formation of these compounds?

At first, you may think that question 1 gives you no clues as to what strategy to use. However, on closer look you will see that the question is asking for a *comparison/contrast*. You must answer by explaining how starch is different from glycogen and cellulose from starch. Here is an excerpt from a student answer to this question:

> Both starch and glycogen are disaccharides, but starch has a d-glycosidic bond that doesn't allow a great extent of H-bonding. Therefore starch is easier to break down than glycogen. Starch is found mainly in plants, whereas glycogen exists mainly in animals. Glycogen is the monomer unit of most fatty acids.

Although this is a technical answer, it is still easy to see that the student is systematically comparing and contrasting. She uses contrasting terms such as *but* and *whereas*. She says how starch and glycogen are similar and how they are different.

Consider the second chemistry question on high-compression automobile engines. Your answer should consist of paragraphs that *divide and classify*—specifying the types of compounds produced—as well as paragraphs that analyze *cause*—saying why high-compression engines produce them.

FROM POLITICAL SCIENCE

Question

In an essay of approximately 300 words, argue for or against this proposition: "If parents choose to send their children to private school rather than public school, then the government should provide them with a voucher equivalent to the cost of a public school education."

This question is clearly asking for an *argumentative* essay. All you have to do is take a side and knuckle down to the work of supporting your argument with the right facts, expert testimony, and logic.

To sum up, although it is not always clear what rhetorical strategy you might best use in writing an essay exam, most of the time you can make a reasonable inference from the wording of the question. Your answer, for that matter, may not always neatly fall into any specific rhetorical strategy. Indeed, most of the time your answer is likely to call for a mixed strategy. In any case, instructors do not judge essay exams on the relative purity of their rhetorical strategies but on such sensible criteria as whether the question is fully answered and the response cites a wealth of factual details.

Sample Essay Exams

To give you an idea of the difference between an A and a C essay written for an exam, we are including two actual student essay answers written for a history class. Notice the instructor's annotations on the essay exams that follow.

Dr. M. Renner   Fall 2008

Glendale Community College

Final Examination Question

History 111--Women in American History

<u>100-point question</u>

Women have not always agreed on their role and function in society. Some women have

emphasized the domestic role, basing their support of this role on religious principles.

Others have cast a wider net and justified their arguments on political, economic,

religious, or other social grounds. Your task is to select four of the women listed below whose attitudes and practices best reveal those differences historically. Discuss the female role(s) they promoted, the values and attitudes that underlay their ideas, and the grounds they used to justify their arguments. End your essay with a discussion of one specific woman who, you believe, has had the most dramatic impact on modern women.

a. Anne Hutchinson

b. Sarah Grimke

c. Judith Sargent Murray

d. Elizabeth Murray Smith

e. Alice Paul

f. Charlotte P. Gilman

g. M. Carey Thomas

h. Elizabeth Cady Stanton

Grade C Answer

74 pts.

C

by Elizabeth Caraballo

1   The role of women in society for the Puritans was being a wife, mother, and home maintainer. Women were supposed to grow up and learn how to cook, clean, keep house, and tend to their husbands' needs. Religion played an enormous part in the Puritans' lives. Women were good and righteous. They went to church and prayed all day on Sunday. Men also went to church and prayed all day on Sunday. Wives had to make their own bread and butter, milk their own cows, and clothe the entire family. These Puritan women also bore many children, one child approximately every two years.

Your opening paragraph is weak. You state the obvious without focusing on the role of women as a challenge.

2   Anne Hutchinson was a Puritan woman who changed or at least sparked an interest in change in the lives of the Puritans. She would gather with other women and speak and teach them things. Hutchinson was a midwife; therefore, she was always with young women and influenced them a great deal. She was a vocal woman who spoke out on what she believed. She was friends with a pastor who was disliked by the Puritan Church. The Puritan Church passed a law forbidding anyone to keep a person in their home. Hutchinson

Not specific enough

What did she believe? What was her challenge?

What was the
issue?

You have
already said
this.
Explain

was keeping this pastor in her home and was caught. Later she was exiled from the Puritan

community, and some followers left with her. ~~Anne Hutchinson was a very outspoken~~
~~woman who spoke out on what she believed.~~ The Puritan Church did not believe that
women should be heard so they got rid of her. She is a clear example of a woman who

believed that she should do something more than stay home and cook or clean.

Vague–Do
you mean his
court trials?

What was the
main content
of her letters?
Again, you
hint rather
than offer
specific
information.
What did she
actually gain?

3   As the years passed, many women began to speak out about how they felt and

what they believed. For instance, the Grimke sisters were the daughters of an attorney

and they learned a lot from situations their father encountered. Sarah Grimke would later

speak about slavery and how wrong it was. She would speak in public. Since this was

not acceptable, the Church wrote her a letter, called the "Pastoral letter." This letter told

Sarah that it was unacceptable behavior for a woman to be doing what she was doing.

This letter told her that her place was in the home and that it would be in her best

interest to do that. She wrote back to the Church and published the letters so everyone

could read them. Grimke came a step closer to becoming someone different from what

she was supposed to be.

4   The Abolition Movement sparked women's interest more than almost any other

issue. Many women believed that slavery was not right. Elizabeth Cady Stanton was

a woman who was educated in private schools. She married Henry Stanton but

You might
have
mentioned the
decades.

What was its
purpose?
Consider
Stanton's fight
for suffrage.
What
specifically
did they want
to change?

remained a very independent woman. She fought for married women's right to own their

own property. She went to court to try to get **it** passed. Finally **it** was passed that

married women could own property, but five years later **it** was reversed. The point was

that she was heard and later on in history women would be able to own property.

Elizabeth Cady Stanton's name appears throughout many years of women's history.

She attended the Women's Convention, which would convene every year with more and

more participants. She would fight for women's education. She and her husband would

spend their lives trying to change things.

Needs further
development.

5   During this same period, Elizabeth Murray Smith had a prenuptial agreement

written so that her husband-to-be could not acquire all of her wealth after they

were married.

6   The ideas that Elizabeth Cady Stanton and Elizabeth Murray Smith portrayed

were ideas suggesting that women could do other things besides just staying home.

The man was not necessarily the boss. These women believed that women were

important as individuals.

Careful! They could have been individuals at home.

7   Religion was the basis of life according to most historical accounts throughout the

eighteenth and nineteenth centuries. In the twentieth century, religion was still important,

but it did not seem as important as in earlier days. Women could gain the right to vote

through the strides of many women in many societies. Now women had a say in what

When?

would happen to them. Many women were opposed to women's voting and so were

many men. Some groups tried to make women believe that good and righteous women

should not vote. They also established voting places in bars, where respectable

women did not dare go. However, matters changed slowly, and by the mid-1900s,

many women were voting.

8   Alice Paul wrote the Equal Rights Amendment. She tried to get women's pay and

education equal to those of men. She also tried to get rid of protective legislation that

harmed women and their goal of equality in general. This amendment was rewritten

many times--the last time in the 1970s--but it has never been passed. The ERA, though,

Who?

put a spark in the government. (They) did agree that women were treated differently.

This kind of brings us up to date.

Do they? "Things happen" because people struggle hard for change.

9   Women in the 1990s are more independent than ever. They still do not have

everything they deserve, but all things happen in due time.

10   I believe that any woman who fights for a cause she believes in is incredible. It is very

hard for me to isolate just one woman who made the most dramatic impact on modern

society, but Elizabeth Cady Stanton was the woman who impressed me the most. It may

be just because her name popped up more than any other woman's name, but she was an

incredible woman.

Nevertheless, the exam requires that you select one woman and explain her dramatic impact.

11   NOTE: We did not discuss Sandra Day O'Connor, the only woman ever to be a justice

on the U.S. Supreme Court, but I admire her and believe her to be the woman who has

made quite an impact on modern women.

Good extra comment

95 pts.

(A)

Grade A Answer

by Melissa Barcelona

1   Through the course of time, women, like men, have held disparate views on what roles a woman should play in society and on what constitutes appropriate conduct for her. Some women have made their point in subtle ways, whereas others have been flamboyant and outspoken. These varying attitudes probably depended on the times in which they were presented and the principles they defended.

2   In the beginning of the Colonial Period here in America, women stood staunchly behind religious principles in defining their roles as women. The world of these women was based on the Bible, which they knew well and taught faithfully to their children. One of these women was Anne Hutchinson, a strong Puritan woman, who based her views of a woman's role on the Bible but who also became a mighty spokeswoman for the theological belief that people were saved by Grace. Although she believed in the Biblical injunctions concerning a woman and her role, Anne Hutchinson did not accept every dogma of the Puritan Church--predestination, for example. But most obvious, she was not a quietly obsequious Puritan woman who remained in the background of public life, the way women of her day were supposed to. By speaking in public on women's issues, she broke the rules of what was expected of a woman. So, although Anne Hutchinson's opinion of a woman's role was based on her understanding of Scripture, her view on how women should function in society contrasted sharply with the Biblical interpretation of her society. Claiming the Bible as her guide, Anne Hutchinson promoted the role of domesticity for women, but one could argue that as a spokeswoman at a time when women were to remain in the background of debate, she clearly broke her own rules.

3   Sarah Grimke was another woman who clearly stood behind religious principles in her view of women's role; however, this belief was tinged with political overtones.

You have responded to the question in an exemplary way, focusing on the roles of four women and what each one specifically contributed to the women's movement in the U.S. Your essay is well organized, and your thesis is well supported.

For instance, when she read the Bible and came across the words "Man and woman are created equal," she took this passage at face value. Sarah Grimke began to write letters on the equality of women. Despite an unfavorable response from her church in the form of a scolding pastoral letter, Sarah Grimke did not back down, just as Anne Hutchinson had not. Grimke not only argued for the equality of women with men, but she also focused on the fair treatment of blacks. It was her strong moral convictions that provoked her to pursue the issue of equality among men, women, and blacks. It is difficult to know whether or not Grimke really supported the role of domesticity for women, but it is easy to see that she believed in a woman's right to choose her role and to have equal rights with men.

4   Alice Paul is another woman who espoused equality for women; however, she did not base her stand on religious principles but on political and economic motivation. She felt that women should have a choice in the role they chose and that they should be treated with equality. Standing squarely behind the Equal Rights Amendment, Alice Paul promoted the idea that women should not have limitations forced on them by the laws of the day. Her argument was that while some of these laws did indeed make life easier for women, so far as job duties and time on the job were concerned, they also limited women by restricting job availability. Paul also took a stand on women's right to vote and thus have a voice in government. She was responsible for reorganizing the National Woman's Party into the League of Women Voters.

5   Like Alice Paul, Elizabeth Cady Stanton was also politically and economically oriented in her views of woman's role and position in society. She stood with the National Woman's Party by writing documents based on the party's platform. She also took a stand on equality in the roles of women and men. Her values were based on the Bible, but she also wrote her own Bible to demonstrate her strong belief in equality, going so far as to change the wording of certain Biblical passages to support her beliefs.

6   Needless to say, women like Elizabeth Cady Stanton and Alice Paul did not support the traditional woman's role of being in the home, as other women of their day did. Instead, they felt women should have a choice and, regardless of their choice, they should be treated fairly and equal with men.

7   Out of these four women, Alice Paul has had the most dramatic and lasting impact on modern women. She was the originator of equal rights. She fought wholeheartedly for the Equal Rights Amendment, long before the battle became a popular cause. Her contribution will not be forgotten by history. I think Alice Paul would fit with ease into today's political arena.

PART IV

The Research Paper

Chapter 17

Doing the Research

A research paper is an essay—longer, more formal, and better documented than essays you are used to writing—but an essay, nonetheless. It is in its length, depth, and documentation that the research paper mainly differs from the usual essay. You are required, in writing a research paper, to collect and incorporate data and the opinions of authorities on your subject and to acknowledge your borrowed sources in either a footnote, an endnote, or a parenthetical reference.

Here is a footnote:

> 1. Caryl Philips, "Doctor Johnson's Watch," in *Foreigners* (New York: Alfred A. Knopf, 2007), 53.

Here is an endnote:

> 1. Jeff Blumberg, "Abandoned Ship," *Smithsonian Magazine* 38 (2007): 20.

And here is an example of a parenthetical reference:

A daily commute in the suburbs of Kingston is measured not in distance but in travel time. Covering the six or seven miles to reach a suburban school from a residence in Red Hills can take as long as forty-five minutes to an hour during the morning rush. Little can be done by traffic engineers to improve this commute. The roadbed descends down the hill at a steep angle, and its twists and turns already devour every available inch of space on the steep hillside. Making more room for a wider road would require massive excavation of the mountain that the government says it can't afford. One small compensation for living on a mountain, as writer Kim Robinson notes in "On the Road," her contribution to *Caribbean Dispatches* edited by Jane Bryce, is the scenic meeting of sky and land where "the lights of the city glint gold, white, red and blue like jewels on the jet-black plain" (7).

The text briefly introduces the author and work, with a page number supplied in parentheses. The entire citation appears only once in the "Works Cited" at the end of the paper:

> Robinson, Kim. "On the Road." *Caribbean Dispatches: Beyond the Tourist Dream.* Comp. and Ed. Jane Bryce. Oxford: Macmillan, 2006. Print.

Footnotes are single spaced at the bottom of the page with double spacing between them. Endnotes are double spaced and placed on a separate page at the end of the paper. All three systems list the citations in a final "Works Cited" page. We shall discuss all the citation styles, but we will concentrate on parenthetical documentation because its ease of use has made it the current most popular style.

Choosing a Topic

You choose a topic for the research paper much as you would for any other essay: You browse the library's book collection, surf the internet, or talk to experts, friends, and fellow students. The only difference is that now you need a meatier topic, one that you can cover in eight to ten pages and back up with reference sources. Sometimes your instructor will make the decision easy by assigning the class a specific topic. Whatever your circumstances, choosing a topic is a relatively straightforward process if you follow this rule faithfully: Always choose a topic that you like. If you hate everything, second-best is to choose a topic that might teach you something useful or a topic in which you have some interest. Liking your topic will make writing about it easier; hating your topic will make writing about it a miserable chore.

A research paper topic does not have to be grand or cosmically significant, but it should be of some substance. The writer Sheridan Baker suggests that every good topic has an argumentative edge that needs to be proved or disproved. For example, the topic "contagious diseases of the past," admittedly overly broad and bland, can be honed to an argumentative edge by a little rewording: "the Black Death: reducer of overpopulation in Europe." This is now a topic with an edge that gives you something to prove. Instead of calling for a summary of major contagious diseases, it hints that they served some useful purpose by controlling the population. This is a controversial outlook that will give your paper the energy of an argumentative edge. People don't whisper when they argue; they shout.

Whatever topic you choose and however you choose it, be sure to clear it in advance with your instructor.

Doing the Research

Doing the research will require you to visit the library either in person or online. You'll have to search indexes and reference works for information about your topic. Most modern libraries have an electronic catalog that makes searching their collections for any topic a breeze. Most likely this catalog will also be linked to one or more databases—information available electronically—that you might find helpful. Ask your librarian what's available in your chosen subject.

Note that your topic at this stage is written in pencil, not etched in stone. The research you do may even cause you to change it. You may have begun with the intention of writing a paper on small poetry magazines. But your reading might have drawn you to a particular poet whose work you'd rather write about. Or, as a psychology major, you had been thinking about writing a paper about the role of foster parents in child care; but when you asked Google to look for "foster parents and child care," the term "ADHS" kept popping up. Coincidentally, you had just seen the play *Distracted*, a satire about ADHS, so you veered toward a paper on the "Attention Deficit and Hyperactivity Syndrome" that seems to afflict so many modern children. Changing a topic or making a slight readjustment to it is fine at this stage so long as you get the approval of your instructor.

A source of information students usually overlook is the presence of experts on campus. Most schools have more genuine experts per square foot than any other comparable ground. Most of these people are available to be interviewed and quoted in your paper. Another treasure on hand for the student is the librarian. He or she can be invaluable in suggesting reference sources that might help you in your research. Don't be afraid to ask the librarian for help.

Using the Personal Interview to Research a Topic

Interviewing local experts about your topic is also a widely underused research tactic. For instance, some teachers consider it a helpful practice to assign students to research a profession or job they would like to pursue after graduating from college. Students are told to look up magazine articles, books, and electronic sources about their chosen profession. But they are also encouraged to interview people who already work in the field of their choice. One teacher at Boston University gave students the following list of questions to ask a prospective interviewee: What are the requirements to enter the field? What are you actually doing on a daily, weekly, monthly, and/or yearly basis? Who works with you (coworkers, clients, patients, vendors, supervisor)? What are the typical working conditions for this career (pay, travel, hours, advancement potential)? What other related careers are out there for people interested in this general area of work? Nothing rivals the personal interview as a way to find out what enjoyment as well as what difficulties are to be had in a particular line of work. Once you have set up the interview, be on time and have a prepared set of questions to ask. Keep in mind that a professional may be too busy to speak with you, so have alternatives in mind. For how to cite a personal interview in your research paper, see Chapter 18.

Using the Internet to Research a Topic

The internet is a self-indexing library of information at your fingertips, which partly explains its popularity. Because the internet is self-indexing, you can use it not only to find information about a specific topic, but also to find out *how to find* information on any topic—a feature beginning researchers often overlook. In any case, you would begin your research on your topic by using a search engine.

Search Engines

Search engines are electronic indexes of the internet. They cost nothing to use because they're supported by advertising. Most people have personal favorites among search engines, but one of the best and most popular is *Google.com,* which uses a special program known as a web crawler to index over three billion web pages.

Most search engines are fairly easy to use. You type what you are looking for in the search field as either a word, phrase, or question. The engine then searches the web for sites that match your entry. A few search engines, however, are specialized and restricted to certain topics. Achoo, for example, is a search engine for medical topics only; its address is *http://www.achoo.com.*

No matter what search engine you use, it will most likely generate more hits (results) than you can possibly sift through. Some search engines will actually search the pages of websites for words in your query and return as a hit any match of a single word regardless of whether it is even remotely connected to the information you are seeking. To narrow your search and yield a manageable number of hits, read the FAQs (frequently asked questions) of the engine. Many engines will search only for a particular combination of words if it is presented within quotation marks. Other engines use the symbols plus (+) and minus (-) to narrow a query to a specific set of words. Exactly how a particular engine works to narrow a query will be found in its FAQs.

If you wish to check books available on your topic, you can go to Amazon.com or its competitor, Barnes & Noble, *http://www.bn.com,* for a comprehensive list of books in print. If your topic is a really rare one, no better place exists for finding books about it than the Library of Congress website found at *http://www.loc.gov.* You can search its collection, which is the mother of all collections, by title, author, ISBN number, or keyword. Some libraries offer access to an electronic version of *Books in Print* through a subscribed database.

Evaluating the Reliability of Websites

If you rely on the internet as your primary source of information and do not conduct the kind of prudent cross-checking of facts you would do for a library source, you are likely to pass on misinformation. A researcher should always be on the lookout for inconsistencies and likely mistakes. For example, one student's search for the national anthem of a certain West Indian country found the wrong lyrics on a website devoted to national anthems.

Errors of this kind are commonplace on the internet. If you are conscientious in your research legwork, you will be more apt to catch them than if you blindly accept every assertion at face value. But how do you evaluate the accuracy of a website?

1. *Determine who owns and operates the website.* Many websites are maintained privately by individuals or special-interest groups pushing their particular agendas. Because propaganda roosts side by side with serious information, you should verify the integrity of any source found on the internet before relying too heavily on it. One way to gauge reliability is to know who or what is behind a website—information that is at least partly revealed in its domain name. The main domain names of internet websites are listed here:

   .com   A commercial site, most likely maintained by a business

   .edu   An educational institution

   .net   A network, probably an internet service provider

   .mil   A site maintained by the military

   .org   A site maintained by a nonprofit organization

   .gov   A government-maintained site

   A source from a site maintained by a respected foundation or university can be trusted, but one plucked from the far reaches of cyberspace should be looked at with suspicion, especially if it makes wild and unsupported claims.

2. *Evaluate the writer's tone.* Reasonable people present their opinions in calm tones without ranting and raving at another point of view. If the writer you're reading on the internet is going off like a stick of dynamite, you would be right to doubt the content of the website.

3. *Consider the opinions of the writer.* That a writer agrees with everyone else is not necessarily a sign of sanity. But if a writer expresses opinions far from the norm and seems unwilling to hear anyone else on the subject, be warned. Like everything else, this observation is merely a caution, not a one hundred percent truth. Galileo, for example, was forced to renounce his theory that the earth revolves around the sun. But he was right, and his inquisitors were wrong.

4. *Check the writer's credentials.* Many an internet source is anonymously authored, making it impossible to find its writer's credentials. But knowing the credentials of a site's creator will give you a general idea of the reliability of a source. People who have invested many years of their lives in a field are not likely to be frivolous about it.

Compiling a Bibliography

You now have a full research topic and know where and how to look for information on it. The next step is to compile a *bibliography,* a list of useful sources on the topic. Purposeful reading is now one of the most important skills you can develop. You must learn to separate useless from useful information without conducting a wasteful and slow page-by-page analysis of possible sources.

Skim book chapters and magazine articles to see if they contain material relevant to the topic. Read tables of contents, index pages, and subtitles of books; read the topic sentences of paragraphs. Mark pertinent passages in pencil if the source belongs to you, or if it is a library source, place a paper clip on the page. When you are reasonably sure that the source will be useful, list it on a 3 × 5 bibliography card. A typical bibliography card looks like this:

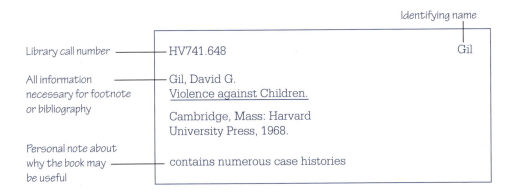

Write the call number of a book and the date and title of a magazine article on the bibliography card. Use a separate card for each source to simplify changes in your preliminary bibliography. To add a source, make a new card; to delete a source, simply remove its card.

Assessing the authenticity and accuracy of sources is part of your job as a researcher. You cannot simply take for granted the fairness and accuracy of a source. Lies appear as often in print and online as they do in speech. The information in some sources (possibly even in most sources) will be found to be truthful, current, and accurate for their time. But there's the rub. Earlier generations were often mistaken. (Our own generation will no doubt appear likewise to our descendants.) And a writer may have published some notion as hard-and-fast fact that was truthful for the time but is now regarded as myth or nonsense. Novice researcher or not, you are the only possible judge of a source's worthiness for inclusion in your paper.

Here are some practical rules that will help you evaluate sources (see also pp. 484–485 on evaluating internet sources):

1. *Check one opinion against others.* As you read on your chosen topic, you'll quickly discover a consensus among the experts that will enable you to separate fact from speculation.

2. *Note the publication date of the source.* The fact of one generation is very often the myth of another. If the source is very old, its views and ideas may be outdated and wrong. If you have two equivalent sources on the same topic, use the later one.

3. *Check your own opinions and evaluations against the views of professionals. Book Review Digest* is a good source for critical opinions on books. The credentials of an author can be checked in the various biographical dictionaries or *Who's Who* volumes.

4. *Beware of statistics.* They can be out of date, and they can also be inaccurate. You should immediately question a source that uses exaggerated numbers, as in "Millions of children are allowed to view pornography on the streets of New York." Make sure that any study using statistics is from a source known to be systematic and careful.

5. *Determine who published the source.* If you have never heard of the publishing house, check its name in *Literary Market Place (LMP)*. This reference work will tell you what kinds of material a house usually publishes, who its audience is, and what its standards are for accepting new work. Another reference work that will help you evaluate books is *Book Review Digest,* which cites selected reviews of works of literature and nonfiction books in all fields.

Taking Notes

Note taking is changing because of the widespread use of computers. Instead of 4 × 6 note cards, many students now use a photocopier or laptop computer to take notes. Some instructors still insist on the use of traditional note cards, however, and you need to ascertain what is expected of you.

The traditional method is to list on 4 × 6 cards any information, data, or quotation to be incorporated into the paper; call numbers and publication information for books or magazine articles should be listed on the bibliography cards. Therefore, there will be both a note card and a bibliography card for each source consulted.

The four primary forms of note taking are *summarizing, paraphrasing, quoting,* and a combination of these.

To *summarize* means to condense. A condensation uses fewer words than the original. A book may be condensed into one paragraph; a paragraph may be condensed into one sentence. For example, a book citing numerous examples of child battering in the schools of Sumer, five thousand years ago, might be summarized like this on a note card:

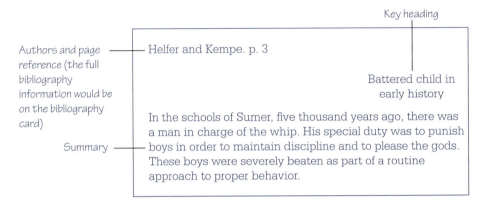

Key heading

Authors and page reference (the full bibliography information would be on the bibliography card)

Helfer and Kempe. p. 3

Battered child in early history

Summary

In the schools of Sumer, five thousand years ago, there was a man in charge of the whip. His special duty was to punish boys in order to maintain discipline and to please the gods. These boys were severely beaten as part of a routine approach to proper behavior.

To *paraphrase* means to restate on original source in your own words using nearly the same amount of space as the original. Here is an example of a paraphrase:

The general public is not fully aware of the seriousness and prevalence of cruelty to children. The knowledge that babies suffer severe injury or death at the hands of their parents is repugnant and extremely hard to accept. Abuse of children, the greatest cause of death among children under the age of three, causes more deaths than auto accidents, leukemia, and muscular dystrophy.

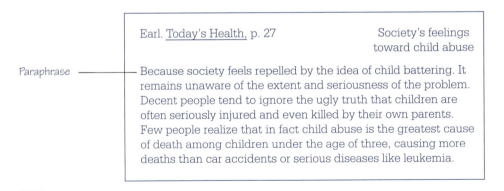

Earl. Today's Health, p. 27

Society's feelings toward child abuse

Paraphrase

Because society feels repelled by the idea of child battering. It remains unaware of the extent and seriousness of the problem. Decent people tend to ignore the ugly truth that children are often seriously injured and even killed by their own parents. Few people realize that in fact child abuse is the greatest cause of death among children under the age of three, causing more deaths than car accidents or serious diseases like leukemia.

Because paraphrasing can lead to accidental plagiarizing, which means stealing someone else's ideas, your paraphrase must follow these strict guidelines: (1) It must be almost entirely in your own words, and (2) your words should remain true to the intent of the original passage. For a more detailed account of plagiarism, see Chapter 18, pp. 494–497.

To *quote* means to use exactly the same words as the original. Many passages may be quoted in the notes, but as few quotations as possible should appear in the actual paper. A good research paper should reveal that the writer has assimilated the information and data and therefore need not rely on the words of others. The frequent use of quotations also gives writing a choppy effect. Use quotations only for these purposes:

1. You want authoritative support for a statement.
2. Something is said with exceptional literary taste.
3. The quotation is needed for accuracy.

Check quotations for accuracy. Quotations must meticulously include every comma and every word in the original. Oddities of spelling or phrasing in the original should be copied exactly and followed by a bracketed [*sic*], which means, "This is the way the text reads in the original." Any omitted portion of the original quotation is indicated by an ellipsis (. . .), as in this example:

> It is thought that because of crowding in small quarters and because of having larger families, "the working-class parent uses . . . punishment more than the middle-class parent."

An ellipsis is not used if the quotation is integrated into a sentence and the omission is made at the beginning or end of the original. Here is an example:

Quotation to be used	Many sociologists have noted that the working-class parent uses physical punishment more than the middle-class parent.
Quotation as it appears in the paper	It is thought that because of crowding in smaller quarters and because of having larger families, "the working-class parent uses physical punishment more than the middle-class parent."

Quotations in the final paper must fit coherently into the flow of writing. Transitional sentences, based on a thorough understanding of both the quotation and its context, should be used to introduce the quotation and move the reader on to succeeding material. A well-prepared note card, with author and subject identified, will help you effectively use a quotation:

Neill. p. 102

An authority's view
on punishment

A. S. Neill suggests that "Perhaps we punish because we are a ——Quotation
Christian civilization. If you sin, punishment awaits you in the
here and now, and Hell awaits you in the future."

Here are some additional suggestions for writing useful note cards:

1. Write in ink, not pencil, so the note cards will not smudge when you shuffle them.

2. Use one card per idea. With one idea on each card, an outline can be created by shuffling the cards and arranging them in a logical sequence. To save money, cut your own note cards from regular paper.

3. In copying or paraphrasing material from more than one page of an original source, indicate all page numbers on the note card. This information will be needed for footnotes or endnotes.

4. Write notes legibly, or you may have to go back to an original source to decipher what you meant. (See also "Plagiarism," pp. 494–497.)

Using a Computer or Photocopier to Take Notes

Many students, especially those who own laptops or electronic notebooks, do not use note cards unless the instructor requires them to. Instead, they prefer to make notes either on the computer or by photocopying the appropriate page of a source they wish to cite. Indeed, making notes directly on a computer bypasses the need for transcribing information from a note card to a paper later and can save the writer time. With a computer, the writer uses the cut-and-paste function of a word processor to insert the notes directly into the paper without having to retype them. If you are among this tech-savvy group who spurns note cards, we have some practical suggestions to help you with your note taking.

First, if you use a photocopier or a computer instead of note cards, be sure to write on each page the source that it came from. Although you may think that you know where any material came from well enough not to have to write it down, as the research progresses and your sources accumulate, it will be difficult, eventually becoming impossible, to name the source of every copied page. If you do photocopy pages and scribble down their sources, you might as well put down all the information that you'll need to include in a formal bibliographic citation. For example, if you took a citation from this book, you would want to do more than just scribble down *McCuen/Winkler* or *From Idea to Essay*. On at least one sheet you should write down the full citation, including the publisher, date, and place of publication—all the information that you would need to complete an entry in the "Works Cited," as shown on page 504.

Pages also have a way of becoming unmanageable. You may think that it is easier to lose a single note card than a single piece of paper, but experience has shown that the opposite is usually true. Note cards can be bundled together with a rubber band and placed in a desk drawer for safekeeping. A piece of paper, on the other hand, tends to get lost among other papers like a single sheep in a flock. Many a student has had to burn the midnight oil because critical citations on photocopied pages have been lost or misplaced.

Second, note cards make management of the sequence of topics easy. You simply shuffle the cards to get a different arrangement if you wish to experiment. Sheets of paper are not as easily shuffled and the sequence of topics consequently not as easy to rearrange.

However, if your instructor has no objections to a paper submitted without note cards and you wish to use another system, you have our blessing. We're from the horse-and-buggy days and like note cards for one very practical reason: They work now as they have for generations of earlier students.

Formulating the Thesis, Outlining the Paper, and Writing the Abstract

The Thesis

Sometime during your note taking, you will begin to lean toward an assumption, an opinion, a point of view about your topic. This leaning will eventually result in your *thesis,* a one-sentence summary of the main idea in your paper. The thesis is, in effect, the conclusion to which you have been brought by your research; it is the imprint of your mind on the paper.

Generally, but not always, the thesis will have an argumentative edge; it will reflect the stand you have chosen to take on the material, the viewpoint you will argue or advocate. But not all research papers are argumentative. Some papers are framed as reports rather than as arguments. The following examples will clarify the difference between the intent of a *report paper* and that of an *argumentative paper.*

> Report thesis   Most Egyptologists today conclude that the Great Pyramid was built by Egyptian citizens using the simplest of tools and technology.

A paper with this thesis will simply report on the techniques used by ancient Egyptians to build the pyramids.

> Argumentative thesis   Although supporters of animal experiments claim that any reduction would jeopardize scientific progress, scientists should stop abusing animals in an attempt to improve human lives.

A paper with this thesis will not report; it will argue in defense of its main idea that cruel scientific experiments on animals should be stopped. The writer of this thesis has clearly taken a stand that the paper must prove and defend.

The thesis is possibly the single most important sentence of your paper. It is literally the scaffolding on which all the ideas in the paper must hang. You should therefore do your utmost to make the thesis sentence as clear and pointed as possible. A muddled thesis starts the paper off on the wrong foot, from which it may never recover.

The Outline

If you are writing a paper for the humanities, the next step is to outline the paper. (See "The Abstract," on the following page 543, if you are writing a social sciences paper.) A simple procedure for creating an outline is to assemble the note cards according to the logical sequence of their major ideas. All information relating to one major idea is placed in the same stack. For example, in the paper on child abuse, the note cards could be logically grouped into three stacks based on the following major ideas:

I. Violence against children by adults has been practiced throughout history.

II. A wide variety of child abuse cases exist today and for numerous reasons.

III. Some effective action has been taken against child abuse, but more social cooperation and legal sanctions are needed to overcome the problem.

These three points could then be condensed into a controlling idea, such as the following:

Adult violence against children, commonly practiced throughout history, occurs today for a variety of reasons in countless cases of child abuse and can be corrected only through social cooperation and legal sanctions.

A controlling idea containing three major divisions is now established. Arrange the note cards within each division into a logical sequence of information, examples, and other data. If necessary, add or delete cards. Translate the logical arrangement of the cards into an outline, as in this example:

Child Abuse

Thesis
Adult violence against children, commonly practiced throughout history, occurs today for a variety of reasons in countless cases of child abuse and can be corrected only through social cooperation and legal sanctions.

I. Adult violence against children has been common throughout history.

   A. The Sumerians beat children with whips to discipline them.
   B. The Romans flogged boys before the altars of Diana as a religious practice.
   C. Early Christians whipped their children on Innocents Day in memory of King Herod's massacre.
   D. During the Middle Ages, children's eyes were gouged and their bodies mutilated to make them effective beggars.
   E. The factory system allowed foremen to beat children mercilessly if they didn't work hard enough.

II. Countless cases of child abuse exist today for a variety of reasons.

   A. Numerous child abuse cases have been recorded.
      1. On record are thousands of cases of planned falls, strangulations, and sexual assaults.

      2. Parents have assaulted children with instruments ranging from plastic bags to baseball bats.

      3. Disciplinary measures may include cigarette burns, plunges into boiling water, or starvation.

   B. Child abuse cases exist for a variety of reasons.

      1. In a study of sixty families with beaten children, all the persecuting parents were beaten as children, indicating a revenge pattern.

      2. Some parents become abusive because they expect more love and affection from their child than the child is able to deliver.

      3. A frustrated parent will use the child's bad behavior to justify abuses.

      4. Unsatisfactory marital relationships are another frequent cause of child abuse.

 III. Social cooperation and legal sanctions are needed to overcome the problem of child abuse.

   A. Although little was heard of the battered child syndrome before 1960, today all the states have adopted legislation governing reporting of battered children.

   B. But only two states, Maryland and New Jersey, have laws specifically prohibiting the use of physical force on children.

   C. Doctors and other people fear slander suits if they notify police of child abuse and an investigation does not support the charge.

   D. The other parent often protects the one inflicting the harm so that proof of battering is difficult to obtain.

   E. Society and its legal system must make further advances toward curbing child abuse.

Avoid creating an overly detailed outline. The rule of thumb is two pages of outline for every ten pages of writing.

The Abstract

An *abstract* is a summary of your paper that, for the benefit of the reader, lists the main points of your research. Unlike the introduction, your abstract is no place to entice, shock, or hint. Use it only to state in the clearest, most concise language what your paper is about.

    To write an abstract, center the heading "Abstract" one inch down from the top of the paper. Then, in a paragraph, clarify the purpose of your paper and state its major points in narrative, not outline, form (see the example in the social science student paper, p. 543). Place the abstract page immediately after the title page but before the paper itself.

Chapter 18

Writing and Documenting the Paper

The best advice we can give the writer of a research paper is this: Be yourself. Don't be overawed by the length and purpose of the paper. Some students have a tendency to overwrite a research paper, feeling that they must put on a more elevated voice for such a serious project. It's as if the writer imagines that formal dress is required for this particular dinner. It is not. What is required is that you express your opinion in a thesis, back it up with your sources, and document the material of your research in an appropriate citation.

Documenting the paper means citing any source from which you have derived information or ideas. You do not have to document your own insights and opinions, obviously. But just as obviously, you should give credit for the ideas of others uncovered in your research and expressed as summaries, paraphrases, or quotations in your paper. A paper containing material improperly documented is regarded as plagiarized (containing stolen ideas), and in many English departments, automatically earns an irrevocable F.

Plagiarism

In its most blatant form, plagiarism is using the words and ideas of someone else without giving that person credit. In the world of scholarship that is the worst offense a writer can commit. But there's another, more subtle kind of plagiarism that involves quoting another writer almost verbatim without the use of quotation marks. This kind of plagiarism almost always involves the paraphrase, with the student making the mistake of paraphrasing the work of a source but staying too close to the original. In paraphrasing, you must use approximately the same number of words as in the original source, but you must digest them so that you can render them in your personal style.

We shall look at three different ways to use someone else's ideas in a paper. The first two are examples of plagiarism, the last an example of proper use. Here is the original passage, taken from an article written by Douglas L. Wilson for the July 4, 2005, issue of *Time* magazine. Wilson is analyzing why Abraham Lincoln's style of writing was not as popular in Lincoln's day as it is today. One reason Wilson gives is Lincoln's rural background and unkempt appearance. Then he provides a second reason:

Original passage:

Another reason Lincoln's writing ability was underrated was that his typically plain diction and straightforward expression were at odds with the public's expectations. The recognized standard for a statesman-like address in mid-19th century America called for considerably more formality and pretension. The prose of acknowledged masters of that kind of writing—such as Lincoln's fellow orator at Gettysburg, Edward Everett, or Massachusetts Senator Charles Sumner—generally featured elevated diction, self-consciously artful expression, and a certain moral unction. Lincoln's insistence on direct and forthright language, by contrast, seemed "odd" or "peculiar."

Blatantly plagiarized student version:

The reason that Abraham Lincoln's writing ability was underrated by his contemporaries was twofold: First, he was considered somewhat of an awkward country bumpkin. Second, his typically plain diction and straightforward expression were at odds with the public's expectation. The public in mid-19th century America wanted far more formality and pretension. It admired elevated diction and moral unction. By comparison, Lincoln seemed a bit odd and peculiar.

Here the student has simply imitated the original passage, using the same language without mentioning the original source, without using quotation marks around copied words, and without giving any kind of credit. This is unabashed plagiarism and, if detected, will land the student an F grade. The following example is the student version attempting to cover the plagiarism:

Historians offer two reasons why Abraham Lincoln's writing was not nearly as admired in his day as it is today. The first reason is that Lincoln's unkempt appearance made him seem like a bungling country lawyer. The second reason is that his plain diction and straightforward expression were not at all what the public wanted from someone who was to rule the country. The public's expectation was that the President would write and speak with great formality and pretension. They wanted him to sound like his competitors—fellow orator Everett Edward or Senator Charles Sumner—who spoke with elevated diction and "moral unction" (*Time*, July 4, 2005).

Despite the source cited in parentheses, this passage is still plagiarized because the student did not assimilate or digest the original passage and then reflect it in his own words and style. The fact that he placed the expression "moral unction" within quotation marks and he also cited the source for his ideas within parentheses shows that the student may have intended to give proper credit, but he did not go far enough.

Here's a student version giving full credit to the original source without plagiarizing:

> It is ironic to realize that while today we consider Abraham Lincoln's words among the most powerful in literature, his contemporaries didn't think that a country lawyer like him could ever live up to the standard they had for the president of the United States of America. According to Douglas L. Wilson, co-director of the Lincoln Studies Center at Knox College, Illinois, two primary reasons exist for this mind-set: The first reason is that Lincoln's public image was of a man who had never outgrown his rail splitter's image. Since he rarely wore elegant clothes and looked rather rumpled most of the time, they couldn't imagine that he could rise above his country-style anecdotes, delivered with a typical Hoosier accent. The second reason had to do with the standards of rhetoric in Lincoln's era. In those days, the public valued brocaded writing and speech, delivered with artificial elegance and expressing a "certain moral unction." Writers and orators like Edward Everett (who spoke at Gettysburg along with Lincoln) and Massachusetts senator Charles Sumner appealed to the popular taste more than did the plain and unadorned Abe (*Time,* 4 July 2005, pp. 68–69).

The student follows the proper protocol for using someone else's ideas and giving the author the required credit. The student has obviously understood and digested the original passage, but in referring to it, she does not copy the language of the original source, preferring to reflect the ideas in her own writing style. When she does quote the author, she places the quoted words within quotation marks, as is acceptable. At the end of the borrowed passage, she places an abbreviated reference note within parentheses.

"Works Cited" at the end of the paper will contain the following citation:

> Wilson, Douglas L. "They Said He Was a Lousy Speaker." *Time* 4 July 2005:
>
> 68–69. Print.

The best way to avoid plagiarism is by making sure that your paraphrases are really paraphrases and not unconscious copying. Remember, when you paraphrase you must use your own words, not your source's. And if you do use exact words from your source, you should put them in quotation marks. All paraphrases must be documented. This stringent requirement, however, does not mean that you can't use another author's work in your research. After all, the whole idea of research is to find out what others have written on a topic and to synthesize their ideas with your own. While you should feel free to use someone else's words, facts, and opinions, any material you use must be given credit. In other words, you cannot pretend that these ideas flew out of your own brain onto the paper. Some ideas are so universally known that they do not require documentation. For example, "Global warming is threatening the habitat of many exotic animals, such as polar bears" is so collectively acknowledged that it cannot be attributed to one source and can thus be used without documentation. So can the comment,

"Recently a number of sports figures have been accused of cheating by using steroids to improve their skills." Popular views for or against some political strategy also belong in the public domain and don't need to be documented unless one author stated them in remarkable language. To guard against unintentional plagiarism, keep careful notes that distinguish clearly between your ideas and someone else's. If you don't take such precise notes, you may stop your research for a few days, and when you return, you will have forgotten which notes are your ideas and which are someone else's.

Two main styles of documentation are now in use:

1. The *author/work system* approved by the Modern Language Association (MLA) and used in most subjects of the humanities. (Art, history, literature, music, and philosophy require MLA style.)

2. The *author/date system* approved by the American Psychological Association (APA) and used in the social sciences. (Anthropology, economics, political science, psychology, sociology, and biology require APA style.)

Both systems are widely used by freshman composition students, who must often write papers for both the social sciences and the humanities. We consequently discuss both the MLA and the APA systems of documentation in the following pages. We do not, however, cover documentation using either footnotes or endnotes because both have been largely replaced by the simpler parenthetical systems.

Documenting the Humanities Paper (MLA)

The suggestions for format and documentation presented here and in the sample student paper generally follow the guidelines recommended in the *MLA Handbook for Writers of Research Papers* (7th ed., 2010). Accordingly, sources are indicated using parenthetical citations in the text of the paper and then listed in the "Works Cited" section at the end. Anything that needs to be explained without interrupting the flow of the paper should be addressed in a numbered content note at the end of the paper (see also pp. 502–503).

Note that the discussion and sample paper in this book vary from MLA style in several respects. Most significantly, MLA style does not require that a research paper have a title page or an outline. Since many instructors do require these elements, however, we have covered them in this chapter. You should verify all the instructor's requirements for each research paper you write, as they will likely vary from instructor to instructor and subject to subject.

Your research paper should include these elements:

Title page (if required)

Outline (if required)

Body of paper

Notes (if you have content notes)

Works Cited

It is not necessary to put your paper in a folder. Simply use a paperclip to keep it assembled.

Using Parenthetical Documentation

The parenthetical style of documentation requires that you provide full documentation only once for each source cited. This will be done in the "Works Cited" section at the end of the paper. Within the paper itself, you will give only brief references, in parentheses, to any sources cited.

Begin the parenthetical documentation one space after the material cited. Except for closing quotation marks, no punctuation of any kind should come between the material cited and the parentheses. Periods, commas, and semicolons go after the parentheses:

> According to William Zinsser, most writers work from a spacious design, trying
>
> to get a lot of material down on paper, but they are not "hung up on starting at
>
> the beginning" (106).

One exception is a quotation set off from the text. In such a case, leave two spaces after the concluding punctuation mark of the quotation and insert the parenthetical reference with no punctuation mark following. Here is an example:

> Writing is never an act conducted in a vacuum. In fact it is a highly personal
>
> transaction that takes place on paper:
>
>> It is one person talking to another person. Readers identify first
>>
>> with the person who is writing, not with what the person is
>>
>> writing about. Often, in fact, we will read about a subject that
>>
>> really doesn't interest us because we like the writer. We like the
>>
>> warmth or humor or humanity that he brings to his subject.
>>
>> (Zinsser 112)

Some guidelines about how to use parenthetical citations follow.

When you give the author's name in the text.   If you give the author's name when referring to a source, then provide only the pagination within parentheses:

> In his best-seller *Restoring the American Dream*, Robert J. Ringer states
>
> emphatically that a fundamental law of economics, one that politicians refuse
>
> to accept, is "There is no such thing as something for nothing" (53).

When you don't give the author's name in the text. If you have introduced a source in text without giving the author's name, give the author's last name and the pagination within parentheses:

> As one great pedagogue put it, "No one can bear young people all the time."
>
> Occasionally every teacher loves to escape into a cool library or garden—away
>
> from the noise of pupils (Highet 27).

When you are citing more than one work by the same author. If you are citing more than one work by the same author but you do not mention the author's name in your text, give the author's name, an abbreviated title, and the pagination within parentheses:

> One point of view is that all writing is "a deeply personal process, full of mystery
>
> and surprise" (Zinsser, *Word Processor* 96).

If, however, you *do* mention the author's name in your text, then supply within parentheses only a short title followed by the pagination:

> William Zinsser insists that the word processor can help writers to achieve
>
> three cardinal goals of good writing—"clarity, simplicity and humanity" (*Word*
>
> *Processor* 112).

When you are using a work by more than one author. When citing a work with up to three authors whose names you have not mentioned in the text, give all last names within parentheses, followed by the pagination:

> It should be pointed out that the God of the Hebrews is distinct from matter
>
> whereas the God of the Babylonians co-existed with matter (McNeil and Sedlar 4).

Use *et al.* or *and others* when citing a work by more than three authors:

> The Norman Conquest united the practical and enterprising qualities of the
>
> Normans and their French instinct for symmetry with the Anglo-Saxon character
>
> to form a new race (Baugh et al. 111). *Or:* (Baugh and others 111).

When you are using a work with a corporate author. If a work is authored by a committee, an institution, a corporation, or a government agency, the full or shortened name of the author should appear within parentheses if you did not mention it in your text:

> "Students are encouraged to attend all worship services and to dress according
>
> to code" (Pacific Union College 6).

In the case of a long and cumbersome corporate name, an abbreviation is acceptable in subsequent citations as long as the name is recognized and understood:

First citation

(National Institutes of Mental Health 22).

Subsequent citation

(NIMH 23).

When you are using a work with more than one volume.   For works with more than one volume, use a colon (followed by a single space) to separate the volume number from the pagination:

Browning's poems often portray "lovers who let the good minute pass without

acting upon it" (Harrison 2: 473).

If, however, you are referring to an entire volume of a multivolume work and there is no need to give pagination, place a comma after the author's name and include the abbreviation *vol.:*

(Durant and Durant, vol. 2).

When you are using quoted material set off from the text.   Quotations longer than four lines must be indented ten spaces (two standard tab indents) from the left margin and set off from the text. In such cases, place the parenthetical citation after the final period of the quote:

Brodie finds an ironic contradiction in Jefferson's so-called agrarian period:

> But if one looks at the private life of Thomas Jefferson in precisely
>
> those years in which he committed himself totally to the rustic life,
>
> some curious contradictions emerge. What exactly did Jefferson
>
> mean by virtue, by corruption, and by morality? For if Jefferson truly
>
> believed, as he wrote in 1781, that laboring in the earth kept a man's
>
> morals free from corruption, how do we square this with the fact that
>
> the finality of Jefferson's settling into rural living in 1767–68 coincided
>
> with his attempt or attempts at the seduction of the wife of his good
>
> friend and near neighbor John Walker? This is an episode that is still
>
> somewhat obscure, and somewhat comic. (73)

When you are using a play cited by act, scene, and line.   When citing a play by act, scene, and line numbers, use arabic numerals divided by periods. For instance, a quotation from Act 1, Scene 3, lines 43–46 of Shakespeare's *The Merchant of Venice* would be treated as follows:

> In an aside to the audience, Shylock reveals his mean character early in the play:
>
> > I hate him for he is a Christian.
> >
> > But more for that in low simplicity
> >
> > He lends out money gratis and brings down
> >
> > The rate of usury here with us in Venice. (*Merchant* 1.3.43–46)

Notice that the final period comes before the parentheses containing the source and that you may use an abbreviated title as long as it is not ambiguous. Some teachers prefer the old-style use of roman numerals. If so, use a capital roman numeral for the act, a lowercase roman numeral for the scene, and arabic numerals for the lines:

> (*Merchant* I.iii.43-46)

When you are using a long classical poem divided into books or cantos.   A poem divided into books or cantos should be treated as follows:

> Pyrochles finds his brother Cymochles in the Bower of Acadia, indulging in a
>
> passionless kind of titillation:
>
> > And now he has poured out his ydle mynd
> >
> > In daintie delices, and lavish joyes
> >
> > Having his warlike weapons cast behynd,
> >
> > And flowes in pleasures and vaine pleasing toyes
> >
> > Mingled emongst loose Ladies and lascivious boyes.
> >
> > (*Fairie Queene* 2.5.5-9)

If your teacher insists on roman numerals, then the parenthetical reference would be as follows:

> (*Fairie Queene* II.v.5-9)

When you are using a poem.   When quoting lines of poetry in stanzaic form, use the words *line* or *lines,* not *l.* or *ll.*

> A feeling of poignant normalcy is asserted by this poem's images:
>
> > When Becky left home
> >
> > the old drought did not break

> the ungainly dragonflies
>
> did not abandon us
>
> the mosquitoes did not lay aside their chopsticks (lines 1-5)

Copy the stanzas, lines, and words exactly as found in the original text. Even a poet's unorthodox capitalization and punctuation must be faithfully reproduced.

When you are using the Bible.   A reference to the Bible is placed within parentheses immediately following the quotation and is cited by book, chapter, and verse; no other documentation is needed:

> Job has reached the nadir of his despair when he cries out, "I am repulsive to my
>
> wife, loathsome to the sons of my own mother. Even young children despise me"
>
> (Job 19.17-18).

When you are citing an indirect source.   Whenever possible, scholars try to deal with the original source of an idea or a quotation; however, sometimes the only source available is an indirect one, as in the case of one author's quoting another. In such a case, place the abbreviation *qtd. in* ("quoted in") before the indirect source in your parenthetical reference:

> Homosexual males experience a high degree of social alienation, caused by the
>
> fact that they are a minority group at odds with the majority of society. In an
>
> interview, after having declared his homosexuality publicly, Congressman Gerry
>
> E. Studds said, "To grow up and enter adulthood as a gay person in this country
>
> is to be in a situation where all the messages one receives with respect to the
>
> deepest feelings inside oneself tell one that those feelings are not legitimate at
>
> best, and that they are sinful and evil at worst" (qtd. in Meredith 59-60).

The parenthetical reference does not give the source of the Studds quotation.

Using Content Notes

Material related to your research but not important enough to be part of the main body of the paper can be placed in a *content note,* either at the bottom of the page to which the information belongs or gathered with other notes at the end of the paper before the "Works Cited" page. The following rules apply to preparing content notes:

1. Indent the first line of each note five spaces (one standard tab indentation).

2. Double-space content notes gathered at the end of the paper and at the foot of a page. Be sure to allow for enough space for the entire note. Begin

the note four lines below the text. Do not insert a solid line between the text and the note because this would indicate a note continued from the previous page when space ran out. Double-space the note. (Most word processors' "footnote" features simplify all this.)

3. In your text insert the note reference number using the automatic insertion in your word processer, or typing the number in superscript followed by one space, as in the following example:

> In the last decade 15 million unborn children have had their lives abbreviated
>
> by someone's decision to have an abortion.[6] All of the combined . . .

The note at the foot of the page adds the following comment without interrupting the flow of the text:

> [6] In 1973 the Supreme Court decision of *Roe v. Wade* made abortions legal.

A content note can be used to explain a term or a procedure, to expand on an idea, to acknowledge assistance, or to refer the reader to another source. If a content note refers to another source, full documentation of that source must appear in the Works Cited section:

> [12] In 1984 President Ronald Reagan directed the Departments of Justice
>
> and Health and Human Services to apply civil rights regulations to protect
>
> handicapped newborns (15).

The "Works Cited" list would then have the following entry:

> Reagan, Ronald. *Abortion and the Conscience of the Nation*. New York: Nelson,
>
> 1984. Print.

Preparing the List of "Works Cited"

At the end of your paper, you must compile a complete list of the sources used in the paper. Title this list "Works Cited," and include in it all sources cited either in the text or in content notes. The entries must be arranged in alphabetical order by the authors' last names. Where several works by the same author appear, list these alphabetically by title. Don't repeat the author's name, but simply use three hyphens, followed by a period. Here is an example:

> Trayers, Scott. "Altered Coins." *Coinage* June 1984: 88-94. Print.
>
> ---. "Counterfeits." *Coinage* Aug. 1984: 64-68. Print.

If the work has no author, as in the case of some magazine articles, alphabetize by the first word of the title, excluding articles, such as *The* or *A*. The format of the "Works Cited" page follows.

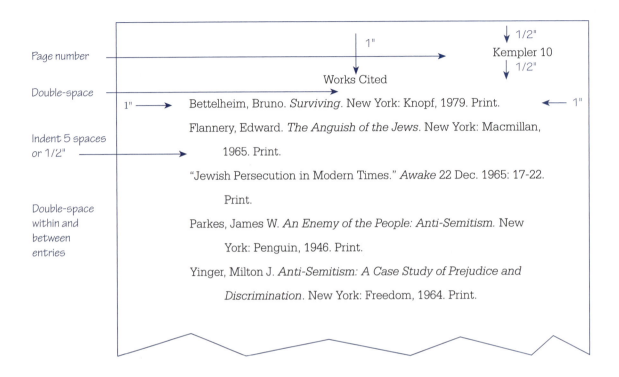

Page number

Double-space

Indent 5 spaces or 1/2"

Double-space within and between entries

1/2"
Kempler 10
1/2"

1"

Works Cited

1"

Bettelheim, Bruno. *Surviving*. New York: Knopf, 1979. Print.   ← 1"

Flannery, Edward. *The Anguish of the Jews*. New York: Macmillan,

1965. Print.

"Jewish Persecution in Modern Times." *Awake* 22 Dec. 1965: 17-22.

Print.

Parkes, James W. *An Enemy of the People: Anti-Semitism*. New

York: Penguin, 1946. Print.

Yinger, Milton J. *Anti-Semitism: A Case Study of Prejudice and*

Discrimination. New York: Freedom, 1964. Print.

Standard Sources.   Listed next are examples of most types of sources you will encounter in your research. Adhere to the formats rigorously. Should you encounter a source for which you find no model, use the format of a similar source or consult your teacher. All sources here follow the MLA style.

Book by a single author

Brodie, Fawn M. *Thomas Jefferson: An Intimate History*. New York:

Norton, 1974. Print.

1. For easy alphabetizing, the author's name is inverted and followed by a period.
2. Then comes the title, given in full, italicized, and followed by a period.
3. A subtitle is separated from the main title by a colon. The full title must be italicized.
4. Next is the place of publication, followed by a colon and the name of the publisher, a comma, the date of publication, and then a period. If more than one place is given, use only the first. Copy the publisher's name as it is listed on the title page of the book. Well-known publishers' names should be abbreviated. For instance, *W. W. Norton & Company, 1973*

should be shortened to *Norton, 1973*. However, always supply the full name of a university press, abbreviating the words *University Press* as *UP: (Oxford UP, 1980)*. Always use the original publication date unless the book is a new edition, in which case you must give the date of the edition being used. If no date is given, use the latest copyright date or state *n.d.* (no date).

5. Finally, note the medium of publication; for books use *Print*.

> Hallberg, Edmond C., and William G. Thomas. *When I Was Your Age.*
>
> New York: Free, 1974. Print.

Book by two or three authors

The names of the second (and third) authors are not inverted. Give the names of the authors in the order in which they appear on the title page.

> Masotti, Louis H., et al. A Time to Burn? An Evaluation of the Present Crisis
>
> in Race Relations. Chicago: Rand, 1969. Print.

Book by more than three authors

Et al. may be replaced by the English *and others* if you prefer. This form for multiple authors should be used only for books by more than three authors.

> American Institute of Physics. *Handbook*. 3rd ed. New York: McGraw, 1972. Print.
>
> Defense Language Institute. *Academic Policy Standards*. Monterey: Defense
>
> Language Institute, 1982. Print.

Book by a corporate author

If the publisher is the same as the author, repeat the information.

> Arnold, Matthew. *Culture and Anarchy*. Ed. J. Dover Wilson. Cambridge:
>
> Cambridge UP, 1961. Print.

Book with an editor

If the editor's contribution is being cited in your paper, his or her name goes first:

> Wilson, J. Dover, ed. *Culture and Anarchy*. By Matthew Arnold. Cambridge:
>
> Cambridge UP, 1961. Print.
>
> Thoreau, Henry David. "Observation." *The Norton Reader*. 3rd ed. Ed. Arthur M.
>
> Eastman et al. New York: Norton, 1973. Print.

Title in an edited collection

> Thomas, Lewis. "The Wonderful Mistake." *The Medusa and the Snail: More*
>
> *Notes of a Biology Watcher*. New York: Viking, 1974. Print.

Title in a collection by same author

> Alighieri, Dante. *The Inferno*. Trans. John Ciardi. New York: New American
>
> Library, 1954. Print.

Translation

As in the case of an editor, if you wish to stress the translator's work, place his or her name first:

Ciardi, John, trans. *The Inferno*. By Dante Alighieri. New York: New American

Library, 1954. Print.

A second or
later edition

McCuen-Metherell, Jo Ray, and Anthony C. Winkler. *Writing the Research Paper:*

A Handbook. 7th ed. Boston: Cengage, 2010. Print.

Other editions could be as follows: *Rev. ed.* (revised edition), *2nd ed.* (second edition), *Rev. and enl. ed.* (revised and enlarged edition).

Republished
book

Knowles, John. *A Separate Peace*. 1959. New York: Bantam, 1966. Print.

The original edition appeared in 1959; the writer of the paper used the 1966 Bantam edition.

A work of
more than
one volume

Harrison, G. B., et al., eds. *Major British Writers*. 2 vols. New York: Harcourt,

1959. Print.

This form is appropriate if you are using all of the volumes in the series; however, if you are using a specific volume, give that number at the end of the entry:

Harrison, G. B., et al., eds. *Major British Writers*. Vol. 2. New York: Harcourt,

1959. 2 vols. Print.

See the two entries below and the following sequence: Author, title of article, name of journal, volume and issue numbers (in arabic numerals separated by a period), year of issue (within parentheses) followed by a colon, the pages of the entire article, and finally the medium of publication. Note that current MLA guidelines no longer make a distinction between journals that are numbered continuously (e.g., vol. 1 ends on page 208, vol. 2 starts on page 209) or numbered separately; that is, each volume starts on page 1. No matter how the journal is paginated, all of them must contain volume *and* issue numbers. One exception are journals with issue numbers only; simply cite the issue numbers alone as though they are volume numbers.

Article in a
periodical with
continuous
pagination
throughout the
year and one
with separate
pagination of
each issue

Paolucci, Anne. "Comedy and Paradox in Pirandello's Plays." *Modern*

Drama 20.2 (1977): 321-39. Print.

Cappe, Walter H. "Humanities at Large." *The Center Magazine* 11.2

(1978): 2-6. Print.

When each issue of a periodical is paginated separately, include the issue number (or month or season). Page numbers alone will not locate the article because every issue begins with page 1.

Article in a
monthly
magazine

Grierson, Bruce. "An Atheist in the Pulpit." *Psychology Today* February,

2008: 80-86. Print.

Barthelme, Donald. "The Captured Woman." *The New Yorker* 28

June 1976: 22-25. Print.

For periodicals that have no volume numbers, supply the exact date:

"Jimmy's Last Ride." *Rolling Stone* 1 April 2010: 51-54. Print.

Robertson, Campbell. "When Scholarship and Tribal Heritage Face Off Against

Commerce." *New York Times* 14 Mar. 2010, A13. Print.

Give the name of the newspaper as it appears on the masthead, omitting any introductory article (*New York Times* not *The New York Times*). Specify the part or section, if one is given. Because different editions contain different materials, give the edition when one is given on the masthead:

Southerland, Daniel. "Carter Plans Firm Stand with Begin." *Christian Science*

Monitor 9 Mar. 1978, western ed.: 1, 9. Print.

Futrell, William. "The Inner City Frontier." Editorial. *Sierra* 63.2 (1978): 5. Print.

Miller, Donald, E. P. Letter. *Time* 14 Jan. 1985: 8. Print.

If the author is replying to a letter, write *Reply to letter of* and the letter writer's name. Do not italicize this information or place it in quotation marks.

Nicholas, Herbert George. "Churchill, Sir Winston Leonard Spencer."

Encyclopedia Britannica. 1968 ed. Print.

or more commonly

"Churchill, Sir Winston Leonard Spencer." *Encyclopaedia Britannica.* 1969 ed. Print.

Also note the following about citing encyclopedia articles:

1. The authors of encyclopedia articles are usually listed by initials at the end of the articles; these initials are clarified in the index.
2. Not all facts of publication are necessary; year and volume number suffice.
3. Watch the various spellings of *encyclopedia.*

Cong. Rec. 10 June 1975: 2520-21. Print.

U.S. Department of Health, Education, and Welfare. *Social Security Programs in*

the United States. Washington: GPO, 1968. Print.

Note that most federal publications emanate from the Government Printing Office (GPO).

Kruger, Jane. *Teaching as an Art.* College Park, University of Maryland, 1970. Print.

1976 Foreign Currency Converter. Los Angeles: Deak and Co., 1976. Print.

Because pamphlets are distributed by many organizations in a variety of nonstandard forms, the best you can do is treat them as much like books as possible, supplying place of publication, publisher, and date.

Critical review

> Hertzberg, Hendrik. "Can You Forgive Him?" Rev. of *Blinded by the Right:*
>
> *The Conscience of an Ex-Conservative,* by David Brock. *The New*
>
> *Yorker* 11 Mar. 2002: 85-89. Print.

If the review is untitled, proceed directly with *Rev. of . . .*

Radio or television program

> *The Hearst and Davies Affair.* Dir. David Rich. Prod. Paul Pompia. Perf. Robert
>
> Mitchum and Virginia Madsen. ABC. KABC, Los Angeles: 14 Jan. 1985.
>
> Television.

The information for a radio or television program should be listed in this order:

1. Title of program, italicized
2. Director, producer, narrator, composer, host, etc.
3. Star performers, preceded by *Perf.*
4. Network (e.g., *CBS*)
5. Local station (followed by a comma) and its city (e.g., *KETC, St. Louis*)
6. Date of broadcast
7. Medium of transmission: *Radio, Television,* etc.

If you want to list an episode, it should precede the title of the program and appear within quotation marks:

Film

> "The Exchange Student." *Schoolbreak Special.* Perf. Neeta Puri. CBS. KCBS,
>
> Los Angeles: 22 Jan. 1985. Television.
>
> *The River.* Dir. Mark Rydell. Prod. Edward Lewis. Writ. Robert Dillon and Julian
>
> Barry. Perf. Sissy Spacek and Mel Gibson. Universal Pictures, 1985. Film.

A film citation requires information in the following order:

1. Title of film, italicized
2. Director, producer, writer—each followed by a period
3. Names of stars, preceded by *Perf.*
4. Name of studio distributing the film, followed by a comma and the year the movie came out
5. Medium of publication

To stress the director, writer, or producer's work, cite his or her name first:

> Rydell, Mark, dir. *The River*. Prod. Edward Lewis. Writ. Robert Dillon and Julian
>
> > Barry. Perf. Sissy Spacek and Mel Gibson. Universal Pictures, 1985. Film.
>
> Roosevelt, Eleanor, narr. *My Life with F.D.R.* Glendale, CA: Glendale Community
>
> > College Library, 1981. Audiotape.
>
> Hampton, Lionel, cond. *Lionel Hampton and His Big Band*. New York:
>
> > Glad-Hamp Record, Inc., GHS 1023, 1983. CD.

Recording or tape

When citing a recording, the order of information listed depends on the desired emphasis. Usually, however, the composer, narrator, or conductor will appear first. Other information to include is the title of the record (italicized), the artist(s) or orchestra, the manufacturer, the catalog number, and the year of issue. Also indicate the medium (e.g., *cassette* or *audiotape*). If you wish to include the titles of individual musical works on the record, then omit the general title and place the work cited in quotation marks; however, do not italicize or place in quotation marks the title of musical compositions identified only by form, number, and key:

> Miller, Glenn, cond. "Moonlight Serenade." Glenn Miller Orchestra. New
>
> > York: RCA, LSP-1192(e), 1960. LP.
>
> Bach, Johann Sebastian. Toccata and Fugue in D minor; Toccata, Adagio, and
>
> > Fugue in C major; Passacaglia and Fugue in C minor. Cond. Eugene
>
> > Ormandy. Philadelphia Orchestra. New York: Columbia, MS 6003, n.d. CD.
>
> Woolley, Morton. Letter to the author. 12 Feb. 1976. TS.
>
> Hirshberg, Jennifer A. Personal interview. 19 Feb. 1976.
>
> Zimmerman, Fred M. "Speculation: Los Angeles-1985." Working paper. Los
>
> > Angeles City Hall: Planning Dept. Library, 1967. TS.

Private letter

Interview

No specific rules exist for the documentation of manuscripts. When using this kind of material, stick as closely as you can to the form for books or magazines. The titles of unpublished works, no matter how long, are enclosed in quotation marks.

Citing Electronic Sources

Electronic sources, which consist of information stored on a computer, have been around for a number of years now, but a standard way of citing them has still not evolved. Although we cannot cover every conceivable kind of electronic citation you might use, we can provide you with a useful rule of thumb for documenting all kinds of electronic sources. It is simply this: *Provide all the information necessary for a reader to locate the source.* As of now, here is the order you need to follow:

1. Give the information concerning the regular print version (if available).
2. Give the title of the internet site (e.g. project, database, online periodical, professional or personal site [italicized]). If the professional or personal site has no title, then provide a description, such as *home page*. For a posting to a discussion list or forum, give the name of the list or forum. For a work from a subscription service, give the name of the service.
3. Give the date of the electronic publication, of the latest update, or of posting when applicable.
4. Give the date when you accessed the service.
5. Supply the URL within angle brackets when it would be difficult for the reader to find the source or your instructor requires it.

Remember that the whole point of including source citations is not to abide by some fussy format but to enable readers to track research and verify supporting documents. The one question you should ask yourself when giving an electronic citation is this: *Could anyone find the source I have cited from the information I have given?* If your answer is yes, then you have adequately documented the source.

A book, periodical, pamphlet, or text.   Provide the same information you would for a regularly printed source. Then add the information for finding it online—the medium (e.g., CD-ROM), if appropriate; the date of access; and the address or path for electronic access. Notice that in this sequence the access date is always the last item before the URL of the site.

CD-ROM	"Boswell, James." *Microsoft Encarta Encyclopedia 99*. Redmond, WA: Microsoft, 1999. CD-ROM.
Online journal	Thompson, Paul. "The Role of Grandparents When Parents Die." *Aging and Society* 19.4 (1 July 1999). Web. 13 Oct. 1999.
Online book	Adams, Henry. *The Education of Henry Adams*. Boston: Houghton, 1918. Web. 8 Oct. 1999. <http://www.bartleby.com/159/index.html>.
Online magazine	Peterson, Scot. "Business: The Smaller the Better." *ZDNet News* 18 Dec. 2001. Web. 5 Jan. 2002.
Online news service	"Six Arrested After Riot on Jet." *CNN News Service* 13 Dec. 2002. Web. 13 Dec. 2002.
Online newspaper	"Israel to Leave Bethlehem for Christmas." *Los Angeles Times* 13 Dec. 2002. Web. 13 Dec. 2002.

A commercial online source. The citation should identify the author, the title (within quotation marks), and the published source and date of the material. In addition, it should indicate that the source is online, identify the name of the database in which the electronic text was found (italicized), include the address or path, and give the date the information was accessed.

> Schaum, Jennifer. "Current D.C. Gun Program Misses Mark." *University Wire* 14
>
> Sept. 1999. Web. 6 Oct. 1999. <http://uwire.com/>.

A forum is an internet site usually organized around a single topic. A posting is an opinion someone has submitted for discussion. Some instructors do not allow postings from a forum to be an essential part of a research paper mainly because the source is often unreliable or even undocumentable. Our advice is that you not use postings from forums in your paper, or if you do, you not cite them as essential evidence for any important point.

The rule of thumb in citing a forum is that you give enough information for the source to be traced. A forum may or may not have an identifiable author. If there's one, mention him or her in the opening. If there's a URL, cite it only if it is unlikely the reader will find the forum without it.

> Poestories.com. A forum on the short stories of Edgar Allan Poe. Ed. Robert
>
> Giordano. Design215, n.d. Web. 25 Feb. 2008.

E-mail. Give the author's name, followed by the descriptive label or subject of the e-mail (within quotation marks). Then state that the document is a message and to whom it was addressed. Also give the date and the notation *e-mail*.

> Cotton, David B. "Gypsy Kings." Message to the author. 26 Feb. 2000. E-mail.

Documenting the Social Sciences Paper (APA)

Everything we have said so far in this chapter about research techniques applies to your social sciences papers. You will need to choose a narrowed topic, get acquainted with the library, collect pertinent information, evaluate your sources, and formulate a thesis, which you then support. The main difference is one of form, rather than approach. For instance, instead of an outline, you will submit an abstract, and instead of using the Modern Language Association (MLA) rules as your style sheet, you will use the rules of the American Psychological Association (APA). Widely used in the social sciences, APA documentation is an author and date system that is parenthetical and similar to the MLA system. If you understand the MLA system, you will find it easy to make the shift to the APA system. The essential difference between them is the APA system's requirement that an author's name be followed by the date of publication—an ever important fact in scientific (especially clinical) research. Full information about the sources cited within the paper will then be contained under a heading called "References" at the end of the paper.

Here are some guidelines for APA style you will want to follow. Most of the guidelines in this section are based on the *Publication Manual of the American Psychological Association* (6th ed., 2010). For the most recent updates on APA style, consult this website: *http://www.apastyle.org/index.aspx.*

Using Parenthetical Documentation

Be clear and uncluttered.   Whenever possible, give the necessary documentation within your main text. If this seems awkward, then give it in parentheses:

> In 1971, Arthur Miller came out with *The Assault on Privacy,* a book pointing
>
> out the problems in a society where private information is so accessible.

> LeMond and Fry (1975) exposed the widespread use of computer records in
>
> various federal agencies.

> All kinds of attorneys, government agencies, and business people have access
>
> to the personal files of individuals because these files are open to people who
>
> know how to get at them (Neier, 1975, p. 190).

If you mention the name(s) of the author(s) in your text, all you need to cite in parentheses is the date and page. But in your "References" list, you must include the names of all authors.

If you are referring to an entire work, you do not need to include a page reference; however, if you are referring to information on a specific page, include the page. It is better to include the page reference whenever helpful for retrieval of information. Give a page number after a direct quotation, for example, *(Peritts, 2002, p. 459).*

When you are using a source with a single author.   As a general rule, place the date of publication as close to the name of the author as possible, followed by the page number to facilitate retrieval of the citation:

> Bachman (1983, p. 86) explains the result of a survey of how American high
>
> school students view the military.

> American high school students generally wish they could avoid the military
>
> (Bachman, 1983).

When you are using a source in which the authors have the same last name.   When a source refers to two different authors who have the same last name (*James Jones* and *Carl Jones*), use each author's first initial to distinguish the two:

> Other authors disagree (J. Jones & C. Jones, 1988).

If the two authors are known to be related, no initial is needed: *(Durant & Durant, 1975).*

Use an ampersand (&) to connect the two names when placed within parentheses. No ampersand is needed for in-text references not within parentheses (see example under the next heading).

When you are using a source with more than two authors. When citing a work by three to five authors, give all names the first time you refer to the work. In subsequent references to this work, use the last name of the first author, followed by *et al.*

> Turco, Toon, Ackerman, Pollack, and Sagan (1983) list the global consequences
>
> of a nuclear explosion.
>
> The global consequences of a nuclear explosion are so immense as to be
>
> indescribable (Turco et al., 1983).

If your reference list has more than one work by *Turco* and any other co-authors, do not shorten any citations to *Turco,* lest you confuse the reader.

For six or more authors, use the name of the first author followed by *et al.,* e.g. *Howdeshell et al., 1967.* In the reference list, for works with up to six authors name all authors. For works with more than six authors, name the first six authors, followed by ellipses and the last author's name:

> Roeder, K., Howdeshell, J., Fulton, L., Lochhead, M., Craig, K., Peterson, R. (1967).
>
> *Nerve cells and insect behavior.* Cambridge, MA: Harvard University Press.

When you are using a source with a corporate author. A corporate author is any organization, such as the *Carnegie Foundation, National Academy of Sciences,* or some governmental agency. Write out the full name of the corporate author for the first citation. You can, however, abbreviate the name in subsequent references:

> Many breeding programs for birds in captivity are proving successful (National
>
> Geographic Society, 1988).

Subsequent references to this source are abbreviated:

> (NGS, 1988).

When you are using a source referred to in a secondary source. In your research, you will often depend on comments or quotations found in your books or journals. For instance, the author of a psychology book you are using as one of your sources may quote Sigmund Freud. The quotation itself comes from a primary source, but the book in which it is quoted is a secondary (indirect) source. When you cite this material in the text of your paper, give the author of the original work first, followed by a parenthetical reference to the work in which you found the citation. Begin the parenthetical reference with *as cited in:*

> Greenway (as cited in Alvin, 1966, p. 24) indicated that . . .

Your "References" list will then contain the following entry:

Alvin, J. (1966). *Music therapy.* New York: Humanities Press.

If you are quoting a statement made by an author in 1862 but contained in a work published in 1949, it is common sense to indicate in your text the time of the original statement. Here is how you can handle it:

In 1862, Otto von Bismarck became chancellor of Prussia. He worshipped force,

saying, "Germany does not look to Prussia's liberalism, but to her power" (cited

in Wallbank & Taylor, 1949, vol. 2, p. 214).

When you are using a multivolume source.   When referring to a work that is part of a multivolume set, include the volume number and page number, separating the volume number from the page number with a comma:

Approval of the project had been unanimous (Harrison, 1988, vol. 3, p. 180).

When referring to a specific table or section of a work, include this information in your citation, as follows:

(Clark, 1988, fig. 5).

(Winstein, 1986, sec. 8).

When you are citing two or more sources within the same parentheses.   If your paper requires you to cite two or more works supporting the same point within the same parentheses, list the citations in the same order in which they appear in the "References" list.

Research during the past two years (Quincy, 1988; Roth, 1987) has given rise to

some serious doubt.

Using Content Notes

Content notes consist of information that does not belong in the main flow of your text. They should be used sparingly, but when they are necessary, they should conform to the following rules:

1. Immediately following the material to which the note refers, place a superscript numeral (elevated one-half space above the line), with no space between the numeral and the last word or punctuation mark (except in the case of a dash, which the footnote precedes, and footnotes contained within parentheses). Here is an example:

In the second experiment, the researchers used voice feedback by recording

all of the vocal protests resulting from the shock that had been introduced.[2] As in

the first situation . . .

A complete reference will then appear on your content notes page.

2. Begin all content notes on a separate page following the last page of your text. Label this page "Endnotes," centering this heading at the top of the page. (See the sample student paper for the social sciences, pp. 542–552.)

3. Here are some typical examples of content notes:

REFERENCES TO OTHER SOURCES

[3] On this point see also P. Marler and S. Peters (1981), who raised 16 male swamp sparrows by hand in acoustic isolation. They were taken from the field as 2- and 10-day-old nestlings.

Your "References" must include any works referred to in your content notes.

COMMENTS RELATED TO THE SUBJECT BEING DISCUSSED

[6] In this paper the term *artificial intelligence* will be used to mean a language developed from a set of rules determined before the language is put into use.

MAJOR SOURCE REQUIRING FREQUENT IN-TEXT CITATION

[12] All quotations of Hubert Dreyfus are from his book *What Computers Can't Do* (1979).

Your "References" must include any version referred to in your content notes.

Preparing the List of "References"

At the end of your paper, you will have a list of all sources actually cited as documentation; this list will be entitled "References." Each entry will contain four units, in the following order: (1) author, (2) year of publication, (3) title, and (4) publication facts. End all units with periods, and separate them from each other by a single space.

Several APA conventions differ from those of MLA. In general, the differences have to do with punctuation and capitalization. Follow these APA conventions:

1. Center the word *References* at the top of a new page. Start the first line of each entry at the left margin, but indent the second and succeeding lines one tab (five to seven spaces). Type the list double-spaced and in alphabetical order by author (or title, if no author is shown). Alphabetize corporate authors by the first significant word in the name.

2. Give the surname and initials of authors, up to six authors. Separate the names with commas, and use an ampersand (&) between the last two names. If there are more than six, list six, followed by elipses and then the name of the last author of the work. List the names in the order listed in the source you are citing.

3. If a book is the work of one or more editors, enclose the abbreviation *Ed.* or *Eds.* in parentheses after the name of the last editor:

Baker, J. (Ed.).

Daniels, M., & Miller, D. (Eds.).

4. Put the publication date in parentheses. For magazines and newspapers, place a comma after the year, then the month—written in full—and the date:

Book

Fishman, J. (1988).

Magazine

Gonzales, P. (1987, January 15).

5. Capitalize only the first word of a book or article title (and the first word of a subtitle, if there is one). Type the remaining words in lowercase letters. However, capitalize each word in the title of a periodical:

Book

AIDS: The ultimate challenge.

Periodical

Journal of Applied Psychology.

6. Italicize the titles of books and periodicals. Do not use quotation marks around the titles of articles within these longer works.

Linden, E. (1988, March 28). Putting knowledge to work. *Time,* 60–63.

7. The actual page numbers on which a newspaper article appears follow the name of the paper and a comma. Use the abbreviation *p.* for single pages or *pp.* for multiple pages. Separate page numbers by commas and end the item with a period:

pp. 50, 51, 63–67.

8. When you are using an essay or chapter within a book, list the author, date, and title of the essay or chapter. Then, place *In* followed by the name of the author or editor of the book, if different, the book title, and then parentheses enclosing the abbreviation *pp.* and the exact page numbers of the article or chapter you have referred to. Finally, give the publisher's location and name, followed by a period. (See the sample in number 10.)

9. Show the state in which the publisher is located, even if city is well-known, such as New York, Chicago, Boston, Paris, or London. Use standard two-letter postal abbreviations for states. Place a colon after the location:

Belmont, CA: Wadsworth.

Be as brief as possible in giving the name of the publisher, omitting such words as *Company* or *Incorporated.* Do spell out the names of associations or university presses:

Macmillan

Oxford University Press

National Audubon Society

10. If your "References" list contains more than one work by the same author(s), repeat the name in every entry. Arrange the entries by year of publication, the earliest year first:

Beardsley, W., & Mack, J. E. (1982). The impact on children and adolescents

of nuclear development. In *Psychological aspects of nuclear developments*

(pp. 54–63). Washington, DC: American Psychiatric Association.

Beardsley, W., & Mack, J. E. (1983). Adolescents and the threat of nuclear

war: The evolution of a perspective. *Yale Journal of Biology and*

Medicine, 56, 79–91.

Standard sources.   Listed next are examples of most types of sources you will encounter in your research. Adhere to the formats rigorously. Should you encounter a source for which you find no model, use the format of a similar source or consult your teacher. All sources that follow are in APA style.

Jackson, S. W. (1988). *Melancholia and depression: From Hippocratic times*   Book by a
                                                                                single author
to modern times. New Haven, CT: Yale University Press.

Cole, D. M., & Scarfo, R. G. (1965). *Beyond tomorrow.* Amherst, WI: Amherst   Book by two or
                                                                                more authors
Press.

U.S. Congress. Office of Technology Assessment. (1982). *World population and*   Book by a
                                                                                corporate
fertility planning technologies: The next twenty years.* Washington, DC: author

U.S. Government Printing Office.

When the publisher is the same as the author, write *Author* where the publisher belongs:

South-Western Publishing Co. (1976). *Fair and balanced treatment of*

minorities and women. Cincinnati, OH: Author.

Friedman, R. J., & Katz, M. M. (Eds.). (1974). *The psychology of depression:*   Book edited by
                                                                                an individual or
Contemporary theory and research. New York, NY: Wiley.   group

Salter, R. M. (1979). Transplanetary subway systems. In F. P. Davidson,   Chapter in an
                                                                                edited book
L. J. Giacoletto, & R. Salkeld (Eds.), *Macroengineering and the*

infrastructure of tomorrow (pp. 50–56). Boulder, CO: Westview Press.

The names of the editors following *In* are not inverted.

Lester, J. D. (1971). *Writing research papers: A complete guide* (4th ed.).   Edition other
                                                                                than first of a
Glenview, IL: Scott, Foresman.   book

| Book in translation | La Boetie, E. (1975). *The politics of obedience: The discourse of voluntary servitude* (H. Kurz, Trans.). Montreal, Canada: Black Rose Books. (Original work published 1971). |

Book in translation

La Boetie, E. (1975). *The politics of obedience: The discourse of voluntary servitude* (H. Kurz, Trans.). Montreal, Canada: Black Rose Books. (Original work published 1971).

Reference to the entire set of a multivolume set

Lindzey, G., & Aronson, E. (Eds.). (1969). *The handbook of social psychology* (2nd ed., Vols. 1–5). Reading, MA: Addison-Wesley.

Reference to an article in one volume of a multivolume set

Moore, W. E. (1969). Social structure and behavior. In G. Lindzey & E. Aronson (Eds.), *The handbook of social psychology: Vol. 4. Group psychology and phenomena of interaction* (2nd ed., pp. 283–322). Reading, MA: Addison-Wesley.

Signed article in an encyclopedia or dictionary

Savitz, L. (2000). Torture. In *Encyclopedia americana* (15th ed., Vol. 26, pp. 868–869). Danbury, CT: Grolier.

Article from a journal paginated continuously

Penfield, W. (1952). Memory mechanisms. *A.M.A. Archives of Neurology and Psychiatry, 67,* 178–198.

The volume number is italicized followed by the page numbers of the entire article.

Article from a journal, each issue separately paginated

Nicholson, T. D. (1988). Down in the dumps. *Natural History, 97*(4), 8–12.

The volume number is italicized, and the issue number is placed within parentheses.

Magazine article in a monthly periodical

Insel, T. R. (2010, April). Faulty circuits. *Scientific American,* 44–51.

APA uses *p.* and *pp.* to indicate pages for newspapers and books but not for magazines and journals.

Magazine article in a weekly

Schnur, S. (1988, March 28). In New Jersey: Day care with a lot of caring. *Time,* 8–10.

Newspaper article with author

Serafino, P. (2010, January 30). Gates foundation promises $10 billion for world vaccines. *San Francisco Chronicle,* p. 9.

Newspaper article without author

Not proved. (1988, April 10). *Los Angeles Times,* Pt. 5, p. 4.

Give the part or section of the paper when it is helpful.

APA does not require that lectures or interviews be listed in "References," but, of course, they must be acknowledged in your text. The general rule for any non-print material is to take down all information available on the source. State the kind of source within brackets following the title. Here are samples for two common types of sources:

Redford, R. (Director), Ward, D., & Nichols, J. (Writers). (1988). *The Milagro*   *Film*

     beanfield war [Motion picture]. United States: Universal.

Jennings, P. (Anchorman). (1988). *Drugs: A plague upon the land*   *Television*

     [Television broadcast]. New York, NY: ABC.   *broadcast*

Citing Electronic Sources

Electronic sources consist of information that must be retrieved from a computer. Some electronic sources, such as CD-ROMs, are easy to cite because they are stored in a permanent format, just like books. Other electronic sources are a little more complicated to cite because the information can change at any time.

With the wealth of electronic information constantly increasing, and the availability of new formats of data (podcasts, blogs, wikis), it is especially important to know exactly where the information was retrieved from, and to cite it in a way that makes it easy for someone else to locate. When you use this kind of information, be sure to capture the data you intend on using in a way that insures it will remain available to you (a screen shot or print out) as you write your paper and cite your sources. Don't trust your browser to keep track of your electronic research—browsers crash, websites go down, wikis are updated and blog posts are removed. Make sure you obtain not only the research data you need, but the information to cite it appropriately as you find the sources.

There are many kinds of electronic sources; the following examples show citation styles for some of the more common ones:

E-Mail. E-mail is cited in text as personal communication (and thus not included in the "References" list, according to APA style). They should be cited parenthetically in your main text, for example:

     (D. M. Petrie, personal communication, June 28, 2000).

Websites. To cite a complete website (not a specific document on that website), give the site's address in text (but again, no "References" entry is needed):

     The Exploratorium provides wonderful resources for teachers of inquiry-

     oriented classrooms (http://www.exploratorium.edu).

Specific Documents on Websites. Begin with the same information that would be included for a print document. Then add a retrieval statement giving the address of the website. For example:

Rand, J. A., & Olson, D. L. (1999, December). The ethics of behavioral research.   *A journal*

     World Scientist, 50, 75–78. Retrieved from http://www.wsa.org/journals/   *article*

     rand.html

Lamont, S. (2000, January 15). UN plots course for the new millennium.

    Global Monitor, pp. 1, 15. Retrieved from http://www.un.org/monitor/

    millen.html

Articles and Abstracts from Databases.   Articles accessed online should be referenced in the same way as an equivalent print source. If the article is not easily accessible, provide database information (*Retrieved from* and then the URL) after the standard citation.

    Costello, R. A. (1999). Interest rates rise as stocks fall. *Midwest Business*

        Journal, 21(31), 281.

    Federal Bureau of Investigation. (1998, March). *Encryption: Impact on law*

        enforcement. Washington, DC: Author. Retrieved from SIRS

        Government Reporter [CD-ROM].

For other examples of various electronic sources, see the sixth edition of the *Publication Manual of the Psychological Association.*

Preparing the Final Copy (MLA)

The final copy of your paper should be clean and free of errors. Do not skimp on revising or proofreading time. Students who use a computer will have an advantage as they edit, but should not rely soley on the spell and grammar checking tools of their word processor. Carefully observe the following rules. (Also see the sample student paper on pp. 542–552.)

1. Print
    a. Print on one side of the paper only.
    b. Avoid using fancy fonts; instead, use a plain type in a readable size (such as 12 point Times New Roman).
2. Paper: Use only white paper, 8½ × 11 inches, of high quality.
3. Margins
    a. Except for page numbers, leave one-inch margins at the top, bottom, and both sides of the paper.
    b. Indent the first word in each new paragraph one-half inch or five spaces.
    c. Quotations must be set off from the text by double-spacing and indenting one inch from the left margin. A colon ends the sentence preceding

them. Double-space the text of the quotation. Skip one space after the concluding punctuation mark of the quotation and insert the parenthetical reference:

> At one point in her life Sylvia Plath was deeply moved by a French motion picture about the temptation of Joan of Arc. She gives this account of her reaction:
>
> > After it was all over, I couldn't look at anyone. I was crying because it was like a purge, the buildup of unbelievable tension, then the release, as of the soul of Joan at the stake. (96)

4. Spacing: Double-space the research paper throughout, including the outline, the heading, the title (if it is longer than one line), quotations, and the bibliography. Also, double-space between the title and the first line of the body of the paper.

5. Title page: MLA style does not require a title page. For examples of how the first page of an MLA paper should look, see the model here and the student sample on page 534.

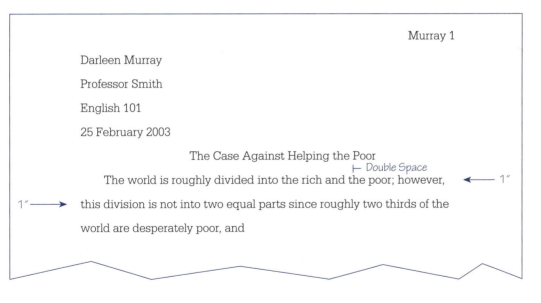

6. Pagination
   a. Number all pages consecutively throughout the manuscript.
   b. Place each page numeral in the upper right-hand corner, one-half inch from the top.

c. Beginning with page 1, place your surname in front of the page number to prevent confusion in case part of your paper gets lost. See below:

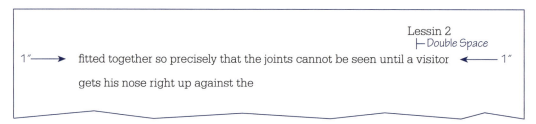

7. Binding: Many students try to make their research papers look attractive by placing them in a folder or cover of some kind; however, such bindings tend to be a nuisance to the teacher trying to analyze the paper and comment on it. Better to submit the paper held together with a good paper clip, which the teacher can remove and replace at will.

8. Submitting your paper electronically: No accepted standards currently exist for the electronic submission of research papers. If your instructor requires you to submit your paper electronically, be sure you understand the formatting you must use and the acceptable model of submission—on disk, by e-mail, or uploaded to a website. To make discussion of a paper's content easier, many instructors also require electronically submitted papers to have numbered paragraphs. If you use this system, place the appropriate number, in brackets—followed by a space, at the start of each paragraph.

9. Outline: MLA does not require an outline. If your instructor does, see pp. 60–62 for a discussion of outlining.

Preparing the Final Copy (APA)

The same basic rules used for typing a research paper for the humanities apply to typing a research paper for the social sciences. That is, use good paper, print on one side only, double-space throughout the paper, observe the proper margins, and so forth. However, a research paper following APA style has three special features: (1) an abstract, (2) a running head (shortened form of the title) on the top right-hand side of each page, and (3) a "References" rather than "Works Cited" list. Here is what your paper will require:

Title page

Abstract

Body of paper

References

Footnotes (if you used content notes)

Some elements of APA style distinguish between a working draft and a published paper. Here are the major differences:

Working draft: The right margin is not justified, titles are underlined (not italicized), and "References" entries are formatted like regular paragraphs.

Published paper: The right margin is justified, titles are italicized (not underlined), and "References" entries are formatted with a hanging indent.

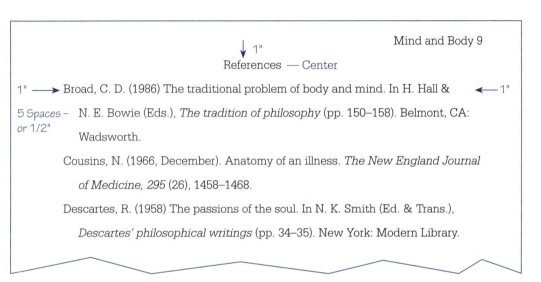

Mind and Body 9

↓ 1"

References — Center

1" ⟶ Broad, C. D. (1986) The traditional problem of body and mind. In H. Hall &   ⟵ 1"

5 Spaces –   N. E. Bowie (Eds.), *The tradition of philosophy* (pp. 150–158). Belmont, CA:
or 1/2"
          Wadsworth.

     Cousins, N. (1966, December). Anatomy of an illness. *The New England Journal*

          of Medicine, 295 (26), 1458–1468.

     Descartes, R. (1958) The passions of the soul. In N. K. Smith (Ed. & Trans.),

          Descartes' philosophical writings (pp. 34–35). New York: Modern Library.

You should find out what your instructor requires for your paper. (Also see the sample student paper on pp. 542–552.)

■ *Exercises*

1. Unscramble the following bibliographical facts, and arrange them in the proper MLA form for "Works Cited."

   a. A book by E. L. Doctorow, published by Random House of New York in 1975. The title of the book is *Ragtime.*

   b. An article entitled "What Is the Federal Cup?" published in volume 23 of *World Tennis,* the August 1976 issue, covering pages 32–34.

   c. "Good Country People," a story by Flannery O'Connor, taken from the second edition of an anthology entitled *The Modern Tradition,* edited by Daniel F. Howard and published in 1972 by Little, Brown and Company of Boston.

   d. Fyodor Dostoyevsky's famous novel *Crime and Punishment,* published by Oxford University Press, Inc., of New York (1953), in a translation by Jessie Coulson.

e. "The Dutiful Child's Promises," a selection from an anthology entitled *Readings from American Literature,* edited by Mary Edwards Calhoun and Emma Lenore MacAlarney, published by Ginn and Company of Boston, 1915.

f. A two-volume work entitled *Civilization—Past and Present,* coauthored by T. Walter Wallbank and Alastair M. Taylor, published in 1949 by Scott, Foresman and Company of Chicago.

g. An unsigned encyclopedia article under the heading "Tiryns," found in volume 22 of the 1963 edition of the *Encyclopaedia Britannica,* pages 247–248.

h. The sixth edition of Karl C. Garrison's book entitled *Psychology of Adolescence,* published in 1965 by Prentice-Hall, of Englewood Cliffs, New Jersey.

i. An article without author from the August 9, 1976, issue of *Time.* The article appears on pages 16 and 19 and is entitled "To Plains with the Boys in the Bus."

j. A feature article by Jim Murray, entitled "The Real Olympian," which appeared in Part III of the *Los Angeles Times,* pages 1 and 7 (Wednesday, August 4, 1976).

2. Unscramble the following bibliographical facts and arrange them in the proper form for APA-style "References."

a. A work put out by the Canadian Tax Foundation. It is entitled *Provincial and Municipal Finances* and was published in Toronto, Canada, in 1979.

b. An article entitled "Boom & Doom on Wall Street," authored by Berkeley Rice. It was published in the April 1988 issue of *Psychology Today* on pages 52–54.

c. A journal article titled "Children and Psychological Testing" and written by the following authors: B. Kerr, J. Davison, J. Nelson, and S. Haley. The article appeared in the year 1982, in volume 34, number 3, of *Journal of Experimental Child Psychology.* The entire article took up pages 526 to 541. The journal numbers its pages continuously throughout a volume.

d. "Beyond Freedom and Dignity," an essay by the psychologist B. F. Skinner, who was born in 1904. The essay is reprinted in an anthology titled *The Tradition of Philosophy,* edited by Harrison Hall and Norma B. Bowie and published in 1952 in Belmont, California, by the Wadsworth Publishing Company. The full article takes up pages 321 to 325.

e. An unsigned article in the *New Columbia Encyclopedia,* published in 1975, entitled "Athlete's Heart." The encyclopedia is edited by William H. Harris and Judith S. Levey. It is published in New York by the Columbia University Press. The article appears on page 176.

3. Using the bibliographical information provided in Exercise 1, convert the following items below into a proper sequence of parenthetical notes according to MLA style.

a. Page 25 of the book by Karl C. Garrison.

b. Page 50 of that same book.

c. Page 30 of volume one of the book by T. Walter Wallbank and Alastair M. Taylor.

d. Page 31 of that same book.

e. Page 90 of the book edited by Mary Edwards Calhoun and Emma Lenore MacAlarney.

f. Page 1 of the *Los Angeles Times* article.

g. Page 248 of the encyclopedia article.

h. Page 48 of Fyodor Dostoyevsky's novel.

i. Page 507 of Flannery O'Connor's story.

j. Page 46 of *Ragtime*.

4. From the works mentioned in this unit, compile a list of sources that you would consult if you were to write on one of the topics below. Make sure that at least a few of them come from electronic sources:

a. The last year of Thomas Jefferson's life

b. Research regarding the education of blind children

c. The novels of William Makepeace Thackeray

d. The myth of Europa

e. The rise of Mao Tse-tung

f. Safety in nuclear plants

g. The art of Jacques Louis David

h. Famous quotations about the value of education

i. The murder of Stanford White by Harry K. Thaw

j. The philosophy of Bertrand Russell

5. Summarize the following paragraph in one sentence:

Those who are awed by their surroundings do not think of change, no matter how miserable their condition. When our mode of life is so precarious as to make it patent that we cannot control the circumstances of our existence, we tend to stick to the proven and the familiar. We counteract a deep feeling of insecurity by making of our existence a fixed routine. We hereby acquire the illusion that we have tamed the unpredictable. Fisherfolk, nomads and farmers who have to contend with the willful elements, the creative worker who depends on inspiration, the savage awed by his surroundings—they all fear change. They face the world as they would an all-powerful jury. The abjectly poor, too, stand in awe of the world around them and are not hospitable to change. It is a dangerous life we live when hunger and cold are at our heels. There is thus a conservatism of the destitute as profound as the conservatism of the privileged, and the former is as much a factor in the perpetuation of a social order as the latter.

—Eric Hoffer, *The True Believer*

6. Summarize the following paragraph into half the length of the original:

Everyone from Drake to Darwin asked the same question: Why would these Yahgan, why would anyone, settle in such a harsh and stingy environment? Since no one would do so willingly, the reasoning went, they must have been driven down here by stronger, more advanced Indians to the north until they fetched up at the very bottom of the habitable world in a place nobody else wanted. Indeed, the Yahgan did have enemies to the north on Tierra del Fuego—the Ona. Whites called them "Foot Indians" to distinguish their way of life from that of the Yahgan, who were "Canoe Indians." The Ona, nomads who occupied the forests, bogs, and pampas on the big island, were statuesque and elegant compared to the "stooped" and "stunted" Yahgan, which seemed to prove the point. Ona culture was in fact richer materially and psychically, partly because they shared their environment with a plentiful prey animal, the guanaco, a smaller cousin to the llama, which supplied a full range of human needs, including clothes.

—Dallas Murphy, *Rounding the Horn*

7. Paraphrase the following paragraph so that it sounds like you:

The urge for a touch of class, for something better than others have, has put new pressure on that classic Russian institution—the queue. Customers the world-over wait in lines, but Soviet queues have a dimension all their own, like the Egyptian pyramids. They reveal a lot about the Russian predicament and the Russian psyche. And their operation is far more intricate than first meets the eye. To the passerby they look like nearly motionless files of mortals doomed to some commercial purgatory for their humble purchases. But what the outsider misses is the hidden magnetism of lines for Russians, their inner dynamics, their special etiquette.

—Hedrick Smith, *The Russians*

8. Paraphrase the following paragraph so that you could not be accused of plagiarizing. If you retain any words from the original, don't forget to place them within quotation marks. Your paraphrase should be approximately the same length as the original.

John Adams was also, as many could attest, a great-hearted, persevering man of uncommon ability and force. He had a brilliant mind. He was honest and everyone knew it. Emphatically independent by nature, hardworking, frugal—all traits in the New England tradition—he was anything but cold or laconic as supposedly New Englanders were. He could be high-spirited and affectionate, vain, cranky, impetuous, self-absorbed, and fiercely stubborn; passionate, quick to anger, and all-forgiving; generous and entertaining. He was blessed with great courage and great humor, yet subject to spells of despair, and especially when separated from his family or during periods of prolonged inactivity.

—David McCullough, *John Adams*

Sample Student Papers

The two student research papers included on the following pages will give you an idea of what good student papers look like. The first paper "As the Japanese Economy Goes Down, Suicides Go Up" (pp. 527–533) offers a close look at a disturbing issue in Japanese society and the first draft provides annotations explaining the general format of humanities papers as proposed by the Modern Language Association (MLA).* The final draft that follows it reflects these annotations. The second paper "Keeping Up with the Joneses" (pp. 542–552) is about the psychological effects of wealth and consumerism on young minds. It is more scientific than the first paper and therefore follows the rules proposed by the American Psychological Association (APA). Your instructor will tell you which format your paper should follow. Both papers were written by college freshmen and demonstrate what any conscientious student can achieve with effort and diligence.

STUDENT PAPER — FIRST DRAFT (MLA)

Polenghi 1

Cesare Polenghi

Professor Edelman

English 101

11 February 2002

As the Japanese Economy Goes Down, Suicides Go Up

1   "And the 47 master-less samurai, after avenging their Lord, committed ritual suicide, and died . . . happily ever after." The closing scene of *Chushingura*, a Japanese drama from the 18th century, mirrors perfectly the way traditional Japanese society glorified suicide. *Chushingura*, or "The 47 Ronin story," is still today the most beloved Japanese tale of all times, and is constantly re-enacted in movies, theatres, and opera houses. Suicide in feudal Japan was seen as nothing more than one of the most elegant ways to part from life, and its tradition continued throughout the centuries. Faith in the divinity of the emperor pushed the Japanese soldiers in the 20th century to

Your last name and page number. You can use the header feature if your computer has one.

Your full name, your instructor's name, the name of your course, and the date on which you submitted the paper.

Title of paper, not italicized

*See the discussion on pp. 521 and 522 about whether to include a title page and an outline.

The most effective place for your thesis is the last sentence of your opening paragraph, as in this student paper.

sacrifice themselves without any doubt or fear. Kamikaze pilots immolated themselves on American vessels, and civilians committed mass suicides from Okinawa to Tokyo. Whereas World War II came to an end more than 50 years ago, suicide is still a big phenomenon in Japan, where stress and failures at work, together with a complete lack of suicide-prevention infrastructure, blend with old tradition and cause an extremely high number of suicides among males.

This paper follows the MLA style, which calls for double spacing throughout the paper. MLA does not require a separate title page.

Indent all paragraphs 5 spaces or ½ inch.

2   Since the Tokugawa period, back in the 17th century, one of the favorite locations for committing suicide was the Aokigahara forest, located next to Mount Fuji. This majestic volcano represents purity and power to all the Japanese. Along the path that crosses through the woods, signs like "Your life is precious," or "Think calmly once again about them: your siblings, and your children," are posted. However, in the year 2000, the local police recovered from the forest 70 corpses of people who had decided to commit suicide there (Hadfield). These were only a few of the 31,957 that took their own lives in 2000 (Asahi 62), when suicides topped 30,000 for the third year in a row (Wehrfritz). A simple calculation leaves us with appalling figures: Japan registers one suicide every 15 minutes, twice the average of the US (Bremner). Seventy-one percent of the suicides are male (Asahi 62), as suicide in Japan is the 13th most common cause of death for men (Lu). Since the Japanese economy hit a recession in 1998, the number of suicides tied to economic reasons escalated enormously. According to the Japanese National Police Agency, they went up 62% in 1998 (Mehri), and another 12% in 1999 (Lamar). There is clearly a close relationship between unemployment and suicide; unemployment is up to a 4.9% record, and growing (Wehrfritz).

Follow the MLA style of parenthetical citation in the text. The period follows the end parenthesis of the parenthetical reference.

3   Why is suicide still so common in a country that has one of the highest GDP and life expectancies in the world? As stated at the beginning of this study, *Seppuku* (traditional suicide) is a legacy of the Bushido, the Japanese

Foreign words are italicized.

Polenghi 3

samurai's medieval code of honor, a process by which one could apologize, prove one's sincerity, or escape from disgrace (Nitobe 116). Centuries later, little has changed in the way the Japanese, as a society, think about suicide.

4   Japanese usually commit themselves to a single cause, and in today's Japan it is commonly thought that work is usually more important than health or family. This is once again a heritage transmitted generation after generation from the feudal era, and what was once the spirit of the samurai was later embodied in the spirit of the "salaryman," the corporate worker. Japanese employees helped the country to perform the real economical miracle of the last century during the 70s and the 80s, and traded their lives, their time, and their health for what they supposed to be a lifelong stability for their family and for them. However, since the Japanese economic bubble burst at the end of the 80s, circumstances have worsened for workers, and failure and disappointment too often resulted in extreme consequences. Most of the registered suicide cases point to middle-aged men in their fifties or sixties. They are the ones that made "Japan Inc." the second economic power in the world, and their workaholic generations were taught not to show weakness. Wataru Suematsu, the director of the Tokyo Life Line (a hot line for people with suicidal tendencies), explains how the victims of suicide in these groups seem to reveal some sad common traits: he describes them as lonely, isolated, and often depressed (Wehrfritz). Freelance journalist Satoshi Kamata asserts that usually, what made the situation irreversible for the victims was their inability to speak about their problems because they feared wage or promotion discrimination (Mehri). Very few of them sought help (Wehrfritz), and statistics show that only 30% of them left suicide notes (Lamar).

5   The most resounding incident in the last few years took place on March 23, 1999, in the Tokyo headquarters of the multinational rubber company

Bridgestone. Employee Nonaka Masaharu, who had worked for his company for 40 years, confronted the president.

Upset about the employer's restructuring program, which had forced him to quit, he demanded fair treatment, saying that the company had betrayed his loyalty. His request was rejected, and Nonaka, after stripping his shirt, locked himself into an office. There, he waited for some other workers and journalists to gather around, and took his life with a kitchen knife (Yamada).

Titles of periodicals must be italicized.

6   However, most opt for a quick, less dramatic suicide. A typical example is the one of Masayuki Tanaka, a vice-president of a smaller company. Stressed by overwork and responsibilities he was not able to handle, he hanged himself in his family's home. In his last note, he wrote: "I chose this way because I couldn't achieve results, even though I worked until becoming completely exhausted" (Fuyuno 78). His widow, Akiko Tanaka (not her real name), interviewed by the *Far East Economic Review*, said that she was reluctant to even file a compensation claim. At the end of her talk, she sadly confessed: "It's already in the past. I am so sorry for my husband, but I feel neither the government nor society will change, no matter what I do" (80). None of her husband's former bosses ever contacted her to offer their condolences (79).

When you copy someone's exact words, they must be placed within quotation marks, followed by the note reference within parentheses. The period is placed after the end parenthesis of the note reference.

Notice how the student carefully documents any important idea resulting from his research, thus avoiding being accused of plagiarism.

7   In Japan mental depression is still regarded as a sign of weakness, and most doctors will not treat mental illness, either because it might hurt the doctor's reputation, or simply because they do not have the necessary skills to treat depressed patients. Today, the government is not planning any special study to try to improve the situation, and it still prohibits the use of antidepressants like Prozac (Wehrfritz). A World Health Organization (WHO) study from the mid 90s threw light on some hard-to-believe realities regarding psychiatry in Japan. Eighty-one percent of the doctors either missed or misjudged mental illness. Even the ones who had been well trained

Polenghi 5

somehow could not assimilate the standard WHO booklet for mental illness. Japanese psychiatry is, sadly, some 20-30 years behind the West (Wehrfritz).

8   The few countermeasures in place to help Japanese people not to commit suicide are clearly inadequate, and implemented only thanks to private, local and limited groups. One of the companies that has been directly affected by suicides is Japan Rail East, which recorded 212 suicides on its network in 1999. Suicides are labeled as a "Human incident," and cause an hour-long stop for trains, resulting in a loss of money and prestige for the rail company. Japan Rail East, after some studies, introduced some "remedies" to reduce suicides. Human-sized mirrors have been placed at the end of many platforms, since they deprive the victim of the intimacy that many people need to commit suicide. Sensors on platforms activate an alarm when someone gets too close to the tracks, and help the personnel to prevent a certain number of accidents. Maybe the most curious countermeasure is newly bright colored stations and crossings. Happier colors supposedly help potential suicides to cheer up a little, and to give up their intentions, at least for the day (French).

9   However, the culture of suicide is still strong, and somehow keeps fascinating the Japanese, who do not seem too worried about organizing and working toward real solutions. In Japanese literature, too, suicide is often part of the plot. For instance, the modern best-selling author Banana Yoshimoto features suicidal characters in almost every one of her books. And not only do literary characters commit suicide, but also some of the most popular Japanese writers of the 20th century did so, like Yukio Mishima, Osamu Dazai, Natsume Soseki, and others.

When references to the names of famous people are the result of the student's own research, no documenta-tion is needed.

10   A search for books on suicide on amazon.com will offer five books on how to prevent suicide. The same exact search on amazon.co.jp—the Japanese version of the online biggest bookstore—will open with the best-seller

Polenghi 6

Titles of
books must
be italicized.

The Complete Manual of Suicide, by Tsurumi Mitsuru. Promoted as "More useful than the Bible as a written suicide aid," it ranks #354 in the Amazon Japan chart. Japanese readers describe it as "Entertaining, even if you are not planning to commit suicide." The manual, that since 1993 sold steadily, going through 50 press runs, clearly explains 12 ways to commit suicide: jumps, rope, gas, water, etc. The author, who has now reached a certain popularity in Japan, and is often invited to be on TV talk shows, put it in these words: "If you want to live, you should live as you please, and if you want to die, you should die as you please. There is not much more to life than that" (Ueda). In other words, Japan has really not yet crept out of the primeval forest of the past, where suicide was often considered an admirable or unavoidable heroic act.

The final
sentence is
a strong
conclusion
because it
restates with
clarity the
student's
thesis.

Works Cited

Asahi Shimbunsha. *Japan Almanac 2002*. Tokyo: Asahi, 2001. Print.

Bremner, Bryan. "A Japanese Way of Death." *Business Week Online* 22 Aug. 2000. Web. 13 July 2001. <http://www.businessweek.com/bwdaily/dnflash/aug2000/nf20000822_176.htm>.

French, Howard D. "Japanese Trains Try to Shed a Gruesome Appeal." *New York Times* 6 June 2000: A4. Print.

Fuyuno, Ichiko. "A Silent Epidemic." *Far Eastern Economic Review* 28 Sept. 2000: 78–80. Print.

Hadfield, Peter. "A Fine Place for Farewell. A Tragic Deadly Toll at Japan's Suicide Central." *U.S. News & World Report* 20 Nov. 2000: 71+. Web. Internet Database Proquest Direct. <http://www.proquest.com>.

Lamar, Joe. "Suicides in Japan Reach a Record High." *British Medical Journal International* 321 (2000): 528. Web. Internet Database Proquest Direct. <http://www.proquest.com>.

Lu, Cathy. "It's a Man's Job: Managing Workplace Stress." *CNN.com*. 11 Jan 2000. Web. 15 Sept. 2002. <http://www.cnn.com/2000/HEALTH/men/01/11/men.workplace.stress.wmd/index.html>.

Mehri, Darius. "Death by Overwork: Corporate Pressure on Employees Takes a Fatal Toll in Japan." *Multinational Monitor* June 2000: 26–28. Web. Internet Database Proquest Direct. <http://www.proquest.com>.

Nitobe, Inazo. *Bushido, the Soul of Japan*. Tokyo: Tuttle, 1969. Print.

Ueda, Yasuo. "Dealing with Death." *Japan Echo* 22 (1995), Online Edition. Web. 10 June 2001.

Wehrfritz, George. "Death by Conformity; Japan's Corporate Warriors Are Killing Themselves in Record Numbers." *Newsweek* 20 Aug. 2001, Atlantic ed.: 183. Web. Internet Database Proquest Direct. <http://www.proquest.com>.

Yamada, Atsushi. "Death of a Salaryman." *Japan Quarterly* July-Sept. 1999. Web. Internet Database Proquest Direct. <http://www.proquest.com>.

"Works Cited" must begin on a new page and is double spaced throughout.

MLA stipulates that authors be listed by their last name, first name, and an initial unless the author is listed otherwise in the original source.

Each entry begins with a hanging indentation (5 spaces or 1/2 inch) for second and subsequent lines.

Entry for an electronic source. See also the other electronic sources cited.

Polenghi 1

Cesare Polenghi

Professor Edelman

English 101

11 February 2002

As the Japanese Economy Goes Down, Suicides Go Up

"And the 47 master-less samurai, after avenging their Lord, committed ritual suicide, and died . . . happily ever after." The closing scene of *Chushingura*, a Japanese drama from the 18th century, mirrors perfectly the way traditional Japanese society glorified suicide. *Chushingura*, or "The 47 Ronin story," is still today the most beloved Japanese tale of all time, and is constantly re-enacted in movies, theatres, and opera houses. Suicide in feudal Japan was seen as nothing more than one of the most elegant ways to part from life, and its tradition continued throughout the centuries. Faith in the divinity of the emperor pushed the Japanese soldiers in the 20th century to sacrifice themselves without any doubt or fear. Kamikaze pilots immolated themselves on American vessels, and civilians committed mass suicides from Okinawa to Tokyo. Whereas World War II came to an end more than 50 years ago, suicide is still a big phenomenon in Japan, where stress and failures at work, together with a complete lack of suicide-prevention infrastructure, blend with old tradition and cause an extremely high number of suicides among males.

Since the Tokugawa period, back in the 17th century, one of the favorite locations for committing suicide was the Aokigahara

Polenghi 2

forest, located next to Mount Fuji. This majestic volcano represents purity and power to all the Japanese. Along the path that crosses through the woods, signs like "Your life is precious," or "Think calmly once again about them: your siblings, and your children," are posted. However, in the year 2000, the local police recovered from the forest 70 corpses of people who had decided to commit suicide there (Hadfield). These were only a few of the 31,957 that took their own lives in 2000 (Asahi 62), when suicides topped 30,000 for the third year in a row (Wehrfritz). A simple calculation leaves us with appalling figures: Japan registers one suicide every 15 minutes, twice the average of the US (Bremner). Seventy-one percent of the suicides are male (Asahi 62), as suicide in Japan is the 13th most common cause of death for men (Lu). Since the Japanese economy hit a recession in 1998, the number of suicides tied to economic reasons escalated enormously. According to the Japanese National Police Agency, they went up 62% in 1998 (Mehri), and another 12% in 1999 (Lamar). There is clearly a close relationship between unemployment and suicide; unemployment is up to a 4.9% record, and growing (Wehrfritz).

Why is suicide still so common in a country that has one of the highest GDP and life expectancies in the world? As stated at the beginning of this study, *Seppuku* (traditional suicide) is a legacy of the Bushido, the Japanese samurai's medieval code of honor, a process by which one could apologize, prove one's sincerity, or escape from disgrace (Nitobe 116). Centuries later, little has changed in the way the Japanese, as a society, think about suicide.

Japanese usually commit themselves to a single cause, and in today's Japan it is commonly thought that work is usually more important than health or family. This is once again a heritage transmitted generation after generation from the feudal era, and what was once the spirit of the samurai was later embodied in the spirit of the "salaryman," the corporate worker. Japanese employees helped the country to perform the real economical miracle of the last century during the 70s and the 80s, and traded their lives, their time, and their health for what they supposed to be a lifelong stability for their family and for them. However, since the Japanese economic bubble burst at the end of the 80s, circumstances have worsened for workers, and failure and disappointment too often resulted in extreme consequences. Most of the registered suicide cases point to middle-aged men in their fifties or sixties. They are the ones that made "Japan Inc." the second economic power in the world, and their workaholic generations were taught not to show weakness. Wataru Suematsu, the director of the Tokyo Life Line (a hot line for people with suicidal tendencies), explains how the victims of suicide in these groups seem to reveal some sad common traits: he describes them as lonely, isolated, and often depressed (Wehrfritz). Freelance journalist Satoshi Kamata asserts that usually, what made the situation irreversible for the victims was their inability to speak about their problems because they feared wage or promotion discrimination (Mehri). Very few of them sought help (Wehrfritz), and statistics show that only 30% of them left suicide notes (Lamar).

The most resounding incident in the last few years took place on March 23, 1999, in the Tokyo headquarters of the multinational rubber company Bridgestone. Employee Nonaka Masaharu, who had worked for his company for 40 years, confronted the president.

Polenghi 4

Upset about the employer's restructuring program, which had forced him to quit, he demanded fair treatment, saying that the company had betrayed his loyalty. His request was rejected, and Nonaka, after stripping his shirt, locked himself into an office. There, he waited for some other workers and journalists to gather around, and took his life with a kitchen knife (Yamada).

However, most opt for a quick, less dramatic suicide. A typical example is the one of Masayuki Tanaka, a vice-president of a smaller company. Stressed by overwork and responsibilities he was not able to handle, he hanged himself in his family's home. In his last note, he wrote: "I chose this way because I couldn't achieve results, even though I worked until becoming completely exhausted" (Fuyuno 78). His widow, Akiko Tanaka (not her real name), interviewed by the *Far East Economic Review*, said that she was reluctant to even file a compensation claim. At the end of her talk, she sadly confessed: "It's already in the past. I am so sorry for my husband, but I feel neither the government nor society will change, no matter what I do" (80). None of her husband's former bosses ever contacted her to offer their condolences (79).

In Japan mental depression is still regarded as a sign of weakness, and most doctors will not treat mental illness, either because it might hurt the doctor's reputation, or simply because they do not have the necessary skills to treat depressed patients. Today, the government is not planning any special study to try to improve the situation, and it still prohibits the use of antidepressants like Prozac (Wehrfritz). A World Health Organization (WHO) study from the mid 90s threw light on some hard-to-believe realities regarding psychiatry

Polenghi 5

in Japan. Eighty-one percent of the doctors either missed or misjudged mental illness. Even the ones who had been well trained somehow could not assimilate the standard WHO booklet for mental illness. Japanese psychiatry is, sadly, some 20-30 years behind the West (Wehrfritz).

The new countermeasures in place to help Japanese people not to commit suicide are clearly inadequate, and implemented only thanks to private, local and limited groups. One of the companies that has been directly affected by suicides is Japan Rail East, which recorded 212 suicides on its network in 1999. Suicides are labeled as a "Human incident," and cause an hour-long stop for trains, resulting in a loss of money and prestige for the rail company. Japan Rail East, after some studies, introduced some "remedies" to reduce suicides. Human-sized mirrors have been placed at the end of many platforms, since they deprive the victim of the intimacy that many people need to commit suicide. Sensors on platforms activate an alarm when someone gets too close to the tracks, and help the personnel to prevent a certain number of accidents. Maybe the most curious countermeasure is newly bright colored stations and crossings. Happier colors supposedly help potential suicides to cheer up a little, and to give up their intentions, at least for the day (French).

However, the culture of suicide is still strong, and somehow keeps fascinating the Japanese, who do not seem too worried about organizing and working toward real solutions. In Japanese literature, too, suicide is often part of the plot. For instance, the modern best-selling author Banana Yoshimoto features suicidal characters

Polenghi 6

in almost every one of her books. And not only do literary

characters commit suicide, but also some of the most popular

Japanese writers of the 20th century did so, like Yukio Mishima,

Osamu Dazai, Natsume Soseki, and others.

A search for books on suicide on amazon.com will offer

five books on how to prevent suicide. The same exact search

on amazon.co.jp—the Japanese version of the online biggest

bookstore—will open with the best-seller *The Complete Manual of*

Suicide, by Tsurumi Mitsuru. Promoted as "More useful than the

Bible as a written suicide aid," it ranks #354 in the Amazon Japan

chart. Japanese readers describe it as "entertaining, even if you

are not planning to commit suicide." The manual, that since 1993

sold steadily, going through 50 press runs, clearly explains 12 ways

to commit suicide: jumps, rope, gas, water, etc. The author, who

has now reached a certain popularity in Japan, and is often invited

to be on TV talk shows, put it in these words: "If you want to live,

you should live as you please, and if you want to die, you should

die as you please. There is not much more to life than that" (Ueda).

In other words, Japan has really not yet crept out of the primeval

forest of the past, where suicide was often considered an admirable

or unavoidable heroic act.

Polenghi 7

Works Cited

Asahi Shimbunsha. *Japan Almanac 2002*. Tokyo: Asahi, 2001. Print.

Bremner, Bryan. "A Japanese Way of Death." *Business Week Online*
    22 Aug. 2000. Web. 13 July 2001. <http://www.businessweek
    .com/bwdaily/dnflash/aug2000/nf20000822_176.htm>.

French, Howard D. "Japanese Trains Try to Shed a Gruesome
    Appeal." *New York Times* 6 June 2000: A4. Print.

Fuyuno, Ichiko. "A Silent Epidemic." *Far Eastern Economic Review*
    28 Sept. 2000: 78–80. Print.

Hadfield, Peter. "A Fine Place for Farewell. A Tragic Deadly Toll at
    Japan's Suicide Central." *U.S. News & World Report*
    20 Nov. 2000: 71+. Web. Internet Database Proquest Direct.
    <http://www.proquest.com>.

Lamar, Joe. "Suicides in Japan Reach a Record High." *British
    Medical Journal International* 321 (2000): 528. Web. Internet
    Database Proquest Direct. <http://www.proquest.com>.

Lu, Cathy. "It's a Man's Job: Managing Workplace Stress." *CNN.com*.
    11 Jan. 2000. Web. 15 Sept. 2002.

Mehri, Darius. "Death by Overwork: Corporate Pressure on Employees
    Takes a Fatal Toll in Japan." *Multinational Monitor* June
    2000: 26–28. Web. Internet Database Proquest Direct.
    <http://www.proquest.com>.

Nitobe, Inazo. *Bushido, the Soul of Japan*. Tokyo: Tuttle, 1969. Print.

Ueda, Yasuo. "Dealing with Death." *Japan Echo* 22 (1995), Online
    Edition. Web. 10 June 2001.

Wehrfritz, George. "Death by Conformity: Japan's Corporate Warriors

Are Killing Themselves in Record Numbers." *Newsweek*

20 Aug. 2001, Atlantic ed.: 183. Web. Internet Database

Proquest Direct. <http://www.proquest.com>.

Yamada, Atsushi. "Death of a Salaryman." *Japan Quarterly* July–Sep.

1999. Web. Internet Database Proquest Direct. <http://www

.proquest.com>.

Page header

Keeping Up with the Joneses 1

Running head, written in capital letters, not to exceed 40 characters

Running head: KEEPING UP WITH THE JONESES

Keeping Up with the Joneses:

Full Title

Psychological Costs of Material Wealth

By line

Danielle Suarez

Course Title

English 1200

Affiliation

East Carolina University

Keeping Up with the Joneses 2

Abstract

While prosperity and health appear as top goals on most social and political agendas, researchers are beginning to question the importance of money as an ingredient in society's pursuit of happiness. The results of the research have been ironic, especially those based on studies concerning adolescents and young adults. For instance, a national survey of teens showed that 75% of youngsters from families with low incomes felt more emotionally tied to their mothers than did wealthier kids. Moreover, as studies by several noted psychologists indicate, children from high economic strata were more likely to internalize their problems and to suffer from depression and drug use than their poorer counterparts. Pressures to excel is another factor leading to problems of self-esteem among the rich whereas the offspring of economically disadvantaged parents feel less pressure to climb to the top of the success ladder and thus tend to be less tense and anxious. The truth is that happiness and inner satisfaction depend on ingredients money cannot buy, such as friendship, family, respect, a place in the community, and the belief that life has a purpose. Unfortunately, as more psychic energy is invested in material goals, less of it is left to pursue other goals vital to personal happiness.

The abstract is a summary of the paper, including its purpose and thesis and a brief reference to the sources used. Center the word "abstract" on page.

Keeping Up with the Joneses 3

Introduction: Recognizing the limited benefits of affluence

1   As we progress into an increasingly sophisticated and well-informed future, prosperity and health are first on our list of priorities. U.S. citizens strive to lead more and more lavish life styles and to acquire more and more material wealth, believing firmly that superior products and services will lead to personal joy. However, recent studies by well-known psychologists have offered reliable observation and statistical data suggesting that, contrary to popular belief, riches offer a false sense of contentment and have no durable effect on troubled frames of mind. In other words, money does not buy happiness.

2   Buying the newest pair of Prada shoes or embarking on a jaunt to the Cayman Islands may offer temporary satisfaction, but has little to do with long-term confidence based on a sense of self-worth. As a matter of fact, wealthy people often grow anxious or even paranoid because they do not feel understood by their peers; thus they form the false belief that money is the best answer to all life's troubles. An increasing number of therapists have found that the psychological effects on children who grow up in wealthy lifestyles can be extremely negative. For instance, Luthar (2005) discovered through research at Columbia University that upper-class children can manifest elevated disturbance in several areas, such as substance abuse, anxiety, and depression because of excessive pressures to achieve and isolation (literal and emotional) from their parents. Family wealth does not automatically confer either wisdom in parenting or equanimity of spirit.

Center all major headings.

Allusion to reliable major studies as support of thesis.

Thesis is the last sentence in opening paragraph.

Author, followed by year in parentheses

Keeping Up with the Joneses 4

Rich versus poor: Who is happier?

3   In recent years, considerable attention has been paid to the problems of disadvantaged children. In fact, studies examining children from families with low income or from disparaged neighborhoods have multiplied, but "there has been almost no research with those at the other end of the socioeconomic spectrum" (Luthar, 2005). A national survey of teens found that 75 per cent of kids from families with incomes below $15,000 felt more emotionally close to their mothers than did kids from families with high incomes (Munger, 2005). Wealthier kids are more overscheduled than middle-class kids, and they are withdrawn from normal adolescent activities, such as developing friendships and "hanging out" (Munger, 2005).

4   One of the first empirical studies to provide a comparative investigation of low-income, urban high school students and their upper socioeconomic, suburban counterparts was performed by Luthar (2005). The study's central aim was to "explore potential differences in links between adolescents' internalizing problems, such as depression and anxiety, and their behavioral competence, such as peer relationships and academic functioning." Caucasian suburban students from white-collar families scored relatively lower than the predominant minority, inner-city students. Affluent youth reported higher levels of depression and substance abuse, reflecting scores three times higher than those among normative samples (Luthar, 2005). These findings suggest that higher-class students endorse substance abuse among friends to maintain popularity and uphold their high status.

This study is based on literature cited in correct APA form throughout the paper. Here the period is placed after the reference end parenthesis.

Growing up wealthy: The psychological effects on rich children

5   Though often the envy of their poorer friends, wealthy children are more susceptible to depression, anxiety, and substance abuse than are poor children. Achievement pressures and isolation from adults are two major reasons for the behavioral trends. "Children are often pressed to excel at multiple academic and extra-curricular pursuits to maximize their long-term academic prospects. It's a phenomenon that may well engender high stress," explains Luthar (2005). To compound the problem, affluent parents are less likely than most to seek professional help, partly because they want to protect the veneer of perfection they feel compelled to maintain. This false pride may constitute a significant impediment to the child's academic and professional future. With regard to isolation, Luthar (2005) elucidates that children from upper income families are often at home alone for several hours a week. Due to the demands of affluent parents' career obligations and the children's many after-school activities, the emotional level of isolation derives from the erosion of family time together. Separation from parental units also leads to sexual promiscuity, a sense of unimportance, and a failure to develop secure attachments. The impression of these feelings follows children into adulthood, and the cycle continues. Thus, while it is imperative that psychologists continue to address the formidable challenges of the poor, they must correct their long-standing lack of concern with the isolation and emotional disturbances unique to wealth (Luthar & Shawn, 2005).

An ampersand is used to separate two authors in parentheses.

Keeping Up with the Joneses 6

Wealthy adults: The effects of moneyed culture and communities

6   The same processes that affect rich adults will also affect their children through exposure to the same subculture. For example, high productivity, associated with affluence, involves little leisure time, and rich adults become prone to distress. In addition, the pressure to work, in order to acquire and consume, tends to deplete personal energies. After studying the effects of wealth on children, Schor (2005) drew the following conclusion: "The more people strive for extrinsic goals such as money, the more numerous their problems and the less robust their well-being." Other scholars have specifically implicated individuals' lack of intimacy in personal relationships, inferring that people who accumulate high wealth are single-mindedly dedicated to their lifestyle, develop materialistic orientations, and seek solace in material goods rather than in internal, intrinsic riches. "People use possessions to define their place in society. . . . Self-worth is being invested in what one owns" (Collett-Whitek, 2001). A majority of rich people live in acclaimed gated communities, which weaken relationships with neighbors and other supportive relationship networks. Luthar suggests that limited engagement of individuals erodes social capital, as exemplified by diminished attendance at PTA meetings, churches, or community development groups (Luthar, 2005).

Note proper citation for quoted material.

7   Furthermore, according to one researcher (Bishop, 2001), wealthy communities are the basis of friendlessness and isolation. Material wealth reduces the need to depend solely on friendships. "Affluent individuals are amply able to purchase various services such as psychotherapy for depression, medical care for physical

illness, and professional caregivers for children" (Bishop, 2001). Bishop goes on to assert the rich are least likely to experience the security of deep social connectedness that is routinely enjoyed by people in communities where mutual dependence is often unavoidable. Moreover, adults develop a phenomenon to want more, build up a shallow sense of greed, and cultivate deep-seated personal unhappiness.

Proposed solution: A step towards diminishing insatiable consumerism

8   As spelled out by the above statements, money cannot buy happiness because the things that really matter in life are not sold in stores. Writing for *Time* magazine, Easterbrook (2005) recognizes that the essentials of human fulfillment include love, friendship, family, respect, a place in the community, and the deep-rooted belief that life has a purpose. "Everyone needs a certain amount of money," admits Easterbrook, "but chasing money rather than meaning in life is a formula for discontent." Americans need to stop transforming their principal goals toward materialism and the cycle of working and spending. Although it may be difficult to make an immediate and comprehensive change, awareness of the psychological costs of overscheduled lifestyles can be effectively promoted via books, workshops, and community groups. However, the first steps begin in family households.

9   Persistent discipline is vital in order to detract the negative effects a rich lifestyle has on an individual. Parents and applied professionals need to remain vigilant to the mental health vulnerabilities of upper class youth. Bishop (2001) reports that some leading private banks offer "sons and daughters" events to educate rich kids about wealth.

If the author is mentioned in the text, only the year appears in parentheses.

Keeping Up with the Joneses 8

Furthermore, a growing number of family partnerships should be created to allow children to work alongside parents in managing the family fortune. In addition, "establishing independence through work is a critical psychological task" for many children of the wealthy, says psychologist McGough (1987). When wealthy parents fail to teach their children the value of work and money, the results can be tragic. McGough suggests that parents require their children to work and do household chores in order to learn and appreciate the value of earning money. Adults should also be careful not to surround their children with overly expensive things. Stein and Brier (2001) believe that it is important for wealthy parents to teach their children to be generous and share their good fortune with other children who have little or nothing. "Philanthropy is a key factor in teaching children to be responsible managers of their money" (Stein & Brier, 2001). Wealth is not an entitlement, and wealthy parents should discourage their children from believing that they are entitled to being rich (Stein & Brier, 2001).

Conclusion

The poor are often characterized as being dishonest, indolent, promiscuous, uninterested in education, and personally responsible for their plight, but this is a parallel set of adjectives commonly applied to the rich (Luthar, 2005). Material affluence inhibits the formation of supportive networks, attracting the dangers of promiscuity, substance abuse, and depression or anxiety. Two sets of potential causes are pressures to achieve and isolation from parents. Disturbances among affluent children and characteristics of

Two authors used in the text are separated by "and."

Two authors in parentheses are separated by an ampersand.

An important irony is pointed out in this paragraph.

Keeping Up with the Joneses 9

their families and neighborhoods reveal a lack of widespread awareness and a blatant lack of knowledge about this serious problem. As Csikszentmihalyi (1999), a scholar at Claremont University, indicates, eventually a person who only responds to material rewards becomes blind to any other kind of incentive and loses the ability to derive happiness from other sources. As more psychic energy is invested in material goals, less of it is left to pursue other goals that are also necessary for a life graced by happiness.

The final sentence concludes the paper by repeating the thesis.

Keeping Up with the Joneses 10

References

Bishop, M. (2001, July). Survey: The new rich, rich man's burden. Retrieved from Yahoo! News: http://www.anycities.com/materialism.html.

Csikszentmihalyi, M. (1999, October). If we are so rich, why aren't we happy? *American Psychologist.* Retrieved from http://www.anycities.com/materialism.html.

Collett-White, M. (2001, July). Materialism link to depression and anger-study. Retrieved from Reuters News: http://www.anycities.com/materialism.html.

Easterbrook, G. (2005, January 20). The real truth about money. *Time 165*: 3, 32.

Luthar, S. (2005, February). The culture of affluence: Psychological costs of material wealth. *Child Development.* Retrieved from ProQuest, Joyner Library, Greenville, NC: http://www.anycities.com/materialism.html.

Luthar, S. & Latendresse, S. (2005, February 14). Children of the affluent. *Current Directions in Psychological Science, 14*: 49–53. Retrieved from ProQuest, Joyner Library, Greenville, NC: http://www.anycities.com/materialism.html.

McGough, R. (1987, October 26). My son, I brought him up like an immigrant. *Forbes, 140:* 58–61.

Munger, D. (2005, March 9). Are rich kids more troubled than poor kids? *Cognitive Daily.* Retrieved from Yahoo! News: http://www.anycities.com/materialism.html.

Keeping Up with the Joneses 11

Schor, J. (1999, March). The overspent American. Retrieved

    from Yahoo! News: http://www.anycities.com/materialism.html.

Stein, H. W. & Brier, M.C. (2001, May 22). Raising responsible

    children of wealth. *Trusts and Estates*. Retrieved from

    Legacy Services: http://www.anycities.com/materialism.html.

Handbook

Chapter 19

Grammar Fundamentals

The Sentence

A *sentence* is a group of words that expresses a complete thought. *Because I'm happy* and *singing in the rain* do not express complete thoughts and are therefore not sentences. The following express complete thoughts and are therefore classified as sentences:

1. Because I am happy, I like to see other people happy.
2. John is singing in the rain.

The Subject and Predicate

Every sentence is divisible into two parts—a *subject* and a *predicate*. The subject is the word or word group about which something is said; the predicate is the word or word group that asserts something about the subject:

SUBJECT	PREDICATE
The bird	fell out of the sky.
It	angered him deeply.
All the boys	left without saying a word.

The *simple subject* of a sentence is the single word—usually a noun or pronoun—about which the sentence says something:

1. The *beggar* suddenly blinked his eyes.
2. The ugly *frog* turned into a handsome young prince.

The *simple predicate* is the verb or verb phrase that makes a statement about the subject:

1. Fred *decided* to play in the tournament.
2. Before dinner we *had welcomed* all the guests.

The Complete Subject and Predicate

The *complete subject* is the simple subject and all the words associated with it. The *complete predicate* is the simple predicate and all the words associated with it. A vertical line divides the complete subject from the complete predicate in each of these sentences:

1. Diseases of the mind | are often caused by the pressures of city living.
2. The regular bus driver | knows his passengers by name.

Learning to distinguish between the simple subject and the simple predicate and between the complete subject and the complete predicate will help you learn to construct and punctuate sentences.

The Compound Subject and Predicate

A *compound subject* is made up of two or more nouns or pronouns tied together; a *compound predicate* is made up of two or more verbs tied together:

1. *Terror and hate* were in their eyes.   COMPOUND SUBJECT
2. The soldier *stopped and saluted*.   COMPOUND PREDICATE
3. *Ghosts and witches* were the main characters in the story.
   COMPOUND SUBJECT
4. In the recesses of his mind, the villain *remembered and felt guilty*.
   COMPOUND PREDICATE
5. *John and Mary laughed and sang*.   COMPOUND SUBJECT/COMPOUND PREDICATE

■ Exercises

Underline the simple subject once and the simple predicate twice in each of the following sentences. Identify the verb first. To find the subject, ask, Who or what performs the action of the verb?

1. The teacher arrived ten minutes after the class was to begin.
2. Mary believes in the intelligence and honesty of dogs.
3. After seeing the movie twice, Alice was sure she was in love with Brad Pitt.

4. At the end of the first act, the big star made his appearance.

5. People all over the world expect the United States to feed them.

6. Ted was elected to run for vice president.

7. We danced in the hallway, in the cellar, and on the patio.

8. Grace, her voice controlled and her head held high, debated the issues with her rival.

9. My father, a business consultant, is going to New York on Friday.

10. At the end of the examination, Bill breathed a sigh of relief.

In each of the following sentences, draw a vertical line between the complete subject and the complete predicate.

1. Jane arranged her schedule to allow for study.

2. As an usher as well as a waiter, Bruce worked to save $300.

3. Alaska, with all of its natural beauty, appealed to the Smiths.

4. Playing a guitar demands skill and sensitivity.

5. Angry and tired, the dean arrived and was hit with a water balloon.

6. Separate wills are recommended for couples who have been married twice.

7. The top of Mt. Whitney offers a breathtaking view of the Sierras.

8. The undefeatable Johnson was dropped from the squad.

9. Horses, covered with flies, stood scratching their backs on the fence.

10. Honor is more important than love.

■ *Self-Grading Exercise 1*

Underline the simple subject once and the simple predicate twice in each of the following sentences. To find the subject, ask, Who or what performs the action of the verb? After completing the exercise, turn to the appendix for the correct answers.

1. Libraries contain the wisdom of civilization.

2. In the district of Wymar, burglars were ransacking the stores.

3. In Hemingway's novels matadors are highly respected.

4. A clear conscience is the best sleeping pill.

5. The silver gray vest suited his quiet personality.

6. Most middle-class homes in the Southwest are built with air conditioning.

7. The outdoor markets in Europe attract numerous tourists.

8. Noise pollution in towns and cities blots out the sounds and silences of the outdoor world.

9. A cup of good tea or coffee must be brought to me early each morning.

10. I wish to describe two kinds of tours available.

■ *Self-Grading Exercise 2*

In each of the following sentences, draw a vertical line between the complete subject and the complete predicate. After completing the exercise, turn to the appendix for the correct answers.

1. Television has contributed to the decline of reading skills.
2. Incensed by their rudeness, the senator left.
3. Michelangelo's work continues to attract admirers all over the world.
4. Wars go on endlessly.
5. Divorce affects children most of all.
6. Professional tennis has become big business in the United States.
7. Most people insist on paying their bills on time.
8. Within five weeks one hundred AIDS victims had been claimed.
9. Spain is no longer a strong world power.
10. Many areas of Saudi Arabia have experienced droughts.

The Clause and Phrase

The Clause

A *clause* is a group of related words that forms part of a sentence. Every clause has a subject and a predicate. There are two types of clauses: *independent* and *dependent.* An independent clause expresses a complete thought by making a complete statement, asking a question, giving a command, or making an exclamation. An independent clause, therefore, could stand alone as a complete sentence, but it is combined with other independent or dependent clauses to form a full sentence, as in the following examples:

1. John was happy at home, but he left to earn a living.

   INDEPENDENT CLAUSE   INDEPENDENT CLAUSE

2. The children played until their parents arrived.

   INDEPENDENT CLAUSE   DEPENDENT CLAUSE

3. Is the soldier happy because he's going home?

   INDEPENDENT CLAUSE   DEPENDENT CLAUSE

4. He preferred friends who were loyal.

   INDEPENDENT CLAUSE DEPENDENT CLAUSE

5. The accused claimed that she was innocent.

   INDEPENDENT CLAUSE   DEPENDENT CLAUSE

There is a crucial difference between an independent and a dependent clause: Standing alone, an independent clause makes sense, but a dependent clause does not. A dependent clause depends for its meaning on an independent clause that either precedes or follows it. Dependent clauses are therefore said to be *subordinate* to independent clauses.

The Phrase

A *phrase* is a group of two or more associated words having neither subject nor predicate. A phrase does not make a complete statement, is never a clause, and is certainly not a sentence. A phrase is only part of a clause or a sentence. The following groups of words are phrases:

1. for his fiftieth birthday
2. practicing the flute
3. under the table
4. after a long time

■ Exercises

Label each of the following passages as *I* (independent clause), *D* (dependent clause), or *P* (phrase).

1. Spring has begun   _____
2. Since their parents died   _____
3. Although Sam is an atheist   _____
4. Follow the main road for a mile   _____
5. Between the two houses   _____
6. Everyone told him to stay home   _____
7. For your country   _____
8. If Mary enrolled in the class   _____
9. You may wish to return the picture today   _____
10. People who attend religious services   _____
11. Begging her to love him   _____

12. Flowers blossom   _____

13. Have you seen the five napkins   _____

14. He seldom speaks his mind   _____

15. Because she grew up in Poland   _____

■ *Self-Grading Exercise 3*

Label each of the following passages as *I* (independent clause), *D* (dependent clause), or *P* (phrase). After completing the exercise, turn to the appendix for the correct answers.

1. Such is my ideal   _____

2. The return from the walk should coincide with the serving of tea   _____

3. Not all books being suitable for mealtime reading   _____

4. What one does not want is a gossipy, superficial book   _____

5. Because self-concern and self-pity filled all their thoughts   _____

6. The letters from his brother, now longer, arrived daily   _____

7. One of the happiest men and most pleasing companions   _____

8. Either condition will destroy the psyche in the end   _____

9. Whenever they have set about correcting the error   _____

10. As if in all ages they had been surrounded by barbarism   _____

11. He has little doubt that they should have succeeded equally well   _____

12. The country was given absolute freedom   _____

13. Plunged into an inferno of torturous extremes   _____

14. Here their methods were the same   _____

15. When I called Cleopatra a "Circe" and her love affairs
    "business deals"   _____

16. But Homer came first   _____

17. Who romanticize the worst poverty   _____

18. My deep appreciation for my parents   _____

19. Some discotheques don't allow clients older than twenty   _____

20. With the lining of her full-length fox coat   _____

Sentence Types

A sentence is punctuated according to its function and form. The examples in this section will assist you in recognizing the function a sentence serves and the forms it can take.

Classification According to Function

A *declarative sentence* states a fact or a possibility and ends with a period:

1. The pilot died in the crash.   FACT
2. The stock market may go up tomorrow.   POSSIBILITY

An *interrogative sentence* asks a question and ends with a question mark:

1. Is it true what they say about Dixie?
2. Have you decided which courses you will take?

An *imperative sentence* makes a request or gives an order:

1. Don't park your car here.
2. Turn over the cash to the cashier.

An imperative sentence ends with a period unless the command is filled with strong emotion, in which case it ends with an exclamation mark:

1. Shut your mouth, you fool!
2. It's an earthquake! Fall to the floor!

An *exclamatory sentence* expresses strong or sudden feeling and ends with an exclamation mark:

1. Oh, the pain is terrible!
2. How cruel you are!

Classification According to Form

A *simple sentence* consists of one independent clause that contains one subject and one predicate and expresses one complete thought:

1. The tree fell.
2. The heavens declare the glory of God.
3. There is no peace in being greedy.

Although a simple sentence has only one subject and one predicate, the subject or the predicate or both may be compound. Not all simple sentences are short, for both the subject and the predicate may have many modifying words:

> Staggering from his wound, inflicted during the heat of battle, and exhausted from the endless trudging through jungles, the young marine found a place near a brook shaded by trees and sat down to rest.

A *compound sentence* consists of two or more independent clauses connected by one of the following coordinating conjunctions: *and, or, nor, but, yet, for, so*. For example:

1. The flowers were blossoming, but patches of snow still covered the earth.
2. He studied hard for the examination, yet he failed.
3. Jim smiled and Fred frowned.

Occasionally, a semicolon separates the independent clauses:

He's superstitious; he never opens an umbrella inside the house.

A *complex sentence* consists of one independent clause to which one or more dependent clauses have been connected:

1. The supervisor ordered the factory employees to work because five days had elapsed.   ONE DEPENDENT CLAUSE
2. Because life is not perfect, we must expect to find that difficulties will confront us as we attempt to achieve our goals.   THREE DEPENDENT CLAUSES

A *compound-complex sentence* consists of two or more independent clauses and at least one dependent clause.

1. The company figured the values of all the pieces of property that lay within the city limits, and the manager then wrote each property owner a letter that explained the cost of curbing.
2. The world's petroleum supply is expected to last about 30 years; although some countries are exploring alternate energy sources, others are not.

■ Exercises

Place the appropriate punctuation mark at the end of each of the following sentences.

1. Oh, crime and violence, how long will you continue to rob us of peace
2. This is the time for all good men to come to the aid of their country
3. Come here this minute
4. Have you, by chance, already met this gentleman
5. Help I am caught in a mousetrap
6. Go to the store and buy me a quart of milk

7. If I need you, will you be available

8. What an exciting evening

9. Should we never meet again, I wish you the best of luck

10. I asked him if he had been paid for his time

Classify each of the following sentences as (A) simple, (B) compound, (C) complex, or (D) compound-complex.

1. At the end of the day, Alice made an appearance;
   however, she did not smile once.   _____

2. Because the winter was nearly over, Maxine arranged to
   be home with her mother, her grandmother,
   and her sisters.   _____

3. After he had reached the end of the road, Mr. Leffingwell
   began to cross the bridge.   _____

4. Big Tom was dropped from the club after one month
   of membership; he now is trying out for the
   swimming team.   _____

5. At the end of the race, Jane let out a yell, for she had
   finished in third place.   _____

6. Maybelle operated an elevator for three years to save
   enough money to go to night school, to buy a new car,
   and to pay her mother's doctor bills.   _____

7. In the top drawer you will find two pairs of old gloves,
   three torn sweaters, and a yellowed picture album.   _____

8. We all believe that the U.S. Constitution must be
   preserved, because our liberties, which our ancestors
   paid for with their lives, must be nurtured with care.   _____

9. After freezing all night, Nancy decided she should have
   worn a sweater.   _____

10. When my family left for New Orleans, I thought
    they would return within two weeks; instead, they
    stayed there a full year.   _____

11. My uncle, a famous poet, gave me a handwritten
    manuscript and asked me to take care of it for him.   _____

12. Your letter was delightful; I am sure that it offended
    no one.   _____

13. Because Tom gave the most forceful pep talk, he was
    asked to represent the senior class at the fine arts festival.   _____

14. The mayor, her voice trembling with rage, denounced
    her opponent, Jack Wilson.   _____

15. He flew to New York, and she drove to Chicago
    because she was afraid to fly with him.   _____

▪ *Self-Grading Exercise 4*

Place the appropriate punctuation mark at the end of each of the following sentences. After completing the exercise, turn to the appendix for the correct answers.

1. We asked him if he would be willing to do it alone
2. Are you usually aware of the problems of older people
3. Sound the alarm Then run for your life
4. I am as angry as a cornered cat
5. Do you mean to tell me that all of the money simply disappeared
6. They inquired as to whether or not we would accompany the performers
7. Heavens What a way to get attention
8. Go straight down the aisle and interrupt his conversation
9. Would you be so kind as to direct me to the British Museum
10. Whew What a terrible odor

▪ *Self-Grading Exercise 5*

Classify each of the following sentences as (A) simple, (B) compound, (C) complex, or (D) compound-complex. After completing the exercise, turn to the appendix for the correct answers.

1. In Paris we lived near the Louvre.   _____

2. The whole school was a great temple for the worship of
   these mortal gods, and no boy ever went there unprepared
   to worship.   _____

3. If you have not visited a German *Gymnasium* (high school),
   you may be confused about the German school system.   _____

4. Their position was emphasized by special rituals;
   nevertheless, we refused to remain in their mansion because
   the atmosphere was stern and depressing.   _____

5. Strength and popularity were not enough to keep them in the
   club if they were not recommended by at least two members.   _____

6. It is vital that they attempt a revolution when the time is ripe.   _____

7. They tried to speed up their social progress by flattering the existing leaders. _____

8. The doors opened into the study, but no one passed through them because the room was too dark to be used. _____

9. As we sat around our table, we felt the silence; however, no one ever spoke up because silence was an absolute rule. _____

10. Each study imitated the cluttered appearance of an Edwardian drawing room. _____

11. They were not like slaves, for their favors were nearly always solicited rather than compelled. _____

12. After games, gallantry was the principal topic of polite conversation. _____

13. I thought about it then, and I am still thinking about it. _____

14. He really insists that the candidate insulted him, yet he remained seated on the podium as if he had received a compliment. _____

15. Dean Metzger has three lovely daughters, a beautiful home, and an airline pass to travel all over the world. _____

16. I became a marked man, but that never stopped me from speaking my mind. _____

17. What takes so much time is waiting in line for the tickets or lining up to get in. _____

18. One must not conclude that the housekeeper's signature was forged, even though two experts testified against her. _____

19. There are two reasons for such an unusual conclusion. _____

20. The modern world is the child of doubt and inquiry, just as the ancient world was the child of fear and faith. _____

Parts of Speech

The Verb

A *verb* is a word that suggests an *action*, a *state of being*, or a *condition:*

1. The cat *leaped* off the roof. ACTION

2. The antique cup *sat* on the lace cloth. STATE OF BEING

3. Her eyes *were* big and luminous. CONDITION

A verb functions as the predicate or as part of the predicate in a sentence:

1. The blind man *hears.*
2. The blind man *has heard.*
3. The blind man *is* still *hearing.*

Note that *verbals* (participles, gerunds, or infinitives) cannot function as the predicates of sentences:

1. Participle: *Heard* melodies are sweet . . .   HEARD FUNCTIONS AS AN ADJECTIVE.
2. Gerund: His *hearing* is bad.   HEARING FUNCTIONS AS A NOUN.
3. Infinitive: *To hear* is important.   TO HEAR FUNCTIONS AS A NOUN.

The Noun

Nouns are *names* of persons, animals, things, places, characteristics, and ideas. The following are nouns:

engineer	Westwood Village
dog	jealousy
box	communism

You should know the following terms that describe nouns:

1. *Concrete nouns:* tangible things, such as *men, cat, towns, teachers, coat*
2. *Abstract nouns:* qualities or concepts, such as *love, justice, hate, credibility, intimacy*
3. *Proper nouns:* specific persons, places, things, organizations, and events, which are capitalized, such as *Mt. Everest, Mary, French, Mr. Jones, the Eiffel Tower*
4. *Common nouns:* general nouns that are not capitalized, such as *chair, kite, happiness, team*
5. *Collective nouns:* words that are singular, but involve a group or imply a plural meaning, such as *jury, group, family, council, committee*

Understanding these terms will help you to avoid common errors in capitalization, agreement of subject and predicate, and agreement of pronouns with their *antecedents*—the words the pronouns stand for.

The Pronoun

Pronouns are words used *in place of nouns.* For example, you may use the pronoun *she* instead of the noun *mother.* You may speak of *the children's toys* or *those* or *theirs*. There are nine kinds of pronouns, listed here. Although it is not important that you be able to name each kind, you should be able to recognize each as a pronoun:

1. Personal   *You* and *they* will help *us*.
2. Interrogative   *Who* is it? *What* do you want? *Which* is best?
3. Relative   The man *who* killed her is the one *that* I saw.
4. Demonstrative   *This* is older than *that*.
5. Indefinite   *Each* of us must accomplish *something*.
6. Reciprocal   Let us help *each other* and trust *one another*.
7. Reflexive   John did it *himself*. I blame *myself*.
8. Intensive   I *myself* heard him. We need money *ourselves*.
9. Possessive   Is that book *yours* or *mine*?

The Adjective

Adjectives are words that *modify* (describe or qualify) nouns and pronouns:

1. The *shiny, black* cat   THE NOUN *CAT* IS MODIFIED.
2. *Morose* and *depressed*, he sat in the corner.   THE PRONOUN *HE* IS MODIFIED.
3. The parking meter took *five* nickels.   THE WORD *NICKELS* IS MODIFIED.

Adjectives usually precede, but sometimes follow, the nouns they modify (*a **tall, handsome** man*). *Appositive adjectives* immediately follow nouns and are set off by commas:

1. The attorney, *pale* with anger, jumped forward.
2. The little boy, *dusty* and *tired*, fell asleep.

Sometimes, the adjective follows the predicate, in which case it is called a *predicate adjective:*

1. The sunset looks *splendid*.
2. The newlyweds seem *happy*.
3. Women are *strong*.

Occasionally, the adjective modifies the object of the sentence, in which case it is called an *objective complement:*

1. The cream sauce made her *sick*.
2. The sun turned him *crimson red*.

Possessive and *demonstrative adjectives* precede the nouns they point out or specify:

1. We visited *their* mansion.
2. She bought *that* coat.

The Article

An *article* is a kind of adjective that *limits* a noun; *the* is a definite article, and *a* and *an* are indefinite articles.

1. *the* people
2. *a* balloon, *an* orange

The Adverb

Adverbs modify verbs, adjectives, and other adverbs. They are next to verbs and nouns in importance. Effective writers tend to use more adverbs than adjectives. Note the use of adverbs in the following sentences:

1. Cecil will work *slowly* and *deliberately.*   ADVERB MODIFYING A VERB
2. My mother inherited a *surprisingly* old clock.   ADVERB MODIFYING AN ADJECTIVE
3. She succeeded *quite* well.   ADVERB MODIFYING AN ADVERB

Most adverbs indicate time (*we must leave **now***), place (*they stayed **over there***), manner (*she walks **awkwardly***), or degree (*all the relatives were **extraordinarily** kind*). Some nouns function as adverbs and are called *adverbial nouns* (*he left home **Monday***).

A special group of adverbs are the *conjunctive adverbs*. The primary conjunctive adverbs are the following:

accordingly	furthermore	instead	still
also	hence	likewise	then
anyhow	henceforth	meanwhile	therefore
besides	however	nevertheless	thus
consequently	indeed	otherwise	

When used to connect independent clauses, the conjunctive adverb is preceded by a semicolon:

1. We doubted their word; *nevertheless,* we went along with the plan.
2. Something about the garden pleased us; *however,* we did not wish to purchase the house.
3. The manager was harsh; *moreover,* he owed us our salaries.

When a conjunctive adverb is used parenthetically, it is set off by commas:

1. You can see, *moreover,* why this is important.
2. She, *however,* denied the truth.
3. This time, *furthermore,* he was forbidden to speak.

When the adverb *there* is used to introduce a sentence, it is called an *expletive:*
There *is a city in Algeria where bazaars appear everywhere.*
   Most adverbs end in *-ly.* The few that do not are called *flat* adverbs:

1. He walked *far.*
2. He walks too *fast.*
3. They work *hard.*

The Preposition

A *preposition* is used to show the relationship of a noun or pronoun to some other word in the sentence. For example, in *The airplane flew **above** the clouds,* the preposition *above* shows the relationship between the clouds and the airplane. Stating anything else that an airplane can do when approaching clouds is likely to involve a preposition:

1. The airplane flew *into* the clouds.
2. The airplane flew *through* the clouds.
3. The airplane flew *across* the clouds.
4. The airplane flew *behind* the clouds.
5. The airplane flew *between* the clouds.
6. The airplane flew *after* the clouds.
7. The airplane flew *by* the clouds.
8. The airplane flew *over/under* the clouds.
9. The airplane flew *with* the clouds.
10. The airplane flew *out* of the clouds.
11. The airplane flew *near* the clouds.

Some prepositions—such as *for, at,* and *of*—will not work in this example.
   Some words—such as *off, on, out, in, over,* and *up*—may be used as prepositions, adverbs, or parts of verbs:

1. He climbed *up* the ladder.   PREPOSITION
2. All of us looked *up.*   ADVERB

3. When I arrived in New York, I *looked* him *up*.   VERB

4. He ran *out* the door.   PREPOSITION

5. Reach *out* with your hand.   ADVERB

6. We must *watch out* for fires.   VERB

The preposition and its object form a *prepositional phrase:*

1. The dog remained *inside his kennel.*

2. Every morning he looked *underneath the table.*

3. The thief lurked *near the car.*

The Conjunction

Conjunctions are connectors and can be classified into two types: *coordinating* conjunctions and *subordinating* conjunctions. Coordinating conjunctions (*and, or, nor, but, yet, for, so*) are used to connect words, phrases, and clauses that are of equal importance:

1. apples *and* oranges   WORDS

2. with them, *but* not with us   PHRASES

3. I love my son, *yet* he must obey me.   CLAUSES

Subordinating conjunctions (*after, although, as, because, before, if, since, until, when, while, than*) are used to connect main clauses with subordinate clauses:

1. That man never looked us straight in the eye *when* he talked with us.

2. *If* you don't believe him, tell him so.

3. The bridge collapsed *because* it was so old.

4. She is stronger *than* any of the men are.

Relative pronouns can function as subordinators:

1. I firmly believe *that* you are wrong.

2. John returned the gift to the person *who* had given it to him.

3. He demands to know *whose* door is squeaking.

Often, subordinating conjunctions consist of more than one word:

1. The sky was pitch black *even though* it was noon.

2. The doctor came *as soon as* he was called.

3. Nothing works out, *no matter* how hard I try.

A special kind of conjunction is the *correlative* conjunction, which is used in pairs:

1. They were *not only* kind *but also* generous.
2. They *neither* complained *nor* cared.

The Interjection

Interjections are words or phrases used to express strong or sudden feelings that attract attention:

1. *Hurray!* They've won.
2. *Ouch!* The horse stepped on my foot.
3. *Whew!* That's hard work.

Context and Parts of Speech

The role of a word in a sentence always determines what part of speech it is. The *context* may change the role of a word:

1. He must *round* the corner at top speed.   VERB
2. The audience gave the orchestra a *round* of applause.   NOUN
3. The baby had a perfectly *round* face.   ADJECTIVE
4. Her fiance lives *round* the corner.   PREPOSITION

■ *Exercises*

Identify the part of speech of each italicized word in each of the following paragraphs.

I[1] went back to the *Devon School*[2] not long ago *and*[3] *found*[4] it looking *oddly*[5] newer than *when*[6] I was a student *there*[7] fifteen years before. It seemed *more*[8] sedate *than*[9] I remembered it, more *perpendicular*[10] and straitlaced, *with*[11] *narrower*[12] windows and shinier woodwork, *as though*[13] a coat *of*[14] varnish *had been put*[15] *over*[16] everything for better preservation. *But,*[17] of course, fifteen years *before*[18] there had been a war going on. Perhaps the school wasn't as *well*[19] kept up in those days; *perhaps*[20] varnish, *along with*[21] *everything*[22] else, had gone to war.

I didn't *entirely*[23] like this glossy new *surface,*[24] *because*[25] it made the school look *like*[26] a museum, and that's exactly *what*[27] it was to me and what I did not want it to be. In the deep, tacit way in which *feeling*[28] becomes stronger than thought, I had always *felt*[29]*that*[30] the Devon School came *into*[31] existence the *day*[32] I entered it, was vibrantly *real*[33] *while*[34] I was a student there, and then blinked out like a candle *the*[35] day I left.

—John Knowles, *A Separate Peace*

1. _____		19. _____
2. _____		20. _____
3. _____		21. _____
4. _____		22. _____
5. _____		23. _____
6. _____		24. _____
7. _____		25. _____
8. _____		26. _____
9. _____		27. _____
10. _____		28. _____
11. _____		29. _____
12. _____		30. _____
13. _____		31. _____
14. _____		32. _____
15. _____		33. _____
16. _____		34. _____
17. _____		35. _____
18. _____		

■ *Self-Grading Exercise 6*

Identify the part of speech of each italicized word in each of the following paragraphs. After completing the exercise, turn to the appendix for the correct answers.

A few years ago, an *Englishman*[1] named John David Potter *was rushed*[2] to the Newcastle General Hospital after suffering *extensive*[3] brain damage *in*[4] a brawl. Fourteen hours *later,*[5] he stopped breathing. Ordinarily, the man *would have been declared*[6] dead, *but*[7] at that moment a kidney was needed *for*[8] transplant, and Potter was an *obvious*[9] donor.

A respirator *was applied,*[10] and *it*[11] *artificially*[12] revived Potter's *breathing.*[13] *This*[14] in turn restored his failing *heartbeat*[15] *and*[16] circulation, *thus*[17] preserving *the*[18] kidneys. These vital organs, *now*[19] strictly *dependent*[20] *upon*[21] the respirator, *were kept*[22] going 24 hours, *even though*[23] the doctors *knew*[24] *that*[25] Potter *had*[26] no chance *of*[27] *recovery.*[28] *Meanwhile,*[29] Mrs. Potter *had granted*[30] permission to remove *a*[31] kidney *for*[32] *transplant.*[33] *When*[34] *this*[35] *was done,*[36] the attending *physician*[37] ordered the respirator *turned*[38] off. For the second time, Potter *ceased*[39] breathing, and his heart stopped *forever.*[40]

—Leonard A. Stevens, "When Is Death?" *Reader's Digest,*
May 1969

1. _____
2. _____
3. _____
4. _____
5. _____
6. _____
7. _____
8. _____
9. _____
10. _____
11. _____
12. _____
13. _____
14. _____
15. _____
16. _____
17. _____
18. _____
19. _____
20. _____

21. _____
22. _____
23. _____
24. _____
25. _____
26. _____
27. _____
28. _____
29. _____
30. _____
31. _____
32. _____
33. _____
34. _____
35. _____
36. _____
37. _____
38. _____
39. _____
40. _____

Chapter 20

Correcting Common Errors

This unit presents the most common errors found in student essays. Most teachers use handwritten symbols to indicate student errors. For an explanation of your own errors and how to correct them, match the symbols in the margin of your paper with those provided in this unit.

Errors with Sentences

<table>
<tr><td>

frag

</td><td>

A sentence *fragment* results when a phrase or a dependent clause is treated as if it were a complete sentence. Correct a fragment either by attaching it to the previous sentence or by adding words to the fragment that will make it a complete sentence:

</td></tr>
</table>

Error	We thought about the weather. Decided to cancel the picnic.
Correction	We thought about the weather and decided to cancel the picnic.
Error	Lonely house on the block.
Correction	There was a lonely house on the block.
Error	A man doesn't call a wall warped. Unless he knows what a straight wall is.
Correction	A man doesn't call a wall warped unless he knows what a straight wall is.
Error	Birds chirping, bees buzzing, the smell of honey in the air. I knew that spring was here.
Correction	Birds were chirping, bees were buzzing, and the smell of honey hung in the air. I knew that spring was here.

<table>
<tr><td>

cs

</td><td>

A *comma splice* occurs when two independent clauses are separated by a comma instead of a period or a semicolon. There are four ways of correcting a comma splice:

</td></tr>
</table>

1. Separate the independent clauses with a period.

Error	I was deeply shaken, my favorite cousin lay ill with cancer.
Correction	I was deeply shaken. My favorite cousin lay ill with cancer.

2. Separate the independent clauses with a semicolon.

  Error   The backyard was full of plums, our family ate them all.

  Correction   The backyard was full of plums; our family ate them all.

3. Join the independent clauses with a comma and a coordinating conjunction.

  Error   Anyone can stick flowers in a vase, few can achieve an artistic arrangement.

  Correction   Anyone can stick flowers in a vase, but few can achieve an artistic arrangement.

4. Subordinate one independent clause to the other.

  Error   You failed to come to dinner, I ate alone.

  Correction   Because you failed to come to dinner, I ate alone.

Don't let a conjunctive adverb trick you into making a comma splice:

  Error   I hate cold weather, however, the Rocky Mountains are good for my asthma.

  Correction   I hate cold weather; however, the Rocky Mountains are good for my asthma.

A *run-together sentence* occurs when one sentence is piled on another without any kind of punctuation, often resulting in an incoherent passage. Correct a run-together sentence by placing a period or a conjunction between the two sentences.

rt

  Error   This map also predicts California's future the San Andreas fault, which underlies Los Angeles, is heading out to sea.

  Correction   This map also predicts California's future. The San Andreas fault, which underlies Los Angeles, is heading out to sea.

  Error   I like her attitude she is a solid person.

  Correction   I like her attitude. She is a solid person.

  Error   The first year of marriage is never easy I made it harder than need be.

  Correction   The first year of marriage is never easy, but I made it harder than need be.

■ Exercises

In each blank at the right, enter *C* if the sentence is correct, *Frag* if it is a fragment, *CS* if it is a comma splice, or *RT* if it is a run-together sentence. Correct any sentence that is incorrect.

1. People must eat.   _____

2. The countless women who need jobs.   _____

3. Chicago being a city riddled with crime.   _____

4. The rivers overflowed their banks the trees were
   swept away.   _____

5. Houses were destroyed, and homes were burned.   _____

6. Pet lovers in our country as well as abroad.   _____

7. In particular the mayor, who had supported a transit
   system when he spoke to the legislature.   _____

8. Irresistible also were the lovely orchards surrounding
   the swimming pool.   _____

9. However, some crowds were vengeful.   _____

10. "I cannot marry you," said the princess, "I am too poor."   _____

11. Every one of us felt the loss.   _____

12. The Vietnam War was senseless it gained us nothing.   _____

13. Run as fast as you can you need the practice.   _____

14. Recalling his visit to Paris, my uncle smiled.   _____

15. All of us visited the statue, few of us admired it.   _____

16. Originally made in Taiwan but then transported to
    the United States.   _____

17. Soon giving up trying.   _____

18. She was as delicate as a butterfly.   _____

19. I want to excel not only as a musician,
    but also as a human being.   _____

20. The car weighed a ton; they could not lift it.   _____

■ *Self-Grading Exercise 7*

In each blank at the right, enter *C* if the sentence is correct, *Frag* if it is a frag-ment, *CS* if it is a comma splice, or *RT* if it is a run-together sentence. After complet-ing the exercise, turn to the appendix for the correct answers.

1. Hardly as big as a powderpuff and no bigger.   _____

2. Quietly this cat dozes by the fire or on her lap.   _____

3. He will not sell himself for any amount of money,
   he will not enter into a contract.   _____

4. Because psychologists have learned a great deal about
   abnormal human behavior.   _____

5. There is nothing difficult here if you found this article
   in a children's book, you would not be surprised.   _____

6. Nevertheless, the writer has prepared you for a
   number of questions.   _____

7. Although necessity is the mother of invention.   _____

8. We believe.   _____

9. Once you have noted the topic sentence,
   the paragraph is easy to follow.   _____

10. Putting your own ideas into words.

11. All creatures living in the wild are subject to attack
    by predators, their survival depends on their ability
    to fend off such attacks.   _____

12. "I'm telling you one last time," said the policeman,
    "Show me your driver's license."   _____

13. The battle lines are firmly drawn between the
    chiropractors and their foes; accordingly, the public
    must decide on which side to be.   _____

14. Everybody knows about Chicago, the "windy city."   _____

15. Consciously ignoring the poor, alienating the old, and
    forgetting the handicapped.   _____

16. Express your thesis concisely, however, do not leave
    out any key words.   _____

17. Of course, there is much more to reading any piece of
    prose, even a popular magazine article, than understanding
    the opening paragraph.   _____

18. The manager taught them time-saving techniques
    and helped them improve their skills.   _____

19. The winter has arrived you should get out
    your snow boots.   _____

20. Many tourists stand admiringly in front of the *Mona
    Lisa,* few leave quickly.   _____

Errors in Agreement

An error in agreement occurs when the subject does not agree with the verb or
when a pronoun does not agree with its antecedent. Agreement means that a subject and verb must both be either singular or plural, as must a pronoun and its antecedent. Avoid errors in subject-verb agreement by learning to recognize the subject
of a sentence. To avoid errors in pronoun agreement, learn which pronouns are
plural and which are singular.

agr

Errors with Verbs

Error	My family, together with numerous other families, were checked for excess baggage.
Correction	My family, together with numerous other families, *was* checked for excess baggage. THE SUBJECT IS *FAMILY*.
Error	The main issue are high taxes.
Correction	The main issue *is* high taxes. THE SUBJECT IS *ISSUE*.
Error	My list of errors were so long that the teacher shook her head in despair.
Correction	My list of errors *was* so long that the teacher shook her head in despair. THE SUBJECT IS *LIST*.
Error	Either John alone or all of the boys together has to show up at the entrance.
Correction	Either John alone or all of the boys together *have* to show up at the entrance. THE SUBJECT IS ALL. WHEN TWO SUBJECTS, ONE SINGULAR AND ONE PLURAL, ARE CONNECTED BY *OR, NOR,* OR *EITHER,* THE VERB MUST AGREE WITH THE NEARER SUBJECT.
Error	Mary is among the girls who has collected funds to build a memorial hall.
Correction	Mary is among the girls who *have* collected funds to build a memorial hall. *WHO,* SUBJECT OF THE DEPENDENT CLAUSE, REFERS TO GIRLS, NOT *MARY*.
Error	Unemployment as well as inflation affect the voters.
Correction	Unemployment as well as inflation *affects* the voters. THE ADDITION OF EXPRESSIONS SUCH AS *TOGETHER WITH, ALONG WITH, AS WELL AS, INCLUDING,* AND *LIKE* DOES NOT ALTER THE NUMBER OF THE SUBJECT.
Error	A pair of scissors and some thread is standard equipment for tailors.
Correction	A pair of scissors and some thread *are* standard equipment for tailors. SUBJECTS JOINED BY *AND* REQUIRE A PLURAL VERB. EXCEPTIONS ARE COMPOUND SUBJECTS REFERRING TO A SINGLE PERSON: "MY LOVER AND BEST FRIEND *HAS* LEFT ME." *LOVER* AND *FRIEND* ARE THE SAME PERSON.

■ Exercises

In each of the following sentences, change the verb that does not agree with its subject. Write the correct form in the blank, or if the sentence is correct, write *C*.

1. Neither storms nor illness delay our newspapers.   _____
2. His five children and their education was his main worry.   _____
3. There's much to be said for simplicity.   _____

4. The importance of words are being stressed in
   all newspapers.   _____

5. My chief concern this summer are my expenses.   _____

6. Taste in books differs from student to student.   _____

7. *The Three Stooges* are a wonderful movie.   _____

8. Mathematics is one of my worst subjects.   _____

9. Either you or I am mistaken.   _____

10. My brothers as well as my sister is coming to visit me.   _____

■ *Self-Grading Exercise 8*

   In each of the following sentences, change the verb that does not agree with
its subject. Write the correct form in the blank, or if the sentence is correct, write *C*.
After completing the exercise, turn to the appendix for the correct answers.

1. Just one error in those endless columns of figures
   make the project unacceptable.   _____

2. These kinds of books is pleasant to read.   _____

3. Everything in this nation, world, and universe
   have a reason for existence.   _____

4. Neither the winner nor the loser was injured.   _____

5. The rate of inflation, along with the scarcity of oil,
   cause people to go into debt.   _____

6. Not only they but also I am unhappy.   _____

7. Either they or he are to drive.   _____

8. There is several active ingredients in the mixture.   _____

9. All three of the courses Mike is taking requires a final
   essay examination.   _____

10. Make sure that either your sister or your brothers go.   _____

11. What is her arguments supposed to prove?   _____

12. The diseases we are investigating cause severe anxiety.   _____

13. Does a man and a woman have to agree?   _____

14. The committee has submitted a fine report.   _____

15. Physics are so difficult when one uses obscure
    problem-solving methods.   _____

16. The main problem are all of the prostitutes in town.   _____

17. No matter how dreadful the weather, a cluster of
    onlookers watch the surfers.   _____

18. The tragedy—and main argument—of the novel is that
    love can fail miserably.   _____

19. There on the park bench sits Fritz and Jane.   _____

20. Surprisingly enough, law, not medicine or architecture,
    appeal to Jim.   _____

Errors with Pronouns

Each of the following pronouns, when used as a subject, always requires a singular
verb: *each, either, neither, another, anyone, anybody, anything, someone, somebody,
something, one, everyone, everybody, everything, nobody, nothing.*

Error	Each of the prizes were spectacular.
Correction	Each of the prizes *was* spectacular. Don't let prepositional phrases trick you into an agreement error. In this case, *each* is the subject.
Error	Behind all the managers stand their president.
Correction	Behind all the managers *stands* their president.
Error	Everyone in that room care sincerely.
Correction	Everyone in that room *cares* sincerely.
Error	Neither of the twins plan to go to private school.
Correction	Neither of the twins *plans* to go to private school.

A pronoun must agree in number with its antecedent:

Error	Everyone who accepted the money knew that they would have to return it.
Correction	Everyone who accepted the money knew that *he or she* would have to return it.
Error	Anyone who visits the principal will find that they are welcome.
Correction	Anyone who visits the principal will find that *he or she* is welcome.
Error	Every woman who wrote demanding a ticket knew that they would get one.
Correction	Every woman who wrote demanding a ticket knew that *she* would get one.

The rule that regards such indefinite pronouns as *everyone, someone, somebody,*
and *everybody* as singular and therefore replaceable by *he* has been challenged by
feminist writers and linguists, who contend that gender-neutral pronouns such as
they and *their* are far better replacements. Feminists argue that while the sentence
Anyone who visits the principal will find that he is welcome may be traditionally correct, it is also sexually biased against the possibility of the *anyone* being a woman.
Many writers are sympathetic to the feminist argument, which carries considerable
logic, and formal usage of *they* and *their* as substitutes for *everyone, someone, somebody, everybody* is becoming increasingly popular. Another acceptable style is to
use *he or she,* as is done in this book.

Collective nouns are replaced by singular pronouns if they denote single units, but by plural pronouns if they denote members of the group acting separately and individually.

> The jury rendered *its* verdict.   ACTING AS A SINGLE UNIT
>
> The jury could not reach an agreement; *they* argued all day.   ACTING INDIVIDUALLY
>
> The whole family gave *its* view.   ACTING AS A SINGLE UNIT
>
> The family have gone *their* separate ways.   ACTING INDIVIDUALLY

Case errors most commonly occur when a writer fails to distinguish between the subjective and objective cases. The subject is always a noun or pronoun that the predicate says something about. The subject answers Who? or What? about the predicate. The object, on the other hand, receives the action of the verb and is not the same as the subject. Study the following diagrams:

case

SUBJECT	VERB	OBJECT
The patient	watches	the sunset.

The patient initiates the action of the verb *watched,* whereas the sunset being watched receives it. Two further examples will reinforce the difference between subject and object:

SUBJECT	VERB	OBJECT
My brother	hit	the dog.
Americans	love	their country.

Problems in case arise when nouns are replaced by pronouns of the wrong case. The following list shows the subjective case of pronouns on the left and the objective case on the right:

SUBJECTIVE	OBJECTIVE
I	me
you	you
he, she, it	him, her, it
we	us
they	them
who, whoever	whom, whomever

Look at these sentences:

1. John bit the dog.
2. The dog bit John.

In each, a pronoun substituted for *John* must reflect in its case whether John is the subject or object of the verb *bit*—whether he initiates the action or receives it:

1. He bit the dog.
2. The dog bit him.

The subjective pronoun *he* is used in place of *John* when *John* functions in the sentence as a subject. The objective pronoun *him* is used in place of *John* when *John* functions in the sentence as an object.

Error	The coach called he and I.
Correction	The coach called *him* and *me*. HIM AND ME ARE OBJECTS BECAUSE THEY TAKE THE ACTION FROM THE VERB *CALLED*.
Error	Ellen and me decided to wear platform heels.
Correction	Ellen and I decided to wear platform heels. *ELLEN AND I* IS A COMPOUND SUBJECT.

Prepositions always require the objective case.

Error	The teacher got a better understanding of him and I.
Correction	The teacher got a better understanding of him and *me*.
Error	Between you and I, the whole matter was a joke.
Correction	Between you and *me*, the whole matter was a joke.

Special care must be taken to use the right case with pronouns in *apposition*. An appositive must be in the same case as the noun or pronoun it qualifies.

Error	They told both of us—my mother and I—that the sale was over.
Correction	They told both of us—my mother and *me*—that the sale was over. *ME* IS IN THE OBJECTIVE CASE BECAUSE IT IS IN APPOSITION WITH *US*.
Error	Let's you and I make sure that the bill is paid.
Correction	Let's you and *me* make sure that the bill is paid. LET US—YOU AND ME. *YOU* AND *ME* MUST BE IN THE OBJECTIVE CASE BECAUSE THEY ARE IN APPOSITION WITH *US*.

The case of pronouns used in clauses must be determined by treating each clause as a separate part.

Error	I shall vote for whoever I like.
Correction	I shall vote for *whomever* I like. *WHOMEVER I LIKE* MUST BE TREATED AS A SEPARATE PART. *WHOMEVER* IS THE OBJECT OF THE VERB *LIKE*.
Error	Give the job to whomever is willing to work.
Correction	Give the job to *whoever* is willing to work. *WHOEVER IS WILLING TO WORK* MUST BE TREATED AS A SEPARATE PART. *WHOEVER* IS THE SUBJECT OF THE VERB *IS*.

Do not allow a parenthetical expression to trick you into a wrong pronoun case:

Error	The Smiths are people whom I think will make good neighbors.
Correction	The Smiths are people *who*, I think, will make good neighbors. *WHO* IS THE SUBJECT OF *WILL MAKE*.

Error	The Pennsylvania Dutch are people who, they say, we can trust.
Correction	The Pennsylvania Dutch are people *whom,* they say, we can trust.
	WHOM IS THE OBJECT OF THE VERB *CAN TRUST.*

A pronoun following *than* or *as* is in the subjective or the objective case depending on the implied verb:

1. He admires him more than (he admires) *her.*
2. He admires him more than *she* (admires him).
3. We are happier than *they* (are).

Use the subjective case when the pronoun follows the verb *to be:*

1. Answer the phone; it may be *she.* (not *her*)
2. It was *they* who rang the bell. (not *them*)

A possessive adjective, not an object pronoun, is used immediately in front of a gerund (noun used as a verb, such as *singing, talking, thinking*). The following are possessive adjectives:

my	our
your	their
his, her, its	whose

Error	Him lying is what tipped off the police.
Correction	*His* lying is what tipped off the police.
Error	Us checking the score helped.
Correction	*Our* checking the score helped.

■ Exercises

Underline the correct form of the pronoun in each of the following sentences.

1. I am more to be pitied than (he, him).
2. The saleslady (who, whom) they think stole the stockings lives next to us.
3. You must praise (whoever, whomever) does the best job.
4. During the Vietnam War some of (we, us) football players felt guilty.
5. Florence insists that I was later than (he, him).
6. Was it (she, her) who called you the other day?
7. The candidate made an excellent impression on us—my Dad and (I, me).
8. (Who, Whom) do you think will set a better example?

9. We were relieved by (his, him) paying the bill.

10. Between you and (me, I), is she innocent or guilty?

11. The coach said that I swim better than (him, he).

12. (Him, His) daydreaming affected his work negatively.

13. Bud doesn't care (who, whom) he gives his cold to.

14. The pinecones were divided among the three of us—John, Bill, and (me, I).

15. (Our, Us) leaving the inner city was a blessing in disguise.

16. Do you remember (me, my) telling you?

17. Can you tell me the rank of the general (who, whom), it is said, struck one of his soldiers?

18. (Whom, Who) the Cubs will play next is unknown.

19. Marilyn Monroe, (who, whom) most women envied, was unhappy.

20. Give the papers to (he and I, him and me).

■ *Self-Grading Exercise 9*

Underline the correct form of the pronoun in each of the following sentences. After completing the exercise, turn to the appendix for the correct answers.

1. No one cares except (he, him).

2. I need to call (whomever, whoever) should be at the celebration.

3. His memory was so bad that he no longer knew (whom, who) she was.

4. Was it (he or she/him or her) who asked the question?

5. Between you and (I, me), the entire plan is vicious.

6. Despite the political problems in the Middle East, (him and I, he and I) traveled to Jerusalem.

7. Do you remember (my, me) getting the measles?

8. The television set was donated to the fraternity for (its, their) members.

9. (Them, Their) escaping the accident was a miracle.

10. By (who, whom) was this fabulous cake baked?

11. They may well ask (you or I, you or me) about the burglary.

12. He has no political views of his own; he will vote for (whomever, whoever) others support.

13. Robert Frost was a poet (whom, who) I admired greatly.

14. After his divorce, he consulted a psychiatrist (who, whom) he had met socially.

15. We admire you every bit as much as we do (she, her).

16. They did not wish to frighten James or (she, her).

17. (Us, We) football players require a great deal of protein.

18. It seems to me that (whomever, whoever) has the biggest car should drive.

19. Both of us—Fred and (I, me)—received an A.

20. (Who, Whom) do you trust completely?

Errors in Point of View

Errors in point of view occur when the writer needlessly shifts person, tense, mood, voice, discourse, or key words.

pv

Person

Error	We have come to the place where one should either fish or cut bait. SHIFT FROM *WE* TO *ONE*
Correction	We have come to the place where *we* should either fish or cut bait.
Error	If you turn right on LaFollet Street, one will see the sign on one's right. SHIFT FROM *YOU* TO *ONE*
Correction	If you turn right on LaFollet Street, *you* will see the sign on your right.

Tense

Error	The weather suddenly turned windy, and clouds arise. SHIFT FROM PAST TO PRESENT
Correction	The weather suddenly turned windy, and clouds *arose.*
Error	William Tell takes the apple, places it on his son's head, and shot an arrow right through the middle. SHIFT FROM PRESENT TO PAST
Correction	William Tell takes the apple, places it on his son's head, and *shoots* an arrow right through the middle.
Error	His face turned purple with rage, and he would strike his friend. SHIFT FROM PAST TO CONDITIONAL
Correction	His face turned purple with rage, and he *struck* his friend.

Mood

Error	People of America, why do you wait? Protect your environment and you should vote against nuclear plants. SHIFT FROM IMPERATIVE TO INDICATIVE
Correction	People of America, why do you wait? Protect your environment. *Vote* against nuclear plants.

Voice

Error	John carried Mary's pack, and her tent was also pitched by him. SHIFT FROM ACTIVE TO PASSIVE VOICE
Correction	John carried Mary's pack, and he also *pitched* her tent.

Discourse

Error	The minister asked Bill if he loved his fiancée and will he treat her with devotion. SHIFT FROM INDIRECT TO DIRECT DISCOURSE
Correction	The minister asked Bill if he loved his fiancée and if he *would treat* her with devotion.

or

The minister asked Bill, "Do you love your fiancée and will you treat her with devotion?"

Key Words

Error	Because everyone has a primary goal in life, I, too, have an outstanding goal. SHIFT FROM *PRIMARY* TO *OUTSTANDING*
Correction	Like everyone else, I have a primary goal in life.
Error	I want to be a perfect human being. God made me, so why not be worthwhile? SHIFT FROM *PERFECT* TO *WORTHWHILE*
Correction	I want to be a perfect human being. God made me, so why not be perfect?

■ Exercises

In each of the following sentences, correct all shifts in (A) person, (B) tense, (C) mood, (D) discourse, (E) voice, or (F) key word. Identify the shift by placing the appropriate letter in the blank at the right.

1. Everyone must live according to your conscience. _____

2. She insisted loudly that "I am opposed to abortions." _____

3. A good meal is enjoyed by all of us and we like fresh air, too. _____

4. She revealed that an unknown intruder is in the room. _____

5. So far we have not mentioned poverty. So let me discuss it now. _____

6. Truth is a principle everyone should cherish because you can be a better person when we cling to it. _____

  7. Lock the door and you should turn out the lights.   _____

  8. The robber stole her jewelry and she was mugged
     by him, too.   _____

  9. Slowly he crept toward me and grabs for my wallet.   _____

 10. A straightforward question to ask the salesman is,
     "Why people should buy his razors?"   _____

 11. He helped me out by pointing out where one could
     find an inexpensive hotel.   _____

 12. The doorman opened the door; then my baggage
     was picked up by a porter.   _____

 13. In his memory he heard the melody of that old song
     and knew that time is passing quickly.   _____

 14. She was a spoiled brat, it always seems to me.   _____

 15. The senator's question was an intelligent one;
     the chair's answer was also a wise one.   _____

■ Self-Grading Exercise 10

In each of the following sentences, correct all shifts in (A) person, (B) tense, (C) mood, (D) discourse, (E) voice, or (F) key word. Identify the shift by placing the appropriate letter in the blank at the right. After completing the exercise, turn to the appendix for the answers. (There is more than one possible way to correct each item.)

  1. As they listened to the music, Sir Peregrine remarked about
     the success of the races while his wife dreams about love.   _____

  2. A person must accept the fact that you can't always win.   _____

  3. Every secretary who worked in the office was asked to give
     their opinion and to say how they felt.   _____

  4. The airline attendants wondered why so many passengers
     were standing in the aisle and who gave them permission to
     leave their seats?   _____

  5. If I were wealthy and if I was living in Washington, D.C.,
     I'd tell the Senate a thing or two.   _____

  6. He pored over all of his notes, and many library books
     were checked out by him.   _____

  7. Mrs. Olson walks into strangers' kitchens and they are told
     by her how to make coffee.   _____

  8. The professor informed us that the test would be given
     and asked if we are ready.   _____

9. First the insane man quoted lines from Richard Lovelace; then he recites a passage from the "Song of Solomon." _____

10. "Raise the property tax—and you must impose rent control!" he yelled with fervor. _____

11. When we buy a foreign car, you have to expect poor service. _____

12. The matter suddenly came to a crisis, but just as suddenly the situation was resolved. _____

13. It is essential that he bring the document with him and that he is here by noon. _____

14. We fear the unknown whereas the known is often welcomed by us. _____

15. Our Constitution protects our right to pursue happiness; however, it does not guarantee that we shall find this satisfaction, no matter how diligently we pursue it. _____

16. The tenant claims that he paid the rent and would I convey this fact to the landlord? _____

17. The skylark gracefully lifts itself into the sky, lets out a joyful warble, and disappeared into a cloud. _____

18. The sea breeze is blowing harder and felt colder. _____

19. As you walked into the slaughterhouse, one could see hundreds of carcasses hanging on hooks. _____

20. Because most of the children loved to go swimming, the group goes to the beach. _____

Errors in Reference

ref

Reference errors occur with the use of pronouns that do not stand for anything specific. Every pronoun must have an unmistakable *antecedent*.

Error	No one is perfect, but that doesn't mean that I shouldn't try to be one. THE PRONOUN *ONE* HAS NO ANTECEDENT, NO SPECIFIC NOUN FOR WHICH IT STANDS.
Correction	No one is perfect, but that doesn't mean that I shouldn't try to be.
Error	She keeps her files well organized; she gets along well with her employers; and she has ethical integrity; however, this is not enough to convince us to hire her. THE ANTECEDENT OF *THIS* IS TOO BROAD; IT NEEDS TO BE PINPOINTED.
Correction	She keeps her files well organized; she gets along well with her employers; and she has ethical integrity; however, these qualities are not enough to convince us to hire her.

Error	Our neighbor, Mrs. Irwin, told my mother that she had not chosen the proper dress. WHO HAD NOT CHOSEN THE PROPER DRESS— MRS. IRWIN OR THE MOTHER? THE REFERENCE IS UNCLEAR.
Correction	Our neighbor, Mrs. Irwin, told my mother, "I have not chosen the proper dress." TURNING THE CLAUSE INTO DIRECT ADDRESS IS THE SIMPLEST WAY TO CORRECT THIS KIND OF REFERENCE ERROR.
Error	His clothes were scattered all across the room which needed folding. CONFUSION ARISES BECAUSE THE MISPLACED *WHICH* IMPLIES THAT THE ROOM NEEDED FOLDING.
Correction	His clothes, which needed folding, were scattered all across the room.
Error	In Europe they often claim that Americans eat too much ice cream. AVOID USING *THEY* OR *YOU* AS A REFERENCE TO PEOPLE IN GENERAL.
Correction	Europeans often claim that Americans eat too much ice cream.
Error	When the Godfather dies, it is due to a heart attack. *IT* HAS ONLY AN IMPLIED REFERENCE.
Correction	The Godfather's death is due to a heart attack.
Error	Arthur swung his racket hard, but it went into the net. *IT* STANDS FOR BALL, BUT THE WORD *BALL* NEVER SHOWS UP.
Correction	Arthur swung his racket hard, but the ball went into the net.
Error	When Elmer Cole's restaurant was opened, he invited all the townspeople for a free meal. A PRONOUN IN THE SUBJECTIVE CASE MUST NOT REFER TO AN ANTECEDENT IN THE POSSESSIVE CASE.
Correction	When Elmer Cole opened his restaurant, he invited all the townspeople for a free meal.

■ *Exercises*

Rewrite each of the following sentences to avoid confusing, implied, nonexistent, or vague pronoun references.

1. Many people are emotional but have difficulty showing them.

   _____

   _____

2. At the factory where I work at night, they say not to ask for salary advances.

   _____

   _____

3. My dad warned my brother that he would not get a promotion.

   _____

   _____

4. She sat by the window knitting, which was too small to let in any light.

   _____

   _____

5. The nuclear bomb was developed in the twentieth century; this completely changed humanity's approach to war.

   _____

   _____

6. The leading baritone didn't show up for opening night, which caused all kinds of gossip.

   _____

   _____

7. In the South, you aren't understood if you have a New York accent.

   _____

   _____

8. Life is a cycle of happiness followed by misery, but I want to have them in equal portions.

   _____

   _____

9. Although it is muddy down by the river, it looks inviting.

   _____

   _____

10. The first chapter awakens the reader's interest in mining, which continues until the Camerons move to America.

    _____

    _____

11. The American colonists refused to pay taxes without being represented. This was the major cause of the American Revolution.

    _____

    _____

12. Tomorrow it may rain and damage our roof, and it should be protected.

    _____

    _____

13. The guests were perspiring and fanning themselves with the printed program; it really bothered them.

    _____

    _____

14. The rose garden in Hoover Park is spectacular. Some of them are deep purple, almost black.

    _____

    _____

15. I went over my check stubs three times, but it never balanced properly.

    _____

    _____

■ *Self-Grading Exercise 11*

Rewrite each of the following sentences to avoid confusing, implied, nonexistent, or vague pronoun references. After completing the exercise, turn to the appendix for the answers. (There is more than one possible answer for each item.)

1. We are now expected to drive less and use public transportation; we are asked to conserve heating fuel. This is realistic.

   _____

   _____

2. They say that a tablespoon of vinegar in some sugar and oil will reduce the appetite.

   _____

   _____

3. In the newspaper it said that a rebirth of great art is taking place in China.

   _____

   _____

4. Byron carried on a lively correspondence with Shelley when he was on the Continent.

   _____

   _____

5. When Golda Meir died, the world was expecting it.

_____

_____

6. My brother is enormously talented, but he does not make full use of it.

_____

_____

7. During lunch John always sat alone while the other students sat together chatting away. This didn't last long, however.

_____

_____

8. In Mahatma Gandhi's room, he wanted only the sparsest of furniture.

_____

_____

9. In an interview with a group of millionaires, the master of ceremonies told the audience that they were very articulate.

_____

_____

10. Melissa invited Ruth to travel to Spain with her because she thought she was interested in Spanish history.

_____

_____

11. Psychologists have no right discussing their patients' personal problems with their friends because they could be embarrassed if their identities were discovered.

_____

_____

12. The passerby noticed a young boy dashing out of the store and running down the street, which made him wonder about it.

_____

_____

13. On our flight across the Atlantic it was beautiful.

_____

_____

14. Inside the Blue Grotto of Capri, the water was rough and dark, but it was splendid anyway.

    _____

    _____

15. My friend John loves to watch basketball for hours on end, but his wife doesn't approve of it.

    _____

    _____

Errors with Modifiers

Dangling modifiers occur when words or phrases are used that have no logical relationship to other elements in the sentence. These words simply "dangle" in front of the reader, causing mystification and mirth. The most frequent dangling errors are caused by (1) misused verbal phrases and (2) misused subordinate clauses. To correct dangling elements, assign the logical subject to all verbal phrases or subordinate clauses.

dang

Dangling	Falling in love with Carole Lombard made me envy Clark Gable.
	FOR THIS SENTENCE TO MAKE SENSE, CLARK GABLE MUST BE THE SUBJECT OF THE PHRASE "FALLING IN LOVE WITH CAROLE LOMBARD."
Correct	I envied Clark Gable's falling in love with Carole Lombard.
Dangling	Upon reaching the age of six, my grandfather took me to school.
	THE SENTENCE IMPLIES THAT THE GRANDFATHER WAS SIX YEARS OLD WHEN HE TOOK HIS GRANDCHILD TO SCHOOL.
Correct	When I reached the age of six, my grandfather took me to school.
Dangling	To understand why fat people eat, a study of self-hatred is necessary.
	IN THIS SENTENCE, *A STUDY* BECOMES THE SUBJECT OF THE INFINITIVE *TO UNDERSTAND,* WHICH IS OBVIOUSLY SILLY BECAUSE A STUDY CAN'T *UNDERSTAND.*
Correct	To understand why fat people eat, we must study self-hatred.
Dangling	Although loved by Americans, historians deny the truth of many anecdotes involving Abraham Lincoln. THIS SENTENCE IMPLIES THAT HISTORIANS ARE LOVED BY AMERICANS.
Correct	Although loved by Americans, many anecdotes involving Abraham Lincoln have been labeled as historically untrue.

Misplaced modifiers occur when modifying words, phrases, or clauses are not placed as close as possible to the words they modify. Confusing, illogical, or awkward sentences are caused by misplaced modifiers.

misp

Confusing	We looked inside the car with our friends for the package. WERE THE FRIENDS INSIDE OR OUTSIDE THE CAR?
Correct	With our friends we looked inside the car for the package.
Illogical	Visitors to France can see the Eiffel Tower floating down the Seine River on a barge. IN THIS SENTENCE, THE EIFFEL TOWER IS FLOATING ON A BARGE.
Correct	Floating down the Seine River on a barge, visitors to Paris can see the Eiffel Tower.
Awkward	My husband and I expect you to instantly pay for the damage to our car. IT IS BEST NOT TO SEPARATE *TO* FROM ITS VERB.
Correct	My husband and I expect you to pay for the damage to our car instantly.

The last error noted here is grounded in the split-infinitive rule, which says that a word should never be interposed between *to* and its verb. This rule evolved from the work of early grammarians, who had in mind the Latin model in which the infinitive is a single word. As arbitrary as it may now sound, these grammarians reasoned that if a Latin verb such as *amare* could not be split, then it was also wrong to split its English equivalent, *to love*. With this logic, they deduced that *to passionately love* must be ungrammatical because passionately comes between *to* and the verb. We think this rule silly, as observing it often leads to incongruous sounding phrases, such as *really to understand* instead of *to really understand*. In classroom usage, however, some instructors remain adamant about never splitting infinitives.

■ *Exercises*

Rewrite each of the following sentences to eliminate the dangling or misplaced modifiers.

1. Looking down in horror the snake crawled away.

   _____

   _____

2. To guarantee their rights, collective bargaining was organized by the teachers.

   _____

   _____

3. She did not realize that he had had major surgery until Friday.

   _____

   _____

4. John had looked forward to getting married for two weeks to Mary Ellen.

   _____

   _____

5. Responding to consumer demands for better gasoline mileage, the Honda was promoted.

   _____

   _____

6. We bought ice cream cones at a small stand that cost 40 cents.

   _____

   _____

7. She decided to immediately telephone her friend.

   _____

   _____

8. Arriving at the pack station, our dried food had been stolen.

   _____

   _____

9. I held my breath as the car slid into the curb that had raced ahead suddenly.

   _____

   _____

10. While dreaming about the future, lightning flashed and the rain began to pour.

    _____

    _____

11. My mother consented to let me use her car reluctantly.

    _____

    _____

12. Continue to whip the cream until tired.

    _____

    _____

13. To understand *The Lord of the Rings,* the classics must be read.

    _____

    _____

14. Drilling my teeth, I could tell he was an excellent dentist.

    _____

    _____

15. He was not willing to completely give up drinking.

_____

_____

16. Looking at the mountain range from the valley, a lovely rainbow could be seen.

_____

_____

17. My uncle had warned me never to leave a gun in my car that had not been unloaded.

_____

_____

18. Now is the time to, if you want a Democrat in the White House, vote for our governor.

_____

_____

19. At the party hors d'oeuvres were served to all of the guests on silver trays.

_____

_____

■ *Self-Grading Exercise 12*

Rewrite each of the following sentences to eliminate the dangling or misplaced modifiers. After completing the exercise, turn to the appendix for the answers. (There is more than one possible answer to each item.)

1. Bowing to the audience, his violin fell to the floor.

_____

_____

2. The tiny kitten sat shivering in the corner filled with terror.

_____

_____

3. Watching from behind a bush, a camera in hand, the bears seemed like harmless pets.

_____

_____

4. What the teacher needs is a list of students neatly typed.

   _____

   _____

5. Students will not need to pass the three conversation examinations that speak French fluently.

   _____

   _____

6. During World War II the Nazis only gave Jewish prisoners cabbage to eat, nothing else.

   _____

   _____

7. Instead of asking forgiveness, a piece of chocolate cake was her sign of repentance.

   _____

   _____

8. Even when confronted with the full truth, the facts were ignored.

   _____

   _____

9. Hearing the bell ring, the boxer's glove was flung to the ground triumphantly.

   _____

   _____

10. Out of breath, the lover ran up the stairs revealing a look of anxiety.

    _____

    _____

11. The day drew to a close with anguish, praying that God would spare the infant.

    _____

    _____

12. We not only enjoy music, but also painting and sculpture.

    _____

    _____

13. After adjourning Congress, the law was enacted immediately.

    _____

    _____

14. Scorched by the sizzling heat, jumping into the river made a great deal of sense.

    _____

    _____

15. We tried on some DKNY pants at a Neiman-Marcus store that cost $150.

    _____

    _____

Errors in Parallelism

//

Lack of parallelism occurs when similar grammatical constructions are not used to express parallel ideas. The result is a disruptive break in the rhythm of writing.

Not parallel	I love swimming, hiking, and to ski. THE SENTENCE STARTS WITH TWO GERUNDS (-ING WORDS) BUT SUDDENLY SWITCHES TO AN INFINITIVE (TO + A VERB).
Parallel	I love swimming, hiking, and skiing.
Not parallel	Community colleges are necessary because they give late bloomers a second chance; they provide free tuition for the poor; and they always encouraged the vocational trades. THE SENTENCE STARTS WITH TWO VERBS IN THE PRESENT TENSE, BUT SUDDENLY SWITCHES TO THE PAST TENSE.
Parallel	Community colleges are necessary because they give late bloomers a second chance; they provide free tuition for the poor; and they encourage the vocational trades.
Not parallel	For days the president of the club wondered whether he should pay the bills or to resign. *HE SHOULD* IS FOLLOWED BY *TO RESIGN*.
Parallel	For days the president of the club wondered whether to pay the bills or to resign.
Not parallel	Whether tired or when he is rested, he reads the paper.
Parallel	Whether tired or rested, he reads the paper.

■ *Exercises*

Rewrite each of the following sentences to improve parallel structure. Join participles with participles, infinitives with infinitives, noun phrases with noun phrases, and so on.

1. Bright sun gleams on the water, dark shadows across the cliffs, and the delicate flowers that blossomed in the desert created a memorable picture.

   _____

   _____

2. I prefer to attend small dinners than going to big banquets.

   _____

   _____

3. What we claim to believe rarely coincides with the things we actually do.

   _____

   _____

4. The anthropologist traveled into heated jungles, along insect-infested rivers, and he ventured up steep mountain trails.

   _____

   _____

5. I tried to explain that time was short, that the firm wanted an answer, and the importance of efficiency.

   _____

   _____

6. Most women's fashions come from Paris, Rome, and also from New York.

   _____

   _____

7. As we watched through the bars of the cage we could see the monkeys eating bananas, scratching their fur, and they swung on rails.

   _____

   _____

8. Most teachers try not only to engage the students' attention, but they also want to say something important.

   _____

   _____

9. Victor Hugo was a statesman and who also wrote novels, including *Les Misérables*.

   _____

   _____

10. Larger Social Security checks would allow senior citizens to pay for decent living quarters, to get proper medical help, and they could afford sound nutrition.

    _____

    _____

11. Basketball, football, and the game of baseball are favorite American specta-
tor sports.

   _____

   _____

12. I admire the songs of Paul McCartney, formerly a member of the Beatles,
but who is now on his own.

   _____

   _____

13. Their divorce was due to his stressful job, his hot temper, and because he
disliked her friends.

   _____

   _____

14. You have two choices: You must take either the exam or to write a research
paper.

   _____

   _____

■ *Self-Grading Exercise 13*

Rewrite each of the following sentences to improve parallel structure. Join participles with participles, infinitives with infinitives, noun phrases with noun phrases,
and so on. After completing the exercise, turn to the appendix for the answers.
(There is more than one possible answer for each item.)

1. He wanted to marry her because she was bright, pleasant, and never placed
herself first.

   _____

   _____

2. The boss fired him because his letters were sloppy, ungrammatical, and he
didn't type well.

   _____

   _____

3. The handbook revealed two ways in which the unity of a paragraph could
be broken: (1) one could stray from the topic sentence, (2) excessive details
obscuring the central thought.

   _____

   _____

4. By exercising daily, by eating proper food, and if he avoids stress, he can regain his health.

5. This simple man did not doubt that after death there was a paradise for good people and a hell for people who had been bad.

6. Most of them were either athletic or had great strength.

7. Handing out oil coupons seemed both intelligent and a necessity.

8. She insisted that he must leave and never to return.

9. The man is either an idealist or foolish.

10. Today pocket calculators are inexpensive, durable, and it is easy to obtain them.

11. The Byronic hero was a man who felt alienated from mainstream society, who withdrew into haughty superiority, loved passionately, and felt an element of self-pity.

12. This is the case not only with police officers but also of firefighters.

13. Here is what you will need to know: how to open a bank account, how to judge a contract, and selling equipment.

_____

_____

14. She climbed Mount Whitney not because she wanted to test her endurance, but out of a sense of arrogance.

_____

_____

15. To err is human; forgiving is divine.

_____

_____

Errors in Diction

d

Poor diction (also called *poor word usage*) refers to the use of a word to mean something other than its dictionary definition or in a way unacceptable according to the standards of users of ideal English. *Ideal English* can be defined as language spoken or written according to the standards of educated people. It is the language of scholastic books, magazines, and newspapers. People who follow precise standard usage rules are using ideal English, although they probably express themselves less formally in day-to-day communication—on the bus, in the laundromat, or at the supermarket.

Ideal English is the language of concentrated formality. Dun J. Li, introducing a textbook on Chinese civilization, uses ideal English when he states, "Of all ideologies that influenced the thinking and life of traditional China none was more important than Confucianism." On the other hand, the irate factory worker complaining about his wages uses colloquial English when he writes, "If you wasn't so darn pigheaded, you'd raise our pay." Both messages are clear; the difference lies in their levels of formality.

Use the Correct Word

Because it is highly precise, ideal English is generally required in student writing. Colloquial, substandard, or slang words are unacceptable in ideal English. If you are unsure about a word's meaning, look it up. The following glossary will help you avoid expressions that are unacceptable in ideal English.

Glossary of word choice

Accept, Except   To *accept* is to *receive;* to *except* is to *exclude.* (We *accepted* her into the group; we didn't let him in because C students were *excepted.*) *Except* is also a preposition meaning *other than, with the exception of.* (Everyone arrived on time *except* Jim.)

Accidently No such word exists. The correct word is *accidentally*.

Advice, Advise *Advice* is a noun; *advise* is a verb. (A person receives *advice*, but one person will *advise* another.)

Affect, Effect *Affect* means to *influence*. (It will *affect* my health.) *Effect* is both a verb and a noun. To *effect* is to *produce, cause,* or *bring about*. (He *effected* a change.) An *effect* is a *result*. (The *effect* of the paint was ugly.)

Aggravate *Aggravate* means *make worse*. It should not be used for *provoke* or *irritate*.

Agree to, Agree with One agrees *to* a proposal but *with* a person. (I agreed *to* his plan. I agreed *with* Nancy.)

Ain't Considered substandard.

All ready, Already *All ready* means that all are ready. (The guests were *all ready*.) *Already* means *previously* or *before now*. (He had *already* moved away from town.)

All together, Altogether *All together* means *all of a number* considered as a group. (She scolded them *all together*.) *Altogether* means *entirely, completely*. (The officer was *altogether* correct.)

Allusion, Illusion *Allusion* means *hint* or *indirect reference*. (The comment was an *allusion* to World War II.) *Illusion* means *false impression* or *belief*. (She is under the *illusion* that she is beautiful.)

Among, Between *Among* is used for more than two people or objects. (We searched *among* the many guests.) *Between* is used for two people or objects. (Divide the money *between* the two workers.)

Amount, Number *Amount* refers to uncountable things (a large *amount* of cement). *Number* refers to countable things (a large *number* of houses).

Any place, No place Corruptions of *anywhere, nowhere*.

Anywheres, Nowheres, Somewheres Corruptions of *anywhere, nowhere, somewhere*.

Appraise, Apprise *Appraise* means *estimate* (the *appraised* value of the car). *Apprise* means *inform*. (*Apprise* me of your decision.)

Apt, Liable, Likely *Apt* means *suitable, qualified, capable* (an *apt* phrase, a man *apt* in his work). *Liable* means *susceptible, prone, responsible* (*liable* to be injured, *liable* for damages). *Likely* means *credible, probable, probably*. (He had a *likely* excuse. It is *likely* to rain.)

Awful Colloquial when used for *disagreeable* or *very*.

Bad, Badly *Bad* is an adjective, *badly* an adverb. (He has a *bad* cold; he sings *badly*.)

Being as Corruption of *since* or *inasmuch as*.

Beside, Besides *Beside* is a preposition meaning *by the side of, in addition to,* or *aside from*. (He sat down *beside* her.) *Besides* is a preposition meaning *except* (he had little *besides* his good looks) and an adverb meaning *in addition, moreover*. (He received a trip and fifty dollars *besides*.)

Blame on   The correct idiom calls for the use of *to blame* with *for,* not *on.* (They *blamed* the driver *for* the accident, not They *blamed* the accident *on* the driver.) *Blame on* is colloquial.

Burst, Bursted, Bust   The principal parts of the verb *burst* are *burst, burst, burst.* The use of *bursted* or *busted* for the past tense is incorrect. *Bust* is either a piece of sculpture, a part of the human body, or a slang expression for *failure.* It is sometimes incorrectly used instead of *burst* or *break.*

But what   Use *that* instead of *but what.* (They had no doubt *that* she won the New York primary.)

Cannot help but   This is a mixed construction. *Cannot help* and *cannot but* are separate expressions, either of which is correct. (*He cannot but attempt it,* or *He cannot help attempting it.*) Do not write, "He *cannot help but* lose."

Capital, Capitol   *Capital* is a city; *capitol* is a building. *Capital* is also an adjective, usually meaning *chief* or *excellent.* As a noun, *capital* means accumulated assets or wealth.

Censor, Censure   To *censor* means to *subject to censorship.* (The Vietnamese military *censored* their mail.) To *censure* means to *criticize severely.* (He was *censured* by the church.)

Choose, Chose   *Choose* is the present tense. (Today I *choose* to stay.) *Chose* is the past tense. (Yesterday I *chose* to stay.)

Cite, Site   To *cite* means to *quote.* (He *cited* Abraham Lincoln.) *Site* means *place* or *location.* (It was a grassy, green *site.*)

Complement, Compliment   *Complement* means *something that completes.* (His suggestion was a *complement* to the general plan.) A *compliment* is an expression of courtesy or praise. (My *compliments* to the chef.)

Considerable   An adjective meaning *worthy of consideration, important.* (The idea is at least *considerable.*) When used to denote a great deal or a great many, *considerable* is colloquial or informal.

Continual, Continuous   *Continual* means *repeated often.* (The interruptions were *continual.*) *Continuous* means *going on without interruption.* (For two days the pain was *continuous.*)

Convince, Persuade   Do not use *convince* for *persuade,* as in "I *convinced* him to do it." *Convince* means to *overcome a doubt.* (I *convinced* him of the soundness of my plan.) *Persuade* means to *induce.* (I *persuaded* him to do it.)

Council, Counsel   *Council* means an *assembly.* (The *council* discussed taxes.) *Counsel* means *advice.* (The teacher gave him good *counsel.*)

Credible, Creditable   *Credible* means *believable.* (His evidence was not *credible.*) *Creditable* means *deserving esteem* or *admiration.* (The male lead gave a *creditable* performance.)

Different than   Most authorities on usage prefer *different from* to *different than.*

Disinterested   Often confused with *uninterested, disinterested* means *unbiased, impartial.* (The judge was *disinterested.*) *Uninterested* means *bored with.* (She was *uninterested* in politics.)

Don't   A contraction of *do not.* Do not write *he, she,* or *it don't.*

Either   Used only with two items, not three or more. *(Either* the teacher or the book was wrong. Not: *Either* the teacher, the book, or I was wrong.)

Emigrant, Immigrant   A person who moves from one country to another is both an *emigrant* and an *immigrant.* He *emigrates from* one place and *immigrates to* the other.

Enthused   The word is colloquial and almost always unacceptable.

Equally as   Do not use these words together; omit either *equally* or *as.* Do not write "Water is equally as necessary as air," but rather "Water is as necessary as air" or "Water and air are equally necessary."

Etc.   An abbreviation of Latin *et* (and) and *cetera* (other things). It should not be preceded by *and,* nor should it be used to avoid a clear and exact ending of an idea or a sentence.

Everyone   This singular pronoun takes a singular verb. (Everyone *is* going.)

Exam   Colloquial for examination. Compare *gym, lab, dorm, soph, prof.*

Expect   The word means *look forward to* or *foresee.* Do not use it for *suspect* or *suppose.*

Fewer, Less   Use *fewer* to refer to items that can be numbered and *less* to refer to amount. (Where there are *fewer* machines, there is *less* noise.)

Formally, Formerly   *Formally* means *in a formal manner.* (He was *formally* initiated last night.) *Formerly* means *at a former time.* (They *formerly* lived in Ohio.)

Funny   When used to mean *strange, funny* is colloquial.

Further, Farther   *Further* is used for ideas. (We studied the question *further.*) *Farther* is used for geographical location (*farther* down the street).

Got   This is a correct past tense and past participle of the verb *to get.* (He *got* three traffic tickets in two days.) *Gotten* is the alternative past participle of *get.* (He had *gotten* three tickets the week before.)

Guess   Colloquial when used for *suppose* or *believe.*

Guy   Slang when used for *boy* or *man.*

Had ought, Hadn't ought   Do not use for ought and *ought not.*

Hardly, Scarcely   Do not use with a negative. "I *can't hardly* see it" borders on the illiterate. Write "I *can hardly* see it" or (if you cannot see it at all) "I *can't* see it."

Healthful, Healthy   Places are *healthful* (conducive to health) if persons living in them are *healthy* (having good health).

Imply, Infer   *Imply* means *suggest.* (His grin *implied* that he was teasing.) *Infer* means *conclude.* (I *inferred* from her look that she was teasing.)

Incidently   There is no such word. The correct form is *incidentally,* which is derived from the adjective *incidental.*

Inside of   In expressions of time, *inside of* is colloquial for *within.* (He will return *within* a week).

Irregardless   No such word exists. Use *regardless.*

Its, It's   The form *its* is possessive. (*Its* cover is gray.) *It's* is a contraction of *it is.* (*It's* your fault.)

It's me   Formal English requires *It is I. It's me* is informal or colloquial.

Kind, Sort   These are singular forms of nouns and should be modified accordingly (*this kind, that sort*). Do not write "*these* kind."

Kind of, Sort of   Do not use these to mean *rather* as in "He was *kind of* (or *sort of*) stupid."

Last, Latest   *Last* implies that there will be no more; *latest* means *most recent.* (After reading his *latest* book, I hope that it is his *last.*)

Leave, Let   The use of *leave* for *let* in expressions like *leave him go* is incorrect.

Like, As   Confusion in the use of these words results from using *like* as a conjunction—"He talks *like* a gentlemen should. She spends money *like* she had a fortune." Use *as* or *as if* instead. (He talks *as* a gentlemen should. She spends money *as if* she had a fortune.)

Loose, Lose   *Loose* means *not tight, not attached.* (The button is *loose.*) *Lose* means to *be unable to keep or find.* (Did she *lose* her diamond ring?)

Lot, Lots   Colloquial or informal when used to mean *many* or *much.*

Mad   The meaning of *mad* is *insane.* Used to mean *angry,* it is informal.

May be, Maybe   *May be* is a verb phrase. (They *may be* late.) *Maybe* used as an adverb means *perhaps.* (*Maybe* they will buy a boat.)

Mean   Used informally for *disagreeable.* (He has a *mean* face.) It is slang when used to mean *skillful, expert.* (He plays a *mean* tennis game.)

Media   *Media* is the plural of *medium*—a means, agency, or instrument. It is often used *incorrectly* as though it were singular, as in "The *media* is playing a big role in political races this year." (the media always seem to side with the underdog.)

Most   Do not use for *almost.* "*Almost* all my friends appeared" is the correct form.

Myself   Incorrect when used as a substitute for *I* or *me,* as in "He and *myself* did it." It is correctly used as an intensifier (*I myself* shall do it) and in the reflexive (I blame only *myself*).

None, No one   Singular pronouns that take singular verbs. (None of his reasons *is* valid. No one *is* going.)

Of   Unnecessary after such prepositions as *off, inside,* or *outside.* (He fell *off* the chair. They waited *inside* the house.)

On account of   Do not use as a conjunction. The phrase should be followed by an object of the preposition *of* (*on account of* his illness). "He was absent *on account of* he was sick" is poor English.

Oral, Verbal   *Oral* means *spoken* rather than written; *verbal* means *associated with words.* When referring to an agreement or commitment that is not in writing, *oral* should be used.

Over with   The *with* is unnecessary in such expressions as "The concert was *over with* by five o'clock."

Past, Passed   *Past* is a noun, adjective, or preposition (to remember the *past;* in the *past* two weeks; one block *past* the pharmacy). *Passed* is a verb. (She *passed* by his house.)

Personal, Personnel   Personal means *private.* (She expressed her *personal* view.) *Personnel* is a *body of employed people.* (The *personnel* demanded higher wages.)

Plan on   Omit *on.* Standard practice calls for an infinitive or a direct object after *plan.* (They *planned to go.* They *planned a reception.*)

Principal, Principle   Principal is both adjective and noun (*principal* parts, *principal* of the school, interest and *principal*). *Principle* is a noun only, meaning *code of conduct, fundamental truth or assumption* (*principles* of morality, a person of *principle*).

Quite   The word means *altogether, entirely.* (He was *quite* exhausted from his exertion.) It is colloquial when used for *moderately* or *very* and in expressions like *quite a few, quite a number.*

Raise, Rise   *Raise* requires an object. (She *raised* the cover.) *Rise* is not used with an object. (Let us *rise* and sing.)

Reason is because, Reason why   These are not correct forms in English. Examples of correct usage are "The *reason* I stayed home is *that* I was sick," "The *reason* (not *why*) they invited us is *that* . . ."

Respectfully, Respectively   Respectfully means *with respect.* (The young used to act *respectfully* toward their elders.) *Respectively* is used to clarify antecedents in a sentence. (The *men and women* took their seats on the right and left, *respectively.*)

Right   In the sense of *very* or *extremely, right* is colloquial. Do not write, "I'm *right* glad to know you."

Same   The word is an adjective, not a pronoun. Do not use it as in "We received your order and shall give *same* our immediate attention." Substitute *it* for *same.*

Set, Sit   *Set* requires an object. (She *set* the cup on the table.) *Sit* is not used with an object. (You must *sit* in the chair.)

Should of, Would of   Do not use these forms for *should have, would have.*

Some   Do not use for *somewhat,* as in "She is *some* better after her illness."

Stationary, Stationery   *Stationary* means *fixed, not moving. Stationery* means paper and other materials for writing letters.

Statue, Stature, Statute   A *statue* is a piece of sculpture. *Stature* is bodily height, often used figuratively to mean *level of achievement, status,* or *importance.* A *statute* is a law or regulation.

Sure, Surely   *Sure* is an adjective, and *surely* is an adverb. (I am *sure* that he will arrive, but he *surely* annoys me.)

Suspicion   This word is a noun and should not be used for the verb *to suspect*. (His *suspicion* was right; they *suspected* the butler.)

Try and   Use *try to,* not *try and,* in such expressions as *"Try to* be kind."

Type   Colloquial in expressions like "this *type* book." Write "this *type of* book."

Unique   If referring to something as the *only* one of its kind, you may correctly use *unique*. (The Grand Canyon is *unique*.) The word does not mean *rare, strange,* or *remarkable,* and there are no degrees of uniqueness: Nothing can be *extremely* (almost, nearly, virtually) *unique*.

Use (Used) to could   Do not use for *once could* or *used to be able*.

Very   Do not use as a modifier of a past participle, as in *very burned*. English idiom calls for *badly burned* or *very badly burned*.

Wait for, Wait on   To *wait for* means *to look forward to, to expect*. (For days, I *have waited for* you.) To *wait on* means *to serve*. (The hostess *waited on* the guests.)

Want in, Want off, Want out   These forms are dialectal. Do not use them for *want to come in, want to get off, want to get out*.

Way   Colloquial when used for *away,* as in "*way* out West."

Ways   Colloquial when used for *way,* as in "a long *ways* to go."

Whose, Who's   The possessive form is *whose*. (*Whose* money is this?) *Who's* is a contraction of *who is*. (*Who's* there?)

Wise   Unacceptable when appended to a noun to convert it to an adverb as in *businesswise*.

Your, You're   The possessive form is *your*. (Give me *your* address.) *You're* is a contraction of *you are*.

■ *Exercises*

Underline the correct term in each of the following sentences.

1. When they arrived at West Point, they received some practical (advise, advice) regarding the honor system.

2. During his lecture, the professor made an (allusion, illusion) to Abraham Lincoln.

3. The prime minister's illness was so (aggravated, irritated) by his drinking that he needed surgery.

4. My aunt does a (credible, creditable) job of sewing evening gowns.

5. In the past, interviewers were (disinterested, uninterested) when they interviewed candidates; now they are biased.

6. I was (enthusiastic, enthused) when they told me about the new director.

7. When we heard about the theft, we immediately (suspicioned, suspected) collusion within the company.

8. They received the news that he would return (within, inside of) a week.

9. Pete Sampras's (latest, last) match gave the world of tennis something to rave about.

10. Be careful not to (loose, lose) the keys.

11. We drank the spring water (as if, like) we would never drink water again in our lives.

12. That information seriously (affects, effects) the decision.

13. The agreement was (oral, verbal), so it will not hold up in court.

14. The reason grades are necessary (is that, is because) they are a point of reference for students.

15. If I had known you were coming, I (would of, would have) baked a cake.

16. Most people improve (somewhat, some) the moment they take one spoonful of Kay's cough syrup.

17. For her birthday, I sent my mother some blue (stationary, stationery) so she could write to her friends.

18. Never use a large (number, amount) of words when (less, fewer) will do.

19. We still had a long (way, ways) to trudge uphill, but none of the students complained.

20. Will the person (who's, whose) wallet this is please claim it at the front ticket booth?

21. Before the tall buildings were built, we (used to could, used to be able) to see the ocean.

22. That scandal in her (passed, past) may keep her from getting the promotion.

23. Many Americans want to return to old-fashioned, religious (principals, principles).

24. (Regardless, irregardless) of the consequences, the ambassador stood by his post.

25. The glint in her eye (implied, inferred) more clearly than words how she really felt.

■ *Self-Grading Exercise 14*

Underline the correct term in each of the following sentences. After completing the exercise, turn to the appendix for the correct answers.

1. After noticing that the watch and the bedspread were gone, they immediately (suspicioned, suspected) his stepdaughter.

2. Dorothy insisted on keeping her (personnel, personal) opinions hidden from her students.

3. The hiring committee preferred communicating by telephone because they believed in (oral, verbal) interviews.

4. I was always told that (this type, this type of) novel was cheap and aimed at the sensation seekers.

5. (Sit, Set) the flower pot in front of the brick wall, where it will look lovely.

6. The (amount, number) of registered students varies from semester to semester.

7. In the upper left-hand corner of his (stationery, stationary) one could clearly discern three modest initials.

8. Earl Warren was considered a Supreme Court justice of immense (stature, statue, statute).

9. The team that climbed Mt. Whitney included (quite a number, a rather large number) of women.

10. Twenty years and six children later, the marriage was finally (over, over with).

11. Day after day his fiancée waited (for, on) him to return from the war.

12. Thank you for the (complement, compliment)—how kind!

13. (Your, You're) either for us or against us.

14. He never returned the suitcase (like, as) he was asked to do.

15. We (can hardly, can't hardly) distinguish one twin from the other.

16. The (farther, further) he delved into St. Paul's theology, the more fascinated he became.

17. When the real estate agent had received a firm bid, he (appraised, apprised) his clients of the fact.

18. He could never be (persuaded, convinced) to travel overseas on an airplane.

19. The (site, cite) for the international hotel was near the center of town.

20. While he was in Vietnam, all of his mail was (censured, censored).

Use Concrete Words

A word is *concrete* when it refers to a *specific* object, quality, or action. *He **limped** across the road* is more concrete than *He **went** across the road*. ***One hundred women** attended the dinner* is more concrete than ***Quite a few people** attended the dinner.* (See also Chapter 8 for use of details in descriptions.)

Vague	I like her because she is such a *nice* girl.
Concrete	I like her because she is *witty* and *vivacious*.
Vague	The lyrics of Paul Simon are *relevant*.
Concrete	The lyrics of Paul Simon *expose many fears felt by the people in our society*.
Vague	I dislike my teacher's *negative attitude* toward old people.
Concrete	I dislike my teacher's *contempt* for old people.

■ *Exercises*

Improve each of the following sentences by replacing the italicized vague word or words with more concrete words or phrases.

1. John *got* on his horse and quickly *went* away.

   _____

   _____

2. Eloise always wears such sloppy *apparel*.

   _____

   _____

3. The streets of Amsterdam are crowded with *vehicles*.

   _____

   _____

4. The lecturer was most *uninteresting*.

   _____

   _____

5. She *ate* her food *quickly*.

   _____

   _____

6. It was fascinating to watch the children *being active* on the school playground.

   _____

   _____

7. I was upset by this whole *business*.

   _____

   _____

8. What a *great* idea!

   _____

   _____

9. We expect to have a *wonderful* time in Palm Springs.

   _____

   _____

10. Penguins are *unusual* in many *ways*.

_____

_____

11. I couldn't follow the complicated *setup* in his church.

_____

_____

12. My psychology class was one of the most *worthwhile* experiences of my college days.

_____

_____

13. Spanking is an important *element* of child rearing.

_____

_____

14. The *negative aspects* of driving huge cars outweigh the *positive aspects.*

_____

_____

15. *All the President's Men* is a *tremendous* movie.

_____

_____

16. Here are the *things* that bother me about assigning grades.

_____

_____

■ *Self-Grading Exercise 15*

Improve each of the following sentences by replacing the italicized vague word or words with more concrete words or phrases. After completing the exercise, turn to the appendix for the answers. (There is more than one possible answer for each item.)

1. To add to our depression, a period of *unfavorable weather* set in.

_____

_____

2. Vicky *showed great satisfaction* as she walked off the stage with her gold medal.

_____

_____

3. I liked *the advantages of living* in the city.

_____

_____

4. His extreme selfishness *had some negative consequences on his life.*

_____

_____

5. He chewed his food noisily, he talked with his mouth full, and he wiped his lips with his hand; in short, his manners were *deficient.*

_____

_____

6. For six days and nights, he *participated in a combat* with fever and death.

_____

_____

7. A delicate seashell is a *nice thing.*

_____

_____

8. All of the fun at Joe's birthday party was ruined because the children *behaved badly.*

_____

_____

9. The Mohave Desert of California and the Sinai Desert of Egypt *have certain characteristics in common.*

_____

_____

10. Every large city *has its problems.*

_____

_____

11. She was a hopeless, withered old lady *going across* the street with her cane, her *entire posture* serving as a symbol of her despair.

    _____

    _____

12. In 1925, a terrible dust storm *went* across the Midwest, *causing considerable destruction*.

    _____

    _____

13. Many of the old Broadway songs reveal poignantly *some regrettable aspects of* American life.

    _____

    _____

14. We tried various cleaning solutions, but the kitchen floor remained *unsightly*.

    _____

    _____

15. People who throw *all kinds of stuff* out of their car windows while they drive along our highways reveal a disgusting kind of vulgarity.

    _____

    _____

Wordiness

Wordiness results when writing is burdened with redundant or wasted expressions. Prune your rough draft of such redundancies.

W

Wordy	He spent all of his entire life in freezing temperatures. *ALL* AND *ENTIRE* ARE REDUNDANT.
Correct	He spent his entire life in freezing temperatures.
Wordy	After the end of the flood, Noah released the dove. *THE END OF* IS WASTED.
Correct	After the flood, Noah released the dove.
Wordy	My dress was pink and yellow in color. THE TERM *IN COLOR* IS WASTED; PINK AND YELLOW ARE OBVIOUSLY COLORS.
Correct	My dress was pink and yellow.

Other redundancies of this kind include:

short *in length*	*necessary* requirements
circle *around*	*and* etc.
still persist	combined *together*
many *in number*	now *at this time*

Wordy	The minivan that was parked behind the supermarket was smeared with mud.
Correct	The minivan parked behind the supermarket was smeared with mud.

Often, relative clauses can be trimmed. Note the following:

the judge *who was seated* on the bench

the judge on the bench

the man *who was* accused

the accused man

■ *Exercises*

Revise each of the following sentences for economy by eliminating redundancies or wasted words.

1. The secretary who sat behind the big mahogany desk of wood seemed to be efficient.

   _____

   _____

2. Most people find it difficult to express the emotion of tenderness toward other people.

   _____

   _____

3. The winner was timid and reticent about accepting the trophy.

   _____

   _____

4. Her coat, which is of the fur type, cost $2,000.

   _____

   _____

5. Worshiping ancestors is a venerable, sacred, old religious tradition among the Chinese.

   _____

   _____

6. My study of history leads me to believe that the Danes were a militant people who loved war.

   _____

   _____

7. Probably paying decent wages is usually the right thing to do in the majority of cases.

   _____

   _____

8. Workers who are employed shouldn't be allowed to collect food stamps.

   _____

   _____

9. If he wants to be president, he had better bring about new innovations in Congress.

   _____

   _____

10. Generally speaking, most of the time it is improper diet that causes gallstones.

    _____

    _____

11. All of the present clothing styles in our day and age reflect a taste for the bizarre.

    _____

    _____

12. At 10:00 P.M. at night a strange knock was heard.

    _____

    _____

13. The consensus of the majority in our class was that we should invite Dr. Boling as our keynote speaker.

    _____

    _____

14. The story dealt with a cruel murder and a tragic ending that was lamentable.

   _____

   _____

15. As a usual rule one should lock one's car while shopping.

   _____

   _____

16. There were three women who decided to volunteer for the job without being forced.

   _____

   _____

17. Neil Simon writes humorous comedies that really make you laugh.

   _____

   _____

18. If we don't cooperate together with the major world powers, a nuclear war could annihilate the world.

   _____

   _____

19. Palestinians and Arabs are very different in various ways.

   _____

   _____

20. In this day and age it is difficult to find a musician in the entire field of music who gets at people's hearts the way Charles Witt does.

   _____

   _____

■ *Self-Grading Exercise 16*

Revise each of the following sentences for economy by eliminating redundancies or wasted words. After completing the exercise, turn to the appendix for the answers. (There is more than one possible answer for each item.)

1. Charles Steinmetz was a man who pioneered in the field of electrical engineering.

   _____

   _____

2. Long-distance runners training for the Olympics run many miles a day, and they cover as many as 20 miles.

_____

_____

3. Each and every person who stood in line received a ticket.

_____

_____

4. Students today demonstrate poor writing skills for one simple reason: The reason is that they are never required to write.

_____

_____

5. My favorite poet is Emily Dickinson among all the women poets that I like best.

_____

_____

6. In the next chapter that follows we will look at and examine a theory held by Charles Darwin dealing with evolution.

_____

_____

7. In this modern world of today, it is difficult to keep up with the most recent and up-to-date advances in science.

_____

_____

8. Made of solid oak material and a rich brown in color, the table has lasted for over a hundred years of time.

_____

_____

9. One of John's most serious faults is the fact that he continuously apologizes for his errors.

_____

_____

10. The method they most often used to grade objective tests was that of using a Scantron machine.

_____

_____

11. One of the most exciting events of the trip was attending a secret burial ceremony never performed publicly.

   _____

   _____

12. Nevertheless, most reasonable judges are rational and do not judge defendants on the basis of feelings or emotions.

   _____

   _____

13. The pilot was in a terrible dilemma because a crosswind was blowing at right angles to his aircraft's line of flight.

   _____

   _____

14. All of the children who were observed by media reporters were tall in height.

   _____

   _____

15. The income from traffic fines is an important source of revenue for New York City.

   _____

   _____

Combining Sentences

The impact of an essay is lessened when its sentences are childishly short and loosely strung together. Here is an example:

> The newspaper recently contained an article. The article was about a man named Lewis Stafford. The man had passed some bogus checks. He was put in jail.

This passage would ring with more authority if its sentences were combined by subordinating the lesser ideas to the greater:

> The newspaper recently contained an article about Lewis Stafford, a man put in jail for passing bogus checks.

Subordination is the art of grammatical ranking. Faced with expressing a series of ideas in a single sentence, the writer arranges them in clauses and phrases that mirror their relative importance. In the preceding example, for instance, the main

sub

clause reports on the newspaper article about Lewis Stafford, and the subordinate clause mentions his jailing for passing bogus checks. The writer has therefore chosen to emphasize the article in the newspaper over the jailing for bad checks. If desired, the reverse emphasis could have been achieved with another subordinate construction:

> Lewis Stafford was put in jail for passing bogus checks, an event recently reported in the newspaper.

The ranking of one event over another through subordination depends entirely on which event the writer deems more important and wishes to emphasize.

Subordination is achieved by combining short sentences into a single, long sentence. This is done by turning main clauses into either phrases or dependent clauses.

Subordination by Phrase

For a definition of *phrase,* see page 559. The following are phrases:

singing in the rain	with its lovely rose garden
left alone with his friend	to lower his taxes

Note how pairs of sentences can be combined by turning one of the sentences into a phrase:

No subordination	The man left. He sang in the rain.
Subordination	The man left, singing in the rain.
No subordination	He was left alone with his friend. He confided his secret to his friend.
Subordination	Left alone with his friend, he confided his secret.
No subordination	Hoover Library stands as a monument to our city. It has a lovely rose garden.
Subordination	Hoover Library, with its lovely rose garden, stands as a monument to our city.
No subordination	He voted for Proposition 13. He did it to lower his taxes.
Subordination	To lower his taxes, he voted for Proposition 13.

Subordination by Dependent Clause

For a definition of *dependent clause,* see page 559. The following are dependent clauses:

although he was confronted with many alternatives

who have lived in the Orient

if the price of gasoline continues to rise

Notice how pairs of sentences can be combined by turning one of the sentences into a dependent clause:

No subordination	He was confronted with many alternatives. He refused to make a choice.
Subordination	Although he was confronted with many alternatives, he refused to make a choice.
No subordination	Many people have lived in Asia. They never learned to like Asian food.
Subordination	Many people who have lived in Asia never learned to like Asian food.
No subordination	The price of gasoline continues to rise. He will probably sell his car.
Subordination	If the price of gasoline continues to rise, he will probably sell his car.

Choosing the Right Subordinator

The word that introduces a dependent clause is called a *subordinator.* Your choice of subordinator will depend on the relationship you wish to establish among ideas. The following list classifies the various subordinators according to the logical relationship they create to the main clause:

Condition
if
provided that
in case
assuming that
unless
whether or not

Cause/Reason
because
since
considering that

Time
when
whenever
as long as
while
before
after
until, till
as soon as

Extent/Degree
although
inasmuch as
insofar as
to the extent that

Place
where
wherever

Noun Substitute
who
that
which
what
whoever
whom
whomever
whichever
whatever

(See also subordinating conjunctions, p. 570.)

Suppose you wish to combine the following two sentences:

> He promised to pay the rent.
> She needed the money.

Several options will be open to you, among them the following:

> He promised to pay the rent
>
> *because* she needed the money.   STRESSES CAUSE
>
> *as long as* she needed the money.   STRESSES TIME
>
> *insofar as* she needed the money.   STRESSES DEGREE
>
> *in case* she needed the money.   STRESSES CONDITION
>
> *to whoever* needed the money.   SUBSTITUTES A PRONOUN FOR A NOUN

Your choice of subordinator depends on the logic you use to link the two sentences.

■ *Exercises*

Combine the sentences in each of the following sets into a single sentence, using either dependent clauses or phrases. Try different subordinators and different combinations to see what logical effect is created.

1. a. The doctor was taking the patient's temperature.
   b. Suddenly a rock came crashing through the window.

2. a. In mid-July he was inspecting the dig.
   b. He was alerted by someone.
   c. Someone was moving along the northern edge of the plateau.

3. a. It was a bright day in May.
   b. The drums exploded.
   c. Two priests from the temple appeared.

4. a. The crowd groaned with disappointment.
   b. They had hoped to see a glamorous young girl.

5. a. Others planned the forthcoming battle.
   b. He remained alone in the shaded grove.
   c. He was meditating and praying to his god.
   d. He needed guidance from his god.

6. a. Members of the city council can ill afford to vote themselves additional fringe benefits.
   b. Their constituents mistrust them.

7. a. Alif was entirely wrong.
   b. He guessed that she was in love with Abdul.
   c. In fact, she was merely bedazzled by his brilliant lyrics.
   d. They reminded her of starry nights in Egypt.

8. a. The fraternity members all over campus carried banners.
   b. They marched back and forth tirelessly.
   c. Their signs called for an end to building nuclear reactors.

9. a. Something occurred to Madeline.
   b. Perhaps she could improve the situation.
   c. She could create an atmosphere of goodwill.

10. a. Give out these sample tubes of toothpaste.
    b. Give one to whoever asks for one.

11. a. Phil Brown regularly attends church.
    b. There he loves to hear the old hymns.
    c. He also loves to hear a rousing sermon.
    d. These make him feel purged.
    e. They give him a new lease on life.

12. a. The specific notes had faded from his memory.
    b. Yet a certain melody remained.
    c. It haunted him for the rest of his life.

13. a. Such facts cannot be ignored.
    b. We want to preserve the wilderness.

14. a. Those of us who are prisoners must face the grim truth.
    b. This truth is that even our spouses and lovers will leave us.
    c. We have shared the most tender and intimate moments with them.

15. a. The scientific establishment now believes that the earth was formed ten to fifteen billion years ago.
    b. It was formed after an explosion, or "big bang."
    c. This explosion set the universe in motion.

■ *Self-Grading Exercise 17*

Combine the sentences in each of the following sets into a single sentence, using either dependent clauses or phrases. Try different subordinators to see what logical effect is created. After completing the exercise, turn to the appendix for the answers. (There is more than one possible answer for each item.)

1. a. The medieval structure collapsed.
   b. Then the beginning of the modern mode of production started.

2. a. Quite a few years ago a stranger came in and bought our small valley.
   b. This was where the Sempervirens redwoods grew.
   c. At the time I was living in a little town.
   d. The little town was on the West Coast.

3. a. Writing skills can be improved.
   b. But English teachers will have to assign more writing than they now do.

4. a. We began to realize something.
   b. Resources in America are not limitless.
   c. We had thought they were.

5. a. We are an exuberant people.
   b. We are also careless and destructive.
   c. We make powerful weapons, such as the atomic bomb.
   d. We then use them to prove that they exist.

6. a. Uncountable buffalo were killed.
   b. The buffalo were stripped of their hides.
   c. They were left to rot.
   d. Thus a permanent food supply was destroyed.

7. a. He was a teacher.
   b. In that capacity he considered objections by students carefully.
   c. To him it was as if these objections had been made by colleagues.

8. a. Its roof was half torn away by wind.
   b. Its walls were blackened by fire.
   c. Its stone floors were covered with mud.
   d. This hotel looked like the ruins of a Gothic castle.

9. a. I was seventeen and extremely shy.
   b. My third-grade teacher came to visit us.

10. a. Television newscasters are victims of the rating game.
    b. They are hired and fired on the basis of how entertaining they make the news.
    c. The rating game is controlled by anti-intellectual viewers.

11. a. All four of my grandparents were unknown to one another.
    b. But they all arrived in America from the same county in Slovakia.
    c. They had experienced a severe famine.
    d. The famine was due to a potato crop failure.

12. a. Most people believed the earth was roughly six thousand years old.
    b. This idea was based on information in the Bible.
    c. It was accepted until the beginning of the nineteenth century.
    d. At that time geologists and naturalists began to suspect something.
    e. What they suspected was that the earth must have existed for a much longer period of time.

13. a. He drove along the highway like a haunted man.
    b. He was stopped by the police.

14. a. The early Incas did not have the wheel.
    b. Their architectural achievements were spectacular.

15. a. Goethe influenced Thomas Mann.
    b. We can surmise that Mann's *Dr. Faustus* is similar to Goethe's *Faust*.
    c. Both works deal with the theme of the demonic.

Errors in Punctuation

Punctuation errors occur with the omission or misuse of one of the following marks:

period	.	dash	—	parentheses	( )
comma	,	question mark	?	quotation marks	" "
semicolon	;	exclamation point	!	italics	___
colon	:	apostrophe	'	hyphen	-

P

The function of punctuation marks is to separate words and phrases within a sentence according to their meanings.

Frequently, meaning may be misinterpreted unless a punctuation mark is provided. Consider the following:

After we had finished the essays were read out loud.

The sentence must be reread with a pause inserted after *finished:*

After we had finished, the essays were read out loud.

The key to effective punctuation is to learn what each punctuation mark means and where it must be used.

The Period .

Periods are used after declarative or mildly imperative sentences, indirect questions, and abbreviations. (See also run-together sentences, p. 575.) Use an ellipsis—three spaced periods (. . .)—to indicate an omission from quoted material.

Declarative	We followed Mr. Smith upstairs to the conductor's room.
Imperative	Visit Old Amsterdam while you are in Holland.
Indirect question	The child asked if it was all right to pick an apple.
Abbreviation	Since we had so little money, we stayed at the Y.M.C.A.
Ellipses	Now is the time for all . . . to come to the aid of their country. (good men)

Current usage permits the omission of the period after these and other abbreviations: TV, CIA, FBI, UN, NBC, USN, URL. If in doubt whether to omit the period after an abbreviation, consult a dictionary.

The Comma ,

The comma is used and misused more than any other punctuation mark. (See also comma splice, p. 574.) A writer of factual prose must learn to master the comma.

Although it is sometimes useful to equate commas with pauses, it is safer to follow these simple rules:

1. Use commas to set off phrases or clauses that interrupt the flow of a sentence or that are not essential to the meaning of a sentence. In this use, the commas sometimes function as the equivalent of parentheses:
   a. Tatyana Grosman, as her first name suggests, is Russian by birth.
   b. Ms. Jones, although charming in every way, held doggedly to her point.
   c. My father, who is a banker, lives in New York.

2. Use a comma after a long introductory phrase or clause:
   a. Near the grove at the top of his block, someone was having a party.
   b. Because I meant my remark as a compliment, I was surprised when my boss became angry.

3. Use a comma to separate the main clause from a long clause or phrase that follows it, if the two are separated by a pause or break:
   a. Certainly no one has tried harder than Jane, although many of her ideas have proved to be disastrous when they have been put into practice.
   b. He awakened something new in me, a devotion I didn't know I was capable of.

4. Use a comma to separate long independent clauses joined by *and, but, or, for, yet, nor, so*:
   a. The tunnel beside the house was very dark, but after school George used it as his imaginary fortress.
   b. If he uses three or four cans of balls, then that's it, and I don't want him to come to me begging for more.

5. Use commas to separate items in a series:
   a. I felt tired, cold, and discouraged.
   b. He raised his head, closed his eyes, and let out a deep moan.

   An adjective that is essential to a noun is not set off from other adjectives with a comma:

   My aunt is giving away some unusual white elephants, including a gigantic Chinese screen, several old Tiffany lamps, and a cracked ironstone platter.

6. Use commas after words of address:
   a. Sir, that is not what I meant.
   b. Do you recall that night, Linda?

7. Use commas to set off *yes* and *no:*
   a. Yes, the flight leaves at midnight.
   b. No, the letter has not arrived yet.

8. Use commas to set off dates and places:
   a. Miami, Florida, is humid in the summer.
   b. November 19, 1929, is my birthday.
   c. They live on 41 Parkwood Drive, Sacramento, California.

9. Use a comma to introduce a quotation:
    a. Patrick Henry said, "Give me liberty or give me death!"
    b. The thief retorted, "You don't need the money."
10. Use commas to set off titles and degrees from preceding names:
    a. John Lawson, Jr., now runs the bank.
    b. Henry Knittle, M.D.
    c. Mark Hamilton, Ph.D.

The Semicolon ;

The semicolon has three basic uses.

1. The semicolon is used to connect independent clauses that are so closely associated in meaning that they do not need to be separate sentences:
    a. He was a wonderful chap; we all loved him dearly.
    b. Loraine left all her money to her stepson; in this respect, she showed considerable generosity.
2. A semicolon may be used to connect independent clauses when the second clause begins with a conjunctive adverb (for a list of conjunctive adverbs, see p. 568):
    a. Joe was not a candidate; nevertheless, the gang chose him as its captain.
    b. Following her to the kitchen, I found that she had made two sand-wiches; however, I was not hungry, so I did not eat.

    If the conjunctive adverb is not the first word in the second clause, the punctuation is as follows:

    The fever had subsided; my mother felt, nevertheless, that a doctor should be called.

3. The semicolon is used to separate phrases or clauses in a series when commas appear within any one of those phrases or clauses:
    a. Her estate was divided as follows: Books, diaries, and notebooks went to her agent; jewelry, furs, and clothes went to her sister; and everything else went to charity.
    b. For three days we followed a strict diet: eggs, grapefruit, and coffee on the first day; lamb chops, toast, and tomatoes on the second day; and fruit with cottage cheese on the third day.

The Colon :

Do not confuse the colon with the semicolon. Colons are used in the following cases:

1. Use colons to introduce lengthy material or lists:
    a. The following quotation from Robert Frost will support my view:
    b. Here is a list of all the camping equipment necessary to climb Mt. Wilson:
    c. Literature can be divided into four types: short story, drama, poetry, and novel.

2. Use a colon after the salutation of a formal letter, between the title and subtitle of a literary work, between a chapter and verse of the Bible, and between hours and minutes in time:
   a. Dear Ms. Landeen:
   b. The Ethnic Cult: New Fashion Trends
   c. I Corinthians 3:16
   d. 10:30 A.M.

The Dash —

To type a dash, use two hyphens without spacing before, between, or after. To write a dash, make an unbroken line the length of two hyphens.

1. Use a dash to indicate a sudden break in thought.
   a. The clerk's illiteracy, his lack of judgment, his poor writing skills—they all added up until the company fired him.
   b. The secret of the recipe is—oh, but I promised not to tell.
2. Use dashes to set off parenthetical material that needs to be emphasized:
   a. Every house in the neighborhood—from Kenneth Road to Russel Drive—was solicited.
   b. She stood there—tall, proud, and unrelenting—daring her accusers to speak.

The Question Mark ?

Use a question mark after a direct question. Do not use it when the question is indirect.

Direct	He asked her, "Have you had lunch?"
Indirect	He asked her if she had had lunch.
Direct	Who am I? Where am I going? Why am I here?

Do not follow a question mark with a comma or a period:

| Wrong | "When will you leave?," he asked. |
| Correct | "When will you leave?" he asked. |

The Exclamation Point !

An exclamation point should be used only to express surprise, disbelief, anger, or other strong emotions:

1. What an adorable baby!
2. What a rat! He couldn't have been that evil!
3. "Jinxed, by God!"

The Apostrophe '

An apostrophe is used to show possession: *John's book* rather than *the book of John.* It is also used to form contractions (*can't, don't*) and certain plurals.

1. Use an apostrophe and an *s* to indicate possession for singular nouns and plural nouns that don't end with *s*. Only the apostrophe is added to plural nouns ending in *s*.
    a. the attitude of the student
        the student's attitude
    b. the party of the girls
        the girls' party
    c. the home of the children
        the children's home
        A possessive pronoun does not require an apostrophe: *the book is theirs,* not *the book is their's.*
        For *inanimate* objects, *of* is preferable to an apostrophe: *The arm of the chair,* not *the chair's arm.*

2. Use an apostrophe to indicate an omission or abbreviation:
    a. He can't (cannot) make it.
    b. It's (it is) a perfect day.
    c. He graduated in '08.
        Caution: Place the apostrophe exactly where the omission occurs: *isn't, doesn't*—not *is'nt, doe'snt.*

3. Use an apostrophe to form the plural of a letter, symbol, or word used as a word:
    a. The English often do not pronounce their *h*'s, and they place *r*'s at the end of certain words.
    b. Instead of writing *and*'s, you can write &'s.

4. An apostrophe is *not* needed for the plurals of a numeral:
    a. Rock groups flourished during the 1960s.
    b. The temperature was in the 90s.

Parentheses ( )

Parentheses always come in pairs. Use parentheses to enclose numbers identifying items in a list, examples, and incidental material:

1. To make good tennis volleys, you must follow three rules: (1) Use a punching motion with your racket, (2) volley off your front leg, and (3) get your body sideways to the flight of the oncoming ball.

2. The big stars of Hollywood's glamor days (Greta Garbo, Clark Gable, Marilyn Monroe) exuded an aura that was bigger than life.

3. Emily Dickinson (often called "the Belle of Amherst") lived a secluded life.

Quotation Marks " "

Quotation marks always come in pairs, with the final set indicating the end of the quotation. The most common use of quotation marks is to indicate the exact spoken or written words of another person. There are several other uses of quotation marks as well.

1. Use quotation marks to enclose the words of someone else:
    a. Montesquieu said, "The first motive which ought to impel us to study is the desire to augment the excellence of our nature, and to render an intelligent being yet more intelligent."
    b. With characteristic bluntness she turned to him and asked, "Are you as old as you look?"

    If the passage being quoted is longer than five lines, indent it but do not use quotation marks:
    The *Los Angeles Times* indicated that actress Estelle Winwood was old but still remarkably spry:

    > She plays bridge for six hours a night, smokes four packs of cigarettes a day, and at 93 Estelle Winwood is the oldest active member on the rolls of the Screen Actors' Guild.

    > Although she professes to be through with acting, her close friends don't believe her. Only recently she joined the distinguished company of Columbia Pictures' "Murder by Death," Neil Simon's spoof of mystery films. And she held her own with the likes of Alec Guinness, Peter Sellers, Maggie Smith, Peter Falk, David Niven, and Nancy Walker.

2. A quotation within a quotation is enclosed by single quotation marks:

    > According to Jefferson's biographer, "The celebrated equanimity of his temper, crystallized in his pronouncement 'Peace is our passion,' extended to his private as well as his public life; his daughter Martha described how he lost his temper in her presence only two times in his life."
    >
    > —Fawn M. Brodie, *Thomas Jefferson*

3. Use quotation marks for titles of songs, episodes of TV programs, and short literary works (essays, articles, short stories, or poems):
    a. My favorite Beatles song is "Eleanor Rigby."   SONG
    b. "The Guest" is a story written by Camus.   SHORT STORY
    c. "Master of My Own Domain" is my favorite episode of *Seinfeld*.   TV EPISODE

4. Use quotation marks for words used in a special way, for instance, to show irony or to indicate that a word is slang:
    a. They killed her out of "mercy."   THE AUTHOR WANTS THE READER TO KNOW THAT IT WAS NOT GENUINE MERCY.
    b. My mother used to refer to the woman down the street as a "floozy."   SLANG

When using other marks of punctuation with quoted words, follow the proper conventions.

1. Place a comma inside the quotation mark. Place a period inside the quotation mark if the quotation ends the sentence.

    a. "Very well," he said, "let's go to the bank."

    If the quotation does not end a sentence but is followed by parenthetical material such as a citation, place the period after it.

    b. "The qualities that make a political leader were less obvious in Lenin than in Gladstone" (p. 451).

2. Place a colon or semicolon outside quotation marks:

    a. He reassured me, "You're a fine boy"; yet, I didn't believe him.

    b. I remember only the following words from Michael Novak's essay "White Ethnic": "Growing up in America has been an assault upon my sense of worthiness."

3. Place a question mark or exclamation point inside quotation marks when they apply to the quoted matter, but outside when they do not:

    a. "Who are the eminent?" he asked bitterly.   THE QUOTED MATTER IS ITSELF A QUESTION.

    b. What do you mean when you describe him as "eminent"?   THE ENTIRE SENTENCE IS A QUESTION; THE QUOTED MATTER IS NOT.

    c. In the movie everyone chants, "I'm mad as hell and I won't take it anymore!"   THE QUOTED MATTER IS ITSELF AN EXCLAMATION.

    d. For heaven's sake, stop calling me "Big Boy"!   THE ENTIRE SENTENCE IS AN EXCLAMATION.

Italics _____

In longhand or typewritten material, italics are indicated by underlining; in print, italicized words are slanted.

1. Use italics for titles of books, magazines, newspapers, TV shows, movies, plays, artwork, and other long works:

    a. Most college students are required to read *Great Expectations* or *Oliver Twist*.

    b. *Harper's Bazaar* is a magazine about fashion.

    c. Although I live in California, I subscribe to the *Wall Street Journal* because it is an excellent newspaper.

    d. Mozart's *Magic Flute* is a long opera.

2. Use italics for foreign words:

    a. Everyone uses the word *détente*.

    b. I found her dress *très chic*.

    c. He gave an *apologia pro vita sua*.

3. Use italics for words, letters, and figures spoken of as such:
    a. Often the word *fortuitous* is misused.
    b. In the word *knight,* only *n, i,* and *t* are actually pronounced.
    c. In the Bible, the number *7* represents perfection.

The Hyphen -

1. Use a hyphen for a syllable break at the end of a line:
    a. sac-ri-fi-cial
    b. nu-tri-tious
    c. lib-er-al

    If in doubt about where to break a word, check a dictionary.

2. Use hyphens in some compound words:
    a. brother-in-law
    b. hanky-panky
    c. self-determination
    d. vice-president (some sources omit the hyphen)
    e. two-thirds

3. Use hyphens in compound modifiers:
    a. well-known movie
    b. blond-haired, blue-eyed baby
    c. low-grade infection

4. The hyphen is omitted when the first word of the compound modifier is an adverb ending in *ly* or an adjective ending in *ish* or when the compound modifier follows the noun:
    a. a deceptively sweet person
    b. a plainly good meal
    c. a bluish green material
    d. is well liked

■ *Exercises*

In the following sentences, insert commas where they are needed. If the sentence is correct, write *C* in the space provided.

1. Professor Grover as all of his students agree is one of the most exciting history teachers on campus.   _____

2. Madam I beg to differ with you; that is my purse.   _____

3. We were asked to check with Mr. Weaver our head custodian.   _____

4. Because the water was murky cold and swift we did not go swimming.   _____

5. In denouncing the hypocritical Truman encouraged honest dealings.   _____

6. Let's not give up until everyone agrees with us.   _____

7. Because they belong to the neighborhood they should pay for part of the damage.   _____

8. Address your letter to Ms. Margerie Freedman 320 N. Lincoln Blvd. Reading Massachusetts.   _____

9. So many memories are connected with the home of my grandparents a big red brick mansion surrounded by a white picket fence.   _____

10. Twice the doctor asked "Have you ever had laryngitis before?"   _____

11. Relaxed and happy Jim ignored the people who were angered by his decision.   _____

12. July 4 1776 is an important date for patriotic Americans.   _____

13. Glistening like a diamond in the sun the lake beckoned us.   _____

14. Readers of the *Times* however were not all equally impressed with the editorial on abortions.   _____

15. All together some ten thousand people filled out the questionnaire.   _____

16. From the mountains, from the prairies, and from numerous villages came the good news.   _____

17. "My most exquisite lady" he said gallantly "you deserve the Taj Mahal."   _____

18. One of her sisters lives in Chicago; the other, in New York.   _____

19. Pat Moynihan who was once the U.S. ambassador to the United Nations was also a popular lecturer.   _____

20. Well Mary are you satisfied with the effect of your crass remark?   _____

21. The laboratory technician has finished the gold tooth hasn't he?   _____

22. Anyone who feels that this is a bad law should write to his representative.   _____

23. Outside a spectacular rainbow arched across the deep blue sky.   _____

24. We walk down this street unafraid, not even thinking of danger.   _____

25. Now his grandparents live in a condominium in Florida where they have no yard.   _____

Punctuate the following sentences so that they read easily and clearly.

1. Shakespeare wrote many plays including the famous *Hamlet*

2. Listen he said if you want we can go to a movie any movie

3. The word renaissance has several pronunciations

4. We can have the party at Johns cabin or the Fieldings apartment

5. Its overtaxed heart failing the race horse collapsed before everyones eyes

6. The most tragic poem I can imagine is Keats Ode to Melancholy

7. Get off my lawn you swine

8. The big bands of the 40s still sell millions of records

9. Last years flowers have wilted they have withered and died

10. As far as the committee is concerned you have lost the grant nevertheless you are to take the exam one more time

11. Just as the situation appeared hopeless a surprising thing happened A number of leading American artists became interested in making lithographic prints

12. Then in the summer of 1976 the counterrevolutionary army took over

13. Do you know the difference between the verbs compose and comprise

14. Wonderful Here comes the beer Cheers

15. He entitled his paper June Wayne Profile of a California Artist

16. He lived a stones throw from Twin Lakes

17. This is what Bertrand Russell says Science from the dawn of history and probably longer has been intimately associated with war

18. Bertrand Russell has said that Science has been intimately associated with war (Refer to item 17.)

19. He received his PhD at 9 am on Sunday June 6

20. My friend asked me Did you read Bill Shirleys article Worlds First Bionic Swim Team published in the sports section of the Los Angeles Times

21. The rule is that you must sign up two days in advance. See Section 25 paragraph 2

22. Dear Sir this is in answer to your letter of May 13

23. A slight tinge of embarrassment or was it pleasure crept across his face

24. The first day we studied later in the week however we relaxed

25. The babies carriages were broken

■ *Self-Grading Exercise 18*

In the following sentences, insert commas where they are needed. If the sentence is correct, write *C* in the space provided. After completing the exercise, turn to the appendix for the correct answers.

1. His daughter a leader among the women had spared her father and set him afloat on the sea in a hollow chest.   _____

2. As for me already old age is my companion.   _____

3. He spoke slowly believing in his heart that he was telling the truth.   _____

4. Great dangers lay ahead and some of the soldiers paid with their lives for drinking so heavily. _____

5. Gently he answered "I have come to my home to recover the ancient honor of my house." _____

6. These fierce women steadfastly refused to surrender to the foreign invaders. _____

7. They scorned them terrorized them and robbed them. _____

8. He insisted that he had been saved by the woman in white who had brought him to Venice an exotic city. _____

9. On November 19 1929 a star bright and luminous shot across the sky. _____

10. Let the taxpayers who reside in the county pay for a new road sign at the intersection of Broadway and Main Street. _____

11. The football players however did not care to linger in such a gloomy narrow place. _____

12. Acheron the river of woe pours into Cocytus the river of lamentation. _____

13. Sir please accept my sincere apologies for the inconvenience this has caused you. _____

14. Because hell is merely an invention of guilty minds why believe in it? _____

15. David Cotton Jr. is doing some important research in the field of high-risk pregnancies. _____

16. On his way to ask his adviser a question about a calculus course Robert arrived at an automatic gate where he blew out a tire causing his Fiat to skid into another car. _____

17. He felt himself degraded by this servile attitude and vowed revenge. _____

18. They told him "Daylight is sweet to the old." _____

19. Yes Chicago Illinois can be windy and freezing cold in the winter. _____

20. Above some perfume bottles filled with exotic bath oils decorated the wall shelves. _____

■ *Self-Grading Exercise 19*

In each of the following sentences, insert all needed marks of punctuation, including italics. Be careful to place quotation marks in proper relation to other marks of punctuation. After completing the exercise, turn to the appendix for the correct answers.

1. According to Mythology a book by Edith Hamilton the Greeks unlike the Egyptians made their gods in their own image

2. Is this an exaggerated view It hardly seems so nevertheless many opponents of the measure dismiss it as unmenschlich

3. The search for a way to stop this vicious cycle has taxed the best minds among the following groups city council members educators and urban planners

4. Let me pose this question Could you love passionately if you knew you would never die

5. Who interrupted me by saying Thats enough for today

6. Dear Mr. Forsythe This is in reply to your request of May 16 2008

7. From now on please cross your t s and dot your i s

8. This is how we propose to assign the various duties The men will scrub the floors ceilings and walls the women will cook mend and garden the children will run errands clean up the yard and pick vegetables

9. But what happens when the national organizations themselves the schools the unions the federal government become victims of a technological culture

10. With his fifth grade education he wrote a marvelous poem entitled Languid Tears

11. The New Yorker is read mostly by people with keen literary interests

12. Students often find it difficult to distinguish between the words imply and infer in fact most people confuse their meanings

13. We currently reside at 451 Bellefontaine Drive Pasadena California

14. One of the delegates was a vegetarian the other was restricted to kosher foods

15. He yelled angrily Get out of my yard

16. Vans boats and campers are not allowed see Regulation #13

17. Have you heard the question asked What can the police department do against the pitiless onslaught of criminal violence

18. This my friends is how I think we can help the world in a time of tyranny by fighting for freedom

19. The age was an age of éclaircissement and self determination

20. You have arrived at your resting place she murmured softly seek no further

21. Inside the antique armoire dominated the room

22. Picture if you please an open space where twenty acrobats stand each locking hands with two different partners then imagine ten acrobats standing on the shoulders of these twenty.

Errors in Capitalization

Capitalization errors result when accepted conventions of capitalizing are not followed. Commonly capitalized are words at the beginning of a sentence and the pronoun *I*. Students tend to ignore rules of capitalization. The most important rules are given here.

cap

1. Capitalize all proper names. The following belong to the group of proper names:
   a. specific persons, places, and things, but not their general classes (*Jefferson, Grand Junction, Eiffel Tower, Harvard University,* and *Hyde Park* are capitalized, but *people, cities, towers, universities,* and *parks* are not)
   b. organizations and institutions (*Rotary Club, Pentagon*)
   c. historical periods and events (*Middle Ages, World War II*)
   d. members of national, political, racial, and religious groups (*Mason, Republican, African American, Methodist*)
   e. special dates on the calendar (*Veterans' Day*), days (*Wednesday*), months (*July*)
   f. religions (*Islam, Christianity, Judaism, Methodism*) but *not* ideologies (*communism, socialism, atheism*)
   g. *Freshman, sophomore, junior,* and *senior* are not capitalized unless associated with a specific event (*The Junior Prom will take place next Saturday.*)

2. In the titles of literary works, capitalize all words except articles, conjunctions, and prepositions: *All the King's Men,* "Who Cares About English Usage?" Conjunctions and prepositions of five letters or more are capitalized: "The Man Without a Country."

3. Capitalize titles associated with proper names: *Mrs. Johnson, Ms. Mary Hanley, Judge Garcia, James R. Griedley, M.D., Henry Hadley, Jr.*

4. The title of a relative is capitalized when it is not preceded by an article, when it is followed by a name, or in direct address:
   a. I gave the keys to Grandmother.
   b. Grandmother Sitwell
   c. Could you help me, Grandmother?
   d. I was deeply influenced by my grandmother.

5. Unless a title is official, it is not capitalized:
   a. Peter Ferraro, President of the Valley National Bank
   b. Peter Ferraro is president of a bank.
   c. We shall appeal to the president (the top executive).

6. Capitalize specific courses offered in school but not general subjects, unless they contain proper names:
   a. I enrolled in Biology 120.
   b. I am taking biology.
   c. I failed Intermediate French.

Avoid needless capitals. For instance, the seasons (*spring, summer, autumn, winter*) are not capitalized unless they are personified, as in poetry (*Where are the songs of Spring?*). *North, south, east,* and *west* are not capitalized unless they are part of an accepted name of a special region (*He is the fastest gun in the West*).

Note that abbreviations are capitalized or not capitalized according to the style of the unabbreviated version: *m.p.h. (miles per hour), M.P. (Member of Parliament), GPO (Government Printing Office), Cong. (Congress), pseud. (pseudonym).*

■ *Exercises*

In each of the following sentences, underline the letters that should be capitalized or made lowercase. If the sentence is correct, write *C* in the space at the right.

1. Our memorial day picnic was canceled because of rain. _____
2. The headline read: "U.S. agent Fired in Investigation of Missing Ammunition." _____
3. Any mayor of a city as large as Chicago should be on good terms with the President of the United States. _____
4. The democrats will doubtless hold their convention at the cow palace in san francisco. _____
5. The tennis courts at Nibley park are always busy. _____
6. If you have to take a psychology course, take psychology 101 from Dr. Pearson, a graduate of harvard. _____
7. There is something elegant about the name "Tyrone Kelly, III, esq." _____
8. Until easter of 1949, they lived in a big, white georgian home. _____
9. During the second world war, Switzerland remained neutral. _____
10. I intend to exchange my capri for a toyota. _____
11. Socrates, the famous Greek philosopher, used Dialogue as a teaching method. _____
12. Some Socialists have joined the Republican Party. _____
13. She said, "the ticket entitles you to spend a night at the Holiday inn in Las Vegas." _____
14. The bible was not fully canonized until the council of Trent. _____

Write a brief sentence in which you use correctly each of the following words.

1. street   _____
2. Street   _____
3. Democratic   _____

4. democratic   _____

5. academy   _____

6. Academy   _____

7. biology   _____

8. Biology   _____

9. memorial   _____

10. Memorial   _____

11. father   _____

12. Father   _____

13. senior   _____

14. Senior   _____

15. against   _____

16. Against   _____

17. company   _____

18. Company   _____

■ *Self-Grading Exercise 20*

In each of the following sentences, underline the letters that should be capitalized or made lowercase. If the sentence is correct, write *C* in the space at the right. After completing the exercise, turn to the appendix for the correct answers.

1. Balloting at both the democratic and republican conventions is by states.   _____

2. He had taken many history courses, but none fascinated him more than introduction to western civilization.   _____

3. Delta Delta Delta, the most active sorority, invited speakers from such organizations as daughters of the American revolution, national organization of Women, and the Sierra club.   _____

4. The subject of the lecture was "The Treasures Of The Nile."   _____

5. John Stuart Mill understood Calculus and could read greek when he was a child.   _____

6. Exodus is the second book of the pentateuch.   _____

7. One of his dreams was to see Mt. Everest.   _____

8. The war of the Triple Alliance was fought between Paraguay on one side and an Alliance of Argentina, brazil, and Uruguay on the other.   _____

9. That is the best photograph ever taken of uncle Charlie.   _____

10. As a capable and tough City attorney, he took action against one of Hollywood's swingers clubs, a place called Socrates' retreat.   _____

11. John toyed with two ideas: joining the peace corps or working without pay for César Chávez's United farm workers of America.   _____

12. Ex-Assemblyman Waldie never ran for Office after the Summer of 1974.   _____

13. Today he is chairman of the Federal Mine Safety and Health Review Commission.   _____

14. The residents of Mammoth Lakes, a mountain resort, are proud of the view of the minarets, a ragged mountain range, seen from highway 395 as one approaches the resort.   _____

15. One of my favorite books is a novel entitled *in the heart of a fool.*   _____

16. Some women have romantic ideas about returning to feudalism, with knights in shining armor and ladies adhering to the manners of the Middle Ages.   _____

17. One of the highest mountain systems in the world is the Hindu Kush, extending 500 miles from north Pakistan into northeast Afghanistan.   _____

18. William S. Levey, S.J., is the vice president of an important men's club.   _____

19. I failed Organic Chemistry 101, but I passed french.   _____

20. A traditional American holiday is Thanksgiving day.   _____

Errors in Spelling

sp

Misspelling occurs when a word is written differently from the way it is listed in the dictionary (*recieve* instead of *receive*) or when the wrong word is used (*loose* instead of *lose*). The following list* of most commonly misspelled words will help weak spellers. Letters in italics are those that cause the most difficulty. For help in selecting the correct word, refer to the Glossary of Word Choice (pp. 602–608).

Commonly Misspelled Words

1. acco*mm*odate	4. al*l*right	7. arg*um*ent	10. bel*ie*ve
2. achi*e*vement	5. am*o*ng	8. arg*u*ing	11. ben*e*ficial
3. acquire	6. ap*p*arent	9. bel*ie*f	12. ben*efit*ed

*From Thomas Clark Pollock, "Spelling Report," *College English*, 16 (November 1954), 102–109.

13. category	35. interest	57. precede	79. separate
14. coming	36. its (it's)	58. prejudice	80. separation
15. comparative	37. led	59. prepare	81. shining
16. conscious	38. lose	60. prevalent	82. similar
17. controversy	39. losing	61. principal	83. studying
18. controversial	40. marriage	62. principle	84. succeed
19. definitely	41. mere	63. privilege	85. succession
20. definition	42. necessary	64. probably	86. surprise
21. define	43. occasion	65. proceed	87. technique
22. describe	44. occurred	66. procedure	88. than
23. description	45. occurring	67. professor	89. then
24. disastrous	46. occurrence	68. profession	90. their
25. effect	47. opinion	69. prominent	91. there
26. embarrass	48. opportunity	70. pursue	92. they're
27. environment	49. paid	71. quiet	93. thorough
28. exaggerate	50. particular	72. receive	94. to (too, two)
29. existence	51. performance	73. receiving	95. transferred
30. existent	52. personal	74. recommend	96. unnecessary
31. experience	53. personnel	75. referring	97. villain
32. explanation	54. possession	76. repetition	98. woman
33. fascinate	55. possible	77. rhythm	99. write
34. height	56. practical	78. sense	100. writing

■ *Exercises*

1. Some of the words you commonly misspell may not appear on either list supplied in this section of the *Handbook*. If not, compile your own list of troublesome words. First, write the word correctly. Then, note your particular difficulty with it:

   bridle   I always spell it bri*dal*, as if it came from *bride*.

   perspiration   I must be sure to pronounce it *per*, not *pre*.

2. Using the dictionary as a guide, study the preceding list of one hundred words until you know (a) what each word means, (b) how it is pronounced, and (c) how it is spelled. Study the words in groups of twenty.

3. In each of the following groups of three, choose the misspelled word and write it correctly in the space provided. Check your answers in the dictionary.

   a. existance, describe, personal   _____

   b. paid, particular, opportunity   _____

   c. benificial, apparent, experience   _____

   d. controversy, concious, occurred   _____

e. preformance, similar, succeed _____

f. probably, marriage, predjudice _____

g. profession, persue, separate _____

h. catagory, paid, disastrous _____

i. effect, disasterous, mere _____

j. preceed, proceed, procedure _____

k. embarrass, exaggerate, envirement _____

l. prevailent, probably, existent _____

m. coming, heighth, professor _____

n. define, fascinate, posession _____

o. repetition, quiet, recieve _____

■ *Self-Grading Exercise 21*

Identify the misspelled word in each of the following sentences, and spell it correctly in the space provided. After completing the exercise, turn to the appendix for the correct answers.

1. After making an appointment with the manager of the firm, he demanded to see his personal file. _____

2. When lovers are seperated for long periods of time, their ardor cools. _____

3. While under the water, he was conscience of the fact that life is fleeting and evanescent. _____

4. Without exageration, he sounded like a genius. _____

5. To him she was a shinning star, a brilliant meteor from heaven. _____

6. Every person on board admitted that it was a most unusual occurrance. _____

7. Sons often feel pressured to enter the same proffessions pursued by their fathers. _____

8. They accused him of being predjudice and reactionary. _____

9. One of the serious concerns of the younger generation is a clean enviroment. _____

10. The mystery novel ends without a clear explenation of how the murder took place. _____

11. The heighth of the building was out of proportion to its width. _____

12. The room was to small for two people. _____

13. The hero was wearing light apparel whereas the villian
    was wearing black. _____

14. One man or women with good typing skills could get that
    manuscript finished in no time. _____

15. They wore similer clothes, but their facial characteristics
    were very different. _____

16. According to the committee, it was quite alright for the men
    to smoke. _____

17. They were lead to believe that he was a victim of his
    own enthusiasm. _____

18. I did not care whether or not I received the money back;
    it was simply a matter of principal. _____

19. Because of blustering winds she kept loosing her hat. _____

20. Just sit quietly and listen to the rythm of your heartbeats. _____

Appendix

Answers to Self-Grading Exercises

The answer keys that follow correspond in number to the Self-Grading Exercises found in Part V.

Self-Grading Exercise 1

1. <u>Libraries</u> <u>contain</u> the wisdom of civilization.
2. In the district of Wymar, <u>burglars</u> <u>were ransacking</u> the stores.
3. In Hemingway's novels <u>matadors</u> <u>are</u> highly respected.
4. A clear <u>conscience</u> <u>is</u> the best sleeping pill.
5. The silver gray <u>vest</u> <u>suited</u> his quiet personality.
6. Most middle-class <u>homes</u> in the Southwest <u>are built</u> with air-conditioning.
7. The outdoor <u>markets</u> in Europe <u>attract</u> numerous tourists.
8. Noise <u>pollution</u> in towns and cities <u>blots</u> out the sounds and silences of the outdoor world.
9. A <u>cup</u> of good tea or coffee <u>must be brought</u> to me early each morning.
10. <u>I</u> <u>wish</u> to describe two kinds of tours available.

Self-Grading Exercise 2

1. Television | has contributed to the decline of reading skills.
2. Incensed by their rudeness, the senator | left.
3. Michelangelo's work | continues to attract admirers all over the world.
4. Wars | go on endlessly.
5. Divorce | affects children most of all.
6. Professional tennis | has become big business in the United States.
7. Most people | insist on paying their bills on time.
8. Within five weeks one hundred AIDS victims | had been claimed.
9. Spain | is no longer a strong world power.
10. Many areas of Saudi Arabia | have experienced droughts.

Self-Grading Exercise 3

1. I	5. D	9. D	13. P	17. D
2. I	6. I	10. D	14. I	18. P
3. P	7. P	11. I	15. D	19. I
4. I	8. I	12. I	16. I	20. P

Self-Grading Exercise 4

1. We asked him if he would be willing to do it alone.
2. Are you usually aware of the problems of older people?
3. Sound the alarm! Then run for your life!
4. I am as angry as a cornered cat.
5. Do you mean to tell me that all of the money simply disappeared?
6. They inquired as to whether or not we would accompany the performers.
7. Heavens! What a way to get attention!
8. Go straight down the aisle and interrupt his conversation.
9. Would you be so kind as to direct me to the British Museum?
10. Whew! What a terrible odor!

Self-Grading Exercise 5

1. A	5. C	9. D	13. B	17. A
2. B	6. C	10. A	14. D	18. C
3. C	7. A	11. B	15. A	19. A
4. D	8. D	12. A	16. B	20. C

Self-Grading Exercise 6

1. noun
2. verb
3. adjective
4. preposition
5. adverb
6. verb
7. coordinating conjunction
8. preposition
9. adjective
10. verb
11. pronoun
12. adverb
13. noun (verbal)
14. pronoun
15. noun
16. coordinating conjunction
17. conjunctive adverb
18. article
19. adverb
20. adjective
21. preposition
22. verb
23. subordinating conjunction
24. verb
25. subordinating conjunction (relative pronoun)
26. verb
27. preposition
28. noun
29. adverb
30. verb
31. article
32. preposition
33. noun
34. adverb (subordinating conjunction)
35. pronoun
36. verb
37. noun
38. verb
39. verb
40. adverb

Self-Grading Exercise 7

1. Frag	5. RT	9. C	13. C	17. C
2. C	6. C	10. Frag	14. C	18. C
3. CS	7. Frag	11. CS	15. Frag	19. RT
4. Frag	8. C	12. CS	16. CS	20. CS

Self-Grading Exercise 8

1. makes	6. C	11. are	16. is
2. are	7. is	12. C	17. watches
3. has	8. are	13. Do	18. C
4. C	9. require	14. C	19. sit
5. causes	10. C	15. is	20. appeals

Self-Grading Exercise 9

1. him	6. he and I	11. you or me	16. her
2. whoever	7. my	12. whomever	17. We
3. who	8. its	13. whom	18. whoever
4. he or she	9. Their	14. whom	19. I
5. me	10. whom	15. her	20. Whom

Self-Grading Exercise 10

1. As they listened to the music, Sir Peregrine remarked about the success of the races while his wife dreamed about love.   B

2. A person must accept the fact that he or she can't always win.   A

3. All secretaries who worked in the office were asked to give their opinions and to say how they felt.   A

4. The airline attendants wondered why so many passengers were standing in the aisle and who had given them permission to leave their seats.   D

5. If I were wealthy and if I were living in Washington, D.C., I'd tell the Senate a thing or two.   C

6. He pored over all of his notes and checked out many library books.   E

7. Mrs. Olson walks into strangers' kitchens and tells them how to make coffee.   E

8. The professor informed us that the test would be given and asked if we were ready.   B

9. First the insane man quoted lines from Richard Lovelace; then he recited a passage from the "Song of Solomon."   B

10. "Raise the property tax—and impose rent control!" he yelled with fervor.   C

11. When you buy a foreign car, you have to expect poor service.   A

12. The matter suddenly came to a crisis, but just as suddenly it was resolved.   F

13. It is essential that he bring the document with him and that he be here by noon.   C

14. We fear the unknown whereas we often welcome the known.   E

15. Our constitution protects our right to pursue happiness; however, it does not guarantee that we shall find this happiness, no matter how diligently we pursue it.   F

16. The tenant claims that he paid the rent and asked me to convey this fact to the landlord. ___D___

17. The skylark gracefully lifts itself into the sky, lets out a joyful warble, and disappears into a cloud. ___B___

18. The sea breeze was blowing harder and felt colder. ___B___

19. As one walked into the slaughterhouse, one could see hundreds of carcasses hanging on hooks. ___A___

20. Because most of the children loved to go swimming, the group went to the beach. ___B___

Self-Grading Exercise 11

1. We are now expected to drive less, use public transportation, and conserve heating fuel. Saving energy is a realistic goal.

2. Some diet experts say that a tablespoon of vinegar in some sugar and oil will reduce the appetite.

3. The newspaper said that a rebirth of great art is taking place in China.

4. When Byron was on the Continent, he carried on a lively correspondence with Shelley.

5. The world was expecting Golda Meir's death.

6. My brother does not make full use of his enormous talent.

7. During lunch John always sat alone while the other students sat together chatting away. John's isolation didn't last long, however.

8. Mahatma Gandhi wanted only the sparsest of furniture in his room.

9. The master of ceremonies told the audience that he found the group of millionaires he interviewed very articulate.

10. Melissa invited Ruth to travel to Spain with her because she thought Ruth was interested in Spanish history.

11. Psychologists have no right discussing their patients' personal problems with their own friends because the patients could be embarrassed if their identities were discovered.

12. The passerby wondered about the significance of a young boy's dashing out of the store and running down the street.

13. On our flight across the Atlantic the weather was beautiful.

14. Despite its dark and rough water, the Blue Grotto of Capri was a splendid sight.

15. My friend John loves to watch basketball for hours on end, but his wife doesn't approve of his doing so.

Self-Grading Exercise 12

1. As he bowed to the audience, his violin fell to the floor.

2. Filled with terror, the tiny kitten sat shivering in the corner.

3. As I watched them from behind a bush, camera in hand, the bears seemed like harmless pets.

4. What the teacher needs is a neatly typed list of students.

5. Students who speak French fluently will not need to pass the three conversation examinations.

6. During World War II the Nazis gave Jewish prisoners only cabbage to eat, nothing else.

7. Instead of asking for forgiveness, she offered a piece of chocolate cake as her sign of repentance.

8. Even when confronted with the full truth, they ignored the facts.

9. Hearing the bell ring, the boxer triumphantly flung his glove to the ground.

10. Out of breath and revealing a look of anxiety, the lover ran up the stairs.

11. The day drew to a close with anguished prayer that God would spare the infant.

12. We enjoy not only music, but also painting and sculpture.

13. The law was enacted immediately after Congress adjourned.

14. Scorched by the sizzling heat, we thought jumping into the river made a great deal of sense.

15. At a Neiman-Marcus store, we tried on some DKNY pants that cost $150.

Self-Grading Exercise 13

1. He wanted to marry her because she was bright, pleasant, and unselfish.

2. The boss fired him because his letters were sloppy, ungrammatical, and poorly typed.

3. The handbook revealed two ways in which the unity of a paragraph could be broken: (1) one could stray from the topic sentence, (2) one could obscure the central thought with excessive details.

4. By exercising daily, by eating proper food, and by avoiding stress, he can regain his health.

5. This simple man did not doubt that after death there was a paradise for good people and a hell for bad people.

6. Most of them were either athletic or strong.

7. Handing out oil coupons seemed both intelligent and necessary.

8. She insisted that he must leave and never return.

9. The man is either an idealist or a fool.

10. Today pocket calculators are inexpensive, durable, and easily obtained.

11. The Byronic hero was a man who felt alienated from mainstream society, who withdrew into haughty superiority, who loved passionately, and who felt an element of self-pity.

12. This is the case not only with police officers but also with firefighters.

13. Here is what you will need to know: how to open a bank account, how to judge a contract, and how to sell equipment.

14. She climbed Mount Whitney not because she wanted to test her endurance, but because she was arrogant.

15. To err is human; to forgive is divine.

Self-Grading Exercise 14

1. After noticing that the watch and the bedspread were gone, they immediately (suspicioned, <u>suspected</u>) his stepdaughter.
2. Dorothy insisted on keeping her (personnel, <u>personal</u>) opinions hidden from her students.
3. The hiring committee preferred communicating by telephone because they believed in (<u>oral</u>, verbal) interviews.
4. I was always told that (this type, <u>this type of</u>) novel was cheap and aimed at the sensation seekers.
5. (Sit, <u>Set</u>) the flower pot in front of the brick wall, where it will look lovely.
6. The (amount, <u>number</u>) of registered students varies from semester to semester.
7. In the upper left-hand corner of his (<u>stationery</u>, stationary) one could clearly discern three modest initials.
8. Earl Warren was considered a Supreme Court justice of immense (<u>stature</u>, statue, statute).
9. The team that climbed Mt. Whitney included (quite a number, <u>a rather large number</u>) of women.
10. Twenty years and six children later, the marriage was finally (<u>over</u>, over with).
11. Day after day his fiancée waited (<u>for</u>, on) him to return from the war.
12. Thank you for the (complement, <u>compliment</u>)—how kind!
13. (Your, <u>You're</u>) either for us or against us.
14. He never returned the suitcase (like, <u>as</u>) he was asked to do.
15. We (<u>can hardly</u>, can't hardly) distinguish one twin from the other.
16. The (farther, <u>further</u>) he delved into St. Paul's theology, the more fascinated he became.
17. When the real estate agent had received a firm bid, he (appraised, <u>apprised</u>) his clients of the fact.
18. He could never be (<u>persuaded</u>, convinced) to travel overseas on an airplane.
19. The (<u>site</u>, cite) for the international hotel was near the center of town.
20. While he was in Vietnam, all of his mail was (censured, <u>censored</u>).

Self-Grading Exercise 15

1. To add to our depression, a period of *driving snow* set in.
2. Vicky *beamed with pride* as she walked off the stage with her gold medal.
3. I liked *going to luxurious restaurants, visiting excellent museums, and attending the ballet* in the city.
4. His extreme selfishness *left him isolated and friendless*.
5. He chewed his food noisily, he talked with his mouth full, and he wiped his lips with his hand; in short, his manners were *disgustingly boorish*.
6. For six days and nights, he *battled* with fever and death.
7. A delicate seashell is a miraculous piece of sculpture.

8. All of the fun at Joe's birthday party was ruined because the children *dropped ice cream on the carpet, left fingerprints on the windows, and broke a chair.*

9. The Mohave Desert of California and the Sinai Desert of Egypt *both experience extreme temperatures and searing winds.*

10. Every large city *suffers from overcrowded conditions, traffic congestion, and lack of green spaces.*

11. She was a hopeless, withered old lady *hobbling across* the street with her cane, her *stooped form* serving as a symbol of her despair.

12. In 1925, a terrible dust storm *swept* across the Midwest, *ripping chimneys off roofs, seeping through closed windows, and ruining entire vegetable crops.*

13. Many of the old Broadway songs reveal poignantly *the poverty of the unemployed, the despair of the old, and the cold arrogance of the rich.*

14. We tried various cleaning solutions, but the kitchen floor remained *streaked with grime.*

15. People who throw *trash* out of their car windows while they drive along our highways reveal a disgusting kind of vulgarity.

Self-Grading Exercise 16

1. Charles Steinmetz was a pioneer in electrical engineering.
2. Long-distance runners training for the Olympics run as many as 20 miles a day.
3. Each person in line received a ticket.
4. Students today demonstrate poor writing skills for one simple reason: They are never required to write.
5. My favorite female poet is Emily Dickinson.
6. In the following chapter we will examine Charles Darwin's theory of evolution.
7. It is difficult to keep up with today's scientific advances.
8. Made of solid brown oak, the table has lasted for over a hundred years.
9. One of John's most serious faults is continuously apologizing for his errors.
10. Most often they graded the objective tests with a Scantron machine.
11. One of the most exciting events of the trip was attending a secret burial ceremony.
12. Nevertheless, most judges are rational and do not judge defendants emotionally.
13. The pilot was in a terrible dilemma because he was flying into a crosswind.
14. All of the children observed by reporters were tall.
15. Traffic fines are an important source of revenue in New York City.

Self-Grading Exercise 17

1. When the medieval structure collapsed, the beginning of the modern mode of production started.
2. Quite a few years ago, while I was living in a little town on the West Coast, a stranger came in and bought our valley, where the Sempervirens redwoods grew.
3. If writing skills are to be improved, English teachers will have to assign more writing than they now do.

4. We began to realize that resources in America are not limitless as we had thought.

5. Although we are exuberant people, we are also destructive and careless, making powerful weapons, such as the atomic bomb, which we then use to prove that they exist.

6. Uncountable buffalo were killed, stripped of their hides, and left to rot, thus destroying a permanent food supply.

7. As a teacher he considered objections by students carefully, as if these objections had been made by colleagues.

8. Its roof half torn away by wind, its walls blackened by fire, and its stone floors covered with mud, this hotel looked like the ruins of a Gothic castle.

9. I was 17 and extremely shy when my third-grade teacher came to visit us.

10. Hired and fired on the basis of how entertaining they make the news, television newscasters are victims of a rating game controlled by anti-intellectual viewers.

11. Although unknown to one another, all four of my grandparents arrived in America from the same county in Slovakia, where they had experienced a severe famine resulting from a potato crop failure.

12. Based on information in the Bible, most people believed the earth was roughly 6,000 years old until the beginning of the nineteenth century, when geologists and naturalists began to suspect that the earth must have existed for a much longer period of time.

13. Driving along the highway like a haunted man, he was stopped by the police.

14. Considering that the early Incas did not have the wheel, their architectural accomplishments were spectacular.

15. Assuming that Goethe influenced Thomas Mann, we can surmise that Mann's *Dr. Faustus* is similar to Goethe's *Faust*, both of which deal with the theme of the demonic.

Self-Grading Exercise 18

1. His daughter, a leader among the women, had spared her father and set him afloat on the sea in a hollow chest. _____

2. As for me, already old age is my companion. _____

3. He spoke slowly, believing in his heart that he was telling the truth. _____

4. Great dangers lay ahead, and some of the soldiers paid with their lives for drinking so heavily. _____

5. Gently he answered, "I have come to my home to recover the ancient honor of my house." _____

6. These fierce women steadfastly refused to surrender to the foreign invaders. ___C___

7. They scorned them, terrorized them, and robbed them. _____

8. He insisted that he had been saved by the woman in white, who had brought him to Venice, an exotic city. _____

9. On November 19, 1929, a star, bright and luminous, shot across the sky. _____

10. Let the taxpayers who reside in the county pay for a new road sign at the intersection of Broadway and Main Street.   __C__

11. The football players, however, did not care to linger in such a gloomy, narrow place.   _____

12. Acheron, the river of woe, pours into Cocytus, the river of lamentation.   _____

13. Sir, please accept my sincere apologies for the inconvenience this has caused you.   _____

14. Because hell is merely an invention of guilty minds, why believe in it?   _____

15. David Cotton, Jr., is doing some important research in the field of high-risk pregnancies.   _____

16. On his way to ask his adviser a question about a calculus course, Robert arrived at an automatic gate, where he blew out a tire, causing his Fiat to skid into another car.   _____

17. He felt himself degraded by this servile attitude and vowed revenge.   __C__

18. They told him, "God's daylight is sweet to the old."   _____

19. Yes, Chicago, Illinois, can be windy and freezing cold in the winter.   _____

20. Above, some perfume bottles filled with exotic bath oils decorated the wall shelves.   _____

Self-Grading Exercise 19

1. According to *Mythology*, a book by Edith Hamilton, the Greeks, unlike the Egyptians, made their gods in their own image.

2. Is this an exaggerated view? It hardly seems so; nevertheless, many opponents of the measure dismiss it as *unmenschlich*.

3. The search for a way to stop this vicious cycle has taxed the best minds among the following groups: city council members, educators, and urban planners.

4. Let me pose this question: Could you love passionately if you knew you would never die?

5. Who interrupted me by saying, "That's enough for today"?

6. Dear Mr. Forsythe: This is in reply to your request of May 16, 1988.

7. From now on, please cross your *t*'s and dot your *i*'s.

8. This is how we propose to assign the various duties: The men will scrub the floors, ceilings, and walls; the women will cook, mend, and garden; the children will run errands, clean up the yard, and pick vegetables.

9. But what happens when the national organizations themselves—the schools, the unions, the federal government—become victims of a technological culture?

10. With his fifth-grade education he wrote a marvelous poem entitled "Languid Tears."

11. The *New Yorker* is read mostly by people with keen literary interests.

12. Students often find it difficult to distinguish between the words *imply* and *infer*; in fact, most people confuse their meanings.

13. We currently reside at 451 Bellefontaine Drive, Pasadena, California.

14. One of the delegates was a vegetarian; the other was restricted to kosher foods.

15. He yelled angrily, "Get out of my yard!"

16. Vans, boats, and campers are not allowed (see Regulation #13).

17. Have you heard the question asked, "What can the police department do against the pitiless onslaught of criminal violence"?

18. This, my friends, is how I think we can help the world in a time of tyranny: by fighting for freedom.

19. The age was an age of *éclaircissement* and self-determination.

20. "You have arrived at your resting place," she murmured softly. "Seek no further."

21. Inside, the antique armoire dominated the room.

22. Picture, if you please, an open space where twenty acrobats stand, each locking hands with two different partners; then imagine ten acrobats standing on the shoulders of these twenty.

Self-Grading Exercise 20

1. Balloting at both the democratic and republican conventions is by states. _____

2. He had taken many history courses, but none fascinated him more than introduction to western civilization. _____

3. Delta Delta Delta, the most active sorority, invited speakers from such organizations as daughters of the American revolution, national organization of Women, and the Sierra club. _____

4. The subject of the lecture was "The Treasures Of The Nile." _____

5. John Stuart Mill understood Calculus and could read greek when he was a child. _____

6. Exodus is the second book of the pentateuch. _____

7. One of his dreams was to see Mt. Everest. ___C___

8. The war of the Triple Alliance was fought between Paraguay on one side and an Alliance of Argentina, brazil, and Uruguay on the other. _____

9. That is the best photograph ever taken of uncle Charlie. _____

10. As a capable and tough City attorney, he took action against one of Hollywood's swingers clubs, a place called Socrates' retreat. _____

11. John toyed with two ideas: joining the peace corps or working without pay for César Chávez's United farm workers of America. _____

12. Ex-Assemblyman Waldie never ran for Office after the Summer of 1974. _____

13. Today he is chairman of the Federal Mine Safety and Health Review Commission. ___C___

14. The residents of Mammoth Lakes, a mountain resort, are proud of the view of the minarets, a ragged mountain range, seen from highway 395 as one approaches the resort. _____

15. One of my favorite books is a novel entitled *in the heart of a fool*. _____

16. Some women have romantic ideas about returning to feudalism, with knights in shining armor and ladies adhering to the manners of the Middle Ages.   C
17. One of the highest mountain systems in the world is Hindu Kush, extending 500 miles from north Pakistan into northeast Afghanistan.   C
18. William S. Levey, S.J., is the vice president of an important men's club.   C
19. I failed Organic Chemistry 101, but I passed french.   _____
20. A traditional American holiday is Thanksgiving day.   _____

Self-Grading Exercise 21

1. personnel	6. occurrence	11. height	16. all right
2. separated	7. professions	12. too	17. led
3. conscious	8. prejudiced	13. villain	18. principle
4. exaggeration	9. environment	14. woman	19. losing
5. shining	10. explanation	15. similar	20. rhythm

Text Credits

p. 113: Copyright © 1957 Condé Nast. All rights reserved. Originally published in The New Yorker. Reprinted by permission.

p. 128: Reprinted with the permission of Scribner, a Division of Simon & Schuster, Inc., from *A Gift of Laughter* by Allan Sherman. Copyright © 1965 by Allan Sherman. All rights reserved.

p. 138: Excerpt from *NIGHT* by Elie Wiesel, translated by Marion Wiesel. Translation copyright © 2006 by Marion Wiesel. Reprinted by permission of Hill and Wang, a division of Farrar, Straus and Giroux, LLC.

p. 156: The poem entitled "Coats" from the book entitled *OTHERWISE NEW & SELECTED POEMS* by Jane Kenyon which was published by Graywolf Press in 1996.

p. 163: From *The No. 1 Ladies' Detective Agency* by Alexander McCall Smith. Copyright © 1998, 2005 by Alexander McCall Smith. Used by permission of Anchor Books, a division of Random House, Inc.

p. 177: Joyce Carol Oates, "Bonobo Momma." Michigan Quarterly Review, Winter 2009. Reprinted in Pushcart Prize XXXIV. Ed. Bill Henderson. N.Y. 2010, pp. 79–89.

p. 185: Sister Flowers from *I Know Why The Caged Bird Sings* by Maya Angelou. Copyright © 1969 and renewed 1997 by Maya Angelou. Used by permission of Random House, Inc.

p. 193: "We're Poor" from *Homecoming: An Autobiography* by Floyd Dell. Copyright © 1933, 1961 by Floyd Dell. Reprinted by permission of Henry Holt and Company, LLC.

p. 196: "Eleanor Rigby" by John Lennon and Paul McCartney. © 1966 Sony/ATV Music Publishing LLC. All rights administered by Sony/ATV Music Publishing LLC, 8 Music Square West, Nashville, TN 37203. All rights reserved. Used by permission.

p. 202: From *Fidelity: Five Stories* by Wendell Berry, copyright © 1992 by Wendell Berry. Used by permission of Pantheon Books, a division of Random House, Inc.

p. 214: Ammon Shea, "The Keypad Solution" from The New York Times, © January 22, 2010 The New York Times All rights reserved. Used by permission and protected by the Copyright Laws of the United States. The printing, copying, redistribution, or retransmission of the Material without express written permission is prohibited.

p. 218: Reprinted by permission of The Estate of Don Farrant.

p. 224: "Arrangement in Black and White," copyright 1927 by The National Association for the Advancement of Colored People, from Dorothy Parker: Complete Stories by Dorothy Parker. Used by permission of Penguin, a division of Penguin Group (USA) Inc.

p. 228: COLOR © 1925 Harper & Bros., NY, renewed 1952 by Ida M. Cullen. Reprinted by permission.

p. 237: "Fundamentalism" by Bert B. Beach, originally appeared in *Adventist Review,* Oct.26, 2006. Copyright © 2006 Bert B. Beach.

p. 257: "Dream House" by Anthony C. Winkler. Copyright © 2005 by Anthony C. Winkler. Reprinted by permission of the author.

p. 265: "The twins" (pp. 23–24; 43 I.) from *BURNING IN WATER, DROWNING IN FLAME: SELECTED POEMS* 1955–1973 by CHARLES BUKOWSKI. Copyright © 1963, 1964, 1965, 1966, 1967, 1968, 1974 by Charles Bukowski. Reprinted by permission of HarperCollins Publishers.

Index